# GUIDE TO COST MANAGEMENT

**Subscriber Update Service**

# BECOME A SUBSCRIBER!
## *Did you purchase this product from a bookstore?*

If you did, it's important for you to become a subscriber. John Wiley & Sons, Inc. may publish, on a periodic basis, supplements and new editions to reflect the latest changes in the subject matter that you **need to know** in order to stay competitive in this ever-changing industry. By contacting the Wiley office nearest you, you'll receive any current update at no additional charge. In addition, you'll receive future updates and revised or related volumes on a 30-day examination review.

If you purchased this product directly from John Wiley & Sons, Inc., we have already recorded your subscription for this update service.

To become a subscriber, please call **1-800-225-5945** or send your name, company name (if applicable), address, and the title of the product to:

mailing address: **Supplement Department**
**John Wiley & Sons, Inc.**
**One Wiley Drive**
**Somerset, NJ 08875**

e-mail: **subscriber@wiley.com**
fax: **1-732-302-2300**
online: **www.wiley.com**

For customers outside the United States, please contact the Wiley office nearest you:

Professional & Reference Division
John Wiley & Sons Canada, Ltd.
22 Worcester Road
Rexdale, Ontario M9W 1L1
CANADA
(416) 675-3580
Phone: 1-800-567-4797
Fax: 1-800-565-6802
canada@jwiley.com

Jacaranda Wiley Ltd.
PRT Division
P.O. Box 174
North Ryde, NSW 2113
AUSTRALIA
Phone: (02) 805-1100
Fax: (02) 805-1597
headoffice@jacwiley.com.au

John Wiley & Sons, Ltd.
Baffins Lane
Chichester
West Sussex, PO19 1UD
ENGLAND
Phone: (44) 1243 779777
Fax: (44) 1243 770638
cs-books@wiley.co.uk

John Wiley & Sons (SEA) Pte. Ltd.
2 Clementi Loop #02-01
SINGAPORE 129809
Phone: 65 463 2400
Fax: 65 463 4605; 65 463 4604
wiley@singnet.com.sg

# GUIDE TO COST MANAGEMENT

Edited by

**BARRY J. BRINKER**

**JOHN WILEY & SONS, INC.**

New York • Chichester • Weinheim • Brisbane • Singapore • Toronto

This book is printed on acid-free paper. ⊚

Copyright © 2000 by John Wiley and Sons, Inc. All rights reserved.

Published simultaneously in Canada.

This publication is designed to provide accurate and authoritative information in regard to the subject matter covered. It is sold with the understanding that the publisher is not engaged in rendering legal, accounting, or other professional services. If legal advice or other expert assistance is required, the services of a competent professional person should be sought.

*Library of Congress Cataloging-in-Publication Data*
Guide to Cost management / edited by Barry J. Brinker.
     p. cm.
  Includes bibliographical references and index.
  ISBN 0-471-31579-6 (cloth : alk. paper)
   1. Cost control—Handbooks, manuals, etc.   2. Cost accounting—Handbooks, manuals, etc.   I. Brinker, Barry J.
  HD47.3.C667     2000
  658.15′52—dc21                      99-043409
                                     CIP

Printed in the United States of America
10 9 8 7 6 5 4 3 2 1

*To two incomparable DBs, Darlene Brinker and Debra Von Bargen,*
*and to the younger Brinker set, Mark and Amy.*

# PREFACE

This book summarizes the topic of cost management and provides an introduction to the many topics people have in mind when they use the term, including:

- Performance measurement
- Strategic cost management
- Total quality management
- Activity-based management
- Target costing

Because I have tilled the cost management vineyards almost as long as there has been such a thing, I hope I will be indulged when I write how amazed I am at the many developments that have occurred in cost management in that relatively short time.

When I started editing the *Journal of Cost Management* in 1988, one of the first contributions I received was an article written by the authors of the cost accounting textbook I had used in business school, which thrilled me. Their willingness to contribute to this developing body of knowledge gave—and still gives—some idea about the virtual revolution that has occurred in managerial (or cost) accounting. Since then, I have edited many publications about cost management—including the *Handbook of Cost Management, Emerging Practices in Cost Management,* and the *International Journal of Strategic Cost Management*—and the pace of change in the field seems only to have accelerated.

**DEFINITIONS**   The first thing to say about cost management is that "cost" is not the exclusive subject. Many topics—such as performance management, time to market, activity analysis, and change management—have little direct connection to dollars and cents. And, although I expect that the main audience for this book will be financial types (e.g., controllers, chief financial officers, cost accountants, and financial analysts), the range of topics is so wide and their effects so profound that almost anybody in business can learn from this book.

Another important point is how truly universal cost management is: Unlike many technical topics (and especially accounting topics), it is international in scope. National boundaries play little role in determining the usefulness or applicability of the tools, methods, and practices written about in this book; important case studies and innovations have occurred all over the world. Quality management, for example, got its start in the United States with men such as Walter Shewhart, W. Edwards Deming, and Joseph Juran, but it was the Japanese who truly developed quality management and made it work. Similarly, target costing developed mainly in Japan, but many companies in the United States and other parts of the world have adopted target costing and made it their own.

Finally, cost management is the wave of the future: Schools that continue to teach traditional cost or management accounting—the old-time religion of purchase-price variances and flexible budgets—are stuck in the past. They do a gross disservice to the next generation. Markets are increasingly global, customers are increasingly demanding, and business is increasingly complex, so what worked in the 1920s (or even in the 1980s) may not work now.

**ORGANIZATION OF THE BOOK**   Because of the dynamic nature of cost management, the challenge will always be to keep an overview comprehensive, usable, and up-to-date. To summarize cost management as it now exists, this book includes 33 chapters, which are divided into the following five parts:

- Strategic cost management
- Performance measurement
- Quality
- Activity-based management
- Management trends and techniques

The chapters are written by both practitioners and academics, all of them acknowledged experts in their fields. Together, the chapters provide wide, yet in-depth coverage of the many management practices, tools, and techniques included in cost management.

**ACKNOWLEDGMENTS**   Many people have made this book possible. Because an editor is nothing without writers, however, my special thanks go to the many authors who worked so diligently and long to write their chapters. Other people who have helped me significantly include Jim Borden of Villanova University (who helped with the outline), Steve Player and Paige Dawson of Arthur Andersen LLP, and Mike Roberts and Pete Zampino of CAM-I. As always, Lori Jacobs did marvels as a copy editor. Sheck Cho and the other editors and staff of John Wiley & Sons (including Rachael Leiserson and Joyce Ting) have been unfailingly pleasant to work with, competent, and also helpful.

Most of all, however, I want to thank Debra Von Bargen, who did a first-rate job in organizing and planning this book, and my wife, Darlene Badal Brinker, who contributed vastly to this large undertaking.

Barry J. Brinker
Valley Forge, Pennsylvania
January 2000

# ABOUT THE EDITOR

Barry J. Brinker, CPA, is a managing editor with The Vanguard Group in Valley Forge, Pennsylvania. From 1988 to 1997, he edited the *Journal of Cost Management.* In 1991 he edited the *Handbook of Cost Management,* the first comprehensive handbook available on the new subject. Other cost management books he has edited include the annual *Emerging Practices in Cost Management* from 1990–1997 (which included special editions about Activity-Based Management and Performance Measurement). He has also launched two other cost management periodicals: *Journal of Strategic Performance Management* and *International Journal of Strategic Cost Management.*

Mr. Brinker has served on the Management Accounting Executive Committee of the American Institute of Certified Public Accountants (AICPA), the AICPA's Business and Industry Executive Committee, and the joint committee that selects the annual accounting literature award sponsored by the AICPA and the American Accounting Association.

# ABOUT THE CONTRIBUTORS

**Tom Albright** is J. Reese Phifer Faculty Fellow at the Culverhouse School of Accountancy at the University of Alabama in Tuscaloosa.

**John Antos** is president of Value Creation Group, Inc. in Dallas, Texas.

**Sergio Beretta** is a professor at Università Commerciale Luigi Bocconi in Milan, Italy.

**James A. Brimson** is president of IPM in Arlington, Texas.

**Wendi Bukowitz** is a director in the Intellectual Asset Management Practice at PricewaterhouseCoopers in Pittsburgh, Pennsylvania.

**Robert J. Campbell** is a professor of accounting at Miami University in Oxford, Ohio.

**David K. Carr** is a partner with PricewaterhouseCoopers' Management Consulting Service in Fairfax, Virginia.

**Lawrence Carr** is a professor of management accounting at Babson College in Babson Park, Massachusetts.

**Carey C. Curtis** is an associate professor of accounting at Southern Connecticut State University in New Haven, Connecticut.

**Stan Davis** is a doctoral student at the Culverhouse School of Accountancy at the University of Alabama in Tuscaloosa.

**Angela Demery** is a manager at the American Productivity & Quality Center in Houston, Texas.

**Dileep Dhavale** is a professor of accounting at Clark University in Worcester, Massachusetts.

**Andrea Dossi** is a professor at Università Commerciale Luigi Bocconi in Milan, Italy.

**Nicholas J. Fessler** is an assistant professor of accounting in the Fogelman College of Business and Economics at the University of Memphis in Tennessee.

**Ross L. Fink** is an associate professor of operations management in the Foster College of Business Administration at Bradley University, Peoria, Illinois.

**Joseph G. Fisher** is the KPMG Peat Marwick Faculty Fellow in the Department of Accounting and Information Systems at the Kelley School of Business at Indiana University in Bloomington, Indiana.

**Richard J. Gargas** is at Eli Lilly and Company in Indianapolis, Indiana.

**Hugh Grove** is a professor of accounting at the University of Denver in Denver, Colorado.

**Don Hansen** is a professor of accounting at Oklahoma State University's College of Business Administration in Stillwater, Oklahoma.

**Ann Hopkins** is a partner with PricewaterhouseCoopers' Management Consulting Service in Arlington, Virginia.

**William Hubbell** is a partner with Arthur Andersen in Boulder, Colorado.

**Neil R. Jones** is an assistant professor at the Richard Ivey School of Business at the University of Western Ontario in London, Ontario.

**Suresh S. Kalagnanam** is an associate professor of accounting at the University of Saskatchewan in Saskatoon, Canada.

**Zafar U. Khan** is a professor of accounting at Eastern Michigan University in Ypsilanti, Michigan.

**Fred A. Kuglin** is a partner with Ernst and Young in Abernathy, Texas.

**John B. MacArthur** is chairperson, Department of Accounting and Finance, and a Kathryn and Richard Kip Professor of Accounting at the University of North Florida in Jacksonville.

**William Maguire** is a senior lecturer in management accounting at the University of Auckland in Auckland, New Zealand.

**Sarah C. Mavrinac** is an assistant professor at the Richard Ivey School of Business at the University of Western Ontario in London, Ontario.

**John A. Miller** is chief financial officer of COMPX in Houston, Texas.

**David Murphy** is an associate professor of accounting at Oklahoma State University.

**Joseph O'Leary** is the partner and co-leader of the Integrated Customer Solutions practice for Arthur Andersen Business Consulting.

**Steven Pedersen** is director, Product Stewardship and Research and Development EHS with Seagate Technology in Shakopee, Minnesota.

**Kenneth Preiss** is the Sir Leon Bagrit Professor in the School of Management at Ben Gurion University of the Negev in Beer Sheva, Israel.

**Martin Putterill** is an associate professor in management accounting at the University of Auckland in Auckland, New Zealand.

**Manash Ray** is the Kane Professor of Business Administration in the College of Business and Economics at Lehigh University in Bethlehem, Pennsylvania.

**Barbara A. Rosenbaum** is an associate director at Ernst and Young in Baltimore, Maryland.

**Harold P. Roth** is a professor of accounting at the University of Tennessee in Knoxville.

**Richard C. Smith** is a partner with PricewaterhouseCoopers' Management Consulting Service in Fairfax, Virginia.

**Christopher H. Stinson** is an associate professor at the University of Virginia's Darden Graduate School of Business in Charlottesville, Virginia.

**Nathan V. Stuart** is a doctoral student in accounting at Indiana University's Kelley School of Business in Bloomington, Indiana.

**Frank O. Sunderland** is a consultant with i2 Technologies of Irving, Texas.

**Ganesh Vaidyanathan** is an associate professor of business at Brandon University in Brandon, Canada.

**Michael Vitale** is a professor at the Melbourne Business School at the University of Melbourne in Melbourne, Australia.

**Jeanine Wilmot** is a consultant with PricewaterhouseCoopers in Guilford, Connecticut.

**Michael J. Wing** is the chief executive officer of U.S. Space & Rocket Center in Huntsville, Alabama.

# CONTENTS OVERVIEW

# CONTENTS

**9  LOGISTICS**                                                                    **144**
FRED A. KUGLIN AND BARBARA A. ROSENBAUM

**10  SUPPLY CHAIN MANAGEMENT**                                                     **164**
TOM ALBRIGHT AND STAN DAVIS

## PART II    PERFORMANCE MEASUREMENT

## PART III    QUALITY

## 17    QUALITY    305
Ross L. Fink

## 28    THEORY OF CONSTRAINTS    521
ROBERT J. CAMPBELL

# PART I

# STRATEGIC COST MANAGEMENT

# CHAPTER 1

# SUPERIOR CUSTOMER SERVICE

## Michael J. Wing
**U.S. Space & Rocket Center**
## Joseph O' Leary
**Arthur Andersen Business Consulting**

## 1.1 KNOWING CUSTOMERS' EXPECTATIONS

*A medium-size professional association located in the Northeast has a national membership base and has experienced a steady, incremental increase in its membership over several years. However, a series of proposed legislative initiatives that are perceived as a threat to the profession have swelled the membership ranks recently. Even though the association endeavors to provide the same type and quality of service to its membership that it has in previous years, it is unable to do so in many areas. Growing increasingly frustrated, the association's top management commissioned an assessment of its membership base to determine its expectations in different areas. It had never conducted such an assessment before.*

*The study revealed that in one area in which the association was seeking to ship publications within 48 hours, members stated that the receipt of such materials within three to four weeks was acceptable. However, members expected the phones to be answered promptly and inquiries to be addressed accurately and efficiently. Armed with this information, the association was able to modify its service level in direct response to member expectations. The result was an increase in member satisfaction and a reduction in cost, despite the increase in the membership base.*

Providing a product or service that customers perceive as excellent requires a company to know what its customers expect. This is the most critical component of delivering excellent customer service.

Virtually every company thinks it knows what its customers want. However, if a company is only slightly inaccurate about its assumptions, it could lose its customers' business to another company that has more accurately filled their needs.

Being only "slightly" inaccurate can lead an organization to spend money, time, and effort on things that are not important to customers. And in a worst-case scenario, it can mean not surviving in an intensely competitive environment.

**(a) Expectation Gap**  At times a gap occurs between what customers expect and what management presumes they expect. This often happens because companies overlook or do not fully understand customers' perceptions and expectations. In spite of a strong commitment and sincere desire to provide quality service, many companies fall dramatically short of the mark, usually because they have an internally directed rather than externally directed focus. An internally directed focus assumes that the company knows what customers *should* want and delivers or produces that. This orientation often leads to providing products and services that do not match customers' expectations—important features and benefits may be left out and levels of performance may be inadequate.

In looking at several different types of organizations, common elements contribute to the gap between customer expectations and the product or service offered. The common elements are:

- Inadequate "bilateral" communication between front-line personnel and management.
- An absence of regular interaction between management and customers.
- An absence of a strong market research program.
- An absence of customer service accountability.

**(b) Communicating with Front-Line Employees**  Front-line employees are in regular contact with customers. As a result, they know a great deal about customers' perceptions and expectations. This information must be regularly passed on to management. When channels of communication are closed or inadequate, managers cannot know about problems occurring in product and service delivery as well as critical information about changing customer expectations.

Communication between front-line employees and management can be enhanced in a number of ways:

- Formal types of communication (e.g., memos, suggestion cards, and open meetings).
- Informal communication (e.g., discussions over coffee, walking around the facility, going out into the field).

It is essential to assess customers' perceptions and expectations regularly, but it is also very important to assess whether managers understand the needs and expectations of front-line employees. Managers who communicate with front-line people not only build morale but also learn a tremendous amount about their customers, thereby reducing the expectation gap.

Some questions to ask concerning the communication between management and front-line employees in an organization are:

- How often do managers have direct contact with front-line employees?
- Do managers encourage suggestions from front-line employees concerning the quality of products or services?
- Are there too many levels of management, causing managers to be cut off from direct contact with and feedback from front-line employees?
- Are there formal or informal opportunities for front-line employees to communicate with management on a regular basis?

- Has management adequately determined and monitored the expectations of front-line employees?
- Do front-line employees feel strongly supported?

**(c) Interaction between Management and Customers**    The larger a company is, the more difficult it is for managers to deal directly with customers. Consequently, managers have less information about customers' perceptions and expectations. However, in smaller companies, managers can receive more direct information concerning their customers.

Even when they are regularly given reports, managers readily lose the customer perspective if they do not have the opportunity for direct customer contact. Theoretical knowledge is a poor substitute for a face-to-face encounter.

To truly understand and appreciate customers' needs and expectations, managers should experience firsthand what really happens in the field—in stores or on the customer-service line—by answering the service line themselves or dealing with customers face to face. Managers can better empathize with employees if they have experienced some of what employees deal with on a regular basis. Here are some questions to consider concerning regular interaction between management and customers:

- Does the company have a program in which managers rotate to different service positions within the organization?
- Does top management make it a priority to get out in the field and see customers?
- Do managers randomly interact with customers (e.g., those waiting in line, browsing in the store, or calling the service desk)?

**(d) Need for a Strong Market Research Program**    Because marketing research is an important tool in assessing customers' perceptions and expectations, a company that fails to regularly collect such information may be more likely to have a significant customer expectation gap.

To effectively deal with expectation versus performance issues, marketing research measurements should focus on product or service quality issues. These might include:

- Which features and benefits are most important to customers?
- How much do customers expect, at what price and in what time frame?
- What do customers think the company should do if problems occur in product or service delivery?

Determining what customers expect is essential to providing superior quality. Regardless of a company's size and resources, there are ways to obtain this kind of information. Questions to consider concerning a company's marketing research efforts include:

- Is research conducted on a regular basis to generate high-quality, reliable information about what customers want and expect?
- Does research focus on quality of service provided?
- Can research findings be readily understood and used by managers?
- Are the research findings integral to the company's strategic planning?
- Are research findings shared throughout the company when appropriate?

**(e) Customer-Service Accountability**     Policies and procedures are important, but when they impede a firm's ability to meet customer needs, they are counterproductive. With many companies experiencing an increase in policies and procedures over the last several years, initiative has been stifled and employees are less willing to get involved.

For companies to compete effectively in an increasingly competitive marketplace, employees must be enabled to identify problems, resolve them, and share suggestions with management. They should not be allowed to withdraw into a bureaucratic environment and assume that someone else will take care of problems. All the while, customers may be migrating elsewhere. The following list provides questions to ask regarding customer service accountability:

- Are employees encouraged to "take ownership" of a problem, and are they supported in their efforts?
- Is the business unduly bureaucratic, and does it encourage an attitude of "someone else will take care of it"?
- Does the business empower its employees to find ways in which customers can be better served?

Any organization, regardless of size, can reduce customer expectation gaps if it improves communication between managers and front-line employees, increases interaction between management and customers, develops a strong market research program, and insists on accountability for customer service.

## 1.2 KEEPING CUSTOMERS

*Jim has an impressive resume. He received excellent training while employed as a brand manager for a Fortune 500 company. For two years, he has been running a small sales-driven company in the Northeast. Because of his experience in a large company, Jim is relentless in his urgent call to employees to attract more customers. Those admonitions have been carefully heeded. More new customers have come to the company in Jim's two years than ever before in its history.*

*However, no measurable increase in revenues or profits has resulted during Jim's tenure. A customer-satisfaction assessment reveals that existing customers feel that the firm's objective is to get new customers. But existing customers do not feel well taken care of, and many choose to leave. When Jim receives this information, he immediately changes the focus of the firm, realizing that pursuing new customers at the expense of customer retention is unprofitable.*

*Within nine months, the number of new customers has fallen, but the number of customers staying with the firm has risen, as have monthly revenues and profits.*

Customer retention is one of the most important strategic issues companies have faced in recent years. Retention is critical for increasing profits and remaining competitive. Studies show that a 5 percent change in the rate of customer retention can shift profits from 25 percent to 100 percent in either direction.

In manufacturing, measuring the number of defects is an important index of quality. In measuring service, the number of *defections* (customers going elsewhere) is important.

Many companies underestimate the cost of customer defections. Few companies track defections (otherwise known as *migration*) or invest in reducing them.

Companies should measure customer migration, and their goal should be customer retention. They must regularly evaluate and modify training programs, information systems, organizational structure, complaint handling procedures, hiring objectives, incentives, and even the company culture. Providing superior customer service is an effective strategy for increasing customer retention, which can lead to an increase in profits, because customers will beat a path to the company that provides superior customer service.

**(a) High Cost of Migration**  Failure to realize the high cost of losing customers stems in part from aggressive selling and marketing. In many companies, the work involved in keeping customers is seen as dull and tedious. Selling is what is truly exciting. Many companies view unhappy customers as chronic complainers who are not worth the effort required to satisfy them.

It is true that some customers are habitual complainers, but too often companies apply this label to every customer who complains. If this attitude permeates a company, dissatisfied customers will probably receive poor treatment and their problems will remain unaddressed.

Prospective and first-time customers usually are treated well during the selling courtship. Many companies aggressively pursue new customers, but these customers go right out the door if service is poor. They come in with great expectations but leave with disappointment, frustration, and possibly resentment.

**(b) Marketing: A Two-Part Process**  The marketing function should be viewed as a two-part process:

1. Getting customers.
2. Retaining customers.

The first part of the marketing process rarely has inadequate resources and seldom suffers from a lack of attention. Sales budgets, advertising campaigns, and promotional efforts usually take a significant percentage of a company's operating budget. However, retention marketing often has little or no budget at all. Research shows that, depending on the specific industry, it costs between five and seven times as much to get a new customer as it does to keep an existing one.

Most companies have little difficulty defending the significant costs of acquiring new customers. But what if the new customers are only replacements for dissatisfied customers? Such companies find themselves barely holding on to customers, or worse, they experience a net loss of customers. Companies that do strive to retain customers have return policies, customer complaint departments, and occasional customer mailings. But few companies engage in aggressive, well-constructed strategies of retention-oriented marketing that keep customers happy and mend relations with dissatisfied customers.

**(c) Moment of Truth**  Every point of contact a customer has with a company (whether by phone, in person, or by mail) is a point at which service is delivered—or not delivered. It is a point at which the customer forms one more impression and makes one more judgment about the company. Some call it the "moment of truth."

Nordstrom's, a department store, operates by the following maxim: "Listen to the customer; the customer is always right. Do anything to satisfy the customer." Every time a company fails to live up to a promise to its customers, it loses some credibility.

Advertising, public relations, architectural design, and other high-profile efforts may create favorable impressions. But the critical difference in customer retention usually occurs in less glamorous areas. For example, customers may be impressed by the behavior and appearance of employees, the way phones are answered, the clarity and accuracy of billings, or the overall promptness and reliability in handling complaints. "Little things" are important, and companies must be vigilant and consistent in their attention to detail. Such vigilance may require redefining the role of marketing, rearranging priorities, and reallocating budgets.

**(d) Obstacles to Superior Customer Service**   There are several obstacles to customer service that at one time or another affect most businesses.

*(i) Attitude That Customers Are Replaceable*   The days of monopolistic enterprises and taking customers for granted have long since passed away. Customers should be considered valuable assets that are obtained only through hard work and at considerable expense. Although employees are often relieved when disgruntled customers leave, this is an unfortunate attitude for any employee or business to have.

*(ii) Insensitive Managers*   The old expression that "no two people are alike" applies to both employees and customers. Problems develop when managers become insensitive to the characteristics or behavior of their employees and customers. Managing the human element is a considerable challenge in providing superior customer service.

Managers must continuously respond to changing situations. They must be able to make instantaneous decisions in an environment in which education, experience, skills, perceptions, values, and prejudices have a direct impact on transactions with employees and customers. Other concerns—such as divorce, financial trouble, or sick children—also affect employee–customer transactions. Given these human idiosyncrasies, companies must monitor, train, motivate, evaluate, and periodically retrain employees so that they are empowered to be of assistance to customers.

*(iii) Budgetary Problems*   Some companies do not properly fund efforts to improve customer service. As a result, they end up with inconsistent customer-service strategies and poor implementation of programs to improve customer service. In a highly competitive economy, budgetary constraints can drive away frustrated customers who may be told, for example, that there are not enough qualified people, or that there simply are not enough people to catch up on back orders. In many companies, the financial resources required to meet customer needs exist, but they are allocated elsewhere. Insufficient funding inherently devalues the importance of customer service in the minds of front-line employees.

*(iv) Lack of Strong Commitment*   In many cases, management lacks a strong commitment to superior customer service. Managers may claim to have a strong commitment, but in reality they pay only lip service to customer service. Unless management undertakes a full-scale effort and requires an intense commitment to superior customer service throughout the organization, the prospects of achieving superior customer service are seriously diminished.

*(v) Inconsistency*   Customers usually measure a product or service by the satisfaction they expect and subsequently receive. If a customer is sold a product or service that fails

to live up to its promises, dissatisfaction is the result. Customers who are oversold or promised undeliverable levels of satisfaction usually forget the salesperson and concentrate instead on the product or service involved and the company behind it. Thus, companies must strive for consistency in the delivery of products and services, in representations made about product and service characteristics, and in the professionalism of all employees who deal with customers.

*(vi) Lack of Listening*   Managers are typically concerned with the big picture, so they seldom have the time to get out and really listen to what customers need and think. Many managers are comfortable believing that if customers are not complaining, things must be going all right. But this can be a dangerous assumption. Managers must be available to both employees and customers. They must observe and listen purposefully and systematically. Most important, they must be open to discussion: They should not be defensive, closed-minded, or apprehensive about being proved incorrect.

*(vii) Inertia*   Computer systems, policy guides, and procedures often take on a life of their own in many companies. Customers usually feel frustrated when they are told, "I'm sorry, but our policy is . . . ," or "There is nothing I can do about it." In some companies, the computer systems are often handy excuses for mistakes. Although computer systems, policies, and procedures are important, they can stifle a company's primary mission—to sell and serve customers—if they are not kept in check. Companies that excel in providing superior customer service focus on the customer and strive diligently not to allow "the system" to interfere with what is best for the customer.

*(viii) Different Frames of Reference*   Words frequently used to describe customer service include "prompt," "reliable," "satisfaction," "courtesy," "professional," "timely," and "quality," along with such phrases as "quick response to customer complaints," "accuracy in billing," "prompt repairs," and "satisfaction guaranteed." For these words and phrases to have relevance, specific definitions, measurements, or other explicitly stated standards have to exist. For example, "quick response to customer complaints" might be defined to mean "within 24 hours," whereas "accuracy in billing" might mean that if errors are identified within seven days of receipt, a correction will be made. When definitions are clearly understood from the start, a company and its customers will have a common denominator for measuring the quality of service.

*(ix) Lack of Perspective*   Providing high-quality customer service is not a program that can be bought and paid for in a short time. High-quality customer service cannot be effectively implemented and sustained through memos, short-lived promotional efforts, or advertising campaigns designed to boost sales.

Management must view high-quality customer service as an ongoing process. The "tyranny of the urgent" often prevents managers from taking steps that will keep customers the company worked so hard to get.

**(e) How to Increase Customer Retention**   Just as there are frequently encountered obstacles to superior customer service, there are also several suggested ways to help a company successfully retain as many of your customers as possible.

*(i) Reliability*   Customers want consistent performance most of all. To be reliable, a company should strive for the following:

- Do what you say you are going to do.
- Do it when you say you will.
- Do it right the first time.

*(ii) Credibility*   Customers will go back to businesses that want to help them and have their best interests in mind. Customers do not want hidden agendas, fine print, hard-sell tactics, or extra charges. They want the products or services they buy to be free of danger, risk, and doubt.

*(iii) Responsiveness*   We live in a time of instant gratification. When customers want service, they usually want it immediately. Being responsive requires being available, accessible, and willing to help customers whenever they have a problem.

*(iv) Empathy*   Being empathetic means putting oneself in the position of a customer. Management must ask itself whether it would do business with the company. Every customer is unique and wants to be treated uniquely. To accomplish this, companies must ask the right questions, listen intently, and then design products or services to meet stated needs.

*(v) Select Front-Line Employees Carefully*   Companies oriented toward customer service should have customer-friendly people in front-line positions. Such positions are not for everybody. Great care should be exercised in selecting prospective employees based on their personality traits and other skills. A psychological consulting firm has singled out the following attributes as especially helpful for employees in front-line positions:

- An ability to make sound judgments in a stressful setting.
- A problem-solving orientation.
- A desire to be liked.
- A naturally optimistic outlook.

*(vi) Provide Sufficient Employee Training*   Customers want to be served by knowledgeable employees. Thus, employees should be well trained before interacting with customers. Employee training should not be viewed as a one-time entrance requirement. Regular training sessions are needed to keep employees updated on new policies and procedures, new product features and benefits, competition, customer needs, new programs, developments in other parts of the company, and core corporate goals.

*(vii) Create a Sense of Belonging*   Employees also need a sense of their company's mission and their role within the company. They need to receive encouragement to enhance their roles while also receiving recognition for contributions made. Regardless of the methods used by different companies, employee recognition is an important motivator and a fundamental tool for nurturing an environment committed to customer service.

*(viii) Avoid Premature Release of Products, Concepts, or Policies*   Taking a new product or service to market before it is ready, changing policies rapidly, or introducing a new computer system before all the bugs are worked out erode customer satisfaction levels. Companies must take great care not to sacrifice customers while trying to achieve progress. Customers want consistency and stability.

*(ix) Make Things Easy for the Customer*    Making things easy for the customer requires careful planning, coordination, and diligence. When companies do not work at these fundamentals, customer service can suffer. Following are ways to make things easier for customers:

- Install a toll-free number.
- Provide adequate incoming phone lines.
- Hire enough employees to answer phones quickly.
- Use business-reply mail (postage-paid).
- Implement easy refund and exchange procedures.
- Provide prompt and accurate information.
- Do not assume that the customers have extensive knowledge about a product or service.
- Speak and write in plain English. Do not use highly technical terms or company jargon.
- Debrief customers who leave the company for competitors.

*(x) If a Customer Leaves, Ask Why*    Whenever the company loses a customer, find out why. Few customers are more honest or candid than a dissatisfied customer.

## 1.3 INVESTING RESOURCES IN THE RIGHT PLACES

*A regionally based accounting firm has grown at a steady rate over a 10-year period. Some of the growth has been fueled by acquiring other firms in the region. The managing partner has been proud of the fact that the firm also has added new services. However, in the last two years, the firm's revenues have been relatively flat. To help assess the situation, the managing partner commissions an assessment of customer satisfaction.*

*The assessment shows that two-thirds of the new services offered are valued highly but that the clients are not very committed to the remaining one-third. With this information, the managing partner cuts the services that customers do not value (thus eliminating the corresponding overhead) and reallocates resources to support the services customers do value. As a result, the firm's revenues and quarterly profits have increased due to the reduction in overhead and expenses associated with cutting one-third of the new services.*

It is important that companies regularly assess their competitive positions. Such an assessment can help identify strengths and weaknesses vis-à-vis the competition, thereby enabling companies to focus on their strengths and eliminate weaknesses.

Few companies can effectively compete against all competitors on all fronts simultaneously. It is important, therefore, to identify key strategic points of difference so that a company can allocate its finite resources optimally. The key areas to evaluate include:

- Markets
- Customers and the products or services offered to them
- Personnel
- Operations, facilities, and technology
- Finances

To be valuable in the marketplace, companies must maximize the return on available and invested capital. They must regularly evaluate their allocation of resources to different areas.

**(a) Markets**  Many companies make decisions about critical components of their operations as if they were in a vacuum: They show little sensitivity to, or awareness of, what other companies are doing in the market. To be effective, they should be asking questions such as:

- What are the trends in the market?
- In which direction is the market headed?
- What do the customers want (versus what they need)?
- Is the company aware of the difference?
- What is the size of other competitors in the market?

To have strategic significance, terms or units of measure should be used that enable companies to compare themselves to competitors. Statistics regarding the number of employees or customers a competitor has may have a marketing impact. Other information—such as the amount of capital invested, asset base, profits, inventory levels, the number of inventory turns, the number of support personnel, and the number of sales representatives—can help a company determine the investment required to compete effectively and identify areas that may not be well served.

**(b) Customers and Products or Services Offered**  Why does a company offer the products or services it offers? Is there a rational process in place by which new products or services are added or deleted from a company's portfolio? Is there a threshold of revenue generation below which a product or service will no longer be carried or offered?

Too often companies offer products or services that management feels *should* be offered, or they continue to offer the products or services that they have historically offered, as opposed to what the market dictates. However, companies should periodically assess their offerings and determine whether customers and potential customers are aware of all the products or services in their portfolios.

Not long ago, a large, well-known law firm disclosed in a meeting that it had budgeted a significant sum toward practice development. Before launching the development campaign, the firm performed an assessment on existing clients to determine their awareness of the services offered. Much to the chagrin of the firm's partners, almost two-thirds of the clients used more than one law firm for their legal work. Further analysis revealed that none of those clients used other law firms because of dissatisfaction but, rather, because they did not realize all the other services available from the firm. Thus, the law firm realized that one of its biggest challenges was to increase the awareness of existing clients before spending significant funds on pursuing new clients.

In another case, a company offered 12 different kinds of services to its customers. Upon careful objective analysis of customer input, the company determined that the customers really had a viable interest in only 7 of the 12 services. At that point, the company had a choice to make: to pursue additional customers that may have an interest in the other services or drop the other services and the costs associated with offering them.

The key point in these examples is that by getting objective information from customers, both organizations could make decisions that enabled them to allocate re-

Dear Valued Client:

Our success at XYZ is built around our ability to meet the needs of our clients. Like any business, it is important that we ask ourselves the question, "How are we doing?"

We believe the best approach is to let our clients answer that question for us. By taking a few moments to complete this survey, you will help us evaluate our performance.

We have enclosed a postage-paid envelope for your convenience. To allow for timely processing, please return the questionnaire within seven days of receipt.

We appreciate your willingness to assist us. Thank you for taking the time to respond to our questions. We'll be listening.

Sincerely,

XYZ


Jane Doe

President


Please indicate your company's awareness of our products and services, utilization of our products and services (as well as products and services from other companies), and interest in the products or services. If you have used a particular product or service from our company, please also rate your level of satisfaction in the products or services. Additional space for comments on any or all of our products or services is provided at the bottom of this assessment.

A box that is not checked will be considered a "no" answer.

### Rate Our Product/Service Quality (where applicable)

| Products and Services | Aware of product or service | Have used this product or service from this company | Have used this product or service from another company | Have used this product or service | High | Medium | Low |
|---|---|---|---|---|---|---|---|
| Product or service A | Q | Q | Q | Q | H | M | L |
| Product or service B | Q | Q | Q | Q | H | M | L |
| Product or service C | Q | Q | Q | Q | H | M | L |
| And so on... | Q | Q | Q | Q | H | M | L |

Additional space for comments:

---

**Exhibit 1.1    Sample Survey of Customer Awareness, Utilization, and Interest in an Organization's Products or Services**

sources where they could generate the greatest return. Without this information, both organizations would have continued operating in a manner that presumed business as usual and thus consumed resources inefficiently. A well-designed customer questionnaire can prove helpful in determining the awareness, utilization, and interest levels of customers. Exhibit 1.1 provides a sample customer questionnaire.

**(c) Operations, Facilities, and Technology**    Companies should periodically assess competitive strategies utilized in terms of operations, facilities, and technology. Information concerning competitors in these key areas can provide important insight regarding their strategic direction. It is particularly helpful to consider how competitors compare in the following areas:

- Locations of branch offices, field offices, and the types of buildings used.
- Creative channels of distribution used.
- Databases, communication networks, and computers employed.
- Technology used downstream with customers, branch offices, field offices, and sales representatives.
- Facility management, overall appearance, and the integration of other offices or facilities.

Because many companies must increasingly compete based on how they allocate scarce capital, a company's ability to profitably compete will increasingly depend on the proper deployment and utilization of operational capabilities, facilities management, and technology. Customer input is a critically important tool in assessing these areas.

**(d) Financial Allocation Decisions**    Customer satisfaction information is helpful in allocating the *financing* and *operating* responsibilities needed to manage a company. Financing responsibilities pertain to how a company obtains the capital needed to provide for assets. Operating responsibilities relate to how a company uses those assets once they have been obtained.

*(i) Return on Total Assets*    One tool that is helpful in making financial allocation decisions is a calculation of the *return on total assets*. The formula for return on total assets can be used in assessing a product or service, overall financial performance, or the re-

---

$$\frac{\text{Net income} + [\text{Interest expense} \times (1 - \text{tax rate})]}{\text{Average total assets}} = \text{Return on total assets}$$

| | | |
|---|---|---|
| Net income | | $1,500,000 |
| Addition of interest expense | | |
| $625,000 × (1 − 0.40) | | 375,000 |
| | Total | $1,875,000 (1) |
| | | |
| Assets, beginning of year | | $26,720,000 |
| Assets, end of year | | $29,000,000 |
| | Total | $55,720,000 |

Average total assets: $55,720,000 / 2 = $27,860,000 **(2)**
Return on total assets: **(1)** / **(2)** = 6.7%

*Note:* This calculation can be done by product or service offering, division, office, the entire organization, etc.

---

**Exhibit 1.2    Return on Total Assets Formula**

---

Date: _____ Product/Service/Organization: _____

**Information required:**
Net income:
Interest expense:
Assets, beginning of year:
Assets, end of year:
Average total assets:

$$\frac{\text{Net income} + [\text{interest expense} \times (1 - \text{tax rate})]}{\text{Average total assets}} = \text{Return on total assets}$$

_____ + [ _____ $\times$ (1 – _____ )] = Return on total assets

---

**Exhibit 1.3    Return on Total Assets Worksheet**

turn on an individual customer. It is a measure of how well assets are utilized—that is, a measure of operating performance. Exhibit 1.2 and Exhibit 1.3 provide the formula and a worksheet for its calculation and analysis.

*(ii) Cost-Benefit Analysis*    Another financial measurement, *cost-benefit* analysis, can prove helpful in allocating a company's financial resources. By carefully measuring specific levels of customer satisfaction on a product-by-product or service-by-service basis, a company can analyze how each element is faring from a customer's perspective.

*(iii) Break-Even Analysis*    Break-even analysis is a tool that helps a company assess whether it should continue providing a particular product or service. Simply defined, the *break-even point* occurs when total sales revenue equals total expenses (whether variable or fixed). Break-even analysis helps a company determine whether to go forward in launching a new product or service or to continue offering an existing product or service.

The calculated break-even point, as illustrated in Exhibit 1.4, determines how many

---

Sales = Variable expenses + Fixed expenses + Profit

At the break-even point, profits will be zero. Thus, the break-even point can be calculated by finding the point where sales just equal the total of the variable expenses plus the fixed expenses.

**Example:**
Sales = Variable expenses + Fixed expenses + Profit
$250x = $150x + $35,000 + 0
100x = $35,000
x = 350 units

where:
x = break-even point in particular product or service units.
$250 = unit price
$150 = unit variable expenses
$35,000 = total fixed expenses

*Note:* This calculation can be done by product or service offering, division, office, the entire organization, etc.

---

**Exhibit 1.4    Break-Even Formula**

units (e.g., products, services, engagements, memberships, patients, or clients) must be successfully engaged for a company at least to cover its costs. While reviewing the numbers derived from a break-even analysis to assess the reasonableness or probability of attaining a particular profit level, a company can factor in valuable customer-based information gleaned from an assessment of awareness, utilization, and interest to aid in the process of determining whether such levels are also realistic in light of customer satisfaction.

## 1.4 PLANNING FOR THE FUTURE

*Although they compete in one of the most cyclical industries anywhere, Alex and his associates always seem to be well organized, in control, and leaders in sales and profitability. When asked to explain his relative calmness and that of his associates, Alex responds that it is because of an untiring commitment to planning the firm's direction—where it has been and where it wants to go—given the dynamics of the marketplace.*

Planning for the future requires a thorough and realistic understanding of existing products, services, markets, margins, profits, return on allocated capital, and availability and skills of employees. When contemplating a company's specific mission, management must have a clear understanding of how well the company is doing today. As has been demonstrated, customer input and assessment of satisfaction can play an enormously important role in setting objectives.

**(a) Prudent Planning**    Prudent planning helps a company, regardless of its size, focus on where it wants to be three to five years in the future. Too often, managers are focused only on short-term needs and prospects, largely because of their immediacy. As a result, long-term problems and opportunities are deferred or given only slight attention. Management must distinguish between current operating challenges and longer-term goals and plans. Some executives search for ways to increase the size, efficiency, and profitability of their company's operations. But if the forecasted performance of existing operations fails to produce expectations of profitable growth, many of them build on the operations that presently exist and accept the status quo.

**(b) Strategic Planning**    Some executives are not satisfied with nominal growth rates into the future. Empowered with well-founded, customer-based information (e.g., measures of customer satisfaction; information about awareness and utilization of products and services; customer wants, needs, expectations; perceived strengths and weaknesses; and suggestions for improvement), they stretch the forecasts and establish new and challenging standards of performance for the future.

Increasingly, companies realize the importance of strategic planning. Several large companies go to the extreme of considering a range of plans that cover simultaneous possibilities across a wide set of assumptions. However, this involved approach usually requires a highly structured strategic planning process and a large planning staff. Although this type of intensive approach has considerable benefits, few companies can afford such a commitment. Smaller companies or larger companies without extensive strategic planning resources can use a simplified approach more effectively. The underlying assumption with this approach is that a person or group can only commit part-time efforts to the strategic planning process. Exhibit 1.5 graphically represents this ten-step process.

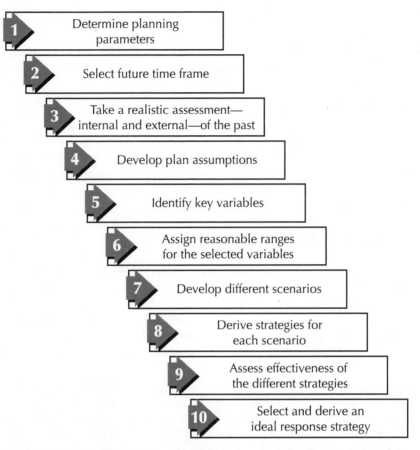

1. Determine planning parameters

2. Select future time frame

3. Take a realistic assessment—internal and external—of the past

4. Develop plan assumptions

5. Identify key variables

6. Assign reasonable ranges for the selected variables

7. Develop different scenarios

8. Derive strategies for each scenario

9. Assess effectiveness of the different strategies

10. Select and derive an ideal response strategy

*Note:* Objectively obtained customer-based data play a critical role in each step of the process. Strategic planning will be seriously flawed if it does not draw extensively on customer satisfaction data when looking at an organization historically and planning for it prospectively.

**Exhibit 1.5    Ten Steps for Business Strategic Planning**

**(c) Call to Action**    A management consultant recently wrote, "Future historians may well describe the 1980s and possibly the 1990s as the era of customer sovereignty. Perhaps 'customer rebellion' is more accurate."[1] To a large extent, which organizations will prosper in today's economy will depend on which organizations recognize the "customer rebellion" and make the preparations necessary to provide superior customer service.

Every organization must vigorously assess the status and quality of its relationships with both external customers (existing, potential, and past) and internal customers (employees). Where do we stand? What do we need to improve? How can we improve? In doing so, remember the following points:

- Customers, potential customers, and former customers perceive value in their own terms. If an organization wants to meet their needs, it must always look at products and services from *their* perspective.

- Customers, potential customers, and former customers think that an organization's reason for being in business is to meet *their* needs.
- If an organization sincerely desires to deal successfully with dissatisfied customers, employees must be empowered to focus on saving the customer, not the sale.
- An organization must strive to provide dissatisfied customers with a positive reason for dealing with the organization again.
- In all likelihood, an organization's employees will not treat customers or potential customers any better than they themselves are treated by the organization.
- Input from customers, potential customers, or past customers is invaluable. An organization should actively seek, appreciate, and review this input.
- The entire process by which an organization creates and delivers its products and services should exhibit superior customer service and support the creation of high levels of customer satisfaction.

Regardless of the size of an organization, it is increasingly difficult to compete primarily on the basis of price or product. In many cases, product differentiation is imperceptible. Thus, in the burgeoning battle for the customer, the key is usually not product superiority (or at least not for long) but service. The quality of service provided has rapidly become the standard by which organizations are judged. Thus, customer satisfaction—and continual improvement in customer satisfaction—has become a primary indication of sustainability.

In a world of increasing complexity and automation, the successful organization must find the means by which it can operate efficiently and profitably while maintaining a commitment to manage with integrity, compassion, intelligence, competitiveness, and an unwavering commitment to providing superior customer service and generating high levels of customer satisfaction. Although not on the balance sheet, customers are the greatest asset that any organization has. They need to be treated as treasured, long-term investments that, if properly nurtured and cultivated, will provide significant dividends.

How does a company know how it is doing with its customers, its prospective customers, and its employees? Are they satisfied? Do they perceive that the company has a strong commitment to providing superior service? The only way to know for certain is to ask—candidly, objectively, and following a good methodology. As Yogi Berra said so well, "The only way to begin is to begin."

Regardless of the type or size of an organization, management can seize the competitive advantage, provide superior customer service, and build high levels of customer satisfaction.

## NOTE

1. *The Arthur Andersen Guide to Talking With Your Customers: What They Will Tell You About Your Business When You Ask the Right Questions* (Chicago: Dearborn Financial Publishing, 1993).

# CHAPTER 2

# VALUE-CHAIN ANALYSIS AND MANAGEMENT FOR COMPETITIVE ADVANTAGE

## Lawrence P. Carr
**Babson College**

**2.1 INTRODUCTION**    This chapter explains the use of *value chain analysis,* at both the industry and firm levels, to evaluate a company's strategy for gaining competitive advantage. The chapter describes the fundamentals of applying value-chain thinking in strategy formulation or the development of management control systems.

*Firm value chains* provide managers a view of their business processes. A firm's value chain starts with the basic elements or components (inputs) of the company's products or services; it then continues through the company's business processes all the way to the satisfaction of final customers after a sale. This view of a firm's value chain is, in turn, embedded into an industry value chain, which traces customer value from basic raw materials to end customers through various intermediary steps, some of which are often controlled by other firms.

An industry value chain is a series of firm value chains that traces the flow of products or services to the ultimate consumers. From the viewpoint of strategic costs, the use of value chains centers on determining the *costs* and *assets involved* in each step of the value chain, then comparing those costs and assets with perceived customer values. If a mismatch is identified, it indicates an opportunity for improvement—or an opportunity for a competitor.

After establishing the basics of firm and industry value chains, this chapter demonstrates how to map a process for a firm value chain, then how to position the firm's process within its industry value chain. The chapter then shows how to add cost and asset structures to each section of the two value chain types. Finally, the chapter discusses how to analyze value and opportunity within the two value chains.

**2.2 VALUE CHAIN APPROACH**    Porter[1] expanded and popularized the value chain approach to strategic planning. He argued that a firm's profitability is a function of:

- The attractiveness of the firm's industry.
- The firm's relative position in its industry.

A firm creates value when buyers of its products or services are willing to pay more than the costs incurred by the firm. Therefore, there are two major forces to consider:

1. The firm's process for delivering value (i.e., the *firm value chain*).
2. The firm's positioning in the industry (i.e., the *industry value chain*).

*Competitive advantage* is created by the performance of each specific activity or process step. Today, much more intermingling of primary and support activities tends to occur in order to improve process flow. The value-creating steps have these activities of the firm embedded in the process. The power of information technology and electronic data interchange combine to help companies manage and coordinate the value-added activities in their processes.

**(a) Strategy**    Every function in a firm contributes in a unique way to the firm's chosen strategy. Areas such as research and development, design, and information technology are key components of a firm's value-creation system. These activities do not occur in a direct linear process flow; rather, they feed and support the firm's process. Competencies and distinctive abilities in these areas often provide the source of differentiation and competitive advantage.

McKinsey and Company, the well-known consulting firm, uses a similar concept—*business systems,* in which each function of a firm (e.g., design, manufacturing, and marketing) is compared with the corresponding function of competitors. McKinsey searches for ways to refine business systems to gain competitive advantage for clients.

**(b) Internal Tasks and Activities**    In a firm value chain, the integration, flow, and cost of sequential internal tasks or activities play critical roles in creating value. To analyze these tasks or activities requires having a process perspective rather than a focus on traditional, functional structures.

For example, good product design can build customer interest and loyalty, but it can also significantly lower manufacturing costs by reducing the number of parts required or the complexity of a product.

The coordination and cross-functional integration of a firm's activities in a delivery system is of vital importance. Value is created through better management of the linkages between process steps. For example, managers go to great lengths to ensure that marketing and manufacturing activities are synchronized for a new product launch. Literature, sales tools, samples, and available products all need to be accessible at the same time. Many consider the firm value chain a value system in which there are both direct and indirect process functions, often with different time phases that work together to create value.

**(c) Adding Value from a Customer's Perspective**    A firm value chain analysis helps a company assess those activities that add value (in the eyes of the customer) and determine which activities might distinguish the firm from its competitors. The firm searches for those activities that create proprietary access to a scarce resource (e.g., patents or distribution networks) or create a cost advantage over other firms (e.g., economies of scale, higher quality, greater productivity, or superior service).

**(d) Linkages with Suppliers and Buyers**    Another focus of a firm's value chain is the external linkages between the firm and its suppliers and buyers. These linkages and relationships describe the way in which a firm's value chain is related to the value chains of its suppliers and customers.

A firm seeks joint optimization and coordination to find a "win–win" situation with both its suppliers (on one end of the value chain) and its customers (on the other end). To sustain a competitive advantage, however, the firm must expand its understanding of the value chain beyond immediate suppliers and customers: The firm must determine how value is created and delivered for the industry as a whole. It is not enough, in other words, for a firm to restrict its focus solely to that portion of the value chain in which it competes. To understand demand, for example, a firm must consider the final customer in the industry chain, because the final customer sets demand rates.

**(e) Formulating and Executing Strategy**    Understanding industry value chain structures is critical to the formulation and execution of strategy. Some observers have compared industry value chains to biological food chains. The ultimate end user or customer is at one end of the industry value chain, while raw material processors are at the other end. In between are all the levels at which value is created and (ultimately) delivered to the end user.

Industry value chains include intermediate levels such as:

- Component supply
- Manufacturing
- Assembly
- Test
- Sales
- Distribution
- Storage
- Retail sales

A firm may compete in all or only a portion of its industry value chain, whereas competitors may control totally different portions of the industry value chain.

For example, consider the personal computer (PC) industry value chain shown in Exhibit 2.1. It begins "upstream" with the various suppliers of components to PC manufacturing and assembly companies. The industry value chain then follows the physical process "downstream" through the industry to the delivery and (theoretically, at least) delight of end users.

**(f) Distribution Channels**    There are three possible channels at the distribution level:

1. Directly to customers (e.g., Dell Computer Corporation).
2. Through retail outlets (e.g., CompUSA).
3. Through *value-added resellers* (VARs), who package PCs into a system.

Different competitors operate in different portions of the industry value chain. Competitor *A* (e.g., IBM in the PC industry) competes at all levels of the industry value chain, whereas Competitor *B* (e.g., Hewlett-Packard, Compaq, and others) starts at assembly and test. Competitor *C* (e.g., AMS Tech) starts at distribution, purchasing the PC from contract manufacturers.

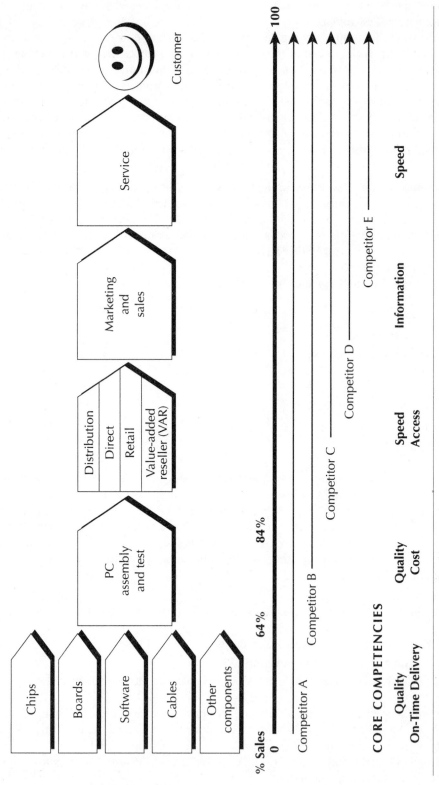

**Exhibit 2.1  Personal Computer Industry Value Chain**

Other players in the industry include Competitor *D*, which performs only marketing and sales functions, whereas Competitor *E* provides only service. Some VARs provide contract services; others furnish application software and service.

Competitors *A*, *B*, *C*, *D*, and *E* all have their own firm value chains, and each is differently positioned within the overall industry value chain. A particular firm's position within the industry value chain offers different sets of opportunities and requires different sets of competencies.

**(g) Attractiveness of an Industry** In addition to looking at the industry process (i.e., understanding industry value chains and positioning), one must also consider the forces that make an industry attractive—in other words, what lets a company earn attractive returns on its investments. Above all, a firm must understand how profitability is attained in an industry, given the costs and assets invested.

In the PC industry, for example, Microsoft must concentrate on marketing and distribution, while Compaq and Dell must concentrate on asset management. Starting with 100 percent of sales at the end user, each sales dollar can be distributed backward through the industry value chain. Ultimately, the goal is to determine where in the industry value chain the best potential return on assets exists.

**(h) Core Competencies** Exhibit 2.1 shows the generic core process steps for an industry. These different steps suggest the diversity of competencies necessary to compete at every stage of the industry value chain. A full understanding of the industry value chain requires identifying where forward or backward integration might enhance performance.

Industry value chains closely resemble biological food chains. Actions in one sector of the industry have business ramifications in other sectors, whether upstream or downstream in the industry value chain. To continue the PC industry illustration, a major change in distribution methods—such as Dell's direct marketing of PCs to end users—has a profound influence on the component manufacturers who supply both Dell and retailers of other PCs.

**2.3 MAPPING VALUE CHAINS** Organizing industry and firm knowledge along value chains gives managers great insight into competitive positions. The process of mapping value chains can be informal (e.g., when it is based mainly on management's knowledge and experience) or formal and detailed (e.g., when it is based on extensive industry and benchmark studies).

The following sections explain the basic steps in mapping value chains for both industry and firm value chains.

**(a) Industry Value Chains** To map industry value chains, a company must take several steps.

*(i) Identify the Process Flow* Follow the process flow from basic raw material inputs through all the intermediate levels of the various process stages (e.g., component manufacturing, subassembly, assembly, and test). Then continue to follow the process through logistics, distribution channels, and retail segments to the final consumer. Note that the flow is similar in service industries, where the "inputs" are people and specific skills. The "process" involves seeking a solution where other service specialists may be used. The "output" is service rendered by solving a customer problem. In both service

and manufacturing, this may involve several handoffs between firms that operate in different segments of the industry value chain. It is important to understand the "value proposition" of the ultimate customer: This force pulls the product or service through the industry value chain. For this reason, it is sometimes easier to start with the end customer, then to work upstream through all the industry stages.

*(ii) Group Activities*    Group activities into logical sets or building blocks. Each activity group should represent a business segment in which revenues are generated, costs incurred, and some level of investment made. Follow the product or service as it passes from one industry participant to another. Each activity set (which should represent a significant percentage of the final sales and final costs) should have the potential for creating differentiation. It may have different cost behaviors or drivers, or it may be performed differently by the competition.

*(iii) Identify Cost Percentages*    Identify the percentage of cost and the percentage of final sales revenue for each level or segment in the industry.

*(iv) Identify Process Stages*    Determine the process stages or levels in which each competitor actively participates. An industry map should resemble the one shown for the PC industry in Exhibit 2.1. The map of an industry value chain ends with the final customer. The starting (or upstream) point should be established at a common base level that is shared by all industry competitors.

*(v) Identify Sources of Industry Data*    Industry data can be obtained from many sources. Talking with final customers provides a good upstream overview. Trade publications and industry newsletters furnish an industry viewpoint that often provides financial information, information about cost structures, and also competitive information. In the plastics business, for example, *Plastics News*, *Modern Plastics*, and *Chemical Week* offer excellent information about the plastics industry.

   Many firms have websites that offer excellent product, firm, and industry information. Many financial institutions and consulting firms also conduct extensive industry research and publish reports. For example, Morgan Stanley recently produced an informative industry report about GE and other *Fortune* 500 firms.

**(b) Firm Value Chains**    To map firm value chains, management should follow several steps.

*(i) Identify the Process Flow*    Management must follow the company's process flow from purchasing and inbound logistics through all of the firm's processes and functional steps that ultimately lead to sales to the customer. In a service business, the value chain consists of inputs, processes, and outputs. In a consulting business, for example, the "inputs" are people, the "process" is solving problems, and the "outputs" are solutions and implementation plans. Processes are usually varied and sometimes customized for specific customers. Nevertheless, certain core skills usually apply to solving an array of customer problems. Exhibit 2.1 serves as a conceptual guide to the various steps.

*(ii) Identify Cost Percentages*    Managers should identify the percentage of costs and assets in each step of the process They should also estimate the percentage of sales rev-

enue represented by each step. Data required for this step can be obtained from the company's accounting information, though some manipulation of the data is usually required to divide the costs into process steps. Make reasonable judgments based on input from process managers. Also, management must analyze both product and period costs to assign the appropriate costs to each of the process steps.

*(iii) Identify Linkages*    In both industry and firm value chains, linkages are critical to the process flow. In a firm value chain, coordination and communication between functions enhance the throughput of the product or service process of the firm. In an industry value chain, the buying and selling relationships between firms and segments of firms in the industry are essential determinants of competitiveness.

Note that industry value chains are simply a set of linked firm value chains. For both firm and industry value chains, management should concentrate on those activities that create value for the end user of the product. This will lead to a better understanding of how to develop sustainable competitive advantage.

**2.4 BUILDING COST STRUCTURES**    The mixture and relationship of four key ingredients are considered in value chain analysis:

1. Process and position
2. Cost structure
3. Level of investments
4. Perceived customer value (as reflected by price)

These ingredients of the value chain "recipe" can change, given competitor actions and changes in market conditions.

The previous section outlined how to establish the process flow and position, the first "ingredient" listed here. The next step is to map the costs and investments related to the activities in the value chain (the second and third "ingredients"). The relative cost of activities can create the basis for distinctive capabilities. The key is to create a firm value chain that gives an advantage in the industry value chain.

In a firm value chain, a distinct cost advantage can arise from purchasing power or efficient logistical networks (e.g., Wal-Mart). A highly efficient and superior sales force can also make a difference in financial results (e.g., Levis). In the industry value chain, direct sales to customers by skipping retail and logistical activities can lead to differentiation and superior performance (e.g., Dell Computers).

**(a) Mapping Costs and Investments**    One significant task in preparing a firm value chain is to map the costs and investments in fixed and working capital into the firm's process activities or steps. Unfortunately, accounting records are not kept based on these activities or steps. However, by using available financial data and applying reason and judgment, managers can estimate cost and investment levels. Usually such an estimate requires close analysis of the firm's income statement, which can be broken down into individual costs and investments (in terms of both dollar amounts and relative percentages). Cost reports and department budgets can aid in reshaping the accounting data to fit the firm value chain. The object is to determine the cost and investments for each step of the firm's critical activities.

Developing cost and investment estimates for industry value chains is more difficult.

It is rare that one company will operate at all levels of its industry and also make the data available. Nevertheless, a good place to start is by collecting and analyzing financial reports of industry competitors.

As a first approximation, cost managers should consider the final sale to end users as 100 percent. They should move backwards, up the stream, through the industry value chain and estimate how the 100 percent is divided among the various levels of the industry value chain. They must start by identifying external markets embedded in the industry value chain. This is where some firms create a market. Then, cost managers should construct an estimated income statement for the firms at each industry value chain process level. They must pay close attention to the margins made at each level of the value chain and match them to published financial reports to verify their estimates. Profitability and cost structures can vary widely among the process levels within an industry. If players at different levels of the industry value chain are part of the same corporation, cost managers should consider the transfer price as market price. For example, when one GE unit sells to another GE unit, a transfer price of cost plus a reasonable return for the seller is used as the market price.

There is an art to this type of strategic analysis, especially when determining which levels in the industry value chain can be meaningfully decoupled. The best economic test is to determine whether some firm can make a business at a specific level of the industry value chain. Calculating the costs and investment levels is also problematic. Cost managers should study the financial reports and determine the competitor's financial footprint at the various industry value chain levels. They must remember to include only the financial data from the business results for the industry under study. They must make reasonable approximations and construct an income statement and using ratios estimate the level of assets needed to support the business activity. Assessing the industry value chain is a meaningful exercise and can be quite instructive. It forces managers to ask how their activities add value in the industry and how their costs and level of assets compare to other players.

Good industry value chain analysis requires good information. It is not just the financial and strategic information of the cost manager's own firm. Cost managers need to collect and monitor competitors' financial reports and keep a pulse on their market moves. Plus, one should monitor the total industry looking for changes in the market. Competitive intelligence is key to value chain analysis.

**(b) Determining Value**    The fundamental idea in value chain analysis is that a product or service gains value (and cost) as it passes through the various steps in the process chain. This can be within the firm (firm value chain) or through the industry (industry value chain). Value is defined as the amount (price) buyers are willing to pay for a product or service. Total revenue is a measure reflecting the price for a unit of goods or services commanded in the market place. Remember the market ultimately determines price, not the cost structure. The goal for firms is to make profit or deliver value to customers that exceed their costs. The generic strategic position is to have efficiencies in process to be the low-cost producer or to have sufficient product differentiation to command a premium price for the activities.

It is essential, therefore, for a firm to know which of its activities are responsible for generating competitive advantage. It is also important to understand at what level in the industry value chain the highest potential for creating value exists. For what activities are the end customers willing to pay a premium and for what activities are the customers indifferent and only want the lowest cost? This section first talks about determining value in the firm value chain and then addresses value creation in the industry value chain.

*(i) Firm Value Chain*    Exhibit 2.1 shows the value activities divided into two broad types: primary and support activities. Primary activities are those involved in the physical creation and delivery of the product. Support activities assist the prime activities in delivering value to the customer. Value is created as inputs are converted to outputs. The customer purchases the outputs at a price that ideally exceeds the cost of the firm's activities. Determining value requires an isolation of each activity and a customer assessment of the value of that specific activity. Management should walk backward from the customer sale through the value chain and determine where value is created in the eyes of the customer. The perceived customer value can then be compared to the cost of the activity to determine the competitive advantage. It is important to take a process view. Management *must* deemphasize the functional structure and follow the business process from input to output.

It is important to note this is not a value-added exercise where selling price less the cost of purchased raw materials is used. Value chain analysis requires external analysis verification. Value can be obtained by exploiting linkages within the firm and the linkages with the firm's suppliers and customers. Firms must focus on cost drivers and examine how various inputs influence the behavior of costs.

The firm needs to understand the cost drivers that regulate each activity. An organization should examine possibilities to build sustainable competitive advantage by controlling cost drivers better than competitors or by reconfiguring the value chain. By driving costs down, firms create better value for their customers. Assessment of value at the firm level requires comparing the customer perceived value and estimated costs of activities of the competition in the industry. Advantage is defined relative to the other players in the industry.

*(ii) Industry Value Chain*    Exhibit 2.1 shows the breakdown in relative activities of the delivery from the upstream basic inputs of raw material to the downstream end customer. The value chain contains processes with levels where value is created and linked to form the industry value chain. Each level of activity incurs costs, generates revenue, and uses assets. Profits, the reflection of value captured, are not evenly distributed across the industry value chain. The set of competitors at each level is different, and each industry value chain level is linked through procurement and sales activities. The bargaining relationships with the buyers and suppliers determine how margins are divided between levels within an industry. A company's ability to differentiate itself reflects the contribution of each value activity toward fulfilling a buyer's need. Determining value requires a view of the full industry from upstream to downstream; comparing customer perceived value to the cost of activities.

To ascertain value, cost managers should work backward through the industry steps from the customer to the raw material. They should estimate the margins and cost at each industry value chain level and compare them to the perceived customer value of the industry value chain end user. Exhibit 2.1 showed the sales of a PC at 100 percent value at 100 percent price (e.g., $2,500). Based on industry analysis, we estimated that the component suppliers represented 64 percent ($1,600) of the price, the assembly and test 20 percent ($500), and distribution plus sales and service as 16 percent ($400) of the price.

Now, compare this breakdown to the value the customers place at each level of industry. Interestingly, the customers categorize PCs based on quality reputation and consider the quality attribute as a requirement. Differentiation and perceived customer value come from the distribution, sales, and service level in the industry. This level is a small part of the total cost, but it creates the most customer value. In some circumstances, the end user may value service the most and consider all other activities as the same commodity or just a PC "box." This is one of the reasons why Dell's move to sell direct to the customer makes a great deal of sense from an industry value chain point of view.

At each level of an industry value chain, there are sets of firms competing. It is important to understand the proper core competencies needed at each level. Efficiency, or superior cost position, is not always sufficient. One needs to determine whether the firm is effective as it competes in an industry. One needs to determine whether the firm has developed the correct set of core competencies that are valued by the customer and then ascertain whether these core competencies are different from those of the competitors.

**2.5 IDENTIFYING OPPORTUNITIES**    Comparing customer value propositions and value chain structures and investments can expose some interesting opportunities. These opportunities are grouped into five categories.

1. *Fashion a major reconstruction of the industry value chain.* A critical assessment of the existing industry value chain can lead to a new way to satisfy the customer while enhancing the firm's core competencies or building new capabilities. Dell, in a very competitive and volatile industry, has achieved outstanding growth and financial returns (69 percent per year growth and an average 43 percent return on equity over the past five years). Dell used a direct selling strategy coupled with a build-to-order process, which was a significant departure from the traditional PC industry value chain. Dell correctly compared customer value to cost structure and determined that inventory, distribution, and retail costs added little or no value but substantial cost for the customers. Its build-to-order and direct sale process has altered the industry value chain and caused firms to rethink their firm value chain.

2. *Enhance the current value chain position by making the firm run lean and fast.* Controlling costs drivers better than the competition requires an evaluation of each value activity. Managers must consider whether they can reduce the cost in activities while holding value (revenues) constant, or whether they can increase revenue in an activity holding costs constant. GE has adopted a Six Sigma program to systematically work out the costs of poor quality (process errors). GE expects the benefit over the first five years of the program to net $5 billion in savings.

3. *Reevaluate the firm's investment intensity at the various levels of the industry value chain.* The challenge to managers is to operate in the industry value chain with an efficient use of assets. Economic value added and return-on-investment calculations highlight the importance of asset management where managers are willing to pay higher cost for lower asset levels. They are seeking to reduce assets required by activities while creating the same value for the customer. On the other hand, firms willingly invest in the value creation portion of the value chain to improve competitive advantage. Firms tend to keep value-creating processes and outsource the non–value-adding but necessary processes.

4. *Build greater differentiation through an enhanced role in the buyer's value chain.* Improved customer value is created when buyers use the enhanced differentiated

products to create their own competitive advantage. Firms are seeking to offer special, custom products to their customers. Information technology has allowed a greater degree of product differentiation and specialization for little relative cost. For example, American Express travel service is able to customize its travel management programs to meet the specific needs of its corporate customers. They use computer models and low fare search routines to track and manage the costs and arrangements of each of its clients on a monthly basis. This has resulted in a profitable business service for American Express.

**5.** *Expand the value chain position through acquisition, joint venture, or other alliances.* The linkages in industry value chains are critical in managing value and the value opportunities differ by industry level. By expanding linkages, firms can participate at higher opportunity levels through some form of partnering within the industry value chain. They are seeking to make the value chains flow better with improved financial returns. A good example is the telecommunications industry, which recently has seen a number of varying partnerships or acquisitions designed to improve a particular firm's position in the industry value chain.

**2.6 VALUE CHAIN DYNAMICS**    Both types of value chains are constantly in a state of flux. Value chain analysis is best performed on a regular basis. The dynamic nature of some industries, such as computers and telecommunications, requires close monitoring. All industries, mature or emerging, are perpetually in a dynamic state. The rates of change are different and some changes are easier to notice. Most firms concentrate their analysis on their immediate market. The challenge is to expand the horizon to include the total industry. Global developments in country economies and relative currency valuations can quickly alter the source of competitive advantage or create new sources for competition. The current business trend toward acquisitions and partnering affects many industries, such as banking, financial services, and entertainment.

At the same time, firms regularly reinvent themselves using reengineering and other techniques to evaluate their processes. Quality programs such as GE's Six Sigma is having a profound effect on the various firm value chains by seeking to understand how customer value is created. This includes a focus on improving the GE customer value and eliminating the costs associated with waste and non–value-added activities. More firms are taking a process focus and working to eliminate non–value-added activities and improve efficiency or the leanness of their business processes. Increasingly, managers are becoming more sophisticated and aware of value chain thinking. Many firms are challenging the current state of their firm value chain and seeking to find a better route to the customer through the industry value chain. Thus, competitor moves are becoming more bold and wise in the search for competitive advantage.

Value chain analysis is conceptually straightforward. It requires a sound understanding of the company and the full industry. One should be comfortable with making reasonable estimates of market and financial result. Good value chain analysis is driven by good information and industry intelligence. Use the power of information technology and keep the business radar operating at short and long range all the time.

## NOTE

1. M. E. Porter, *Competitive Strategy* (New York: Free Press, 1980); M. E. Porter, *Competitive Advantage* (New York: Free Press, 1985).

## SUGGESTED READINGS

Porter, M. E. *Competitive Strategy.* New York: Free Press, 1980.

———. *Competitive Advantage.* New York: Free Press, 1985.

Rayport, J., and J. Sviokia. "Exploring the Virtual Value Chain." *Harvard Business Review* (November–December 1995): 75–85.

Shank, J. "Strategic Cost Management: The Value Chain Perspective." *Journal of Management Accounting Research* (Fall 1992): 179–197.

———. *Strategic Cost Management.* New York: Free Press, 1993.

Shank, J., and V. Govindarajan. *Strategic Cost Analysis.* Homewood, IL: Irwin, 1989.

# CHAPTER 3

# TARGET COSTING

## Nicholas J. Fessler
**The University of Memphis**
## Joseph Fisher
**Indiana University**

**3.1 INTRODUCTION**    Target costing is a market-driven cost management technique that can be used by businesses early in a product's life cycle to maximize overall product profitability. The purpose of this chapter is to acquaint readers with target costing and to suggest how financial managers might contribute to the target costing process.

Historically, most cost-reduction and cost-control efforts have focused on the production stage of the product life cycle. Budgeting and standard cost systems are prime examples of this type of cost control, which focuses on production processes. The chief concern at the product planning and design stages has been product specifications and scheduling, with little attention paid to product cost. Unfortunately, most production capabilities and costs are set during production planning and design and are, for the most part, relatively fixed once production begins. Estimates vary, but approximately 80 percent of a product's life-cycle costs are designed into a product and committed once the first unit of product is manufactured. Thus, efforts to reduce a product's costs once production begins may be of limited effectiveness.

By ignoring costs during a product's design stage, managers are effectively allowing design engineers—who typically have little motivation to care about the cost implications of their designs—to determine the bulk of a product's cost. Indeed, it is not uncommon for engineers to include in their product designs "pet" features that are "nice to have" but not cost-effective features actually needed by the firm's customers. The addition of such features unnecessarily increases the production cost of a product.

Lack of concern about product cost during the product planning stages can reduce profitability. There may be far greater opportunity for cost reduction early in the product life cycle (during the planning and design stages) than there is later in the life cycle (during the production stage). Thus, effective efforts to control cost must focus on the design phase of the product life cycle.

Strategy theory has suggested that a company can create a strategic advantage either by differentiating its product from competitors' products or by establishing a position of cost leadership.[1] In the past, companies that were first to market with a new product could charge a premium to early users of the product and could thus expect to have some time during which they could make the product profitable. But the competitive environment has changed. Low-cost imitators can now bring products to market so rapidly that most companies have little time to develop brand loyalty, let alone recover development costs. Innovations that are rapidly copied by competitors cannot lead to a sustainable competitive advantage.

The long-term financial success of any business depends on whether its prices exceed its costs by enough to yield a satisfactory return to its stakeholders and to finance continued growth. In a highly competitive climate, target costing is a tool that companies can use to help ensure that the firm's financial goals are achieved.

Target costing, then, is a systematic process that begins in the product planning stage for reducing product costs and meeting product profit targets. The Japanese are generally credited with the first consistent use of target costing. Toyota is often credited with inventing it in the mid-1960s.[2] Since then, Japanese companies such as Toyota, Nissan, Sony, NEC, Olympus, Daihatsu, and Matsushita—along with many U.S. and European companies—have used target costing with great success. Target costing is most common in companies that have discrete manufacturing processes, relatively short product life cycles, and regular model changes. For example, in 1992, target costing was being used extensively in Japan by companies in the automotive industry (100 percent of the companies in that industry), the electrical industry (88.5 percent of the companies), the machinery industry (82.8 percent of the companies), and the precision equipment industry (75 percent of the companies).[3]

Fundamentally, target costing is a planning tool and a constructive way to establish product prices and determine product costs. Conceptually, all businesses can benefit from such forethought. For example, service-oriented companies incur costs to deliver services to customers, so target costing can be used to manage the costs of their "products." Similarly, target costing can be used to facilitate discussions about whether a new service should be offered by a company.

**3.2 TARGET COST DEFINITIONS**  Most definitions of target costing describe a process that occurs in a competitive market environment in which cost minimization is an important component of profitability. Cost planning, cost management, and cost reduction must necessarily occur early in the design and development process of the product to minimize the total life-cycle cost of the product. Cost control must occur early in the product life cycle in a target costing framework.

Although a generally accepted definition of target costing does not yet exist, examples of target costing definitions include:

- Sakurai says, "Target costing can be defined as a cost management tool for reducing the overall cost of a product over its entire life cycle with the help of the production, engineering, research and design, marketing, and accounting departments."[4]
- Cooper suggests, simply, "The purpose of target costing is to identify the production cost for a proposed product, such that the product, when sold, generates the desired profit margin."[5]
- Horváth writes on behalf of the Consortium for Advanced Manufacturing-International (CAM-I), "Target costing is a set of management methods and tools to drive the cost and activity goals in design and planning for new products, to supply a basis for control in the subsequent operations phase, and to ensure that those products reach given life cycle profitability targets."[6]

- Kato argues, "In reality, target costing is not a cost quantification technique, but rather a complete cost reduction program, starting even before the first drawings of the product have been prepared. It is an approach aimed at reducing the cost of new products throughout their life cycle, while meeting consumer requirements in terms of quality and reliability among others, examining all conceivable ideas relating to cost reduction at the planning, development and prototyping stage. Target costing is not a simple cost reduction technique, but a complete, strategic profit management system."[7]

These definitions illustrate a variety of viewpoints regarding target costing, but there are common themes. Taken together, the definitions have three things in common:

1. They emphasize the importance of target price and profit determination before calculating the target cost.
2. They emphasize the importance of early cost planning to reduce costs incurred over the product's entire life cycle.
3. They indicate that a cross-functional team is needed to successfully implement target costing.

Fisher contrasted a target costing sequence as recommended in the previous definitions with a traditional costing sequence.[8]

The lefthand side of Exhibit 3.1 shows the typical steps in determining a target cost for a product. First, a company develops a preliminary product concept. Then the company determines a target price and product volume based on the perceived value to the customer. A product's target profitability is derived from a long-range profit plan, which in many Japanese companies is based on a return-on-sales metric.

Given estimated sales and a desired profit margin, calculating total (or per-unit) profitability is straightforward. The price derived by the perceived value of the product to the customer minus the long-range profit equals the target, or allowable, cost. Employees responsible for product design are given the target cost as one of the design

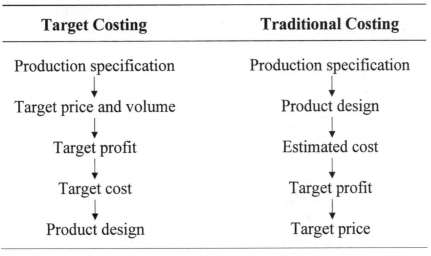

| Target Costing | Traditional Costing |
|:---:|:---:|
| Production specification | Production specification |
| ↓ | ↓ |
| Target price and volume | Product design |
| ↓ | ↓ |
| Target profit | Estimated cost |
| ↓ | ↓ |
| Target cost | Target profit |
| ↓ | ↓ |
| Product design | Target price |

**Exhibit 3.1    Sequence of Price and Cost Determination**

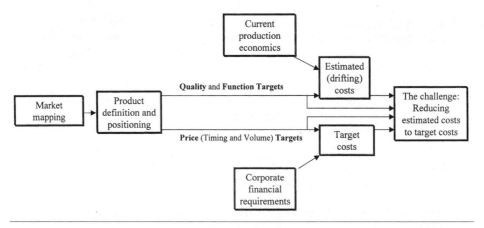

**Exhibit 3.2    Target Costing Process.** *Source:* **Adapted from R. Cooper and B. W. Chew, "Control Tomorrow's Costs Through Today's Designs,"** *Harvard Business Review* **(January–February 1996).**

specifications of the product. Note that cost information plays a minimal role in determining the target price or target profit.

Target costing contrasts markedly with the sequence shown on the righthand side of Exhibit 3.1 as the traditional costing method. Like target costing, traditional costing begins with product specification, but product design follows immediately after product specification. Product cost is not a major factor in product design, and production costs are estimated only after product design occurs. Instead, the focus at the design stage is on product specifications and product scheduling. Price is set by means of a markup over estimated cost to return—or so the company hopes—a satisfactory profit. The major flaw in the traditional costing method is the relatively late consideration of product cost in the product life cycle.

These points are elaborated in the sections that follow. Exhibit 3.2, which is the basis for further discussion, shows the typical steps in a target costing process.

As Exhibit 3.2 shows, *market mapping* (i.e., the process of defining the product that customers want) leads to function and price targets before considering product costs. The outcome of the target costing process is the reduction of a product's estimated costs so that they meet the product's target cost.

**(a) Price-Based Cost Targets**    Cooper and Chew argue that the logic of target costing is simple.[9] A company starts by predicting the marketplace of tomorrow. In doing so, the company attempts to draw a "map" of customer segments and target the most attractive segments. The company then focuses on these attractive market segments to determine what level of quality and function will succeed within each segment and what price customers will be willing to pay for the product (i.e., the target price). Then the company designs the product and the associated production process that will enable it to achieve its desired profit at the target price. "In effect, the company reasons backward from customers' needs and willingness to pay instead of following the flawed but common practice of cost-plus pricing. Target costing ensures that success with the customers will yield economic success for the company."[10]

Most simply, target costing is a process that changes the order of the traditional methods used to determine product price. A target selling price is established *first,*

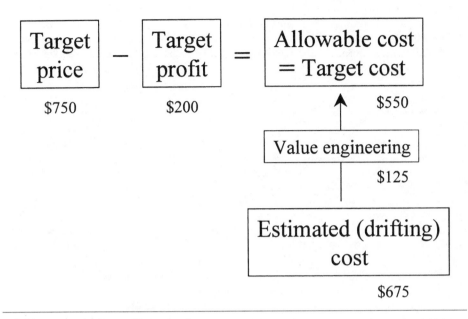

**Exhibit 3.3    Target Costing Example**

based on the perceived value of the product to the customer, then a target profit or profit margin is determined. As Yukato Kato notes: "The target profit, for products in particular, must be derived from corporate strategic profit planning and be based on medium-term profit planning (3 to 5 years). It is then necessary to imagine the future product portfolio. Allocation of a target profit to each product in the portfolio is a critical activity in its own right."[11]

The target cost is thus the cost that allows a company to realize its target profit when selling the product at its target price. Consequently, "target cost" is sometimes described as the "allowable cost," or the cost that allows the company to earn its desired profit. The estimated cost of a product is what it would cost to produce the product using existing technology and production processes. The estimated cost to produce the product typically is higher than the target cost because market forces require a company to lower its cost or lose profits. Product redesign and value engineering are used to reduce the estimated cost to the target cost. Some refer to the estimated cost as the "drifting cost" because, through target costing, the company is working to reduce this cost to the allowable (target) cost.[12]

Exhibit 3.3 provides a numerical example of a simple target cost calculation. The target price of the hypothetical product is $750, the hypothetical target profit is $200, and the target cost of the product can be calculated as $550. The estimated (drifting) cost of the product is $675. Cost reduction efforts by the target costing team focus on reducing the estimated cost of the product by $125 so that the product can be sold at a profit the company deems acceptable.

**(b) Early Cost Planning**    A major benefit of target costing is that that it forces the company to plan its prices, profits, and costs much earlier than is typical for most companies. Target costing requires that considerable cost calculations be made before a product is introduced. In a manufacturing company, for example, once the target cost is

| Production Component | Current Product Cost | + | Cost of New Features | = | Estimated Cost | − | Target Cost | = | Desired Cost Reduction |
|---|---|---|---|---|---|---|---|---|---|
| Body | $A_1$ | | $B_1$ | | $C_1$ | | $D_1$ | | $E_1$ |
| Batteries | $A_2$ | | $B_2$ | | $C_2$ | | $D_2$ | | $E_2$ |
| Machine mechanism | $A_3$ | | $B_3$ | | $C_3$ | | $D_3$ | | $E_3$ |
| Direct labor | $A_4$ | | $B_4$ | | $C_4$ | | $D_4$ | | $E_4$ |
| Indirect labor | $A_5$ | | $B_5$ | | $C_5$ | | $D_5$ | | $E_5$ |
| Packing materials | $A_6$ | | $B_6$ | | $C_6$ | | $D_6$ | | $E_6$ |
| . | . | | . | | . | | . | | . |
| . | . | | . | | . | | . | | . |
| . | . | | . | | . | | . | | . |
| Depreciation | $A_{t-2}$ | | $B_{t-2}$ | | $C_{t-2}$ | | $D_{t-2}$ | | $E_{t-2}$ |
| General overhead | $A_{t-1}$ | | $B_{t-1}$ | | $C_{t-1}$ | | $D_{t-1}$ | | $E_{t-1}$ |
| Total | $A_t$ | | $B_t$ | | $C_t$ | | $D_t$ | | $E_t$ |

**Exhibit 3.4    Target Cost Calculation Sheet. *Source:* Adapted from J. Fisher, "Implementing Target Costing," *Journal of Cost Management* (Summer 1995): 50–59.**

established, the cost must be allocated to the product's parts and subassemblies. Companies should allocate target costs to *components* for a new product similar in design to previously manufactured products, but they should allocate target costs to *functional areas* for new, innovative products.[13] A functional allocation method attempts to allocate target cost to product characteristics that directly satisfy customer requirements.

*(i) Component Allocation Method*    Exhibit 3.4 presents an example of a *component* allocation method. The exhibit shows an abbreviated version of the target cost form used by the Japanese company Matsushita Electric. This form is completed formally at three different points during the product life cycle:

1. During product planning.
2. Before ordering product molds and dies.
3. Just before full-scale production begins.

The five columns with numerical data in Exhibit 3.4 represent the reconciliation of estimated product cost to target cost. The rows in Exhibit 3.4 represent a detailed list of component costs.

The first column in Exhibit 3.4 contains actual product costs (A) from the current product. Typically, an existing product is replaced by a new product. By using the current product as the starting point for cost estimation, Matsushita tailors the target cost for incremental product change (i.e., model changes) rather than revolutionary products. The advantages of using the cost of an existing product as the starting point for estimated cost include:

- Ease of calculation
- Reduced calculation cost
- Decreased need for detailed product specifications

The second column estimates the cost changes due to new product specifications and features (B). Typically, these are cost increases that are estimated jointly by the engineering department and the cost management department. Increases in cost can be compared with the value added by the new product features to determine whether the new features can be cost justified. The sum of columns A and B equals the estimated cost for the new product and is shown in column C.

The total target cost, $D_t$, is calculated before determining the target cost for each component. The next step is to spread the total target cost to the various component categories. The difference between columns C and D represents the cost reduction needed to reach the target cost, as shown in column E. Column E is thus the cost reduction that value engineering must provide to achieve target cost. The total in column E, $E_t$ (i.e., the difference between target and estimated cost), is spread to the various production components under the direction of the chief engineer, who works in tandem with the cost management department to determine where costs can be reduced. A target cost is generally set so that it cannot be reached without extra effort.

The rows in Exhibit 3.4 are production component categories. At Matsushita, these product categories represent subassemblies of the new product, labor, and overhead. The rows begin with direct materials.

Consider a cassette recorder, for example: The direct materials in a cassette recorder may include the body, batteries, machine mechanism, wiring, and other components. These materials are followed by direct labor, indirect labor, and packing materials.

The last two rows of Exhibit 3.4 represent fixed charges for depreciation and other overhead items. Because target costing focuses on production costs, further divisional and corporate allocations are not considered.

*(ii) Functional Allocation Method*    Some argue that the component method of assigning costs illustrated in Exhibit 3.4 is most applicable when the new product is similar in design to previously manufactured products.[14] The component method allocates a target cost to component "blocks," which typically consist of subassemblies. But the component method may not work as well for innovative products, because designers may become material oriented rather than function oriented.

For innovative products, target cost should be allocated to *functional* areas of the new product. A functional allocation method attempts to allocate target cost to product characteristics ("functions") that directly satisfy customer requirements. A functional area allocation differs from the component method by having functional areas rather than components listed in the lefthand column.

*(iii) Value Engineering*    Value engineering, or *value analysis*, is the primary means by which a company can reduce the estimated cost to the target cost. Value engineering is a process whereby each component of a product is examined to determine how costs can be reduced while maintaining the overall functionality, quality, and performance of the product. For instance, value engineering would determine whether it is possible to reduce the number of parts used in a product or to simplify the production process. Examples of changes based on value engineering include:

- Changing the quality or grade of the materials
- Reducing the number of components in a part
- Using a common component instead of a unique or specialized component
- Changing the method of production[15]

Companies that use target costing ideas have implemented their systems in different ways, and it would be a mistake to conclude that there is one "right" way to install target costing. How a particular company uses target costing is likely to vary by the nature of the product being produced and the business environment in which the company operates.

Although target costing is implemented at the design stage, its benefits accrue throughout a product's entire life cycle. Target costing is not a daily or monthly production cost control technique; rather it is a cost planning tool that addresses cost considerations through product specifications and product design. However, the successful use of target costing requires participation from a wide variety of organizational functions.

**(c) Cross-Functional Involvement**    Target costing is a cross-functional company exercise. As Horváth states: "Target costing is essentially a multi-functional activity. A basic requirement is the use of interdisciplinary teams."[16] The finance organization alone cannot implement target costing. Target costing requires the simultaneous involvement of marketing, technical, and economic skills. It is important to have an organizational link between the market research team and the other departments involved in the development of the product. Similarly, it is important that design engineers communicate with managers and employees familiar with the production process, because "[t]he best designers are superfluous if they do not integrate production techniques in full. Design engineers frequently lack concrete experience of production. They must therefore work in close collaboration with the production departments."[17]

Cross-functional involvement requires good communication. At the beginning of the target costing process, a cross-functional team must be assembled to address the inevitable trade-offs that will occur whenever a company tries to develop a product and establish a target cost for it. This team should work together from the concept stage until production begins. The first decisions made by the team can be the most decisive—and the most difficult to reverse. Paradoxically, the beginning of the target costing process is when the information available is most limited, yet that is precisely when cooperation and decision making are most important.

Generally, a target cost team includes people from the following functions:

- Production technology
- Design
- Purchasing
- Development
- Marketing
- Manufacturing
- Product planning
- Finance or accounting

In many companies, the team has matrix-management responsibility to a product manager responsible for the overall development of the product.

**3.3 TARGET COST PROCESS (IMPLEMENTATION)**  In many companies there are at least three distinct points in a product life cycle at which a target cost is formally calculated and evaluated:

1. The product planning stage.
2. The product design stage.
3. The preproduction stage.[18]

While the conceptual basis of target costing is fairly straightforward, the implementation and operation of target costing can be both time-consuming and difficult. Exhibit 3.5 shows the typical sequence of product development using target costing.

*Product planning*   • Product concept
                     • Product specifications
                     • Development schedule
                     • Target price and volume
                     • Target profit and target cost
                     • Estimated (drifting) cost

*Product design*       • Target cost allocated to components
                       • Concept design
                       • Basic design
                       • Detail design
                       • Order product molds and dies

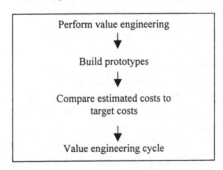

*Preproduction*        • Set product price
                       • Set up manufacturing process
                       • Experimental runs
                       • Compare estimated cost to target cost

*Production*           • Cost maintenance phase
                       • *Kaizen* costing if necessary

**Exhibit 3.5  Sequence of Product Development and Target Costing.** *Source:* Adapted from J. Fisher, "Implementing Target Costing," *Journal of Cost Management* (Summer 1995): 50–59.

For each stage identified in Exhibit 3.5, the following sections provide a general description of how a target cost is calculated and evaluated in a typical company.

**(a) Product Planning**    Target costing begins with a concept for a new product. The chief engineer develops a proposal with help from a new product committee, which includes employees from different functional areas. In Japanese companies, the members of the committee have typically rotated through several functional departments before being named to the new product committee.[19]

A new product proposal includes:

- Product concept
- Product specifications
- Development schedules
- Features and options

In preparing a proposal, the committee evaluates whether the product specifications meet customer requirements. Information on customer requirements can be obtained from:

- Customer surveys
- Market forecasts
- Research studies
- Comparisons with competitors
- "Best in class" analysis

After a basic product concept and specifications are approved, the chief engineer's committee works with a divisional manager to determine product price, desired profitability, and volume. In many companies, the basic concept for the product is the chief engineer's responsibility, whereas the target profit is primarily the responsibility of the divisional general manager.

The divisional general manager sets a target price based on input from the sales and marketing department. The major input in determining product price is the perceived value to the customer. Again, product cost has little impact on product price at this stage in product development. After a target price is set, the divisional focus is on determining desired or target profitability. In many Japanese companies a return-on-sales metric is used. Finally, after the basic product concept, target price, target profit, and target volume are decided, the target cost can be calculated.

The chief engineer is also responsible for estimating product cost. This estimate is usually based on the current production model. The difference between estimated and target cost represents the *cost-reduction target*. Consequently, the estimated cost and target cost are calculated in separate departments in the organization. The planning stage culminates in an approved plan that includes these elements:

- Product specifications
- Target price
- Profit and volume
- Target cost

Prior research has shown that the planning stage can range from 10 to 36 months, depending on company and industry characteristics.

*(i) Target Costing Tools for Product Planning*     For many companies, target costing is an extremely valuable—perhaps the most important—tool in reducing product cost. For companies that have effectively used target costing, it is a mind-set and a management philosophy about prices and costs and about when and how decisions regarding price and cost should be made.

Target costing is not a simple toolbox. It is an ambitious management approach of strategic proportions. However, a number of tools are often used in tandem with target costing processes. The first three—market assessment, competitive analysis, and reverse engineering—focus on information and events outside the company, whereas the fourth—activity-based costing—focuses on information inside the company.

*(ii) Market Assessment*     Target costing begins with an assessment of the market. Market assessment is a tool that companies can use to answer the question, "What do our customers want?" The answer to this question must be known before a company can satisfy its customers with a proposed new product.

A company may want to ask customers what they like and do not like about its product. *Surveys* of customers and prospective customers can provide useful information. *Focus groups* can enable representatives of the company to interact with customers and to learn what they like and dislike about existing products, what they want in new products, and how much they would pay for the presence or absence of various features. This information is essential in setting a target price.

For example, when Olympus performs market research to learn what camera models to sell and at what prices, it uses questionnaires, group interviews, interviews at fashion centers, and interviews with photographers. In addition, Olympus benchmarks itself not only against other camera manufacturers but also against the makers of CD players and Walkman-type products. Olympus realizes that it is competing against all these products for the discretionary funds of its customers. It is not competing just against camera manufacturers but against the manufacturers of all kinds of consumer gadgets.[20]

*(iii) Competitive Analysis*     Understanding the competitors in an industry can be very important to a company's survival, particularly when an individual competitor or a group of competitors is increasing market share, selling its product at a lower price, or applying competitive pressure in some other way.

*Competitive analysis* may include assigning a team to study competitors and sending representatives to visit a competitors' production plants. For example, when Olympus performs competitive analysis, it examines such areas as competitors' capabilities, likely price points, and filed patents.[21] And, as noted previously, Olympus defines its competition rather loosely as any company that produces a product that might be purchased instead of an Olympus camera. Knowledge of a competitor's practices can stimulate improvement and change in one's own company. Competitive analysis can also be helpful in product specification and setting the target price.

*(iv) Reverse Engineering*     Another name for reverse engineering is *teardown analysis,*[22] which involves acquiring competitor's products and then disassembling them to learn about:

- Materials used to manufacture their products.
- The design of products.
- The likely manufacturing processes for the products.
- The quality of the product.
- Estimates of how much the products will cost.

When used effectively, reverse engineering can give a company valuable knowledge about its competitors' products. Learning about competitors' products can provide a target costing team with ideas for its own value-engineering and cost-reduction efforts.

*(v) Activity-Based Costing*   Activity-based costing (ABC) is a tool companies can use to better understand product costs. (Part Four of this book contains five chapters about various aspects of ABC.) The greatest strength of ABC lies in its ability to trace fixed costs to processes and products—a chief weakness of traditional costing systems. As production facilities become more automated, more production costs are fixed in the short run, so it becomes more important than ever that the firm's cost accounting system be capable of accurately assigning fixed costs to products.

As Horváth states: "As indirect costs become increasingly important their management has to be included in the target costing process. Activity-based costing is an ideal instrument to meet this requirement. It can support target costing in determining the drifting [estimated] cost, calculating the product costs under strategic considerations and in supporting the reduction of overhead costs."[23]

ABC can provide valuable support—through more accurate cost information—to target costing efforts. *Product cost analysis* is the process that estimates two things:

1. What it would cost to produce the proposed new product under existing process characteristics.
2. How costs would change given the implementation of new production process characteristics.

Accurate cost estimation of both the target cost and the estimated cost is essential to the success of target costing, because its entire architecture is based on the comparison of estimated cost to target cost and on the implementation of actions designed to eliminate the difference between them. The reliability and relevance of cost information are therefore essential for the effective use of target costing techniques.

As Douglas Webster has observed, "Precise cost data is essential. Costs compiled by conventional accounting methods provide a poor answer to the needs of designers and managers."[24] ABC can provide the precise cost data that are critical to the success of target costing efforts.

**(b) Product Design**   In the product design stage, product specifications from the product planning stage are used to engineer a working prototype. Target costing techniques in the product design stage focus on value engineering, which proposes design and production methods for attaining the target cost. Though value engineering can be applied at any time during production, Toyota and Matsushita, for example, exert most of their value engineering efforts during the product design phase.[25]

The evaluation of target cost attainment is possible only with a timely flow of product cost estimates, and prototypes are an essential component in estimating product cost. Cost reductions are incorporated into product design and tested by producing prototypes. This phase includes concept design, basic design, and detail design. *Concept design* formulates the preliminary design based on the design specifications determined in production planning. *Basic* and *detail design* refine the basic concept into a product that can be manufactured. Throughout the design stage, estimated and target costs are compared. The designers are instructed not to proceed with a design without achieving the target cost reduction at each design point. This stage culminates with a working prototype.

**(c) Preproduction**  The preproduction—or manufacturing preparation stage—consists of configuring the assembly line and performing experimental runs. The target cost is typically calculated one final time in preproduction before a selling price is fixed. Because the prototypes are produced with the actual production process, actual costs can be estimated with great precision. If the estimated cost is greater than the target cost, the value engineering department must again make changes in the product or manufacturing process to achieve the target cost. Only after the target cost can be achieved is the new model approved for production.

**(d) Production**  Once production begins, formal target costing ends; the start of production signals the beginning of the *cost maintenance* phase. Because there are multiple checks on a target cost in the product planning and design stages, the target cost is typically achieved. For many companies, a standard cost system is the chief form of cost control in the maintenance stage. Nonetheless, target costing continues to be important during production for two reasons:

1. Standards used in the standard cost system are based on the target cost numbers.
2. Actual costs from an existing product are the starting point for estimating costs for the next generation of products.

Therefore, the standard cost system is tied directly to the target cost numbers previously calculated and feeds forward into the next product generation.

**3.4 ROLE OF THE FINANCIAL (ACCOUNTING) MANAGER**  Financial managers are essential to implementing target costing. A financial manager should take an active role as a business partner with other areas of the organization that participate in the target costing effort. Like any effort to change and improve organizational processes, target costing requires the full support of management and the support and cooperation of all areas of the company involved in the target costing team.

In Japanese companies, a member of the accounting and finance organization (hereafter a "financial manager") is on the cross-functional target cost team. Financial managers are particularly skilled at gathering, analyzing, and reporting cost information—information that is critical to the success of any target costing effort. The participation of financial managers improves the reliability of the financial information and adds credibility to the financial implications of any decisions the team makes during the target costing process. Cost information is the glue that holds together all stages of the target costing process, so financial managers should be involved at each step.

**(a) Establishing Target Prices**  The first step of the target costing process is to establish a target price. The marketing organization must help to assess the market and determine the value of the proposed product to the customer. Competing products should be evaluated and their prices noted. Financial managers can help the team estimate competitors' production costs. In addition, the team must evaluate the customers' cost-benefit trade-offs about different features of the product. Before a final target price is established by the team, strategic considerations must be considered. For example, is the company attempting to gain market share with this product, trying to maximize short-term profitability, or something else? Financial managers are qualified to perform the cost-volume-profit analysis that can help the team decide on a target price, taking into consideration the proposed product's position in the market relative to competing products and their prices.

**(b) Determining Target Profit**    The second step of the target costing process is determining the target profit. The business understanding and analytical skills of financial managers will again prove valuable as members of the team distill overall organizational financial goals and apply them to the proposed product.

Financial managers can access information unavailable to others in an organization to help establish profit goals and determine how much profit a proposed product should contribute to the overall profits of the company. Different products have different levels of profitability, so it must be decided how much is required for *this* particular product. Some products require high profits to recover the cost of investments to develop and produce them whereas other products cannot be as profitable because market competition limits the price flexibility of their manufacturers.

**(c) Determining Target Cost**    The third step of the target costing process is to determine the target cost for the proposed product. The estimated cost of producing a proposed product is an important comparison to the target cost. Financial managers can help estimate how much it would cost to produce a proposed product given the product specifications and manufacturing processes currently used by the company. By using an ABC system, financial managers can more easily identify the cost of direct materials, direct labor, overhead, and nonmanufacturing costs (e.g., freight charges and product-specific sales costs) associated with a proposed product. If the company does not have an ABC system in place, financial managers can help implement one. All too often, companies' existing cost accounting systems are inadequate for determining the level of cost detail required by target costing. In addition, financial managers can facilitate breaking down the allowable cost for each of the components and parts used to make a product.

A financial manager is the expert on accounting systems for the target costing team, so a financial manager can help to establish both the target cost and the estimated cost of the proposed product and its components. Financial information is key when the team undertakes the value engineering process and explores the trade-offs between different product designs, manufacturing processes, and make-versus-buy decisions to reduce the estimated cost to the target cost. The financial manager on the team can help estimate the cost impact of any given combination of choices and record progress that is made toward achieving the target cost.

Only when the target cost is achieved should production begin. When production begins, the actual costs of the product (and its parts and components) must be collected and recorded by the financial manager, so management and the target costing team can monitor any variances between the target cost and the actual cost. This analysis can also direct further cost-reduction efforts by the company and enable the success of those efforts to be monitored. Finally, current cost information recorded and analyzed by the financial manager can be useful to future target costing efforts.

**3.5 SUMMARY**    Target costing is a management control technique based on the proposition that most production costs are determined before production ever begins. Therefore, production costs can also be managed—and thus reduced—most effectively before production ever begins. The central notion of target costing is that the future selling price for a given product will be set by the marketplace. The profit that a given product needs to earn is determined by the company's strategy, including information about rate and type of growth, funding, and marketing and sales strategy. Cost can then be calculated and viewed as a constraint that must be achieved if the company is to meet its strategic objectives. Target costing requires companies to consider cost and price issues during the product design stage of the product life cycle. A cross-functional team is essential. The use of target costing should increase in importance as companies become more automated, as costs are determined earlier in the product life cycle, and as competition becomes more intense.

# NOTES

1. For example, M. E. Porter, *Competitive Strategy: Techniques for Analyzing Industries and Competitors* (New York: Free Press, 1980).

2. M. Tanaka, "Cost Planning and Control Systems in the Design Phase of a New Product." In *Japanese Management Accounting: A World Class Approach to Profit Management,* ed. Y. Monden and M. Sakurai (Cambridge, MA: Productivity Press, 1990); T. Tanaka, "Target Costing at Toyota," *Journal of Cost Management* Vol. 7 (1993): pp. 4–11.

3. P. Horváth, *Target Costing: State of the Art Report* (Arlington, TX: Computer-Aided Manufacturing International, 1993).

4. M. Sakurai, "Target Costing and How to Use It," *Journal of Cost Management* (Summer 1989): 39–50.

5. R. Cooper et al., *Implementing Activity-Based Cost Management* (Montvale, NJ: The Institute of Management Accountants, 1992).

6. Horváth, op. cit., p. 2.

7. Y. Kato, *Target Costing Support Systems: Lessons from Leading Japanese Companies, Management Accounting Research,* Vol. 4 (1993).

8. J. Fisher, "Implementing Target Costing," *Journal of Cost Management* (Summer 1995): 50–59.

9. R. Cooper and W. B. Chew, "Control Tomorrow's Costs Through Today's Designs," *Harvard Business Review* (January–February 1996): 88–97.

10. Cooper and Chew, op. cit., pp. 88–89.

11. Kato, op. cit.

12. Horváth, op. cit.

13. M. Tanaka, op. cit.

14. M. Tanaka, op. cit.

15. R. W. Hilton, *Managerial Accounting* (4th ed.) (New York: Irwin/McGraw-Hill, 1999).

16. Horváth, op. cit., p. 5.

17. T. Tanaka, op. cit.

18. Fisher, op. cit.

19. Fisher, op. cit.

20. Cooper and Chew, op. cit.

21.  Cooper and Chew, op. cit.

22.  Howell, op. cit.

23.  Horváth, op. cit., p. 13.

24.  D. W. Webster, "Activity-Based Costing Facilitates Concurrent Engineering," *Concurrent Engineering* (1992).

25.  Fisher, op. cit.

## SUGGESTED READINGS

Cooper, R., and W. B. Chew. "Control Tomorrow's Costs Through Today's Designs." *Harvard Business Review* (January–February 1996): 88–97.

Fisher, J. "Implementing Target Costing." *Journal of Cost Management* (Summer 1995): 50–59.

Sakurai, M. "Target Costing and How to Use It." *Journal of Cost Management* (Summer 1989): 39–50.

# CHAPTER 4

# NEW PRODUCT DEVELOPMENT

**Manash Ray***

**Lehigh University**

**4.1 INTRODUCTION**   It is recognized that decisions made at the product design phase cause a high proportion of manufacturing costs to be committed, yet cost management for the new product development process has not received the attention it deserves. This stems partly from the complexity of the process and the fact that development teams stay focused solely on attaining target specifications (product performance attributes) and meeting time-to-market deadlines. The changing operating environment and strategic decisions related to technology choice, manufacturing location, and timing of new product introductions create additional pressures. However, managing the new product development process with attention to downstream processes can yield substantial benefits to manufacturing companies.

This chapter discusses issues and tools related to managing new product development. Although the term "cost management" is used throughout the text, note that cost, quality, and time are all required and interrelated metrics that need to be managed throughout the process.

**(a) Integrated Product Development**   Manufacturing companies are currently recognizing the potential integrative role of *integrated product development* (IPD). A well-implemented IPD process:

- Recognizes the impact of product development decisions on other parts of the value chain.
- Includes management processes that enable such assessments.
- Utilizes innovative tools in the areas of cost, quality, cycle time, and information management to help make decisions and realize gains across the value chain.

**(b) Key Themes**   Accordingly, this chapter has the following four elements as its key themes:

1. Role of product development in the extended enterprise.
2. Product development goals and performance assessment.

---

* The author wishes to acknowledge the Summer Research Support received from the College of Business and Economics at Lehigh University.

3. Tools for managing new product development and implementation guidelines.
4. Prescriptions to manufacturing executives regarding prioritization of initiatives and practical approaches to deployment of tools.

**4.2 NEW PRODUCT DEVELOPMENT IN THE EXTENDED ENTERPRISE**    New product development usually spans elements of the company's value chain, which includes research and development (R&D), design, and engineering. Depending on the nature of the industry and the firm, the R&D function may be deployed to develop a combination of the following outputs:

- Technology
- Products
- Process technologies

Until recently, R&D, design, and engineering functions were focused inward (i.e., they were engaged in activities specific to the individual company).

**(a) Extended Enterprises**    Market forces have recently forced companies to rethink this firm-specific strategy. Increasingly, companies collaborate to develop enabling technologies (e.g., for microchips and operating systems), design new products, and deliver them using shared resources.

Today, we have industry value chains that compete against one another. These industry value chains are closely integrated and include design partners, several tiers of suppliers, alternative delivery-channel allies (e.g., retail, Internet, Federal Express, or UPS), customers, and their customers. This chain that links a company's suppliers and its customers has been referred to as the "extended enterprise" or the "interprise."[1]

The *extended enterprise* has emerged as a solution for the new realities of the market. Shortened life cycles, high rates of technological obsolescence, short windows of opportunity, and high investment requirements for developing and deploying new technologies and processes have combined to force companies to pool their resources so that they can compete through this extended enterprise. Yet another driver of change has been the emphasis on customized products, which forces companies to seek alliance partners in design, manufacturing, and delivery.

**(b) Virtual Organizations**    One form of such alliances has been referred to as the virtual organization.[2] Given the market realities, the operational solution often adopted is to form *virtual organizations* by partnering with other companies (sometimes including even competitors) to take advantage of emerging market opportunities that cannot be addressed by one company alone.

A virtual organization is a specific project-based alliance among two or more companies with a specific operational objective of developing or delivering a product or service. Virtual organizations are formed to enable companies to accelerate product development, access new markets, develop customized products, and add value to products and services. This project-based federation of corporate teams and the inherent uncertainty about financial arrangements distinguishes a virtual organization from *mergers and acquisitions* and more routine *strategic alliances*. A virtual organization is a subset of strategic alliances in that it represents one possible configuration of alliances that are strategic in nature but involve integrated, intercorporate operation.

New product development can no longer be considered in the context of a single company. Whether it is strategic alliances, mergers and acquisitions, a virtual organization, or a regular channel alliance, new product development will span multiple organizations at both the design and delivery ends of the value chain. For example, product development may need to consider several factors:

- Menus customers will choose from over the Internet
- Information management system used to schedule production
- Types of storage or packaging requirements for outbound logistics
- Electronic commerce partners

**(c) Applications in Service Industries**    Note that the concept of the extended enterprise and its implications for new product development apply to nonmanufacturing companies as well. In the financial services area, credit card transactions that appear seamless to the consumer are orchestrated by an apparatus that is actually a configuration of different corporate partners enabled by *information technology* (IT). The development of data warehouses, imaging systems, and enterprise integration systems have enabled partnerships in the financial services arena that have facilitated niche marketing, PC banking, and on-line trading.

Ray and Beidleman, while investigating the feasibility of mass customization in financial services, provided many examples of such practices already at work.[3] Bank One, for example, is a financial services company that made use of a partnering arrangement to design its TRIUMPH software system for processing credit card transactions. Bank One entered into collaborative arrangements with Arthur Andersen to develop TRIUMPH. The system includes regional databases, image processing, and expert systems that enabled the development of target marketing strategies. Results from the initiative included:

- Accelerated new product development
- Successful implementation of targeted marketing strategies
- Development of new markets and business opportunities

Similarly, Intuit, Inc., developed an on-line financial service, "Investor Insight," to provide tailored, on-line investment management for individual portfolios. The company provides a daily, customized newsletter with details of all items relevant to the individual. Intuit has recently established partnerships with Bank of Boston, American Express Co., First National Bank of Chicago, and Smith Barney.

Capital One is yet another financial services company that has used alliances to its benefit. Formed in 1994 as an independent company (Credit Card Division of Signet/Bank of Virginia), it views itself as being in the information business. Capital One has mastered the processing of credit evaluation and credit extension business. Using large databases, Capital One conducts tests that help identify the best set of product characteristics to enable the customization of products at the individual account level. Capital One has formed alliances with a targeted group of issuers of credit cards and is part of a virtual organization that is invisible to the consumer.

**(d) Extended Manufacturing Enterprises**    In the manufacturing arena, recent examples of extended enterprises include the following:

- *Sony and Toshiba.* Collaboration on making a central processing unit (CPU) for the next generation of PlayStation games.
- *IBM and Dell.* Formation of a technology pact.
- *IBM and Caldera Systems.* Collaborative agreement to recruit systems integrators and work closely with third-party companies to help speed up a wide range of IBM-based solutions for Caldera's OpenLinux operating system.
- *Motorola and MIT Media Lab.* Joint development of "smart appliances."
- *AT&T.* Provision of a suite of communication services by linking the capabilities of many different companies.
- *AT&T and NBC.* Alliance to distribute NBC broadcast, cable, and newer digital services over AT&T's cable network.

**(e) Role of Information Technology**    IT is an important factor in new product development. This aspect of new product development comes into play because of interoperability requirements for partners in the alliance as well as the emphasis on customized products and services.

David Anderson[4] provides several examples of such "mass customization" and the use of enabling IT components. Levi Strauss & Co., which now offers the Personal Pair™ jeans to its customers, had to manage the following options and outcomes when entering the mass customization market:

- Number of manufacturable sizes increased from 40 to more than 4,000.
- Five additional options on color or finish.
- Enabling PC-based technology developed by Custom Clothing Technology Corp.
- Custom orders transmitted to manufacturing unit in Mountain City, Tennessee.
- Delivery in less than two weeks.

Andersen Corporation, the maker of Andersen Windows, recently offered customers the opportunity to order custom windows by using the company's interactive software system. Andersen's foray into mass customization had the following highlights:

- There were millions of possible window configurations.
- The number of unique end items shipped increased from 10,000 in 1980 to more than 188,000 in 1995.
- The enabling technology used was a multimedia system called Window of Knowledge™.
- Distributors collaborate with end users in designing their own windows.
- The system generates error-free quotes and transmits orders directly to factory.

ChemStation, Inc., manufactures customized industrial soap. Its success in the car-wash market was based on providing a unique service to its customers—that of managing inventory for them and providing refills as needed. The highlights of Chem-Station's approach to customization were:

- The company studied customer needs and developed products customized by concentration strength, pH level, enzyme concentration, foaminess, color, odor, and similar considerations.
- Products were supplied in ChemStation plastic storage tanks, then the company monitored the tanks to signal reorder points.
- The enabling technology was a system that generates reorders and makes overnight delivery possible.

Similarly, Ross Controls, Inc., is a company that manufactures pneumatic valves and air control systems. Its approach to customization involves active collaboration with customers to design products that meet varying needs. The highlights of Ross Controls' mass customization efforts are:

- Collaboration with customers on precisely tailored designs.
- Replication of customers' designs across various production lines.
- An enabling technology called the "ROSS/FLEX" process, which learns customer needs and integrates this knowledge with manufacturing capability.
- An "integrator" position that combines marketing, engineering, and manufacturing.

**(f) Beyond the Single-Firm Model**    Clearly, then, changing market forces have created a model of new product development that has progressed far beyond the single-firm model of innovation. Today, it is possible to have two or more alliance partners at each of the following stages of new product development identified by Souder:[5]

- *Exploratory*. Search and inquiry activities.
- *Concept development*. Concept elaboration, extension, and substantiation activities.
- *Prototype development*. Identify and target commercially relevant prototype.
- *Prototype testing*. Evaluation of prototype for manufacturability, functionality, and the like.
- *Market development*. Market generation, demand simulation, and market analyses.
- *Manufacturing start-up*. Initial production runs and manufacturing ramp-up.
- *Marketing start-up*. Preparation for market entry.
- *Technical service*. Follow-up marketing and service activities.

At each stage, companies may have to invest in IT enablers that allow interoperability, seamless sharing of information, and features or options that add value to the customer. Managing the new product development process will also increasingly involve transaction costs—the costs of communicating with and coordinating the efforts of multiple work forces belonging to different organizations. This additional transaction cost, the IT investments, and the focus on customization create additional demands on the how the process of new product development should be managed. The nature and intensity of each variable will be driven by some strategic decisions and by operational objectives that flow from those strategic decisions—issues discussed in the next section of this chapter.

**(g) Defining Characteristics of the New Environment**   The new product development process requires focus on the extended value chain, or the extended enterprise. In addition to managing the process, companies have to evaluate and invest in IT solutions, control transaction costs, and develop products that are aligned with flexible manufacturing and customization objectives.

Following are some of the defining characteristics of this new environment:

- Rapid technological obsolescence.
- High level of uncertainty regarding technology and standards.
- Shortened product life cycles.
- Focus on accelerated product development.
- Investment in IT solutions.
- Heavy use of alliances and other arrangements throughout the process.
- Expectation of cost reductions soon after introduction.
- Expectation of continuous cost reduction.
- High proportion of life cycle cost (up to 85 percent) can be committed in the design phase.
- Relative emphases on different objectives during different phases of the new product development process.
- Market shifting to customized products or customer solutions.
- High information content in all areas of product delivery and use.

**4.3 MANAGING THE NEW PRODUCT DEVELOPMENT PROCESS**   As discussed earlier, the nature of the specific issues that need to be managed depends on some strategic and operational decisions. The full set of decisions may be classified into primary and secondary categories:

- *Primary:*
  —Strategic.
  —Technological.
  —Design.
  —Operational.
- *Secondary:*
  —Extended enterprise (extended value chain level).
  —New product development process level.
  —IT level.

In the *primary* category, strategic issues relate to the product or service strategy of the company (or business unit). Strategic choices relate to the sources of competitive advantage. Strategic decisions in this category may be represented by the following questions:

- Will the company (or business unit) be a low-cost producer or a manufacturer of differentiated products?
- Will the company be a player in niche markets?

- Will the company have customized products? What will be the degree of customization? Will customization involve design?
- Will the company be the technological leader in the industry?
- What is the industry value chain for the product family?
- What is the company's (or business unit's) core competency?
- Will the company actively seek alliances to attain its objectives?
- Will the alliances involve collaborative product development?

**(a) Technological, Design, and Operational Decisions**  Technological decisions relate to three aspects of technology choice:

1. *Present and future products.* The technology choice for present and future products needs to be articulated.
2. *Develop or buy.* Technology decisions during new product development will involve the "develop or buy" question. A company (or business unit) has to decide whether it will develop technology in-house, develop it through a collaborative arrangement, or use existing technology available in the marketplace. A company (or business unit) could also buy a controlling interest in another company that has developed the needed technology.
3. *Timing.* The timing of introduction of new or next-generation technology has to be determined.

Design-related decisions also involve three specific product-related features:

1. *Features.* Identification of features valued by focus groups or identified through the use of quality tools such as a *quality function deployment* (QFD) matrix.
2. *Model range.* "Model range" refers to the number of models—and the specific functions—to be made available in each model.
3. *Customization.* Decisions related to the level of customization affect the management of new product development.

Operational decisions, for the purpose of this chapter, are defined as decisions related to the goals of the new product development process. These goals include:

- Specified performance features
- Specified factory standards
- Development schedule
- Development project budget

**(b) Trade-offs**  Ray[6] discusses how every decision about a design, feature, or development activity can lead to trade-offs among objectives. For example, time to market can be speeded up by spending more on the development project. A decision to add a product feature may increase the time to market.

A common trade-off is between development time and development budget. In high-technology industries, speeding up product development while increasing devel-

| Objectives | Product Cost | Development Cost | Development Time |
|---|---|---|---|
| Product performance | ✘ | ✘ | ✘ |
| Product cost | | ✘ | ✘ |
| Development cost | | | ✘ |

**Exhibit 4.1   Trade-offs among Objectives**

opment spending is considered a viable goal. It is commonly believed that high-technology products may earn up to 33 percent less over their life cycle if all other objectives are met except that the introduction occurs six months too late. Exhibit 4.1 illustrates the six possible trade-offs during the new product development process.

**(c) Time to Market**   Time to market is seen as a primary goal for high-technology companies because a "pioneer" can charge premium prices until competitors manage to bring their own products to market. Although these premium prices have to be cut later, the pioneer is further along the learning curve and can use process improvements to cut costs further.

In an earlier study, Souder compared the relative emphasis on cost versus time for each stage of the product development process across eight industries.[7] Souder collected life-cycle cost and life-cycle duration data from 289 new product development innovations. Comparing cycle time and cost data for each stage, Souder concluded that time is not the dominant factor in all phases of new product development. He found that whereas time is a dominant factor in exploratory research, prototype development, and prototype testing, other phases (e.g., concept development and market development) are more often cost-intensive. Finally, depending on the industry, manufacturing start-up, marketing start-up, and technical services may be more time-sensitive. Therefore, operational decisions involving each stage of the process have to be made with caution. Whereas time to market is an overall goal of the process, individual stages may have the need for effective management of cost.

**(d) Secondary Decisions**   *Secondary* decisions deal with the value chain, the new product development process, and IT levels. The value chain level involves decisions regarding other parts of the value chain that are driven by design. For example, a particular design decision could lead to vendor search, qualification, and selection in the purchasing area. Other decisions could create the need for custom manufacturing equipment, make some equipment obsolete, or create excess capacity in other areas. A design decision could also trigger decisions in packaging and warehousing by creating nonstandard material-handling and storing requirements. Finally, design changes late in the development cycle could lead to unanticipated decisions related to tooling requirements for manufacturing and testing equipment for product testing.

Process-level decisions relate to each stage of the process. These involve routing work, personnel decisions, equipment investment decisions, and overall cost and cycle time management. Important investment decisions need to be made in the development process itself. For example, design choices may require investments in special testing equipment during the prototype testing phase.

IT-level decisions pertain to the need for managing information. Prior field studies have shown that substantial inefficiencies exist in the design stages of the product-realization process.[8] Information regarding customer requirements, for example, is seen to "erode" as it moves from one end of an organization to another. Often design changes or changes in customer requirements are not communicated to people in a timely manner. At other times, teams at other parts of the value chain (e.g., purchasing or manufacturing), at the supply chain (first-tier and second-tier suppliers), and at alliance-partner locations engage in redundant activities because they lack access to the most recent design and customer-requirements information. Such inefficiencies in information exchange create iterations in the product development process, which (in turn) add to cost and cycle time.

Iterations in design and engineering are rarely caused by genuine technical problems. Usually they result from information-related problems and poor policy decisions. Examples include:

- Inaccurate communication of customer requirements.
- Incompatible computer-aided design or computer-aided manufacturing (CAD/CAM) systems.
- Changes in key product characteristics, which generate expensive engineering-change notices.

Decisions at the IT level deal with IT solutions to ensure that accurate, timely information is provided to the product developments group, to suppliers, and to alliance partners involved in the process.

**(e) New Product Development Competencies**   The previous discussion of decisions relating to new product development leads to 12 desirable competencies of a new product development process:

1. Identifying individual activities at each stage of the new product development process.
2. Quantifying cost, quality, and time attributes of each activity.
3. Identifying non–value-added activities and targeting them for elimination.
4. Assessing the impact of design decisions on other parts of the value chain.
5. Anticipating the impact of design and customer-requirement changes both downstream (i.e., to the company's own value chain) and upstream (i.e., to supplier and design-partner locations).
6. Providing distributed access to design and customer-requirements information for upstream and downstream alliance partners, as well as for the company's own value chain.
7. Identifying parts of the process that contain a high frequency of iterations.
8. Determining the sources of iterations and identifying corrective action steps.
9. Evaluating the cost and time impact of iterations to prioritize iterations for improvement or elimination.
10. Anticipating the overall cost impact over the life cycle and making changes to design.

11. Generating decision rules that help make trade-off decisions.

12. Assessing the risks related to assumptions used to generate decision rules.

These are the process-management competencies associated with effective management of the new product development process. There are several tools available to help companies to take steps toward attaining these competencies. These tools, which need to be adapted for use in the new product development environment, include:

- *Activity-based management.* For competencies 1 through 5.
- *Intranets and other IT solutions.* For competency 6.
- *Design structure matrix.* For competencies 7 through 9.
- *Target costing.* For competency 10.
- *Financial modeling.* For competencies 11 and 12.

Tools are also necessary to make strategic decisions and alliance-management issues, which are discussed earlier in this section. The next section discusses these tools, along with the competencies listed previously.

**4.4 TOOLS FOR MANAGING NEW PRODUCT DEVELOPMENT**    This section provides an overview and applications of five tools that can be adapted for use in the new product development arena, as well as several issues related to managing alliances. These alliance-management dimensions of new product development are seen as critical to the success of collaborative design and technology development. The five tools that enable companies to gain process management competencies are discussed first.

**(a) Activity-Based Management**    "Activity-based management (ABM) is a discipline that focuses on the management of activities as the route to improving the value received by the customer and the profit achieved by providing this value. This discipline includes cost driver analysis, activity analysis, and performance measurement. Activity-based management draws on activity-based costing as its major source of information."[9]

ABM is commonly understood as the application of activity-based costing (ABC) techniques to other parts of the value chain. Using the principles of cost-driver analysis and activity analysis, companies can derive important information about processes that yield reports related to:

- Customer profitability analysis.
- Distribution channel analysis.
- Supplies analysis.

In these applications, *cost objects* may be defined as individual customers, distribution channels, or suppliers. The implementation of such projects involves four steps:

1. Development of expense data from the general ledger. These data contain the people cost (labor), equipment depreciation, and cost of supplies.

**2.** Interviews or other information-gathering methods are used to identify activities. Resource drivers are used to assign dollar amounts to individual activities.

**3.** Costs are assigned to cost objects (e.g., customers, channels, or suppliers) based on the proportion of (or actual) activities consumed by them.

**4.** Activity driver rates are considered as candidates for performance measures.

**(b) Use of Activity-Based Management for New Product Development**  The use of ABM in the new product development arena requires some adaptations and modifications. Cost, quality, and time are critical attributes in this part of the value chain, and they need to be considered together. In addition, the focus of attention ought to be "management of the process" rather than the costing of cost objects. Obtaining maximum value from such an exercise requires an understanding of the downstream impacts of product development activities.

Management of the new product development process should include an understanding of information-exchange patterns. As discussed in the previous section, cost and cycle time are added to the process because of inefficiencies in information exchange. Therefore, identification of activities (during an ABM implementation) should be expanded to include collecting information, waiting for information, updating or correcting information, and disseminating information.

The recommended application of ABM in new product development includes the following initial steps:

- Identification of different stages of the new product development process.
- Identification of new product development goals.
- Identification of individual transactions and major activities.
- Ownership of downstream impact by each team.
- Documentation of outside influences.
- Mapping of information exchange patterns.

**(c) Information Exchanges**  Several of the individual steps require further elaboration. The distinction between "individual transactions" and "major activities" is an important one. ABC and ABM implementations include identification of individual "tasks" that are later aggregated into activities. Transactions are elements of tasks, which include the exchange of information. The inclusion of information exchange makes "transaction analysis" (as compared to activity analysis) a powerful tool for documenting the product-realization process.[10]

Ownership of some downstream activities by individual design teams is useful because it encourages the timely exchange of information and discourages frequent change notices. For example, if design teams had ownership of "rework cost" for tooling and testing equipment, they would ensure that changes (if any) are communicated as quickly as possible. Documentation of outside influences refers to the fact that cycle time is often driven by internal policy or external influences, such as the approval process by the Food and Drug Administration in the pharmaceutical industry.

Mapping of information-exchange patterns provides a method that may be used to represent the various units inside and outside an organization that exchange information during the development of a new product. Creating these information-exchange maps helps identify:

- The complexity of the process.
- Possible sources of problems.
- The various units that should be part of an IT solution to improve information exchange.

Such maps are particularly useful in situations in which technology development or design is being undertaken jointly with two or more alliance partners.

**(d) Activity Analysis**    Once these preliminary steps are taken, activity analysis can be performed for selected stages of the new product development process. The particular stage (or stages) selected for analysis depends on the strategic decisions (discussed in the previous section) and on the cost or cycle-time intensity of each stage.

The process in each stage needs to be broken down into activity categories. The next step involves assigning dollar amounts (cost), determining quality levels, and deriving cycle times for each individual activity. Once this information is obtained, the new product development process may be expressed as a collection of sequential stages, with cost, quality, and time attributes available for each stage. The availability of such information makes a significant difference in decisions that have to be made in this area.

Cost, quality, and cycle time information can be used for the following purposes:

- Identification of non–value-added activities.
- Pareto analysis on non–value-added activities by cost and cycle time.
- Pareto analysis of value-added activities by cost and cycle time.
- Pareto analysis of information-exchange-related activities by cycle time.
- Identification of root causes of selected activities.
- Reduction or elimination of activities.
- Redeployment of freed-up resources.
- Identification of upstream (i.e., supply-chain and alliance partners) and downstream (e.g., purchasing and manufacturing) activities.
- Identification of activities that have high costs or high cycle times because of iterations in the process, then determining the root causes of the iterations.

**(e) Supporting the Shift toward Customization**    ABM implementation for the new product development process supports the shift toward customization in three important ways:

1. *Impact on design processes.* For each customized option, companies can identify activities in product development. Because ABM implementations provide cost, time, and quality attributes of these activities, the cost impact on design can be easily generated. If these costs and cycle times are substantive, adjustments need to be made to the design process, the options being offered, and the price charged to the customer.
2. *Impact on manufacturing.* Part of an ABM implementation involves identification of downstream (e.g., purchasing or manufacturing) activities. Therefore, each customized option may be evaluated in terms of activity costs and adjustments made to pricing or option offerings.

3. *Impact on supply chain.* Because ABM implementations involve identification of upstream activities (i.e., activities involving the supply chain or design collaborators), customized options may be evaluated against activities generated and adjustments made to offerings and price.

The shift toward customization has created additional opportunities for companies to charge premium prices for customized, value-adding products and services. However, customization comes with a burden of complexity (because of unique processes and low volumes) that must be managed.

If complexity is not managed effectively, the costs incurred in design, the supply chain, and other parts of a company (in addition to manufacturing) will exceed the premium prices. ABM analysis of design processes is an appropriate place to begin such efforts to manage complexity.

Each configuration of customer options may be associated with corresponding design activities, which can then be linked to upstream and downstream activities. An evaluation of each configuration in terms of activities may be used to generate approximate estimates of cost and appropriate adjustments to options and prices.

ABM has the following distinguishing characteristics:

- It is totally focused on the process and does not include costing of cost objects.
- It includes cost, quality, and cycle-time information.
- It facilitates identification of iterations and their root causes.
- It includes activities related to information exchanges.
- It promotes identification of activities with upstream and downstream impact.

ABM for product development does pose some challenges and limitations. Some stages of the new product development process are not routine and, hence, not repetitive in nature. These stages (e.g., exploratory research or basic research aimed at development of new technologies) should not be subjected to activity analysis. ABM is best applied to the *development* end of R&D, along with general guidelines that basic research, to the extent possible, should be aligned with the strategic interests of the company.

**(f) Intranets and Other Information Technology Solutions**   As discussed earlier, cost and cycle time are largely influenced by inefficiencies in information exchange. The information-exchange maps and root-cause analysis (for iterations and non–value-added activities) conducted as part of ABM may be further analyzed for efficient IT solutions. Some possible tools and application scenarios are discussed next.

Intranets can be used as a repository of updated design and customer requirements. Teams throughout the value chain, including suppliers and alliance partners, should be given access to this information. Such a strategy provides distributed access to accurate, updated information on critical variables concerning design and customer requirements. The intranets and databases for supplier selection may be used to drive cost-sensitive design decisions by accessing global supplier databases. One downstream impact of design changes is the need for new parts or raw materials, which in turn creates a need for supplier search, evaluation, certification, and selection. An Intranet-based query of global databases may provide names of vendors that have the capability to deliver the required parts. To reduce downstream transaction costs, design engineers can select parts for which precertified vendors already exist.

Intranets may be used to access ABC or ABM process-level information to make strategic decisions. For example, ABM data on the product development process may be used to determine whether an alliance partner or outsourcing is needed for a new product development initiative. Such technology can also be used to manage customization. ABC data related to parts of the manufacturing process may be used to evaluate various customization options. Once the cost of processing is known for each option, design engineers can use the information to decide on the number of models and range of options across model ranges that will yield the lowest total cost over the life cycle of the product.

Other IT solutions enable designers to identify interrelated processes and alert other teams whenever a design change takes place. Yet other systems allow customers to directly customize their solution and get a quote on the price of the customized product. The highest-leverage IT solutions in the product development area are those that deal with information exchange. Because information exchange is a prime driver of cost (through rework and unanticipated investments) and cycle time (through multiple iterations), making accurate, updated information available to teams throughout the organization has to be a high-priority item for the effective management of this process.

**(g) Design Structure Matrix**  *Design structure matrix* (DSM) is a tool introduced first by Steward and later extended by Eppinger et al.[11] The tool uses transaction analysis to identify and manage iterations in complex product development processes.[12] As discussed earlier, transaction analysis is activity analysis at the task level that includes information exchange.

ABC or ABM implementations begin with identification of individual tasks that are clustered into separate *activities*. Transaction analysis is conducted at a greater level of detail—at the task level. The level of detail is increased because it includes tasks related to collecting, organizing, and disseminating information.

Van de Ven defined "transactions" as exchanges that tie people together, forming a complex and interdependent "web" of interpersonal contacts occurring in the product realization process.[13] Van de Ven concludes that the following phenomena act in concert, resulting in suboptimal innovation performance:

- Poor communication among functional areas.
- Unexpected errors or delays in upstream transactions that complicate downstream efforts or cause rework in them.
- Incompatible organizational support.

DSM is a graphical depiction of information flow and dependencies through activities or processes. The product development process, with its interdependent parts and accompanying iterations, is an appropriate area for DSM applications. The DSM methodology was developed as a tool for "analyzing parametric descriptions of designs and has recently been used to analyze development projects modeled at the task level."[14] The authors, after discussing various project management methods, offer several key ideas:

- "Projects consist of tasks linked to each other by dependencies. Tasks can be sequential, parallel, or coupled.

- Collection of tasks linked by dependencies define a critical path, whose duration defines the minimum possible completion time of a project.
- The design structure matrix can be used to represent dependencies. Gantt charts are used to represent the timing of tasks. PERT charts represent both dependencies and timing and are frequently used to compute the critical path."[15]

DSM can be used as a tool for:

- Documenting existing procedures.
- Identifying areas for improvement in work flow.
- Highlighting opportunities for coordination.
- Identifying iterative loops.
- Aiding in the design of new work flows.

Exhibit 4.2 provides an example of a DSM. The same activities are represented in the rows and columns. Any off-diagonal "X" on the right represents an iteration (loop) back to an earlier step. Thus, in the example shown, we conclude that there is an iteration at the very end of the process ("Decision to go") back to an earlier step ("Establish candidate product/processes"). Another possible iteration is from the last step, again, to the step "Develop 'ballpark' estimate."

Typical process flow charts of the product development process are complex, and it is difficult to reveal iterations and feedback loops that exist. Often these iterations are not even documented in process manuals. However, analysis of transactions from an ABM implementation can be used to construct a DSM and thus highlight iterations. In addition, ABM information may be used to derive cost and time data related to each activity in the DSM. When this information is available, iterations displayed by the DSM may be used to compute the activity cost and the cycle-time estimates for each iteration.

Exhibits 4.3 and 4.4 provide two more examples of a DSM, using generic activity labels. Exhibit 4.4 shows that there is an iteration loop from activity A4 back to activity A1. Indeed, Exhibit 4.4 shows three iterations: A4 to A1, B3 to A1, and B5 to A1. The use of DSM to cost iterations is recommended only if an ABM implementation is already under way in the product development area. Maps can be very complex, and it is often difficult to unearth iterations. Some iterations are seen as regular accepted practices. The DSM allows managers to focus on iterations by providing a simpler representation.

Because the activity descriptions and cost and time data are collected during an ABM implementation, constructing a DSM requires some incremental effort. However, the payoffs can be substantial. Iterations, for example, may be ranked by time and cost, then a root-cause analysis may be done to determine the cause of the iterations. For example, iterations may occur because of policies or because of problems with information exchange. If so, new policies may be formulated or IT solutions implemented to remove iterations from the process. As with any implementation, only areas that traditionally have delays or cost overruns should be targeted for a DSM analysis.

Benefits of the DSM methodology may be summarized as follows:

- Level of detail of linkages available.
- Sequences or flow problems may become visually evident.

| A Real-World Example | Identify business opportunities | Acquire customer background info | Establish candidate product/processes | Collect business requirements | Determine volumes and applications | Review market research data | Develop "ballpark" estimate | Establish relevance to business process | Estimate resource requirements | Identify product teams | Establish program timing | Decision to go: PDTs formed |
|---|---|---|---|---|---|---|---|---|---|---|---|---|
| **Activity** | | | | | | | | | | | | |
| Identify business opportunities | ▓ | | | | | | | | | | | |
| Acquire customer background info | ✗ | ▓ | | | | | | | | | | |
| Establish candidate product/processes | ✗ | ✗ | ▓ | | | | | ✗ | | | | ✗ |
| Collect business requirements | ✗ | | | ▓ | | | | | | | | |
| Determine volumes and applications | ✗ | | | | ▓ | | | | | | | |
| Review market research data | ✗ | | | | | ▓ | | | | | | |
| Develop "ballpark" estimate | | ✗ | ✗ | ✗ | ✗ | ✗ | ▓ | | | | | ✗ |
| Establish relevance to business process | | ✗ | ✗ | ✗ | ✗ | | ✗ | ▓ | | | | |
| Estimate resource requirements | | | ✗ | | ✗ | | | | ▓ | | | |
| Identify product teams | | | | | | | | | ✗ | ▓ | | |
| Establish program timing | | | | | | | | | | ✗ | ▓ | |
| Decision to go: PDTs formed | | | ✗ | ✗ | ✗ | ✗ | ✗ | ✗ | ✗ | ✗ | ✗ | ▓ |

**Exhibit 4.2    Design Structure Matrix**

- May assist in locating unknown dependencies.
- Shows complete range of iterations possible in the process.
- Can enable process design or improvement.
- Can be integrated with ABM to remove iterations and improve cost and cycle-time performance.

**(h) Target Costing**    Target costing has gained popularity in recent years as a cost management tool. It is a methodology aimed at ensuring that manufacturing costs come at or under target cost levels. This section discusses how target costing methods may be

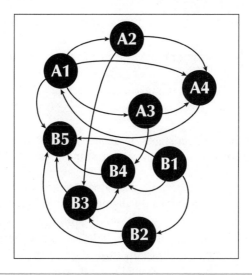

**Exhibit 4.3    Design Structure Matrix with One Iteration Loop**

enhanced through the use of activity-level information regarding the new product development process.

Target costing involves the following sequence of activities:

- Select pricing strategy.
- Derive market-driven price.
- Deduct an allowable margin (the target return).
- Deduct an additional allowance for cost overruns.
- Arrive at a target cost.
- Evaluate cost based on a prototype.

| Task | A1 | A2 | A3 | A4 | B1 | B2 | B3 | B4 | B5 |
|------|----|----|----|----|----|----|----|----|----|
| A1 | | | | ✗ | | | | | |
| A2 | ✗ | | | | | | | | |
| A3 | ✗ | | | | | | | | |
| A4 | ✗ | ✗ | ✗ | | | | | | |
| B1 | | | | | | | | | |
| B2 | | | | | ✗ | | | | |
| B3 | | ✗ | | | | ✗ | | | |
| B4 | | | ✗ | | ✗ | | ✗ | | |
| B5 | ✗ | | | | ✗ | ✗ | ✗ | ✗ | |

**Exhibit 4.4    Design Structure Matrix with Three Iteration Loops**

- If the cost exceeds the target cost, then reevaluate the options using value analysis.
- Modify the product design, making decisions about features based on value to customers.
- Modify the process to attain the target cost.
- Continuously improve cost performance.

ABM implementation at select stages of the new product development process can enhance the goals of target costing in three important ways:

1. Use activity-based information to generate more accurate estimates of life cycle costs by including costs incurred during product development.
2. In the redesign stage of target costing (modify product design), activity-based information regarding the impact of design decisions may be used to select appropriate options that minimize downstream costs. In high-technology companies, it may be decided that the development cost of redesign, when compared to lost revenue because of late entry, requires that the product be launched at a level higher than the target cost, though with targeted improvements identified for the future.
3. Target costing for customized products can greatly benefit from activity-level information about design and engineering functions. As discussed earlier, such information can be used to select options based on the impact of design.

**(i) Financial Modeling**    Previous sections of this chapter discuss operational decisions that need to be made during the new product development process, including decisions that involve trade-offs among the four goals of target specifications, target cost, time to market, and development budget. Smith and Reinertsen have developed a financial modeling tool that may be used to quantify trade-off rules to help such decisions.[16] The methodology involves the following steps:

- Identify and document all assumptions, then construct a financial statement for the life cycle of the product. The life cycle includes the development time and the development budget. Assumptions are made about price, cost, cost-reduction rates, and the volume of sales over the life cycle. The cumulative *profit before taxes* (PBT) is computed: This is the "baseline profit."
- The model is now rerun by perturbing each of the four product development goals. For example, the development budget is increased by 50 percent, product cost is increased by 10 percent, sales is reduced to reflect failure to meet target specifications, then again reduced by 10 percent to reflect failure to meet time-to-market goals. In each of these four simulations, all other variables in the model are held constant.
- The analysis yields four different cumulative profit figures in addition to the initial baseline estimate. These profit figures are each subtracted from the baseline profit to quantify the profit impact of the failure to attain each goal.

The method behind deriving these decision rules is illustrated using an example. Assume that baseline profit is $10,000,000 and that the four simulations yield the following results:

- Assume that a six-month delay in introducing a product results in $800,000 in profits. This figure, when subtracted from the $10 million baseline profit, shows a profit impact of $2 million. Spread over six months, the impact is $333,333 per month.
- Assume that a 50 percent overrun in development expense results in $9.5 million in profits. The profit difference of $500,000, spread over 50 percentage points, yields an impact of $10,000 per percent overrun.
- Assume that failure to attain target specifications results in sales reduction of 10 percent and profits of $9.2 million. The profit difference of $800,000, spread over 10 percentage points, yields an impact of $80,000 per percent decrease in unit sales.
- Finally, assume that failure to attain the target cost results in a 10 percent cost overrun and a profit of $9.4 million. The profit difference of $600,000, spread over 10 percentage points, yields an impact of $60,000 per percent cost overrun.

The rules of thumb for each category may be summarized as follows:

- Delay in product introduction: $333,333 per month.
- Development budget overrun: $10,000 per month.
- Failure to meet specifications: $80,000 per percent decrease in unit sales.
- Failure to meet target cost: $60,000 per percent product cost overrun.

Smith and Reinertsen provide several examples of operational decisions that could benefit from these rules of thumb.[17] These decision rules, though approximate, are powerful decision aids and incentives to influence behavior. The quantification of failure to attain goals serves as a strong incentive to implement activity analysis methods to identify cycle times for each development activity and to reduce development time. Companies considering the use of this tool should consider the following guidelines:

- Decision rules are "approximate," but far better than having no information.
- The modeling results from cross-functional effort.
- The effect of launch delays is the most difficult to predict.
- Assumptions need to be documented after a consensus is reached.
- Sources of assumptions (e.g., the data and analysis used) need to be documented and made accessible to decision makers.
- Activity-based analysis of the new product development process enhances the financial modeling tool. Many decisions involving trade-offs require costs of particular product development activities. Activity analysis provides accurate estimates of such costs.
- Specific *risks* associated with assumptions in the model should be identified, and plans for managing these risks should also be put in place.
- Action steps related to assumptions (e.g., cost reduction) need to be identified.
- Individuals or groups should take ownership of goals related to individual assumptions (e.g., cost reduction).
- The model should be updated periodically, and goals should be revised and communicated.

**(j) Managing Alliance Partners**    Management of alliance partners in product development is a concern of general management. Such decisions are made at a strategic level after consideration of technological and product-design competencies. However, some issues need to be managed at the product-development end. These issues pertain largely to management of transaction costs. Transaction costs are costs of communication and coordination related to the development partnership.

While managing such alliances, companies need to rein in transaction costs through the use of IT solutions that provide distributed access to updated information and tracking of such costs. Other issues relate to the evaluation of the relative contribution of the partners. Activity analysis can help by providing accurate estimates of development costs as they relate to the collaborative project.

Investments made in collaboration with partners need to be tracked, because they are often taken into consideration during the dissolution stage of the partnership. Although such alliances are usually managed at the corporate level, the product-development group may find value in managing and tracking all transaction costs and tracking the use of investments made in the project.

**4.5 GUIDELINES FOR IMPLEMENTATION**    Manufacturing executives who consider using the tools outlined in this chapter have to approach them in a systematic manner, while being sensitive to perceptions about the impact of control on innovative activities. Basic research and other exploratory activities should not be subjected to activity analysis. Using ABM and other tools requires participation from product-development engineers and scientists, and if they perceive an atmosphere of excessive control, it will inhibit their participation.

Stages of the new product development process that will be analyzed need to be evaluated in light of the technology and product strategy of the company. Wherever possible, a decision that will benefit from the analysis should be identified. During the data-collection stage, clear and unambiguous communication is needed between members of the project team and development personnel. The project should not be seen as an "accounting or finance" project but, rather, as a project that will lead to operational benefits. To this end, the strategic and operational significance of these projects needs to be communicated to participants. During the data-analysis stage, engineers and scientists should be kept informed about progress. The best use of these tools occurs when development personnel take ownership of them and continue to maintain and use them. Therefore, communication is a critical element in any implementation.

Prioritization of areas and initiatives is equally important. An organization has finite resources that can be devoted to these initiatives. One approach to prioritization is to investigate the problems associated with the most recent product launch. Once these problems are identified, the root causes of the problems may be identified. These root causes usually point toward two or more stages of the process, along with issues related to policy and information exchange. These are the stages and areas that need to be addressed first.

Cost management for new product development is, as this chapter suggests, not restricted to cost analysis: It must include cycle-time and information-exchange management. Managing new product development is challenging because not every stage is appropriate for the tools and methodologies that are available, and not every stage should be subjected to such analysis. Despite the challenges, effective management of new product development can yield substantial benefits across the entire extended enterprise and over the life cycle of new products.

# NOTES

1. K. Preiss, S. L. Goldman, and R. N. Nagel, *Cooperate to Compete: Building Agile Business Relationships* (New York: Van Nostrand Reinhold, 1996).

2. S. L. Goldman, R. N. Nagel, and K. Preiss, *Agile Competitors and Virtual Organizations: Strategies for Enriching the Customer* (New York: Van Nostrand Reinhold, 1995).

3. M. R. Ray and C. Beidleman, *The Agility Revolution: A New Paradigm for the Financial Services Industry Report* (Bethlehem, PA: Agility Forum, 1996); M. R. Ray and C. Beidleman, "The Agility Revolution," *Bloomberg Magazine* (February 1997): 29–33.

4. D. Anderson, *Agile Product Development for Mass Customization* (Chicago, IL: Irwin Professional Publishing, 1997).

5. W. E. Souder, *Managing New Product Innovations* (Lexington, MA: D. C. Heath & Co., 1987).

6. M. R. Ray, "Cost Management for Product Development," *Journal of Cost Management* (Summer 1995): 52–60.

7. Souder, op. cit.

8. M. R. Ray, M. Anderson, G. Johnson, and D. Marquette, "Measurement/Metrics Development Methodology for Agile Organizations," *Proceedings of the 4th Annual Conference on Creating the Agile Organization: Models, Metrics and Pilots* (March 1995): 383–393; D. Whitney, et al., "Agile Pathfinders in the Aircraft and Automobile Industries—A Progress Report," *Proceedings of the 4th Annual Conference on Creating the Agile Organization: Models, Metrics and Pilots* (March 1995): 245–268.

9. N. Raffish and P. B. B. Turney, "Glossary of Activity-Based Management," *Journal of Cost Management* (Fall 1995): 53–63.

10. D. Whitney, et al., "Agile Pathfinders in the Aircraft and Automobile Industries—A Progress Report," *Proceedings of the 4th Annual Conference on Creating the Agile Organization: Models, Metrics and Pilots* (March 1995): 245–268; M. R. Ray, M. Anderson, G. Johnson, and D. Marquette, "Measurement/Metrics Development Methodology for Agile Organizations," *Proceedings of the 4th Annual Conference on Creating the Agile Organization: Models, Metrics and Pilots* (March 1995): 383–393.

11. D. V. Steward, *Systems Analysis and Management Structure: Strategy and Design* (New York: Petrocelli Books, 1981); S. Eppinger, D. Whitney, R. Smith, and D. Gebala, "A Model-Based Method for Organizing Tasks in Product Development," *Research in Engineering Design,* Vol. 6, No. 1 (1994): 1–13.

12. The author acknowledges work done by graduate student Steven R. Roth in integrating DSM tools with activity-based information. S. Roth, "Process Analysis Tools: Activity Chains and DSM," *Report,* Lehigh University, Management of Technology Program (1995), provided a comparison of DSM and other project management tools and outlined areas for future work. Parts of this section are based on Roth's 1995 report.

13. A. Van de Ven, "Central Problems in the Management of Innovation," *Management Science,* Vol. 32, No. 5 (1986): 590–607.

14. K. T. Ulrich and S. D. Eppinger, *Product Design and Development* (New York: McGraw-Hill, 1995): 262.

15. Id. at 280.

16. P. G. Smith and D. G. Reinertsen, *Developing Products in Half the Time* (New York: Van Nostrand Reinhold, 1991).

17. Id.

# CHAPTER 5

# TIME-BASED COSTING

## Kenneth Preiss*

**Ben Gurion University of the Negev**

*If the truth were self-evident, eloquence would be unnecessary—Cicero.*

**5.1 INTRODUCTION**   From a financial perspective, a company represents an asset that is expected to give a good return, meaning a good *return per unit of time,* whether monthly, quarterly, or yearly. However, when choosing products or projects, those with a better *margin per unit of product* are usually preferred. If we are interested in a good return per unit of time, why do we use the margin per unit of product as a prioritization measure? The answer is that if the rate of sales is unchanged with time, the product or project with the best margin per unit of product also gives the best return per unit of time. In the early days of modern business, sales were indeed usually steady over time, so the product having the best margin also gave the best return per unit of time. Not so today. When the rate of sales changes with time, the product or service with the best margin per unit may in fact not give the best return per unit of time.

The mix of the many different products and services sold by a company changes, often sharply, as time goes by. This observation is behind the development of time-based costing. Before considering in detail the problems caused by the varying times required to make and sell different products, consider an analogous question: the problems caused by failure to recognize the variable consumption of overhead resources by various products.

Johnson and Kaplan[1] in their well-known book give a fine description of the historical development of costing practice. They point out a fact that is today well appreciated: When using a fixed overhead rate for a product or project, the real cost of the product or project may be under- or overestimated. This is because a specific product may in fact use more overhead resources than the amount allocated to it by the overhead rate (in which case it is subsidized by other products), or it may use fewer overhead resources than allocated (in which case it subsidizes other products).

The description of Holden Evans, a naval contractor around 1900, quoted by Johnson and Kaplan, shows that even then, the fact that overhead expenses were allocated based on the assumption that they were uniformly used was causing problems for some businesses.

---

*The useful comments of Professor Manash Ray of the College of Business and Economics at Lehigh University are gratefully acknowledged.

"In some of the large establishments with numerous shops the expense burden is averaged and applied on the basis of direct labor—notwithstanding the fact that in one shop the shop expense percentage is nearly a hundred while in another it is less than twenty-five. Frequently such establishments are called on to bid for work which is almost exclusively confined to the shops where the expense is low, and by using the higher average rate the bids are high and the work goes to other establishments where costs are more accurately determined. Thus profitable work is often lost."

Experience with many companies today suggests that an analogous quote for today's practice would follow from neglect of the difference of times required to produce and sell different products.

In some of the establishments with numerous products the expense burden is averaged and applied on the basis of activities or direct labor—notwithstanding the fact that for one product the time required to produce $100 of profit is much more than the time required to produce the same profit with another product. Frequently such establishments are called on to bid for work that is almost exclusively confined to products that require little time to make.

By using the average overhead rate, the company's bids are high, so the work is awarded to other establishments that can determine the costs of time more accurately. Thus, profitable work is often lost. Conversely, products that use more time than average are thought to cost less than they in fact do, so bids are made at prices that are too low. Many companies then take on projects that require much time and lose money because their bids are too low, while at the same time they do not win fast, profitable work because their bids are high.

Costing data are generally used for two purposes: (1) to analyze the past performance of a company, and (2) for predictive reasons (i.e., to make prioritization decisions based on anticipated cost and income from a product or project). For the first, historical, purpose, even if the cost computed does not match what the real cost was, the erroneous cost data cannot change what was done. It may change the conclusions reached about the historical actions, and therefore influence further actions, but the amount of money made or left on the table will not change. Not so with predicted costs. When analyzing predicted costs, it is important that computed costs match reality. Because action has not yet been taken, errors in the computation can lead to wrong prioritization decisions: Money will be made or lost by the actions to be taken. Correct cost data are therefore central to operational management of a company, because management prioritization decisions follow from that cost data. To make the correct cost and income estimates, two items need to be in place.

1. The computation method used has to match business reality.
2. The computation method must be correctly used.

The methodology of activity-based costing (ABC), discussed elsewhere in this book, was developed following the understanding that general, or overhead, resources are not used uniformly across products or projects, as is implied by using the usual allocation methods.

Time-based costing goes further than ABC. It has been developed following the understanding that time is spread unevenly across products and projects. In today's commercial world, activities in companies ranging from retailing to manufacturing to services are characterized by sharp changes in money flows with time. In other words, the amount of money flowing into a company per unit of time from sales is not steady, and time is not allocated evenly over the income flow.

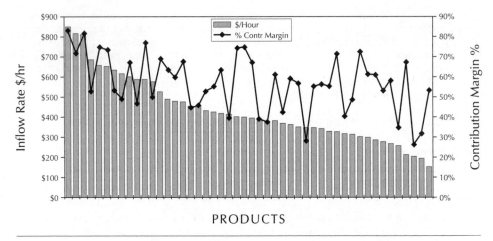

**Exhibit 5.1    Prioritization of Products: Margin vs. Inflow Rates Per Unit of Time**

The fact that the income per unit of time is not steady has a marked impact on how costs are computed. If unit costs are computed while neglecting the uneven use of time (and hence the unevenness of income flow rate), the computed unit costs of products will not match the real costs, so decisions that flow from that data will be faulty. For example, as shown later in the chapter, if one neglects the time factor when computing the margin per unit of each of a group of products, the product with the better computed margin may in fact be the product that produces the least real profit. This is true even if one uses ABC, because ABC takes no account of time. By neglecting the change in income flow rates, ABC computations do not match the reality of business, which is characterized by uneven income flow rates.

Exhibit 5.1 shows prioritization of products for a plant of the Rhône Poulenc Corporation. The points give the margin per unit of product; the bars show the inflow rates per unit of time. We see that there is no correlation between the two types of data. When the manager and personnel of this plant understood the approach of time-based costing, they rearranged their sales efforts and budget allocations according to the money inflow rate achieved. Then "In two years . . . by the company's own cautious reports, this generated a combined contribution margin increase and capital expense savings in excess of $7 million."[2]

The subject of this chapter is how to deal with costs when income flows are dynamic, or changing, over time. This will be explained with the help of several computed examples. The question that immediately comes into most people's minds is, "What is the appropriate time interval for calculating costs?" A week, a day, an hour, or a minute? We will see that, according to the methodology of time-based costing, this question becomes irrelevant.

This chapter first reviews principles of money flow. Because the flow of income into a company depends on the flow of goods and services out of the company, the outflow of goods and services is then discussed. Discussion of the flow rate of goods and services necessarily brings up the subject of bottlenecks in that flow, which prompts a discussion of the theory of constraints[3] and its relationship to time-based costing. Finally, the chapter discusses implementation questions, the effect of time-based costing on prioritization of product and service offerings, and its effect on investment decisions.

**5.2 MONEY FLOW RATES**    To deal with time, one needs to go back to the origins of cost accounting and develop a path abandoned many years ago but relevant again. The ensuing methodology is not difficult—in fact, it is surprisingly easy to perform—but it differs from the traditional methods of cost accounting that developed over the last century. We, of course, want to know how much money a particular product or project makes or loses. The correct way to phrase that question is, "How much is the rate of money inflow increased by the sale of a unit of product?" not "How many net dollars do I make from the sale of a unit of product?" That this is the correct question will become clear as the chapter progresses further.

It is first necessary to make the terminology clear: The word "time," on its own, refers to the generic idea of time that goes by. A time interval, such as a quarter or a week, is a *time period,* or *interval.* The time basis for a flow rate is the *time unit.* Money flows are measured in dollars per unit of time, such as dollars per week (in which case the time unit is a week), dollars per day, dollars per hour, or the like. This is analogous to reading the speedometer of a car. The unit of speed is distance per unit time, measured in miles per hour (if the time unit is an hour), kilometers per hour (if the time unit is an hour), feet per second (if the time unit is a second), and so on. We all understand the two ideas of speed and total distance covered in a given time period. The ideas of money flow rate and total money collected in a given time period are analogous.

Time-based costing is based on use of money flow rates—dollars per day, dollars per hour, or the like. When we want to know how much money is made over some time interval, say a quarter, we obtain that by summing the money flows over the required period. If we wanted to know how much money is made by selling units of product, we would find the answer by summing the flows over the period of time relevant for producing and selling the units of product. The following paragraphs are designed show how one relates money flow rate to the total amount of money that has flowed through in a given period. This is discussed in a more formal way in the appendix, for readers who prefer a mathematical discussion.

Imagine that one could know the net amount of money that flows into a company per day. Imagine also that for each week we know the average inflow rate per day for that week. Because there are seven days in a week, the money flowing in, in any week, is seven times the average dollar inflow per day for that week.

To know the net quantity of money flowing in for a week we would sum the daily inflow for the days of the week. For a month, we would sum the daily inflows for the month, similarly for a quarter, and so on. Whatever the basic time interval, whether a week, a day, an hour, or a minute, the procedure would be the same. The money flowing in per interval of time is the *money inflow rate.*

For example, assume that Exhibit 5.2 shows the average weekly inflow rate for a company or profit center, measured in dollars per day for the 13 weeks of a quarter. The factor on the "total" line in Exhibit 5.2 is used because there are seven days in a week. Note that one cannot know the total for the quarter from the data of any single week; one has to sum the income from each week.

The units of day, week, and quarter here are used only as examples. This computation can be used whatever the units chosen. We could choose to measure the inflow rate in dollars per hour, for intervals of a month each, to determine the total sum of money flowing in over a quarter. The previous approach would still be valid.

Now imagine that the inflow per day were constant. The table would then look as shown in Exhibit 5.3. Because the daily income is constant, there is in fact no need to sum up the weekly incomes. We could know immediately that the income for a week of

| Week | Average Daily Inflow Rate $ per Day |
|------|-------------------------------------|
| 1    | 150,000                             |
| 2    | 190,000                             |
| 3    | 220,000                             |
| 4    | 180,000                             |
| 5    | 140,000                             |
| 6    | 120,000                             |
| 7    | 110,000                             |
| 8    | 140,000                             |
| 9    | 156,000                             |
| 10   | 187,000                             |
| 11   | 205,000                             |
| 12   | 213,000                             |
| 13   | 199,000                             |

TOTAL INFLOW PER QUARTER =
$2,210,000 * 7 = $15,470,000

**Exhibit 5.2   Weekly Inflow Rate (Varying Daily Rate)**

| Week | Average Daily Inflow Rate $ per Day |
|------|-------------------------------------|
| 1    | 170,000                             |
| 2    | 170,000                             |
| 3    | 170,000                             |
| 4    | 170,000                             |
| 5    | 170,000                             |
| 6    | 170,000                             |
| 7    | 170,000                             |
| 8    | 170,000                             |
| 9    | 170,000                             |
| 10   | 170,000                             |
| 11   | 170,000                             |
| 12   | 170,000                             |
| 13   | 170,000                             |

TOTAL INFLOW PER QUARTER =
$2,210,000 * 7 = $15,470,000

**Exhibit 5.3   Weekly Inflow Rate (Constant Daily Rate)**

seven working days is seven times the income for a day, that is $170,000 * 7 = \$1,190,000$ per week, which is $1,190,000 * 13 = \$15,470,000$ per quarter. If we were assured that the inflow per day would be constant, the income for any period would be known directly after the first day.

The implicit, but unstated, assumption in today's allocation methods, including ABC, is that the inflow rate is constant. That assumption today does not match reality, and for that reason we need to look at costing from the perspective of time—as time-based costing.

**5.3 FROM FIRST PRINCIPLES**   The contribution margin per unit of product is such a common measure that we seldom pause to consider what its significance really is. In fact, that measure is, of itself, not fundamental. It is a stepping-stone to figuring out whether a specific project or product is sufficiently profitable for a company.

Although cost accounting methods developed in a way that made the profit or margin per unit the center of attention, that development was not inevitable. It was a historical accident, made possible by the fact that income flows were assumed to be constant. Customers are surely interested in how much they pay for a unit of product. However, suppliers are interested in making a reasonable profit every day, week, month, and quarter.

The flaw in the use of gross margin or contribution margin to predict the contribution of a product or process to the profit of a company is that the usual computation of margin assumes that the time required to provide a product or service is spread uniformly over all projects. It is not. That is presumably why the well-known business thinker Peter Drucker[4] writes that "the worship of high profit margins" is one of the five deadly business sins. The numerical example that follows in section 5.4 illustrates this point.

An enterprise represents an investment of capital, and management strives to increase the rate of return on that investment. The return on any investment is measured in dollars per time. For a company that provides units of service or units of product, equation 1 shows the simple relation between margin per unit of product and return per unit of time. In this equation, the lefthand side measures the financial success of the enterprise, which is the factor in which management of the company is interested.

$$\frac{\$}{\text{time\_unit}} = \frac{\$}{\text{unit\_of\_product}} \times \frac{\text{units\_of\_product}}{\text{time\_unit}} \tag{1}$$

The factor \$ / unit_of_product is recognized as the unit margin, or contribution margin per unit of product. The factor units_of_product / time_unit is the velocity of products moving through the systems in the enterprise. We can therefore write:

$$\frac{\text{net earnings}}{\text{time\_unit}} = \text{unit margin} \times \text{product velocity} \tag{2}$$

Return on investment (ROI) is expressed as net earnings divided by the average operating assets. The net earnings flow rate expressed as a proportion of average operating assets becomes the rate of inflow of net earnings, as explained in the following:

$$\text{ROI} = \frac{\text{net earnings}}{\text{average operating assets}} \tag{3}$$

$$\text{ROI velocity} = \frac{\text{net earnings}}{\text{average operating assets} \times \text{time\_unit}} \tag{4}$$

$$\text{Expected ROI in a given period} = \text{ROI velocity} \times \text{time period} \tag{5}$$

We see that the use of money flow rate data is applicable to ROI computations, and in fact to all the usual overall measures used to assess the financial efficiency of a company.

**5.4 RESOURCES, MATERIAL, AND PROCESSES**    The flow rate of money into a company depends on the flow rate of goods and services out of the company. Goods and services are manufactured and shipped by resources. Operation of the resources consumes both time and money. Consumption, or use, of the resources is therefore responsible for an outflow of money. Note also that the resources cannot use more time in a day than is available. Time is the one irreplaceable resource. It should be used to maximize the money inflow rate.

Resources are used in a process or activity in order to convert material from an input state to an output state. Time is used by the resources, and only by the resources. The material may be the components of a physical product, such as a household machine (from the whitegoods industry), in which case the resources would then be the production machines in the factory. Alternatively, the material may be electronic data and the resources computers and networks. Or the material may be part of a service that is provided—for example, an insurance or financial service—in which case the resources are then the computer networks and people who provide the service. A transportation process changes the state of material from being in one location to another by using trucks and other resources. An industrial manufacturing process uses machinery to convert input materials into some new configuration, and so on. Time is used by all the resources in the activities that do the conversion. To do time-based costing for a collection of products or services, one needs to understand the time used by the resources during that flow. Without such data, it is would be impossible to perform a time-based costing computation. Here is where time-based costing connects with the well-known theory of constraints.

Exhibit 5.4 shows a simple diagram that is commonly used to characterize a process or activity. It shows an input that is converted to output by an activity which uses resources and is subject to controls or limitations. Examples of inputs, outputs, and resources were discussed earlier. A control or limitation may be a legal requirement such as those of the Occupational Safety and Health Act (OSHA), a law of nature (such as the laws of chemistry), or a company policy.

An activity or process flow diagram shows the flow of material from one activity to another. Exhibit 5.5 shows an example of an activity flow diagram for four resources named A, B, C, and D. The four resources working together process material to make two products: U and V.

In the diagram, the letter in each block gives the name of the resource. Here, units of products U and V are manufactured from units of raw material by resources A, B, C, and D. The activity flow diagram shows that a unit of raw material costing $20 per unit is processed by resource D for 12 minutes, then by resource A for 7 minutes, before it is passed to assembly process B. A unit of raw material costing $25 per unit is processed by resource C for 8 minutes, then by resource A for 5 minutes before it is passed to resource B, where it is combined with the first piece of raw material in work that requires

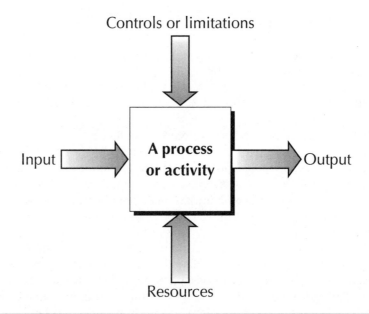

**Exhibit 5.4   Process or Activity Flow**

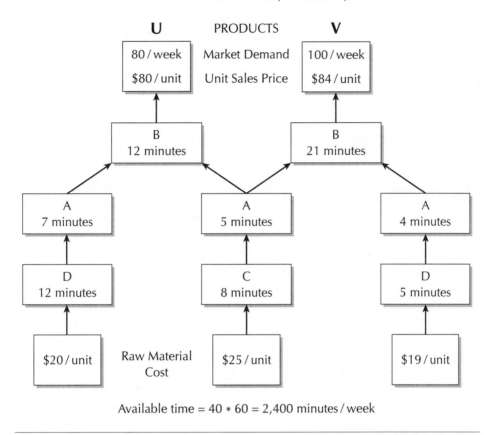

Exhibit 5.5    Activity Flow Diagram for Four Resources That Manufacture Products U and V

12 minutes, before appearing as product U. Note that resource A that processes the items is one and the same. In the diagram there are three blocks named A because the single resource A is used for three streams of work flow. The diagram shows that the market can absorb 80 units of product U per week, with a sales price of $80 per unit. Similarly, the diagram shows how two items of raw material, one costing $25, the other $19, are processed by the four resources, ending up as product V. The variable, raw material cost associated with a unit of raw material is shown at the bottom of the diagram, whereas the sales revenue for a unit of product is shown in the upper blocks. The diagram shows that in this example, no resource is devoted to one product only; each resource is part of the flow for production of both products, U and V. Each resource modifies the material moving through it using an amount of time in minutes, as shown for each process.

For products U and V, Exhibit 5.6 shows data that would usually be used to choose between the products.

V appears to be a more profitable product than U because:

- V requires less direct time than U.
- V has a lower material cost than U.

| | U | V | Percent Difference |
|---|---|---|---|
| Total direct time | 44 minutes | 43 minutes | 1/43 = 2.3% |
| Variable expense cost | $45 | $44 | 1/44 = 2.3% |
| Sales price | $80 | $84 | 4/84 = 4.8% |
| Contribution margin | $35 | $40 | 5/40 = 12.5% |

**Exhibit 5.6    Computed Traditional Data Per Unit of Product for Prioritizing Products U and V**

- V has a higher sales price than U.
- V provides more contribution margin than U.

We can compute the times required from resources A, B, C, and D to satisfy the total market demand of both products U and V (see Exhibit 5.7). We see from this computation that resource B is overloaded, as only 2,400 minutes are available in a 40-hour week. We therefore need to decide which of the two products is more profitable. Based on usual allocation costing criteria mentioned previously, product V is to be preferred. Following this through, if we decide to make all the V we can on resource B, then make U with any remaining time:

- We will make 100 units of V.
- The time needed to do so at resource B is 100 * 21 = 2,100.
- The amount of time at resource B then available for product U will be 2,400 – 2,100 = 300 minutes.
- In this time we will be able to make 300/12 = 25 units of U.
- The net income for a week will then be 100 * $40 + 25 * $35 = $4,875.

Now let us adopt the counterintuitive prioritization of making all the U that can be taken by the market, then making V in any time left over.

| Resource | Time Required for One Unit of U | V | Minutes for 80 Units of U and 100 Units of V |
|---|---|---|---|
| A | 12 | 9 | 80 * 12 + 100 * 9 = 1,860 |
| B | 12 | 21 | 80 * 12 + 100 * 21 = 3,060 |
| C | 8 | 8 | 80 * 8 + 100 * 8 = 1,440 |
| D | 12 | 5 | 80 * 12 + 100 * 5 = 1,460 |

**Exhibit 5.7    Unit Times Required at Each Resource**

- We will then make 80 units of U, using 80 * 12 = 960 minutes of resource B to do so.
- The weekly time remaining for resource B will be 2,400 − 960 = 1,440 minutes. In this time we will make 1,440/21 = 68.57 units of V.
- The net weekly income is then 80 * $35 + 68.57 * $40 = $5,543.

By the usual criteria mentioned previously, V seemed to be a more profitable product, but these calculations show that product U is in fact the more profitable, yielding $5,543 instead of $4,875. Why does the counterintuitive approach give more profit? Because it took into account the *velocity* of product through the system, a factor that other costing methods ignore.

**5.5 FLOW OF MONEY**   We may regard a company as a process that takes an input of money and produces an amplified output of money. For time-based costing we deal with money flows: dollars per hour (or some other unit of time).

At any instant in time, the total flow is considered to be the sum of two types of flow: a constant and a variable flow. For analysis, the money flows are divided into those two categories. The variable flow is a flow that follows the activity of a particular project or product. The constant flow is a flow that does not change over the time period being considered. These notions of variable and constant flow are discussed in detail later.

In the early days of modern industry, a century ago, many people were paid by piece rate. They were paid exactly according to the work they produced: The expense for their pay was variable because it varied with their output. As expensive machines and systems were introduced, compensation changed to weekly or monthly salaries. In other words, one was paid because the clock had ticked, regardless (in the short run) of how much work one had done. The variable outflow changed to a constant outflow. This is a constant outflow rate, because it is unrelated to the output for a specific project or product.

In most companies today, most workers continue to be employed whatever the daily inflow rate of money to the company. Most daily corporate expenses are also incurred without reference to exactly how much work is performed each day. Downsizing, the sale of units of the business, the replacement of unsuccessful people, and similar actions are usually taken based on overall performance data, not based on the short-term changes in project or product mix sold.

Payroll and many other expenses are constant over a time period much longer than the time period in which the sales figures fluctuate up and down. If people are paid by piece, that expense rate is linked exactly to the production rate of a product, so it is a variable expense. Similarly, raw materials, shipping, shipping insurance, and percentages paid to facilitate a specific sale are examples of variable expenses because they are linked to the money inflow rate deriving from a specific sale. If production workers or customer service people are paid a monthly salary, regardless of how much work they happen to do each day, they are part of the constant outflow rate.

The inflow of money is generated by the flow of goods and services. This leads to Exhibit 5.8, which shows the company as a process. The flow of product or service is in one direction and the flow of money in the other.

To do time-based costing, we divide the money outflow rate into two streams: the constant outflow and the variable outflow. The constant outflow is the rate in $/time_unit of money being expended that is constant, whatever the product or project

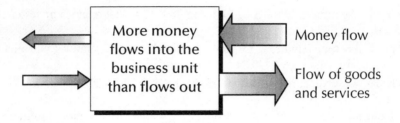

**Exhibit 5.8    Flow of Money**

mix. If workers are paid, or material or energy consumed, whatever the business unit does, they are part of the constant outflow. The computations for time-based costing are carried out without the allocations common to other methods of costing. Allocations, if wanted, are allocations of the flows of money, not of the money itself. To compute allocations, the flow rates are first computed, then allocated by their timewise behavior, considered as variable and constant flows.

Every outflow that is not constant is a variable outflow (see Exhibit 5.9). The method by which to determine whether the cost of an item is part of a constant flow is to imagine that the product or project mix changes by any arbitrary amount. Consider the true outflow of money, with no allocations, for one product or project of the mix. Part of that outflow will continue to be constant even though the flow of product or project slows or speeds up. For example, the total payroll expense may be constant whatever the rates of sales of various products. Those outflows of money that continue to be incurred at the same rate even if the rates of sales for products or projects change are part of the constant outflow.

The variable outflow changes as the product or project mix changes. We can apply the following test to find the variable costs associated with a product or project:

- If the product is being made or the project being carried out, imagine that it would be suddenly stopped. Any cost that would be saved is a variable cost.

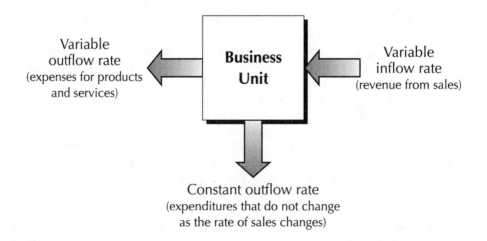

**Exhibit 5.9    Money Flow Rates**

- If the product is not yet being made or the project not yet being carried out, imagine that it would be started. The additional product or project-specific cost that would be incurred is a variable cost.

**5.6 IMPORTANCE OF A BOTTLENECK**    Because time-based costing is based on the flow rate of money, it takes into account both money and time. The flow of money is generated by the flow of goods and services, and usually the money flow is inseparably linked to the flow of goods and services. Therefore, to understand the times involved in the money flow, we must follow the timings of the flow of product or service. One of the concepts that has become rooted in management ideas, but which implicitly assumes that the flow of material (and hence money) is constant. is that of the fully utilized balanced facility. In fact, *the idea of a balanced facility where each resource is utilized 100 percent of the time is erroneous* and can never be achieved.

It seems intuitively correct that if the line were designed so that the capacities of each workstation were balanced, each station could be utilized for an equal amount of time. In that case, we would want to use each station 100 percent of the available time. In fact, that is not possible, because small statistical effects are enormously magnified in such a line. For example, imagine a customer order processing system, where at the first station we see a computer system taking orders, then a station processing the payments, then a station scheduling the orders, then a packing station, and so on. Even if the capacities of each station were exactly matched, it is inevitable that there would be a statistical variation of capacity over time at each station. Different orders require different times to process, machines and computers break down or malfunction temporarily, the pace at which people work changes, and so on.

A well-known game illustrates this point[5]: Ten people sit in a row, each with a die. Their job is to pass something (a match, say) from one to another at a preset pace—for instance once every 30 seconds. Each person is given one match to start with, and a new match is fed in at the beginning of the line every 30 seconds. However, before passing the match, each person rolls a die. If the number "2" shows, the person does not pass the match along. Each die will come up with a "2" a fraction 1/6 (16.7 percent) of the time. You may expect that if a match were passed into the line every half minute, then after 30 minutes the number of matches passed out of the line would be 60 * 5/6, which is 50. However, that is not so.

We can calculate the outcome of this game. The average utilization of each station is 5/6 = 83 percent. The maximum number of units of work a perfectly operating station could process in 50 minutes is 100, so this station will process on the average 83 units in 50 minutes.

Workstations have delays and breakdowns at unrelated times. When a workstation is "down" or delayed, it will starve the subsequent station, which, although capable of working, will not have material fed into it, so it will not be able to produce. The time lost is never recovered, because the starved station will not be able to produce at a capacity exceeding 100 percent when it resumes working. The temporarily starved station will thus have lost some production that will never be recovered. As a result, the capacity of the whole process will be reduced, so it will be lower than 83 percent. What will the capacity of the system of 10 stations be? To compute that precisely is exceptionally difficult, but we can find the lowest possible value of the capacity, which is called a lower bound. The lower bound is the time during which all the stations will definitely be working together and the line will surely be producing. For a 10-station line with each station working at 83 percent capacity, that lower bound is 0.83 ∗ 0.83 ∗ 0.83 . . . ten times, in other words, 0.16.

So if in a 40-hour week any one station is functioning 5/6 of the time (or 33.3 hours), the whole line will be productive for some value of time between 0.16 ∗ 40, which is 6.4 hours and 33.3 hours. The result is around 20 hours for the data used here. This explains an enormous frustration of managers: that a work system as a whole is much less efficient than any one process in the system.

It is interesting to note that Henry Ford, the entrepreneur of mass production, knew this well. At the River Rouge plant, a classical mass-production plant, each process was arranged so that it operated at less than 100 percent of its individual capacity, in order that the flow in the total process would not be impeded. For Ford, the timing of the individual flows to keep the entire process coordinated was more important than the efficiency of any single activity. That is a far cry from today's requirement—often applied blindly—that each process be 100 percent utilized. As Henry Ford knew, statistical variation is unavoidable, even when producing many identical copies of a single product. When providing a constantly changing mix of products and services, variation will be even greater.

We come now to an important principle of time-based costing, which is the influence of a *bottleneck* (also called a gate, constraint, or flow control point) on the money-making capability of a company. A bottleneck occurs because there is not enough time to do the work. Time is the same for everyone and every process—everywhere. As a result, time-based costing and the understanding that bottlenecks occur give a common time basis to the many processes that contribute to the money-making flows in a company.

A company may be in a position where it could sell everything it made, yet still could not meet the market demand. Because it cannot fulfill the market demand, there must necessarily be a bottleneck somewhere within its own work processes, or within the work processes of a supplier. The bottleneck possibly may not be at one fixed location, and it may even move around from time to time, but a bottleneck there surely is. On the other hand, there may be insufficient market for the output of the company, in which case the productive capacity in the company is underutilized. In that case, the bottleneck that controls the flow of money is not within the company itself but somewhere further along the value-providing chain—perhaps at a customer, a customer's customer, or further downstream the chain. This issue is further discussed in section 5.9.

**5.7 NET EARNINGS PER UNIT TIME**    Time-based costing deals with the flow rates of money through a company. As discussed previously, this flow passes through a bottleneck, either within the company or outside it. Exhibit 5.5 showed a flow of activities in which the product U, which appeared less profitable than product V by all conventional criteria, actually created a higher flow rate of income than did V. Product U required more direct time for production than did product V, it had higher material cost than V, had a lower sales price than V, and provided less margin per unit than V. Why was it the more profitable product? The reason is that when we deal with the flow rate of money, the best product or project is the one that produces the *greatest flow of money per unit time* at the bottleneck activity. When inflow rates were reasonably steady with time, as they used to be, the best product or project (according to the prioritization criteria based on a unit of product or service) was indeed the product or project that gave the highest inflow rate in dollars per unit of time. But when the inflow rate varies with time, as it often does in today's business world, the two criteria—one per unit of product and the other per unit of time—give different results.

For the previous example, product U creates a flow rate of $35/12 = $2.92 per minute at B, and V creates a flow rate of $40/21 = $1.9 per minute. U is, in fact the better product in this flow system. The conventional prioritization parameters in Exhibit 5.6 indicate that the profit to be expected from products U and V is close, less than 13 percent apart for any one of the four factors. But, in fact, product U is much more than marginally better. It is *very* much better, producing 54 percent more earnings per minute than V—not 13 percent more. However, U is not always or universally the better product: It is more profitable only in this network and given these numbers.

## 5.8 MONEY FLOW CONTROL DIAGRAM    The data used for the example discussed previously can be written as a set of easily understood equations. The data are the following:

- Timing data:
  —The time required from each of the four resources A, B, C, and D to produce one unit of U or V.
  —The time per week that each of the four resources is available for productive work.
- Market data:
  —The maximum sales (market limit) for U and V in the period (a week).
- Financial data:
  —The variable cost per unit of product U or V. (In this simple example, the variable cost was shown as raw material only.)
  —The sales income per unit of product.

Four equations will represent the time used at each of the four resources A, B, C, and D. The time used by resource A is shown in equation 6, where the number of units of U sold in the time interval of a week is represented by U and the number of units of V sold by the letter V. In deriving the equation, 12 minutes are required to produce each unit of U, 9 minutes are required for each unit of V, and resource A is available for 2,400 minutes per week. Similar reasoning gives equations 7, 8, and 9.

$$12 * U + 9 * V \leq 2,400 \text{ minutes at resource A} \tag{6}$$

$$12 * U + 21 * V \leq 2,400 \text{ minutes at resource B} \tag{7}$$

$$8 * U + 8 * V \leq 2,400 \text{ minutes at resource C} \tag{8}$$

$$12 * U + 5 * V \leq 2,400 \text{ minutes at resource D} \tag{9}$$

For this example, the contribution margin per unit of U is $35 and per unit of V is $40. Thus we can write an equation for the net revenue from production and sale of a quantity U units of product U and V units of product V.

$$\text{net revenue} = 35 * U + 40 * V \tag{10}$$

The limits of the market demand are written in the following equations:

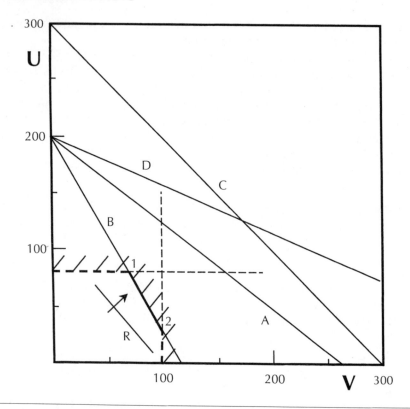

**Exhibit 5.10    Money Flow Control Diagram**

$$U \leq 80 \qquad \text{market limit} \qquad (11)$$

$$V \leq 100 \qquad \text{market limit} \qquad (12)$$

These equations are plotted graphically in Exhibit 5.10. The lines for equations 6 to 9 are labeled with the symbols of the relevant resources. The market limits of equations 11 and 12 are shown as dashed lines. The line R shows constant revenue for all combinations of U and V, which is equation 11. As the revenue line moves up and out on the diagram, it represents increasing sales of U and V, hence an increasing inflow of money. Exhibit 5.10 shows the limitations to the money inflow and is known as the *money flow control diagram*. The common factor behind all the lines shown is time, and the diagram shows how well time is used to create a flow of money into the organization from the flow of products and services out of the organization.

If one has a single value for the quantity of product U and a single value for the quantity of product V made and sold in a week, one obtains a single point in the diagram of Exhibit 5.10. For example, assume that, in a particular week, 20 units of U and 30 units of V are made and sold. The point corresponding to U = 20 and V = 30 can be plotted on the diagram. We see that it falls in a region for which the following statements hold:

- The quantity of U and V can be absorbed by the market.
- The quantity of time needed by each resource is less than the limit of 2,400 minutes.

It is thus feasible to make and sell 20 units of U and 30 units of V in a week.

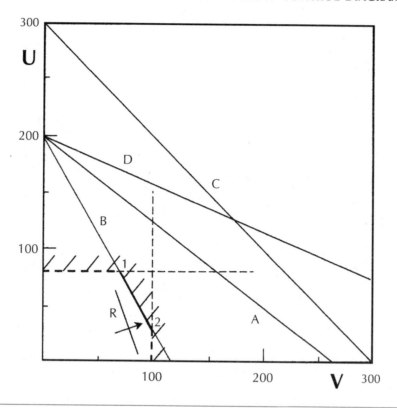

**Exhibit 5.11    Money Flow Diagram with Different Contribution Margins**

Now imagine that one wants to make and sell 80 units of U and 100 units of V in a week. The market can absorb those quantities, but we see on the diagram that this point falls above the line for resource B, indicating that resource B does not have enough time in the week to make those quantities of products.

In summary we see that the diagram shows a closed region within which the combination of U and V must fall to be feasible. This region is the allowed operating region, where all the equations 6 through 11 are satisfied. If the revenue line R were to move beyond the boundary of the operating region, it would move into a region where there is insufficient time or insufficient market to manufacture and sell all the quantity of U or V. The highest rate of money inflow is achieved when the line R moves up so that it touches the boundary of the operating region, which in this case is point 1 on the diagram. We see that at point 1, the quantity of product U is 80 and of product V is 68.57, just as was computed previously in section 5.5.

Exhibit 5.11 is the same as Exhibit 5.10, but the contribution margins of the two products have been changed. The contribution margin values do not affect the time used by, or available to, any of the resources, nor do they change the market demand. They affect only the factors in equation 10, so they affect only the slope of the line that shows the revenue from sales of the two products. Notice, however, that because of the change in the slope of the revenue line, it may reach the border of the operating region at point 2 rather than at point 1 (as before). We may therefore conclude that product V (rather than product U as before) now gives a higher inflow rate of money. That con-

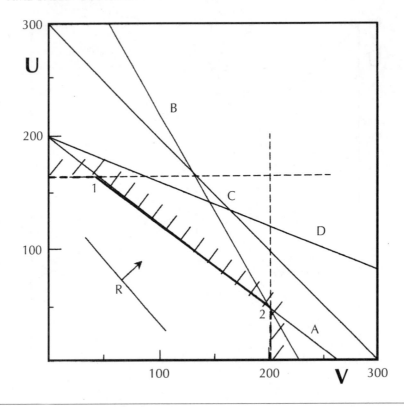

**Exhibit 5.12    Money Flow Diagram With Changed Capacity and Market Demand**

clusion could not be reached from the financial data alone: It requires knowledge of both the financial data, expressed in the revenue line, and the timing data, expressed in the sloping lines that represent the time used by the four resources.

Exhibit 5.12 resembles Exhibits 5.10 and 5.11 except that the available capacity of resource B has been doubled, as has the market demand for the two products. Doubling the capacity of resource B could have been achieved by investing in a new resource B, by adding a second shift in a single-shift operation, or by outsourcing. We see that the lines that represent the market demands for U and V move to new positions, and the line representing the use of resource B moves up. In doing so, the shape of the operating region changes, and the resource that now borders the region is A, not B. A has become the bottleneck. This shows us that every time the market demand changes, or every time we add or remove capacities of resources, borders of the operating region may change, which means that we must again evaluate the operating region's shape and find out which resource is the bottleneck.

The diagram shown here is for two products or services. Note that for three products the diagram would be three-dimensional. For more than two products the diagram cannot be plotted on a sheet of paper and must be constructed and analyzed in a computer. Prototype software to do so has been developed.

**5.9 EXTENDED ENTERPRISE**    When dealing with the time-dependent flows of money, we should view the flow as a single "river" of money flowing through all the companies in the value-providing chain of the "extended enterprise."

A company is a legally recognized entity with defined boundaries of responsibility and authority. In that sense, each company is indeed an independent entity. However, operational terms do not need to be identical with the legal concepts. Companies in the past perceived themselves as stand-alone in both the legal and the operational contexts. A company would make its plans based on orders from customers, data about developments in the marketplace, and information from suppliers and other sources. Whatever the sources of information, the plans and management decisions were made autonomously by the company alone, and implementation of those plans made no provision for modification caused by real-time information sent from sources external to the company. If such changes were needed, they were considered interruptions and required management intervention and decision.

Times have changed. Today companies begin to perceive themselves as part of value-providing chains. They operate under conditions where the ability to change is as important, and perhaps even more important, than the ability to be unchangingly efficient. Jack Welch, the successful chief executive officer of General Electric, says that when change imposed from outside the company is faster than the ability of the company to change internally, the company is doomed. It may be doing its work very efficiently, quickly, and at good quality and low cost, but it is nevertheless doomed.

These changes in perceptions, structure, and management focus derive from developing concepts of the world as a network and also from concrete business reasons. Many companies have discovered that a major proportion of their costs derive from suppliers, whether those provide raw material, machines, services, or anything else that a company uses. In many manufacturing companies, if the costs of shipped product are analyzed, the fraction of the cost going to suppliers varies from 50 percent to 95 percent. As these companies have become more efficient and have reduced costs internally, they have found that the major opportunity to reduce cost is in the supply chain. If one holds the supplier at arm's length and fails to coordinate work processes between companies, the cost reduction will be a grudging few percentage points. However, if the work processes are coordinated between companies in such a way that the customer changes its demands to allow the supplier to save money, and the supplier does things differently so that the customer can also save money, significant savings are possible. If a supplier makes a change that saves money internally for Harley-Davidson, the motorcycle manufacturer, Harley can share the savings with the supplier, as a motivation to generate the savings.

Hence, competitive pressures for reduced cost and time, together with the requirement that companies enhance their ability to change under the pressures of unavoidable drivers, have created a new and dynamic system within which companies interact. We thus perceive the emergence of companies that interact in a network instead of the isolated nodes that existed before. This new system is the extended enterprise. No deliberate decision or action created this new system; competitive pressures did.

When business processes interact in real time they necessarily become dynamic. We all have experienced a system that changes from being arm's length and static to being interactive and dynamic. Road traffic is such a system. We can consider the car in front to be operating on a piece of road, then passing that piece of road on to the car behind. The amount of road between the cars is analogous to the inventory placed between the companies—in warehouses or somewhere else inside the logistics system. Consider travel on a road on which the traffic is spread out widely. On such a road, the driver of a car does not have to look in the mirror at the car behind and also does not have to pay attention to the brake lights of the car ahead. The situation can be summarized as follows:

- No real-time information from the cars behind or ahead is needed to drive.
- Each driver can autonomously choose any speed, without being influenced by cars ahead or behind, until the entire road (which represents material) between the cars is used up.
- On the open road, the rates of acceleration and deceleration have no importance. The quality of the braking system is unimportant.

Now consider driving in an interactive traffic system—a crowded freeway. In such a situation, a driver must pay careful attention to the brake lights of the car ahead and to the car behind. The situation can be summarized as follows:

- Exchange of real-time information between cars becomes essential.
- Whereas a driver on an open road can make an autonomous decision about driving speed, no single driver on a crowded freeway can make that decision.
- The speed of traffic becomes a system characteristic that is defined by the complex and dynamic interactions between the cars.
- In crowded traffic, the ability to accelerate or decelerate is very important to avoid accidents and to succeed, and the quality of the braking system is very important indeed.

The real-time interaction of the cars on a crowded road creates a single system. In this system, dynamic effects (e.g., the ability to accelerate and decelerate) become primary characteristics of survival and success. This is in contrast to the open road, where each car is managed independently in a static environment in which the ability to accelerate is unimportant. Similarly, the commercial world has evolved from being a collection of independent business units with static behavior to being a single system operating in a dynamic mode. Today's industrial and commercial world, being interactive and dynamic, behaves fundamentally differently than the past arm's-length, static system of the past. As a result, it requires fundamentally different management approaches.

Exhibit 5.13 shows the flows of money down the value-providing chain of an extended enterprise, along with the products and services that justify that money flow up the chain. As the flow corresponding to a single product (or product family) gets closer to the end customer, the value of a unit of the product increases and so does the money flow rate corresponding to the flow of units of product.

**5.10 INTERNAL AND EXTERNAL BOTTLENECKS**   The flow of money and the corresponding flow of goods and services extend through the entire value-providing network. To think of the money flow in one company alone without considering the flows upstream through its suppliers and their suppliers and downstream through its customers and their customers is to neglect an important piece of reality. Theoretically, the entire value-providing network should be considered, though in practice one must restrict one's attention to a manageable part of the network. When a business plan is prepared at Texas Instruments, the motto is "two up, two down."[6] The business plan is

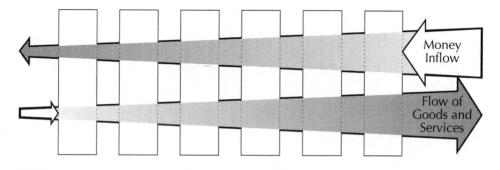

**Exhibit 5.13    Money Flow in an Extended Enterprise**

expected to consider the effects of five companies in the value-providing chain relevant to Texas Instruments.

A bottleneck that impedes the flow of goods and services—and hence of money—may therefore be either within a company or somewhere else in the extended enterprise chain. If the bottleneck is within a company, the market could take more goods but the company's ability to provide them is limited. If the bottleneck is somewhere along the chain of suppliers, the limitation is in one of the suppliers. If the bottleneck is in the customer side of the chain, the production capacity of the company (and probably also of the suppliers) is underutilized.

We see that a bottleneck that impedes the flow of money *always* exists, but it may not exist inside the company. It always exists because there are seven days in everyone's week, and 24 hours in everyone's day. The beat of the clock ties everyone together in the web of interaction of modern commerce.

When managers face a decision whether to produce and sell a new product or service, they commonly ask, "Is there a market?" This is the "push" question, which is usually generated by innovative product development. Asking this question implies that the bottleneck is in the market and that the systems of the extended enterprise can supply the demand. A "pull" question, by contrast, starts in the marketplace, when one sees an opportunity to sell a product or service. The question to ask then is "Is there enough time?" The meaning of this question is that one should ensure that the sales effort will not be impeded by a bottleneck somewhere along the value-providing chain that would limit the supply of product.

The implications of such observations are many and pervasive. For instance, if a company is producing when there is no internal bottleneck, management must work hard both to increase markets and to reduce expenses. On the other hand, the bottleneck may be within a supplier, in which case it will not help to look for a bottleneck in one's own organization. It may even be worthwhile to spend some of the company's money to help the supplier overcome its bottleneck (e.g., by making a loan or some other arrangement).

If there is an internal bottleneck that cannot be overcome and remains in place, the company has to decide which of its projects or products are to be preferred, because there is not enough capacity to produce the entire market demand of every product. The use of gross margin for this decision is erroneous. The parameter for prioritizing the choice is the dollars produced per unit time of constrained resource (bottleneck) used by the product or project. This simple rule, which is understood by only a few man-

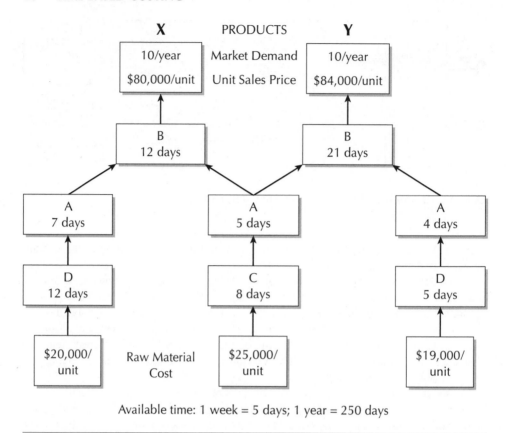

**X**        PRODUCTS        **Y**

Exhibit 5.14   Activity Flow Diagram for an Extended Enterprise

agers who previously prioritized products by gross margin, has yielded millions of dollars in real profit to their companies. The question they asked themselves was not "how much margin do I make on a unit of product X?" but "how much money per hour does a sale of one unit of product X bring me?" That is the question one asks when faced with today's changing world.

The flow of money needs to be seen as extending throughout the extended enterprise: Thus, a bottleneck outside one's own company may inhibit one's own inflow of money. Exhibit 5.14 shows an activity flow diagram for an extended enterprise of four suppliers, A, B, C, and D, which together produce two products, X and Y. Product X is made up of two items of raw material that cost $20,000 and $25,000 each. The item that costs $20,000 takes 12 days to pass through supplier D, then 7 days to pass through supplier A; then it is sent to supplier B. The item that costs $25,000 takes 8 days to pass through supplier C, then 5 days to pass through supplier A; then it meets up with the $20,000 item at supplier B, which takes 12 days to assemble the final product X. The raw material item that costs $19,000 passes through supplier D, requiring 5 days, then supplier A, taking 4 days, then gets to supplier B, which takes 21 days to assemble the $19,000 item with the $25,000 item to produce final product Y. The diagram shows that the maximum sales of product X is 10 per year at $80,000 per unit and of product Y is 10 per year at $84,000 per unit. Furthermore, the maximum time available to all the suppliers for this work is 250 days per year.

The data for the activity flow diagram of Exhibit 5.14 can be shown as a series of simple equations that are plotted on Exhibit 5.15. These equations are:

$$12 * X + 9 * Y \leq 250 \text{ days at resource A} \tag{13}$$

$$12 * X + 21 * Y \leq 250 \text{ days at resource B} \tag{14}$$

$$8 * X + 8 * Y \leq 250 \text{ days at resource C} \tag{15}$$

$$12 * X + 5 * Y \leq 250 \text{ days at resource D} \tag{16}$$

For this example, the contribution margin per unit of product X is $80,000 – ($20,000 + $25,000) or $35,000. The contribution margin per unit of product Y is by a similar calculation, $84,000 – ($25,000 + $19,000), or $40,000. Thus, we can write the equation for the net revenue from production and sale of a quantity X units of product X and Y units of product Y as follows:

$$\text{net revenue} = 35{,}000 * X + 40{,}000 * Y \tag{17}$$

The limits of the market demand are written in the following equations:

$$X \leq 10 \qquad \text{market limit} \tag{18}$$

$$Y \leq 10 \qquad \text{market limit} \tag{19}$$

We see in Exhibit 5.15 that the operating region for this setup is bounded by the market demand and by the capacity of supplier B. When moving the revenue line to the boundary of the operating region we see that it meets the boundary at point 1. Therefore, the maximum money inflow rate is attained when the market demand for X, 10 per year, is met. Supplier B assembles as many Y as possible in the remaining time, which turns out to be 6.2 per year. For supplier A in that activity flow, if supplier B would manage to speed up its work, the money inflow rate for all the extended enterprise, including supplier A, would increase. If supplier A would do his work differently to save time at supplier B, even if time were added at supplier A to do so, the money inflow would increase to all four suppliers.

Exhibit 5.16 shows the money flow control diagram for another situation in which each supplier works on one product, so there is no interaction between products and suppliers. In this example, the sales of product family P2 are limited by the capability of supplier S3, but both suppliers S1 and S2 have more than enough time to produce the market demand of product P1. The diagram illustrates that the line for supplier S3 is exactly horizontal, meaning that it invests time only in product family S3, whereas the lines for suppliers S1 and S2 are exactly vertical, indicating that they invest time only in product family P1. In this case, if supplier S3 would increase his rate of production, that would have no effect at all on the other suppliers. Management efforts to improve the conversion efficiencies of a company often neglect the fact that a supplier may have to share his time between different products. They implicitly assume that each supplier uses his time for one product only, as shown in this example. Time-based costing can deal with the case in which the supplier is a shared resource because it starts off from the premise that time is the one resource common to all the suppliers, and no supplier has available more than 168 hours in a week or 52 weeks in a year. It is a more reliable method for prioritizing efforts between suppliers than costing methods that ignore the effect of time.

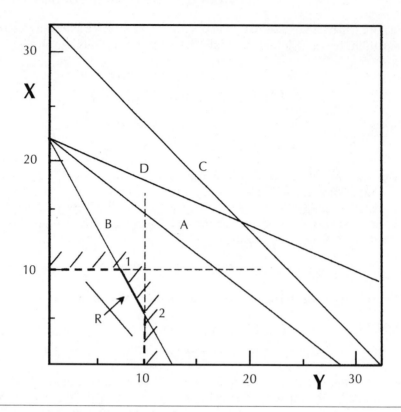

**Exhibit 5.15   Money Flow Control Diagram**

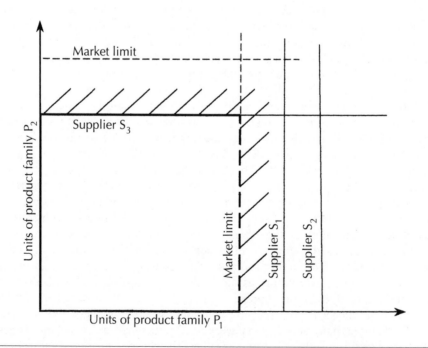

**Exhibit 5.16   Money Flow Diagram (Each Supplier Makes Only One Product)**

**5.11 FLOWS AND ALLOCATIONS**    Time-based costing divides money flows into constant and variable flows. We now consider those flows in more detail.

Under what conditions is an outflow termed "constant"? Nothing lasts forever. Companies upsize and downsize: They sell and buy divisions. Actions such as these do affect money outflow, but they themselves are influenced only in a general way by changes in the rate of sales. They, instead, are the result of managerial decisions that are usually not directly tied, hour by hour or day by day, with sales and, hence, with money inflow. The *variable* outflow is tied directly to the rate of sales of products and, hence, is directly related to the money inflow from sales. The *constant* outflow, however, is not directly tied to inflow from sales.

The flow that is considered constant depends on the managerial level within a company. Someone responsible for a production line within a plant would consider the expenses incurred by the plant surrounding him to be constant, because he would not be able to affect those outflows, and they are not affected by sales from the production line. For this manager, variable flows change over a short period, maybe days. The time perspective of a plant manager who has within his responsibility several production lines will be longer than that of a production-line manager. And the time perspective of a group manager responsible for several plants will be longer than that of a plant manager. He may think in terms of the revenue from each single plant, just as a production line manager thinks of the time-based inflow rate from a single product, or the plant manager for a single production line.

Considering an activity flow diagram such as the one shown in Exhibit 5.5 from the perspective of a line manager, a single resource such as A, B, C, or D might be a process machine. From the perspective of a plant manager, A, B, C, or D might represent a production line. From the perspective of a divisional manager responsible for several plants that contribute to a product or service that is shipped and sold, each resource A, B, C, or D might represent a whole plant.

To allocate the flows, then, we allocate them not on the basis of the products to which they contribute but on the basis of the time period over which they appear to be variable. Over the time that one deals with a single unit of product within a batch, the outflows related to the batch appear to be constant. Over the time that one deals with a batch, the outflows related to the product line appear constant, and so on.

Exhibit 5.17 shows the inflow rate from sales along with four outflow rates. The unit-

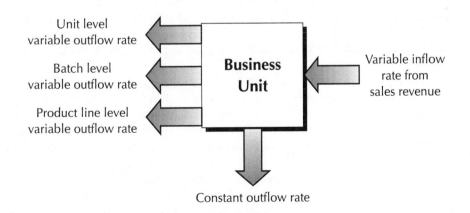

**Exhibit 5.17    Inflow Rate from Sales**

level outflow changes more rapidly than the batch-level outflow rate, which changes more rapidly than the product-line-level outflow rate. And there are always even more slowly changing flows, which are grouped under the arrow called constant outflow rate. These are all types of outflow commonly used in accounting practice: They show one approach for allocating the outflow according to the rate of change of the flow rate. The variable outflow may be divided up according to these or even other categories, but it is always based on the rate of change in the money velocity.

To sum up:

- Unit-level outflow will be incurred for each unit of product. It includes material, freight, insurance, and other costs incurred directly for each unit of product. This is the traditional variable cost.
- Batch-level outflow will be incurred whenever batches are made. It varies over time—as does the demand and, hence, the production of batches of product.
- Product-level variable outflows are cost flows incurred at the product level that are not part of either the unit-level or the batch-level outflow. This outflow rate may be attributable to a family or collection of products or projects. The organization or setup costs to produce a new product family would be a product-level variable outflow.

**5.12 ORGANIZATIONAL IMPLICATION**    The central and most important implication for the organization derives from the fact that time and financial data are tied together inseparably. In most organizations, time data is the province of operational personnel, whereas financial data is the province of the finance department. This separation follows from the methods of conventional financial management, in which timing data had no influence on computed profitability, which (as we have seen) was valid only in a world of slow change. But in today's rapidly changing world, we can no longer separate timing data from financial data. When people dealing with timing data work separately from those dealing with financial data, misunderstandings often ensue. Financial people and operations people should work together. Joint teams should be charged with the responsibility of improving the net inflow of money per unit time from each product or project rather than focusing only the net margin per unit of product.

It is not feasible to know all the timing data in great detail for every resource in every process in a company. However, it should be clear that one needs accurate data for processes that are bottlenecks or that are close to the operating region in the money control diagram: For processes far from the operating region, the data can be approximate. This observation is helpful in prioritizing the efforts of any team dealing with time-based costing.

This recommendation can be seen in the context of the money flow control diagram. In that diagram, the slope of the revenue line depends only on variable costs. The slopes and locations of the resource lines depend on speeds and capacities of the resources. Money is traditionally the province of cost accounting, whereas speeds and capacities are the province of operations and production engineering. But all these issues affect the operating region and must all be dealt with in a coordinated way. Consequently, members of both cost and process management must be one team.

The effect of time on overhead rates is often neglected. A typical case occurred in 1996, when a division of one well-known defense company was bought by another well-known defense company. Executives of the division that was bought had been used to a policy of investing to save time at bottleneck resources. Executives of the new owner insisted on seeing an ROI computation before committing to a project. Moreover, they insisted on using the fixed corporate overhead rate in that computation.

In fact, as the velocity of products through the company increases, the overhead rate should go down. Imagine, for example, that the overhead rate in a company is 50 percent and that the money outflow rate for overhead expenses is constant. In other words, overhead personnel and other expenses per week are constant, whatever projects are being worked on. Now imagine that a project with a direct cost of $1 million could be completed in a year. In that year, the project would thus use $0.5 million of overhead resource. But if the time required to finish the project can be reduced to six months— and if there is enough useful work in other projects to take up the freed-up overhead resource—the project now would use only $0.25 million of overhead resource. The overhead rate should thus be reduced to 25 percent.

In the case of the defense company referred to, the new executive group insisted on using a fixed overhead rate; they would not allow for a reduction in the overhead rate corresponding to a reduction of time. They thus neglected a major benefit of time reduction and actually eliminated projects that would have made the company more profitable.

**5.13 PRIORITIZATION OF PRODUCTS, PROJECTS, AND IMPROVEMENTS**    The money flow control diagram shows that the payoff available from improvements differs for different resources or processes. In Exhibits 5.10, 5.11, and 5.15 we can see that B is the bottleneck process, because the line for B is a border of the operating region. If we reduce the time taken by work at resource B, or if we increase the amount of resource B available, the line for B will move up, the operating region in the diagram will increase, and the money inflow rate will increase. However, making such improvements for resources A, C, or D will have no effect on the border of the operating region; in fact, it will be a waste of effort. Improvement efforts should therefore focus on bottleneck processes, and each time an improvement is made, one should check what now limits the inflow rate of money and whether another process has become a new bottleneck.

The steps to be taken can be summarized (with the aid of the money flow control diagram) as follows:

- *Focus cost-cutting efforts on the nonbottleneck processes.* For those processes, reducing the amount of resource or increasing the amount of time spent by them will have no effect on the money inflow rate.
- *Focus improvement investments on the bottleneck process.* Check the value of making such an investment by computing the expected increase in inflow rate, then compare that with the amount of investment to compute the payback time.

Exhibit 5.18 shows money flow data regarding a proposed investment of $1 million.

- The net inflow rate before the investment is, according to the data, $1,200,000 − ($600,000 + $500,000) = $100,000.
- The net inflow rate after the investment is, according to the data, $1,400,000 − ($620,000 + $585,000) = $195,000.
- The increase in net inflow rate is $195,000 − $100,000 = $95,000.

|  | Before Investment | After Investment |
|---|---|---|
| Gross inflow rate from sales | $1,200,000 per month | $1,400,000 per month |
| Variable outflow rate | $500,000 per month | $585,000 per month |
| Constant outflow rate | $600,000 per month | $620,000 per month |

**Exhibit 5.18    Data to Compute Payback Time of Investment to Increase the Money Inflow Rate**

- The payback time for the investment of $1,000,000 is then $1,000,000 / $95,000 = 10.5 months.

If there is a bottleneck in an organization, management should remember that the most valuable resource it has is time at the bottleneck. Every product or project prioritization decision should first be subject to the question, "Does this generate the best use of time at the bottleneck?"

If a bottleneck exists in an organization, no product is always, under all circumstances, more profitable than another. Deciding which product produces the greatest money inflow rate depends on where the bottleneck is and how it is used. The factor governing prioritization is the money flow per unit time at the bottleneck.

If one changes only the financial unit margin data for a product or process but not the timing data, the prioritization of products or projects might change also. This was illustrated in Exhibit 5.11 compared with Exhibit 5.10. In Exhibit 5.10, the point that gives the greatest money inflow rate in the money flow control diagram is 1; in Exhibit 5.11 it is 2. At point 1 the product that produces the greater inflow rate is U; at point 2 it is V.

Having decided that a particular product gives the highest money inflow rate based on a given bottleneck, one should ensure that everyone in the company understands that priority. Practices of operational personnel should ensure that the bottleneck resource is never idle, and sales personnel should be instructed to prioritize their efforts so that the mix of products sold, which generates the inflow rate of money, should give the greatest possible money flow at the bottleneck.

If the market can absorb more products and there is no bottleneck within one's own organization, the bottleneck must be within a supplier. Therefore, one must work with suppliers to identify and overcome this bottleneck, remembering that overcoming a *supplier's* bottleneck increases the money inflow rate into *your* organization.

If there is no bottleneck in the company and, given the current mix of products and services, the sales cannot be increased, one must find ways to change what is offered in order to increase sales. Such efforts may include segmentation or mass customization. In figuring the cost benefit of such proposed efforts, the criterion is how much the net inflow rate of money will be increased, not the margin per unit of product or service.

**5.14 SUMMARY**    One is always interested in the financial return per unit of time (e.g., a quarter or year) of a company. Prioritization of products or services according to the margin per unit of a product implies that money flow rates are constant. This assumption may have been reasonable in the past, but it is not reasonable in today's volatile world, where sales rates often fluctuate considerably. As a result, when management considers the cost of producing and selling a product or service, the question to ask is not, "How many net dollars do we make from the sale of a unit of product?" but "By how much is the rate of money inflow increased by the sale of a unit of product?" Computed examples and published data from the Rhône Poulenc Corporation illustrated that the use of margin per unit can give an erroneous prioritization, because it can cause management to prefer a product or service that does not give the best return per unit of time.

The rate of sales may be limited by the flow rate of products within one's organization because of the presence of a bottleneck. Time-based costing therefore takes into account the effect of a bottleneck by using concepts from the theory of constraints. The rate of money inflow into a company or profit center is computed from the margin per unit of product multiplied by the flow velocity of products and services. That flow velocity is limited by one of two factors:

- Insufficient market demand.
- Insufficient time at a needed resource, which then becomes a bottleneck unable to meet the market demand.

The product or service that contributes most to the profitability of a company is the one that uses time to the best effect. In other words, the best product is the one that produces the most margin per unit of time at the bottleneck.

To perform a time-based costing analysis one needs both financial and timing data. Examples in this chapter show that the most profitable product, given one set of timing and cost data is not always, under all circumstances, the most profitable. As the times used by different resources or the margin per unit of product change, the product that gives the greatest money inflow rate may change.

The interaction and influence of the two factors that limit money flow can be represented as a money flow control diagram. When considering two products this is conveniently plotted on paper; for more than two products one uses a computer program. That diagram shows that there is a bounded operating region that controls the flow rates of the various products. The feasible flow rates of the different products and the optimum flow rates that give the greatest return per unit time can be determined from the diagram.

The principles of time-based costing are not limited to a single company only. They apply also to an extended enterprise or value-providing chain. In this case, each supplier can be considered a "resource." It then becomes clear that the rate of money inflow to one company may be restricted by a bottleneck at a supplier that limits the money inflow rate to all the players in the extended enterprise. Overcoming that supplier's bottleneck will then increase the money inflow rate to the entire extended enterprise. Such an undertaking, in which all the companies in the extended enterprise benefit, requires negotiation and coordination of efforts and investments. The aim is to make the effort worthwhile for everyone, even though the bottleneck may be at one company only.

Time-based costing provides a framework for prioritizing improvement and reengineering efforts. In short, if a process is a bottleneck, one should overcome it, even if this requires investment. The places to save money are the nonbottleneck processes, because even if work slows down in those areas, the money inflow rate will not be affected. Of course, all these actions should be accompanied by careful analysis, because whenever changes occur in financial or process timing data, the shape of the operating region in the money flow control diagram can also change.

The most important implementation recommendation is a people issue. It follows from the fact that time and money are dealt with together, not separately. As a result, the people who deal with money, usually in a finance department, and the people who deal with timings, usually in an operational department, need to work together on the same team, to develop a detailed understanding of the interaction between timing and cost data on money flow rates.

## NOTES

1. T. Johnson and R. Kaplan, *Relevance Lost: The Rise and Fall of Management Accounting* (Harvard Business School Press, 1987).

2. R. Shulman, "Rhône-Poulenc Uses Profit Velocity to Pave the Way to Agility," *Agility & Global Competition,* Vol. 1, No. 1 (1997): 42–58.

3. E. M. Goldratt and J. Cox. *The Goal: A Process of Ongoing Improvement* (North River Press, 1994); E. M. Goldratt. *The Haystack Syndrome: Sifting Information Out of the Data Ocean* (North River Press, 1991).

4. P. F. Drucker. *Managing in a Time of Great Change* (New York: Truman Talley Books/Plume, 1995).

5. S. L. Goldman, R. N. Nagel, and K. Preiss. *Agile Competitors and Virtual Organizations: Strategies for Enriching the Customer* (New York: Van Nostrand Reinhold, 1995).

6. K. Preiss, S. L. Goldman, and R. N. Nagel, *Cooperate to Compete: Building Agile Business Relationships* (New York: Van Nostrand Reinhold, 1996).

## APPENDIX

The chapter showed the relation between flow rate and money entering the system as a summation of time intervals. Anyone familiar with high school calculus will recognize that the mathematical method of dealing with this is to understand the money flow rate as an instantaneous value. The amount of dollars accumulated in any time period is a mathematical integral over that period. The total amount of dollars fed into the system over a time period from t1 to t2, from any one product or service, is obtained by mathematical integration. Because the product velocity is not constant, it cannot be separated from the contribution margin. The total amount of money flowing into the system from a single product or project, denoted as i, in a time period from t1 to t2, is, in general, then:

$$\$_i = \int_{t1}^{t2} (\text{flow rate})_i \, dt$$

$$= \int_{t1}^{t2} (\text{unit margin})_i * (\text{product velocity})_i \, dt$$

(A1)

The contribution margin for a product is usually constant over time period t1 to t2, so it may be extracted from the integral above to obtain equation A2:

$$\$_i \ = \ (\text{unit margin})_i \ * \ \int_{t1}^{t2} (\text{product velocity})_i \, dt$$

(A2)

$$= \ CM_i \ * \ \int_{t1}^{t2} v_i \, dt$$

To extend this equation to all the products or services passing through the system, the value obtained from equation A2 must be summed over all products or projects, obtaining equation A3, where $CM_i$ denotes the unit margin or contribution margin of product i.

$$\text{Total Inflow Sum \$} \ = \ \sum_{\text{products } i} \left( CM_i \ * \int_{t1}^{t2} v_i \, dt \right)$$

(A3)

# CHAPTER 6

# SHAREHOLDER VALUE AND ECONOMIC PROFIT

## William Hubbell
### Arthur Andersen

**6.1 INTRODUCTION** The global economic landscape was transformed in the 1990s by U.S.-style capitalism. Shareholder value became the mantra of business on every continent. In today's connected, global economy, boards and managers increasingly recognize that their primary responsibility is to maximize the total wealth-creating potential of the enterprises under their direction. For today's senior executives, finding the answers to the following three questions has become critical:

1. Are managers creating or destroying wealth?
2. How are managers creating or destroying wealth?
3. How can managers increase wealth creation?

The purpose of this chapter is to help answer these questions.

**6.2 MEASURING WEALTH CREATION** When asked how the typical company measures whether wealth is being created or destroyed, most managers would point to the company's financial statements. Most would cite earnings or earnings per share (EPS). They would, in fact, be referring to the accounting model of wealth creation. This model assumes that the market determines a stock's price by establishing some multiple of earnings, known as the *price earnings* (P/E) ratio. Thus, the stock price for a company with EPS of $1 and a P/E ratio of 10 is $10. A fundamental assumption of wealth creation in this accounting model is that as earnings growth increases, the company's stock will demand a higher P/E ratio. For example, as the company's earnings grow 100 percent to $2 per share, the P/E ratio should increase to something higher than 10, which means that the price per share would be higher than $20.

**(a) No Correlation Between Earnings Growth and Price/Earnings Ratios** If the accounting model were a good description of how share prices are set, a statistical relationship—or *correlation*—would be found between the growth in EPS and P/E ratios. Have market observers found such a correlation? The answer is a resounding no. In fact, several studies have shown that the correlation between earnings growth and P/E ratios is almost <u>zero</u>.[1] This result makes the accounting model virtually useless as a good predictor of share prices. More complete information is needed to explain the movement of share prices.

**(b) Problems with Accounting Earnings**    Traditional accounting earnings present the following problems:

- The amount of capital required to generate the earnings is ignored.
- The only financing cost reflected in accounting earnings is interest expense.
- Equity is treated as if it were cost free.
- Accounting earnings are affected by accruals and reserves that are recorded in order to conform to generally accepted accounting principles (GAAP). These adjustments distort the true economic reality of a company's financial transactions and results of operations.

Managers need a measure that corrects for these problems. The measure that best solves these problems is *residual income* or *economic profit* (EP).[2]

The stock market recognizes that earnings are necessary—but not sufficient in themselves—to measure wealth creation and set share prices. Investors also take into account how much capital is required to generate a stream of earnings. For example, consider the comparison in Exhibit 6.1 of two companies that compete in the same industry.

Which company is performing better? On first inspection, their performance is identical. Neither company is doing better than the other based on the revenues, costs, and profits shown. However, an important piece of information is missing. Company *A* has invested $100 million in capital, whereas Company *B* has invested only $50 million. Company *A*'s return on capital (profit/capital) is 12 percent. Company *B*'s return on capital is 24 percent. Company *B*'s performance therefore is two times better than Company *A*'s. The managers of Company *B* require only half as much capital as Company *A* to produce the same results.

**(c) Measuring Capital as Well as Earnings**    Investors need to measure not only earnings but also a company's use of capital to make informed investment decisions. The measure that combines all the relevant economic factors is EP. EP is defined as *operating profits after tax less a charge for the capital employed.* For example, assume that Exhibit 6.2 shows the financial statements of ABC Company.

To calculate EP, the amount of capital employed by ABC company must first be calculated, as shown in Exhibit 6.3.

|  | Company A | Company B |
| --- | --- | --- |
| Revenues | $100,000,000 | $100,000,000 |
| Operating costs | $ 80,000,000 | $ 80,000,000 |
| Pretax profits | $ 20,000,000 | $ 20,000,000 |
| Taxes | $  8,000,000 | $  8,000,000 |
| After-tax profits | $ 12,000,000 | $ 12,000,000 |
| Profit margin | 12% | 12% |

**Exhibit 6.1    Company Comparison**

**Income Statement**

| | |
|---|---|
| Revenues | $ 1,000,000 |
| Costs | $ 700,000 |
| Profit before tax | $ 300,000 |
| Taxes | $ 120,000 |
| Profit after tax | $ 180,000 |

**Balance Sheet**

| Current assets | | Current liabilities | |
|---|---|---|---|
| Accounts receivable | $ 250,000 | Accounts payable | $ 75,000 |
| Inventories | $ 90,000 | | |
| Total current assets | $ 340,000 | Long-term debt | $ 442,750 |
| Net fixed assets | $ 1,000,000 | Equity | $ 822,250 |
| Total assets | $ 1,340,000 | Total liabilities and equity | $ 1,340,000 |

**Exhibit 6.2 Financial Statements for ABC Company**

Exhibit 6.4 shows the calculation of EP for the ABC Company.

The calculation in Exhibit 6.4 is often referred to as the *residual income method*. EP can also be calculated by the *spread method*, as shown in Exhibit 6.5.

The residual income method is a useful format for reporting results of operations. Managers are used to seeing financial results in a profit-and-loss format. Now they can see the additional cost of managing the capital they have been entrusted with—the capital charge. However, the spread method is a good teaching device for viewing investment opportunities. In the example, the company is earning a positive EP of $51,413 because the spread is a positive 4 percent.

More EP can be earned in one of two ways:

1. By increasing the spread on the current capital base.
2. By increasing the capital invested while still maintaining a positive spread.

**6.3 ADJUSTMENTS** Today's financial statements conform to GAAP, whose accounting principles are highly conservative. One of the main objectives of GAAP is not to

**Capital Employed**

| | |
|---|---|
| Current assets | $ 340,000 |
| Current liabilities | $ 75,000 |
| Net working capital | $ 265,000 |
| Net fixed capital | $ 1,000,000 |
| Total capital | $ 1,265,000 |

**Exhibit 6.3 Capital Employed at ABC Company**

| Residual Income Method | |
| --- | --- |
| Revenues | $ 1,000,000 |
| Operating costs and expenses | 700,000 |
| Taxes | 120,000 |
| Net operating profits after tax (a) | $    180,000 |
| Capital employed | $ 1,265,000 |
| Cost of capital | 10% |
| Capital charge (b) | $    128,587 |
| Economic profit = (a) – (b) | $      51,413 |

**Exhibit 6.4    Economic Profit Calculation for ABC Company: Residual Income Method**

overstate net income or asset values on the balance sheet. The result is that GAAP-based financials do not truly reflect the economic value created by a business. Creditors use these financial statements to determine a company's debt-servicing ability and the liquidation value of assets should bankruptcy occur. Investors and money managers make many adjustments to the financial statements in order to understand the economic value being created by the company and the value of the stock.

**(a) Types of Adjustments**    Adjustments that convert accounting financial statements into a comprehensive and accurate economic framework fall into several categories, which include:

- Accrual to event.
- Cash flow to economic life.
- Accrual to economic life.
- Nonrecurring events.

The sections that follow explain these categories in more detail.

*(i) Accrual to Event*    Accounts receivable are an example of accrual to event. Accountants reduce the gross book value of receivables through an allowance for doubtful accounts. This allowance, or reserve, is established because the company does not expect all of its customers to pay what they owe. Consequently, a gross receivables of $100 with an allowance of $5 results in net receivables of $95. Thus, investors see receivables of

| Spread Method | |
| --- | --- |
| Net operating profit after tax (a) | $    180,000 |
| Capital (b) | $ 1,265,000 |
| Return on capital = (a) / (b) | 15% |
| Cost of capital | 10% |
| Spread = ROC – C | 4% |
| Economic Profit = spread x (b) | $      51,413 |

**Exhibit 6.5    Economic Profit Calculation for ABC Company: Spread Method**

$95 of total receivables reported in assets, not $100. And, because of double-entry bookkeeping (a very good idea), the increase in the allowance is also shown as an expense on the income statement.

When an economic perspective is adopted, the accountant's adjustment is reversed. Investors want managers to collect everything that customers owe them. Economic value is not realized until the cash is received from the customer. Managers, especially those whose bonus plan is tied to economic value, should be accountable for the *gross book value* of receivables, not the *net* book value. The capital statement therefore carries accounts receivable at the full value of $100. If a customer goes into bankruptcy and cannot pay, then gross receivables are reduced by the amount that will never be collected. The net operating profit after tax (NOPAT) statement must also be adjusted (to maintain the integrity of double-entry bookkeeping). The $5 of expense shown in the account's income statement is added back—that is, expenses are increased by $5. This makes sense. The original $5 expense came from the accountant's *estimated* accrual of likely unpaid invoices, which is not true economic reality. Economic reality is when the customer *actually* goes bankrupt and cannot pay.

*(ii) Cash Flow to Economic Event*    The next example illustrates adjustments that convert the current year's cash expenditures to a long-term economic perspective. For example, research and development (R&D) is an expense incurred by many companies, especially those in the high-technology and pharmaceutical industries. These expenditures are incurred to create future products for the company. GAAP requires that R&D expenditures be fully recognized (expensed) in the period in which they are incurred on the grounds that intangible assets such as R&D are difficult to place a value on. This results in a more conservative figure for both net income and the balance sheet. However, a more accurate (and realistic) economic perspective recognizes that these expenditures are an investment today that will yield returns in future years.

The economic approach is to capitalize these expenses by putting them in the capital statement, then amortizing them over some probable economic life, say, five years. This treatment induces R&D managers to recognize—and feel accountable for—the long-term nature of the investment. They realize that adjusting this year's expenditures to meet artificial budget and EPS targets does not create value in the long run. For companies whose future depends on significant R&D efforts for new products, investments in R&D have to occur continuously regardless of current business conditions.

*(iii) Accrual to Economic Life*    An example of an adjustment that changes a simple accounting life to a more accurate economic life involves *depreciation*. The true cost of owning an asset is both the depreciation on the asset and the capital charge. Depreciation is an attempt to account for the decline in value of an asset over its useful life. A capital charge represents the opportunity cost for investing in a particular asset rather than in some other opportunity. Investors require managers to cover both of these costs, just as a banker requires a mortgagee to repay both the principle on a mortgage (depreciation) and also interest (the capital charge).

Accountants typically depreciate assets on a straight-line basis over some assumed asset life for purposes of the income statement and on a declining-balance basis for purposes of income tax reporting. (Declining-balance methods result in higher reported expenses and thus lower taxes.) The net effect is that managers usually view older assets as cheaper because they are mostly (or possibly even completely) depreciated. This creates a bias toward acquiring new assets, as the new assets raise both the capital base—

and thus the capital charge—and depreciation expense. The cost of ownership of new assets is viewed as more expensive than older assets. In other words, managers sometimes avoid retiring old assets and acquiring new ones because the (undepreciated) new asset base is higher than the (fully depreciated) old asset base. Managers should make the asset-investment decision based on the prospective income from the asset.

Economists agree with accountants that assets have a limited useful life. Also, depreciation of asset values is an economic reality recognized by both groups. Ultimately, therefore, the solution is to develop a depreciation method that eliminates the built-in bias of straight-line and declining-balance methods. One way to accomplish this is to create a cost of ownership that is constant rather than declining. Using assumptions about the economic life, required rate of return, and salvage value, the annual repayment amount required to keep the cost of ownership constant can be calculated. The annual amount calculated is analogous to a mortgage: The monthly payment is constant, but the amounts going to principle (depreciation) and interest (capital charges) vary. This approach is often referred to as the *sinking fund method*.

For example, consider purchasing an asset for $100,000. Assume the facts shown in Exhibit 6.6.

Exhibit 6.7 shows the cost of ownership under straight-line depreciation.

The cost of ownership under the traditional accounting method of straight-line depreciation declines from almost $20,000 in year 1 to just over $10,000 in year 10.

Exhibit 6.8 shows the cost of ownership under the sinking fund depreciation method.

The cost of ownership under the sinking fund method remains constant each year.

*(iv) Nonrecurring Events*   The last example involves nonrecurring events (e.g., restructuring charges). Typically, an accountant charges all restructuring expenses to the year in which the decision to restructure takes place. If a charge of $100 million is taken, pretax earnings will be reduced by that amount.

The economist, however, takes a slightly different view. Restructuring charges can be viewed as an investment in the organization's ability to earn higher levels of economic value in the future. A simple adjustment puts the $100 million in the capital account and amortizes it over some future period, say, three years. The capital account will continue to carry a capital charge until the $100 million is fully amortized. This will encourage managers to earn the required rate of return on the remaining capital balance rather than expensing the $100 million all in one year and forgetting about it the next.

**(b) Guidelines for Adjustments**   The previous sections provided simply a few examples of the many potential adjustments that convert GAAP-based financial statements to an economic framework. The types of adjustments needed vary by industry. Oil and gas and mining exploration companies need to include the value of oil and gas reserves in their annual measures of value creation. Another industry, such as utilities, must cope with the unique issue of including "stranded" assets. Financial service companies must already deal with reporting of risk-based capital for federal agencies in addition to GAAP-based measures. The topic is far too large and complex to adequately cover here.

Managers must consider several trade-off criteria in deciding how many adjustments are appropriate. They should consider four guidelines regarding the subjectivity of the process:

| Assumptions: | |
|---|---|
| Required return | 12% |
| Asset cost | $ 100,000 |
| Asset life | 10 |
| Salvage value (%) | 10% |
| Salvage value ($) | $ 10,000 |

Exhibit 6.6    Asset Purchase

| Period | Annual Cost of Ownership | Straight Line Depreciation | Capital Charge | Net Book Value |
|---|---|---|---|---|
| 1 | $19,920 | $9,000 | $10,920 | $91,000 |
| 2 | $18,840 | $9,000 | $ 9,840 | $82,000 |
| 3 | $17,760 | $9,000 | $ 8,760 | $73,000 |
| 4 | $16,680 | $9,000 | $ 7,680 | $64,000 |
| 5 | $15,600 | $9,000 | $ 6,600 | $55,000 |
| 6 | $14,520 | $9,000 | $ 5,520 | $46,000 |
| 7 | $13,400 | $9,000 | $ 4,440 | $37,000 |
| 8 | $12,360 | $9,000 | $ 3,360 | $28,000 |
| 9 | $11,280 | $9,000 | $ 2,280 | $19,000 |
| 10 | $10,200 | $9,000 | $ 1,200 | $10,000 |

Exhibit 6.7    Cost of Ownership Using Straight Line Depreciation

| Period | Annual Cost of Ownership | Sinking Fund Depreciation | Capital Charge | Net Book Value |
|---|---|---|---|---|
| 1 | $17,128.57 | $ 5,128.57 | $12,000.00 | $94,871.43 |
| 2 | $17,128.57 | $ 5,744.00 | $11,384.57 | $89,127.42 |
| 3 | $17,128.57 | $ 6,433.28 | $10,695.29 | $82,694.14 |
| 4 | $17,128.57 | $ 7,205.28 | $ 9,923.30 | $75,488.86 |
| 5 | $17,128.57 | $ 8,069.91 | $ 9,058.66 | $67,418.95 |
| 6 | $17,128.57 | $ 9,038.30 | $ 8,090.27 | $58.380.65 |
| 7 | $17,128.57 | $10,122.90 | $ 7,005.68 | $48,257.75 |
| 8 | $17,128.57 | $11,337.64 | $ 5,790.93 | $36,920.10 |
| 9 | $17,128.57 | $12,698.16 | $ 4,430.41 | $24,221.94 |
| 10 | $17,128.57 | $14,221.94 | $ 2,906.63 | $10,000.00 |

Exhibit 6.8    Cost of Ownership Using Sinking Fund Depreciation

| | % Weight | Cost | Weighted Cost |
|---|---|---|---|
| Cost of debt (after tax) | 35% | 4.9% | 1.7% |
| Cost of equity | 65% | 13% | 8.5% |
| Cost of capital | | | 10.2% |

Exhibit 6.9    Calculating Cost of Capital

1. *Materiality*. Does the adjustment make a significant difference in the correlation between EP and share prices (market value added)?
2. *Availability of data*. Are the data available from existing financial and operating reporting systems, or can they be made available with minor modifications?
3. *Simplicity*. Is the adjustment relatively simple to calculate and explain to nonfinancial managers?
4. *Motivational impact*. Will the adjustment cause managers to make decisions in a different way that has significant impact on EP?

Each of the potential adjustments under review by managers should be tested against these criteria. The deciding factors should be simplicity and motivational impact. If the adjustment is material and the data are available but will not change the way managers make decisions, then why bother?

For example, a company that has an aggressive, experienced credit department may be doing everything possible to collect receivables in a timely manner. Making the adjustment from net receivables to gross receivables may further complicate the measurement system while adding little to future results. In general, most companies that have implemented these new economic-based measures find that six to eight key adjustments are all that are necessary to create an economic perspective that is still manageable and simple to understand.

**6.4 COST OF CAPITAL**    One of the major differences between accounting earnings and EP is the cost of capital. This number is the weighted average of debt cost and equity cost. The cost of debt is very straightforward. It is the marginal borrowing rate for the company. For example, if the company can borrow funds at 7 percent and has a tax rate of 40 percent, the after-tax cost of borrowing is $.6 \times 7$ percent, or 4.2 percent.

**(a) Opportunity Cost**    Economists refer to the cost of equity as an *opportunity cost*. This is the cost investors require to compensate themselves for undertaking the risks of investing in the company. A good approximation of the equity cost can be made by starting with the risk-free rate of return (e.g., 30-year government bond rates) and adding a risk premium sufficient to compensate investors for the added risk associated with equities. If the risk-free rate is 6 percent and the equity risk premium is 7 percent,[3] the full cost of equity is 13 percent.

Calculating the weighted average cost of capital requires one more assumption: the target capital structure of ABC Company—that is, the proportions of debt and equity used to finance the company. If management's goal is to use 35 percent debt financing, then the cost of capital would be as shown in Exhibit 6.9.

**(b) Market Value Added**    A measure of wealth creation that takes into account market values is market value added. ABC Company's market value added is calculated as shown in Exhibit 6.10.

Market value added represents the stock market's assessment of how much value the company has created with the capital provided by investors and lenders. In this case, ABC managers have created more than $20 of additional value for every dollar of capital invested. Statistical studies show that variations in market value added (i.e., stock price variation) are closely correlated with EP: They yield a correlation of almost 50 percent.[4]

| Market Value Added | |
| --- | --- |
| Number of shares outstanding | 1,000,000 |
| Price per share | $      21.00 |
| Market value of equity | $ 21,000,000 |
| Debt | $      442,750 |
| Total market value of company | $ 21,442,750 |
| | |
| Capital | $   1,265,000 |
| Market value added | $ 20,177,750 |

**Exhibit 6.10    Market Value Added**

EP is a superior internal performance measure that relates to movement in share prices and wealth creation. This measure is far more important than traditional accounting EPS. It is the measure by which managers' performance in creating wealth should be assessed. With this performance measure as a tool, managers now must ask how wealth is created.

**6.5 HOW WEALTH IS CREATED**    The clearest truth in business is that companies create shareholder value—or wealth—by addressing the needs of customers. A company must offer superior value to convince customers to return with repeat business rather than to take their business elsewhere. Wealth cannot be created—or shared with employees or owners—unless it is first obtained from customers. Analyzing how wealth is created requires understanding which customer segments create economic value and which ones destroy it.

**(a) Use of Activity-Based Costing**    One of the most widely adopted tools for understanding which customer segments are creating value is *activity-based costing* (ABC). Historically, ABC has been used to trace costs to customer segments in order to understand the profitability of particular customer segments. Exhibit 6.11 illustrates this process.

All the costs found in the general ledger can be traced through activities to cost objects such as customer segments. However, there is an important cost missing from the general ledger: the capital charge. Clearly, there is nothing in the general ledger such as a capital charge for elements of working capital (e.g., receivables and inventories). Often, managers think that the capital charge for fixed capital is depreciation. However, depreciation expense is insufficient to repay investors fully (see section 6.3(a)(iii)). Depreciation is similar to repaying the principal on a loan. The capital charge is like the interest on the loan. Simply accounting for depreciation is like repaying the loan principal without paying any interest.

Within the shareholder value framework, managers need to know how much EP is created by each customer segment. Capital charges need to be added to the ABC model in order to calculate customer profitability as measured by EP. Thus, the process shown in Exhibit 6.11 needs to be modified as shown in Exhibit 6.12.

The ABC Company example illustrates how managers can be misled in understanding how wealth is created if capital charges are left out of the equation. Assume that ABC Company has the following five major business processes, or activities:

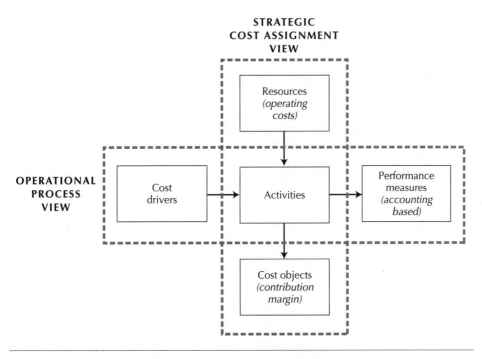

**Exhibit 6.11    Using ABC to Trace Costs to Customer Segments**

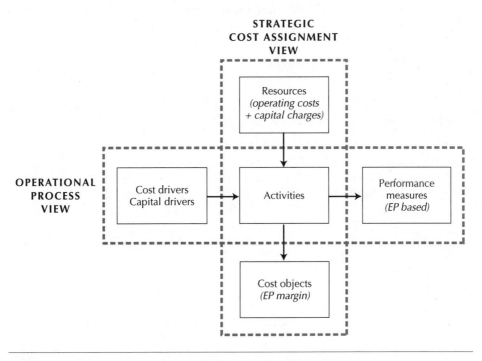

**Exhibit 6.12    Using ABC and Capital Charges to Trace Costs**

1. Identify customer needs.
2. Design products.
3. Manufacture products.
4. Sell and distribute products.
5. Provide corporate support.

Assume now that the ABC Company has completed an activity-based costing project. Total operational costs have been traced to each process and then to the three major customer segments. Exhibit 6.13 shows the results.

Given these results, managers believe that segments C and A are the most profitable. Segment B, although profitable, does not provide as much contribution margin as C or A.

Now consider the results after capital charges are included in the analysis. First, process costs are adjusted to include capital charges, as shown in Exhibit 6.14.

Now the customer segment analysis is updated for capital charges, as shown in Exhibit 6.15.

Customer segment C is still the big winner, and, although customer segment A is still profitable, A's profit margin is now much weaker. The big surprise is customer segment B. This segment has gone from profitable to unprofitable. Managers need to decide whether this segment is worth keeping. If there is a strategic necessity to continue servicing this segment (perhaps customers from other segments look to this segment for referrals), the company needs to investigate which processes need to be improved to make customer segment B profitable.

**(b) Example of an Activity-Based Costing Project: Profit Contribution**   An actual situation that demonstrates the usefulness of this type of analysis occurred recently at a

| | | | | Percent of Process Cost | |
| | Percent of | Process | | By Customer Segment | |
| Core Business Processes | Total Cost | Cost | A | B | C |
|---|---|---|---|---|---|
| Identify customer needs | 10% | $ 70,000 | 30% | 50% | 20% |
| Design products | 20% | $140,000 | 10% | 70% | 20% |
| Manufacture products | 40% | $280,000 | 20% | 50% | 30% |
| Sell and distribute products | 20% | $140,000 | 30% | 40% | 30% |
| Corporate support | 10% | $ 70,000 | 30% | 50% | 20% |
| Total costs by customer segment | | $700,000 | $154,000 | $364,000 | $182,000 |
| Revenues | | | $200,000 | $400,000 | $400,000 |
| Contribution margin | | | $ 46,000 | $ 36,000 | $218,000 |
| Margin percent | | | 23% | 9% | 55% |

**Exhibit 6.13   ABC Project by Process and Customer Segment**

| Core Business Processes | Process Cost | Receivables | Inventories | Payables | Fixed Assets | Economic Cost |
|---|---|---|---|---|---|---|
| Identify customer needs | $ 70,000 | | | | | $ 70,000 |
| Design products | $140,000 | | | | | $140,000 |
| Manufacture products | $280,000 | | | $(7,624) | $81,320 | $353,696 |
| Sell and distribute products | $140,000 | $25,413 | $9,149 | | $10,165 | $184,726 |
| Corporate support | $ 70,000 | | | | $10,165 | $ 80,165 |

**Exhibit 6.14    ABC Project with Capital Charge Adjustment**

large midwestern printing company. The publishing division of the company, which printed books for large publishers, wanted to better understand the profit contribution from its largest customers, so it conducted an extensive ABC project.

The ABC model did a much better job than traditional costing approaches at tracing shared and overhead costs to activities and to the various customers. The top 10 profit contributors were held up before management as key accounts that helped to sustain the financial performance of the division. However, division managers were not satisfied that they had identified which customers were creating value and which were not.

At that time, the company was beginning to adopt value-based management, including EP as the number-one financial performance measure. Consequently, the ABC model was further refined by including capital charges. As it turned out, working capital investment had a significant impact on the economic value contributed by each customer.

Traditional terms for book publishers were 90 days. However, terms for one the largest customers had been extended to 150 days. Also, the company used its buying power to purchase paper at better prices than its customers could negotiate. This paper

| Core Business Processes | Percent of Total Cost | Process Cost | A | Percent of Process Cost By Customer Segment B | C |
|---|---|---|---|---|---|
| Identify customer needs | 10% | $ 70,000 | 30% | 50% | 20% |
| Design products | 20% | $140,000 | 10% | 70% | 20% |
| Manufacture products | 40% | $353,696 | 20% | 50% | 30% |
| Sell and distribute products | 20% | $184,726 | 30% | 40% | 30% |
| Corporate support | 10% | $ 80,165 | 30% | 50% | 20% |
| Total costs by customer segment | | $828,587 | $185,207 | $423,821 | $219,560 |
| Revenues | | | $200,000 | $400,000 | $400,000 |
| Economic value contribution | | | $ 14,793 | $(23,821) | $180,440 |
| Margin percent | | | 7% | –6% | 45% |

**Exhibit 6.15    Customer Segment Analysis with Capital Charge Adjustment**

stayed in inventory until it was required by the customer. The ABC cost model was updated to include the capital charge associated with accounts receivable and the paper inventory. These extra costs caused 3 of the top 10 customers to become unprofitable in terms of economic value contribution.

Clearly, allocating charges for fixed capital (i.e., the printing machines used to print each customer's jobs) would cause the results to look even worse. Managers now had a much better perspective on the total economic costs needed to service each customer. Two decisions were made immediately:

1. The pricing models used by the sales department would include the cost of receivables and paper inventory as part of the value provided the customer. This would help offset the effects of price discounting used to win competitive bids.
2. Sales commissions would be based on economic value contribution—not on contribution margin, as in the past. This would encourage salespeople to appreciate and sell the full value of services offered—including printing, financing (receivables) and availability of paper—instead of just selling printing.

Another example of the strategic difference offered by this type of analysis occurred at a large consumer database marketing company. The company sells database information and target marketing services to direct marketers such as catalog retailers, magazine publishers, and financial services companies. Over the years, the company continued to add new information products to satisfy every customer demand. The product lines proliferated until the update and maintenance of the overall systems became a substantial financial burden. Managers had adopted EP as the primary performance measure. The question became: Which product lines are contributing to EP and should be kept, and which ones are destroying value and should be abandoned?

ABC was used to calculate product costs. Capital charges were included so that economic value contribution was identified. The results of the study showed that only 30 percent of the product lines contributed to value. Fully one-half of the product lines contributed no value or were marginally negative. The remaining 20 percent destroyed value. Managers made the following three decisions based on the results of the analysis:

1. Several product lines were eliminated.
2. Pricing was increased to improve value contribution on some product lines.
3. One customer segment was abandoned altogether.

The analysis also led to some long-term reengineering decisions. Data processing had always been considered a core competency. After considering the amount of capital committed to these processes, managers decided that outsourcing the entire data center to another organization was a quantifiably justified economic choice, because capital investment was reduced, operating costs were reduced, and cycle times for updating the database were reduced. Customer service options increased because of the availability of entirely new technologies. As a result, the EP of the company began to increase significantly.

**6.6 CONTINUOUS IMPROVEMENT OF WEALTH CREATION**    Applying the methodologies just described answers the first two questions posed at the beginning of the chapter:

- Are managers creating wealth?
- How are managers creating wealth?

The remaining problem is how to give managers the incentives to continuously improve shareholder value. Three approaches to this issue are described.

First, the information systems that are used by managers to make day-to-day decisions must include relevant economic information. Legacy cost systems must be updated so that they include capital charges.

Second, each manager should have access to the *capital statement*. This statement shows the types and amounts of capital managers are responsible for. Strategic planning and annual budgeting forms should be revised to include capital, capital charges, and EP.

**(a) Value Drivers**   Finally, new reports need to be created that show the trend of key value drivers.

Value drivers are classified as either financial drivers or operating drivers. Financial drivers are derived from the elements of the EP calculation. For example, recall that EP can be calculated as:

$$(\text{Return on Capital [ROC]} - \text{Cost of Capital}) \times \text{Capital}$$

$$\text{where ROC} = \text{NOPAT} / \text{Capital}$$

ROC can also be rewritten as:

$$\text{ROC} = (\text{NOPAT} / \text{Sales}) \times (\text{Sales} / \text{Capital})$$

$$\text{or, NOPAT margins} \times \text{capital efficiency (turnover)}$$

The two key drivers of profit margin and capital efficiency have now been calculated. To use the ABC Company example:

$$\text{NOPAT margin} = 18 \text{ percent}$$

$$\text{Capital Turnover} = .79$$

$$\text{ROC} = 18 \text{ percent} \times .79 = 14 \text{ percent}$$

NOPAT margin is a healthy 18 percent. However, capital turnover is a rather anemic .79—the company turns its capital less than one time per year. Because total capital is composed of both working capital and fixed capital, the turnover of these two components can also be calculated:

$$
\begin{aligned}
\text{Working Capital Turnover} &= \text{Sales} / \text{Working Capital} \\
&= \$1,000,000 / \$265,000 \\
&= 3.8 \text{ times} \\
\text{Fixed Capital Turnover} &= \text{Sales} / \text{Fixed Capital} \\
&= \$1,000,000 / \$1,000,000 \\
&= 1.0 \text{ times}
\end{aligned}
$$

Turnover of working capital appears to be in good shape. Further investigation into "accounts receivable days sales outstanding" and inventory turnover—compared to benchmark statistics for the industry—would reveal any problems with the productivity of these capital investments.

The major problem seems to be with fixed capital. Turnover of fixed capital of only one time a year is quite low. Based on this statistic, managers should determine current capacity utilization of plant and equipment. They should also study future expected utilization based on forecasted industry demand.

**(b) Operating Drivers**    Whereas the analysis of value drivers starts with financial drivers, the effort should be expanded to include operating drivers. Operating drivers are nonfinancial metrics such as customer satisfaction, quality, cycle time, and productivity (cost per unit output). Productivity in the economic framework is defined as total economic costs (operating costs plus capital charges) divided by total output. For example, customer satisfaction may be linked to the terms of sale, which is measured by accounts receivable days sales outstanding (DSO), and product availability, which is measured by inventory turns and stockouts. All these factors must be managed simultaneously to achieve growth in EP.

**6.7 TRAIN EARLY, TRAIN OFTEN**    Training and education regarding the concepts and methodologies of economic value analysis are also critical to ensure continuous process improvement. Improving processes often requires capital investment. This means an increase in capital charges. The decision will produce more EP only if the increase in NOPAT margin more than offsets the increase in capital charge. Managers need to learn how to make this trade-off decision in the areas for which they are responsible.

One example is a company in the oil services industry. The company manufactures drill bits for drilling oil and gas wells. To increase market share, managers decided to increase the level of bit inventories in the field at major stocking points and even at the drilling rig site. The increased capital investment in inventories and distribution facilities significantly increased the company's capital charge. However, customer service depended on the timely supply of bits and immediate response to the customer's drilling needs. By responding to these needs, the company increased its market share to become the number-one provider of drill bits in the United States. Because the gross margin on drill bits exceeded 60 percent at the time, the increased NOPAT more than offset the increase in capital charge. Total EP increased, as did the company's stock price when investors saw the results of the strategy. The lessons learned from this example were put into a case study for managers throughout the company.

Training and education are of such importance that they must begin before the company implements the concepts and systems of *shareholder value-based management* (SVBM). Asking managers to attend three or four classes is simply not enough. Training must continue to stress that SVBM is part of the company's working philosophy. Also, SVBM is an evolving discipline. Managers will improve in their expertise by keeping abreast of new methods and research findings for SVBM if training is viewed as ongoing.

**(a) Incentive Compensation**    A final and excellent inducement for managers to continuously improve processes—and thereby increase EP—is incentive compensation. Managers used to think that "what gets measured gets managed." Certainly this was true 20 or 30 years ago when performance measurement was hampered by the difficulty of col-

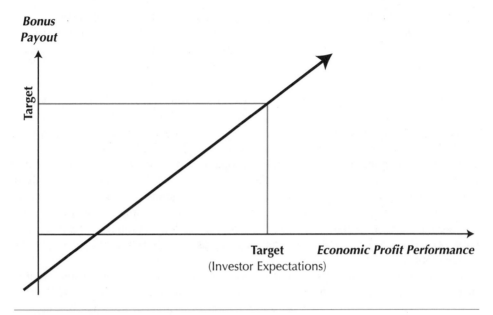

**Exhibit 6.16    EP-Based Incentive Compensation Plan**

lecting data for analysis. Because data were so hard to collect, companies had relatively few performance measures.

Today, with the help of personal computers, managers routinely collect and display thousands of performance measures on even a daily basis. Clearly, not all these measures are getting managed. However, it is still true that managers tend to do what they are paid to do. If they are paid for increasing market share or EPS, they will strive to increase these measures—even if total EP decreases as a result. If they are paid on the basis of increasing EP, they will focus on accomplishing just that.

**(b) Characteristics of Economic Profit-Based Compensation Plans**   The typical EP-based incentive compensation plan has the payout profile shown in Exhibit 6.16.

These plans have several important characteristics. First, the performance target incorporates investor expectations about the company's growth in EP. This is different from most traditional compensation plans. In most plans, the target is a negotiated budget. Why pay managers bonuses for achieving the budget if that budget actually results in value destruction? In EP-based plans, managers are paid for achieving or exceeding investor expectations—not budgets.

The second characteristic is that there is no upside or downside to the bonus payout opportunity. In most traditional plans, there is a minimum performance level (below which no payout occurs) and a maximum performance level (above which no additional payout is made). But if managers can exceed investor expectations, why not continue to pay them much more than the target bonuses? These large payouts are usually approved by boards of directors because they know that investor expectations have been exceeded. Investors are well compensated by an increasing stock price. The company can afford to share in the increment of EP over target, and managers deserve it. More important, managers will continue to drive up EP if they are routinely rewarded for exceeding EP targets.

The final characteristic of these plans is that the payout profile for the managers matches the risk-reward profile faced by investors. This aligns the economic interests of the managers with the investors, or owners, of the company. Under this plan, managers are more likely to think and act as if they were true owners.

**(c) Compensating Lower-Level Managers**    Compensating managers based on consolidated company EP or business unit EP makes sense. But what about a situation in which lower-level managers are responsible only for one department or business process? In this situation, calculation of "departmental EP" may not be easy or even meaningful. The best approach is to pay these managers for improving the value drivers under their control that are linked to EP. The overall bonus pool should be funded out of company or business-unit EP. The payout can be made for individual drivers if there is money in the pool. Payouts are not possible when the pool is empty. This prevents the situation in which a lower-level manager is a paid target bonus for improving measures, such as quality or cycle time, while the company as a whole is still not meeting its financial targets.

Linking incentive compensation to measures of shareholder value is a trend that is increasing in the United States. A recent *Wall Street Journal* article states that "virtually every major company in North America is in some stage of investigating, designing or implementing a shareholder value-based incentive plan."[5]

James Wallace, from the Graduate School of Management, University of California at Irvine, conducted research on companies that have adopted compensation plans based on residual income (another name for EP) to determine the effects of these plans on managers' actions.[6] The study abstract contains the following:

> Managers, consultants, and the financial press have asserted that compensation plans based on a residual income performance measure help mitigate dysfunctional behavior associated with plans based on accounting earnings. This assertion is empirically tested by selecting a sample of companies that have begun using a residual income performance measure in their compensation plans and comparing their performance to a control sample of companies that continue to use traditional accounting earnings-based incentives. The results generally support the prediction that residual income-based performance measures lead managers to take actions that are consistent with increasing shareholder wealth.[7]

Wallace summarizes his findings as follows:

"Relative to the control companies, companies that adopted a residual income performance measure:

1. Decreased their new investment and increased their dispositions of assets, leading to a decrease in net investment; and
2. Increased their payouts to shareholders through share repurchases. These actions are consistent with managers overcoming a free cash flow agency conflict."[8]

The evidence seems to indicate that companies that adopt EP as the primary performance measure—and reward managers for improving EP—are able to achieve increased capital efficiency and shareholder wealth relative to companies that still use traditional accounting measures.

**6.8 SUMMARY**    This chapter begins to answer the following questions:

1. Are managers creating or destroying wealth?
2. How are managers creating or destroying wealth?
3. How can managers increase wealth creation?

The best performance measure to address these questions is EP. Holding managers accountable for improving EP ensures that they are managing the key value drivers in the business: growth, revenues, costs, and capital. Managing costs means managing all economic costs, both operating and capital costs. Cost management systems, such as ABC systems, need to include the full cost of capital (capital charges). Without this critical cost component, managers will be unable to fully address and resolve the questions posed above. Finally, managers who are rewarded for improving EP will consider that creating shareholder value should always be their primary goal.

## NOTES

1. Tom Copeland, *Valuation: Measuring and Managing the Value of Companies* (New York: John Wiley & Sons, Inc., 1995): page 78.

2. The term Economic Profit, or EP, will be used throughout the chapter. EP has been in general use for many years. It is more easily remembered and understood by nonfinancial managers than other terms such as Residual Income or Economic Value Added.

3. Stocks, Bonds, Bill, and Inflation, Ibbotson & Associates, 1998.

4. William Hubbell, "Combining Economic Value Added and Activity-Based Management," *Journal of Cost Management,* Warren, Gorham & Lamont, Vol. 10 No. 1, Spring 1996, page 20.

5. Joseph B. White, "The 'In' Thing: Value-based pay systems are the fad of the moment in compensation circles", *Wall Street Journal,* Dow Jones & Company, Inc., 4/10/97, page R10.

6. James S. Wallace, *Adopting Residual Income-Based Compensation Plans: Evidence of Effects on Management Actions* University of California, Irvine, Revision 1 1996.

7. Free cash flow agency conflict is characterized by managers who hold onto free (net) cash flow rather than distributing it to owners. They do this for many reasons. They are worried that they will be unable to finance future investments, so they hold onto free cash when they have it. They like to add to the capital and employee base in order to build personal empires.

# CHAPTER 7

# MANAGEMENT OF CAPACITY COSTS

## Dileep Dhavale
**Clark University**

**7.1 INTRODUCTION**   One major category of costs faced by any manufacturing or service organization relates to acquiring and maintaining the resources it needs. Most of these resources are purchased in discrete "bundles." These bundles have certain capacities to perform the desired work. Idle capacities reflect wasted opportunities either to improve the output of goods and services or to reduce costs.

This chapter describes the characteristics and behavior of capacity costs. Idle capacity can result from having acquired excess resources or from continuous improvement in a company's efficiency. The complex nature of idle capacity is exemplified by the caveat that not all idle capacities (and their costs) need to be eliminated. The chapter discusses a method for estimating the cost of idle capacities. It also discusses the advantages of excluding the cost of idle capacities from product or service costs.

**7.2 RESOURCES**   Organizations need resources to manufacture the products or provide the services customers need. A manufacturing company, for example, needs raw materials, subassemblies, labor, machinery, and plant buildings to transform materials into finished products. A retailer needs an inventory of goods, buildings for stores, and salespeople. A service organization may need expert personnel, a support staff, and tools to provide the service.

Without resources, organizations cannot function. Because resources are generally purchased from external sources, understanding the behavior of the costs of acquiring resources will help in controlling their costs.

**(a) Types of Resources**   This chapter distinguishes between two types of resources:

1. Resources that an organization purchases when required are *buy-as-needed resources*.
2. Resources that an organization must purchase ahead of their intended use are *committed resources*.

Understanding this distinction can help managers decide how to control the acquisition and consumption of different resources.

Committed resources are by far the most common type. Usually it takes substantial effort and investment to acquire committed resources; some have long lead times. Examples of committed resources include the following:

- Machinery
- Equipment
- Buildings

Contrary to popular belief, most hourly employees also fall in this category. They are hired based on an annual or a long-term projection of labor needs; weekly or daily fluctuations in the need for their services do not affect their employment. Most companies try to maintain a level work force because layoffs cause significant costs to be incurred, including costs related to public relations and morale problems. The idea that labor is a committed resource is especially true in countries that have rigid labor laws, which can make layoffs next to impossible. Skilled employees such as engineers—who are difficult to hire and expensive to train—are another clear example of a committed resource.

**(b) Idle Capacity**  Committed resources have capacities. A machine, for example, might make 10,000 components in a year, or a plant building might have 30,000 square feet of usable space. If business operations do not make use of these capacities, they remain idle, and idle capacities cost money.

Buy-as-needed resources do not have capacities; they are purchased as they are used. Examples of buy-as-needed resources include:

- Electricity
- Materials
- Temporary workers (e.g., workers hired through an agency)

Materials are a buy-as-needed resource because only the amount used is charged to the cost of a product or service. If the actual amounts of material purchased exceed the amount used, the unused portion is inventoried and not charged immediately to completed goods. Buy-as-needed resources do not have idle capacities.

**7.3 CAPACITY OF A RESOURCE**    Textbooks often define different types (or categories) of capacities, such as the following:

- Theoretical capacity
- Ideal capacity
- Practical capacity

*Theoretical capacity* is obtained by ignoring all operating constraints. *Ideal capacity* assumes optimal operating conditions (e.g., no unexpected breakdowns). *Practical capacity* assumes real-life operating conditions (i.e., expected and unexpected downtime, delays, and shortages can occur). For purposes of this chapter, practical capacity is the most useful measure. It is defined as the maximum output of a productive system under normal operating conditions.

**(a) Changes in Practical Capacity**    Practical capacity should not be considered a fixed number. In fact, managers must make deliberate changes in practical capacities to control costs. Other than an overt management action to increase or decrease capacity—by adding a new shift, expanding an assembly line, selling a plant, or shortening the workday, for example—there are many indirect ways to increase capacity. These indirect methods include the following:

- Reductions in setup times
- Continuous improvement programs
- Improved quality
- Improved worker training and skills
- Learning curve effects
- Increased automation
- Elimination of non–value-added activities

**(b) Multiple Capacities in an Operation**    Each committed resource has its own capacity, and the capacities of all resources used in a given manufacturing or service operation may not be equal. These unequal capacities can create problems. A company may not be able to use idle capacity of machines, for example, if its manufacturing engineering department has insufficient capacity to process engineering change orders in a timely fashion. Similarly, a hospital cannot use all its beds if it has a shortage of nurses.

It is often misleading, therefore, to consider a manufacturing or service entity as having a single practical capacity. Even though one often hears statements to that effect, they usually refer to the capacity of the most expensive or most committed resource while ignoring all the other capacities.

In manufacturing, practical capacity generally refers to the capacity of machines or direct labor; in hospitals it refers to patient beds. In analyses of capacity costs, however, it is important to consider capacities of all resources, because to use idle capacity of the main resource, significant investment may have to be made to obtain additional capacity in one or more secondary resources.

**(c) Cost Drivers for Capacity Costs**    Capacities of committed resources can be measured by their *cost drivers*. For example, direct labor capacity can be measured by the number of labor hours available for work. The capacity of a setup department can be measured by using either the number of setups the department can perform or the number of hours of it can work.

For some committed resources, however, no causal relationship can be found between the resources and any manufacturing or service variables. For these resources—which are called *facility-level resources* in activity-based costing (ABC; see Chapter 5)—the capacities cannot be expressed in terms of a manufacturing or service variable. Their usage does not depend on the volume or level of any particular manufacturing or service activity.

**7.4 COST OF CAPACITY**    The *cost of capacity* is defined as the cost of establishing and maintaining a given capacity for a certain period. It includes all recurring costs incurred to maintain an installed capacity as well as allocations of capital costs (i.e., depreciation) related to that capacity. For example, the capacity cost of machines in a department includes the cost of maintenance and repairs plus depreciation expense for the machines.

Cost of capacity changes when capacity itself changes. In almost all situations, the

| | |
|---|---|
| Salaries and benefits | $320,000 |
| Support, occupancy, and supplies | 400,000 |
| | $720,000 |

**Exhibit 7.1    Capacity Cost of the Engineering Department**

cost of capacity will increase as capacity increases, although the relationship is not always linear. In many instances, the capacity for a resource can be increased only in discrete steps. Thus, no continuous, smooth, mathematical relationship between the capacity and its cost is possible.

**(a) Example of Capacity Cost**    Consider the case of a hypothetical small manufacturer, which has a team of four engineers to handle production and manufacturing duties. For the sake of simplicity, assume that the engineers' work is always initiated by a request for assistance called an *engineering change notice* (ECN). Also assume that all ECNs are of the same type and require about the same level of attention. Exhibit 7.1 shows the annual budget for the company's engineering department.

During the current year, the engineering department expects to process 3,600 ECNs. The practical capacity of the department is 4,000 ECNs. The cost of one ECN based on practical capacity is $180 (i.e., $720,000/4,000), whereas the cost of one ECN based on the expected activity level is $200 (i.e., $720,000/3,600).

**(b) Questions about the Capacity of the Resource**    Many questions may be raised about the engineering department as a resource used in manufacturing. For example, is the resource fully utilized? What should the company do with the excess capacity? Should the company reduce the excess capacity? How should it charge the products that are manufactured for use of the engineering resource? Should the charge be based on the expected activity level (i.e., 3,600 ECNs) or the practical capacity (4,000 ECNs)? What are the advantages of using the expected activity level rather than the practical capacity for product costing (or vice versa)? The answers to these questions form the framework for an analysis of capacity costs.

**(c) Cost of Consumption of Resources**    When resources are used in manufacturing products or providing services, the costs of the resources consumed are allocated to products and services. Many organizations use sophisticated methods such as ABC to fairly allocate the cost of consumed resources.

Costs are charged to entities (such as a production batch) for their use of resources. The consumption cost is computed based on predetermined overhead rates for resources. For resources that are not included in the overhead, rates similar to the overhead rates (e.g., hourly rates for labor) are used to determine the consumption cost.

At this juncture, it is important to understand that the cost of *acquiring* a resource (i.e., the cost of capacity) differs from—and is independent of—the cost charged for the *consumption* of that resource. Many textbooks, cost studies, and reports fail to distinguish clearly between the cost of capacity and the consumption cost. Implicitly, they assume that the cost of consumption (as determined by a cost system or by flexible bud-

|  | Committed Resource | Buy-as-Needed Resource |
|---|---|---|
| Resource capacity | Resource has installed capacity. | Resource does not have installed capacity. |
| Ease of acquisition | Additional capacity is costly and has a longer lead time. | Available as needed. |
| Costs | Cost of capacity and cost of consumption are not equal. | Cost of capacity equals the cost of consumption. |
| Examples of resources | Equipment, plant building, support departments, labor. | Electrical power, natural gas, materials, temporary employees. |

**Exhibit 7.2    Comparison of Committed and Buy-as-Needed Resources**

geting) equals the cost of capacity. Later, this chapter discusses how current accounting practices and tax regulations may actually encourage such thinking.

In fact, cost of capacity and consumption costs are equal only for buy-as-needed resources. For the vast majority of resources—namely, committed resources—the cost of capacity and the cost of consumption are different. As for the cost that appears on the income statement and that affects the bottom line, it is the cost of capacity and not the cost of consumption. Consumption cost is merely an accounting technique to allocate capacity costs to the users.

**(d) Committed and Buy-as-Needed Resources Compared**    Exhibit 7.2 summarizes the differences between the two types of resources.

**7.5 IDENTIFICATION OF RESOURCES**    The method described next provides managers information about the cost of idle capacity for each resource used in manufacturing products or providing services. The first step in this analysis is to identify all resources. Some of them are quite obvious—for example, direct material and direct labor—although managers may need to deliberate to identify and define others.

For example, what degree of detail is necessary to analyze the capacity cost of an engineering department? Does this resource need to be separated by the department's various functions (such as process planning, tooling, engineering)? Or should this resource be segregated by product lines so that there is not one department but several "subdepartments" within the department? Answers to questions such as these will help managers decide whether there should be one resource called "engineering" or whether the department should be split into several smaller resources, each with its own capacity and cost.

Detailed cost information allows managers to obtain a clearer picture of a situation. But from a practical perspective, the number of resources must be kept at a manageable level because of the cost of collecting and maintaining data, but also because unnecessarily detailed information can be distracting. It may be worthwhile to divide resources that have large costs into subcategories, just as it may facilitate matters to combine several small-cost resources into one category. The best persons to make determinations such as these are those who will be using the capacity cost information.

Because cost drivers will be used to analyze the costs, resources must be defined such that they are mutually exclusive and contain costs that vary predominantly with respect to only one kind of cost driver (unit-, batch-, or product-level). As an example, consider setup resource. If all setups on all machines were approximately similar in terms of time needed, then a unit-level cost driver, such as number of setups, would be appropriate. On the other hand, if there were some direct numerical control (DNC) machines whose setup needs were much different from the rest, then number of setups would not be a good cost driver.

**7.6 DETERMINATION OF CAPACITY COSTS**  To obtain capacity costs, general ledger accounts and budgets have to be analyzed. For example, to determine the salaries of employees in the setup department and their fringe benefits, payroll accounts have to be disaggregated. To determine occupancy costs of the department, perhaps a formula based on square footage occupied should be used, given depreciation expense for the building as determined from the appropriate accounts.

In a few instances, no hard data may be available for making cost allocation from general ledger accounts to resources, in which case estimates may have to be used. Once an initial analysis disaggregates accounts into resources, the same relationships may generally be used in succeeding years unless changes in technology or processing require updates.

Disaggregation of general ledger accounts to obtain cost pools for resources is the first step in ABC. If a company is already using ABC method, this step may be unnecessary; alternatively, the company may only have to make slight adjustments or modifications (e.g., in resource definitions and corresponding costs) to prepare an analysis of capacity costs.

**(a) Cost Computations**  Exhibit 7.3 shows an analysis of capacity costs that would be performed at the end of a year. Column 1 shows resources used in a small manufacturing firm. Based on the earlier discussion, these resources are designated as either committed ("C") or buy-as-needed ("B") in column 2.

Practical capacities of resources are measured in terms of appropriate cost drivers, as shown in column 3. Column 4 shows cost of capacity, which was defined as the recurring costs of maintaining capacity plus any depreciation (or allocation) of capital-layout costs.

Because the first three resources are buy-as-needed resources, they have no installed capacity or cost of capacity. The last two, which are facility-level resources, are not influenced by manufacturing variables, so they have no cost drivers.

Cost of capacity per unit (column 5) is based on the practical capacities of the resources. Because the two facility-level resources have no cost drivers, their unit capacity costs cannot be measured. For the buy-as-needed resources, the cost of purchasing a unit is listed in this column.

The consumption of capacity column (column 6) shows the amount used of each resource. Based on this consumption and the unit capacity cost shown in column 5, the cost of consumption is computed in column 7. Finally, column 8 (the "Cost of Idle Capacity") shows the difference between the cost of capacity (column 4) and the cost of consumption (column 7). A positive value indicates idle capacity, whereas a negative value indicates that the resource was used beyond its capacity. Only some committed resources can be used beyond their practical capacity.

| Column 1 Resources | 2 Type | 3 Practical Capacity | 4 Cost of Capacity | 5 Cost of Capacity per Unit | 6 Consumption of Capacity | 7 Cost of Consumption | 8 Cost of Idle Capacity |
|---|---|---|---|---|---|---|---|
| Electricity | B | N/A | N/A | $.08/KWhr* | N/A | $80,000 | $0 |
| Materials | B | N/A | N/A | $5/lb* | N/A | $350,000 | $0 |
| Temp. Workers | B | N/A | N/A | $25/hr* | N/A | $30,000 | $0 |
| Setups | C | 2,000 setups | $250,000 | $125/setup | 1,700 setups | $212,500 | $37,500 |
| Direct Labor | C | 20,000 hours | $300,000 | $15/hr | 19,000 hours | $285,000 | $15,000 |
| Material Handling | C | 2,000 moves | $100,000 | $50/move | 2,100 moves | $105,000 | ($5,000) |
| Ordering and Receiving | C | 2,500 orders | $200,000 | $80/order | 2,525 orders | $202,000 | ($2,000) |
| Engineering | C | 4,000 ECNs | $720,000 | $180/ECN | 3,600 ECNs | $648,000 | $72,000 |
| Plant Administration | C | N/A** | N/A | N/A | N/A | $120,000 | N/A |
| Property Tax | C | N/A** | N/A | N/A | N/A | $20,000 | N/A |

Types: B = Buy as needed
C = Committed

N/A = Not applicable
* These are costs of purchasing a unit, since they don't have capacities.
** For these facility-level resources, practical capacities cannot be measured in manufacturing-related variables.

**Exhibit 7.3   Capacity Cost Analysis**

**(b) Analysis of Idle Capacity Costs**   As Exhibit 7.3 shows, the buy-as-needed resources have zero cost of idle capacity. This is because these resources have no installed capacity: The amounts purchased are also the amounts consumed in operations (or, in the case of materials, the unused amounts are inventoried).

But with committed resources, managers have to decide what should be done with the idle cost of the resources. The choices are as follows:

- Decrease the capacity of a resource, thus decreasing or eliminating the cost of idle capacity.
- Do nothing (i.e., simply treat the cost as a cost of doing business).

The first choice, of course, is the obvious one. If the engineering department has a practical capacity for 4,000 ECNs and is currently doing 3,600 setups, a 10 percent reduction would eliminate any idle capacity. Even though the reduction necessary to achieve full utilization is obvious, actually reducing capacity in this way requires a thorough analysis of the demand for the resource and its current capacity. Some of the considerations related to the engineering department are:

- An exact 10 percent reduction may be impossible. If one of four engineers is laid off, capacity may drop by 25 percent. The same would be true of most resources whose capacities can be increased or reduced only in discrete "bundles" or "chunks."
- If the engineers specialize in different areas of work, it may not be possible to lay off even one person.
- Quick turnaround time—which is basic to flexible manufacturing—is possible only if support departments such as the engineering department can handle their work expeditiously, which may require having some idle capacity.
- Engineers are highly skilled and trained; a layoff would cause a permanent loss of the employee. If the company expects future growth or attrition, the layoff would be ill advised.

Any one of these considerations might influence managers to retain all four engineers and write off the cost of idle capacity as a necessary business cost. As this scenario points out, it may not always be possible to eliminate the cost of idle capacity. In fact, after careful analysis a manager may opt to retain idle capacity for some resources in order to maintain operational flexibility. In some instances, doing so might prove to be the lower-cost choice in the long run.

The moral is that not all idle capacity costs are inappropriate or candidates for reduction. Some idle capacities can be eliminated, others are probably unavoidable, and yet others may be needed simply to maintain flexibility. Only a careful review of idle capacities in light of all the variables can tell a manager the right course of action.

**(c) Impact of Efficiency Improvements**   The most fruitful avenue managers have for reducing capacity costs is to use resources more efficiently. The continuous improvement philosophy has helped many companies achieve significant efficiency improvements. These efficiency gains are incremental, whereas the introduction of a new technology or a new process (e.g., through reengineering) provides a large, one-time jump in efficiency. Efficiency improvement has a different impact on buy-as-needed and commit-

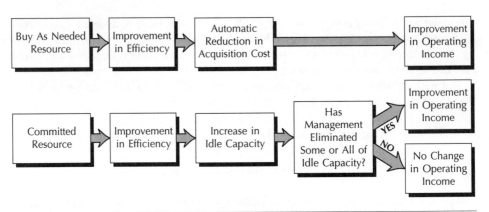

**Exhibit 7.4   Impact of Efficiency Improvements on the Bottom Line**

ted resources. Understanding this difference can help managers take appropriate further action.

When buy-as-needed resources are used more efficiently, fewer resources are needed, so the cost of acquiring them decreases immediately: A manager does not have to take any further action. Not so with committed resources. Improving efficiency decreases the corresponding cost driver activity and *increases* idle capacity—and its cost.

At this point, it is interesting to point out a common fallacy often heard at discussions on budgets and even unintentionally supported by many textbooks—that by merely reducing cost driver activity, the related operating cost is reduced. What is actually reduced is the cost of consumption of that resource, not its cost of capacity.

Unless action is taken to slash idle capacity, there is no savings from improved efficiency. In some situations, the additional step required to reduce idle capacity is never carried out, arguably for very good reasons. In such instances, the improved efficiency does not increase the operating income of the company. Exhibit 7.4 summarizes this concept.

**7.7 PRODUCT COSTING AND CAPACITY COSTS**   Most manufacturing companies use predetermined overhead rates computed by tracking expected annual activity levels (whether a conventional cost system or an ABC cost system is used). Use of an expected annual activity level ensures that a minimum amount of over- or undercharging of overhead to the manufactured units will occur. This is important if the objective is to have the minimum variance for the overhead account at the end of the year.

But when the annual activity level is used, the idle capacity costs are included in the overhead rates and product costs. Because the cost of idle capacity is not segregated, product cost may provide misleading information to managers.

**(a) Use of Practical Capacity for Overhead Rates**   The solution to this problem is to compute predetermined overhead rates based on practical capacity rather than expected activity level. One of the advantages of using practical capacity is a costing system that provides stable product costs unaffected by annual fluctuation in activity levels.

Without this stability, it becomes difficult to judge the impact of changes in operations or of continuous improvement on product costs. Another advantage is that product costs based on practical capacity provide managers a benchmark. These are the minimum costs at which products could be made with existing equipment and processes if the current idle capacity is fully utilized.

The disadvantage of using practical capacity to compute predetermined overhead rates is that products will be perennially undercosted, because their costs will not include the cost of idle capacity. The undercosting only worsens as idle capacity increases. The cost of idle capacity—even if it is the cost of unused or wasted resources—must eventually be recovered from customer orders. Such undercosting, however, is usually not a problem, because most companies do not determine selling prices based strictly on unit costs.

Tax rules in the United States pose another problem for the use of practical capacity in costing. The Tax Reform Act of 1986 imposed uniform capitalization rules for purposes of costing inventories. One of those rules prohibits the use of practical capacity in allocating indirect manufacturing costs (Treasury Regulations Section 1.263A-2(a)(4)) for tax purposes, though not (of course) for purposes of managerial accounting.

**(b) Special Orders and Bids**   Exhibit 7.3 provides valuable information for special orders (i.e., orders that are not part of a company's ongoing business). These orders, which are generally accepted on a one-time-only basis, are expected to cover only variable costs, thus providing some profit. Without the information shown in Exhibit 7.3, a manager preparing a bid will include only direct labor, direct materials, and variable overhead as the variable costs.

But Exhibit 7.3 shows that direct labor has idle capacity, so no additional labor cost would be incurred by accepting the order. Thus, a manager could accurately estimate the true cost of accepting the order by examining the resources that would be used to fill the order—in particular, whether those resources have idle capacities. The actual cost of the order to the company would be only for use of the committed resources that have no idle capacity and must be purchased plus any buy-as-needed resources used for the order.

**7.8 COST BURDEN OF IDLE CAPACITY**   It is possible to provide an estimate of the cost of idle capacity even when expected activity levels (instead of practical capacities) are used for predetermined overhead rates. Exhibit 7.5 computes this estimate of additional manufacturing cost resulting from idle capacity (which is called *cost burden of idle capacity*). (Data are for the same company described in Exhibit 7.3, but for a different year.)

Column 2 of Exhibit 7.5 shows budgeted amounts for all the resources, column 3 shows practical capacity, and column 4 shows expected activity levels. These levels are used in determining the predetermined overhead rates (which are not shown here). Column 5 expresses idle capacity as a percentage of practical capacity. Based on these percentage values and the budgeted costs for resources, the last column calculates the expected cost burden of idle capacity.

The sum of the last column shows that an expected $120,950 worth of resources would remain idle during the year. In full-absorption costing using an annual activity level for overhead rates, the cost burden of idle resources would be charged to production. Information in Exhibit 7.5 shows that the overall idle capacity cost burden for products is $120,950/$1,765,000 = 6.85 percent. This figure means that 6.85 percent of the manufacturing cost of a product is due to idle capacity. Had practical capacity been

| Column 1 | 2 | 3 | 4 | 5 | 6 |
|---|---|---|---|---|---|
| Resources | Budgeted Cost Capacity | Practical Capacity | Expected Activity During the Year | Idle Capacity in Percent | Expected Cost Burden of Idle Capacity |
| Electricity | $85,000 | N/A | N/A | 0% | $0 |
| Materials | $360,000 | N/A | N/A | 0 | 0 |
| Temp. Workers | $20,000 | N/A | N/A | 0 | 0 |
| Setups | $245,000 | 2,000 setups | 1,760 setups | 12 | $29,400 |
| Direct Labor | $280,000 | 20,000 hours | 19,000 hours | 5 | $14,000 |
| Material Handling | $120,000 | 2,000 moves | 2,000 moves | 0 | 0 |
| Ordering and Receiving | $220,000 | 2,500 orders | 2,500 orders | 4 | $8,800 |
| Engineering | $275,000 | 400 ECNs | 300 ECNs | 25 | $68,750 |
| Plant Administration | $140,000 | N/A | N/A | 0 | 0 |
| Property Tax | $20,000 | N/A | N/A | 0 | 0 |
| Totals | $1,765,000 | — | — | — | $120,950 |

**Exhibit 7.5  Cost Burden of Idle Capacity**

used to compute the overhead rates (rather than the expected annual activity), the cost burden of idle capacity would not have been charged to the products.

When an ABC system is used, it would be possible to obtain an estimate of the cost burden of idle capacity separately for each product. Because products use different resources, the products that use resources having more idle capacity will have a higher percentage of the cost burden.

To illustrate, assume that the total manufacturing cost of a product is $2,400. The product was charged the following amounts for use of four resources that have idle capacities:

- Setup, $140.
- Direct labor, $50.
- Ordering and receiving, $280.
- Engineering, $950.

The cost burden of idle capacity for this product is obtained by multiplying the percentage idle capacities from Exhibit 7.5 and the respective costs of the resources consumed, as shown previously. The cost burden turns out to be $268, and the percentage amount is $268/$2,400 = 11.2 percent ($2,400 is the total manufacturing cost, including the costs of buy-as-needed resources, committed resources with idle capacity and committed resources without idle capacity; $1,420 is only the cost of idle committed resources). Therefore, this product carries a higher burden of idle capacity cost than the average.

**7.9 SUMMARY** Managing the cost of capacity is an important aspect of cost-containment efforts. Providing segregated costs of idle capacity highlights problem areas and indicates possible management responses. This information is also useful in determining the incremental cost of new orders.

Product costs based on practical capacities provide benchmarks because they show the lowest costs that could be achieved given current operating constraints but assuming the full use of all resources. These benchmarks can help managers focus on controlling capacity costs and using assets more efficiently.

# CHAPTER 8

# CHANGE MANAGEMENT

## David K. Carr
## Richard C. Smith
PricewaterhouseCoopers

**8.1 INTRODUCTION AND DEFINITION OF CHANGE MANAGEMENT**  Astronauts, when launched into space in rapidly accelerating rockets, suffer tremendous gravitational forces. However, astronauts can look forward to zero-gravity relief once they are in orbit.

But the rapid increase in the rate of change in most industries promises no such comfort to those who work in them. No one predicts an end to the pressure; all say that the pace of change increases every day. What seems certain is that those who hope to survive and thrive in the future have to enter into a partnership for change.

Creating this partnership is the job of advanced change management, which we define as the process of aligning the human, organizational, and cultural dimensions of an organization with new ways of doing business.

**8.2 DIMENSIONS OF CHANGE**  Most executives think of new ways of doing business in two dimensions: operations (or work processes) and technology (including information systems). But there are an additional three dimensions that relate to people and the environment in which they work:

- The human dimension.
- The organizational dimension.
- The cultural dimension.

These new ways of doing business—*innovations*—may be specific to a process or broadly applied throughout an organization. (There could also be additional dimensions, depending on the nature of an organization and its work. For example, public agencies must sometimes consider the political dimension; that is, how elected officials and interest groups will react to changes in policy or operations.)

Attempts to change only the operations or technological dimensions may succeed if the change is small and if it is aligned with the people dimensions. However (as suggested in the next sections), a major change in any one dimension usually requires making changes in some or all of the other dimensions. A key task in change management, therefore, is to understand the effect of a change on *all* dimensions.

**(a) Human Dimension**    The following are the focus of the human dimension:

- Process operators
- Managers
- Customers
- Suppliers

Considerations relating to the human dimension include:

- How people accept a new way of working, its effect on their lives, and their ability to operate under the new way of working (taking into account their skills, the possible rewards, their attitudes, and their motivation).
- What knowledge, ability, and skills people need to use, operate, or continuously improve the new methods (and how they will obtain these).
- What new personnel (or new types of personnel) will be needed.
- Whether people will be displaced by the innovation (and, if so, who).

**(b) Organizational Dimension**    The focus of the organizational dimension includes structure, infrastructure, and management behaviors. The considerations for this dimension include:

- How the organization is structured to accommodate new ways of working (including authority levels, lines of communication, and basic infrastructure).
- How people will operate under the new way of working (e.g., as individuals or in teams).
- What the relationship between supervisors and employees will be (e.g., whether supervisors will be coaches, inspectors, or team leaders).
- What new tasks managers and supervisors will need to perform (including any new management skills or abilities they will need).

**(c) Cultural Dimension**    The focus of the cultural dimension relates to formal versus informal norms, values, and beliefs held by employees. The considerations involved in this dimension include:

- How an organization's culture fosters or hinders changes in the other dimensions.
- Whether the innovation will require workers to think and act independently (e.g., will they be rewarded or punished for making the right or wrong decisions).
- Whether managers and supervisors will see the innovation as causing them to lose power and authority (and, if so, how best to overcome their resistance to this loss).
- Whether the innovation will require continuous learning by all employees (e.g., will continuous learning be valued and rewarded, and how will it be encouraged).

**(d) Levers of Change**    One way of looking at change dimensions is to consider them "levers" that may be "pulled" to transform an organization's performance. Effective change management is the process of knowing which levers to pull—and understanding that a major change often requires that all of them be pulled.

One way to categorize the "levers" is:

- *New views of markets and customers.* Such views include how different groups in an organization perceive and segment customers.

- *Changes in scope or variety of products and services.* Changed market views may lead to new products and services. Product innovations may, in turn, lead to new views of markets and customers, or to new business processes. Changes in this area may also lead to new strategic alliances with key customers and suppliers.

- *New business processes and performance measures.* Every organization has (or will have) gaps between its current process capabilities and customer requirements. How performance is measured changes the behavior of the people who are measured.

- *Differences in types of people needed, the skills they require, and how they are rewarded.* New processes require new skills—and possibly people having different abilities. New performance measures may lead to new ways of rewarding those people.

- *New organizational structure or facilities.* There is usually a gap between an organization's current structure and the way it should be configured in the future to accommodate new processes, to get closer to customers, and to provide a proper environment for employees.

- *Opportunities offered by new technology.* New technologies require new ways of working and new skills, so they often lead to new relationships with employees.

Viewed from the perspective of dimensions or levers, change is a complex undertaking. It has become even more complicated because of the rapid pace of change for both businesses and not-for-profit organizations.

**8.3 WHY CHANGE IS DIFFERENT NOW**    Sometime in the 1970s, the rocket took off: The business world (which, for purposes of this chapter, includes the business-like aspects of governmental entities and not-for-profit organizations) changed in ways that put a high premium on the ability to innovate, then to apply those innovations quickly. New products, new services, and new ways of doing business arose so frequently that people came to expect—and sometimes to dread—them.

By the year 2000, new ideas by themselves ceased to provide competitive advantage. Well-managed companies with ample capital, large research and development (R&D) departments, and sound but traditional ways of doing business have lost market share to nimbler competitors. These competitors—although they have fewer resources—can rapidly transform their processes in order to bring products to market faster and to provide better customer service, higher quality, and more cost savings.

This is not an isolated phenomenon that affects a few sectors of the economy. Instead, innovation permeates nearly every industry. It has transformed some to such an extent that their basic products and operations no longer resemble their earlier incarnations.

**(a) Change as a Constant**    Change is such a constant in the information technology field that we accept as a given "Moore's Law," which posits that the performance of microprocessors will double every 18 months. In the information age, the management corollary to Moore's Law is that any competitive advantage accruing from doing business as usual can decrease just as rapidly.

Frequency and rapidity are only two characteristics of change that make it different than the change that prevailed in earlier eras. Another is the attitude of those who need to change, especially employees.

In 1911, for example, Frederick W. Taylor described the model employee in his *Principles of Scientific Management*: "A high priced man does just what he's told and no back talk. . . ."[1] Such hierarchical organizations as automobile factories were considered the ideal way to control "high-priced men." Similarly, centrally planned economies were thought the best way to control societies. In both cases, change was formulated and designed from on high by specialists, then pushed down by cadres of managers and commissars.

**(b) Advanced Information Technologies**    Today, the environment for control and change has changed in fundamental ways. For example, advanced information technologies have forever altered the balance of power in organizations—and, therefore, how change occurs. To be able to respond quickly to customer demands and gain competitive advantage, organizations make information of every type available to everyone throughout their enterprises. The rising popularity of data warehouses and enterprise resource planning management systems are manifestations of this need.

What has the effect on management been? As political scientist Francis Fukuyama (author of the controversial book *The End of History and The Last Man*) writes:

> The arrival of cheap and ubiquitous information has had a profoundly democratizing impact; it is much less easy for hierarchies of various sorts, from governments to corporations to unions, to use their control over information to manipulate those over whom they have authority. It is not accident, then, that authoritarian regimes began to collapse all over the world just as the global economy started to shift to the information age.[2]

Today's high-priced man is the so-called knowledge worker. Armed with ample information and the technology to use it, knowledge workers have much more control over their work than Taylor's model employee. Initiatives to "empower" such employees often come long after they have already been empowered by the changing nature of their work. Each day they make decisions without supervisors looking over their shoulders, and they understand their processes better than managers, executives, or analysts with stopwatches. As corporations pared layers of middle management in their attempts to streamline operations and cut costs, they left power vacuums soon filled by trained, skilled workers.

**(c) Mobility**    Not the least of these new powers is mobility. Dissatisfied with their current situation and in high demand elsewhere, many knowledge workers can easily move on to other employers. Because they have portable benefits plans and have worked in organizations that showed little loyalty to them or their colleagues, they are not at all reluctant to make the move.

Because of demographic reasons, mobility will only increase over the next few decades. An aging population in developed countries means that the percentage of working-age adults will decline, so increased job opportunities will exist for those who work, which should give rise to even more mobility.

One response to this increased mobility will be more initiatives to improve productivity, which will generate more changes in the way work is done. If executives do not manage the changes well, the result will be lower productivity and increased worker stress and dissatisfaction, which (as discussed) can lead to low employee loyalty and high turnover.

**(d) Partnerships for Change**    To retain their most valuable people, organizations must accept that their success at introducing new ways of working will depend on those who do the work. Hence, the participation of knowledge workers in change is essential (and, more important, their acceptance of—and "ownership" in—the new ways of working).

Just a few years ago, those who specialize in change management talked in terms of *change targets* (i.e., the groups of employees and managers who *must* accept innovations). Now, because change has become fairly constant, change targets have come to think of themselves as sitting ducks. Organizations must alter their approach to these employees by working with them to create what Peter Drucker calls "long-term partnerships in the process of change."[3] Otherwise, organizations risk lost opportunities because of failed change projects—but they also risk losing a valuable resource: a superior, committed work force.

The word "partner" implies ally—someone with whom we have a common bond and purpose. Thus, there has to be some universal goal to unite partners. This common goal, we believe, is adding value that customers want and for which they will pay (or, in the case of governments and not-for-profits, achieving societal goals).

Partners treat each other with respect; they involve other partners in decisions and make sure that they get what they need to do their work. One of those needs is *predictability* about overarching goals. This predictability is supplied, in part, by making the universal goal clear and showing the links between it and major changes—thus aligning (or "connecting the dots" between) the many change management initiatives planned and under way.

**8.4 CHANGE BARRIERS AND SUCCESS FACTORS**    In 1997, PricewaterhouseCoopers and Market and Opinion Research International interviewed key managers associated with the change processes of 500 companies. This was a global survey. In all, 150 interviews were held in each of the United Kingdom, the United States, and Europe, while

| Change Barriers | % of 500 Companies Citing Barrier |
|---|---|
| Competing resources | 48% |
| Functional boundaries | 44% |
| Change skills | 43% |
| Middle management | 38% |
| Long IT lead times | 35% |
| Communication | 35% |
| Employee oppostion | 33% |
| HR (people/training) issues | 33% |
| Initiative fatigue | 32% |
| Unrealistic timetables | 31% |

**Exhibit 8.1    Ten Greatest Barriers to Change**

| Success Factor | % of 500 Companies Citing Factor |
|---|---|
| Ensuring top sponsorship | 82% |
| Treating people fairly | 82% |
| Involving employees | 75% |
| Giving quality communications | 70% |
| Providing sufficient training | 68% |
| Using clear performance measures | 65% |
| Building teams after change | 62% |
| Focusing on culture/skill changes | 62% |
| Rewarding success | 60% |
| Using internal champions | 60% |

**Exhibit 8.2    Greatest Success Factors for Change**

another 50 were held in the Far East and Australia.[4] Exhibit 8.1 summarizes what the respondents reported as the major barriers to change in their organizations.

These findings and our personal experience in major change projects indicate that almost all the problems involved in introducing innovations to organizations occur because of poor management of the people dimensions of change. This is reinforced by the survey's findings about the success factors in the change process, which are shown in Exhibit 8.2.

**8.5 PLANNING FOR CHANGE**    Organizations are used to making plans for introducing the process and technology dimensions of change, but they have less experience with planning in the other three dimensions (see section 8.2, "Dimensions of Change").

An effective change-management plan for the three people dimensions requires a written document that outlines objectives, tasks, schedules, responsibilities, performance measures, and budgets. Components of the plan may include:

- A statement of the case for the change to help people visualize the new way of working and a compelling need to adopt it.
- An analysis of the effect of the change on different stakeholders and their probable reaction to it. Stakeholders may include individuals or groups of managers, employees, customers, suppliers, and others.
- Activities needed to gain the commitment of key stakeholders (including how to involve them in the change process).
- A communication plan that sends relevant, consistent messages to stakeholders and encourages them to respond with their concerns and suggestions.
- Actions needed to align a change initiative with other change initiatives.

Why a written plan? The main reason is that executives tend to "assume their way past" many of the issues raised by the plan outline just given. Basically, they assume that they understand all aspects for the change or that someone else down the chain of command will. In a complex, sophisticated organization, however, it is improbable that any one group can, without a concerted effort, grasp the impact of major change on all parts of the enterprise. Also, work force diversity means that employees' perception of their roles and of the effect of change may not be homogeneous; this is exacerbated in a multinational organization.

Thus, an examination of change must be disciplined and comprehensive, which is the work of teams of people from various parts of an organization, who are often trained and advised by a specialist in change management. Before going into the details of the change-management plan, section 8.6 reviews the types of people needed for these positions. The end of the chapter (section 8.9) then discusses how to align (or "connect the dots" between) various plans.

**8.6 WHO IS INVOLVED IN THE CHANGE INITIATIVE?**    "Change partners" are the individuals or groups involved in or affected by a change initiative. Within an organization, they vary during the life of a change project, but they typically follow this progression:

- Executives
- Middle managers
- Line supervisors
- Employees

Customers and suppliers may also be change partners when it is necessary to change their behavior to fit into a new process or system. Each group must, in its turn, make a commitment to change.

Sections 8.6(a) through 8.6(d) explain the roles that each group may play during a change initiative.

**(a) Executives and Other Leaders**    Leadership is the linchpin for effective change management. Another study by PricewaterhouseCoopers (this one done with Opinion Research Corporation International in 1997) surveyed 410 executives from Fortune 1000 companies and governmental organizations that were undergoing major transitions. If executives were satisfied or highly satisfied with the measurable results of change (such as return on investment or profitability), their change efforts were rated as successful. The 47 "most successful" organizations were identified by means of multivariate analysis.[5]

According to this research, in 94 percent of the most successful organizations, the behavior of senior managers supported change (versus 76 percent for the other organizations). In 87 percent of the organizations, respected managers were advocates of change (versus 71 percent for the others). And in 70 percent of the organizations, leaders of different units worked together to help make change happen (versus 54 percent for the others). This type of leadership takes several forms. For example, top executives may do most or all of the following:

- Work together as the premier change-management team (also called the *change sponsors*) to plan at a high level how change will be carried out in all five dimensions.
- Put organizational structures in place to support change (e.g., establish streamlined reporting relationships and rewards strategies).
- Remove obstacles to change (e.g., require cooperation across functional boundaries and removing outmoded policies).
- Provide visible and vigorous leadership of their change initiatives.
- Ensure intensive communication of change goals.
- Commit adequate resources to change management.

In most successful change efforts, a single executive will emerge as the *change champion*. According to Peter Drucker, this is "somebody within the enterprise who really wants the new. [E]verything new gets in trouble. And then it needs a champion. It needs somebody who says, 'I am going to make things succeed,' and then who goes to work on it. And this person needs to be somebody whom the organization respects."[6]

Without an executive leader, a major change effort will not hold the attention of the other executives who need to support it. Among middle managers and employees, lack of a top-level leader may be perceived as a message that a change is not that important. An executive can cut across the functional boundaries of an organization, pulling together support from diverse offices and departments when needed.

**(b) Middle Managers**   Solid support from middle management is required for change that conforms closely with the change enunciated by top executives. Middle managers tend to be somewhat more conservative about change than either executives or employees—perhaps because they may have much to lose in terms of power and authority as a result of some types of changes. Middle managers also have to do much of the hard work required when executive managers fall subject to "flavor-of-the-month" management fads—including picking up the pieces when these fads fizzle out.

But if middle managers can be convinced and made part of a change project, they can be highly effective *change agents*. They do the detailed work of developing and introducing a change:

- Working with technical staff to identify the effect of an innovation on the people dimensions.
- Collecting assessment information on an organization's readiness for change.
- Developing communication strategies and tactics.

Change agents provide coaching and mentoring to employees; they use training to communicate new work expectations and to equip people with the skills to meet the new expectations.

**(c) Line Supervisors and Employees**   Together with middle managers, some key line supervisors and employees should become part of the team that conducts research related to a specific change and does the detailed planning and implementation discussed earlier.

Beyond this, change plans need to be designed to elicit feedback (i.e., reactions to the proposed innovation) from all employees affected by change. Mechanisms for obtaining this feedback include surveys, focus groups, and responses to communications from management. Employees also need to be open to participating in training and other skill-building activities that will prepare them for a new way of doing business.

**(d) Customers and Suppliers**   Customers and suppliers play interesting roles in change management. To begin with, they sometimes have to change the way they interact with an organization. If so, they may be in much the same position as line supervisors and employees. When executives from customers and suppliers line up with an organization's own top leaders, they are effectively part of the change-sponsor team.

Customers are, either actively or passively, powerful allies in building a case for change. Serving customers is a powerful common denominator in any organization. Employees often respond more readily to the fact that customers want what a change will produce—and will pay for it—than to any other proposition. Indeed, if things get stalled during a major change effort, it is helpful to bring a customer into the picture. Management can hold a focus group of customers and have key stakeholders in the organization listen to any dissatisfaction expressed. Alternatively, managers and key employees can visit customers and listen to their complaints. This external impetus can help get things back on track.

**(e) Change-Management Specialists and Consultants**   Organizations that are new to change management or that face particularly challenging changes may need to call on the service of outside change management specialists and consultants. These specialists provide training and coaching in the tools of change management; they can facilitate focus groups and handle the sometimes difficult dynamics of meetings. Some consultants specialize in communication about change, and they may coach executives on how to develop and deliver effective change messages. They may also offer objective feedback, the voice of experience, and best practices from other organizations.

Change management should become a permanent capability within every organization. Therefore, wise organizations will hire consultants who agree to, and have the methods for, transferring their change management skills to executives and middle managers.

**8.7 MAKING THE CASE FOR CHANGE**   A case for change is a reasoned yet persuasive justification for planned changes. To be effective, a case for change must be brief, clear, logical, compelling, and well documented (both qualitatively and quantitatively). The case must enable people throughout the organization to have a common vision of how the future will differ because of a change. Above all, a case for change must build a strong sense of urgency that drives people to action.[7]

Making the case involves several activities.

- *Describe and understand the planned change and how it will affect the five dimensions of change within an organization.* This part of making the case is research, not communication. It helps top executives understand what is going to happen. Why do this first step? Ask a dozen people about what a change in their organization will entail and expect a dozen different answers. Many will envision new technologies dominating the change effort, and they may support such one-dimensional change. They may not realize that there will also need to be changes in work processes, in reward systems, and in management styles until much later during the change process—and they may be upset by these aspects of change. This can be as true in the executive suite as on the shop floor. Therefore, it is critical to perform a multidimensional analysis of all proposed changes, simply to understand what is going to happen and to avoid leaving out anything that is necessary to support gaining the desired results.

- *Paint the big picture.* When an organization understands change in this way, it is much easier to communicate the new way of working *in its entirety* to everyone concerned. This is first done by creating a vision of what the future will be like, once the goals of the change are achieved. Details are added later, but they should be consistent with the initial vision.

- *Identify stakeholders and their needs, concerns, and levels of commitment.* Stakeholders include anyone who has a vested interest in the change process, especially change partners. Understanding where they stand and what they need makes it possible to devise strategies for helping them adopt the new way. This is discussed more in section 8.8.

- *Link to corporate strategy.* An organization's strategy provides context and direction for major change. Showing that a proposed change is aligned with actual business, market, and organizational strategies creates legitimacy for activities and lays the foundation necessary for accomplishing them. If that connection is not made *and maintained*, no amount of communication can compensate. For example, in the study of 410 Fortune 1000 organizations mentioned previously, 77 percent of the most successful organizations said that employees' roles were aligned with goals and objectives (versus 47 percent of the other organizations); also, 74 percent said that employees clearly understood the vision and strategy (versus 44 percent of the others). Making the strategic link shows that management is being consistent as it moves toward the future.

- *Show proof that change is needed.* Sinking sales, competitor gains, dissatisfied customers—documenting and sharing such facts with stakeholders helps them to understand the need for change. Other ways include benchmarking the practices and performance of an organization against those of similar organizations (including competitors), which can—if the performance gap is significant—convert a merely plausible case for change into a call to arms. As discussed earlier, having customers state their dissatisfaction with the status quo is a qualitative method of proving that change has to happen.

- *Set forth the compelling need.* This is a succinct statement of the case for change that incorporates the proofs identified earlier. A compelling need may be a "burning platform" or a "sunlit uplands" issue. The platform metaphor suggests that an issue is a bit like standing on a burning oil platform in the middle of the ocean, with the choice of jumping off and into a new, risky situation or staying put—and dying. It means that the cost of maintaining the status quo is prohibitively high, perhaps because of pressures from competitors or disaffection by customers. A burning platform issue is a mixed blessing. Although serious, the problems are recognizable and most people, once they understand them, will agree on the need to change. "Sunlit uplands" issues are driven by business strategies that seek to avoid burning platforms by actively taking advantage of opportunities. (The metaphor "sunlit uplands" refers to the higher aspirations of a company that is already doing well—so well that its people may be complacent.) Here, a market leader who wants to stay in front of the competition must make major changes in anticipation of evolving markets, technologies, and other external business drivers. People may be less likely to agree on the need to change when the status quo seems fine, so that sunlit uplands issues require extra attention to articulating the need to change.

**8.8 STAKEHOLDER ANALYSIS**   Stakeholders tend to ask one basic question about a change initiative: "How will this affect me?" To answer the first question, stakeholders will be evaluating the change project in terms of their own potential wins and real or feared losses. It is unwise to second-guess their answers; it is wise simply to ask them, whether through surveys, focus groups, or interviews.

Stakeholders are not a homogeneous group; they can include everyone from executives through employees, and they can be located both within an enterprise or outside it. Identifying internal stakeholders can be done during process mapping, which is typically done as part of the development of plans for change in the process and technical dimensions. People who work in processes to be changed are likely to be stakeholders, as are those who work in processes that supply targeted processes or receive their outputs.

The next step is to segment stakeholders into manageable groups for analysis and communication. For example, people in each process or function that will be affected by a change form a group; subgroups may include managers and employees, or people in different plants, offices, or professions.

The final segmentation is into two more groups: Those who support the change and those who are indifferent, lukewarm, or downright opposed to it. Learning why people feel the way they do, and the strength of their feelings, helps to create a much-needed map of where to focus attention for change management. Exhibit 8.3 shows an example of this map.

According to the map in Exhibit 8.3, the chief financial officer can be counted on to be a key supporter and advocate for the contemplated change: Not only is he on board, but he obviously has a strong stake in a positive outcome. Corporate accounting personnel are also affected, but on the opposite extreme when it comes to support. Division accounting personnel fall somewhere in the middle. Different approaches at different levels of effort are needed to help form partnerships for change with each group.

Having identified stakeholder segments, an organization must quickly get their issues out into the open. Only when these are voiced and understood can they be addressed. However, the views of initial stakeholders may change over time as the prospects for change loom closer. Therefore, it is important to continue a dialogue with stakeholder groups throughout the change process—and for some time after a change is introduced.

**(a) Plan to Address Each Stakeholder**   After an organization understands its stakeholders, the next step is develop a formal plan for securing the commitment of each stakeholder or stakeholder group. This plan should outline the perceptions and positions of each, including a means for involving them in the change process. For enthusiastic supporters, the plan should indicate how their support will be leveraged (e.g., by securing their involvement, gaining access to their communication channels, or obtaining funding from them). Possible ways of securing the commitment of stakeholders are explained in the following paragraphs.

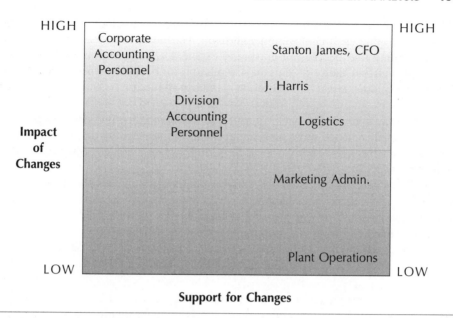

**Exhibit 8.3    Mapping Stakeholder Support for Contemplated Changes**

*(i) Mitigate Risk*    Clearly, the less enthusiastic stakeholders perceive either that there is a risk involved if they go along with the proposed change or that there is no risk to their careers if they do not.

A plan should address how negative risk can be mitigated (e.g., by providing special training for employees who lack the skills required to operate a new process). If jobs will be eliminated by a change, the plan should address how to help displaced workers make the transition to new jobs (whether inside or outside the organization). In some cases, the plan should address how to make it risky for people, especially managers, to cling to the status quo (discussed later).

*(ii) Offer Rewards*    What types of rewards or other compensation will move people to accept change, especially if this involves new behaviors (e.g., having to work cross-functionally, share closely held information, or take more risks)?

Studying this question stakeholder by stakeholder may yield different motivators for each group. The plan should address how best to reward people for both helping the change happen, then "living the change" afterward.

*(iii) Involve Stakeholders*    Involving people is one of the best ways to obtain their support. One type of involvement is to engage people in doing the work of planning for and implementing a change. There is a misconception that the number of people in an organization engaged in making change happen must necessarily be kept small, in order to more easily coordinate and direct their efforts. But one chemical manufacturer that had a total of 4,000 employees engaged 500 of them in its reengineering initiative.[8] Engaging many people in the actual work of change helps to create a critical mass of acceptance that, once achieved, accelerates receptivity in all other parts of an organization.

A second way of engaging people is to help them envision the new way of working.

This can be done through pilot projects, demonstrations, simulations, visits to other organizations that use an innovation, and so on. The idea is to turn an idea into a reality—something that people can grasp and experience. Advances in computer-based training and virtual reality systems make it possible for people to experience a new way of working before it is put into operation—and can be far less expensive than trying to deal with delays and resistance from people who simply do not understand.

A third way is to get feedback from people. Listening, hearing, and acting on this feedback helps convince some that management is sincere in its desire to meet their needs. Even if this fails to convince people to support the change, it often makes them at least neutral.

A fourth way is to be firm with executives and middle managers about top management's intent to make change happen, to invite their positive support for a change effort, and to counsel those who are not forthcoming that this failure on their part could be a career breaker. Firing or reassigning the most recalcitrant—even if they are executives—is something that many top chief executive officers (CEOs) have had to do to convince everyone else that the change envisioned is serious business.

*(iv) Keep in Touch*    Stakeholders' commitment may change over time. Therefore, an organization must keep communication channels to all stakeholder groups open and active; silence from a group probably means that there are problems.

**(b) Communication**    It has to become routine for any enterprise to ask about any change, even the most minor one: "Who needs to be informed about this?" In the study of executives from 410 Fortune 1000 companies and governmental agencies mentioned previously, all the executives interviewed said that articulating a clear vision was vital to success. However, among the most successful organizations, most gave their visions a practical and operational voice through open and honest communication about change (81 percent, versus 71 percent of other organizations). They also issued frequent progress reports (66 percent versus 42 percent), and they felt that they had an effective communication strategy (64 percent versus 44 percent). The most effective messengers of change communication were identified as senior-level executives, such as the CEO, chairman, or president. In-person meetings and discussions were rated as by far the best channels for communicating change plans to employees.[9]

Effective communication about planned change has to be well planned. A sound communication plan identifies and addresses:

- *Who the stakeholders are, and communications objectives for each.* A communication objective in change management is nearly always action oriented. It describes what the stakeholder is expected to do as a result of receiving the communication. If no action or outcome can be associated with a communication objective, it could be the wrong objective.
- *Communications activities for each stakeholder group.* This is a list and schedule of the events and other actions that will be used to reach different stakeholder groups. Although all events and actions may share common themes and messages, it is likely that at least part of each must be tailored to specific stakeholder groups.
- *Messages to be sent and the tones of the messages.* Messages may include basic information (e.g., "This is the problem and this is our approach to solving it"), calls for action (e.g., "Learn about this new resource and use it for your and our bene-

fit"), and information that gives context to messages (e.g., the "big picture," which adds relevance to a change project). The tone should fit the seriousness of the change; humor should almost always be avoided, because it is so easily misunderstood.

- *Media to be used.* The most common channels are public presentations, newsletters, and memos, but an organization must also think about how people are used to getting information. Management should consider using creative channels that will get people's attention or provide extra communication capabilities. Some of these media include:
  —Phone messages with daily updates.
  —Messages in paycheck envelopes.
  —Websites.
  —Electronic mail or groupware.
  —Computer-based training.
  —Videos.
  —Personal correspondence sent to people's homes.
  —Hotlines or bulletin boards to counteract rumors.
  —"War rooms" with charts, posters, and works in progress that everyone can see.
  —Off-site workshops or seminar.
- *Who will serve as spokespersons.* For nearly all major change projects that involve an entire organization, the main spokesperson should be the CEO. However, routine communications may come from the change sponsor. One way to involve other executives and managers is to have them be spokespersons for their respective units, functions, or lines of responsibility.
- *Optimal frequency of messages.* The more, the better. It is far safer to communicate too much than to be accused of not sharing enough information.
- *How feedback will be channeled and responded to.* Any change-management initiative that does not actively seek feedback from change partners is not using communication effectively. The only thing worse is to seek feedback and not respond to it quickly and credibly.

Here is a good example of high-tech communication and feedback. In one major change project, we helped a client set up an Intranet site that its sales force checked daily. The site had complete descriptions of planned changes, including copies of all memos and other communications; it allowed people to send e-mail queries and comments directly to the change sponsor. The sponsor answered all questions within 24 hours, even if the response was nothing more than "We're working on your answer and will get back to you by [a specific date]." Feedback was also channeled to people working on the change. Questions and comments from their change partners gave additional insights and helped avoid problems later on.

Finally, managers must always tell the truth and shun secrets. Usually, employees know if a manager or organization is truthful, and one untruth will undermine the credibility of all other messages. Nobody likes surprises, which is what secrets are once they become known. One good policy for all communications should be *no surprises.*

The most effective combination of message and medium occurs when the top executive in an organization meets personally with all the managers and employees that can possibly be reached. Just having the CEO take the time to explain the change communicates the message that it is important; his or her personal participation also says that change partners are important.

### 8.9 ALIGNING CHANGE INITIATIVES WITH OTHER CHANGE INITIATIVES    According to Exhibit 8.1, about one-third of the companies surveyed reported "initiative fatigue." This condition happens when too many changes occur at once or in rapid succession. The condition is a management mandate to analyze, set priorities for, and integrate all ongoing change programs.[10]

In some cases, it may be possible to merge some change programs or, at least, to establish better lines of communication and cooperation among them. Done well, this will create synergy in the programs. Managers should avoid, however, making change programs compete with each other for the same scarce resources. Eliminating a specific change initiative may be done for reasons such as incompatibility with the big picture of where an organization wants to go. More often, however, it happens (or should happen) because of priorities. Having too many high-priority change programs going on at once can weaken them all, cause conflicts, and undercut an organization's real work, which is to serve customers.

Developing a coherent, priority-driven change agenda requires "connecting the dots" of the many past, current, and planned change initiatives in an organization. The only person who can take charge of this process is the top leader in an organization, although that leader may get help from other executives. Job number one is for the leader to understand each major change initiative to the point where he or she can see the connection of all of the initiatives to customers and also to each other.

Much of the conflict in major change programs arises because people do not understand the rationale, methodology, and objectives involved. This is especially true for change initiatives not related to a specific work process but, instead, to organization-wide work policies or culture. Examples of these include Six Sigma, quality management, ISO 9000 series, knowledge management, restructuring, mergers, activity-based costing, mentor programs, and so on. However, it also holds for the frequent changes that occur in the basic operation of the core business processes that make and deliver products and services to customers.

Having understood the change programs, a leader can look for their similarities and compatibilities. Usually, such efforts are more alike than not (although the advocates of each may claim differently). Leaders can take several actions based on the similarities. These actions include integrating the teams involved in some initiatives and removing obstacles that have inadvertently (or deliberately) kept the programs apart. It may not be practical to integrate some programs, but their conflicts and overlaps must be resolved.

In some cases, one or two programs may need to be killed because they fail to support the organization's goals. Besides, in the Darwinian environment of most businesses, a few projects just do not make it.

The steps just mentioned only sort out, coordinate, and set priorities for multiple improvement efforts: They do not create a big picture of the reason and direction for all change initiatives in an organization. The background of this picture is the overall vision of the future for the entire organization, which is based on customer focus and made real through strategy. The foreground is a map that shows past and present change programs and underscores both their rationale and commonalities. If the map does not make sense despite an honest effort to "connect all the dots," the organization must rethink its approach to managing change. This rethinking includes developing policies and practices that help set priorities for change initiatives and lines of communication among initiatives.

When employees, managers, customers, suppliers, and other change partners understand the map, an organization has probably arrived at highly effective change management. Future success depends on understanding the complexities of change, maintaining trust with partners, and making a continuing commitment to planned changed.

## NOTES

1.  F. W. Taylor, *Principles of Scientific Management,* New York: W. W. Norton, 1998.

2.  F. Fukuyama, "Second Thoughts: The Last Man in a Bottle," *The National Interest* (Summer 1999): 27.

3.  P. Drucker, *Management Challenges for the 21st Century* (New York: HarperBusiness, 1999), 91.

4.  S. Redwood, C. Goldwasser, S. Street, and R. Tanner Pascale, *Action Management: Practical Strategies for Making Your Corporate Transformation a Success* (New York: John Wiley & Sons, 1999).

5.  D. Smith, "Invigorating Change Initiatives," *Management Review* (May 1998).

6.  Drucker, op. cit., 87–88.

7.  The Price Waterhouse Change Integration Team, *Better Change: Best Practices in Transforming Your Organization* (Chicago: Irwin Professional, 1995), 30.

8.  Ibid., 136–137.

9.  Smith, op. cit.

10.  *Better Change,* op. cit., 113.

# CHAPTER 9

# LOGISTICS

## Fred A. Kuglin and Barbara A. Rosenbaum
**Ernst & Young**

**9.1 INTRODUCTION**　In the current global business environment, the business process of *logistics*—or *supply chain management* as it has evolved to today—has taken on ever-increasing importance. Supply chain management includes all activities within or across extended enterprises that involve planning, buying, making, moving, or selling—from raw materials to consumers—to produce products and services that customers want and are willing to buy.

The key performance metrics of any enterprise (e.g., revenues, costs, shareholder value, market share, asset productivity, and customer satisfaction) are heavily influenced by effective supply chain management. Studies have shown that logistics costs range from 5 to 50 percent of sales, depending on the industry, products, geography, and company. Revenues are in large measure influenced by a supply chain's ability to deliver to customers the right product, to the right place, at the right time, in the right condition, and at the right cost. Because the objective of an effective extended-enterprise supply chain is to provide the highest level of customer service at the lowest possible cost, the effective functioning of a supply chain requires an accurate understanding of costs and the factors influencing those costs.

**9.2 EVOLUTION OF LOGISTICS INTO SUPPLY CHAIN MANAGEMENT**　The logistics process has seen a dramatic evolution over the last 20 years. In the early 1980s the process was often called Distribution and comprised those processes dealing with the physical movement of product—for example, transportation and warehouse management. These activities were typically segmented into "functional silos." Costs were suboptimized within the individual processes as opposed to being considered across the enterprise. During the 1980's, globalism and the deregulation of transportation provided forces that expanded the role of logistics in an enterprise.

In the late 1980s and early 1990s, technology provided an additional force of change for logistics. Forward-looking enterprises such as Wal-Mart, Frito-Lay, Procter & Gamble, Dell, and Toyota began to see the value of looking across processes for synergy and cost optimization. Logistics organizations were formed which, in addition to transportation and warehouse management, included demand-and-supply planning, purchasing, and customer-service processess. This organizational structure allowed a broader range of costs to be considered when making key decisions. For example, when considering shipment modes such as air versus truck shipments, the decision could be made considering not only transportation costs but also the customer-service and inventory implications of a quicker mode of transportation.

The most recent evolution of this process has encompassed an increased breadth of function both within and between enterprises. The term "supply chain management" now refers to all processess involved with planning, buying, making, moving, and selling. It encompasses the entire extended enterprise—from raw materials to the final customer. With the recent advances in technology and the Internet, it has now become possible to collaborate across enterprises, thus achieving a win-win situation for trading partners by reducing the total overall cross-enterprise costs to the ultimate consumer and thus improving customer service.

An understanding of each of the components of the supply chain is required before examining the relevant costs.

**(a) Plan**   Demand-and-supply planning is the process of understanding customer demand and matching that with supply so that inventory levels can be minimized and customer service needs met. The process components include:

- Sales and operations planning.
- Demand forecasting.
- Inventory management.
- Production planning.

The key objectives of this process are to understand the customer demand requirements to ensure that the right product is in the right place at the right time to meet those requirements at the right cost. Some companies, particularly in the high-tech industries, have been able to eliminate the uncertainty of the forecasting process and move entirely to a make-to-order environment, thus eliminating the need for costly inventory. A prime example of such a company is Dell Computer, which operates with almost no inventory. In other industries (e.g., consumer products packaged goods) a make-to-stock environment remains the norm. In those industries, therefore, companies must continue to forecast consumer demand and manage inventory effectively to control costs.

In a make-to-stock environment, a key component of the sales and operations planning process is an understanding of the profitability of a product line and the cost of that stocking strategy. The Pareto 80/20 rule is evident when the product lines of many companies are analyzed. Often 20 percent of the products account for 80 percent of the sales revenue and, correspondingly, 80 percent of the products account for 20 percent of the sales. Often, moreover, 50 percent of a company's products account for only 5 to 10 percent of its total sales. A question that should then be analyzed is the profitability of the bottom 50 percent of the product line. An accurate analysis of costs is essential to determining the cost of stocking and selling these items versus their profitability.

**(b) Buy**   Sourcing and supplier management make up the process of managing supplier relationships and the acquisition of all goods and services required for the enterprise.
Key components of this process include:

- Sourcing strategy.
- Supply base management.
- Product requirements definition and specification.

- Procurement planning and control.
- Service and supplies acquisition.

Sourcing and supplier management must accomplish two primary objectives:

- Establishment of a supplier base to replenish all goods and services to required specifications at the lowest total delivered cost.
- Collaboration with suppliers to reduce costs and time to market and to ensure high quality.

A company's sourcing strategy is critical to the overall effectiveness of an enterprise supply chain. A few companies believe that single sourcing is needed to truly partner with suppliers, eliminating wasted positioning time and purchasing bids. And a single sourcing strategy can be effective in a developing supplier relationship: Automotive companies, for example, will work with a "developing supplier" for brake systems. Brake systems take approximately two years to develop, and there are only a handful of brake system suppliers around the world.

Often, however, companies will embrace a dual or multisourcing strategy. A dual-sourcing strategy involves splitting the purchase of an item between two suppliers—usually either a 50–50 or an 80–20 split of the purchases—and is usually determined through an annual bid. These items are usually critical to a company but can be furnished by several suppliers. Certain electrical systems for automobiles fall into this category. The presence of a second supplier usually works to ensure a competitive market price.

A multisourcing strategy usually involves commodity-like items that can be supplied by numerous suppliers. Water pumps for automobiles are an example of a multisourced item. The supply of water pumps usually exceeds the demand, thus driving the price to a natural competitive level.

Product specifications are needed to determine both the complexity of an item and the number of sources for the item. Frequently, sharp purchasing professionals can make minor specification changes to an item that may affect its form but not its content yet provide significant cost savings. For example, a global automotive company was sourcing water pumps in Europe for an automotive production line in Brazil because water pumps made by suppliers in Brazil did not match the specifications for the automobile being produced. By altering the specifications a few centimeters, the automotive company was able to source these water pumps from Brazil. The savings for each water pump was over $50—a lot of money when one considers that the automotive company produced up to 125,000 automobiles a year in the one plant.

The key is to use product specifications to position items to be purchased in a sourcing quadrant (see Exhibit 9.1). This quadrant is developed using the supply market challenges (complexity) for the X axis and the business impact for the Y axis. Items in the lower left are noncritical, like office supplies and water pumps. Items in the upper left are leverage items, such as packaging. These two left-side quadrants fall into the sourcing approach of "leverage buying power."

Items in the lower right are bottleneck items, like third-party logistics services. The upper-right quadrant includes strategic items like brake systems. These two right-side quadrants fall into the sourcing approach of "create marketplace differentiation."

It is important to categorize the items to be sourced into the correct quadrant. The

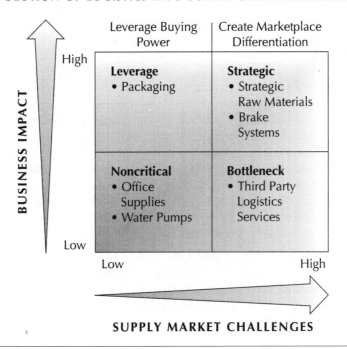

**Exhibit 9.1    Sourcing Positioning Quadrant**

marketplace approach in working with suppliers must incorporate the combination of business impact and supply market complexity in order for the purchasing professional to maximize the value and minimize the cost when contracting for these items. As most astute purchasing professionals know, purchasing items is much more sophisticated than just sending out request for bids and selecting the lowest-cost bidder.

Procurement guidelines also have significant cost implications for enterprises. For example, Wal-Mart requires its suppliers to replenish its distribution centers within 72 hours of receiving a "replenishment-pull" signal. However, 24 hours is preferred. Many enterprises incorporate quality, delivery, and issue-resolution expectations in purchasing contracts. These procurement guidelines are in the purchasing contracts with suppliers, and they are measured using a balanced scorecard (see Chapter 13).

**(c) Make**    Manufacturing and operations involve optimizing the processes involved in manufacturing a product or completing operations so that the process is completed on time at the least cost. Key processes include:

- Manufacturing strategy.
- Lean manufacturing implementation.
- Total productive maintenance.
- Industrial material management.
- Process control.
- Production material process.

The key components of lean manufacturing strategies have been adopted by many companies to allow for continuous production flow, quick product changeovers, minimal work-in-process inventories, short cycle time, and high quality. The objective is to produce high-quality products quickly and at low cost. By using lean manufacturing principles, Honda recently cut the costs of producing the new and larger Accord at its plant in Marysville, Ohio, by an estimated 20 percent. Toyota exceeded that when remodeling its Camry, slicing prices by $750 as well.

In the consumer products industry, the importance of production planning is increasing significantly. The more customers want continuous replenishment and customized packaging, the more pressure suppliers feel to add flexibility to their production processes. This is changing the old paradigm of long production runs (e.g., "run the production line 168 hours of the same item to minimize the manufactured cost per item"). The more flexibility there is, the more cost that is added to an item. It is therefore critical for an enterprise to know its costs and to price customized services to recapture the added cost caused by flexibility. It is also critical to use advanced factory planning tools to minimize overall costs wherever possible.

**(d) Move**    The transportation and distribution process involves the movement and storage of raw material, work-in-process inventories, and finished goods. Therefore, it includes both transportation management and warehouse management components, as follows:

- Physical network optimization.
- Freight cost and service management.
- Private fleet management.
- Fleet routing and scheduling.
- Transportation load planning.
- Warehouse management.

The key objectives of this process are to meet customer requirements at the least cost by either performing the processes internally (using an internal private fleet and company-owned warehouses) or outsourcing the transportation and warehouse processes. An accurate understanding of all the relevant costs is required to effectively make outsourcing decisions. For example, Kmart has outsourced its private fleet to third-party logistics companies. Wal-Mart continues to use a private fleet from its distribution warehouses to its stores. Which is right? The answer is that both are.

Another role of transportation and warehousing is to provide the least-cost network for companies to ship their products from manufacturing plants to customers. All manufacturing plants have varying cost structures and production capacities. It is essential that they leverage the fixed-cost investment in plant and equipment by using the lowest-cost combination of manufacturing, warehousing, and transportation costs. Because customer demand is variable, the key to achieve this fixed-cost leverage is to have a variable service area within the distribution network. In many industries, the cost to manufacture a product ranges from 35 to 65 percent of the total landed cost of the product to the customer. Warehousing and transportation costs usually average 5 to15 percent of total cost. Therefore, it is necessary to place the flexibility in warehousing and transportation to enable the least-cost network combination and still meet customer expectations and requirements.

**(e) Sell**   Customer service and order management are components of the process of understanding customer requirements and fulfilling those requirements in a timely, cost-effective manner. A key concept here is the idea of customer segmentation—that is, understanding the requirements and profitability of various customer segments, then adjusting the services provided to ensure profitability in each segment. An understanding of costs is essential in this process. Key subprocesses in this area are:

- Customer segmentation/value strategy.
- Customer service organization and operations.

The objectives of this process are to ensure customer profitability and satisfaction at minimal cost. One objective is to provide excellent service to customers that a company wants to attract and retain. These customers usually are repeat buyers that understand the "value exchange." Another goal in this area is to avoid "unnecessary excellence." Excellent—yet costly—supply chain services should be avoided for customers that are unprofitable. The long-distance telephone customers that switch long-distance carriers monthly just to receive a check in the mail are examples of customers that should be avoided for high value-services. An understanding of total delivered cost and profitability (by customer type and by product) will help professionals make strategic decisions about which customers to serve and how best to serve them.

**9.3 EFFECTIVE SUPPLY CHAIN MANAGEMENT DRIVES SHAREHOLDER VALUE**   In the past, distribution or logistics processes were often viewed as cost centers that had little impact on the overall performance of an enterprise. Today, however, the concept of a supply chain has brought greater understanding of the large potential that supply chain processes have to influence corporate profitability and shareholder value. As a general rule, companies with high-performing supply chains (Compaq, Cisco Systems, Dell Computer, Procter & Gamble, Wal-Mart, and Becton-Dickinson, to name a few) also have high-performing stocks. These companies work continuously to address five value drivers[1]:

1. Profitable growth.
2. Working capital minimization.
3. Fixed capital minimization.
4. Tax minimization.
5. Cost minimization.

Effective management of the supply chain can have a significant impact on each of these five drivers. For example, high-quality manufacturing and high-quality customer service directly affect a customer's willingness to buy—and thus the profitable growth of a company. Note that an enterprise is interested in *profitable* growth, not just growth. One of the keys to profitable growth is an understanding of customer profitability, as previously discussed.

Working capital minimization is in large part achievable through effective planning of demand and supply, which should lead to reductions in inventory levels and days sales outstanding (DSO). Fixed capital minimization is achieved largely through optimized network planning and optimizing the utilization of manufacturing resources.

Tax issues should play a significant role in the planning of overall supply-chain strategy. Location of manufacturing facilities and distribution centers has a significant effect on the worldwide effective tax rate for a company. Globally, the impact is particularly significant, because tax rates vary significantly from country to country. For example, the tax rate in Germany is 47 percent, whereas the tax rate in the Netherlands ranges from 20 to 35 percent, depending on a favorable tax ruling. The tax savings on value-added supply chain activities performed in the Netherlands versus Germany can produce *below-the-line* tax savings of 12 to 27 percent. Therefore, any value-added activities (such as sorting, kitting, subassembly, free trade zone warehousing of in-bond imports, and special packaging) that can be performed in the Netherlands and then shipped into Germany for final sale or consumption will produce significant tax savings. Where a company captures and realizes the "value-added" portion of a product in a global supply chain can have a significant *below-the-line* impact on profitability.

We focus here on the key cost elements that should be considered across the supply chain. An integrated supply chain requires an understanding of the key cost trade-offs across processes and the minimization of those costs across the enterprise and in fact across the entire supply chain, from supplier to customer. The key cost elements in a supply chain include the following:

- Warehouse operations costs.
- Purchasing and procurement costs.
- Excess and obsolete inventory costs.
- Cost of purchased items.
- Information technology costs.
- Inbound, outbound, and interenterprise transportation costs.
- Direct manufacturing costs.
- Indirect manufacturing costs (MRO, maintenance, utilities).
- Return logistics costs.

Following are the key factors affecting these costs:

- Product life cycles.
- Order-to-cash cycle times.
- Location of demand and supply points.
- Interdependability of purchasing, manufacturing, warehousing, and transportation costs.
- Number of stock keeping units (SKUs) sold and stocked.
- Raw material and finished goods inventory levels versus needed levels.
- Number and location of manufacturing facilities.
- Transportation modes and carriers.
- Customer order patterns.
- Customer-service requirements.
- Information technology used.
- Manufacturing flexibility and efficiency.
- Warehouse operational efficiency.

- Number of suppliers.
- Quality of delivered material.

Examining these costs and the factors that affect them makes it clear that to optimize the costs across the supply chain, an enterprise must understand and work collaboratively with its customers and suppliers. All the factors affecting costs can be viewed as being driven by several elements.

- *Customer-service requirements.* The requirement to meet customer needs drives many of these costs. Many of the drivers on the previous list are affected by customer requirements. For example, the number and location of distribution centers, the number and location of manufacturing facilities, the number of SKUs stocked in each distribution center, and the choice of transportation modes are all heavily influenced by the need to meet a customer's order-to-delivery and cash-cycle-time requirements. A key point, therefore, is the need for a clear understanding of customer requirements. Too often distribution strategies are developed around perceived customer needs without first surveying customers to determine their real needs. For example, management may perceive that customers require a two-day order-to-delivery cycle, whereas a survey of key customers may reveal that three days is acceptable. Working toward a strategy of two days can result in significant dollars being spent to achieve "unnecessary excellence."

- *Enterprise operational efficiency.* Once customer requirements are understood, a firm must strive to meet those requirements as efficiently and cost-effectively as possible. The efficient operation of a warehouse and the efficient operation of a manufacturing facility using lean manufacturing principles are significant cost drivers. In addition, information technology can produce significant efficiencies and cost savings. There are a number of software packages currently on the market that work with enterprise resource planning (ERP) systems such as SAP or PeopleSoft to yield significant efficiencies in supply chain processes. These packages include warehouse management systems, transportation management systems, advanced planning and scheduling systems, component and supplier management systems, and manufacturing execution systems. (These are discussed in section 9.4.)

- *Supplier relationships.* The final influence is the firm's relationship with its suppliers. A key element of effective supplier management is to reduce (or in a few cases increase) the number of suppliers and to develop strategic relationships with key selected suppliers (e.g., developing suppliers). A reduction in the number of suppliers provides greater leverage in terms of price negotiations because more is bought from fewer vendors. It also reduces the administrative costs caused by dealing with many vendors. The development of a strategic relationship also allows requirements definition discussions with key vendors during product development, which should lead to enhanced quality and lower overall manufacturing costs.

**9.4 ACTIVITY-BASED COSTING**   Activity-based costing (ABC) is a management and financial system, not just an accounting system. The objective in utilizing ABC is to restate costs based on how the supply chain consumes resources. This approach differs from the traditional accounting approach that uses a chart of accounts within functional or vertical groups of a company.

The case study in section 9.6 shows that the series of logistics activities that make up supply chain management are all interrelated. The key is to understand the drivers of these activities, the linkages between these drivers and other activities created by these drivers, and the resources consumed by each activity.

Direct costs are the easiest to measure. Traditional manufacturing direct labor or raw material costs are fairly easy to assign to a product being produced. But many companies have a difficult time allocating indirect costs without a proper operational and financial system. Manufacturing utility costs, transportation management overhead, warehouse management overhead, facility maintenance costs, and customer-order management costs are examples of functional costs in the supply chain that transcend specific product costs. Selling, general and administrative (SG&A) costs also fall into this indirect cost category.

For example, order management may fall into a "salaries and benefits" account in a traditional accounting approach. The ABC approach would be to show this expense as an "order management" cost and allocate the expense to products based on an agreed-on method. The ultimate goal is to develop a "true" allocated cost for each product so that a product portfolio profit and loss (P&L) can be developed.

ABC can also be used to assign costs based on shipping containers, distribution channels, and even major customers. The intent here is to focus on those specific drivers of supply-chain activities that disproportionately consume supply chain resources.

Wal-Mart is such a large customer for many consumer products companies (frequent estimates are 15 to 30 percent of a consumer products company's business may now be with Wal-Mart) that specific supply chain activities relating to Wal-Mart can be (and often should be) tracked and measured. For example, a special size bundling of products for Sam's Club or a specific continuous replenishment program for Wal-Mart consumes supply chain resources at a different rate than do other customers. Identifying and tracking these costs are essential if a company hopes to understand the costs (and profits) associated with doing business with Wal-Mart. Companies will be required to have this information during negotiations with Wal-Mart. Without this information, erroneous decisions may be made on a significant portion of a company's business base.

Another example of how costs can be displayed in a horizontal or supply chain format is the bread customer supply chain (see Exhibit 9.2). The costs for each process are shown along the top line, while the supply chain buildup costs for the product are shown on the bottom line. This helps the company's executives to view functional efficiency cost performance as well as the overall supply chain cost performance for the selected product.

In this example, a loaf of bread (branded, not private label) costs $1.00 to $1.08 per pound (16 ounces). The largest cost components are indirect (manufacturing and SG&A), suggesting that plant capacity utilization and direct store-door delivery systems represent significant fixed cost investments that need to be leveraged. Ingredients (at $.15 per pound) are the next highest cost component, which suggests having a sharp focus on strategic sourcing strategies. Packaging, transport of raw materials, and general and administrative costs (separate from distribution/selling) represent smaller cost components, so they should command less management attention.[2]

One note on this example. The thrift stores for stale bread (bread has an average shelf life of three days with traditional packaging) returns $.04 per pound to the bread company. Insiders in the industry say that the thrift stores' profit (or negative cost) frequently represents *the* profit margin for a bread company! With a three-day shelf life

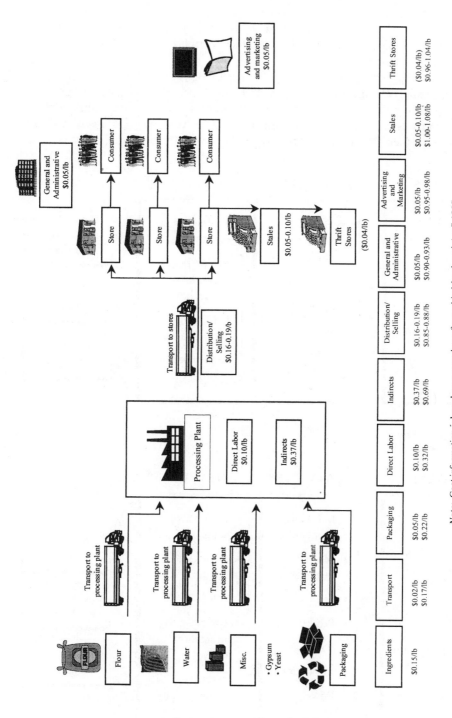

*Note:* Cost information is based on research performed in March and April 1997

**Exhibit 9.2  Bread Customer Supply Chain**

and razor-thin margins, this is truly an industry that must have a handle on its functional and supply chain costs.

The critical success factors are to know costs, track costs, and assign supply chain costs to product, channel, or customer activities. Once accomplished, the resultant financial information can be used to drive product portfolios, investments, and strategic decisions about major customers.

In Exhibits 9.3 through 9.6, the major costs, activities, and cost drivers are identified for the key supply chain processes of buy, make, move, and sell. (The fifth supply chain process, plan, is not included here because this process deals with the planning of the other four processes.) Each exhibit first identifies the key cost categories associated with the process. It then lists the key activities associated with the process. Finally, each ex-

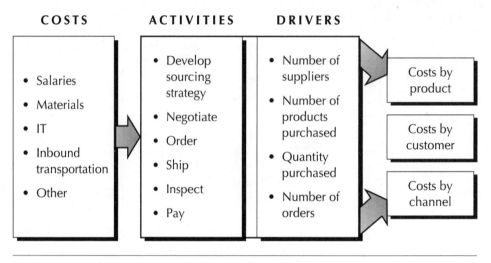

**Exhibit 9.3    Buy**

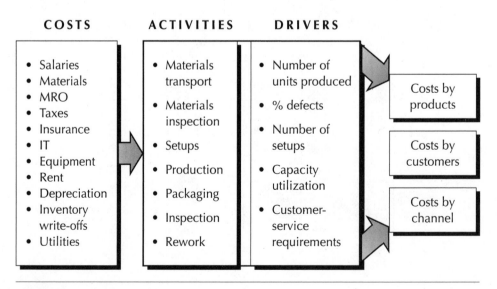

**Exhibit 9.4    Make**

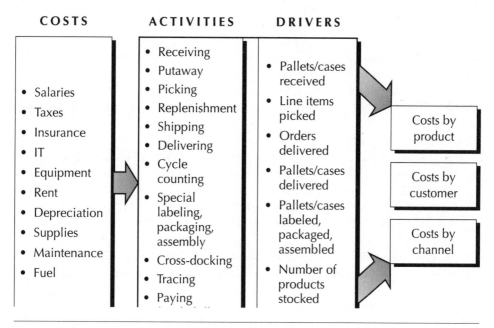

**Exhibit 9.5 Move**

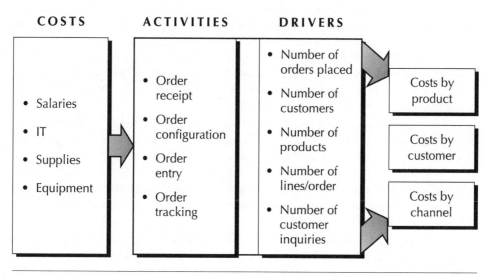

**Exhibit 9.6 Sell**

hibit identifies the cost drivers to be used in assigning the costs to the activities. The assignment of costs to activities ultimately provides information that can be used to develop costs by product and by customer. An enterprise then has the tools to understand which products, channels, and product lines are profitable. It can also understand the profitability of various types of customers and the types of services that can be profitably offered to various segments of customers.

One of the keys to implementing an effective ABC system is the availability of accurate data for the costs and the cost drivers. In recent years many firms have implemented ERP systems, which have had a dramatic effect on increasing the quality and consistency of data throughout an enterprise. One common database is used throughout the firm, thus allowing for timely and accurate information regarding products, orders, and inventories. In addition, in the supply chain area, a number of "bolt-on" packages have become available to fill in gaps in process areas where ERP functionality may be incomplete. These supply chain software packages can be generally grouped in several categories.

- *Advanced planning and scheduling systems.* This class of systems generally enables the processes discussed previously in the plan area of the supply chain. Forecasting, inventory management, and production planning functionality are covered. This system generates the plan in terms of what products should be produced, when, and in what manufacturing facilities. It then suggests where that planned production should be shipped.

- *Component and supplier management systems.* This class of systems deals with the buy process. It assists an enterprise in rationalizing its supplier and product base. The system can examine the purchasing records of a firm to determine the quantity of product being purchased from each vendor. This may seem like a simple task. However, records may indicate purchases from IBM, I.B.M., International Business Machines, etc., all of which—from a system's point of view—appear to be distinct companies. The system even identifies subsidiaries operating under different names that are actually part of the same corporation. A firm can thus understand and thereby leverage purchases made from one supplier. The system can also identify multiple parts that perform the same function. Companies may find that they are purchasing 10 different screws that perform the same function. By modifying their purchasing to buy one type of screw instead of 10, they can significantly reduce the costs of purchasing and stocking parts. The system then maintains a catalogue of preferred parts for use by product designers.

- *Warehouse management systems.* Within the move process, warehouse management systems control all the operations within the four walls of the warehouse. On the receiving side, that involves tracking a product from receipt to directed put-away. From the standpoint of order picking and shipping, the system directs the work flow in terms of product picking, marshaling, and shipment. The system maintains data on the flow of work in and out of a warehouse in terms of orders, lines, cases, and pallets.

- *Transportation management systems.* Also within the move process, transportation management systems manage the load planning and consolidation of shipments for delivery. For example, a transportation management system will determine the most effective way to ship a group of orders by considering alternate modes, stopoffs, back-hauls, and pool points. The system can then cost the shipment and pay the freight bill.

This brief discussion provides some guidance on the types of systems that may be needed to gain the data required for the implementation of activity-based costing with the supply chain.

**9.5 PERFORMANCE MANAGEMENT**   Supply chain performance measurement is a process to define and measure operations to support a company's mission, strategy, and operations. It is an extension of cost management that enables managers to monitor, evaluate, and improve operations. Performance measures must be linked with a company's overall business strategy and with performance goals. The design of a performance measurement system should take into account responsibility and accountability beginning at the lowest possible level and flowing up to top management. The crucial element of an effective performance management system is to ensure that performance measures at all levels support the overall goals of the enterprise.

In a manufacturing environment, for example, an often-used performance measure is machine utilization. However, maximizing machine utilization can have a detrimental impact on overall enterprise costs. Producing product that is not needed builds unneeded inventory and creates unnecessary costs. The principles of lean manufacturing indicate that product should only be produced when required to meet customer demands. When demand goes up, utilization should increase; when demand goes down, utilization should decrease. A more appropriate measure is on-demand utilization factor (i.e., the machine is available when required.) This measure implies that the manufacturing operation has minimized machine breakdowns, defects, setup time, adjustments, and loss of speed.[3] A manufacturing manager working toward the goal of maximizing machine utilization could do significant harm to the firm's overall profitability.

A first key step in the design of a supply chain performance measurement system is an understanding of the enterprise-level critical success factors. As discussed earlier, every enterprise has as its overall goal the maximization of shareholder value. However, there may be a variety of strategies for achieving that goal. These may include:

- Cost minimization.
- Customer satisfaction.
- Quality.
- Market share.
- Innovation.
- Quick time to market with new products.

These measures must then be translated into measurements specific to the supply chain. For example, customer satisfaction from a supply chain perspective can translate into the following more specific goals:

- Orders can be placed easily.
- Sufficient inventory is on hand to fill orders.
- Delivery date promises are kept.
- Products are delivered undamaged.
- Rush orders are filled promptly.
- Orders can be easily changed after they are placed.
- Company is flexible and responsive.
- Orders are delivered complete.
- Order-to-delivery times meet customer requirements.
- Information on order status is readily available.

The challenge is to determine the relative importance of these factors for each customer (or group) and for each product (or group).

Once critical success factors are identified and their relative weights determined by appropriate categories, estimates of the current state of performance and performance goals can be established for each supply chain activity.

**9.6 CASE STUDY**    A major consumer packaged goods manufacturer represents a solid example of how cost can be integrated into the management of a supply chain. This case about a consumer packaged goods manufacturer also weaves the concept of time into the cost considerations in its supply chain. Let us take a look at the concept of time in the supply chain and how this company integrates the driving forces of its supply chain with the elements of time and cost.

**(a) Concept of Time**    The concept of time within the supply chain has four critical elements that tie to increased costs and lower profits. Three of those critical elements are:

- Product "shelf life."
- Adding value to the product as close as possible to the sale to customers.
- The movement of material through stages of the supply chain governed by time restrictions based on date of prior-stage manufacture.

The fourth critical element, time to market for new product introductions, is not discussed here but is covered in Chapter 16.

*(i) Shelf Life*    Many manufactured products have a "shelf life," or amount of time from the date of manufacture to a date of diminished value. For example, automobiles have their "model year." When a new model comes out in late summer, unsold new vehicles from the old model year become "last year's model" and are subject to clearance sales. Personal computers (PCs) have a shelf life (or life cycle) of four to six months before they are replaced with upgraded PCs. Consider a recent purchase of a Dell 350MHz desktop computer on sale with a 10 percent discount that was four to five months in production. Within two months, Dell came out with a 400MHz and a 450MHz desktop computer.

Food companies have an assortment of shelf life products. Milk has a 7- to 10-day shelf life, whereas beer has a 4- to 6-month shelf life, and bread approximately 3 days. Unsold food products become "stales" that are either sold at a discount or thrown away (and often written off as negative sales). Regardless of the product, one key success factor is for the enterprise to maximize the time the product is available to be sold to customers to minimize the risk of lost value through obsolescence or stale product.

Many manufacturers measure their products on a cost basis until these products arrive at the next or final stage of their supply chain. Frequently, this final stage involves wholesalers or retailers. These products are then converted to a "retail" cost, with a final sale registered for the manufacturer. This final sale includes the margin added to the cost basis for the product and is built into the delivered "store door" or retail price. Thus, when a product does not sell, many retailers and some wholesalers return the unsold, obsolete, or stales to the manufacturer for credit. This credit is frequently shown in the form of a "negative sale," and it includes the cost of the product *and* the margin.

*(ii) Time from Adding Value to Sale*   A second element in the concept of time involves the time frame between the enterprise adding value to a product and sale of the product to a customer. Another key success factor is for the supply chain executive to minimize the amount of time costs that "reside" within the supply chain by adding value to products as close to the sale as possible. For example, Dell Computer frequently has its computers assembled and shipped *after* they are sold to the customer. This situation, combined with Dell's payables and receivables practices, produces a situation that comes close to a negative working capital situation. Thus, a flexible and time-sensitive supply chain allows Dell to enjoy a working capital and free-cash-flow situation that is the envy of most companies today!

*(iii) Time Restrictions Based on Date of Prior-Stage Manufacture*   The third critical element of time involves the movement of material through stages of the supply chain. Each supply chain participant is governed by time restrictions based on the date of prior-stage manufacture.

For discrete manufacturers, this critical element of time helps enable the second critical element. For example, in the automotive industry, when a Tier 1 supplier provides completed "systems" (e.g., brake systems) to original equipment manufacturers (OEMs), Tier 2 suppliers provide subsystems to a Tier 1 supplier, and Tier 3 suppliers provide basic parts or materials to the Tier 2 supplier, conversion of parts into subsystems and subsystems into systems requires the placement of value on *products* that become *materials* for new products. The compression of time between the placement of value at each stage of assembly helps allow for the compression of time between the final point of added value and the sale to the ultimate customer.

Assuming that cost and material ownership transfers with each movement in the supply chain, it is important that inventories of parts, subsystems, and systems be held to a minimum while maintaining perfect order-fill rates. The sale of the automobiles associated with these products are dependent on numerous factors. Unless a guaranteed sale contract with an automotive OEM exists, these suppliers are at risk if automobile sales fall short of forecasted levels. By compressing the time between each stage of value added, the response time of the overall supply chain improves while inventories at each stage decrease. Otherwise, Tier 1 suppliers can have an investment in parts, subsystems, and systems that plummets significantly when the final automobile sales falter. There are only two major effects to a company when this occurs. The first is lower profits due to obsolete material write-offs. The second is higher prices for the OEM—and the final customer—to cover the risk exposure of the Tier 1 supplier. Both of these effects are unacceptable to shareholders and security analysts, and they can be avoided through sound supply chain management practices.

Whether it is managing the "shelf life" of the product, the timing of the placement of value in the product as close as possible to the final sale to the customer, or the compression of time between each stage of product conversion in the supply chain, the concept of time has major implications for cost within the supply chain.

**(b) Consumer Products Company Case Study**   The ABC Company, a consumer products company, has products that have 35 to 90 days of shelf life. The company's whole supply chain is driven on the movement of raw materials and finished products within established time frames for each component of the supply chain. The cost for the material move with the material as it progresses through each component of the supply chain. The major supply chain components with this company are:

- Delivery to the store shelf and product ordering.
- Purchasing/procurement.
- Production scheduling and manufacturing.
- Warehousing.
- Transportation.

*(i) Delivery to the Store Shelf and Product Ordering*    ABC has designed its whole supply chain around the replenishment of its allocated store shelf space. The store shelf, which has been designed with a category management focus, uses plan-o-grams that mix high-velocity and high-margin products. The company demands zero stockouts from its supply chain partners, which translates into perfect order-fill rates.

ABC's salesmen are assured that the product delivered to them will have at least 28 to 83 days of shelf life remaining on the product. This means that the supply chain has only seven days from the date the product is manufactured until the date that the salesman can place the product on the store shelf. Any product delivered with less shelf life and outside the allowable seven days is subject to refusal by the salesman. When this happens, the delivering entity is forced to absorb the cost of the product. In addition, the perfect order-fill expectation remains in effect. The route salesman is required to have no more than four days' worth of inventory on hand (not on shelf) at any given time.

In this case, the delivering entity is the company's own private fleet for approximately 90 percent of the deliveries. There is no budget allowed for "stales" or refused product. There is also little tolerance for failures in customer deliveries and less than perfect order-fill rates. The manager of each entity must account for the variances to the budget and customer service levels. The urgency behind delivering the product to the salesman and the store shelf within seven days and with perfect order-fill rates is high.

For noncompany delivery entities, a specific delivery date ties to the date of manufacture and the seven allowable days. Nonperformance by outside delivery entities (that are not caused by acts of God) is subject to chargebacks for the freight charges and the inventory cost of the merchandise. However, there is still accountability for the merchandise and the delivery by the internal supply chain department that arranged for the alternate delivery entity.

The route salesmen and the stores submit their orders one week in advance of desired delivery. These orders are modified by area personnel to adjust for promotions and product portfolio changes. These orders are then accumulated by demand points, sorted by production commodity type, and allocated to plants and distribution centers. These orders are allocated based on the least-cost combination of manufacturing and distribution costs. As such, the lowest-cost plants and distribution centers are scheduled for 100 percent utilization, which results in leveraging the lowest-cost asset base of the company. It also pressures the highest-cost plants and distribution centers to lower their costs or face closure.

*(ii) Purchasing/Procurement*    ABC purchases most of its commodities on long-term contracts. In selected cases, future trading is done to ensure a consistent supply of commodities at a consistent price. The corporate office purchasing staff's costs are allocated to each commodity as the commodity is used by the production plants.

The raw materials or commodities are "called out" against the master contracts by the production plants after the demand is allocated. The purchase price of the raw materials, including the overhead allocation from the purchasing department, is then moved with the raw materials to the requesting plant. It then becomes part of the production cost for the associated finished product.

Inbound freight is separated from the purchase price, and it also moves with the raw material to each production plant. Although the suppliers route the raw materials to each plant, the rates are negotiated annually by the company.

*(iii) Production Scheduling and Manufacturing*   Once the demand is allocated to each plant, it must be scheduled for production. Raw materials are requested, and plant production schedules are set. Costs are categorized into fixed, semifixed, and variable costs. The fixed and semifixed costs are allocated to the finished product cost on a total-volume-produced basis. The key variables to measure variances in each category are set and reviewed annually.

The finished product, along with the production cost (which includes both the purchasing or procurement cost and the plant fixed, semifixed, and variable costs), is moved to a warehouse controlled by a supply chain department. The manufacturing plant has three days from receipt of the order and one day from date of manufacture to the time it must transfer the finished product to the warehouse and the cost to the supply chain department. Any finished product moved after three days is subject to refusal by the supply chain department. In addition, the requirement for perfect order-fill remains in effect.

*(iv) Transportation and Distribution*   The *transportation* schedule must be completed within 24 hours after orders are entered. The service area can be (and often is) variable to allow for the 100 percent utilization of the lowest-cost plant/distribution combination. However, efforts are made to balance out shipments by day of week to balance equipment utilization and manpower planning.

Orders are routed with fixed service windows that can range from 1 hour to 24 hours, depending on the delivery location's needs. All truckloads are then routed with a least-cost constraint, contingent upon service commitments which must be satisfied before any other routing optimization. A mix of private fleet and common/contract carriers is used for these transportation deliveries.

Cost comes into play in three ways in transportation. The first way involves efficient and effective routing of drivers and assets. The allocation of fixed, variable, and overhead costs is measured on a cost-per-product-unit-shipped basis. The more product shipped at the least cost possible, the lower the cost component becomes for transportation. In addition, the avoidance of using "sales" or "revenue" as a denominator to measure transportation cost efficiency helps avoid the confusion and impact of pricing. (All costs will eventually be combined with all revenues on the P&L statement. However, it is important to measure the efficiencies of each function independently as well.)

The second way for cost to come into play is the balancing of shipments throughout the week. The company balances transportation dispatches over a seven-day work week. (Trucks and trains have wheels, and they are made to move: Assets cannot sit idle without creating an "unused asset opportunity cost.") The seven-day dispatch week keeps the private fleet transportation assets moving and helps lower the overall fixed asset allocation to the product moved. It also avoids higher rates that dedicated contract carriers may charge if their assets sit idle evenings or on weekends.

The third way for cost to come into play in transportation is the decision between private fleet and common/contract carriers. Outsourcing transportation services may or may not be in a company's best interest. Wal-Mart maintains its private fleet for shipments from its distribution centers to its stores, but it uses contract and common carriers for shipments into their distribution centers. Kmart uses third-party logistics companies to handle most of its transportation needs. For each company, these different decisions could be the right ones.

The company in this case study uses a mix of private fleet and common/contract carriers, depending on service and cost. The company knows its costs and makes its decisions accordingly. In addition, the company reviews the total outsourcing option every two to three years to have a handle on the "gap" between its private fleet cost and an outsourced cost. This "gap" is used as an incentive to drive down internal costs to maintain the core of the private fleet and the flexibility it provides to the company's operations.

Once the transportation schedule is completed, it is then turned over to the *warehousing* department. The transportation schedules are sorted and assigned to warehousemen in the overall warehouse schedule. The warehouse has 24 hours to complete every load and must meet all dispatch times. This time frame includes the completion of the administration forms (shipping orders, bills of lading, invoices, and shipping manifests) on line and in paper form, if applicable.

The warehouse operation appears to be simple, but it is a critical operation with the company. The product is physically and financially transferred from the production department to the warehouse on a continuous basis. The production value added is moved with the product. This company is intense about the accuracy in the movement of the product and the movement of the associated financial responsibility. This is true both from production to warehouse and also from warehouse to transportation. Remember, there is no budget allowed for "old" product and for inventory shrinkage due to loss, damage, or miscounting.

The warehouse is measured on a cost-per-product basis. However, readers must be careful in this example. Less sophisticated companies may try to "load up" a warehouse to lower the warehouse cost per unit handled. There are numerous examples in which companies have saved significant dollars by shipping directly to customers or consumers and avoiding the warehouse altogether. In fact, this concept is at the heart of the savings for companies in e-Commerce or electronic retailing (e-Tailing).

The warehousing department receives the product on day 1 and loads the product on day 2 of the shelf life (days 4 and 5 of the order cycle). The transportation department dispatches and delivers the product on days 3 and 4 of the product shelf life (days 6 and 7 of the order cycle.) Thus, of 35 to 90 days of shelf life, the salesmen have approximately 28 to 83 days to place the product on the shelf for sale. Given the fact that the three-day salesmen inventory replicates replenishment orders from the stores themselves, it is a frequent occurrence that the company product will have at a minimum 25 to 80 days on the shelf to sell.

*(v) Case Study Summary*    Cost and time within supply chain management play a significant role for high-performing companies. The process disciplines; the roles, responsibilities, and training of people, and the effective use of technology all contribute to the "high performance" of leading companies. However, the one key success factor that motivates and influences the behavior of all companies in the extended enterprise supply chain is cost.

The company utilizes the concepts of time and cost to create a supply chain capability that differentiates it in the marketplace. To some, it can be considered a core competency. Regardless, the results could not have materialized unless the company had truly known its costs and understood how to assign and allocate these costs.

**9.7 SUMMARY**    Effective supply chain management has become a key differentiator and competitive advantage for enterprises in today's global economy. As this chapter discusses, those companies that are most successful are actively managing their supply chain and have an understanding of the key costs and cost drivers in the supply chain. As competitive pressures have grown in recent years, many companies have an increased understanding of the need to understand and manage costs. A study completed in 1998 by the Ohio State University's Supply Chain Management Research Group captures changes regarding the use of ABC within the supply chain over the previous five years: 72 percent of respondents indicated that they were currently using ABC in their supply chain and 49 percent indicated that ABC had been in use for less than two years.[4] Companies have learned that the supply chain's objective of integration both within and between enterprises makes it a prime candidate for ABC applications, which allow for an accurate understanding of the costs and cost trade-offs.

## NOTES

1. G. Tyndall, C. Gopal, W. Partsch, and J. Kamauff, *Supercharging Supply Chains* (New York: John Wiley & Sons, 1998).
2. F. Kuglin, *Customer-Centered Supply Chain Management* (New York: Amacom, 1998).
3. K. Suzaki, *The New Manufacturing Challenge* (New York: Free Press, 1987).
4. B. LaLonde and T. Pohlen, *1998 Survey of Activity-Based Costing Applications within Business Logistics,* presentation to the 1998 annual conference of the Council of Logistics Management, Anaheim, CA (October 12, 1998).

# CHAPTER 10

# SUPPLY CHAIN MANAGEMENT

## Tom Albright and Stan Davis*
### The University of Alabama

**10.1 INTRODUCITON**  Supply chain management (SCM) has received increased attention as companies seek to gain and maintain a competitive advantage in the market. SCM encompasses not only planning and controlling the flow of materials from suppliers to end users (*logistics-based SCM*), but also the philosophy adopted by a company toward supplier relationships (*strategic SCM*). Thus, SCM is a philosophy that seeks to unify skills and resources of business functions found both within an enterprise and outside. The thrust is to develop relationships and to synchronize the flow of products, services, and information.[1]

This chapter addresses both logistics-based SCM (LSCM) and strategic SCM (SSCM). The section on SSCM includes a discussion of the supply chain as an integral component of an organization's value chain, the importance of alliances with suppliers, and the importance of SCM to a successful implementation of business initiatives such as just-in-time (JIT), total quality management (TQM), electronic data interchange (EDI), outsourcing, and target costing. The section that addresses LSCM focuses on value-added opportunities and current trends. The final section offers points that companies beginning an SCM program should consider. Although illustrations from various successful SCM practices are cited, the chapter identifies the supply chain practices taking place at Mercedes U.S. International in developing the new M-class sports utility vehicle.

**10.2 SUPPLY CHAIN MANAGEMENT AT MERCEDES-BENZ**  During the recession that began in the early 1990s, Mercedes-Benz (MB) struggled with product development, cost efficiency, material purchasing, and problems in adapting to changing markets. In 1993, these problems caused the worst sales slump in decades, and MB lost money for the first time in its history. Since then, MB has streamlined its core business and reduced both its parts and system complexity. Mercedes-Benz also established simultaneous engineering programs with suppliers, a key element of the company's SCM strategy.

In a search for additional market share, new segments, and new niches, MB started developing a range of new products. Perhaps the largest and most radical of MB's new projects was the M-class. To design vehicle and production systems, Mercedes-Benz U.S. International (MBUSI) used functional groups that included representatives from

*The authors thank Ola Kallenius and Bob Birch of Mercedes for their generous contributions.

every area of the company (marketing, development, engineering, purchasing, production, and controlling). A modular construction process was used to produce the M-class. First-tier suppliers provided modular systems (rather than individual parts or components) for production of approximately 65,000 vehicles annually.

**(a) M-Class Project Phases**    The M-class moved from concept to production in a relatively short time. The first phase (or concept phase) was initiated in 1992 and led to a feasibility study that was approved by the board. The project realization phase began in 1993, and production began in 1997. Key elements of the various phases are described below.

*(i) Concept Phase: Early Supplier Involvement*    From 1992 to 1993 team members compared the existing product line with various market segments to discover opportunities for new vehicle introductions. The analysis revealed opportunities in the rapidly expanding sports utility vehicle (SUV) market that was dominated by Jeep, Ford, and GM. Even at this early stage of development, key suppliers worked with MB team members to develop cost estimates for the concept vehicle.

*(ii) Project Realization Phase*    From 1993 to 1996, MB held regular customer clinics in which potential customers could view the prototype and hear the company's concept for the new vehicle. Mercedes-Benz engineers and external suppliers organized by functional groups designed systems to deliver essential characteristics as discussed in the clinics. Mercedes-Benz did *not* use target costing and supply chain management to produce the lowest-priced vehicle. On the contrary, the company's strategic objective contemplated delivering products that were slightly more expensive than competitive models, but the additional cost had to translate into greater perceived value on the part of the customer.

*(iii) Production Phase*    Achieving the target cost for the M-class vehicle began with an estimate of the existing cost for each functional group. Next, components used for each functional group were identified, along with their associated costs. Cost-reduction targets were set by working closely with suppliers, then comparing the estimated existing cost with the target cost for each functional group. Next, cost-reduction targets were established for each component.

The M-class manufacturing process relied on high-value-added systems suppliers to provide components such as the cockpit. Thus, systems suppliers were also made part of the development process from the beginning of the project. Mercedes-Benz expected suppliers to meet established cost targets.

**(b) Results**    Managers at MB used indexes during the concept design phase to understand the relationship of the *importance* of a functional group to the *target cost* of a function group. Thus, opportunities for cost reduction (consistent with customer demands) could be identified and managed during the early stages of product development. Choices made during the project realization phase were largely irreversible during the production phase, because approximately 80 percent of the production cost of the M-class was for materials and systems provided by external suppliers. Using target costing and supply chain management as key elements, MB manufactured the first production vehicle in 1997.

**10.3 STRATEGIC SUPPLY CHAIN MANAGEMENT**    Supply chain logistics is a primary activity in an organization's value chain. To engage in strategic cost management, managers must identify and assess primary and secondary activities and the processes necessary for the organization to compete. These activities and processes are an organization's *value chain*.

The value chain for a company includes primary activities that create value for customers both *inside and outside* the firm. Understanding the costs associated with each activity of the value chain provides an understanding of the organization's cost structure, which allows a firm to set cost or niche strategies. Typically, a value chain includes six primary activities:

1. Purchased supplies and inbound logistics.
2. Operations.
3. Outbound logistics.
4. Sales and marketing.
5. Service.
6. Profit margin.

Supply chain management is integrally involved in the first three links in the chain and is becoming integrated into a firm's strategy.

In developing a strategic plan, a company should carefully analyze potential relationships with suppliers. Because successful supply chain management is a key element in other management techniques such as JIT, TQM, EDI, target costing, and outsourcing, assessing the power relationship is important. Given the demands placed upon suppliers by these programs, proper relationships with key suppliers are essential.

**(a) Alliances with Suppliers**    Successful supply chain management practices begin with the selection of key suppliers, then the development of trusting, mutually beneficial relationships that last over long periods. Alliances with suppliers are usually necessary only for vendors that supply integral (strategically important) components to the manufacturing process. The objective of aligning closely with suppliers is not to acquire the lowest possible price but, rather, to secure acceptable prices in return for superior service and reliability. Another benefit of developing strong alliances with suppliers of key components is the assistance suppliers can offer in production-process design and innovations. But developing strong alliances often is difficult because of mistrust from both sides of the purchase arrangement. The supplier-purchaser relationship has long been an arm's-length transaction, with both sides seeking as much short-term gain as possible. Thus, developing long-lasting ties and sharing sensitive information often is difficult for managers. Seeking to develop alliances built on trust and mutually beneficial outcomes requires a change in mind-set at many companies. Four practices help foster improved relations with suppliers of strategic parts: (1) power balancing, (2) cospecialization, (3) target costing, and (4) personal ties.[3]

*(i) Power Balancing*    In buyer-supplier relationships in which the buyer represents a large proportion of the supplier's business, the buyer may be in a position to demand price (or other) concessions. Such an uneven power distribution is not conducive to building a healthy strategic alliance. Equal dependence between partners occurs when the proportion of a supplier's total output that is sold to a customer is roughly equal to

the proportion of total purchases acquired by a customer from that supplier. For example, if a supplier sells approximately 25 percent of its total output to a strategic partner, a power balance is achieved if the buyer's proportion of total purchases is 25 percent for that supplier. Maintaining relative dependence between suppliers and buyers increases the likelihood that both parties will have a vested interest in the success of the other partner as the degree of relative dependence increases. Aside from making both parties less vulnerable, the buyers and sellers increase their experiences with other businesses and can then share learned innovations with a strategic partner.

*(ii) Cospecialization*   Apart from balancing the power in a supplier-buyer relationship, developing a codependency in the relationship can benefit the alliance. When a supplier commits substantial specialized resources to meeting the demands of a purchaser, and the purchaser chooses to single-source with that supplier, both parties have a vested interest in the success of the purchaser. This relationship reduces maneuvering for short-term gains by suppliers and strengthens the desire for mutually beneficial outcomes for both parties.

*(iii) Target Costing*   Instead of seeking the lowest bid, establishing target costs for components, then rewarding suppliers when those targets are reached, encourages joint problem solving.

*(iv) Personal Ties*   Developing trust between supplier and purchaser usually begins at the individual level. Establishing joint teams consisting of purchaser and supplier employees helps to develop important working relationships. Trust increases as each side begins to feel more comfortable with members from the other organization.

Many organizations often single-source many of their strategic components but fail to establish the trust and partnership ties that can provide additional benefits for both parties. As the following example illustrates, treating suppliers as partners in strategic alliances provides long-term benefits other than obtaining low costs on supplied components.

Mercedes-Benz included suppliers early in the design stage of the vehicle. By including suppliers as functional group members, MB was able to take advantage of their expertise and advice on matters such as supplier capability, cost, and quality. The synergy generated by these cross-functional groups also allowed the group to solve larger design issues, such as how to more efficiently and economically switch from manufacturing left-side-drive vehicles to right-side-drive vehicles. Significant time savings were recognized because of the design improvements implemented by the functional groups. Because supplier personnel were at the MB plant on a full-time basis during the launch, other issues (e.g., quality problems or slight modifications to the product) can be addressed in a more timely fashion.

**(b) Supplier Involvement in Just-in-Time and Total Quality Management**   As discussed in the previous section, initiating cost savings and quality programs requires a commitment not only from an organization itself but also from parties outside the organization, such as transporters and suppliers of goods. Management initiatives such as JIT, TQM, target costing, and outsourcing require significant cooperation between suppliers and purchasers.

The JIT philosophy advocates *waste elimination*, including wasted materials resulting from a manufacturing process and wasted time in delivery and movement of goods. Additional sources of waste include machine setups, rework, warehouse space required by large inventories, and capital required to carry large inventory levels (which can mask production problems).

The success of JIT and TQM depends on developing innovative performance measures for suppliers. These measures include quality, response time, and number of delivery points. The ability to sustain a long-term relationship enables purchasers to work with suppliers over time to achieve acceptable performance on such measures. Buyers that frequently change suppliers constantly purchase from companies that are at the beginning of the learning curve. Thus many benefits of a long-term relationship are foregone.

In addition to quality issues, lower inventory levels require suppliers to provide more shipments in smaller quantities. Suppliers must be able to respond quickly to orders and ship in lot sizes desired by the purchaser. In some cases, manufacturers may also require delivery of goods *to the point of production*, thus reducing the need for inventory and reducing the expense and time of moving materials from a receiving dock to a holding area and to the point of production. These demands have caused a different type of relationship to develop between purchaser and supplier. Many purchasers and suppliers are forging relationships based on long-term commitments, thus saving negotiation, inspection, and other costs associated with contracting with many suppliers. Properly orchestrated, the relationship between supplier and purchaser can be a win-win situation when organizations initiate programs such as JIT and TQM. Buyers receive high-quality goods delivered on schedule and suppliers gain long-term commitments that enable them to plan for future orders with the understanding that buyers will continue to assist them in improving quality and service. These quality and service improvements can then be transferred to other customers that the supplier may serve.

Mercedes-Benz designed its manufacturing facility consistent with the JIT philosophy, so there is little warehouse space at the site. Instead, MB relies on "in-sequence delivery," a system whereby supplies of preconstructed modules arrive in a prescribed sequence so that the modules are ready to be placed on the manufacturing line.

For example, from the moment a new vehicle order is initiated, manufacturers of the cockpit module have 169 minutes to manufacture (to specifications) and deliver the module to the proper place in the manufacturing line at the MB plant. Mercedes and its suppliers stay in constant contact through EDI facilities that transmit order specifications and other information between the plant and first-tier suppliers.

Exhibit 10.1 illustrates MB's in-sequence delivery system. When an order is initiated, suppliers are notified through an EDI transmission of the specifications for the new vehicle. Suppliers are then expected to deliver their products in a predetermined order as each module is needed in the manufacturing process. This system moves one step beyond the simple JIT philosophy by requiring various suppliers to synchronize their efforts so that production can occur uninterrupted.

**(c) Target Costing**    Because most costs are designed into a product, target costing must begin at the design stage of product development. It is at this stage that supplier selection becomes most critical. The indexes developed by Mercedes allowed the company and its suppliers to work closely to align the cost of a functional group with its perceived value, as defined by customers. All numbers provided here have been altered for proprietary reasons; however, the exhibits illustrate the actual process used in the development of the M-class.

During the concept development phase MB team members used various indexes to help determine critical performance, design, and cost relationships for the M-class. To

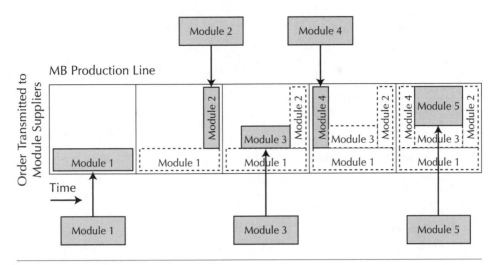

**Exhibit 10.1   In-Sequence Delivery**

construct the indexes, team members gathered various forms of information from customers, suppliers, and members of the design team. Though the actual number of categories used by MB was much greater, Exhibit 10.2 illustrates the calculations used to quantify customer responses to the M-class concept. For example, values shown in the *importance* column resulted from asking a sample of potential customers whether they consider each category extremely important when considering the purchase of a new Mercedes product. Customers could respond affirmatively to all categories that applied.

To gain a better understanding of various sources of costs, functional groups were identified together with target cost estimates. (Mercedes also organized *function groups,* teams whose role was to develop specifications and cost projections.) As shown in Exhibit 10.3, the relative target cost percentage of each functional group was computed.

Exhibit 10.4 summarizes how each functional group contributes to the consumer requirements identified in Exhibit 10.2. For example, potential customers identified safety as an important characteristic of the M-class; some functional groups contributed more to the safety category than others did. Mercedes engineers determined that chassis quality was an important element of safety (50 percent of the total function group contribution).

Exhibit 10.5 combines the category weighting percentages from Exhibit 10.2 with

| Category | Importance | Relative Percentage |
|----------|------------|---------------------|
| Safety | 32 | 41% |
| Comfort | 25 | 32 |
| Economy | 15 | 18 |
| Styling | 7 | 9 |
| Total | 79 | 100% |

**Exhibit 10.2   Relative Importance Ranking by Category**

| Function Group | Target Cost | Percentage of Total |
|---|---|---|
| Chassis | $x,xxx | 20% |
| Transmission | $x,xxx | 25 |
| Air conditioner | $x,xxx | 5 |
| Electrical system | $x,xxx | 7 |
| Other function groups | $x,xxx | 43 |
| Total | $xx,xxx | 100% |

**Exhibit 10.3    Target Cost and Percentage by Functional Group**

| Function Group | Category | | | |
|---|---|---|---|---|
| | Safety | Comfort | Economy | Styling |
| Chassis | 50% | 30% | 10% | 10% |
| Transmission | 20 | 20 | 30 | |
| Air conditioner | | 20 | | 5 |
| Electrical system | 5 | | 20 | |
| Other systems | 25 | 30 | 40 | 85 |
| Total | 100% | 100% | 100% | 100% |

**Exhibit 10.4    Function Group Contribution to Customer Requirements**

| Function Group | Category | | | | |
|---|---|---|---|---|---|
| | Safety | Comfort | Economy | Styling | Importance Index |
| | .41 | .32 | .18 | .09 | |
| Chassis | .50 | .30 | .10 | .10 | .33 |
| Transmission | .20 | .20 | .30 | | .20 |
| Air conditioner | | .20 | | .05 | .07 |
| Electrical system | .05 | | .20 | | .06 |
| Other systems | .25 | .30 | .40 | .85 | .35 |
| Total | 1.00 | 1.00 | 1.00 | 1.00 | |

**Exhibit 10.5    Importance Index of Various Functional Groups**

the functional group contribution from Exhibit 10.4. The result is an importance index that measures the relative importance of each functional group across all categories. For example, potential customers weighted the categories of safety, comfort, economy, and styling as .41, .32, .18, and .09, respectively. The rows in Exhibit 10.5 represent the contribution of each functional group to the various categories. The importance index for a function group is calculated by multiplying each row value by its corresponding category value, then summing the results. For example, the chassis importance index of .33 is computed as follows: $((.50 \times .41) + (.30 \times .32) + (.10 ( .18)) + (.10 ( .09)) = .33)$.

As shown in Exhibit 10.6, the target cost index is calculated by dividing the importance index by the target cost percentage by function group. Managers at MB used indexes such as these during the concept design phase to understand the relationship of

| | Index | | |
| Function Group | (A) Importance Index | (B) % of Target Cost | (C) A/B Target Cost Index |
|---|---|---|---|
| Chassis | .33 | .20 | 1.65 |
| Transmission | .20 | .25 | .80 |
| Air conditioner | .07 | .05 | 1.40 |
| Electrical system | .06 | .07 | .86 |
| Other systems | .35 | .43 | .81 |
| Total | | 1.00 | |

**Exhibit 10.6    Target Cost Index**

the *importance* of a functional group to the *target cost* of a function group. Indexes less than one may indicate a cost in excess of the perceived value of the function group. Thus, opportunities for cost reduction, consistent with customer demands, may be identified and managed during the early stages of product development.

**(d) Outsourcing**    A popular trend among manufacturing organizations is to minimize on-site value-added activities by outsourcing significant portions of the assembly processes. Original equipment manufacturers (OEMs) increasingly have begun to outsource their production processes to contract manufacturers (CMs) in an effort to reduce costs. OEMs now outsource some of the manufacturing processes that were formerly considered core competencies. OEMs are focusing their efforts on design and innovation issues. It has been estimated that CMs will achieve a cumulative annual growth rate of 25 percent between 1996 and 2001. EDI and partnering with suppliers are essential for OEMs that seek to reduce costs by using CMs.[4]

Although many manufacturers contract with suppliers for parts and manage assembly in-house, MB has taken a different strategy. Mercedes outsources assemblies to suppliers. Engineers divided the M-class into systems that were combined to form a completed vehicle. As many as 18 modules to be delivered in sequence have been outsourced to suppliers, which purchase the subcomponents and assemble the module for Mercedes. By assembling the modules off-site, MB has reduced plant and warehouse space requirements. In addition, the number of suppliers used has been drastically reduced by this outsourcing of systems. For example, the cockpit requires more than 150 parts from approximately 35 vendors. By outsourcing the cockpit to one vendor, MB has reduced its involvement from potentially 35 vendors to only 1.

Relative to modules, Mercedes has developed a two-tier supplier network. First-tier suppliers provide finished modules to MB. Second-tier suppliers are the vendors from which first-tier suppliers purchase parts. At the beginning of the production process, MB maintained strict control over both first-tier and second-tier suppliers with respect to cost and quality issues. As the level of comfort and trust grew between MB and first-tier suppliers, MB gave first-tier suppliers more freedom to make their own arrangements with second-tier suppliers. Exhibit 10.7 illustrates Mercedes' two-tier relationship with suppliers.

The benefits to MB are numerous. By outsourcing over 80 percent of vehicle components to a limited number of first-tier suppliers, MB reduces the overhead associated with purchasing activities. In addition, MB saves on labor and employee-related costs.

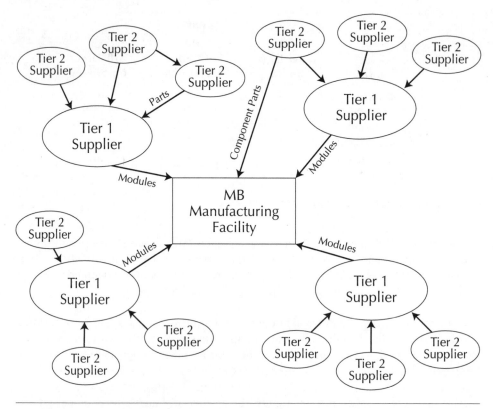

**Exhibit 10.7    Mercedes Two-Tier Supplier Network**

Further, by having established strong alliances with these first-tier suppliers, MB enjoys a higher level of service from suppliers and benefits from the expertise developed by suppliers as they seek ways to improve current operations. Finally, because much of the product is manufactured off-site, suppliers of major modules are encouraged to work together to continuously improve not only their module but the integrated product as well.

**(e) Developing Supplier Relationships**    As discussed previously, strategic alliances with suppliers is a key element of successful supply chain management. Although each organization's experience with building supplier relationships is unique, three suggestions to make the venture more likely to succeed are considered here.

   **1.** *Commit to partnering before seeking partners.* Because developing strategic alliances with suppliers will change many current practices, top management must be committed to establish these relationships and to accept changes they will bring. Some of these changes include:

- Accepting a smaller vendor base from which to purchase supplies.
- Including suppliers in the early stages of design and development of new products.
- Developing the ability to share information with vendors that will make their jobs easier.[5]

An organization's commitment also may include agreeing to train supplier personnel in various areas of importance (including the organization's production practices), developing joint objectives with suppliers (e.g., establishing joint profit levels), and striving to be a better customer.[6]

**2.** *Select appropriate suppliers for alliances.* Because the best partner may not be among the current set of suppliers, it may be necessary to sever long-term business relations if existing suppliers are unwilling or unable to commit to a partnering relationship.[7]

Due diligence is required to ensure that new suppliers can provide the required level of service and quality. Customers can provide information about a supplier's dependability, quality, and service. Another important point to consider is the supplier's commitment to entering into a partnership arrangement. Because a strategic alliance requires two-way commitment, suppliers should be willing to accept the responsibilities imposed by TQM, JIT, or continuous improvement initiatives.[8]

**3.** *Be prepared to sell the relationship.* Ask the question, "Why would a supplier want to align themselves with this organization?" Agreeing to the requirements of TQM or JIT may leave the vendor asking, "What's in it for me?"—a valid question. A supplier's willingness to enter into such a relationship depends, in part, on its ability to meet increased service requirements.[9] A key selling point includes increased volume for supplier partners. Other rewards include business, technical, production, and training assistance and the ability to take advantage of any production/technological gains in doing business with other customers. If the arrangement is not mutually beneficial, the prospects of entering into a helpful strategic alliance are greatly reduced.

**10.4 LOGISTICS-BASED SUPPLY CHAIN MANAGEMENT**    Logistics-based supply chain management has long held a prominent place within operations management as an area for cost savings. This discussion defines LSCM, evaluates how LSCM can add value to an organization, and reviews current trends and future directions of LSCM.

Traditionally, LSCM has involved management of material flow from supplier to manufacturer (inbound logistics) or from manufacturer to customer (outbound logistics). This approach, however, was restricted because it ignored material flow *within* an organization. Recent approaches have encompassed total materials flow: from the supplier of materials, through the manufacturing organization, to purchasers of finished goods.

Specifically, LSCM activities include:

- Sourcing and purchasing.
- Conversion (manufacturing), including capacity planning, operations management.
- Production scheduling, and materials planning.
- Distribution planning and warehouse operations.
- Inventory management (including inbound and outbound transportation).
- The linkage with customer service, sales, promotion, and marketing activities.[10]

LSCM can provide value-added activities in many areas including transportation, inventory, and information.[11] Each is discussed in more detail.

**(a) Transportation**    The primary goal of transportation is to have goods delivered on time, undamaged, and cost-effectively. Deregulation of the transportation industry has made contracting for the delivery of inbound and outbound freight more beneficial. Although a common practice is to contract with the lowest bidder for transportation services, many shippers are beginning to demand not only low prices but also a higher level of service. Given the increased importance of JIT deliveries and maintaining low inventories, managers often incorporate the cost of missed delivery schedules into the cost of transportation.

Two philosophies exist toward selecting carriers:

1. Repeatedly soliciting bids for individual transportation engagements.
2. Developing a relationship with certain carriers to encourage higher-quality performance.

By sharing shipment responsibilities, sellers and buyers can include carriers in negotiations and reach agreements on such issues as traffic volume, frequency and quality of service, rates, and the carrier's liability for loss, delay, or damage. The resulting agreement that arises from including all three parties (buyer, supplier, and transporter) will likely be more beneficial to all parties. The buyer gets to specify its issues of importance (on-time delivery vs. cost; damaged goods vs. on-time delivery) whereas the seller gets to specify its issues of importance. The transporter gains a better understanding of what is expected by both buyer and seller, as well as what services are most important to its customers and what services it is willing to pay for.[12]

**(b) Inventory**    LSCM can aid in controlling inventory levels and ensuring that goods are delivered in good order to other manufacturing units as well as to buyers outside the organization. Marketing, manufacturing, and purchasing personnel should all participate in forecasting material needs to achieve an effective purchasing and delivery plan. Traditional solutions for inventory management include mathematical formulas such as the economic order quantity (EOQ) formula and materials requirement planning (MRP) techniques, which are used to optimize production schedules. Many computerized programs exist to aid manufacturers and wholesalers in maintaining an effective inventory management system (software packages used for SCM are discussed later in the chapter). In managing inventory levels, it is essential for businesses to know with as much certainty as possible the lead time for delivery of supplies and for the production of goods. Without understanding the time required between recognizing the need for a good and its production, maintaining an optimal inventory balance is difficult. Unknown lead times increase the chance of over- or understocked inventory, both of which are costly to the business.[13]

At Hewlett-Packard (HP), benchmarking is used to aid its LSCM planning. Inventory is an insurance against uncertainty. HP attacks this uncertainty at three sources: suppliers, manufacturing, and customers. Although all sources of uncertainty cannot be eliminated, tracking certain measures enables manufacturing organizations to reduce their exposure to uncertainty. At HP, benchmark indicators include:

- *Suppliers.* HP tracks on-time performance, average days or hours late, and the degree of inconsistency (the standard deviation of late measures). Tracking these measures helps HP know how much extra stock to keep on hand per supplier while minimizing the probability of stockouts.

- *Manufacturing.* Downtime (for the process, not just a machine), repair time, and variation in repair time are key performance indicators. HP uses a probability distribution of performance and focuses on the reliability of the process.
- *Customers.* Greater levels of order variation require greater levels of safety stock. HP tracks average demand and the variability of demand by customer.[14]

To control costs and improve the supply chain, leading companies use vendor-managed inventory (VMI). By yielding (or at least sharing) the responsibility of managing inventories with suppliers, buyers reduce inventory carrying costs and receive improved service from suppliers.[15] Suppliers benefit by gaining better insight into buyers' requirements and processes and also from the increased information flow concerning future demands. By entering into a VMI agreement with a supplier, one wholesaler reduced delivery and administrative charges and also average inventory (from 10 days to 6 days) while keeping service levels constant. In addition, the company reduced the time from order to delivery from 48 hours to 10, and gained a competitive advantage by sharing some of the associated cost savings with customers.[16]

Organizing suppliers into a consortium can enable manufacturers to control inventory costs. Coordinating the activities of first- and second-tier suppliers can yield lower transaction costs by sharing operating insights and best practices. The increased cooperation among consortium members facilitates the sharing of information learned about third-tier suppliers and thus helps identify substandard suppliers. FedEx, among other organizations, has begun offering management services explicitly to help other companies set up consortium buying arrangements. Toyota has also developed supplier associations that foster communication and cooperation across major suppliers. The associations do the following:[17]

- Standardize quality control.
- Facilitate supplier interaction.
- Provide forums that build trust.

**(c) Information Technology**  With shorter turnaround times and smaller orders becoming the norm, the ability to withdraw information from a logistics management system is crucial. Many buyers and suppliers are arranging EDIs that provide unfettered information flow to ensure that orders and inventory levels are constantly monitored and maintained. Characteristics of an LSCM system include:

- Rapid and accurate transaction processing.
- Real-time technologies integrated to other functions within the organization.
- Advanced decision-support capabilities.

These systems also should include modeling, transportation, routing, and scheduling capabilities that are linked to suppliers and purchasers to be as effective as possible.[18]

By choosing to link with suppliers through some form of EDI, firms can share long-term and short-term forecast demands to aid upstream suppliers in their scheduling requirements. One Volvo plant uses EDI hookups with a supplier to share forecasts of goods three to four days in the future. The EDI system then creates sales orders and initiates purchase orders so that the forecast can be met. Further, EDI links are planned for suppliers of Volvo's suppliers (second-tier suppliers) to further expedite the transfer of information and maintain proper materials flow among suppliers and Volvo.[19]

Other organizations use the Internet to share information with key suppliers. Using secure websites, manufacturers such as Boeing, Dell, and Thompson Consumer Electronics have designed ways to improve communications with suppliers and customers. Boeing allows customers to browse its catalog and order spare parts from an Internet site, which processes about 4,000 transactions per day. This has reduced order processing costs by 25 percent and also shortened delivery time.

Thompson Consumer Electronics receives customer demand forecasts on its secured Internet site. This information is entered into Thompson's SCM software for scheduling and production requirements (Thompson uses SCM software manufactured by i2 technologies). Further, Thompson posts its demand forecasts on line, thereby allowing suppliers to know when components are needed. As a result, Thompson has shortened lead times from three or four weeks to as little as one week in many cases. Dell has taken information sharing one step further. By customizing approximately 30 web pages for top suppliers, Dell allows its suppliers to view its customers' demands, so that suppliers can better plan for future demands. Dell also has linked websites to bulletin boards where suppliers can post messages and share information. Manufacturers on the leading edge of SCM continually seek ways to increase information flow between suppliers and its customers.[20]

SCM software integrates external communications (with suppliers and purchasers via either the Internet or EDI) and internal communications. SCM software includes (but is not limited to) products from Manugistics, Inc., American Software, Inc., i2 Technologies, Inc., Numertrix Ltd., and Red Pepper Software Co. Using the PC-based Manugistics Routing and Scheduling Version 10 (MRS 10), Domino's Pizza updates and optimizes its routing schedules for delivery to production sites on a daily basis. Domino's previous system allowed updates only on a semiannual basis. Given dramatic changes in demand, Domino's hopes to save $1 million during its first year by optimizing its trucking routes on a daily basis.

By linking with suppliers and purchasing an integrated SCM software package, Molson Breweries not only notifies suppliers in various manufacturing locations of upcoming demand but also gains valuable information about margins for particular production sites. Production scheduling and transportation now are handled more efficiently based on profit margins of products, demand in given areas, and supplier capabilities at a given time.

3Com Corp., a network equipment supplier, relied on linked Excel spreadsheets to keep production lines near target utilizations. As volume grew, planning and scheduling became more difficult. Therefore, 3Com acquired Red Pepper's ResponseAgent to aid in its SCM efforts. Now, schedules that balance material and capacity constraints are generated and what-if scenarios are run in a matter of hours. Previously, what-if scenarios had taken days.[21]

By utilizing Internet technology, EDI, and SCM software, suppliers know what a customer needs before they ask (or even realize they need it). Thus, technology has made the concept of a seamless supply chain a reality. Developing creative links with suppliers and customers appears to be a rich opportunity for innovative manufacturers to enjoy a competitive advantage over competitors that are unwilling or unable to invest the time and resources into improving their supply chains.

**(d) Future Trends in Logistics-Based Supply-Chain Management**    Trends in LSCM include:

- A greater emphasis on establishing a balance between cost and service in the logistics function.
- Increasing third-party services for LSCM activities.
- Increasing emphasis on channel integration.
- Expanding roles for EDI relationships between suppliers and purchasers.

The transportation and warehousing industry is slowly transforming itself into a full-service logistics manager for manufacturing organizations that outsource logistics functions. Successful third-party providers of logistics services will tailor their services to specific industries and manufacturers to develop an expertise and relationship not offered by ordinary transportation providers. Included in these services are EDI hookups linking suppliers and purchasers to further facilitate transactions among organizations.[22] Competition among third-party transportation providers (transporters of goods other than the supplier or the purchaser of the goods) is increasing. Thus, customers can demand not only lower prices but also expect more extensive services, furthering the benefits to businesses deciding to outsource logistics functions.[23]

Channel integration is the management of inventory, warehousing, and transportation across corporate boundaries.[24] SSCM and LSCM techniques discussed in this chapter enable managers to reduce interorganizational barriers. Segmenting product offerings into channels allows manufacturers to better determine profitable and unprofitable product lines, differentiate between the level of service required by these channels, and possibly eliminate unneeded layers within some channels.

Another major trend in LSCM is an increased dependence on EDI. Organizations are just beginning to realize the vast array of benefits available from EDI and advanced information systems capabilities. Unfortunately, a recent survey conducted by KPMG as part of a Global Supply Chain Benchmark Study reports that many organizations are not taking advantages of recent information technology advances. The report indicates that organizations are making more use of SCM software for internal purposes, but the exchange of information between organizations is still far behind where it could be with the capabilities of today's information technology.[25]

**10.5 SUMMARY**    This chapter has discussed several important components of SCM. Examples from successful practices employed by MB and other companies illustrate how organizations can reduce cost and create competitive advantages. Consideration of the supplier-buyer relationship is necessary as organizations implement initiatives such as JIT, TQM, and target costing. Developing and sustaining long-term relationships with suppliers is necessary, as is utilizing communication links through EDI or the Internet. Software packages exist that can coordinate supply-chain activities within an organization and also help bridge communication channels between buyer and supplier, thus moving organizations toward a seamless supply chain. As information technology continues to improve, the possibilities for improving the supply chain will increase, providing an opportunity for those companies willing to invest in practices that strengthen their supply chains.

## NOTES

1. D. F. Ross, *Competing Through Supply Chain Management: Creating Market-Winning Strategies Through Supply Chain Partnerships* (New York: Chapman & Hall, 1998).

2. A. A. Thompson and A. J. Strickland III, *Strategic Management Concepts and Cases* (9th ed.) (Chicago: Irwin, 1996).

3. J. T. Landry, "Supply Chain Management," *Harvard Business Review* (November–December 1998): 24–25.

4. B. Roberts, "Ties that Bind," *Electronic Business* (August 1998): 62–68.

5. J. Morgan, "Building a World Class Supply Base from Scratch," *Purchasing* (August 19, 1993a): 56–61; D. Tait, "Make Strong Relationships a Priority," *Canadian Manager* 23(1998): 21, 28.

6. M. Kepp, Relationship-Building," *Business Latin America* 29(1994): 6–7.

7. E. J. Hay, "Implementing JIT Purchasing: Phase III—Selection," *Production and Inventory Management Review and APICS News* 10(1990): 28–29.

8. E. J. Hay, "Implementing JIT Purchasing: Phase IV—Relationship Building," *Production and Inventory Management Review and APICS News* 10(1990): 38, 40.

9. Tait, op. cit.

10. C. Copacino, *Supply Chain Management: The Basics and Beyond* (Boca Raton, FL: St. Lucie Press, 1997).

11. Ross, op. cit.

12. J. R. Carter and B. G. Ferrin, "The Impact of Transportation Costs on Supply Chain Management," *Journal of Business Logistics* 16(1996): 207.

13. Ross, op. cit.; Copacino, op. cit.

14. T. Davis, "Effective Supply Chain Management," *Sloan Management Review* (Summer 1993): 35–46.

15. G. Tyndall, C. Gopal, W. Partsch, and J. Kamauff, "Ten Strategies to Enhance Supplier Management," *National Productivity Review* (Summer 1998): 31–44.

16. J. Holmstrom, "Implementing Vendor-Managed Inventory the Efficient Way: A Case Study of Partnership in the Supply Chain," *Production and Inventory Management Journal* (3rd Quarter 1998): 1–5.

17. I. Stuart, P. Deckert, D. McCutcheon, and R. Kunst, "Case Study: A Leveraged Learning Network," *Sloan Management Review* 39(1998): 81–93; Tyndall et al., op. cit.

18. Copacino, op. cit.

19. Anonymous, "Make Supply Chain Technology Work for You," *Works Management* (July 1998): 37–41.

20. T. Stein and J. Sweat, "Killer Supply Chain," *InformationWeek* 708(1998): 36–41.

21. J. H. Mayer, "Supply-Chain Tools Cut Inventory Fat," *Applications Software Magazine* (May 1996): 77–80.

22. Copacino, op. cit.

23. R. C. Mireles, "Supply Chain Management Trends," *Transportation and Distribution* (July 1998): 75.

24. Copacino, op. cit.

25. Anonymous, "Key Trends and Analysis," *Stores* (April 1988): S9–S20.

# PART II

# PERFORMANCE MEASUREMENT

# CHAPTER 11

# PERFORMANCE MEASUREMENT OVERVIEW

## Nathan V. Stuart and Joseph G. Fisher
**Indiana University Kelley School of Business**
## Richard J. Gargas
**Eli Lilly and Company**

**11.1 INTRODUCTION**    This chapter provides an overview of performance measurement issues. The way companies calculate measures of customer satisfaction, shareholder value, product quality, product costs, and employee effectiveness is critical to the decision making and management of all organizational employees.

Successful managers choose performance measures that encourage employees to make decisions and take actions that benefit not only themselves but also the organization as a whole. This chapter provides a general process that managers can use to identify and implement appropriate performance measures for their businesses.

**(a) What Is Performance Measurement?**    Performance measurement can be defined as the assessment of whether individuals, groups, and organizations are achieving their stated objectives. It requires the *measurement* of the *performance* of someone or something. Measurement involves assigning a score, whether it is a qualitative score (such as "poor" or "good") or a quantitative number (such as "$100 in sales" or "95 out of 100 shipments made on time"). Performance involves the process and outcomes of organizational activity; it is the realization of efforts to complete organizational tasks. Performance measurement, therefore, is an important component of an organization's management control system. Managers use performance measurement information to reward and encourage employees, to develop strategy, to make and revise implementation decisions, and to take corrective action if the company is not achieving its desired goals.

**(b) What Is a Performance Measurement System?**    A company's management control system has several components. A performance measurement system must interact with the company's strategic planning process, budgeting process, personnel policies, structure and culture, and information technology to support implementation of the company's strategy and achievement of its objectives. The performance measurement system defines:

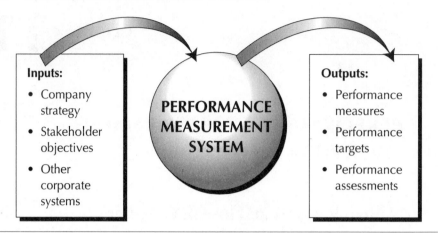

**Exhibit 11.1    Potential Inputs and Outputs of a Performance Measurement System**

- The sequence of managerial activities and decisions that establish performance objectives.
- The measures that employees will use to assess whether the objectives have been met.

Exhibit 11.1 depicts the potential inputs (e.g., the company's strategy) and outputs (e.g., specific performance targets) of a performance measurement system.

There is no one best performance measurement system or performance measure: Each company must determine its own most effective approach to performance measurement. The discussions in this chapter are intended to help managers learn to address performance measurement problems. Section 11.2 describes the importance of performance measurement and discusses the behaviors that performance measurement can create. Section 11.3 provides a general managerial process for selecting specific performance measures. The process begins with the company's strategy and involves specifying the purpose for a measurement, determining what characteristics the measurement should have, selecting a specific measure, setting a performance target, assessing actual performance, and taking appropriate managerial action. Section 11.4 summarizes the chapter and highlights the critical learning points.

**11.2 IMPORTANCE OF PERFORMANCE MEASUREMENT**    Managers and employees routinely base operational and managerial decisions on information about organizational performance: costs, cycle times, market share, productivity, and error rates are just a few of the possible performance measures. These decisions include which investments to make, which markets to enter, at what price to introduce a new product, and how to reward employees for their contributions to the company. Given the importance of such decisions, companies must ensure that performance measures motivate behavior that helps the company meet its objectives.

Exhibit 11.2 tells the story of how a poorly designed performance measurement system may motivate dysfunctional behavior. Why did the crew rush to place one bag on the baggage-claim carousel well before any of the other luggage? The answer lies in the baggage-handling performance measurement system. In an effort to decrease the time that passengers had to wait for their luggage, airline managers decided to evaluate

Picture a busy international airport. A large passenger jet rolls slowly in toward its gate: A member of the ground crew guides it in with hand signals. Nearby, a baggage-handling crew waits for the plane to stop so that it can begin unloading luggage. The crew has all the equipment ready—a connected series of empty carts for carrying the baggage and a conveyor ramp to access the plane's cargo hold.

The plane stops, and the baggage-handling crew springs into action. One member drives the conveyor ramp up to the plane and positions it at the opening to the luggage compartment. Another member hurries up the ramp and opens the compartment door, disappearing inside. The worker tosses the first bag out of the plane as the conveyor begins to move, bringing the smallish duffel bag down to the tarmac. Another baggage handler grabs the duffel and sprints across the tarmac to the access doors to the baggage claim carousel for this flight. The baggage handler places the duffel bag on the carousel and turns it on, watching as the bag disappears inside the terminal.

The baggage handler saunters back to the plane where the rest of the crew is now routinely unloading the remaining suitcases and stowing them in the mini-train of empty carts. When the last bag is removed, the crew accompanies the cart train to the carousel and puts all the luggage on the slowly turning belt. Its task completed, the crew heads for its next assignment.

*The authors are indebted to David Otley for this example.

**Exhibit 11.2    Dysfunctional Behavior in Baggage Handling**

baggage-handling crews on the time it took them to place the *first* bag on the carousel after the plane stopped at the gate. As the story indicates, the baggage-handling crew found a way to make this particular performance measure look very good without actually improving service to most passengers (and if the owner of the one bag has more luggage checked, the crew has not improved service to *any* passengers).

Exhibit 11.2 highlights the complex nature of performance measurement. The seemingly simple managerial task of determining how well an employee carries out a task becomes much more difficult when managers must make that assessment within the overall context of the organization. Many factors influence the information that managers use to assess performance and make decisions. These factors include:

- The firm's information technology.
- Its organizational structure and culture.
- Its personnel policies (including compensation practices).
- Its other control systems (e.g., the annual budget process or the use of total quality management).
- Its performance measurement system.

Poorly designed performance measurement systems can motivate dysfunctional behavior that decreases company performance. Exhibit 11.3 describes a scenario in which a manager's desired outcome—improved employee health and safety—is not achieved. The manager's safety program measures the number of near-miss accidents *that em-*

For several years, a medium-size manufacturing plant has had a consistently poor safety record. The record is so consistent that the manager in charge of health and safety can predict how many employees will experience a major incident (a lost-time accident) within the coming year.

The manager is convinced that smaller near-miss accidents are a predictor of the larger safety issues. To work safely, the manager believes employees must adopt a mind-set that not even small accidents or injuries are acceptable. Therefore, remembering that "what gets measured gets done," the manager begins a program that carefully measures and widely publicizes the number of near-miss accidents. This attention to smaller incidents, the manager expects, will encourage employees to be more careful in their actions, thus reducing the number of major accidents as well.

Several months later, the number of reported near-miss accidents in the plant falls from 15 per month to only 2 per month. The safety manager is not at all pleased, however, because the plant's lost-time accident rate has actually *increased* over the same period. The safety manager wonders whether his assumption about the behavioral connection between near-miss and lost-time accidents was erroneous. He concludes that the plant's safety measurement needs to focus on both lost-time accidents and near misses.

**Exhibit 11.3   Misreporting and "Gaming" of a Performance Measurement System**

*ployees chose to report as near-miss accidents.* The focused measurement of this statistic motivated employees to act in ways that would reduce the near-miss accident rate. The employees had several options: behave more safely, stop reporting near-miss accidents, or report near-miss accidents as more severe incidents. The results after several months suggest that employees chose not to make the difficult behavioral changes but chose instead to "game" the performance measure. Many near-miss incidents went unreported, while others became lost-time accidents in the records. Thus, not only did the number of lost-time accidents not fall in concert with the near-miss accidents, they actually increased because of misreporting. More important, overall health and safety did not improve despite the measurement system.

This example and the airline baggage-handling story in Exhibit 11.2 both emphasize the importance of considering the motivational effects of performance measurement. Two factors that managers must consider when they design performance measures are goal congruence and goal conflict.

**(a) Goal Congruence**    *Goal congruence* exists when the goals of all interested parties are satisfied by the same set of actions. Effective performance measures will lead employees to make decisions that result in positive rewards for them and also outcomes that other company stakeholders desire, such as improved quality, greater market share, better reliability, cleaner and safer neighborhoods, and higher share prices. Exhibit 11.4 describes Lincoln Electric's piece rate system, an example of a performance measurement system that achieves high goal congruence.

A situation in which actions support the goals of one party (e.g., employees) without supporting those of another party (e.g., management) *lacks* goal congruence. An old saying in the performance measurement literature, "you get what you measure," is

A famous example of a performance measurement system that establishes organizational goal congruence is Lincoln Electric's "piece-rate" compensation system. The company's employees (who produce electric motors and other products) receive a standard piece rate for each unit they produce. The workers have a financial incentive to work as quickly and efficiently as they can to produce as many units per shift as possible, thus maximizing their compensation. The output also benefits Lincoln Electric's managers, who enjoy lower overall costs and increased profitability, and its customers, who pay lower prices because of the lower costs. In turn, Lincoln's shareholders are better off because Lincoln is able to maintain market share through competitive pricing.

A simple piece-rate system, however, might encourage Lincoln's workers to produce so quickly that they fail to maintain product quality at an acceptable level. Therefore, Lincoln modifies the piece-rate system to exclude off-quality units and also requires that workers repair off-quality units *without additional compensation.* This approach mitigates the incentive workers might have to work too fast, which helps managers and shareholders achieve goals of maintaining a high-quality reputation in the market, by assuming that customers obtain the highly reliable equipment they desire.

Finally, Lincoln's system encourages workers to learn and innovate by sharing improvements in productivity and efficiency with the workers. Workers are motivated to improve production methods because they share in the financial benefits of innovation. If workers improve a production method so that they can make more parts per hour, the company does not immediately change the standard to reflect the new potential rate. If the company did so, the workers could never make more than the standard amount, and they would have no incentive to innovate and improve productivity and efficiency. By not changing the standard to fully reflect the improvement, the company is in effect sharing the financial benefit with the worker.

**Exhibit 11.4    Goal Congruence in a Performance Measurement System (Lincoln Electric)**

based on the frequent lack of goal congruence in performance measurement systems. In Exhibit 11.2, for example, the airline measured the time for the first bag to arrive on the claim carousel; that time was made very short in the example, to the sole benefit of the baggage handlers. Similarly, in Exhibit 11.3, the safety manager measured the number of reported near-miss incidents and found a low number of reported incidents but no corresponding reduction in lost-time accidents. In both of these cases, the employees' goal was to look good according to the performance measure (to make the time as short as possible and the number of reported incidents as low as possible). The managers' goals, however, were entirely different: to improve customer service at the airline and to improve employee health at the plant. Exhibit 11.5 provides yet another example of low goal congruence and the disastrous outcomes that can result from poor performance measurement.

**(b) Goal Conflict**    Goal conflict can occur when several goals (e.g., two or more different performance measures that do not move together) exist simultaneously in an organization. Frequently, these goals may be at odds with one another, in which case they

In 1991, executives at Sears Roebuck & Co. changed their evaluation process for Sears's automotive operation. They set rigorous targets for the number of parts sold per shift and included quotas for specific parts (e.g., shock absorbers). They also set targets for overall automotive repair revenues. The executives wanted the new performance measures and targets to lead to greater productivity in the division.

Automotive division employees could have met the new targets by improving internal efficiency and capturing a larger share of the auto repair market. Instead, they began overcharging customers for needed repairs and claiming that customers needed repairs that were in fact not required. (Not surprisingly, they recommended many unnecessary replacements of shock absorbers.)

When the deceptive practices became public, Sears suffered financial losses. Even more significant was the loss of trust that had existed between the company and its customers. Poorly designed performance measures can indeed have disastrous effects.*

*T. Yin, "Sears is Accused of Billing Fraud at Auto Centers," *The Wall Street Journal,* June 12, 1992, p. B1.

**Exhibit 11.5    Unwanted Outcomes of Poor Performance Measurement Systems (Sears Roebuck & Co)**

may lead to dysfunctional behaviors. Exhibit 11.6, for example, describes a typical scenario in which short-term performance goals conflict with long-term objectives.

Manager *A* meets the (short-term) production and budget goals not by managing the plant's assets intelligently but by producing constantly while ignoring machine maintenance, employee training, and new technologies. The company's reward system, which motivates short-run performance, leads to a conflict that Manager *A* resolves by maximizing short-term performance.

Manager *B* resolves the conflict differently: Unable to meet product quality and cost goals with the existing equipment and work force, Manager *B* invests in new equipment and training. These investments, however, also create costs that show up in the plant's short-term performance measures. Trapped within this conflict, Manager *B*'s performance appears to be much worse than Manager *A*'s, when in fact, Manager *B* positioned the plant for effective operations in the future.

In conclusion, performance measurement is an important aspect of any organization. Managers use performance measures to evaluate how well the organization and its employees are performing. Because employees will most often act in their self-interest, managers must establish performance measures that enable employees to maximize their own interests in ways that lead to positive organizational outcomes. Ill-considered performance measures will motivate behavior detrimental to the firm. Well-designed performance measures, however, fully align the efforts of all organizational stakeholders to produce outcomes that benefit all members of the organization.

**11.3 PERFORMANCE MEASURE SELECTION PROCESS**    Exhibit 11.7 depicts a managerial process for selecting performance measures. This section discusses each of the steps shown in Exhibit 11.7 as part of a general approach that managers can adapt to

The main widget plant of the Acme Corporation is critical to the company's success, so the company typically promotes plant managers who perform well there. The widget business is very competitive, so the ability to hold down costs and produce good quality is important. For the past two years, the plant has been breaking all productivity records while consistently beating its budget. Manager A, who earned significant attention because of the plant's results during his tenure as plant manager, was promoted to division head of one of Acme's other businesses.

Manager B, the new plant manager, makes some difficult decisions in the first month. Manager B replaces several important machine tools, which appear to have been poorly maintained for some time and can no longer produce acceptable quality. Manager B also slows down production so that operators can attend classes in statistical process control and computer operations. This training will enable the plant to take advantage of new technology that has become available over the past two years. Finally, Manager B installs the new production technology on the main assembly line, thus allowing workers to keep pace with competitors that have begun using the new technology.

Unfortunately (for Manager B), these decisions increased the plant's expenses because of higher depreciation, maintenance, and technician charges. They also reduced productivity markedly because of start-up costs and employee training time. Acme's divisional vice president is not pleased with this performance, so he reassigns Manager B to a position in "special projects" after 10 months. Manager C, the next plant manager, having observed how the two previous managers acted and were rewarded, begins to run the new equipment continuously. He also reduces training and maintenance.

**Exhibit 11.6    Goal Conflict: Short-Term vs. Long-Term Goals (Acme Corporation)**

their particular businesses. The steps of the performance measurement selection process are:

- Identification of *critical success factors* (CSFs) for the company.
- Selection of a business process or outcome to measure (this should be a component of a CSF).
- Determination of the purpose for which the performance measurement will be used.
- Identification of the desired characteristics of the measure.
- Selection of the specific performance measure.
- Establishment of a target or goal for the measure.
- Assessment of actual performance outcomes.
- Adaptation of the performance measurement system for continuous improvement.

Readers familiar with total quality management and the work of W. Edwards Deming will recognize the Plan-Do-Check-Act cycle embedded in this performance measurement process.[1]

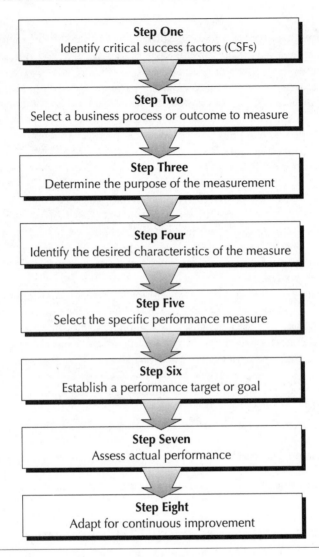

**Exhibit 11.7   Performance Measure Selection Process**

An important consideration for managers is the development of *ownership* of performance measures and goals among employees. The most effective way to create such ownership is to include employees in as much of the selection process for performance measures as possible. Although it may not be appropriate to have line operators identifying CSFs, their experience may make them better than managers at identifying the most appropriate performance measures and targets (steps two through six). Given the chance to influence the selection process, employees may become more committed to achieving the firm's goals by meeting the performance measurement targets.

**(a) Step One: Identify Critical Success Factors**   The first step of the performance measurement selection process involves ensuring that the effort that managers exert in measuring performance is aimed at business processes and outcomes that are strategi-

For organizations to successfully deploy their competitive strategies, they must identify the *critical success factors* (CSFs) for their businesses and adopt performance measures to ensure that they excel at the CSFs. Eli Lilly and Company, a pharmaceutical producer, understands that its ability to rapidly identify and develop new drug products that provide increased health-care benefits is one of its CSFs. The company adopted a specific target for the amount of time it takes to move a new product through the regulatory approval process and into the marketplace. The focus on this strategically important performance measure helped the company reduce this development cycle time by 30 percent in the 1980s.

Similarly, in the 1990s Motorola began to custom-design pagers for its customers and provide the finished product within one or two business days. To succeed at this market approach, one CSF for Motorola was *order-filling cycle time:* the amount of time it took the factory to build the specified pager once the order arrived. This cycle time had to be significantly less than one day for the company to meet its marketing obligation. Factory managers had to make decisions about the production system that allowed factory workers to achieve the cycle-time requirements.

**Exhibit 11.8    Critical Success Factors (Time)**

cally imperative for the organization. This section defines CSFs and briefly describes two frameworks that can help managers connect performance measures to the business's competitive strategy.

*(i) Critical Success Factors*    A CSF is either a business process (such as new product development or order delivery) or a business outcome (such as market share) at which a company must excel to achieve its strategic objectives. An organization must have a clearly defined business strategy before it can identify CSFs; managers must understand this strategy before they can use the performance measure selection process. Exhibit 11.8 describes CSFs that Eli Lilly and Company (a pharmaceutical manufacturer) and Motorola (a consumer electronics producer) use in their performance measurement systems.

*(ii) Performance Measurement Frameworks*    Exhibit 11.7 provides a general process for identifying performance measures. There are also several formal frameworks that address performance measurement selection. This section briefly discusses two of these frameworks: the balanced scorecard and the performance hierarchy.

(1) The Balanced Scorecard    The balanced scorecard (known in Europe as the *tableau de bord,* or dashboard), was developed in response to managerial concerns that companies were placing too much emphasis on traditional accounting-based financial performance. A well-designed balanced scorecard, therefore, provides not just a snapshot of an organization's current financial results but also a selection of other performance measures (both financial and nonfinancial) that are *leading indicators* for the business's financial health.[2] Exhibit 11.9 depicts a modified balanced scorecard framework.

These leading indicators typically fall into categories that involve *customer-related measures,* measures of how well a firm is performing its most important internal busi-

**Vision
and
Strategy**

**Financial Perspective**

Measures that:
(1) Assess how well a firm is providing for its shareholders;
(2) Represent the more traditional, currency-denominated performance measures.

**Customer Perspective**

Measures that:
(1) Are highly correlated with the measures in the financial perspective;
(2) Assess how well the company is providing for its customers.

**Internal Business Perspective**

Measures that:
(1) Are highly correlated with the measures in the financial or customer perspectives;
(2) Assess how well the company is executing its business processes (CSFs).

**Learning and Growth Perspective**

Measures that:
(1) Are highly correlated with the measures in the customer or internal business perspectives;
(2) Assess how well the company is institutionalizing new knowledge and skills.

**Exhibit 11.9   Balanced Scorecard Framework**

ness processes, and measures of the extent to which the firm and its employees are learning and growing. It is critical, however, for managers using the balanced scorecard framework to make sure that the performance measures displayed in the scorecard are truly indicative of the company's CSFs. If the scorecard contains measures that are not relevant to the firm's strategy, the scorecard framework may lead to dysfunctional behavior (see section 11.2).

Firms that have implemented the balanced scorecard caution that the framework does not eliminate the trade-offs between short-term and long-term results. The relationships between the measures in Exhibit 11.9 are long-term relationships. It may prove impossible to avoid short-term reductions in some financial outcomes while making investments that improve customer, internal business, or learning and growth indicators. One benefit of the balanced scorecard is the mere fact that these other perspectives are represented, because it means that managers must consciously address the trade-offs as they make operating decisions.

(2) The Performance Measure Hierarchy    The performance measure hierarchy is a framework based on the traditional hierarchical organization of many firms.[3] It emphasizes the importance of linking strategic objectives at the business unit (or firm) level with tactical objectives at lower organizational levels. The linking of objectives flows down the corporate hierarchy from top management to the operating levels, while performance measure outcomes flow up the organizational hierarchy from operations to top management.

This framework categorizes measures according to whether they address how well the firm is performing in its chosen external (market) environment or how well the firm is executing its internal operations. It is important for the firm to consider measures of both effectiveness and efficiency at all hierarchical levels. Exhibit 11.10 shows the performance measure hierarchy.

The performance measure hierarchy begins with the firm's strategic vision and objectives; all performance measures should support this mission. Business unit level measures involve financial assessments of the firm's activities (e.g., net income or Economic Value Added EVA™))[4] and assessments of the firm's position in its strategic markets.

The performance measure hierarchy then addresses the cross-functional activities with which the firm produces and delivers its products. Measures of activity at this level fall into three general categories: customer satisfaction, flexibility, and productivity. The chosen measures in each category should support the business unit's goals. Managers must choose these measures to ensure goal congruence and avoid goal conflict.

| Organization Level | External Effectiveness | Internal Efficiency |
| --- | --- | --- |
| Top Management | Corporate Mission | Corporate Mission |
| Business Units | Market Measures | Financial Measures |
| Business Operating Systems | Customer Satisfaction<br>Flexibility | Flexibility<br>Productivity |
| Departments and Work Centers | Quality<br>Delivery | Cycle Time<br>Waste |

**Exhibit 11.10    The Performance Hierarchy**

The last level of the performance measure hierarchy involves the individual departments and work centers that interact to conduct the business processes of the firm. Each department has efficiency measures that address the department's cycle time, waste, and expenses. Each department also has measures that assess its performance with respect to its external environment, which can be another department or work center in the firm or an external organization. Specific measures will depend on the department's critical activities, and will relate to the quality and delivery reliability of the department. The measures at the departmental/work center level must also connect logically to the operating system measures to ensure that activity at the lowest level aligns with the objectives at the top.

**(b) Step Two: Select a Business Process or Outcome to Measure**   In step two, managers select a specific component of a CSF that requires measurement. If speed is a CSF, for example, a firm might select the new product development process, the production process, or the order-filling process. All these business processes influence how quickly a firm can place its products in the hands of its customers.

**(c) Step Three: Determine the Purpose of the Performance Measure**   There are several uses to which managers can put performance measurement, and the specific purpose for a given measurement may help determine the most appropriate measure to use. In step three, managers determine the purpose for a measure; measures that are used for more than one purpose often create goal conflict. Some typical purposes for performance measurement are:

- Strategic support.
- Effort allocation.
- Operational monitoring.
- Decision support.
- Employee evaluation.

*(i) Strategic Support*   Each organization has a strategy that serves as a boundary marker for decision making. Managers cannot choose alternatives that involve products, markets, and projects outside the company's established strategy. Within the chosen strategy, however, managers need performance measures to ensure that:

- The strategy is appropriate for the business's strengths and opportunities.
- Employees are implementing the strategy effectively.

Organizational-level measures such as EVA, return on assets, net income, and sales growth may be appropriate for evaluating an organization's strategy. Section 11.3(e) (step five) provides more details on these and other performance measures.

*(ii) Effort Allocation*   Performance measures can act as a signal to employees of what managers believe to be most important and deserving of attention. For example, Eli Lilly and Company's choice of drug development cycle time as a critical performance measure (see Exhibit 11.8) sent a strong signal to researchers that the company was willing to balance obtaining the most scientifically elegant solution with reaching the marketplace more quickly.

Managers must be careful when they use performance measures to direct employee effort, however. Effort-directing performance measures must ensure goal congruence among employees, managers, and other stakeholders; they must avoid goal conflict. For example, although a manufacturing vice president might want plant managers to focus their efforts on containing costs and even tie annual bonus payments to cost results, a marketing vice president might prefer slightly higher costs due to overtime if the overtime ensures that customers receive their orders on time. The plant manager and vice president need to discuss these priorities carefully and agree about which outcomes are acceptable for the entire organization.

*(iii) Operational Monitoring*    On a day-to-day basis, operational monitoring is probably the most common use of performance measures. Every organization is composed of various business processes—tasks that it must complete to acquire resources (e.g., materials, labor, and capital), convert those resources to products, and then sell those products to customers. Companies must have systems in place that provide feedback regarding how well they perform these business processes.

For example, a manufacturing firm wants to minimize the number of times a machine fails in the middle of a production run. To do so, it implements a preventive maintenance (PM) program that entails routine checks of the machine at specified intervals, regular replacement of parts that receive extensive wear and tear during operation, and an annual disassembly and overhaul of the entire machine. All these activities take place at scheduled times between production runs.

To monitor the effectiveness of a PM program, which represents an investment of labor and machine time, a firm might keep track of the number of times the machine fails during production, the severity of these failures, and the percentage of the scheduled PM activities that occur as planned. A marked decrease in the amount of unplanned downtime signals that the PM program is having the desired effect. A lack of improvement might signal either that the PM program is not addressing the proper machine components *or* that the program has not been properly implemented.

*(iv) Decision Support*    Managers use performance measurement as inputs in decision making. Perhaps the most prevalent use of performance measures in decision making is in the context of deciding in which project to invest, including both capital investments and improvement projects. Performance measures can identify processes that consistently produce poor-quality products and hence are ripe for improvement. Performance measures can also detect processes that produce excessive waste and may thus be violating environmental regulations. Performance measures can also indicate which business units are returning their cost of capital and are therefore the best places to invest additional funds. As should be evident by now, however, managers must ensure that the information they use as inputs for decisions is truly reflective of the performance of the business and not instead a misleading signal caused by dysfunctional employee behavior.

A less frequent yet important use of performance measures is in the evaluation of past decisions. A true "learning organization" will measure the performance of each type of investment decision over time to make sure that the decision process used leads to a positive outcome for the organization. The appropriate performance measures in this case are those that indicate whether a firm actually realizes the expected benefits from an investment. Did costs decrease as expected? What was the actual improvement in product or service quality? What was the return on investment?

Unfortunately, few firms take the time to assess their decisions and investments in this fashion. The benefits for future decision making are obvious: The firm can learn how realistic its assumptions were about potential cost savings, new cash inflows, and effects on service and quality. Managers can then use their improved understanding of the company's economics to make future decisions. In essence, the decision-making process requires performance measurement and feedback (just like any other business process). Both firms and managers will find value in assessing the quality of their decisions via such feedback. In addition, if managers expect that their decisions will undergo such evaluation, they will be motivated to make realistic assumptions when making decisions.

*(v) Employee Evaluation*    A final use for performance measurement is in the evaluation of employee performance. Employees generally believe that the better their scores on performance measures, the higher their evaluations will be, the greater their raises or bonuses will be, and the more likely they will be to win promotions. Consequently, managers can rely on employees to act in ways that will show improvement in the chosen *performance measure,* regardless of whether those actions actually improve company performance.

**(d) Step Four: Identify the Desired Characteristics of the Measure**    There is a wide variety of performance measures. At step four, managers narrow their possible selections by deciding on several characteristics of the measure. These characteristics include whether the measure is financial or nonfinancial, oriented toward process versus outcome, and diagnostic versus interactive.

*(i) Financial versus Nonfinancial Measures*    Performance measures can either be financial (i.e., measured in dollars or some other currency) or nonfinancial (i.e., measured on some other basis). In the past, organizations have made extensive use of financial performance measures.

Firms implement financial measures at multiple organizational levels. At the divisional or profit-center level, financial control is usually based on financial metrics such as profits, return-on-investment, or EVA™. Budgeting and standard cost systems then break down the profit goal into smaller components. Upper management often assigns responsibility for these smaller components to managers of lower-level divisions, *or business units.*

A conventional financial performance measurement system has several major components. It includes some form of long-range (usually five-year) financial forecasting. It also includes an annual budgeting process based on the long-range forecast, with both top-down and bottom-up negotiation processes.

In a typical company, budgeting begins with a sales forecast that leads to a production plan. On the basis of the production plan, managers estimate the firm's material, labor, and inventory needs and build a cost-control system around standard costs and standard cost variances. The final phase compares actual financial results with the forecasted or budgeted amounts. Managers often give significant attention to these variance reports. They attempt to explain large unfavorable variances and act to "correct" or "understand" their causes.

Recently, the traditional practice of focusing on financial results to measure performance has come under increased criticism. Financial measures are *lagging* indicators of performance; they reflect the results of past decisions and fail to focus on the actionable steps needed for surviving in a given firm's competitive environment. Uneasiness about using financial measures to guide and evaluate performance is nothing new: The intensity of the concern has increased, however, so many firms now carefully examine the links between their strategies and performance measures.

Historically, accounting-driven systems (e.g., standard cost systems) were designed for operating conditions characterized by long production runs, standard products, a relatively static external environment, and a production process that used both direct labor and direct materials intensively. Product price was a relatively important competitive driver, and product cost was an important component of profitability.

Financial control systems may operate relatively well under such conditions. A static environment with standard products implies that performance standards need to be updated only infrequently, and system timeliness is relatively unimportant because any opportunities that the system generates can be pursued over long product life cycles. The fact that today's competitive environment is steadily moving away from these conditions has important implications for financial control and performance measurement systems.

The quality movement was an important milestone in the reconsideration of financial control systems. The success of Japanese manufacturing in the 1980s and the Japanese emphasis on quality fostered a global concern about quality. As firms implemented total quality programs, they began tracking quality measures such as scrap rates, defect rates, and response times. Managers viewed financial performance measures as less relevant in the new quality initiatives. Recently, companies have been adopting other strategic initiatives, such as customer satisfaction and time-based competition. Managers now question the relevance of financial measures in the implementation of these programs.

Time is becoming an increasingly important strategic driver, because many market opportunities can be exploited only briefly. Many firms that compete on the basis of time have difficulty controlling a time-based strategy with their financial measures. In response to time-based competition, firms track measures such as cycle times, time-to-market, response times, and delivery commitments (see Exhibit 11.8 for an example). The difficulty in reconciling new strategic realities with the exclusive use of financial measures has led companies to conclude that their financial control systems are inadequate. They have therefore designed and integrated new nonfinancial performance measures into their strategic control systems.

Nonfinancial measures may include cycle time, defects, observed behaviors, rates of flow, and many others. By definition, nonfinancial measures include all measures not denominated in financial terms. Proponents of nonfinancial measures often argue that they are *leading indicators* of financial performance, and that they can help provide a balance between short-term and long-term objectives. Another benefit of nonfinancial measures is that front-line employees can more readily observe their influence on the measures. Exhibit 11.11 provides an example of how an organization might use both financial and nonfinancial measures of the same phenomenon: production scrap.

*(ii) Process versus Outcome Measures*    Outcome measures, which indicate the end results of a firm's activities, can be either financial or nonfinancial. Net income, for example, is a financial outcome measure whereas the number of finished vehicles is a nonfinancial output measure for an automobile assembly plant.

Process measures monitor the activities of a process and indicate how well a company performed as it was producing its output. Process measures can help a company

Acme Corporation uses both financial and nonfinancial measures for different purposes and at different levels of the organization. Acme's main widget factory uses measures of scrap production in its performance measurement system.

On the production line, each operating team is responsible for the weight of scrap material produced each shift. The teams strive to minimize this nonfinancial measure by maintaining the production process at its most efficient settings. Training and experience allow the operators to understand how variations in operating pressure and temperature increase scrap, so they have a clear understanding of how their actions affect the performance measure.

At the process engineering level, however, Acme uses financial measures of scrap to direct engineering activity to the most costly processes. Processes A and B, for example, might each produce an average of 200 pounds of scrap per shift. The materials involved in Process A, however, are more expensive than those in Process B, so the company benefits by investing engineering resources in lowering the scrap rate of Process A. The financial measure (the dollar cost of scrap produced per shift) directs attention to Process A; the nonfinancial measure (pounds of scrap per shift), by contrast, would indicate no difference between the processes.

**Exhibit 11.11    Different Uses for Financial and Nonfinancial Measures of the Same Phenomenon**

detect operational problems before they have a significant effect on the company's outcome measures. Process measures are usually nonfinancial. Examples include manufacturing cycle time and customer response time.

Process indicators may predict outcome measure. The number of finished automobiles coming off a production line at the end of a shift is an *outcome* measure. The rate at which the production line is moving during the day is a *flow* or *process* measure. If the flow measure during the course of the first half of the shift is consistently 10 percent under target, one knows by midshift that the likelihood of making the outcome goal is poor. Firms often assess process measures using the concepts of statistical process control (see Chapter 20).

*(iii) Diagnostic versus Interactive Performance Measures*    Companies can choose to use performance measures in a diagnostic or interactive fashion.[5] Diagnostic measures provide performance information about the firm's activities. Managers can use this information to take the actions necessary to ensure that the firm achieves its objectives. Interactive measures, on the other hand, provide information about the company's environment. Managers can use this information to detect competitive threats and determine effective responses.

Diagnostic control systems help managers maximize the likelihood that the company will achieve its specific goals. They typically address the firm's operational processes and require a measurement of the processes' outputs, standards against which to compare the actual results, and means to address deviations from the standard. Typical diagnostic control systems include business plans, budgets, and standard cost systems.

Diagnostic control systems provide information about how a firm is performing with regard to crucial competitive variables. The effectiveness of diagnostic control systems for the firm depends on an appropriate choice of performance variables; managers must consider how they will use the information that the system provides and select measures accordingly. A firm that markets a commodity product, for example, should implement diagnostic systems that involve product quality and cost rather than new product innovations. Firms that want to use diagnostic information for employee motivation and evaluation must select measures that create goal congruence.

Finally, diagnostic control systems allow managers to identify competitive strengths and weaknesses so that they can take action to leverage strengths and improve on weaknesses. The process and outcome information that the system provides enables members of the company to identify operating deficiencies, determine the root cause of weak performance, and take corrective action.

Whereas diagnostic control systems tend to constrain management activity by creating a focus on a known standard, interactive control systems encourage managers to search for competitive threats and opportunities. Their primary benefit is to help an organization avoid threats and prepare to respond to possible contingencies. As such, an organization's ability to adapt readily and decisively to changes in the competitive environment might be the best measure of effective interactive control systems.

The critical aspect of these systems is that they are interactive. Managers at all levels must be able to routinely interact with the systems to develop alternative courses of action in response to strategic uncertainties. The control systems must contain useful information about these uncertainties; they must also update that information frequently. The specific measures and information that a firm's interactive control system uses will depend on the company's chosen competitive arena. For example, the measures might address trends in technology, in regulation, or in consumer preferences.

An example of an interactive control system is a market intelligence program that identifies competitor activities that threaten the company. Consider a sales manager whose ability to meet performance targets is a function of customer preferences, pricing and quality of competitors' products, and the economy in general. Assume that during the year, the market intelligence program alerts the manager to a 30 percent price reduction by one competitor and a new product launch by another. Based on this information, the manager can use various analysis tools to predict how these external events will affect the firm's ability to achieve its annual goals. The interactive market intelligence system allows the manager to identify a serious threat and to consider several possible responses, perhaps even simulating the outcome of each. Based on these results, the manager can implement the response that enables the firm to best meet the competitive challenge.

**(e) Step Five: Select the Specific Performance Measure**  Having specified the desired characteristics of the performance measures, managers can then select the specific performance measures to use. This section provides brief descriptions of some measures commonly used in manufacturing and service organizations. The list is by no means exhaustive; managers should select (or develop) specific measures that best address the activities critical to achieving the strategic objectives of their own firms.

When selecting or developing performance measures, managers should bear two things in mind:

1. Most CSFs will require measurement along at least one of three dimensions: cost, quality, and time. The descriptions that follow address all three of these dimensions.

2. The best measure of a CSF will have an appropriate level of time and organizational aggregation. For example, monthly sales data are not helpful for measuring the quality of daily production output, nor are divisional expenses useful for assessing the efficiency of a single department.

*(i) Productivity Measures*    Productivity measures can address how efficiently a company uses its financial resources, capital equipment, or work force. There are several measures of a company's financial productivity.

EVA (also known as residual income) attempts to quantify the performance of a firm based on its ability (or inability) to create value with the capital resources it employs. EVA is simply after-tax operating profit minus the total annual cost of capital. If EVA is positive, a firm is creating value. If EVA is negative, a firm is destroying value. Many firms adopted EVA in the 1990s, not only as a measure of organizational success but as a basis for executive compensation.

*Return on investment* (ROI) is simply a firm's net income divided by the investment in the company. In practice, there are many definitions of return and investment, which can make comparisons difficult. *Return* is typically defined as net income. *Investment* may be defined as shareholder's equity, gross assets, net assets, or invested capital (long-term debt plus equity). Note that this discussion involves the postimplementation assessment of how well a project met its projected goals, *not* the assessment of whether the project should be implemented. The investment decision requires a consideration of the time value of money and a measure such as net present value. The assessment, which occurs after the project cash flows are realized, requires only comparison to the expected outcome.

Equipment productivity measures keep track of the operational productivity of specific capital resources. *Utilization*, for example, measures time employed to time available. Minutes (or hours) of unplanned downtime is a specific utilization measure that:

• Accounts for planned downtime such as preventive maintenance.
• Allows for Pareto analysis of the causes of unplanned downtime.

Managers and employees can take corrective action to address the causes that create the greatest unplanned downtime.

Effective preventive maintenance programs can greatly improve operational effectiveness by minimizing or eliminating equipment breakdowns. A measure of conformance to a preventive maintenance schedule can help ensure that PM activities receive appropriate priority and identify if, when, and how the schedule was not adhered to in the event of excessive breakdowns.

One simple productivity measure for any process is the number of units produced in a given period. It is possible to define this measure for all types of organizations: manufactured output for manufacturing companies, customers served for front-office activities (e.g., bank tellers), and units completed for back-office activities (e.g., insurance claims processing). This measure should be balanced with an appropriate quality indicator as well; some companies, for example, count only acceptable units.

Personnel productivity measures attempt to capture the quantity of productive output that each employee generates. Two typical examples are "unit output per employee" and "sales per employee." These measures divide total output (in units or in sales dollars) by the number of employees who worked to produce that output. Increasing the measure typically signals higher productivity, but it is important to apply this type of measure in conjunction with measures of quality and employee well-being to ensure that productivity is not increasing at the expense of the organization's long-term survival.

*(ii) Customer-Service Measures*   Measuring how well an organization meets the needs of its customers is becoming an increasingly important strategic task. Firms often use measures of customer satisfaction, on-time delivery, and the overall relationship with the customer to assess customer service.

Customer satisfaction is a qualitative measure that companies typically collect by conducting customer surveys. A customer satisfaction measure indicates customers' overall perception of how well a firm meets their needs. This measure can be assessed on an absolute satisfaction scale (How satisfied are you with our product?) or on a relative scale (Compared to your satisfaction with Competitor $X$, how satisfied are you with our product?).

Another measure of customer satisfaction is the level of repeat business. This measure assumes that customers who are satisfied with a firm's product or service will purchase it again. In addition, many firms contact former customers to understand why these purchasers chose another supplier.

Some firms assume that satisfied customers will shift more of their purchases to products or services of the firm, so they measure the proportion of customer purchases captured by their products. This measure is expressed as a percentage of total customer purchases of similar products or services. For example, a customer might have a monthly requirement of 100 units. The "proportion of purchases" measure is 20 percent if the customer buys 20 units from the company and 80 percent if the customer buys 80 units from the company.

Delivery measures assess another important dimension of customer service. The percentage of deliveries that are on time provides an indication of the frequency with which the company meets its promised delivery dates. Many companies use an aging schedule to weight different time delays, ensuring that the latest orders receive appropriate attention. Another delivery measure, cycle time, is the span of time from customer order to receipt. Clearly, the firm must understand its delivery-cycle-time capability in order to make promises it can keep.

Finally, many firms include customers in the development process for new products and services. Firms should measure the success and effectiveness of these relationships. One simple way to do so is to measure the percentage of development projects with customer representation on the design team. Another is to track the number of product or feature ideas that customers add to the development agenda.

*(iii) Quality Measures*   Measures of quality can be categorized as either measures of the quality of conformance (i.e., how well a produced product meets its design specifications) or measures of the quality of design (i.e., how well the design of a product meets the needs of users).

Measures of conformance quality include process capability indices, mean time between failures (MTBF), scrap rates, rework levels, warranty expense, and customer complaint rates. Process capability measures provide an indication of the ability of a particular process or machine to produce products that fall within established specifications. If a selected process capability index is not acceptable (i.e., the process cannot produce an acceptable proportion of outputs that meet customer specifications), the firm must change the process to reduce its natural variability. The six sigma standard popularized by Motorola is based on a process capability index.

MTBF measures the average time that passes from one incident of failure to the next; a larger MTBF indicates a more reliable product. This measure can be used to track the reliability of a firm's equipment as well as of its products. The amount of scrap an operation produces is also an indicator of its quality, as is the percentage of units that require rework.

Many products are sold with warranties, a commitment by the seller to incur repair costs for certain types of failures during a specified length of time. A company's warranty expense, or the money it spends meeting its warrantee commitments, provides an indication of product reliability and of customer satisfaction, because the customer must exert effort to make a warranty claim.

A customer complaint rate provides an indication of how often customers encounter problems with a firm's products or services. It is often reported in terms of the number of complaints per time period. When tracking this measure, the firm must be certain to distinguish between complaints caused by conformance failures and complaints caused by design failures. A firm that chooses complaint rates as a measure must also keep in mind that many customers who encounter problems with its product or service may never complain but may simply switch suppliers.

Several measures discussed in previous sections can also serve as indicators of the firm's design quality. In particular, customer satisfaction, repeat business, and customer complaint rates can all be interpreted in terms of design quality. Yet another measure of design quality is the growth rate of sales for new (and particularly innovative) products, which can indicate how well a product, as designed, meets customer needs.

*(iv) Cycle-Time Measures*    A *cycle time* is a measure of the elapsed time from the beginning of a process until its completion. Although there are many measurable cycle times, firms have focused on three common measures:

1. Manufacturing cycle time typically measures the elapsed time between when raw materials are released into production and the time when the finished product moves into finished goods inventory.
2. Product development cycle time measures the elapsed time between when a new product idea is identified and the time when the product is introduced into the market.
3. Delivery cycle time measures the elapsed time between when a customer places an order and the time when the product is delivered to the customer.

A firm's CSFs will help determine which cycle times are most important for it to measure.

*(v) Internal Personnel Measures*    To achieve its strategic goals, a firm must build and maintain the necessary abilities in its work force. Managers can use either subjective or objective measures to address this critical aspect of performance. Subjective measures address general employee attitudes such as morale or satisfaction.

There are ways to directly measure employee skills and abilities; these methods should be used in careful conjunction with the clearly stated skill requirements for each job. Standardized tests can evaluate employees' reading, writing, and mathematical skills. Firms often choose indirect measures, however, such as hours spent in training or the percentage of employees certified to perform various tasks.

**(f) Step Six: Establish a Performance Goal or Target**    Once managers have selected specific performance measures, they need to set targets for performance outcomes. There are several possible standards on which managers can base targets, including budget expectations, past performance, industry norms, and best practices. There are two important characteristics of targets: clarity and ease of attainment.

*(i) Clarity*    Performance targets need to be as clear as possible. Quantitative targets expressed in precise terms are most clear: "98 percent of line-item orders shipped within 24 hours of receipt of order" is clearer than "98 percent on-time delivery" or "improve on-time delivery performance." When specifying targets, however, managers must keep in mind the issues of goal congruence and goal conflict. Heavy emphasis on one measure and its target may lead to behaviors that undermine the company's ability to succeed at other CSFs. According to James March, the more precise the measure of performance, the greater the motivation to find ways of scoring well on the measurement index without regard to the underlying goals.[6]

*(ii) Ease of Attainment*    When establishing goals and targets, managers must decide how challenging the targets should be. Targets that are easy to achieve may not motivate employees to work very hard, because they know they will be able to meet the goals with minimal effort. Targets that are too difficult to achieve, however, may cause low employee motivation, because if the employees believe they have little chance of meeting the goal, they probably will not to exert much effort toward achieving the target. Research has not led to an obvious answer about the best level at which to set targets. Managers and employees must therefore learn together what level of difficulty leads to positive outcomes for the employees and the company.

**(g) Step Seven: Assess Actual Performance**    As employees accomplish their tasks within a performance measurement system, they will produce realizations (outcomes) of specific performance measures. With some regular frequency, employees and managers should review these outcomes and determine whether or not they are satisfactory. This assessment often involves a comparison between targeted and actual values of the performance measure. A difference between the targeted value and the actual outcome is known as a variance, and the comparison and analysis process is called variance analysis.

If a variance exists for a particular performance measure, it is important to determine which of several alternative reasons causes the variance. The first possibility is that performance was actually better (a favorable variance) or worse (an unfavorable variance) than could be reasonably expected. In this case, it is appropriate to work with the employees involved to identify the causes for the abnormal performance, then either to institutionalize them or to correct them, as appropriate.

A second possibility is that the estimate of performance that could be reasonably expected at the time the target was set was inaccurate: either too low (a favorable variance) or too high (an unfavorable variance). In this case, it is appropriate to work with the employees involved in setting the performance targets to improve their understanding of the capabilities of the business system.

Finally, it is possible that environmental factors (e.g., the price of a raw material) that affect performance changed significantly between the time managers set the targets and when they evaluated actual performance. If so, it is appropriate to factor out the environmental change in evaluating employee or process performance, then take actions to reduce the likelihood of such a change recurring (e.g., signing a long-term contract for raw materials).

It may also be beneficial to use relative performance evaluation (RPE) when assessing performance. RPE compares one individual's or group's performance results against those of comparable entities. These relative comparisons allow managers to factor out common effects on the performance measure and focus on the contribution of the individual or group.

Consider a small manufacturing company that has three plants, each producing the same type of product. A recent surplus of oil has significantly reduced energy costs, so all three plants have met cost-reduction targets. Two plants, however, have reduced costs an additional 30 percent. A relative cost measure among all three plants can offer insight into the plants' performance that a simple comparison to plant targets would conceal.

**(h) Step Eight: Adapt for Continuous Improvement**    The final step involves adapting business and performance measurement processes for continuous improvement. (Firms can implicitly or explicitly tie rewards to performance measures. Compensation design and its connection to performance measurement are extremely complicated and important issues but beyond the scope of this chapter.) There are several possible responses when performance outcomes differ from expectations:

- Change employee expertise or attitude.
- Change the business process itself.
- Change the level of expectations to a more appropriate level.
- Take steps to reduce environmental uncertainty.

Of course, if the results indicate that some type of goal conflict exists, managers must change the performance measurement system to eliminate these problems.

When adapting the performance measurement cycle based on realized results, however, managers must be careful not to reduce employee motivation. If employees are able to achieve an outcome that exceeds the target, only to see managers set the next target at the demonstrated (higher) level of performance, employees may conclude that there is no point in trying to beat the goals because they will only receive harder goals in return. Managers and employees have to find effective ways to share any surplus created when employees find creative ways to produce truly better than expected performance.

**11.4 SUMMARY**    This chapter discusses the general principles of performance measurement. It also describes a process for selecting performance measures that managers (and employees) can follow when designing performance measurement systems. Performance measurement is both extremely important for an organization's success and extremely complex. The examples in this chapter indicate that well-meaning managers can design performance measurement systems and performance measures that motivate employees to act in dysfunctional ways. Managers who design performance measures that motivate effective behaviors through high goal congruence and low goal conflict, however, will help their organizations achieve strategic objectives. The process outlined in this chapter provides managers with a general procedure for designing effective performance measurement systems.

# NOTES

1. Readers familiar with total quality management and the work of W. Edwards Deming will recognize the Plan-Do-Check-Act cycle embedded in this performance measurement process. See, e.g., W. Edwards Deming, *Out of the Crisis* (Cambridge, MA: Massachusetts Institute of Technology Center for Advanced Engineering Study, 1986).

2. S. Kaplan and D. P. Norton, *The Balanced Scorecard* (Boston, MA: Harvard Business School Press, 1996).

3. This framework is an adaptation of the performance pyramid described in R. L. Lynch and K. F. Cross, "Performance Measurement Systems," in *Handbook of Cost Management,* ed. B. Brinker (New York: Warren, Gorham, & Lamont, 1996), Ch. E3.

4. EVA™ is a trademark of Stern Stewart & Company.

5. R. Simons, *Levers of Control* (Boston, MA: Harvard Business School Press, 1996).

6. J. G. March, "Bounded Rationality, Ambiguity, and the Engineering of Choice," *Bell Journal of Economics* 9 (Autumn 1978): 587–608.

# CHAPTER 12

# COUNTING CHANGE: PERFORMANCE MEASUREMENT SYSTEMS IN THE INFORMATION AGE

**Sarah C. Mavrinac and Neil R. Jones**

**Richard Ivey School of Business, University of Western Ontario**

**Michael Vitale**

University of Melbourne

> *Water, water, everywhere,*
> *Nor any drop to drink.*
> Samuel Taylor Coleridge, *The Ancient Mariner*

**12.1 INTRODUCTION**   Since the introduction of the computer as a managerial tool in the mid-1960s, the cost of cataloging, storing, and retrieving performance data has fallen steadily. The cost of computing is now so low that every organization, even the smallest, can collect and report performance data on a scale not previously feasible for even the wealthiest companies. With this change, however, an irony has emerged:

More data do not necessarily yield improved performance measures.

Technology may have transformed our ability to gather data on the businesses around us, but computing power alone will never solve the performance measurement problem. The key issue for management today is *not* more data, faster data, or cheaper data. On the contrary, the ease with which data can now be collected may actually compound the performance measurement problem by encouraging managers to "solve" problems by collecting more data rather than leveraging new ideas. In many organizations, increased computing power is too often used simply to automate existing systems. Automation allows wider circulation and finer analysis of traditional measures, but the outcome is merely faster distribution of generic, and increasingly irrelevant, performance metrics.

The solution to the performance measurement problem will never be found through technological advance alone but will come only with better metrics and better, more tailored systems for organizing them. Ultimately, the critical task is not measuring per se but developing meaning out of what is measured. Effective performance measurement systems foster insight into the critical operating dimensions of the organization and provide actionable knowledge, not simply a ranking of historic achievement.

This chapter attempts to provide managers some perspective on how such performance measurement systems might be constructed and, more important, how these systems can be used to foster continuous improvement and growth. The chapter begins with a brief discussion of traditional accounting measures and some of the reasons why they are increasingly inadequate for both managerial and investors' decision making. We argue, for example, that the declining usefulness of financial measures is due partly to the weaknesses of conventional accounting practice and also—more significantly— to changes in the global economy and in the processes through which companies create value.

Next, the chapter examines nonfinancial performance measures as an adjunct to traditional cost and profit measures. We believe that nonfinancial measures can play a role both in leveraging current operations and in predicting future performance—and dozens of research studies investigating the performance measurement question back us up. Some of these are large-sample studies that offer a high-level perspective on trends over time and across industries; others rely on field research methods to detail the experiences and lessons learned by a single company. Both types exhibit interesting patterns that will be relevant to managers who are concerned with improving their measurement capabilities.

Having argued for the potential value of expanded measurement systems, the chapter then considers the essential components of a performance measurement system: its purpose, its optimal structure, and its consequences for organizational functioning. To illustrate the arguments, the chapter describes the paths taken and the lessons learned by senior managers at 10 companies that were among the first in the United States to experiment with performance measurement reform. Their experiences should be enormously instructive.

The chapter concludes with a summary of lessons learned for systems implementations and with a call for continued experimentation.

**12.2 "IRRELEVANCE" OF EARNINGS**    For generations, investors and managers have relied heavily—and often exclusively—on financial measures for insight into performance. Measures of cost, revenue, and profitability have been used to define success, to distinguish winners from losers, and to separate high quality from low quality. But over the past 5 to 10 years, managers have grown frustrated with the limitations of traditional financial measures.

**(a) Calls for Accounting Model Reforms**    There have been enough complaints about the failure of traditional accounting systems to prompt organizations like the Association for Investment Management and Research (AIMR),[1] the American Institute of Certified Public Accountants (AICPA),[2] the Conference Board,[3] and even the Securities and Exchange Commission to investigate reforms. The AICPA's Jenkins Committee, for example, has published a detailed report that calls for an overhaul of the entire financial accounting model. It argues that today's investors need information above and beyond what is contained in financial statements if they are to fully understand a corporate entity.

Dissatisfaction and frustration with existing measurement systems is also clearly felt by front-line managers in a range of industries. According to a 1995 study by researchers from the Harvard Business School, most managers believe that financial accounting disclosures are insufficient for communicating long-term business performance potential.[4] They, too support reform.

Of course, this is not the first time in history that managers have opted to shift or "modernize" accounting systems. Since Luca Pacioli, an Italian monk, first codified the logic behind double-entry bookkeeping some 500 years ago, performance measurement practices have continually evolved to accommodate regular shifts in the structure of business. Both external financial accounting practices and internal management accounting systems have become more sophisticated over time. Early in this century, for example, the E. I. Dupont de Nemours corporation invested heavily in a new system of ratio analysis in an attempt to better measure and monitor the success of its divisional managers. In the early 1950s, General Electric invested in a radical new system of "nonfinancial" measures to improve its internal processes. Some 20 years later, GE was to experiment again with one of the first *economic-value-added* (EVA™)-type systems.

**(b) Need for Reform** System changes in large organizations are expensive, disruptive, and not likely to be made without good reason. Presumably, these changes, and others like them, were prompted by significant shifts in the business environment, internal processes, or customer demands, and they were preceded by the same frustrations managers experience today.

Much of the current frustration with traditional measurement tools is understandable. The claim that financial measures have outlived their usefulness is not simply the latest business fad or the outcome of some simple shift in managerial priorities. There is convincing statistical evidence to support managers' intuition that traditional financial measures really do not offer the same insight into performance that they used to.

Some of this evidence can be found in a working paper produced by Baruch Lev for a 1998 conference on performance measurement sponsored by the Intangibles Research Center.[5] Using data on some 5,000 publicly traded companies over the period 1977–1996, Lev assessed the relationship between annual returns to shareholders and corporate earnings. Describing the findings of his study, the author writes: "My main conclusion . . . is that the informativeness of financial reports has decreased over the last 30 years and is currently rather low." In other words, earnings numbers simply are not as useful as they used to be in predicting corporate performance, at least when performance is defined in terms of returns to shareholders.

**(c) Importance of Intangible Assets** The decline in relevance is not limited to the earnings number, or even to the numbers on the income statement. Similar "weaknesses" can be identified with the balance sheet as well. Consider, for example, the balance sheet of any hot new Internet company. Although the company's share price might be hitting record highs, it is unlikely that its balance sheet could offer much insight into the source of shareholder value. The assets listed on the company's financial statements are probably limited to some personal computers, leased communications lines, office furniture, and perhaps some prepaid advertising. Clearly, the value creation process at such a company is not dependent on investment in tangible assets.

For many companies in today's knowledge-based economy, future earnings and current share values are based on the strategic management of *intangible* assets—the talent of employees, the ability to anticipate consumer needs, a network of corporate relationships, and perhaps some trade secrets, for example. None of these assets appear anywhere on the balance sheet.

Another vivid illustration of the newfound problem with corporate balance sheets can be found in a second study by Lev, this one coauthored with Z. Deng.[6] Lev and Deng make their case for the irrelevance of financial reporting largely by offering evidence of the increasing significance of intangible assets and of the complexities caused by the traditional treatment of these intangibles. Their study examines the consequences of expensing in-process research and development (R&D) and considers the relevance of R&D estimates reported at the time of an acquisition. In the process of applying the purchase method of accounting, which is generally required in such cases, fair market values must be assigned to in-process R&D and to a host of other tangible and intangible assets as well.

One of the purposes of the study is to provide data on the magnitude of in-process R&D as a component of acquisition value. The examples that Deng and Lev offer are striking. Consider, for example, the acquisition of Lotus Development Corporation by IBM in 1995. IBM "allocated" Lotus's $3.2 billion acquisition price as follows:

| Line-items on Lotus's balance sheet | (in millions) |
|---|---|
| Tangible net assets | $   305 |
| Identifiable intangible assets | 542 |
| Current software products | 290 |
| **Software under development** | **1,840** |
| Goodwill | 564 |
| Deferred tax liabilities | −305 |
| Total purchase price | $3,236 |

Note that *software under development* (i.e., *in-process R&D*) is valued at $1,840 million, which constitutes more than 50 percent of the acquisition price. Overall, for the 375 companies included in this study, the average value of in-process R&D was 72 percent of the acquisition price and was thus the largest asset included in the acquisitions. Because—under current accounting principles—these values must be expensed within the acquisition quarter, the average company was left with a postacquisition loss of almost $8 million and a same-year decrease in profit of almost $25 million.[7]

Clearly, the size of the R&D in these acquisitions is impressive, but so is the increasing *frequency* of these acquisitions. Although the authors studied all acquisitions of R&D-intensive public companies between 1985 and 1996, 85 percent of the cases occurred during the three years 1994 to 1996.

**(d) Why Traditional Measurement Systems Are Inadequate**    In the first paper mentioned above, Lev asks a provocative question: "How can it be that the regulations enacted by the various Accounting Research Bulletins, Accounting Principles Board Statements, Emerging Issues Task Force Reports and SEC Technical Bulletins, and in particular the standards set by more than 120 FASB statements over the past 20 years, have not resulted in a substantial *improvement* in the usefulness of financial reports?"[8] (emphasis in original). Why, indeed, have our traditional measurement systems begun to fail us?

The answers are not definitive, but there are some speculative explanations. One explanation is the pace of change in the business environment. Industrial changes, technological shifts, increasing global competition, and regulatory reform all contribute to the dynamic context of our times. Consider, for example, shifts in product design and the increasing pace of product development. A 1992 study by the American Quality Foundation and Ernst & Young reported that the computer industry shortened the time needed to introduce a new product by an average of 15 percent over the period 1989–1992 and anticipated a further 30 percent reduction in the coming three years. A similar survey of European manufacturers reported an 8 percent improvement over the years 1985–1987.[9] It is only logical to believe that as the pace of change increases, historically based accounting measures will lose at least some of their ability to predict future performance.

Along with these product-related advances have come shifts in competitive advantage and organizational restructurings. In the past, these events were rare and radical. Now corporate restructurings are quite frequent—and expensive. Indeed, the magnitude of the corporate restructurings, and the requirement that they be expensed in their entirety in the year in which they occur, must certainly have an impact on the usefulness of earnings as a predictor of future returns. In fact, Lev argues that restructuring charges are one of the primary reasons why earnings now have so little relationship to shareholder value.

Restructuring, the increasing significance of intangible assets, and fundamental change certainly appear to be among the reasons the that measurement processes should change. But there is a potential fourth reason, too. Fundamental business changes are prompting a reconsideration and reconceptualization—or redefinition—of what a business should set out to achieve, what its goals are, and which constituencies it should serve. None of these fundamental governance or social issues are considered by traditional, financial measurement systems.

**12.3 NONFINANCIAL ALTERNATIVES**    Although no one would suggest that traditional financial measures should be abandoned entirely, an increasing number of organizations (including the AICPA) have encouraged the business community to expand its measurement set.

Obvious complements to traditional financial measures are the nonfinancial measures that have been the mainstay of shop-floor supervisors for centuries: units produced, rejects or returns per thousand, cycle time, inventory size, head count, units produced per employee, and so on. These are among the metrics by which processes and action can be understood, analyzed, and improved. For many managers, these nonfinancial measures provide an immediacy and specificity that financial measures never can.

If nonfinancial metrics can improve operational decision making, might they also do the same for investment decision making? Can current nonfinancial performance provide insight into future financial performance?

**(a) Findings from the U.S. Department of Labor Report**    The U.S. Department of Labor (DOL) recently commissioned a report to investigate these very questions.[10] The answer, based on a review of some 300 academic and practitioner articles, was a qualified "yes." Nonfinancial measurements, when used in the appropriate way, *can* provide insight into future financial performance.

Most of the articles reviewed for the DOL suggested strongly that new ways of measuring and managing can indeed drive improvements in both firmwide financial performance and in intermediate outcomes, such as product quality and customer satisfaction.[11] The results included the following:

- Companies noted for their progressive use of *process management and measurement practices* had price-to-book valuation ratios significantly higher than their industry peers that had not invested in these workplace practices.[12]
- An international comparative study of the returns to *process management* and *employee training and involvement practices* found that the use of "lean" produc-

tion practices (involving cross-training, expanded measurement, and employee participation) was strongly associated with lower indirect labor levels and overhead costs.[13]

The review of the returns to investments in workplace and customer outcomes provides compelling evidence that there is a relationship between intermediate product and customer outcomes (on the one hand) and financial performance (on the other). This, in turn, argues strongly for the use of nonfinancial measures as leading indicators of future financial performance. Consider the following, for example: A comprehensive study analyzing survey data collected from 632 companies over two-year operating periods found that higher levels of *product quality* were significantly associated with higher levels of financial performance in three of six industry groups studied. Mediating the quality-profitability link were such intermediate variables as cost, price, and market position.[14]

A second study investigated stock market reactions to firms' announcements of *quality award receipt*. Companies receiving such awards were found on average to enjoy one-day excess returns of .59–.67 percent.[15]

One study investigating the profit impact of improved *customer satisfaction* levels concluded that an annual one-point increase in customer satisfaction could return $7.48 million over five years to the typical company in Sweden. As the authors wrote: "Given the sample's average net income of $65m, this represents a cumulative increase of 11.5 percent. If the impact of customer satisfaction on profitability is similar for companies in the Business Week 1000, then an annual one-point increase in the average firm's satisfaction index would be worth $94m or 11.4 percent of current ROI."[16]

A central message of the DOL report is that improved measurement practices *can* foster improved financial returns and measures of workplace and customer outcomes *can* serve as leading indicators of future financial performance. The report suggests that managers should now turn to questions of when these results will be most obviously seen, under what conditions value is maximized, and how the value of various practices can be enhanced.

**(b) Investors Use Nonfinancial Data**   Although earlier studies made clear that *managers* can profit from changes in their measurement set, there is still a good deal of uncertainty about whether *investors* might also benefit from such an expansion. One of the earliest studies to address this issue was conducted in 1996 by Sarah Mavrinac and Terry Boyle.[17] In an attempt to better understand the role and consequence of measurement use in a capital markets context, these investigators focused on the relationship between financial analysts' use of nonfinancial data and their ability to predict future corporate earnings.

The study was based on a content analysis of some 300 investment reports and an inspection of the frequency with which the analysts considered nonfinancial performance issues. The results of the study suggest that analysts consider a wide range of nonfinancial factors, although the types of issues considered vary greatly across industries. The results of the study also provide modest support for the hypothesis that analysts who consider nonfinancial data frequently generate more accurate earnings predictions. In short, the results of the study suggest that analysts *do* treat nonfinancial performance data as leading indicators of future financial performance.

Mavrinac presents even more compelling evidence of the value of nonfinancial measures in a paper coauthored with Tony Siesfeld, a senior research fellow at the Ernst & Young Center for Business Innovation.[18] This study focused on such key questions as the following:

- When and under what conditions do investors find value in nonfinancial data?
- Which types of nonfinancial data do they value most?
- To what extent do changes in nonfinancial performance influence the investment decision?

What distinguishes this study from earlier analyses is its methodology, its direct assessment of investors' information requirements, and its assessment of their decision-making routines and value priorities. This study was also among the first to offer an explicit assessment of the valuation impact of nonfinancial performance improvement.

Using data collected from over 250 institutional portfolio managers, the investigators compiled evidence that strongly supports the study's basic hypothesis that nonfinancial performance data are relevant to shareholder evaluations and investment decisions. Based on these results, the authors concluded that the typical institutional investor does devote substantial attention to nonfinancial performance issues. In fact, the study data suggest that for the typical investor, approximately 35 percent of the investment decision is driven by the evaluation of nonfinancial data. For a handful of others, it drives almost the entire decision.

The study participants did not consider all nonfinancial data equally useful, however. According to the respondents, measures of strategy implementation, management credibility, innovativeness, market share, and the firm's ability to "attract and retain talented people" were substantially more useful than measures of customer complaints, quality award programs, employee training programs, or environmental and social policies. Interestingly, all types of investors perceived the importance of particular types of nonfinancial data in about the same way. This may be an indication of the general applicability of nonfinancial data. That is, the value of nonfinancial data appears not to be specific to any particular investment strategy or investor type.

In the last phase of analysis, the investigators used experimental data collected through investment simulations to draw an association between financial and nonfinancial data in an attempt to "value" the nonfinancial data. Specifically, they investigated the relationship between nonfinancial performance and the propensity of an investor to acquire company shares. This experimental approach effectively allowed nonfinancial performance improvements to be "priced." Results of the analysis—conducted specifically for companies in the pharmaceuticals industry—showed strong variation in the estimated "value" of certain types of nonfinancial performance improvements. Improvements in the "quality of products and services" were valued more highly than improvements in "investor communications," for example, but the data still suggested strong returns from improvements in investor communications. The authors wrote:

> According to the estimates, a "one unit"[19] improvement in the quality of investor communications by a large company operating in the pharmaceuticals industry would be equivalent in the minds of shareholders to a 0.5 percent increase in share price. For a company like Merck, this measure could translate into a market valuation gain of $140 million.[20]

**12.4 BUILDING NEW PERFORMANCE MEASUREMENT SYSTEMS**    The research findings discussed previously should certainly motivate managers to begin experimenting with new systems and metrics. The evidence collected to date suggests that although many of our traditional measures may have lost some of their relevance, a host of new measures can replace them—measures that offer insights into process and customer outcomes that financial measures alone could never provide. But the measures themselves are not the solution to the measurement problem. As suggested in the introduction, to be truly useful, new measures must be embedded in a new system. This system, in turn, should be designed specifically to foster the company's own unique goals.

The intent of this section of is to offer some suggestions on how to begin exploring new measurement alternatives and how, ultimately, to build new measurement systems. This section describes the paths taken and the lessons learned by senior managers at 10 companies that were among the first in the country to invest in a radical extension of their measurement activities. Not all these companies have succeeded in changing their systems. Some have stumbled along the way. One, after an abortive first try, has had to return to the drawing board to chart a new course. However, most of the companies *have* succeeded, and their histories show interesting patterns that suggest important lessons to be learned.

**(a) Balanced Scorecard**    All the managers whose stories are told here were members of a group that participated in Kaplan and Norton's development of the balanced scorecard.[21] The balanced scorecard is an appealingly straightforward framework for describing and managing corporate performance that was first introduced in 1992. In its original form, the balanced scorecard displays corporate performance along four dimensions: financial, customer, internal, and innovation. The four dimensions acknowledge the interests of customers, employees, and shareholders, and they incorporate both long-term and short-term goals. Exhibit 12.1 offers a (disguised) example of an actual balanced scorecard designed for a fast-food franchising organization. (The balanced scorecard as a particular measurement system is described in detail in Chapter 13 of this volume.)

The balanced scorecard has proved itself to be a powerful and flexible concept that can be interpreted, modified, and implemented to suit the particular needs of almost any organization. It is thus little wonder that the balanced scorecard is appealing to senior executives who are concerned about the effectiveness and accuracy of their existing performance measurement systems.

**(b) Experience with the Balanced Scorecard**    What follows are descriptions of these pioneers' experiences with the balanced scorecard, their interpretations, and their advice about what works best and when. These suggestions are organized around certain questions that have been posed by many executives interested in initiating change in the performance measurement systems of their own companies.

Although these people are dissatisfied with their current performance measurement systems and interested in the balanced scorecard, they also have important concerns about some of the details—and some of the effects—of implementing the balanced scorecard. Among their most frequent questions are the following:

- What process should be used to select new measures?
- What sorts of measures are best?

**Financial**

Comparative sales increases
Projected first-year real estate return on assets
Operator profitability
Gross margin/customer type
Visits per customer

**Customer**

Overall customer satisfaction
Order accuracy
Order service time
Product quality
Roadside market share

**Internal**

Total G&A cost/transaction
Total operating cost/transaction
Profit per initiative
Profit per employee
Employee satisfaction

**Innovation**

Number of profitable ideas generated
Number of profitable ideas implemented
Profits and sales from new venues
Number of successful new products
Number of cost reduction breakthroughs achieved

**Exhibit 12.1    Balanced Scorecard in Operations: An Illustration**

- If individual scorecards are developed for divisions or strategic business units, should these scorecards be aggregated, and if so, how?
- Should a corporate-level scorecard be rolled down to individual employees? If so, how should it relate to individual evaluation and compensation plans?
- Is it realistic to think of the balanced scorecard as a complete replacement for an existing performance measurement system? If not, how should the balanced scorecard be integrated with the old system?
- Should some nonfinancial performance information be released to shareholders, financial analysts, portfolio managers, and other interested parties? If so, which information should be disclosed, and how?

The final question, and ultimately the most important, is always: What are the benefits of using a balanced scorecard?

**(c) Lessons on the Design Process**    Almost any performance measurement "how-to" article will argue that the starting point for development must be the firm's strategy. Certainly, a key purpose of any performance measurement system is to link day-to-day operations with the organization's strategic intent and business strategy.

Kaplan and Norton's second balanced scorecard article[22] describes the process for developing a balanced scorecard as one that should start with an articulation of "vision, mission, and strategy." Other how-to articles talk about starting with customer goals or needs, using those to develop the *customer quadrant* of the scorecard, and then working through the rest of the scorecard. In any event, all these articles describe the development of the scorecard as an approximately linear process that should be, and probably will be, roughly the same from one organization to the next.

Interestingly, experienced executives rarely describe such an explicit or straightforward development process. Their comments suggest that the "linearity" of the development process is highly dependent on the existence of a clearly specified corporate strategy and on some existing skill with performance measures. But fewer than half the companies we studied had a concise strategy; most had only a vague mission statement, and others were experiencing a profound shift in strategic direction. For these companies, the process of developing the balanced scorecard had as much influence on strategy as strategy had on the scorecard. The development process was often iterative, requiring conscious movement from perceived strategy to measures and back again. Although these companies inevitably took longer than expected to develop their scorecard, one invaluable result of their work was a clearer understanding of strategic intent.

Those companies that did not have extensive experience using nonfinancial performance measures first had to come to terms with what "good" measures were, why they might be used, and what insights could be realized from them. Typically, these companies had a strong tradition of financial measurement. Breaking out of the financial mind-set was difficult for them, but the process of creatively considering nonfinancial measures opened up an entirely new set of management possibilities and, significantly, allowed a new set of voices into the development process.

Although traditional measurement systems are often the purview of senior executives and accountants alone, the balanced scorecard process demands the participation of a wider range of "experts." Those individuals who are most familiar with a particular process are also most likely to know how it should be measured. Clearly, then, they should have input into the process regardless of their status or position in the organization.

*(i) Selecting Implementation Teams*   Although there were striking differences across organizations, there were also some similarities in the balanced scorecard development structure. Virtually all the organizations in the sample identified a team (of about three members) and charged it with developing the initial version of a balanced scorecard. In 6 of the 10 companies, a company's chief financial officer or vice president of finance assumed direct responsibility for the team. Several of the companies added an outside consultant as a facilitator, but most did not. One particularly conscientious group actively recruited advisers for itself: They chose midlevel managers from various functional areas who were well acquainted with current procedures and who could inform the implementation team of the real value of particular measures.

Regardless of their membership, all the teams began their work by becoming familiar with the overall concept of the balanced scorecard. After that, their first decision was whether to accept the balanced scorecard framework intact, to create a new framework, or to modify the existing framework by adding or—less commonly—by subtracting categories. As discussed in greater detail later, the group's definition of the project goal invariably determined which option the team selected.

*(ii) Using the Financial Scorecard Without Modification*   Four companies in the sample chose to use the scorecard framework without substantive modification. These companies all had a clearly defined strategy and some experience with process measures. Their explicit goal was to use the balanced scorecard to drive bottom-line performance improvements. The intent was to measure, control, and improve the value-added returns

to major corporate processes. For them, the four original scorecard quadrants were sufficient.

*(iii) Modifying the Scorecard Framework*    The other companies modified the scorecard substantially. They used new measurement categories that represented the interests of important stakeholders or, in some cases, the overarching "values" of the company. Whereas each of these companies hoped the modified balanced scorecard framework would lead to bottom-line improvements in the long run, the goal of the project in the short run was to drive organizational and cultural change. Some companies hoped to realize new levels of innovation and flexibility. Others were pushing for a new "quality" or "customer" consciousness, but all of them planned to use the balanced scorecard as a tool for signaling who and what should be important to the company. Accordingly, these companies devoted special attention to the definition of the scorecard categories.

One company ended up with only three categories: employees, customers, and the community. Another had five, representing the firm's interest in innovation, employees, customers, shareholders, and key suppliers. Still another organization established a business mission with six "pillars," including recruiting and training, the development of new service offerings, and improved pricing. Although measurements for the "stones" that make up these pillars could have been distributed across the four boxes of the traditional balanced scorecard, the organization found it more appealing to expand its scorecard to include a distinct category for each pillar.

Discussions with corporate executives and analysis of the interview data confirmed that these companies were using their new balanced scorecards not just as a measurement tool but primarily as a communications device. The measurement system was intended to introduce and nurture a new set of values—values focusing on customer satisfaction, environmental safety, production safety, or, in several cases, employee development. For companies that had not had much experience with process measurement, this innovative way of using the balanced scorecard also allowed employees to become familiar with the new measurement focus. Any inhibitions or insecurities employees might have felt initially were relieved by the fact that the measures were tied to values and goals they could understand and support.

*(iv) Implementation Processes*    There is undoubtedly no "best" process for developing a balanced scorecard, but the team approach seems to work well in most organizations. A full-time skilled facilitator, whether from inside the organization or outside, also seems useful, while the explicit support of senior managers is essential.

A few companies in the sample developed balanced scorecards as a staff exercise, hoping that the content of the finished scorecard would convince top management that implementation would be advantageous. Using this "backstairs approach" to developing the balanced scorecard has not proved successful. A more effective strategy includes an active campaign to publicize the scorecard project before too much time and energy are invested. Such a publicity campaign should include clear and concise statements about why the new performance measurement system is being developed and how (if at all) it will be linked to individual evaluation and compensation.

If the organization has an explicit vision, strategic intent, or business strategy, that should be the starting point. Then the company can develop specific statements of how things will be better for customers, shareholders, employees, and other stakeholders when success is achieved. Occasionally such an attempt to operationalize a strategic intention or a corporate vision reveals a lack of agreement or understanding about its content and implications. This is a signal for the scorecard development team to seek clarification from senior management. Such clarification, if achieved, is a down payment on the overall value to be derived from the process of developing the scorecard. If clarification cannot be obtained, it is a clear signal to stop the project, for even if a scorecard is constructed, it is unlikely to be accepted. It may even be dangerous, because it is based on unclear assumptions about what the organization needs to do.

No company should feel it has to start exclusively with its strategy, however. As discussed previously, a number of innovative companies have used their balanced scorecard to communicate and reinforce corporate values or to drive organizational change. Making the balanced scorecard work in general is not the question—making it work for *your* company is.

**(d) Selecting Measures**   The companies in the study used a wide variety of measures. Some companies were strongly opposed to the use of information from customer or employee surveys or from any other "subjective" source; others were comfortable with such information when it was gathered and reported in a consistent way. Senior executives at some companies vetoed the use of activity measures such as "hours of training delivered" and allowed only outcome or results measures to appear on their scorecards. Executives at other companies favored measures of results but accepted measures of activity in areas in which outcomes were either difficult to measure or difficult to connect indisputably with outcomes.

*(i) Index Measures*   Some companies were also comfortable with index measures and actively sought to construct such measures. An example of an index measure is as follows: "Compare current activities or outcomes with activities or outcomes in a fixed previous period" (e.g., "days lost due to accidents this month compared to days lost to accidents in January 1996"). Other companies thought index measures were inherently difficult to understand and therefore difficult to incorporate into performance management.

*(ii) Prioritizing Measures*   When they had reduced their initial group of measures to a final short list, the teams had to prioritize the measures that were left. They used a variety of prioritization tools and techniques. Companies that had been using only one or two measures (these were inevitably financial measures and typically included revenues, costs, or profits) generally retained those familiar few as part of their new scorecard.

If the company or division had an explicit business strategy, the development team generally worked to ensure that the proposed measures covered all elements of that strategy. In other words, they attempted to construct a set of measures that would ensure that the goals of the business strategy were met.

If the company's strategy were not so explicit, another translation step was required. For example, one company had published the following mission statement: "Be number one in overall customer satisfaction." Its scorecard development team drew on existing corporate research that showed that customer satisfaction was based on price, service, quality, consistency, and product variety. Measures for each of these elements could then be discussed.

*(iii) Measurement Quality Checklist*   One specific tool that various companies used to assist in final selection was a measurement quality checklist. This evaluation tool allowed

team members to consider, for example, the availability of data for the measures, their accuracy, their precision and clarity, and their general *validity*—that is, how well they measure what they purport to measure. Exhibit 12.2 presents a sample checklist, collected from one of the subject companies. It is rare that any one measure will receive high marks on every one of the quality criteria. However, the strength of the balanced scorecard as a whole is dependent on the quality of its components. Knowing the pluses and minuses of each of the measures is essential to the evaluation of the finished product.

Despite the contingencies of corporate culture and style, the definition of every measure on the balanced scorecard must be understandable by every member of senior management. Each must be able to say, without analysis or even much thought, whether—all other things being equal—it is better for the organization if the value of a given measure gets larger or smaller. Measures that are not understandable in this straightforward way have no place on the scorecard. Companies should follow the lead of those who use measurement quality checklists like the one presented in Exhibit 12.2. There is no point to building a scorecard around measures that are not routinely available or whose accuracy is suspect.

**(e) Questions of Aggregation**    Between the top floor and the shop floor are a host of organizational units or entities. Depending on the history and strategy of the broader organization, these units may be structured around product line, location, customer base, or functional expertise. These units typically have their own unique performance agendas, and many units may have their own performance measurement systems.[23] Naturally, when companies begin to consider launching a performance measurement project, the question of tying these various sets of measures together arises.

Please evaluate all current and nominated measures using the five criteria identified below. Performance along each dimension should be identified using the adjacent scale. Please circle the most appropriate rating.

Recommended measure _____

| Criteria | Description | Poor → → → Excellent | | | | |
|---|---|---|---|---|---|---|
| Availability | Who has the data? Is it readily accessible? Will a new IT system have to be built? | 1 | 2 | 3 | 4 | 5 |
| Accuracy | Do you trust the measures? Are they consistent from month to month? Does change reflect change in the underlying activity? Or is it noise? | 1 | 2 | 3 | 4 | 5 |
| Precision | Not arithmetic but logical. Are you measuring what needs to be measured? Are you focused on the right level of analysis? Where can change be implemented? | 1 | 2 | 3 | 4 | 5 |
| Clarity | Is the measure understandable? Will employees understand it? | 1 | 2 | 3 | 4 | 5 |
| Validity | Are you actually measuring what you want to measure? Or just what you *can* measure? | 1 | 2 | 3 | 4 | 5 |

**Exhibit 12.2    Measurement Quality Checklist: A Disguised Illustration**

Traditional financial measures can be denominated in the same units (Canadian dollars, for example) and, generally, defined in the same way across divisions. Their aggregate values can therefore be formally calculated and reported at many levels—for example, by region, business unit, or sector—regardless of whether this aggregation actually makes sense or results in better decision making. Nonfinancial performance measures, on the other hand, often apply only to the business unit for which they are defined. For example, the property and casualty division of one company, a large multiline insurance and financial services organization, uses its *combined ratio* (the sum of operating expenses and claims paid divided by premiums paid) as a key internal measure. Other parts of this same company (the investment division, for example) would find this measure meaningless.

Even when identical measures are used across divisions, aggregating the results can obscure the facts. The same multiline insurer has decided to move away from its traditional indemnity health insurance product toward a newer managed care product. It wants sales of the traditional product to decrease and sales of the managed care product to increase. Aggregating the scorecards for the two health insurance product divisions would deliver a precise—but useless—number for "total sales." This company has decided instead to measure and report results for the two divisions separately.

The frustrations inherent in linking unlike measures can throw off even the most carefully organized development process. Consider the company that produces over-the-counter drugs: This company ended its attempt to build a balanced scorecard when it realized that new corporate goals for building market share could not be distributed to the product divisions in a way that guaranteed that achievement of divisional market-share goals would lead to reaching the corporate goal as well.

Eventually, all the "balanced scorecard pioneers" found some way out of this conundrum. Some of the companies developed scorecards for some or all of their *business units*—groups that have their own "customers, distribution channels, production facilities, and financial performance measures"—and made no attempt to aggregate the scorecards. Others developed a corporate-level scorecard only and made no formal attempt to roll the measures down to business units. In short, these companies have dealt with the issue of aggregation by not doing it! Still another company has made a conceptual leap away from the standard, mathematical form of aggregation to develop another, less formulaic type of connection. This company opted for a "logical" rather than an arithmetic linking.

Each year, the process of building the balanced scorecard starts at the top of the organization. The president of this billion-dollar division creates his objectives and defines two or three measurable goals for each of the five scorecard categories.

His staff has its turn next. Using their boss's goals as a guide, each staff member defines in measurable terms what to do to ensure that the president reaches his goals. And so the scorecard rolls its way down through the organization—through the senior executive level to the management and supervisory levels through the administrative functions and even to the shop floor. At the end of the planning period, each individual has a unique set of performance objectives that are expressly linked with those of his or her superiors. In this way, each member of the organization can feel tied to the company's strategy, mission statement, and, ultimately, its performance.

In many companies, the annual process of setting corporate financial goals that are then distributed to organizational subunits on a take-it-or-else basis is an exercise in mutual self-delusion and political maneuvering. Corporate strategic planners develop goals that they have no idea how to meet, and business units—after some ritual skirmishing—accept formal responsibility for their piece of the pie with no real intention of producing it. Each month or quarter the divisional results roll together smoothly into a neat, simple, and probably misleading statement about progress toward the corporate goals. By the end of the year, circumstances have inevitably changed, blame and praise are shared, and the process starts anew. Along the way, divisional managers have probably gained little from measuring themselves against allocated targets.

Instead, each business unit should eventually have a balanced scorecard of its own. These scorecards should be logically—if not arithmetically—linked with the corporate vision, strategic intent, or—if it exists—the corporate balanced scorecard to be sure that the accomplishment of divisional goals will contribute to the success of the organization as a whole. A simple table of divisional measures compared with corporate intention can be used to test the alignment.

Functional groups below the business-unit level—for example, information systems, marketing and sales, or manufacturing—should also have their own performance measurement systems. Ideally, these will be linked to business-unit balanced scorecards. Indeed, for a balanced scorecard measure to be useful to managers, it must be linked down through the organization to the actions that have produced the results being measured. Without this linkage, it will be difficult to know how to respond to results, whether favorable or unfavorable. These linkages need not be fully in place at the time a balanced scorecard is introduced, but in order to be successful with the balanced scorecard, an organization must be willing to use analysis as well as exhortation as a stimulus to better performance.

**(f) Link to Performance Evaluation and Rewards**    Fewer than half the companies studied explicitly linked performance on the balanced scorecard measures to individual financial rewards. For those that did, a typical approach was to use success in achieving corporate or divisional scorecard objectives to determine the size of a bonus pool that would be shared by a group of employees. The makeup of this group varied from corporate senior executives only to most of the employees in a particular division. The bonus pool was then divided among all those eligible, often on a largely subjective basis.

When asked about the philosophy underlying their approach, all the companies responded that they were treating the new balanced scorecard system in the same way that they had treated previous performance measurement systems. Companies that had explicitly linked performance to pay continued to do so; those that had not did not change their approach after they developed a balanced scorecard. The companies that did opt for pay-for-performance programs tended to be those that had an explicit strategy and a well-articulated value chain. They also tended to be those whose project goal was to drive value creation and improvements in the bottom line.

Although the pay-for-performance philosophy is woven deeply into the fabric of U.S. business, companies vary widely in their beliefs about how explicit the link should be. And, despite the rhetoric about executive stock options and shareholder value creation, a growing school of thought strongly opposes the idea of explicit pay-for-performance links. This debate is clearly beyond the scope of this chapter. However, when strategy is explicit and when the employee task is well understood, a pay-for-performance system can be useful for encouraging both short-term productivity and longer-term process improvements.

At the same time, if the purpose of the scorecard is to support innovation and cultural change, the most appropriate reward plan might involve no pay-for-performance link or at most some broad-based gain- (and risk-)sharing plans rather than a specific link between pay and balanced scorecard performance. When an organization changes its culture and ways of doing business, employees must learn an entirely new set of organizational routines. Such learning should be real and positive. By linking cultural change to pay, organizations run the risk of twisting, and perhaps even preventing, that learning.

**(g) Letting Go**    Organizations that are contemplating the development of a balanced scorecard or any other new performance measurement system are naturally interested in knowing what will happen to their existing system once the new one is in place. In fact, letting go of existing measures has been difficult for many of the early balanced scorecard companies, and this is an issue that should be recognized at the outset of a balanced scorecard project.

No matter how thoroughly an existing system can be faulted on theoretical and practical grounds, its features are likely to be well understood across the company, in particular by those who have learned to manipulate the system for the benefit of both themselves and their organizational units. The existing system is also likely to be intertwined with evaluation, compensation, and other human resource processes that are of considerable personal interest to senior management as well as to those in charge of administering them. An infrastructure of information systems is probably also in place to gather, consolidate, and report performance measurement information. Against this backdrop, it is easy to understand why letting go of the existing system can be difficult.

From a content perspective, the balanced scorecards developed by the pioneers generally included many of the measures that were already in place. This was true despite the team leaders' description of the development process as "starting with a clean sheet of paper." Two companies that had historically paid a lot of attention to performance measurement and already had reasonably satisfactory systems, basically converted those systems into balanced scorecards that contained many of the same features. Other companies that had been focused initially on just one or two measures included those measures among the considerably larger sets that make up their scorecards. Only two companies could be said to have replaced their systems; in both cases those earlier systems were complex, widely disliked, and inconsistently used.

**(h) Scorecard and Disclosure**    Whether companies should disclose their scorecards is a question that is being asked with increasing frequency. Only 1 out of the 10 organizations studied included nonfinancial measures from its balanced scorecard in its published annual report. Although almost all of the annual reports include some nonfinancial measures (if only counts of employees), only one company explicitly produces its balanced scorecard in its annual report.

Most companies probably will not soon disclose either the measures on their balanced scorecards or the values of those measures. Although there might be some advantage in illustrating the quality of management and the thoughtfulness with which strategic intent is being communicated to employees, the balanced scorecard concept may be still too new for companies to risk legal exposure by revealing it.

**(i) Benefits of Change**    For at least half the companies in the sample, the balanced scorecard project was considered a resounding success. Had it improved the bottom line, identified waste, or revealed ways to reduce cost? Well, "yes" for some companies and "not yet" for others. For most of the sample companies, bottom-line improvement did not matter that much. Instead, the balanced scorecard allowed them to realize substantive change in organizational functioning.

Many of the pioneering companies found the balanced scorecard effective in helping employees prioritize multiple change projects—which occasionally conflict in terms of goals and often conflict in terms of demands for time and attention. This prioritization can be carried out both for existing projects (some of which may be canceled or curtailed as a result) and for proposed new projects. In one company, the sponsor of each project is now asked to illustrate explicitly how the project will contribute to the achievement of one or more of the key organizational goals included on the balanced scorecard. For the growing group of companies suffering from project overload, this form of "organizational detoxification" can be helpful indeed.

Companies that were undergoing some form of business reorganization (e.g., reengineering) frequently found themselves enjoying a second type of benefit. For these companies, the balanced scorecard provided their employees a commonly understood and accepted way of measuring the "success" of the reengineering initiative. Because of its focus on nonfinancial metrics that can be accepted and understood by virtually every employee, the balanced scorecard can get people from formerly different units—or formerly different companies—talking the same language and striving to reach the same goals. And, although a surprisingly large number of reengineering projects avoid specifying in advance what results are being sought, that approach can backfire. At some point during the inevitably unsettling, often painful process of reengineering, someone is bound to ask whether all the turmoil is worthwhile, and how anyone will know when it is over. The balanced scorecard can be used to answer these questions and to help determine which reengineering projects to undertake in the first place.

The pioneering companies realized a variety of other benefits as well, including increased employee morale, improved customer satisfaction, and increased product quality. Some of these benefits were realized by all the companies and other benefits by only one or two companies. Eventually a pattern emerged that matched a particular type of company with each benefit. Analysis of the data showed that there were actually two groups in the sample:

1. Companies that had an explicitly defined and well established strategy.
2. Companies that either had no strategy or were significantly reconfiguring their strategy.

The motivation, implementation, and benefits of the scorecard varied dramatically across these two groups.

The companies that had an explicit strategy tended to implement the balanced scorecard in a manner very much like that described in the Kaplan and Norton articles. In every case, the scorecard was designed—just as the *Harvard Business Review* articles suggest—to reflect corporate strategy, with the categories of measurement mimicking the original balanced scorecard categories. In every case, the purpose of the implementation process was to drive improvement in bottom-line performance by focusing employee attention on strategic priorities and the leading indicators of future financial performance. There was no subtlety in the process. Management knew clearly what the value chain looked like and which customer and internal factors were most likely to drive improvements in revenues and profits. The scorecard was used to communicate management's insight to lower-level employees by making evident the levers of control.

For these companies, the benefits were first and foremost a new visibility of the value chain and a new tool with which to manage it.

In contrast with these strategy-oriented companies, other subject companies either had no explicit strategy or were attempting to dramatically shift their strategic orientation. Analysis suggests that these companies did not implement the scorecard to drive improvements in profitability per se. These companies were looking instead for changes in employee orientation and in the corporate beliefs system more generally. Their intent was to create a new series of corporate values, values that their senior managers believed were fundamental to the company's future and to the successful implementation of any future strategy. These values were considered to be a necessary foundation for later development of strategy.

The values-oriented companies tended to develop their own framework for the scorecard. They opted for categories that reflected closely held values or the needs of the constituencies that were most important to the company. The measurements used to populate these categories were not as precise or as "valid" as the measures used by the first group, but that apparently did not matter. These measures were chosen primarily for symbolic purposes and were used to influence outlook more than behavior. Not surprisingly, these companies were less likely to tie performance on the scorecard measures to financial compensation.

What were the benefits for these companies? Although these companies did not enjoy substantial change in profitability, their managers were generally pleased with the results of the implementation process. To them, the noticeable shifts in organizational culture, the improvements in employee satisfaction, and the new energy in the company substantially outweighed the costs of implementation.

The benefits of improved performance measurement, like the benefits of a clear corporate vision or of an explicit business strategy, are often difficult to quantify. If an existing measurement system is of such poor quality that it causes erroneous decisions to be made, it should be replaced for reasons of cost and efficiency alone. In most cases, however, the development of a balanced scorecard should be considered part of a larger corporate change effort. This change effort can involve minor changes in operating structure or in strategic focus or major changes in outlook and culture. But the company must understand what type of change it is attempting to make and why. Success is realized only when these *expectations* are realized.

**12.5 NEXT STEPS**   In a 1991 article, Robert Eccles predicted a coming revolution in performance measurement. "At the heart of this revolution," he wrote, "lies a radical decision: to shift from treating financial figures as the foundation for performance measurement to treating them as one among a broader set of measures."[24] His prescription for managing the new age of competition was to develop new and more comprehensive systems of measurement, systems that were more focused on process and more supportive of long-term investments in change and capability.

Nearly a decade has passed since the appearance of that article, but the revolution is still nowhere near maturity. Almost daily, the number of companies pledging allegiance to the movement grows. But as those managers who have already joined the movement know, this is no trivial commitment. Significant effort is required to develop measurement systems that help the organization truly learn. But the learning can be rewarding, even offering competitive advantage to the extent that it nurtures and enhances the company's core competencies.

Indeed, to the extent that there is any similarity in the development processes used by the pioneering companies described in this chapter, it is that the design process attended to the *unique* capabilities of the companies. All the pioneering companies that realized success in measurement had four things in common:

1. A well-specified project goal.
2. A clear vision of organizational processes and patterns of value creation.
3. Support of top management for the project.
4. Most significantly, a development plan that took explicit account of the organization's current performance levels, its "performance measurement history," and its cultural environment.

This last success factor is an important one. As discussed previously, effective performance measurement systems are critical to the management of an organization. They are the essence of control—they shape understanding and attitudes, prioritize goals, and encourage improvement. If these systems are to foster success, they must be uniquely tailored to the goals and objectives of each individual organization. They must also be capable of adapting to change, for certainly every organization will change. And, with every change will come the need to realign, rethink, and reorganize.

As any manager knows, measures can have a profound behavioral impact on those who use them. They are the "lens" through which people see, evaluate, and manage the activities of a company, and they are the language with which the company translates its strategic purpose and direction into action.

Measures are symbols of what is important and what counts. When measures change, a firm's view of itself and of its place in the world changes as well. So, as new measures are developed to accommodate external changes occurring in our environment and internal changes in the company, it would not be unusual for the company to want and value still more change—change in performance, change in value, and further change in measures. These changes, in turn, could prompt the company to rethink what and how it manages, which encourages still more change in measurement.

Essentially, what is required of effective measurement systems is a dynamic adaptability, an ability to change routinely within the confines of a certain structure (in this case, the corporate strategy). An effective system not only ensures connection between inputs and outputs or financial and nonfinancial components, but also some connection between system and strategy. Perhaps these connections should be thought of as positive feedback loops that allow links between those generating the strategy of the organization and those designing its system for assessment and motivation. (See Exhibit 12.3 for a graphic illustration of this system.) These systems should operate to ensure that a company is simultaneously attuned to both its environment and its internal processes, that it matches capability with opportunity, and that it responds rapidly to each shift in competition.

An organization can assess the adaptability and effectiveness of its systems only through careful analysis and experimentation. The point is to sketch the business model and then use the data and measures collected to test the model by evaluating the relationships between the various value-creation stages and by looking for weaknesses or unexploited strengths. Such analysis can be enormously rewarding. Indeed, the very process of articulating a performance model can reveal hitherto unspoken assumptions about strategic priorities, corporate assumptions, and the integrity of functional and divisional interactions.

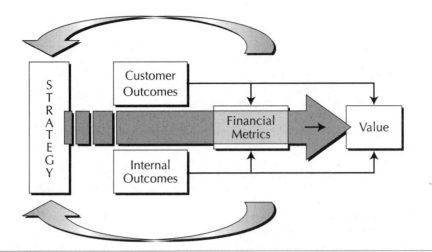

**Exhibit 12.3    Performance Measurement Schema with Feedback Loops**

The learning from this exercise requires time and repeated experimentation and production of data. However, over time, patterns will emerge. With frameworks, scorecards, and benchmark data, managers should begin to see more clearly the mechanisms underlying the value-creation process and to understand the nature of those mechanisms, their relation to outcomes in the workplace, and their response to workplace practices. It will be time-consuming and, at times, frustrating, but most managers will find it more than worth the effort.

## NOTES

1. See P. Knutson, *Financial Reporting in the 1990s and Beyond: A Position Paper of the Association for Investment Management and Research* (Charlottesville, VA: Association for Investment Management and Research, 1992).

2. See AICPA, Special Committee on Financial Reporting, *The Information Needs of Investors and Creditors* (New York: American Institute of Certified Public Accountants, 1993).

3. See Brancato, *Communicating Corporate Performance: A Delicate Balance* (New York: The Conference Board, 1997).

4. See R. G. Eccles and S. C. Mavrinac, "Improving the Corporate Disclosure Process," *Sloan Management Review* 36 (1995): 11–25.

5. B. Lev, "The Boundaries of Financial Reporting and How to Extend Them," Working Paper, Stern School of Business, New York University, 1996.

6. Z. Deng and B. Lev, "The Valuation of Acquired R&D," New York University, Working Paper, 1998.

7. The significance of these write-offs has not gone unnoticed. The Financial Accounting Standards Board has plans in place now to modify the accounting for R&D acquired through acquisitions.

8. Lev, op. cit., p. 3.

9. A. De Meyer and K. Ferdows, "Influence of Manufacturing Improvement Programmes on Performance," *International Journal of Production Management* 10 (1989): 120–131.

10. See S. C. Mavrinac, N. R. Jones, with M. M. Meyer, *Competitive Renewal Through Workplace Practices: The Financial and Nonfinancial Returns to High Performance Workplace Practices* (Washington, DC: Ernst & Young LLP and the U.S. Department of Labor).

11. Because the majority of studies reviewed for the report generated their findings using large samples of firms, the conclusions must be viewed as representing a portfolio effect. Not every firm will or should expect to generate financial returns from workplace investment. However, on average, a group or portfolio of firms using innovative workplace practices should perform well—if not continuously better than a portfolio of comparable firms not using the practices.

12. See Lilli A. Gordon, J. Pound, and Todd Porter, *High-Performance Workplaces: Implications for Investment Research and Active Investing Strategies* (Waban, MA: The Gordon Group, May 30, 1994).

13. See C. D. Ittner and J. P. MacDuffie, "Exploring the Sources of International Differences in Manufacturing Overhead," Working Paper, The Wharton School, University of Pennsylvania, March 1994.

14. See L. W. Phillips, D. R. Chang, and R. D. Buzzell, "Product Quality, Cost Position and Business Performance: A Test of Some Key Hypotheses," *Journal of Marketing* 47 (Spring 1983): 26–43.

15. See K. B. Hendricks and V. R. Singhal, "Quality Awards and the Market Value of the Firm: An Empirical Investigation," Working Paper, April 20, 1994.

16. See E. W. Anderson, C. Fornell, and D. R. Lehman. "Customer Satisfaction, Market Share, and Profitability: Findings from Sweden," *Journal of Marketing* (July 1994).

17. See S. C. Mavrinac and T. Boyle, "Sell-Side Analysis, Nonfinancial Performance Evaluation, and the Accuracy of Short-Term Earnings Forecasts," Working Paper, Ernst & Young LLP, 1996.

18. S. Mavrinac and T. Siesfeld, "Measures That Matter: An Exploratory Investigation of Investors' Information Needs and Value Priorities." In *Enterprise Value in the Knowledge Economy: Measuring Performance in the Age of Intangibles* (Ernst & Young LLP, 1998).

19. In this study, a one-unit change in nonfinancial ranking (e.g., a movement from a rank of 6 to 7) represents a relative change of less than a half a standard deviation.

20. To calculate this hypothetical return, the authors used share price and earnings numbers collected for September 1996. At the end of this month, Merck's share price was approximately $70 while its earnings were $3.50 a share.

21. See R. S. Kaplan and D. P. Norton, "The Balanced Scorecard—Measures that Drive Performance," *Harvard Business Review* (1992): 71–79.

22. R. S. Kaplan and D. P. Norton, "Putting the Balanced Scorecard to Work," *Harvard Business Review.*

23. C. Gold, "IS Measures—A Balancing Act," Research Note CITA27, Ernst & Young Center for Business Innovation, May 1992.

24. Eccles, R., "The Performance Measurement Manifesto," *Harvard Business Review,* January/February, 1991, pp. 131–137.

# CHAPTER 13

# THE BALANCED SCORECARD

## Stan Davis
## Tom Albright
**University of Alabama, Tuscaloosa**

**13.1 INTRODUCTION** The balanced scorecard is rapidly becoming the strategic management tool of choice for companies seeking to improve the performance of employees and business units. The balanced scorecard is a performance measurement system that focuses employee behavior on actions that directly or indirectly relate to achieving business-unit strategic objectives. In a survey of management accountants conducted in 1998 for the Cost Management Group of the Institute of Management Accountants, 35 percent of responding companies indicated they either already had a balanced scorecard program or had plans to implement one.[1] Since Robert Kaplan and David Norton introduced the concept of the balanced scorecard in the early 1990s, it has quickly grown into a management tool that enables managers to align the interests of employees and business units.

The three sections of this chapter that follow discuss different aspects of the balanced scorecard. The first section (13.2) presents basic information about the balanced scorecard, including a brief history of the balanced scorecard, the underlying concepts and components, and strategic categories for classifying most business units. The next section (13.3) illustrates key components of the balanced scorecard by describing a balanced scorecard program recently implemented by a banking institution. The chapter concludes with a section (13.4) on the motivational effects of the balanced scorecard and suggestions for companies that are considering implementing a balanced scorecard program.

**13.2 BALANCED SCORECARD** Beginning in the early 1980s, researchers and practitioners in management accounting began to note the increasing irrelevance of traditional control and performance measurement practices. The failure of cost systems to remain useful can be traced to several different sources, including:

- A failure to link performance measurement to the strategic initiatives of organizations.
- An emphasis on accounting for external reporting rather than reports useful for internal decision making.
- A failure to account for advances in technology that change how manufacturing firms operate.[2]

225

The growing importance of service industries and increased global competition have intensified the need for alternative control and performance measures for organizations seeking to remain competitive. Unfortunately, accountants remained trapped in practices whose development could be traced back to the 1920s.[3]

**(a) History**   During the late 1980s and early 1990s, management accounting practitioners and academics began laying the foundations for what became known as the balanced scorecard. Most of the concepts can be traced back to a practice called (in French) the *tableau de bord,* a measurement system developed by process engineers in the early 1900s that linked strategy to financial and nonfinancial performance measures.[4] The term "balanced scorecard" became prevalent after Robert Kaplan and David Norton published an article in the *Harvard Business Review* in 1992.[5] Kaplan and Norton drew their observations from a year-long project that studied the performance measurement systems of twelve companies. Although both practices are similar in many aspects, *tableau de bord* systems typically place a greater emphasis on financial measures, include more measures than a balanced scorecard system, and focus on internally generated measures rather than externally generally measures (such as customer driven measures).

From 1992 to 1996, numerous articles in a wide variety of journals described the balanced scorecard and its benefits to an organization. The scorecard was proposed as a means for disseminating strategy throughout an organization to achieve and sustain long-term success. In 1996, Kaplan and Norton published their book, which provides an extensive description of the balanced scorecard.[6] The discussion of the balanced scorecard that follows is based on the work of Kaplan and Norton.

**(b) Important Concepts of the Balanced Scorecard**   The balanced scorecard focuses on four concepts:

1.  Performance at the business-unit level.
2.  Cause-and-effect relationships.
3.  Both nonfinancial and financial measures.
4.  Dissemination of corporate strategies to employees.

The sections that follow discuss each of these concepts in more detail.

*(i) Performance at the Business-Unit Level*   Because companies frequently operate simultaneously in different markets with different products, different strategies may be appropriate, depending on the competitive environment or capabilities of a particular business unit.

Tailoring scorecards to individual business units allows companies to maximize performance by a particular business unit. The balanced scorecard approach recognizes the fact that goals may differ among various business units within an organization, so performance measurement systems are adjusted accordingly.

*(ii) Cause-and-Effect Relationships*   When a balanced scorecard is first designed, top management decides on the strategic objectives of each business unit in an organization. Unfortunately, many companies fail to define their missions or core values. Use of

a balanced scorecard requires management to define success in achieving strategic initiatives.

By identifying *what* a business unit's measures of success are (these measures often called "lag indicators," because they occur or change as a result of other actions), management can begin to determine *how* to affect these measures. Through this process, causal relationships between the actions that employees take and the desired outcomes that result from those actions can be identified.

By asking, "What causes our measures of success to improve," managers begin to identify key performance "drivers." These key performance drivers (called "lead indicators" because they often precede the achievement of strategic objectives) are translated into a series of measurable performance indicators and become a part of a business unit's balanced scorecard.

Cause-and-effect relationships are then identified or established between specific employee actions and the key performance drivers identified previously. Managers ask themselves, "What actions should our employees undertake to affect these key performance drivers?" These actions, which should be quantifiable in nature, become the basis for an employee's individual scorecard for performance measurement.

The success or failure of a balanced scorecard depends on the following factors:

- Identification of lead indicators.
- The quality of the cause-and-effect relationships used to link employee actions to key performance drivers.
- The quality of the cause-and-effect relationships that link key performance drivers to strategic objectives.

Exhibit 13.1 depicts the relationship between lead and lag indicators.

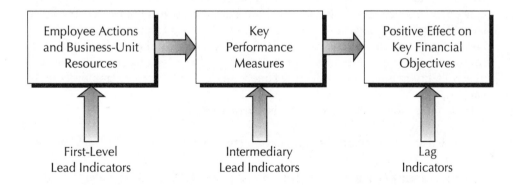

Employee actions and business-unit resources serve as lead indicators of key performance measures. *If* first-level lead indicators take place, *then* intermediary lead indicators will be positively affected. *If* intermediary lead indicators are positively impacted, *then* key financial performance measures will be positively affected.

The strength of a balanced scorecard program lies in the ability to identify lead indicators of success. After identifying lead indicators of success, managers can develop measures against which employee and business-unit performance can be judged.

**Exhibit 13.1   Lead and Lag Indicators and Cause-and-Effect Relationships**

*(iii) Both Nonfinancial and Financial Measures*    A balanced scorecard is a performance measurement system that measures the performance of both individuals and business units by using a combination of financial and nonfinancial measures. Traditional performance measurement systems focus solely on financial measures, but this can foster decision making that benefits a business unit's short-term financial performance at the expense of its long-term well-being.

To address this weakness in traditional performance measurement systems, a balanced scorecard uses a combination, or balance, of nonfinancial measures and financial measures to judge the performance of individuals and business units. An objective of the balanced scorecard is to shift the focus of the performance measurement system from the short term to the long term.

A key concept of the balanced scorecard is to reward employees and business units on the basis of nonfinancial measures. However, Kaplan and Norton contend that motivating financial performance should, in most cases, continue to be the overall goal of a performance measurement system.[7] Lag indicators can be the same financial measures that were emphasized under a traditional system. An advantage of the balanced scorecard is that it lessens rewards for individuals and business units for actions that benefit the short-term interests of a business unit and increases rewards for actions that benefit its long-term interests.

*(iv) Dissemination of Corporate Strategies to Employees*    The balanced scorecard translates the often nebulous goals found in corporate mission statements into strategy.

By detailing specific actions and outlining cause-and-effect relationships between those actions and key financial objectives, a balanced scorecard serves not only as a performance measurement system but also as a means for communicating long-term strategic initiatives to business units, then tracking their performance. Although companies now routinely share mission and vision statements with employees, many would have difficulty describing how these mission or vision statements contribute to employees' understanding of how their individual actions affect the company. Including front-line employees in the development of the balanced scorecard contributes to higher-quality causal relationships and better "buy-in" on the part of employees to the company's goals.

In summary, four concepts support the balanced scorecard:

1. A balanced scorecard should focus on strategies appropriate for each business unit.
2. By assessing *how* to improve lag indicators, an organization can identify cause-and-effect relationships. These, in turn, suggest key financial and nonfinancial performance measures that can be included on scorecards for both individuals and business units.
3. Including both financial and nonfinancial measures in balanced scorecards encourages employees to pay attention to actions that improve the long-term well-being of a business unit.
4. Communicating the specifics of a balanced scorecard to employees helps employees embrace the performance measures, because they will better understand how they can contribute to the organization's success.

The next section discusses how to develop key performance drivers of long-term success.

**(c) Four Business Perspectives**    Kaplan and Norton classified performance measures into four business "perspectives":

1. The financial perspective.
2. The customer perspective.
3. The internal business perspective.
4. The learning and growth perspective.

For each perspective, a question guides those who develop the system toward performance measures that will make a strategic difference to the organization.

*(i) Financial Perspective: "How Do We Look to Shareholders?"*    The first perspective from which to view a business unit should be the financial perspective. This step allows managers to link business-unit objectives to overall corporate strategy. To identify key performance measures in this perspective, managers should ask, "How do we look to shareholders?" This assessment will usually take place during a strategic planning session early in the development of a balanced scorecard; it is closely linked to business-unit strategic initiatives.

Examining strategic initiatives from a financial perspective leads to determining whether these initiatives are being met. For example, if a company adopts a "sustain" strategy for a particular business unit, a financial measure related to this strategy may be maintaining gross revenues.

Although a key advantage of the balanced scorecard is that it does not rely solely on financial measures to judge performance, financial measures remain the central focus of most balanced scorecard programs. As Kaplan and Norton note, "[e]very measure selected for a scorecard should be part of a series of cause-and-effect relationships, ending in financial objectives, that represent a strategic theme for the business unit."[8] The financial objectives chosen at the onset of the balanced scorecard implementation should serve two purposes:

1. To provide definite performance expectations from chosen strategies.
2. To provide a focus for objectives and measures in each of the other three perspectives.

*(ii) Customer Perspective: "How Do Customers View Us?"*    The second perspective from which to view a business unit is that of its customers. In this stage, companies identify customers and market segments in which they compete and also the means by which they provide value to these customers and markets.

In identifying why customers choose a particular business unit, managers identify lead indicators for the customer perspective. Continuing with the example used in section 13.2(c)(i), one way of maintaining a constant level of gross revenues is to maintain the current customer base. If customers value on-time delivery, then on-time delivery becomes a lead indicator for a key performance driver such as customer retention.

Examples of lead indicators may include any number of customer considerations, including:

- On-time delivery
- Defects per shipment
- Cost
- Service

By delivering quality as defined by the customer, business units can improve outcome measures such as customer satisfaction, retention, acquisition, and loyalty.

The theme for the customer perspective is that without customers to provide revenue for an organization, its financial objectives cannot be met: "Clearly, if business units are to achieve long-run superior financial performance, they must create and deliver products and services that are valued by customers."[9]

*(iii) Internal Business Perspective: "At What Must We Excel?"*    For the internal business process perspective, companies identify processes necessary to achieving customer and financial objectives outlined in the first two perspectives. The process of developing key internal drivers may involve reassessing a business unit's value chain and making changes to existing operating activities.

Kaplan and Norton[10] point out that deriving objectives in this perspective represents the sharpest distinction between the balanced scorecard and other performance measurement systems that use nonfinancial measures. In seeking to define how to best achieve objectives set for the customer and financial perspectives, the balanced scorecard establishes measures that integrate nonfinancial objectives across departments within business units. By contrast, traditional performance measurement systems that include nonfinancial measures typically seek to improve the performance of individual departments rather than business processes:

> Conventional performance measurement systems focus only on monitoring and improving cost, quality, and time-based measures of existing business processes. In contrast, the approach of the Balanced Scorecard enables the demands for internal process performance to be derived from the expectations of specific external constituencies.[11]

Continuing the previous example, if maintaining gross revenue is a company's financial objective and the company determines that on-time delivery increases customer retention, the internal business perspective requires asking how to improve on-time delivery. This may involve decreasing the number of production stoppages or reducing off-specification production.

*(iv) Learning and Growth Perspective: "How Do We Continue to Improve and Create Value?"*    In the learning and growth perspective, the goal is to determine what is necessary to achieve the objectives set in the previous three perspectives. Kaplan and Norton point out three primary categories into which objectives in this perspective normally fall[12]:

1. Employee capabilities.
2. Information system capabilities.
3. Motivation, empowerment, and alignment.

Because the balanced scorecard is intended to improve long-term performance, managers may invest in resources needed in the short-run without their business unit being penalized for having made the investments. To increase expectations in the other three perspectives without providing adequate resources would be detrimental to any effort to use the balanced scorecard:

> Ultimately, the ability to meet ambitious targets for financial, customer, and internal-business-process objectives depends on the organizational capabilities for learning and growth. . . . Strategies for superior performance will generally require significant investments in people, systems, and processes that build organizational capabilities.[13]

Continuing the previous example, to maintain a certain level of gross revenues (a financial-perspective lag indicator), a company might determine that customer retention (a customer-perspective lead indicator) is important. One factor in customer retention is providing on-time delivery (a lead indicator to customer retention). To achieve on-time delivery, a business unit might focus on decreasing production stoppages and off-specification production (a lead indicator for on-time delivery for the internal business perspective). To achieve on-time delivery, the business unit might decide on two courses of action:

1. Purchase logistics software to help optimize delivery schedules (a learning-and-growth lead indicator of on-time delivery).
2. Empower employers to override production schedules to ensure that they meet orders of preferred customers.

Exhibit 13.2 illustrates the cause-and-effect relationship for this example across the four business perspectives.

In summary, by developing objectives based on the four perspectives of the balanced scorecard, organizations can identify causal relationships between performance drivers (lead indicators) and outcome measures (lag indicators). By assessing and rewarding performance based on scorecard measures, companies motivate employees toward specific actions that are tied to specific rewards.

A company achieves balance in the measures included in a scorecard by focusing on the four business perspectives from which measures are derived—the financial perspective, the customer perspective, the internal business processes perspective, and the learning and growth perspective. After considering each perspective, managers can develop scorecards that include complementary measures to encourage actions that will support the company's strategic initiatives. As a result, employees obtain a scorecard of performance measures tailored specifically for them, and they should also gain an understanding of why each measure exists and how it relates to the strategies of their particular business units.

**(d) Business-Unit Strategies Based on Life Cycles** To facilitate the development of strategy, business units may be placed in one of three broad strategic life-cycle stages[14]:

1. The growth stage.
2. The sustain stage.
3. The harvest stage.

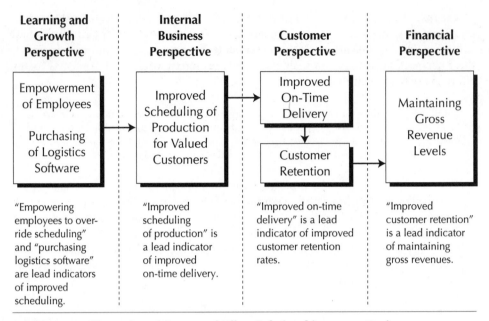

| Learning and Growth Perspective | Internal Business Perspective | Customer Perspective | Financial Perspective |
|---|---|---|---|
| Empowerment of Employees  Purchasing of Logistics Software | Improved Scheduling of Production for Valued Customers | Improved On-Time Delivery  Customer Retention | Maintaining Gross Revenue Levels |
| "Empowering employees to over-ride scheduling" and "purchasing logistics software" are lead indicators of improved scheduling. | "Improved scheduling of production" is a lead indicator of improved on-time delivery. | "Improved on-time delivery" is a lead indicator of improved customer retention rates. | "Improved customer retention" is a lead indicator of maintaining gross revenues. |

**Exhibit 13.2    Illustration of Cause-and-Effect Relationships across Business Perspectives**

These three strategies are not all-inclusive, but they at least provide a general framework companies can use when they develop strategies. Because different business units within an organization may have different strategies based on their stage of development, one scorecard for an entire company may be impossible.

*(i) Growth Stage*    Growth-stage business units are typically in the early years of their life cycle and have numerous opportunities for expanding their product offerings or output capacity.

Key financial measures for growth-stage business units typically include percentage changes in revenues for existing products or the percentage of revenues generated by new products. Growth-stage business units usually need (and receive) large investments to enable them to grow. Negative cash flows and low rates of return on employed capital are common for growth-stage business units.

*(ii) Sustain Stage*    Sustain-stage business units are concerned with maintaining and improving their performance; less emphasis is placed on new markets or new products.

Most business units can be classified in the sustain stage. Key financial measures for sustain-stage business units typically include profit measures, such as operating income or gross margin. Although capital outlays in the stage are significant, they are far lower than the capital outlays required for growth-stage business units. Capital investments focus on process improvements and moderate growth opportunities.

*(iii) Harvest Stage*    Harvest-stage business units have reached a more mature stage of development. Management no longer desires to make large capital investments. In-

| | LIFE CYCLE STAGE | | |
| --- | --- | --- | --- |
| | **Growth** | **Sustain** | **Harvest** |
| **Capital Expenditures** | High | Moderate | Low |
| **General Financial Objectives** | Revenue and sales growth rates in targeted areas | Profitability measures related to capital, such as ROI or ROCE | Cash flow measures and cost-containment measures |
| **Performance Expectations** | Low cash flow and returns | Satisfactory returns and cash flows | High cash flows |

**Exhibit 13.3    Life Cycle Development Effects on Business-Unit Strategies**

stead, the goal is to reap the benefits of investments that were made when the business unit was in one of the two earlier phases.

Key financial measures for harvest-stage business units include cash flow and working capital indicators. Exhibit 13.3 summarizes the effects of life-cycle development on business-unit strategy.

**13.3 EXAMPLE OF THE BALANCED SCORECARD**    To illustrate how key concepts and components of the balanced scorecard can be translated into actual scorecard measures, this section uses the disguised example of an actual banking organization that recently implemented the balanced scorecard as its performance measurement system.

**(a) Background**    Acme Bank has 30 branches located in communities that range from small rural areas to cities of more than 200,000 persons. The bank employs about 300 persons—about 250 in branch operations and the remaining 50 at a central administrative location that serves as bank headquarters.

Branches are divided into two geographical regions. The Northern Division has 16 branches; the Southern Division has 14 branches. Employees in a typical branch include:

- A branch president.
- A branch vice president/chief loan officer.
- Customer service representatives.
- Loan representatives.
- Mortgage loan originators.
- Head tellers.
- Tellers.
- Administrative assistants.

Acme Bank's top management team decided to roll out the balanced scorecard in the branches of its Southern Division first, though they intended to add the Northern Division's branches later. The Southern Division's branches were treated as independent business units: Each was to have a scorecard developed to suit its unique set of goals.

Acme Bank had enjoyed strong financial success over the preceding six years; it had expanded its operations by acquiring several branches over the preceding four years. Each year the bank's strategic direction was reviewed at a meeting that included the bank's top officials and outside consultants. The purpose of the annual meeting was to outline the vision and mission of the bank and to ensure that all the top managers understood and agreed on the bank's strategic direction.

In 1997, Acme Bank adopted the master strategy of balancing profits with growth to ensure that the bank remained an independent entity that existed to provide quality service and products to an increasingly diverse customer base. From this master strategy came the basis for key financial measures that were to be used in assessing branch performance.

The Southern Division's president conducted a series of interviews with front-line employees and discovered that they did not understand or know the bank's mission or goals; the employees also lacked an understanding about how their specific jobs contributed to the overall success of the bank. These interviews, coupled with the need to sustain the positive trend in performance, prompted the Southern Division's president to gain approval to implement the balanced scorecard. The president wanted a performance measurement system that would be designed to direct employee efforts to take specific actions associated with reaching the bank's strategic objectives.

The process of implementing the balanced scorecard began in early 1998, when all branch presidents in the Southern Division received a copy of Kaplan and Norton's book.[15] Shortly afterward, all these branch presidents met with the division's president to begin identifying key performance drivers and the causal relationships that affected key financial indicators of their branches. During the first half of 1999 the president met with all employees in all the branches to outline strategic initiatives, solicit feedback, and begin the educational process of introducing the balanced scorecard to branch employees.

**(b) Key Financial Performance Indicators**    When Acme Bank began considering the balanced scorecard, it was using the following seven financial measures as a gauge of the bank's success:

1. *Loan volume.* The outstanding loan balance for each branch (in dollars).
2. *Noninterest deposit volume.* The balance of all deposits (in dollars) by customers on which the bank pays no interest to the depositor.
3. *Loan yield (%).* The portfolio interest rate earned by the bank for outstanding loans.
4. *Noninterest income.* Income unrelated to interest revenue on outstanding loans. This category included service charges on deposits, credit insurance income, gains or losses on securities, and sales commissions on annuities.
5. *Net chargeoffs.* The dollar amount of loans determined uncollectable and written off by the bank (net of collateral recoveries).
6. *Cost of funds (%).* The average interest rate the bank paid on customer deposits.
7. *Noninterest expense.* Expenses unrelated to interest paid on customer deposits in demand and savings accounts. These expenses include salaries and benefits, occupancy expense, equipment and data processing expense, and other miscellaneous operating expenses.

The bank applied these measures—which it considered strategically important—not only to the bank as a whole but also to each individual branch. For the early phases of its balanced scorecard process, the bank's management decided to retain these measures as the financial targets on which its balanced scorecard initiatives would be based.

**(c) Measures for the Growth Stage** The importance of each key financial measure varies depending on the strategic focus of an individual branch. The bank's management determined that two balance sheet categories—loan volume and noninterest deposit volume—were more important for branches in the growth stage of development. These measures are important for branches in the growth stage because they indicate the acquisition of new customers or the retention of existing customers.

**(d) Measures for the Sustain Stage** The bank's management determined that three measures of profitability should serve as key financial measures for branches in the sustain stage of development:

- Loan yields.
- Noninterest income.
- Net chargeoffs.

Loan yield is closely linked to loan volume, because the cost of borrowing money affects the number of loans made by the bank. Bank management determined that loan yield is more important for branches in the sustain stage, because the emphasis for these branches is not so much to attract new customers as to maintain a certain level of performance. Whereas branches in the growth stage may be willing to offer lower loan rates to borrowers, branches in the sustain stage are more concerned with the return on loans.

**(e) Measures for the Harvest Stage** Bank management determined that three measures should serve as key financial measures for branches in the harvest stage:

1. Cost of funds.
2. Noninterest expense.
3. Net chargeoffs.

Cost of funds is an important measure in the harvest stage, because harvest-stage branches are seeking to profit from an existing customer base while deemphasizing deposit growth. Chargeoffs are more important for branches in the sustain and harvest stages, because the emphasis is on maintaining an existing customer base.

**(f) Employee Bonuses** Employee bonuses at Acme Bank had previously been awarded based on both branch performance and the bank's overall performance. This system frustrated many of the bank's employees, however, because outstanding performance by a particular branch could be outweighed (and sometimes was outweighed) by poor performance of the bank as a whole. Consequently, the bank designed its balanced scorecard to eliminate much of the frustration arising from its former system for awarding performance bonuses.

Despite the fact that the bank's management decided to continue using the same key financial measures to assess the performance of individual branches, these financial measures were to be supplemented by other measures. Although these key financial measures would serve, under the balanced scorecard, as lag indicators, they would represent only some of the measures used. To evaluate the performance of both employees and branches, the bank would also use lead indicators, which were based on specific actions that employees needed to perform to help achieve the strategic goals of each branch.

**(g) Cause-and-Effect Relationships**    The key to a successful balanced scorecard implementation is the strength of the cause-and-effect relationship that exists between the targeted financial outcome and actions employees are supposed to perform based on their individual scorecards.

For example, three financial objectives suitable for a branch in the growth stage are:

1. To increase loan volume.
2. To increase deposit volume.
3. To increase the number of products each customer purchases from the bank.

The cause-and-effect diagram in Exhibit 13.4 illustrates five causal relationships for a loan officer that should lead to achieving these three goals.

As shown in Exhibit 13.4, if an employee receives adequate training in appropriate areas, the employee should be more effective when working with new prospects. If, in turn, the employee is more effective when working with new prospects, higher-quality interactions should result. These higher-quality interactions should help the employee do a better job of assessing each prospect's needs in terms of services the bank offers. Assessing prospects' needs better should help the employee recognize opportunities for cross-sales and referrals. Each relationship ends with a desired outcome measure directly related to one of the three key financial measures used by a growth-stage branch.

Many intermediate links in the causal relationship are measurable and appear on the loan officer's scorecard. For example, measurable components of this cause-and-effect relationship (which stems from the learning-and-growth initiative "increase training received by employees") include:

- The number of training hours.
- Results of customer-service surveys.
- Number of referrals.
- Number of successful referrals.

By measuring intermediary linkages in the causal relationships, the bank's balanced scorecard differs markedly from the bank's previous performance measurement system. Under the old system, the branch was measured only on the key financial measures. The balanced scorecard, by contrast, encourages employee actions that improve the key financial measures, then measures an employee's (and a branch's) performance based on these actions.

Exhibit 13.5 shows a simplified scorecard for a loan officer in a growth-stage branch. The scorecard consists of several directives (i.e., explicit actions the loan officer should perform) as well as measures of intermediate and end goals for the employee or branch.

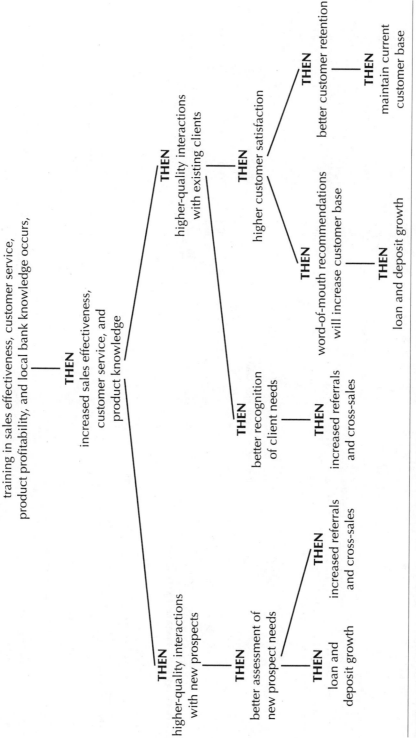

**IF**
training in sales effectiveness, customer service,
product profitability, and local bank knowledge occurs,

**THEN**
increased sales effectiveness,
customer service, and
product knowledge

**THEN**
higher-quality interactions
with new prospects

**THEN**
better assessment of
new prospect needs

**THEN**
increased referrals
and cross-sales

**THEN**
loan and
deposit growth

**THEN**
higher-quality interactions
with existing clients

**THEN**
better recognition
of client needs

**THEN**
increased referrals
and cross-sales

**THEN**
higher customer satisfaction

**THEN**
word-of-mouth recommendations
will increase customer base

**THEN**
loan and deposit growth

**THEN**
better customer retention

**THEN**
maintain current
customer base

**Exhibit 13.4   Cause and Effect Relationships: Loan Officer in Growth Branch**

237

**Branch A**
**Employee B—Loan Officer**
**January–June 1999**

**DIRECTIVES:**

(1) Two hours of training per month in appropriate areas
(2) Twelve referrals per month
(3) Twenty sales calls or follow-ups per month
(4) Twenty in-person calls per month

## INDIVIDUAL PERFORMANCE MEASURES:

|  | Weight | YTD Performance | % of Goal | Scorecard Performance |
|---|---|---|---|---|
| Training hours | 15.00% | 1.92 | 95.83% | 14.38% |
| Sales calls | 15.00% | 19.83 | 99.17% | 14.88% |
| Referrals | 10.00% | 20.67 | 103.33% | 10.00% |
| Shopper survey results | 10.00% | 4.80 | 96.00% | 9.60% |
| Past dues | 6.00% | 1.31% | 75.00% | 4.50% |
| Document exceptions | 6.00% | 1.92% | 100.00% | 6.00% |
| Net charge-offs | 8.00% | 0.30% | 75.00% | 6.00% |
| Loan volume | 10.00% | 8,275 | 110.33% | 11.03% |
| Loan yield | 3.00% | 8.31% | 100.73% | 3.02% |
| Origination fees/CL | 4.00% | 295 | 98.22% | 3.93% |
| Upward evaluation | 4.00% | 5 | 100.00% | 4.00% |

## BRANCH-WIDE PERFORMANCE MEASURES:

|  | Weight | YTD Performance | % of Goal | Scorecard Performance |
|---|---|---|---|---|
| Customer satisfaction | 3.00% | 5.00 | 100.00% | 3.00% |
| Referral sales | 3.00% | 24.00 | 100.00% | 3.00% |
| Branch-wide score | 3.00% | 92.00% |  | 2.77% |
| | 100.00% | | | 96.10% |

## INDIVIDUAL PERFORMANCE MEASURES:

|  | Baseline | Target | Jan | Feb | Mar | Apr | May | Jun |
|---|---|---|---|---|---|---|---|---|
| Training hours (hours per month) | 0 | 2 | 2 | 3 | 2.5 | 0 | 2 | 2 |
| Sales calls (calls per month) | 15 | 20 | 20 | 17 | 21 | 21 | 20 | 20 |
| Referrals (per month) | 10 | 20 | 20 | 18 | 18 | 21 | 20 | 27 |
| Shopper survey results (average) | 4 | 5.0 | 5.0 |  | 4.7 |  | 4.7 |  |
| Past dues | 2.00% | 1.25% | 1.25% | 1.30% | 1.40% | 1.10% | 1.00% | 1.80% |
| Document exceptions (average) | 5.00% | 2.00% | 2.00% | 2.00% | 2.10% | 1.70% | 1.80% | 1.90% |
| Net charge-offs (average) | 3.50% | 0.25% | 0.25% | 0.27% | 0.28% | 0.34% | 0.36% | 0.27% |
| Loan volume (current balance or average) | 5,000 | 7,500 | 8,000 | 8,150 | 8,147 | 8,149 | 8,150 | 8,275 |
| Loan yield (YTD) | 0.075 | 8.25% | 8.25% | 8.25% | 8.30% | 8.31% | 8.31% | 8.31% |
| Origination fees (average) | 275 | 300 | 300 | 300 | 314 | 279 | 276 | 299 |
| Upward evaluation average score | 4 | 5 | 5 |  |  |  |  |  |

**Exhibit 13.5  Sample Balanced Scorecard**

Whether the branch or employee achieves these measures depends on whether the employee performs the directives listed at the top of the scorecard.

Each performance measure listed on the scorecard is given a weight based on its importance (as determined by the president of the Southern Division and the branch president). An employee's individual performance level is calculated as follows:

$$\Sigma \, [\text{Performance Measure Weight}] \times [\% \text{ of Goal Met}]$$

Note that the weights assigned to the measures must sum to one. Each scorecard consists of both individual and branchwide measures (customer satisfaction is an example of a branchwide measure). By including a branchwide measure on an individual's scorecard, the bank hopes to foster an attitude of teamwork and cooperation that will benefit both the bank and its customers. Branch performance on the scorecard is a function of:

- The employees' scores.
- Branchwide measures such as customer satisfaction (as determined by surveys) and the number of successful referrals made by branch personnel.
- Key financial measures for the branch.

**13.4 SUMMARY**    The balanced scorecard has proven to be a powerful motivational tool for management. Traditional performance measurement systems use financial outcomes as a basis for rewarding performance. The balanced scorecard, by contrast, can reward outstanding performance regardless of the short-term financial outcomes.

**(a) Balanced Scorecard as a Motivator of Employees**    Under a traditional performance evaluation system, management tells employees (in effect), "Work as hard as you can, then—provided our financial performance is good for the period—you'll get a bonus." With the balanced scorecard, management says (in effect), "Excel at these tasks, and we will reward you in the specified manner."

The balanced scorecard also focuses on teamwork within and across functional segments of a business unit. If group or business-unit targets are shared by employees within a functional department, greater coordination between individuals will lead to better performance. To continue the previous example, the Acme Bank may use "number of referrals" as a measure for the balanced scorecards of individuals and "successful referrals" as a branchwide measure. By following this measurement scheme, the bank encourages quality referrals and a heightened interest in recognizing opportunities where other functions within the bank might be able to sell a financial product.

A final motivating element of a balanced scorecard is the organizational commitment it fosters. When employees are allowed to share in the development of scorecards and get the opportunity to understand the business unit's strategic direction, employees can develop a commitment to the organization that causes them to strive for improved performance. The combination of objectively defined tasks and an understanding of how jobs relate to the strategic goals of the business unit improves employees' focus and commitment.

**(b) Suggestions for Balanced Scorecards**    Because not all scorecard initiatives succeed, it is important to follow certain guidelines when beginning a balanced scorecard program. A recent survey by KPMG Management Consulting[16] lists the following ideas to consider when implementing a balanced scorecard:

- Ensure that strategic objectives are well defined before beginning. Making up strategy as you go may unintentionally cause the system to encourage unwanted employee behavior.
- Both financial and nonfinancial managers should be committed to the project to establish credibility for the balanced scorecard and to show that it has priority over other management initiatives.
- Solicit the support of line managers, because they can often identify key performance drivers and also causal links between actions and outcomes.
- Implement a pilot study before attempting to devise a companywide balanced scorecard.
- Communicate the goals and timelines for the balanced scorecard. Employees need to understand why they are being measured on certain objectives. They also need to understand how the balanced scorecard will benefit them if they excel at these measures.
- Do not underestimate the resources necessary to initiate and maintain a scorecard program. Everyone should understand the substantial administrative duties associated with having a balanced scorecard.

Managers of balanced scorecard programs should continually identify lead indicators and causal relationships so that they can improve the company's performance measurement system.[17] Although the concepts and components of a balanced scorecard are simple, they provide a powerful tool for managers who are willing to implement a program that focuses on long-term success.

## NOTES

1. M. L. Frigo and K. R. Krumwiede, "Balanced Scorecards: A Rising Trend in Strategic Performance Measurement," *Journal of Strategic Performance Measurement* (February/March 1999): 42–48.

2. R. J. Palmer, "Strategic Goals and Objectives and the Design of Strategic Management Accounting Systems," *Advances in Management Accounting* 1 (1992): 179–204; B. H. Spicer, "The Resurgence of Cost and Management Accounting: A Review of Some Recent Developments in Practice, Theories, and Case Research Methods," *Management Accounting Research* 3 (1992): 1–37.

3. R. S. Kaplan, "The Evolution of Management Accounting," *The Accounting Review* (July 1984): 390–418; E. G. Flamholtz, "Relevance Regained: Management Accounting—Past, Present, and Future," *Advances in Management Accounting* 1 (1992): 21–34; Palmer, op. cit.

4. M. J. Epstein and J. F. Manzoni, "The Balanced Scorecard and Tableau de Bord: Translating Strategy Into Action," *Management Accounting* (August 1997): 28–37.

5. R. S. Kaplan and D. P. Norton, "The Balanced Scorecard—Measures That Drive Performance," *Harvard Business Review* (January–February 1992): 71–79.

6. R. S. Kaplan and D. P. Norton, *The Balanced Scorecard: Translating Strategy into Action.* Boston: (Harvard Business School Press, 1996).

7. Ibid.

8. Ibid., 62.

9. Ibid., 63.

10. Ibid.

11. Ibid.

12. Ibid.

13. Ibid., 146.

14. Ibid.

15. Kaplan and Norton, *Translating Strategy into Action,* op. cit.

16. P. McCunn, "The Balanced Scorecard . . . the Eleventh Commandment," *Management Accounting* (December 1998): 34–36.

17. M. L. Frigo and K. R. Krumwiede, "Ten Ways to Improve Performance Measurement Systems," *Cost Management Update* (April 1999): 1–2.

# CHAPTER 14

# BENCHMARKING

## Sergio Beretta and Andrea Dossi
Universita Bocconi
## Hugh Grove
University of Denver

**14.1 INTRODUCTION**   Cost management has always been a basic component of any successful business strategy. But companies that want to survive in today's competitive environment can no longer focus on cost reduction at the expense of quality and service. Competition requires continuous improvement of each component of a product or service system: price, level of quality, and delivery time.

To accomplish such a challenging goal, companies must simultaneously manage the key business processes through which products and services are provided to the customer: product design, manufacturing, distribution, and both pre- and postsales assistance. Companies may have to rethink how their business processes are designed and managed, and this change in mind-set must be incorporated into management mechanisms. Only companies that can combine an ability to manage routine activities efficiently with an ability to innovate in their own business processes will survive.[1]

**(a) Breaking with the Past**   A critical point is that successful companies, which are usually in the best position to face this challenge, are often prisoners of their own success. They tend to replicate solutions and behaviors that worked in the past. But because the context in which they operate changes constantly, solutions that worked in the past will probably not be optimal in a changed business environment.

Also, continuous improvement of existing processes and practices usually yields diminishing returns over time. Although competitors may have less experience, they usually also have fewer constraints, so they are more likely to achieve quantum-leap improvements to gain competitive advantage. Thus, a key question for any successful company is how to break with the models and ways of doing business that dominated their past without making leaps into the dark.

One reasonable answer is to learn from companies that have found successful new solutions, although there are some risks. Apart from possible ethical and legal problems that could arise from imitating solutions developed by direct competitors, learning from competitors also raises the risk of excessive uniformity (*industry homologation*): Because business practices often result from demands expressed by customers and by the technology that exists for satisfying those demands, a company that compares its own practices only with those of companies in the same industry may become convinced—often mistakenly—that existing industry practices are the best ones possible.

It is important, therefore, to compare business practices with the best practices available, regardless of the industry. Benchmarking was developed mainly by Japanese companies, then later refined and formalized by Xerox, which developed ways to make efficient and effective comparisons between companies in various industries.[2] The Xerox way of benchmarking has proved to be an effective tool for learning and for disseminating best practices.[3] Benchmarking has also become a popular management tool. According to a study conducted by Ernst & Young with the American Quality Foundation, more than 60 percent of the companies in four important industries (computers, automobiles, banks, and hospitals) regularly benchmark their products and services.[4]

**(b) Defining Benchmarking**    A starting point for developing a successful benchmarking strategy is to define benchmarking. One well-known definition was given by David T. Kearns, the former chief executive officer of Xerox, who institutionalized benchmarking there: "Benchmarking is the continuous process of measuring products, services and business practices through the comparison with the strongest competitors or with companies that are recognized as industry leaders."[5]

The Westinghouse Productivity and Quality Center has provided a definition that complements the one by Xerox: "Benchmarking is a continuous search for and application of significantly better practices that lead to superior competitive performance."[6]

According to these definitions, benchmarking implies the following:

- *A nontraditional perspective in performance measurement.* Because benchmarking stimulates an objective-setting process that begins with the identification of excellent performers, the historical scorecard of a company for a given process is no more than a starting point from which to move incrementally. Target setting must be aimed at obtaining quantum-leap improvements.

- *A focus on business processes.* Business performance can be fully appreciated only if a company's management focuses on business processes. Traditional organizational performance measurement systems drive management attention only to the cost side of the performance measurement process; time and quality are usually deemphasized. For benchmarking to drive companies toward excellent performance, companies have to reconsider the traditional ways things are done. A process focus is needed.

- Performances must be linked to practices. Performance measurement is seen as the method that enables companies to search for best practices by quantifying the gaps between their own performance and that of the best performers. Benchmarking should balance this performance measurement aspect with the quest for best practices.

For each of these reasons, benchmarking has introduced new elements in the managerial search for continuous improvement. But benchmarking has also been accepted in many companies as a tool for promoting *business process reengineering* (see Chapter 27).

Any methodology for structuring the benchmarking process has to blend two complementary aspects:

1. Performance measurement (in order to quantify *credible* performance gaps).
2. Identification of best practices (in order to focus management attention on those practices that have proved to be effective as drivers of performance improvement).

A 1996 survey of firms in the United Kingdom confirmed that 85 percent used benchmarking. This high figure seems questionable, perhaps on the basis of the definition of benchmarking used. If benchmarking is seen as merely a mix of management curiosity, business tourism, and subjective analysis of business practices, the risk is that it could be considered just another management fad.[7] But if benchmarking is seen as a way to institutionalize the search for continuous improvement through identification of performance gaps and the discovery of sound business practices to be adopted, benchmarking can become a strategic management tool.

Accordingly, for benchmarking to become part of a company's management system, the company must carefully define what benchmarking is and what management expects from it. An effective definition of benchmarking as a rigorous and productive tool is as follows: "Benchmarking is a continuous, systematic process for evaluating the products, services and work processes of organizations that are recognized as representing best practices for the purpose of organizational improvement."[8]

Any benchmarking project must be planned in a rigorous manner because two basic principles seem to be in conflict. On the one hand, a context for benchmarking is needed. The primary objects of benchmarking are work processes, each of which depends on the technology applied and the peculiarities of customers' demands. The temptation is to consider each benchmarking project as unique.

On the other hand, the need for a systematic approach drives the search for reliable methodologies. The reliability of any benchmarking process largely depends on the way it is structured and the methodologies adopted in each phase. A successful benchmarking methodology must balance these two conditions. The need for context means that managers must consider customer needs and specific technologies when choosing performance indicators and analyzing the practices that correlate with best (or worst) performance. The need for a systematic approach must be designed into a benchmarking process.

**(c) Benchmarking Methodology**    The basic aspects of benchmarking methodology are usually the same. They can be presented as follows:

- *Sequential phases.* Certain obligatory phases should be completed before the next phases begin. The quality of each phase largely conditions the quality of the total process.
- *Comparability.* Benchmarks will be accepted only if they are credible, so benchmarking methodologies should ensure comparability.
- *Correlation.* The identification of best practices should go beyond an initial correlation with performance. A best practice should survive the test of stress by demonstrating significant, ongoing correlation with superior results.
- *Transferability.* Whether best practices can be adopted by companies having different contexts is a question that should be carefully evaluated.

**(d) Basic Steps**    Conceptually any benchmarking process should move through six basic steps[9]:

1. *Understand and measure critical success factors.* This step identifies critical management processes and areas.

2. *Search for appropriate companies for comparison.* A company should compare its performance only with companies whose processes and areas are worth considering.

3. *Measure process performance and analyze performance gaps.* A company must be able to quantify the potential for improvement.

4. *Determine the root causes of performance gaps.* A company should focus on those practices that have to be modified or abandoned to improve performance.

5. *Select best practices.* After a company identifies best practices, the company must modify those practices so that they are appropriate to the company's own environment.

6. *Integrate best practices into management.*

This description of the benchmarking process is sufficiently generic to apply to any project. Unfortunately, it is also too abstract to be used as a detailed methodological guide for a project.

**(e) Organizational and Informational Dimensions**  To design a practical but flexible methodology requires that two dimensions of the benchmarking process be analyzed:

1. The *organizational dimension* (i.e., how to manage the benchmarking process).
2. The *informational dimension* (i.e., which inputs the process requires and which outputs must be expected).

*(i) Organizational Dimension*  The *organizational dimension* can be reduced to the following five-phase process framework[10]:

1. *Determine what to benchmark* (i.e., identify customers for benchmarking information, identify their needs, and then define the specific object to be benchmarked).
2. *Form a benchmarking team* (i.e., identify people in the company who can take charge of the benchmarking project, assign specific roles and responsibilities, and then introduce project management tools to ensure control over the project).
3. *Identify benchmarking partners* (i.e., get information about best performers from business literature, industry reports, government sources, consultants, and analysts).
4. *Collect and analyzing benchmarking information* (i.e., find benchmarking partners, analyze their performance, and synthesize management practices for a benchmarking report). This is the core of the project.
5. *Take action* (i.e., adapt the best practices to the new context, then implement them).

*(ii) Informational Dimension*  Because benchmarking is concerned with analyzing, measuring, and reporting, a benchmarking process should be viewed as a system; that is, information in each phase starts as an input from the previous phase and (in turn) becomes an output for the next phase. Accordingly, the *informational dimension* of a

benchmarking process has to be designed before the project begins. Exhibit 14.1 summarizes the five-phase, systematic perspective.[11]

The idea of benchmarking as a learning process is embedded in the scheme illustrated in Exhibit 14.1. By moving from the recognition of unmet customer needs or from identification of a negative performance gap, a company can take advantage of benchmarking to review its key processes and to check its performance. Through comparison with external companies, performance gaps can be quantified so that better practices can be identified and change can be implemented.

One important feature of this approach is that each of the five phases of the process must be aimed at generating additional elements of knowledge. The first phase shown in Exhibit 14.1 (identify core issue) should lead to a clear diagnosis of the key performance areas and to identification of the key processes that have to be compared with those of the best companies. In this framework, learning is internal once an area of interest has been selected.

The second phase shown in Exhibit 14.1 (internal baseline data collection) is the identification of the processes to be benchmarked and a detailed analysis of their structure and their performance. The expected outputs are a clear and shared view of the processes and their performance drivers. Considering the general lack of knowledge about how processes are performed on a functional basis, the output of this phase is by itself an extremely important element of change. Looking at an organization through the lens of a shared process view generally leads to simplification and reengineering, because it provides an integrated view of how a company works and a clear understanding of how malfunctions can result from poor integrating mechanisms.

The third phase shown in Exhibit 14.1 (external data collection) exposes a company to the wide variety of new practices adopted by benchmark companies. The success of this phase is largely grounded on the quality of the analysis conducted in the two previous phases. A sound analysis of a company's processes gives a specific focus for comparisons with other companies that would otherwise be generic and, often, unproductive.

The fourth phase shown in Exhibit 14.1 (analysis) is aimed at comparing and contrasting benchmarking data. Performance gaps have to be measured and analyzed so that best practices can be identified.

The fifth phase shown in Exhibit 14.1 (change implement) is aimed at driving the company to capitalize on these opportunities for improving current performance by reengineering.

**(f) Critical Aspects of Benchmarking Methodology**    Combining these two organizational and informational dimensions for the design and management of the benchmarking process reinforces three critical aspects of the benchmarking methodology:

1. *Comparability of performance.* Comparability provides credibility for performance benchmarks and gaps identified. If external performance measures are perceived as being irrelevant because of contexts or environments that cannot be reproduced or even validly compared, they will probably be rejected, and the benchmarking project will probably fail. Comparability must therefore be explicitly analyzed, codified into procedures, and incorporated into the benchmarking methodology. Otherwise, comparability merely becomes a matter of subjective judgment or internal negotiation.

2. *Identification of best practices.* Measurements of performance gaps should lead to a search for best practices. Identification of best practices should not be left to

| | Identify Core Issue | Internal Baseline Data Collection | External Data Collection | Analysis | Change Implement |
|---|---|---|---|---|---|
| **INPUT** | Issue<br>– Unmet customer needs<br>– Performance gap<br>– Problem areas<br>– Strategic advantage | • Overview of process<br>• Current measures<br>• Potential drivers and external organizations | • Benchmark questionnaire | • Compare and contrast benchmark data | • Implementation plan<br>• Issues |
| **OUTPUT** | • Defined benchmark area<br>• Overview of key processes to be benchmarked<br>• Selected performance<br>• Identify potential drivers and external organizations | • Process flow mapping<br>• Validate drivers<br>• Benchmark target companies<br>• Short-term operational improvement<br>• Benchmark questionnaire | • External companies<br>• Process analysis, performance assessment, and measures | • Gap<br>• Process improvements or reengineering opportunities<br>• New<br>– Flows<br>– Policies<br>– Procedures<br>• Implementation plan<br>• Outstanding Issues | • Plan to close the gap<br>• Actions to close the gap<br>• Recalibrate benchmarks<br>• Additional analysis or benchmarking to address issues |

**Exhibit 14.1   Framework for Benchmarking**

informal, generic site visits or to subjective judgment. An effective benchmarking methodology should lead a benchmarking team toward those areas of practice that appear directly correlated with superior performance.

3. *Transferability of best practices.* For benchmarking to be more than an academic exercise, measures of successful adoption must exist. Despite the importance of comparability of performance, comparability alone is not enough to guarantee that practices that work well in one specific context will also work elsewhere. To reduce the risk of unsuccessful implementations of new practices, the identification of such best practices should be followed by an analysis of any structural constraints that could prevent their successful adoption.

Many false starts and failures of benchmarking projects result from the lack of reliable benchmarking data and to a poor methodological approach. For this reason, the rest of this chapter focuses on benchmarking methodology more than on the benchmarking process.

**(g) When and Where to Use Benchmarking**    Benchmarking can help initiate change when resistance to change exists for some reason, particularly when reliable standards do not exist. Benchmarking has been used for most business processes and can be particularly useful in analyzing activities and departments that have the traditional combination of inefficiencies accompanied by weak (or nonexistent) performance measurements.

The finance (accounting) area is one of the areas in which benchmarking can demonstrate its potential for improvement. Mounting demands for better performance of accounting processes (including containment of accounting costs) have put strong pressure on the finance and accounting departments of many companies.

**14.2 BENCHMARKING IN THE UNITED STATES**    It is never simple to plan and manage a benchmarking project. Apart from the difficulty of attracting benchmarking partners that may be best practitioners, the number of companies that can be managed in a single project is necessarily low—usually between three and five companies. The restricted number of participants inevitably limits the reliability of performances that emerge from analysis and comparison. It is especially hard to define the best performer from such comparisons as having the "best practices" in absolute. For these reasons, many companies prefer to start their benchmarking experience by participating in benchmarking databases and by attending related workshops.

Benchmarking databases offer companies widespread access to operating information that has been summarized and sorted to preserve the confidentiality of the participating companies. Companies must agree to provide their own confidential operating data to participate in benchmarking databases. According to the Society of Management Accountants of Canada, there are more than 60 such benchmarking database clearinghouses in the world.

**(a) Hackett Study Benchmarking Database**    The largest benchmarking database of knowledge-worker functions in the world is the Hackett Study, which was begun in 1991 by the Hackett Group, a management consulting firm.[12] The Hackett Study is sponsored by the American Institute of Certified Public Accountants and now has about 700 participating companies, including AT&T, AlliedSignal, Bank of America, Conoco, General Motors, IBM, McDonald's, Owens-Corning, Ralston Purina, Texas

Instruments, US WEST, and Westinghouse Electric. This benchmarking database provides operating data in six functional areas:

1. Finance (accounting)
2. General administrative
3. Human resources
4. Information systems
5. Procurement
6. Treasury

In finance alone, there are about 30 functions, which are sorted by three types of processes:

1. *Transactions,* whose functions include accounts payable, travel and entertainment, accounts receivable, collections, and payroll.
2. *Control and risk management,* whose functions include budgeting, forecasting, business performance reporting, tax planning, and cash management
3. *Decision support,* whose functions include business performance analysis, pricing, cost analysis, and strategic planning support.

Only companies with revenues of more than $50 million may join. Workshops and software are provided to participating companies to help with data gathering, analysis, and technical support. The time commitment involved is about two to three person days per collection location.

Companies participating in the Hackett Study receive a customized report and a database for further analysis for each of the six functional areas they choose to participate in and pay for. Each report tells the company how its functions compare to those of other companies, to what extent it employs best practices, its efficiency and effectiveness, and potential improvements.

A sample report for the finance (accounting) functional area would include a comparison of the company's operating performance, with quartile and average performances in the following general areas:

- Finance cost as a percentage of revenue.
- Full-time equivalent (FTE) employees in finance.
- Productivity per employee for various functions or processes (e.g., accounts payable, accounts receivable, and payroll).
- Number of processing locations.
- Number of systems per process.
- Budget cycle in days.
- Closing cycle in days.

This sample report for the finance functional area would also compare a company's costs to quartile and average costs in the following categories: overall, staffing, systems, and miscellaneous finance costs.

Staffing or labor costs are then separated by the following four drivers: wage rate, staff mix, organization structure (spans of control), and productivity measures (e.g., transactions per FTE). Productivity is analyzed by reference to best practices in the various functional areas. In the finance functional area, best practices would relate to processes such as accounts payable, accounts receivable, and payroll. Potential cost savings for each of these functional area processes are then calculated by comparison to first-quartile companies. Thus, participating in a benchmarking database study allows a company to observe and learn best practices from a summary of other participating companies' operations without having to repeat all of the same mistakes.

**(b) Other U.S. Benchmarking Sources**   For smaller companies, a good starting point is the Benchmarking Exchange, an Internet access service, which has over 2,000 participating companies and provides an on-line, menu-driven system for benchmarking and literature searches. The Benchmarking Exhange features an electronic exchange of information among member companies, including interest groups for various benchmarking topics. All the large accounting firms have also compiled benchmarking information that they make available to their clients.

Once operating performance gaps are identified and analyzed through the use of benchmarking databases, both large and small companies may want to identify specific companies to partner with in order to obtain detailed information about best practices. Two organizations in the United States meet such needs:

1. The American Productivity and Quality Center has created the International Benchmarking Clearinghouse, which has about 500 corporate members.
2. The Strategic Planning Institute has created the Council on Benchmarking, which has about 60 corporate members.

Both organizations provide networking groups for all major business operations, not just the support functions provided by the Hackett Group. They identify potential benchmark partners and manage benchmark exchange relationships. They also focus on process improvement and reengineering by sponsoring workshops and training sessions.

**14.3 BENCHMARKING INTERNATIONALLY**   An Italian benchmarking database project provides additional examples of how participating companies may develop cost management and other strategies for competitive advantage. This international accounting benchmark project was established in 1994 at the business school of Bocconi University in Milan, Italy. It is called the Benchmarking Clearinghouse Project (BCP) and is sponsored by the Centro Studi di Amministrazione e Direzione Aziendale (CESAD) of Università Commerciale L. Bocconi. This BCP study has grown from 30 of the largest Italian and international companies operating in Italy to more than 50 companies, including Agip Petroli, Alitalia, Digital, Fiat, Hewlett-Packard, IBM, Italtel, 3M, Pirelli, Roche, Siemens, and Telecom Italia.[13]

As with the Hackett Study in the United States, the BCP database exists for purposes of sharing confidential operating information.[14] The general goal of the BCP project is to provide participating companies a comprehensive understanding of the reasons for any performance gaps identified.

Managers of the participating companies can learn about specific management practices by the BCP companies in different industries and countries. These business managers also develop various strategies for competitive advantage. Thus, the BCP project combines features of general information sharing by the Hackett Study's benchmarking database and more specific information sharing with business partners from U.S. benchmarking groups.

**(a) BCP Cost-Management and Benchmarking Strategies**   The BCP project has always considered its participating companies customers, so it continuously involves them in choices made about benchmarking, performance measures, and analyses. This participation has proved fundamental to the credibility of BCP's operations and analyses. In fact, from various BCP benchmarking studies to date, the following strategic cost-management and benchmarking guidelines have been developed with the participation of the BCP companies:

- *Create economies of scale* by processing accounting items with high transaction volumes (i.e., centralize finance and accounting operations if possible).
- *Reduce inefficiencies* ("diseconomy of variety") by processing accounting items whose activity complexity is low (i.e., simplify finance and accounting operations, if possible).
- *Decrease non–value-added or compensating accounting activities*, such as verifying invoices or payments by using appropriate technology (e.g., electronic data processing or electronic funds transfer, when possible).
- *Develop nontraditional benchmarks* (e.g., delivery time, cycle time, quality, and customer satisfaction) for strategic cost management and evaluation of business processes.
- *Make appropriate comparisons* by benchmarking with companies having similar levels of centralization, complexity, and structure in their accounting operations (or other process of interest). Traditionally, companies have compared themselves just to "best practice" or "world class" companies.

**(b) Trends and Strategies**   Both the Hackett Study and the BCP have identified the following trends and key strategies for accounting operations:

- Transaction processing is moving back to central locations to reduce accounting costs.
- Centralized transaction processing and shared services can lead to significant reductions in accounting staff—reductions of about 50 percent.
- Business analysis activities will expand by about 50 percent and be dispersed from corporate headquarters to divisions and departments to meet the local decision-making needs of operational managers.

**(c) Cost-Management and Benchmarking Strategies**   The BCP studies have been guided by the American Productivity and Quality Center's definition of benchmarking as a process of continuously measuring and comparing an organization's business against business process leaders anywhere in the world to gain information for improving performance. Accordingly, the long-term BCP plan has emphasized the benchmarking of business processes, not organizational units, as its member firms collect such process data.

This BCP plan is consistent with the management strategy now current to gain competitive advantage by improving business processes. These processes have been defined as series of *activities* that are cross-functionally linked to achieve specific objectives.

The BCP goals have been to develop benchmarking for strategic cost management, for value generation, for purposes of identifying and spreading the use of best practices among companies.

The initial BCP benchmarking studies have analyzed performances of the participating companies' accounting departments, including functions or activities such as the general ledger, accounts payable, credit management, collection, and accounts receivable. Data partitions or clusters of the participating companies' accounting activities have been created for strategic cost management. The data have been divided by transaction *volume* (as a key determinant for assessing economy of scale) and by *activity complexity* (as a key determinant for assessing diseconomy of variety). The BCP studies have also used accounting benchmarks for value-added analysis.

Because the companies participating in these BCP studies were viewed as customers, they were involved in choosing BCP's benchmark measures and analyses. For example, the companies requested a long-term focus on business process measures. This involvement on the part of the participating companies has been fundamental to the credibility of BCP's benchmarking approach and analyses.

**14.4 BENCHMARKING FOR COST-MANAGEMENT STRATEGIES**    The following four Exhibits (14.2, 14.3, 14.4, and 14.5) summarize key benchmarking analyses from the initial Italian BCP studies and provide examples of how participating companies can use benchmarking to develop cost management strategies for finance and accounting processing.

Assume that managers of Company A (disguised for confidentiality purposes) would like to develop cost-management strategies based on the results of the BCP studies in which Company A participated. Exhibit 14.2 shows a cost-control benchmark for total costs of the finance/accounting department as a percentage of the company's total sales.

**(a) Transaction Volume and Activity Complexity**    Note that BCP data were partitioned by transaction volume and activity complexity. Transaction volume was used to investigate potential economy of scale for controlling accounting costs. However, the participating companies indicated that it was not feasible to track their exact numbers of financial transactions. They agreed instead to a surrogate, normalized measure composed of three indicators:

1. Company sales.
2. Number of customers.
3. Number of suppliers.

This measure was designated as an indicator of transaction volume for classifying the participating companies into one of the two clusters or cells on the vertical axis of Exhibit 14.2.

Activity complexity was used to investigate potential diseconomy of variety for controlling accounting costs. The participating companies contended that much of the variety or complexity of their accounting transactions and reports was a result of the number of different product lines. They agreed to a surrogate, normalized measure composed of the number of product lines multiplied by a diversity factor. This measure was designated as an indicator of activity complexity for classifying companies into one of the two clusters or cells on the horizontal axis shown in Exhibit 14.2.

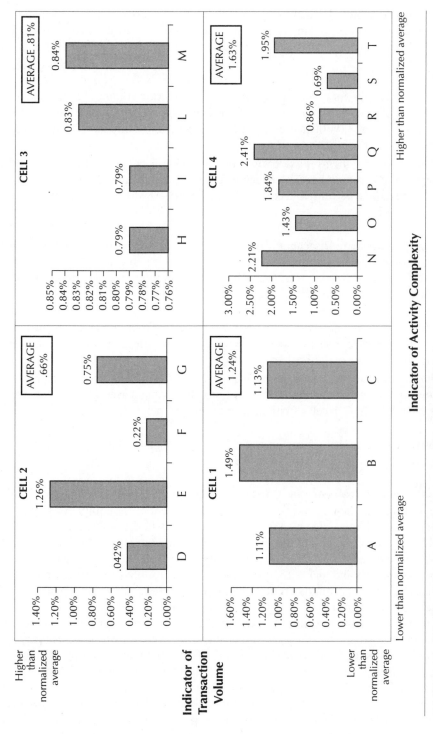

**Exhibit 14.2   Finance Department Costs as a Percentage: Total Sales**

**(b) Centralize to Achieve Economy of Scale**    Exhibit 14.2 illustrates a strategy to reduce accounting costs by centralizing operations to achieve economy of scale. The vertical axis shows the importance of creating data clusters or cells by transaction volume for economy of scale:

- *Higher costs for low-volume companies.* The transaction volume cluster shows distinctly higher costs for all the low-volume companies. These include companies *A*, *B*, and *C* in cell 1 (with an average of 1.24 percent) and companies *N* through *T* in cell 4 (with an average of 1.63 percent).
- *Lower costs for high-volume companies.* Much lower costs are shown for all the high-volume companies. These include companies *D* through *G* in cell 2 (with an average of 0.66 percent) and companies *H* through *M* with an average of 0.81 percent in cell 3.

**(c) Simplify to Eliminate Diseconomy of Variety**    Exhibit 14.2 also illustrates a second strategy for reduce accounting costs—to simplify activities to eliminate diseconomies of variety. A weaker cost control cluster by activity complexity is shown on the horizontal axis for diseconomy of variety:

- *Higher costs for high-complexity companies.* The activity complexity cluster shows distinctly higher costs for the high-complexity companies: *N* through *T* in cell 4 (with an average of 1.63 percent).
- *Lower costs for low-complexity companies.* Much lower costs are shown for all the low-complexity companies: *A*, *B*, and *C* in cell 1 (with an average of 1.24 percent) and *D* through *G* in cell 1 (with an average of 0.66 percent).

However, there were also lower costs for the other high-complexity companies: *H* through *M* in cell 3 (with an average of 0.81 percent).

**(d) Strategy to Reduce Accounting Costs**    In reviewing these results, managers in Company *A* can see that their accounting costs are 1.11 percent of the company's sales. Cell 1 includes low-volume and low-complexity companies, whose average cost is 1.24 percent. The lowest average cost (0.66 percent) was for companies in cell 2, which had high transaction volumes and low activity complexity. Companies in cell 3, which have high transaction volumes and high activity complexity, also produce a low average cost (0.81 percent).The highest accounting costs (1.63 percent) corresponded to companies in cell 4, which have low transaction volumes and high activity complexity.

If both cell 2 attributes cannot be achieved, the Exhibit 14.2 benchmarking results indicate the following strategic choice for cost control. Economy of scale (transaction volume) is a stronger factor than diseconomy of variety (activity complexity) for reducing accounting costs (i.e., 0.66 percent in cell 2 and 0.81 percent in cell 3 versus 1.24 percent in cell 1 and 1.63 percent in cell 4). If possible, therefore, Company *A*'s managers should try to centralize their accounting operations. Doing so could reduce their accounting processing costs by about 50 percent (i.e., from an average of 1.24 percent in cell 1 to 0.66 percent in cell 2).

**(e) Accounts Payable Function**    Exhibit 14.3 provides a cost control benchmark for the accounts payable function. The benchmark is the average cost per invoice processed.

This invoice processing was defined as the chain of activities that starts with receipt of a purchase order and ends with reconciliation of the accounts payable database.

Again, the two major factors—economy of scale (transaction volume) and diseconomy of variety (activity complexity)—were used to divide or cluster the data. The participating companies agreed to the following two measures:

1. *Transaction volume* was measured on the vertical axis as the number of purchase invoices and the total number of invoice lines (these two measures were normalized).

2. *Activity complexity* was measured on the horizontal axis with a normalized indicator composed of the percentage of foreign invoices out of the total number of purchase invoices and the percentage of invoices referring to services acquired (on the total number of invoices).

The vertical axis of Exhibit 14.3 illustrates the importance of creating data clusters (or cells) by transaction volume for economy of scale:

- *Higher costs for most low-volume companies.* The transaction volume shows a higher cost (in lira) for most low-volume companies: *O, A, I, L, B,* and *S* in cell 4 (with an average of 28,662).
- *Lower costs for most high-volume companies.* There was a lower lira cost for most high-volume companies: *P, F, G,* and *M* in cell 2 (with an average of 18,162).
- *Exceptions.* The low-volume companies (*H, R,* and *C*) in cell 1 had average costs (17,196) that resembled those of the high-volume companies in cell 2 (18,162). Also, the high-volume company (*Q*) in cell 3 had the highest costs of all companies (43,548).

**(f) Simplify the Accounts Payable Function**   The horizontal axis of Exhibit 14.3 shows a stronger cost control cluster by activity complexity for diseconomy of variety:

- *Higher costs for high-complexity companies.* The activity complexity shows a higher lira cost for all the high-complexity companies (*O, A, I, L, B,* and *S* in cell 4, with an average of 28,662, and Company *Q* in cell 3, with a cost of 43,548).
- *Lower costs for low-complexity companies.* There was a lower lira cost for all the low-complexity companies (*P, F, G,* and *M* in cell 2, with an average of 18,162, and *H, R,* and *C* in cell 1, with an average of 17,196).

**(g) Benchmarking for Strategic Cost Management**   In reviewing these results for the accounts payable function, Company *A*'s managers can see that Company *A* has the highest accounts payable processing costs (53,333) of any company in the benchmarking study. These high costs result can be attributed to the fact that Company *A* has a very expensive processing combination of high activity complexity and low transaction volume.

Thus, Company *A*'s managers need to simplify the company's accounts payable processing, because the less complex companies had the lowest average processing costs (i.e., 17,196 in cell 1 and 18,162 in cell 2). Once a company has simplified its accounts payable processing, however, a centralization strategy showed no significant difference in average costs (i.e., 18,162 in cell 2 versus 17,196 in cell 1).

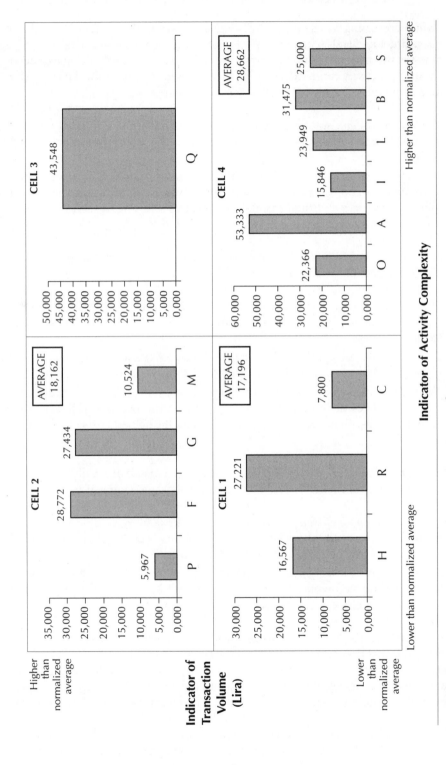

**Exhibit 14.3    Average Cost per Purchase Invoice Processed**

From the benchmark analyses shown in Exhibits 14.2 and 14.3, a cost management strategy was indicated for Company *A*. The lowest accounting costs were generally achieved through economy of scale (high transaction volumes) and economy of variety (low activity complexity). Conversely, the highest accounting costs were generally associated with diseconomy of scale (low transaction volumes) and with diseconomy of variety (high activity complexity).

Thus, a general strategy to reduce accounting costs is to develop a transaction processing structure that can achieve both economy of scale and economy of variety.

**14.5 BENCHMARKING FOR VALUE-ADDED ANALYSIS**    Because Company *A* had the highest accounts payable processing costs (53,333) of any company in this study, its managers should be interested in additional benchmarking analysis to provide guidance in reducing such costs.

**(a) Value-Added Analysis**    To identify another strategy for reducing accounting costs, value-added analysis was performed in the BCP benchmarking study. The accounts payable activity was investigated with the process reengineering strategy of eliminating non–value-added activities. A key criterion for defining a non–value-added activity was used: compensating work (i.e., verifying or correcting someone else's work).

Four major activities for accounts payable were identified and costed:

1. Filing
2. Verifying
3. Recording
4. Closing

The verifying or checking activity was determined to be the only non–value-added or compensating activity and was investigated in Exhibit 14.4.

In Exhibit 14.4, the verifying or checking activity was measured as a percentage of time spent verifying versus total time spent on invoice processing (filing, verifying, recording, and closing). Once again, the poor accounts payable processing of Company *A* can be seen in Exhibit 14.4. The highest processing costs (53,333) of Company *A* were associated with the second highest percentage (50 percent) of non–value-added checking activities. A direct association or relationship between the checking activity and the average cost per purchase invoice processed was found. Thus, a strategy for Company *A* (and other) managers to reduce their accounts payable processing costs is to decrease the non–value-added activity of checking or verifying.

**(b) Use of Electronic Data Interchange to Reduce Costs**    One way to reduce non–value-added activities may be to use newer technologies, such as electronic data interchange (EDI) and electronic funds tranfer (EFT). The BCP study investigated this strategy in following up on the accounts payable processing activities of its member companies. As Exhibit 14.5 shows, companies that use EDI extensively for their purchase invoice processing (i.e., for more than 25 percent of their invoices) reduced their costs by about 50 percent (i.e., from an average of 27,870 to an average of 14,462).

In Exhibit 14.5, companies are grouped based on whether they use EDI systems to process 25 percent or more of their annual purchase invoices. The three companies (*P*, *M*, and *G*) with more than 25 percent EDI usage had an average lira cost per purchase

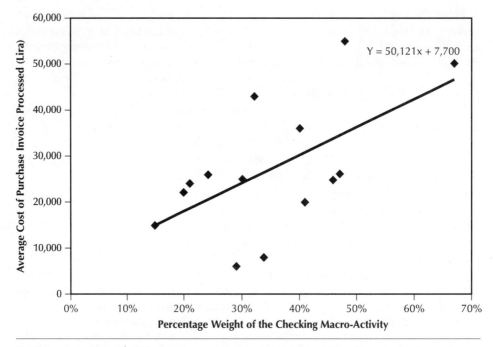

**Exhibit 14.4    Relationship Between Percentage Weight of Checking Activities and Average Cost per Invoice Processed**

invoice (14,642) that was about 50 percent lower than the average of the remaining companies (27,870).

Again, the highest accounts payable processing costs on Exhibit 14.5 (53,333) belong to Company *A*. Company *A*'s managers may decide to establish benchmarking partnerships with companies *P*, *M*, and *G* as one way to learn how EDI systems can successfully reduce the costs of processing accounts payable.

In summary, one strategy to reduce accounts payable processing costs is to use EDI accounting systems. Other BCP studies found that two other common strategies did not succeed in reducing accounting costs: outsourcing and using information systems departments to assist accounting departments.

**14.6 STRATEGIC BENCHMARKING PERSPECTIVES**    Both the Hackett and the BCP studies have been developing a business process perspective to provide more strategic benchmarking information for participating companies. Managers in these companies have indicated a need for benchmarking information on business processes, especially for reengineering purposes.

This view is consistent with the recent trend in the United States of managerial accountants providing decision support and analytical information from process reengineering and activity-based management. For example, a recent Hackett Group benchmarking study of treasury departments discussed advantages of reengineering better links between the treasury and accounting processes.[15] Cost savings of 20 to 50 percent were found to result from reengineering such linkages. Exhibit 14.6 illustrates this trend toward a business process approach.

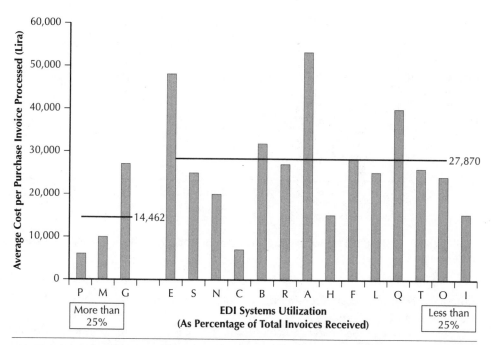

**Exhibit 14.5    Relationship Between Use of EDI Systems and Average Cost per Invoice**

**(a) Emphasis on Business Processes**    On the vertical axis in Exhibit 14.6, the traditional approach has concentrated on the *organizational unit* or *department* as the primary measurement focus. The new process approach emphasizes *activities* and *processes* instead. On the horizontal axis, the traditional approach has concentrated on the organizational unit's mission as the preservation of functional technology. This traditional focus of managerial accounting has not been oriented toward supporting the process of value generation.[16] The new process approach emphasizes value generation, either by increasing customer utility or by reducing costs, in providing services and products to both internal and external customers.

**(b) Using Technology to Free Up Accounting Resources**    A related managerial accounting strategy has been to process the same level of transactions with fewer accounting resources. This strategy has been achieved through newer technology, such as desktop computers, networked computers, EDI, and EFT. These freed-up accounting resources have then been used to generate customer value by providing more decision-making and problem-solving information to internal customers (i.e., business managers).[17]

**14.7 MODEL FOR BENCHMARKING**    Exhibit 14.7 summarizes the ongoing BCP studies by presenting a model for benchmarking accounting processes.[18] The model starts with data clusters, or cells, which represent the cost-management strategies for econ-

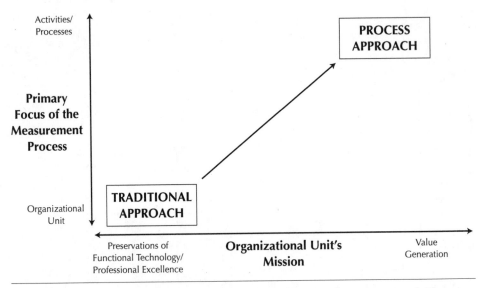

**Exhibit 14.6    Toward Performance Improvement of Accounting Processes: A Change in Perspective**

omy of scale (transaction volume) and economy of variety (activity complexity), as shown in Exhibits 14.2 and 14.3.

The next phase in the model shown in Exhibit 14.7 is a multidimensional performance evaluation with measures of cost, time (delivery and cycle), and quality. This focus is consistent with process reengineering and business process measures of performance, such as cost, quality, service, and speed.

Finally, this process approach is expanded with structural choices, accounting practices, and enablers, as shown at the bottom of Exhibit 14.7. Examples of structural choices that affect resources employed because of activity complexity (as analyzed in Exhibits 14.2 and 14.3) are the number of product lines and foreign operations. Exhibit 14.4 analyzes an organizational activity (verifying) and categorizes it as a non–value-added activity. However, a structural choice for a value-added activity was using EDI in accounting information systems (as analyzed in Exhibit 14.5). An organizational profile example was the number of customers and suppliers used in the transaction volume analysis (see Exhibit 14.2).

Qualitative and quantitative accounting practices are included in the traditional and process approaches of Exhibit 14.6. Enablers are factors external to the specific process that make the process more or less efficient. An example is the importance of nonaccounting personnel who provide data necessary for the closing of the general ledger by the specified cutoff time. Another example of an enabler is a well-managed customer database file, which provides correct information for invoice management. Correct information from the database reduces or eliminates discrepancies between customer orders and invoices.

**14.8 BENCHMARKING METHODOLOGY IN ACTION**    Because benchmarking presents more methodological issues than organizational issues, this section analyzes the key methodological steps for achieving effective results. The starting point is obtaining accurate knowledge of the process that will be compared.

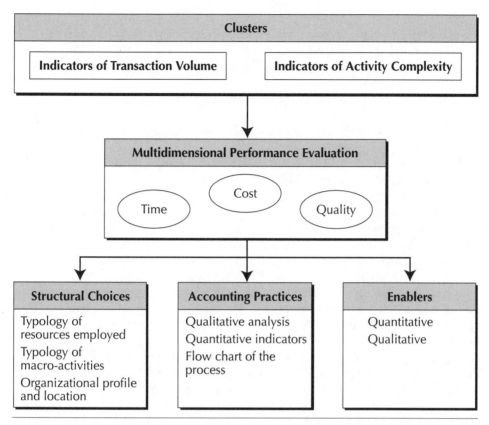

**Exhibit 14.7   Model for Benchmarking the Accounting Process**

In benchmarking activities, companies search for a process model that links process activities to organizational resources. The questions of interest are:

- How do process activities absorb resources from organizational units?
- Which resources are needed, and how much of each?
- How can organizational units control the acquisition and use of resources used in processes.[19]

Because benchmarking projects seek better solutions from better process models being used by companies that have better performance, companies must first define their own processes and their own management model. The BCP experiences suggest that several key methodological steps (as explained in the sections that follow) are needed to achieve best practices.

**(a) Define Process Boundaries**   The first step is to define boundaries of the process. Each company can define its processes from different perspectives. The differences may be driven by technologies used, strategies, or organizational structures.

For example, consider the accounts receivable (A/R) process. The complete A/R process is a sequential flow of activities that starts with credit approval for a new customer (or a credit check for a new order from an existing customer) and ends with receipt of payments from the client (or the writeoff of the receivable).

But it is not usual to find a broad perspective. Typically, the "accounting" A/R process is confined to the collection phase or, in a transactional view of the process, from the order through the invoice management phase. A definition of the boundaries of the process is needed in order to make clear comparisons between benchmarking companies.

A process approach may create the following benchmarking opportunities:

- An opportunity to identify cross-functional best practices that connect activities and integrate various processes.
- An opportunity for a value-based analysis that covers the cost, time, and quality dimensions of various processes.

A broad definition of the A/R process facilitates these two improvement opportunities because it involves many business units and departments (e.g., management information systems, finance, and distribution). These units and departments may also identify cost, time, and quality goals for process performance measurement.

**(b) Segment the Process**    The second step is segmenting the process. There are two basic alternatives, segmenting by *phases* or by *macroactivities*. Segmenting a process into phases emphasizes the process flow and helps identify the connections between activities that are most critical for efficient processes. Segmenting a process by macroactivities aggregates tasks that are homogeneous for technology applications, independent of their sequence. This helps identify areas for improvement in cost, time, and quality.

For example, the entire A/R process can be segmented into five phases:

1. Credit check and approval.
2. Order/invoice management.
3. Discrepancy management.
4. Credit management and collection.
5. Cash management.

Process segments are not single activities depicted through a flow-charting methodology. There are two reasons for not using an analytical mapping approach in the search for a common view of the process to benchmark. First, companies perform processes in very different ways, so it is difficult to share a process map among companies. Second, a model articulated by segments and related macroactivities is adequate for purposes of gathering data.

**(c) Define the Performance Vector**    The third step is the definition of the performance vector or composite performance measure. This step presents three critical choices to be made:

1. The value-related process performance measure (the primary indicator).
2. The comparability of the primary indicator among different companies.
3. The structure for a multilevel performance measurement system.

*(i) Value-Related Process Performance Measure (the Primary Indicator)*    The first choice concerns the value-related process performance measure (the primary indicator). The

foundation for effectiveness of a performance indicator is the activation of behaviors that are congruent with the generation of value for a client. Because processes represent a logical bridge between the value-generation strategy and the daily operations of a firm, performance measures should be process based.[20] This implies an expansion of the traditional one-dimensional perspective (typically cost) toward a multidimensional perspective (i.e., to include cycle time and quality as well as cost).

In the case of the A/R process, performance may be measured in two main ways. The first alternative emphasizes the cost/productivity dimension. Typical measures include:

- Average cost per order or invoice processed.
- Number of A/R accounts per FTE.
- Number of invoices issued per FTE.
- Total cost of the process as a percentage of total sales.

The second alternative stresses the financial flows connected to the A/R process. Typical measures include:

- Days sales outstanding (DSO).
- Aging of past-due accounts.
- Percentage of current accounts receivable within payment terms.

Time-based performance measures may also be useful (e.g., total cycle time from shipping to invoice or from the receipt of an order to invoice).

The multiple metric of process performance implies that strategies for value generation and the process mission should be clearly defined before any performance measures are chosen. Only the value-generating criterion should drive both the identification of useful performance indicators for each single dimension (cost, time, or quality) and the composition of a well-balanced, multidimensional vector (one that integrates cost, time, and quality) for target setting and benchmarking.

Each performance indicator should be given differentiated importance, according to its impact on other business processes and on the firm's value. For example, the A/R process mainly affects value generation through cash inflows and the amount of capital invested in receivables. Any reduction in DSO increases working capital turnover and cash flows. According to this measurement strategy, both gap analysis and best practices identification in A/R management process should focus on DSO reduction.

*(ii) Comparability of the Primary Indicator among Different Companies*    The second critical choice refers to the *comparability of the primary indicator among different companies*. In the A/R process example, the DSO was chosen as the primary performance indicator, but it is affected by some comparability limitations. Because DSO reflects the terms of payment stated by the company, a higher DSO does not mean per se a lower effectiveness in the management of A/R process. It may simply reflect a policy of longer payment terms. To make meaningful comparisons between different companies, such comparability issues must be considered. Thus, in benchmarking the A/R process, the distance between the *actual DSO* and the *theoretical DSO* should be measured. This distance may be calculated in days or in percentage (with reference to theoretical DSO). The percentage measure has been designated the DSO performance ratio (DPR). The BCP 1996 study found that the DPR measure ranged from 20 percent to 105 percent.

This evidence indicated potential value improvement by increasing the effectiveness of the A/R process (e.g., by changes in the way human resources are organized and information technology is used).

However, the peculiarities of the process environment (or context) must be considered for purposes of comparability. External elements may affect the performance and comparability of the process, including:

- The type of customers (e.g., direct versus through wholesalers; new vs. old customers; private vs. public customers).
- The method of payments (e.g., EFT vs. mail; foreign vs. local currency).
- The geographical sales mix (e.g., local vs. regional or international).

External elements such as these, which derive from different business characteristics, may be defined as *structural performance drivers* (i.e., factors that are external to the process but that influence the resources and the types of activities carried out to satisfy a client's demands).

Different levels of performance can be affected not only by different management practices but also by different contextual or environmental conditions. Thus, the identification of structural performance drivers that influence the context in which a process is managed is a basic step in the process of grouping participating companies for purposes of comparing their performance. For comparable benchmarking to occur, companies must be identified and clustered according to these structural performance drivers. Each process has its own structural performance drivers, which are usually process specific rather than industry specific.

*(iii) Structure of a Multilevel Performance Measurement System*    The third critical choice concerns how to structure a multilevel performance measurement system. Given a set of performance indicators for the A/R process, DPR should be correlated with other performance measures. Thus, for example, higher productivity in invoice management may lead to lower DPR, and more resources allocated to the process may increase DSO performance.

This correlation analysis should determine which type of performance improvements will advance the goal of reducing DPR, the primary objective of the process. The BCP data for the A/R process show a strong negative correlation between number of invoices issued per FTE and DPR; in other words, less bureaucracy and more information technology usage are correlated with the effectiveness of the process. The data also show a strong positive correlation between the total cost of the process as a percentage of total turnover and DPR; in other words, more resources dedicated to the process do not ensure better performance.

In summary, the key to better performance is the practice, not resources. Performance indicators can be correlated to the whole process or to single segments. The goal is to construct a multilevel performance vector that can facilitate the search for, and the identification of, best practices (see Exhibit 14.8).

**(d) Analyze Best Practices**    The fourth step is a detailed analysis of the practices adopted in the management of the critical areas of the process. If benchmarking is not limited to gap measurement, it can help managers identify the drivers and practices that underlie the best performances. The starting point is a clear definition of a *practice*.

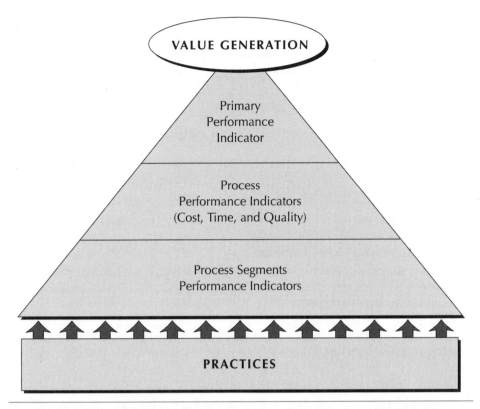

**Exhibit 14.8    Connections between Value, Process Performances, and Practices**

A practice can be defined as an organizational solution structured either to manage single activities or to connect different activities. An example of a practice to manage single activities is how a company manages data entry for client orders, which could range from manual data entries when customers call to direct data entry by salesmen over modems. For an example of a practice to connect different activities, consider the documents produced in the sales order-fulfillment process (e.g., order acceptances, picking lists, packing lists, shipping notes, and invoices), which may be integrated by a software application or manually produced by different units in the company.

Much more difficult is the task of defining what is a *best* practice. As value generation is the generally accepted criteria for the overall performance evaluation of a firm, a best practice can be defined as one that contributes to value generation or that prevents the destruction of value. As each process is connected to (and influenced by) other processes, aid or obstacles to the effective management of a process can come both from inside and from outside the boundaries of the process.

As an example of an external factor, a negative impact on the complexity of the A/R process may come from independently managed customer files. This factor, which is external to the process, can be defined as an *enabler*. In this example concerning customer files, file managers (which are typically located in the sales department) are external to the A/R managers (which are mainly located in the accounting department).

The location of enablers is critical. Modifying the way things are done (or the way activities are connected) is more difficult when the levers of control reside outside the boundaries of a process. For this reason, practices need to be differentiated from *en-*

*ablers.* Practices reside inside a process, whereas enablers are external factors that ease or disturb the management of a process or the connection between different processes.

In the A/R process example, activities can now be performed to successfully conduct the best-practice analysis. First, it is necessary to run a correlation analysis between primary performance indicators, secondary indicators, and *process trim.* (Process trim is the system of choices regarding the structuring of human resources and technology.) An understanding of the roots of superior performance demands not only the identification of best practices and enablers but also the analysis of the *process trim* in the specific process to explain:

- The quality and quantity (mix) of resources employed (including human resources, information systems, automation, and outsourced activities).
- The resources absorbed by each of the macroactivities or phases into which the process is articulated. This analysis should highlight the resource allocation strategies pursued by best practitioners.
- The organizational profile of the process (i.e., which activities are located inside and outside the finance department) to identify key roles, responsibilities, and organizational connections.

The BCP 1996 study found that discrepancies are the major cause of delays in payment by customers. The study identified four main causes of discrepancies:

1. Pricing errors (28 percent of the total discrepancies).
2. Returned or refused merchandise (23 percent of the total discrepancies).
3. Adjustments, allowances, and rebates (16 percent of the total discrepancies).
4. Advertising and promotional claims (9 percent of the total discrepancies).

This analysis of best practices suggests that distance—or a lack of communication and coordination—between sales departments and accounting departments accounts for a large part of the discrepancies. Specifically, the analysis reveals a strong contrast between the flexibility adopted in sales negotiations (which is driven by demands from customers and by the complexity of the markets served) and the rigidity of the accounting transaction process (which is driven by financial procedures and by regulations).

Once the area (or process segment) correlated with performance has been identified, the existing level of integration among activities can be analyzed. Discrepancy management in the BCP example shows that some practices have a clear connection with different levels of efficiency and of effectiveness (see Exhibit 14.9).

**(e) Redesign Management Practices**    The management practices reported in Exhibit 14.9 may have to be redesigned as follows to improve discrepancy management:

- *Elimination of root causes* (i.e., a sound capacity to identify the causes of each discrepancy, to track the development of discrepancies over time, and then to eliminate the root causes). In this example, the root cause was the lack of information flows among the different units that contributed to customer deliveries (i.e., informational integration).

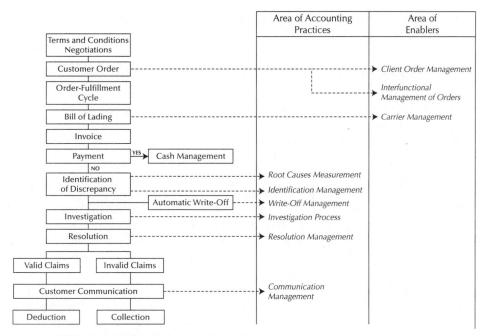

*Source:* CESAD, Università L. Bocconi, Milano, 1996.

**Exhibit 14.9    Identifying Best Practices: Discrepancy Management.** *Source:* CESAD, Universita L. Bocconi, Milan, 1996.

- *Reduction of the distance between operating units and the number of exchange points inside the process.* In this example, there was little integration between the different professional expertises required to manage the process (i.e., commercial expertise, administrative expertise, financial expertise, and logistic expertise). Agreement on customer complaint procedures can be achieved only if the different operating units share the same goals and definitions. Such cooperation can accelerate the cycle time of the identification, investigation, and resolution processes.

- *Reducing the distance from customers.* Cooperation is facilitated if every expertise, or functional competence, can reduce the distance from customers. If cooperation between different departments is needed, the way that performance indicators for the process are defined can help achieve goal congruence among departments. This managerial integration (i.e., when all the departments share the same DSO goal) is facilitated by understanding customer needs. For discrepancy management, managerial integration calls for a definition of a credit policy that considers customers' needs in providing direction to the resolution of customer complaints.

Practices are solutions that boost informational, cognitive, and managerial integration. Benchmarking can help in the identification of best practices. Consider the practices connected with reducing the distance of operating units from customers. Some BCP companies have adopted the following best practices, which focus on making accounting people aware of discrepancies and disputes as soon as possible:

- A contact person named on the invoice.
- Formal requests for debit memos or remittance information from customers to support all claims.
- Formal requests of proof of deliveries to carriers and a formal link of payment to the service level assured by carriers.
- Information systems for understanding and documenting customers' accounts payable practices.
- Information systems for understanding and documenting customers' criteria for preferred vendor payment ranking.

Common to all these solutions is the effort to improve the quality of the connections with the customer or between the different units involved in the A/R process.

For identifying best practices in management processes, an effective benchmarking methodology should clearly identify and compare the different accounting practices, but it should also highlight the functionality required of accounting processes by nonaccounting processes and practices (*enablers*).

Superior performance relies both on the effectiveness of specific practices and enablers and on the quality of the organizational context (process trim). Building a system of qualitative and quantitative indicators that depicts the organizational context has proved to be a sound basis for useful comparisons. If based on a shared model of analysis, benchmarking processes can offer participating companies a unique opportunity to learn the reasons underlying performance gaps and best practices that are worth adopting.

**14.9 SUMMARY**   This chapter presents an approach to benchmarking based on Exhibit 14.1. Developing accounting benchmarks for process management and strategic cost management is a major long-term goal for various benchmarking projects, including the Hackett and the BCP study.

Key strategic findings to manage processes better and to reduce accounting costs were determined as follows:

1. Centralize for economy of scale by processing items with high transaction volumes.
2. Simplify for economy of variety by processing items with low activity complexity.
3. Decrease non–value-added or compensating activities by using technology, including EDI, to reduce checking activities

Both the Hackett and BCP studies are also developing nontraditional benchmarks for the evaluation of business processes, as summarized in Exhibit s 14.6, 14.7, and 14.8. These benchmarks are responsive to the needs of participating companies, which need benchmarks to assess their competitive strategies that attempt to improve business processes to differentiate their products or services and gain cost control advantages. Process benchmarks include nontraditional performance evaluation measures (i.e., cycle time, delivery time, quality, and customer satisfaction) as the data become available from the participating companies.

Such measures can be used to help identify best practices for discrepancy management in the accounts receivable process, as shown in Exhibit 14.9. Benchmarks for economy of scale, economy of variety, and business processes are already providing valuable information for process management and for strategic cost management in the BCP studies. These strategic uses of accounting benchmarks should help make the information that managerial accountants provide to managers more relevant.

The BCP classification matrix shown in Exhibits 14.2 and 14.3 works well as a clustering device for assessing the comparability of accounting processes, because its two axes (volume and complexity) reflect structural differences in business characteristics. These volume and complexity characteristics can be defined as structural performance drivers or factors that are external to the accounting process but that significantly influence the resources and types of activities needed to complete the accounting processing.

For example, in the accounts payable process, the number of invoices and number of lines per invoices can be used to define the volume driver. The number of service (as opposed to raw material and product) purchases and the percentage of invoices without a formal purchase order can be used to define the complexity of accounts payable processing. Thus, member companies need to know these volume and complexity characteristics before making detailed benchmarking comparisons (such as those shown in Exhibits 14.4 and 14.5).

More sophisticated benchmarking comparisons also imply new perspectives and major challenges for performance analysis and management control, as shown in Exhibits 14.6 through 14.9. A fundamental management control guideline is changing the perspective from organizational units (e.g., the accounting department) to organizational processes (e.g., accounts receivable, accounts payable, and other business processes). Accordingly, performance measurement needs to expand from a one-dimensional, cost-based focus to a multidimensional view that includes nonfinancial measures such as cycle time and quality of services.

In summary, this chapter provides guidance on using benchmarking database analyses for at least four methodological issues critical to the success of benchmarking projects:

- How to define performance measures.
- How to achieve comparability of performances.
- How to identify best practices.
- How to evaluate the transferability of best practices.

Managers need to carefully consider these methodological issues before embarking on benchmarking in an effort to gain competitive advantage through business process management and strategic cost management.

## NOTES

1. P. M. Senge, *The Fifth Discipline* (New York: Doubleday, 1990).

2. Japanese companies are generally given credit for inventing the concept of benchmarking through their practice of sending managers to visit companies to get a deep understanding of sound business practices. See P. Ahmed and M. Rafiq, "Integrated Benchmarking: A Holistic Examination of Select Techniques for Benchmarking Analysis," *Benchmarking for Quality Management and Technology* 5 (1998): 225. Xerox's experience of benchmarking with L. L. Bean is well documented in Robert Camp, *Benchmarking: The Search for Industry Best Practices That Lead to Superior Performance* (Milwaukee, WI: ASQC Quality Press, 1989), 73–79.

3. A. Cox and I. Thompson, "On the Appropriateness of Benchmarking," *Journal of General Management* 23 1998): 1–20.

4. Ahmed and Rafiq, op. cit., p. 225.

5. R. Camp, *Benchmarking: The Search for Industry Best Practices that Lead to Superior Performance* (Milwaukee, WI: ASQC Quality Press, 1989), 29.

6. Westinghouse Productivity and Quality Center, *Proceedings of Benchmarking Week 92* (Houston, TX: APQC, 1992).

7. R. Boxwell, *Benchmarking for Competitive Advantage* (New York: McGraw Hill, 1994).

8. M. Spendolini, *The Benchmarking Book (*New York: Amacom, 1992), 9.

9. G. Watson, *The Benchmarking Workbook: Adapting Best Practices for Performance Improvement* (Cambridge, MA: Productivity Press, 1992), 11–12.

10. M. Spendolini, op. cit., pp. 46–49.

11. K. Leibfreid and C. J. McNair, *Benchmarking: A Tool for Continuous Improvement* (New York: HarperBusiness, 1992), 38–40.

12. The Hackett Group, *Developing World-Class Organizations Through Benchmarking* (New York: American Institute of CPAs, 1996).

13. During five years of activity, the BCP project benchmarked the finance department and the performances and practices of the following accounting processes:

- General ledger.
- Accounts payable management process.
- Accounts receivable management process (including collection and cash management).
- Budgeting and forecasting process.
- Internal auditing.

A typical benchmarking project is developed through four main phases lasting about six months:

1. *A first workshop* (generally, half a day with participating companies), which explains the business processes, the performance measures, and the critical practices. The output of this phase is the structure of the questionnaire.

2. The data collection and analysis phase, which helps companies fill out the questionnaire (which was previously sent by mail).

3. *A second workshop*, which presents a first version of the final report and discusses findings.

4. *A third (optional) workshop*, which examines specific practices correlated with best performances.

All the projects end with the delivery of a final report to each company. The results helped develop a questionnaire that has been sent to the major companies operating in Italy (1,000 companies). This survey research (called 1.000 imprese) is now in the data collection phase concerning critical practices.

14. S. Beretta, A. Dossi, H. Grove, and T. Obremski, "Benchmarking: Beyond Comparing Performances to Identifying Best Practices," *International Journal of Strategic Cost Management* (Autumn 1998): 35–49.

15. J. Rosengard, "The Missing Link in Reengineering," *Financial Executive* (March/April 1995): 15–20.

16. S. Beretta and A. Dossi, "La Misurazione Delle Prestazioni Delle Unità Erogatrici Di Servizi Generali: Vincoli Strategici e Implicazioni Progettuali," *Sviluppo e Organizzazione* (Maggio–Giugno 1994): 1–15.

17. S. Coburn, H. Grove, and C. Fukami, "Benchmarking With ABCM," *Management Accounting* (January 1995): 56–60.

18. S. Beretta, A. Dossi, and H. Grove, "Methodological Strategies for Benchmarking Accounting Processes," *Benchmarking for Quality Management and Technology* (1998): 165–183.

19. T. Greenwood and J. Reeve, "Process Cost Management," *Journal of Cost Management* (Winter 1994): 1–10.

20. P. Lorino, *Comptes et Recits de la Performance* (Paris: Les Editions d'Organisations, 1995).

# CHAPTER 15

# BEST PRACTICES IN PERFORMANCE MEASUREMENT

## Angela Demery
### American Productivity & Quality Center

**15.1 PERFORMANCE MEASUREMENT BEST PRACTICES**  Performance measurement systems and the processes that regulate and control them are used as decision-making models and as tools to affect employee behavior. Yet much of what we now know and practice about performance measurement is based on opinions and anecdotal evidence rather than on clear facts and demonstrated practices.

Organizations today face new challenges in influencing employees and creating incentives for them. Performance measurement systems require modern mechanisms for modifying employee behavior to achieve organizational goals.

Leading organizations have recognized the need to improve their performance measurement systems, other companywide systems, and improvement mechanisms in order to maintain a competitive advantage. No longer can managers expect that the traditional methodologies for measuring performance will enable organizational growth. Managers have also learned that empirical forms of testing performance measurement systems can be costly and time-consuming, particularly when they have no end objective in mind. Thus, a carefully orchestrated and carefully planned performance measurement approach is what gives organizations today the inspiration to carry out such efforts, because they promise value-added, measurable results.

This chapter discusses performance measurement best practices in the context of the latest available research. The purpose of the chapter is to help companies plan benchmarking programs and ensure that proper channels and linkages are in place within the organization.

**15.2 BEST-PRACTICES ADAPTATION**  Organizations are beginning to use *best practices adaptation,* a new strategy to encourage growth and avoid expensive testing periods. The notions of *best practices* and *benchmarking* go hand in hand and are highly correlated. Benchmarking is essentially the tool used to promote and facilitate the sharing of best practices. Simply put, best practices are proven techniques and approaches that are "leading edge" with respect to a particular organizational process or function.

Companies elect to benchmark the best practices of other leading firms for many different reasons. The better planned (and more successful) a company's attempts at benchmarking are, the more successful the company's subsequent adaptation of best practices is likely to be. Companies must recognize the need for a formal, structured approach to benchmarking in order to uncover—and later implement—best practices.

**(a) Why Companies Benchmark**   One of the leading reasons for benchmarking best practices is to develop and manage human resources, of which measuring performance is a critical component. In most instances, benchmarking saves time, money, and effort, in pursuit of approaches and successes that other companies have already experienced. Exhibit 15.1 offers a chart that lists the top reasons companies give for why they benchmark best practices.

An effective performance measurement or cost-management system can be attained through continuous improvement and refinement processes. Benchmarking and best-practices adaptation also make it possible. The key to benchmarking other organizations for best practices is simple—networking. As its name implies, networking is the practice of meeting and communicating with professionals who work within a specific process and function, then maintaining an ongoing relationship that includes sharing practices. Networking proves particularly helpful when building a relationship with a company known for its best practices in a certain area (e.g., performance measurement, activity-based management, or quality). Networking is also used as a forum for discussing lessons learned or practices to avoid. Using this approach, companies can determine certain practices or approaches that should be avoided in implementing a particular system or solution. The value proposition for networking is that it eliminates

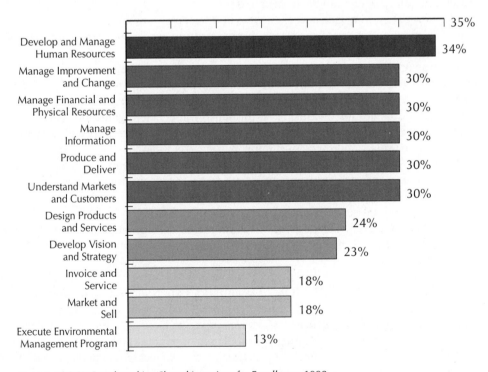

*Source:* APQC's *Benchmarking Shared Learnings for Excellence,* 1998.

**Exhibit 15.1   Why Companies Benchmark for Best Practices**

"rework" of an approach that has already been tested. Networking typically occurs in small focus groups that meet three to four times per year. These groups decide upon specific topics that will be discussed for each session, then use those topics to guide conversation and dialogue around best practices. The company representatives are then given the task of transferring the best practice approaches and learnings internally throughout their respective organizations.

Firms benchmark other leaders in specific process or functional areas in pursuit of emerging practices. Companies have begun to realize that duplicating proven, successful approaches that other companies are using is much more efficient than wasting valuable time and resources piloting new strategies. In this way, companies can duplicate successful approaches without having to experience the pitfalls or relearn the lessons from a pilot project to implement a particular practice or methodology.

In essence, a successful adaptation of best practices (and avoiding major pitfalls) allows companies to streamline their processes and drive down costs. Companies that have participated in best practice benchmarking activities report breakthrough improvements by directly and indirectly improving cost control, quality, cycle time, customer satisfaction, and profits. Equally important to note is that these improvement initiatives require intense concentration, dedication, and focus to be effective and successful.

**(b) Choosing What to Benchmark**    Regardless of the effort expended, a company can never implement all the best practices uncovered. Firms must prioritize their objectives and develop criteria for what will be benchmarked and what will be implemented in terms of learnings and leading practices. Benchmarking does not provide apples-to-apples comparisons because companies differ in terms of their size, composition, and business needs. What works in one firm may not work or transfer equitably given the conditions, competitive issues, and environment of another firm. Therefore, managers must make decisions about which components or processes are likely, given their organizational culture, to be successful when they are adapted from the company being benchmarked. Likewise, they must consider lessons learned, or obstacles, in the same fashion. One company's failure or opportunity may not necessarily translate into a problem for a firm considering the same (or a similar) practice. This is what makes best practices adaptation an art, not a science.

Another important consideration is that best practices can be found in an organization of any size in any industry. Best practices identified for the development and implementation of performance measurement systems represent a continuum of performance measurement systems. They range from "underdevelopment" to truly stellar and leading practices. Similarly, companies having best-practices performance measurement programs include such industries as automotive, chemical, financial, nonprofit, transportation, and many others, and the companies range in size from as few as 20 employees to hundreds of thousands.

The principles supporting best-practices adaptation suggest that organizations gain and sustain a competitive advantage by duplicating proven approaches with regard to measurement from various organizations and by using a combination of all of the collected practices.

**15.3 SURVEY RESULTS**    In 1995, the American Productivity & Quality Center (APQC), a nonprofit organization located in Houston, Texas, began to research best practices in performance measurement. As part of this important research, APQC surveyed 30 best practice organizations from all over the world over a span of four years about their performance measurement strategies and approaches.

The research found that although these leaders differ significantly in terms of their size, industry, revenues, and objectives, their approaches are similar. Leading organizations achieve phenomenal levels of success and savings by adopting best practices.

Companies that exhibit best practices in performance measurement have the following characteristics and strengths with respect to their systems:

- Organizational alignment and commitment.
- Leadership involvement.
- Priority and focus.
- Communication and education.
- Feedback.
- Support technology.
- Links to incentives and compensation.
- Links to quality and improvement.
- Links to strategy.
- Self-directed work teams.
- Internal business assessments (based on criteria of the Malcolm Baldrige National Quality Award).

The rest of this chapter discusses each of these key attributes of best-practices performance measurement systems.

**15.4 ORGANIZATIONAL ALIGNMENT AND COMMITMENT**    Today's top managers recognize the importance of developing and implementing well-aligned performance measurement systems that foster participation, commitment, and buy-in from employees at all levels of the organization. Ongoing research in this area shows that performance measures, when properly aligned to vision and corporate objectives, greatly affect performance, which (in turn) has a great bearing on strategic direction. Simply put, one cannot improve what one cannot measure.

Most of the performance measurement systems that exist today were initiated and designed by financial professionals—an interesting fact, given the shift that has occurred toward *nonfinancial* and *operational* performance measurement. Now management is forced to include virtually all employees, especially senior leaders and managers, in measurement and cost-management exercises to ensure that those who have the most comprehensive information about organizational vision and objectives are involved. Many best-practices organizations report that the participation and commitment of key people in the organization contributes to a well-balanced performance measurement system whose goals and measures complement the organization's strategy.

These leading organizations have also articulated the compelling need to align performance measures with corporate goals and strategy. The first—and perhaps most important—step is to ensure the commitment of senior management and all other employees to promote excellence in institutionalizing and implementing effective performance measurement systems.

Another important approach to achieve alignment of measures with corporate goals and strategy is to form quality circles. Quality circles are small groups of individuals embedded within various locations throughout an organization to achieve organizational objectives locally. These groups examine organizational goals and mission with respect to performance measurement and cost management data to ensure that they are properly aligned. By far, this approach is the best in terms of ensuring that goals and measures complement one another. Alignment is absolutely critical to a successful performance measurement effort.

**15.5 LEADERSHIP INVOLVEMENT**   Best-practices companies exhibit a strong commitment by top management to their performance measurement systems. Most leading organizations have performance measurement systems that have been in use for many years (the ages of the systems ranged from 3 years to 84 years in the survey), so these systems have become an integral part of the daily operation and culture of the company. Leadership involvement requires that corporate goals be "cascaded down" from top management to bring focus to a "vital few" set of measures that drive organizational excellence.

Leading executives at best-practices companies use a variety of methods to show their commitment to the performance measurement system. Many become actively involved in annual training sessions about the performance measurement system. This promotes and showcases to all employees the commitment of top management to the measurement principles used, and it also demonstrates the importance and value of the system itself. Top management is responsible for helping to design the performance measurement system in best-practices companies and also for helping to maintain and improve the system.

To further promote leadership involvement, best-practices companies use frequent, collaborative meetings (e.g., planning boards, executive quality councils, and strategy boards) as forums to analyze the results generated by measurement system, to make decisions based on the data, and to implement actions designed to improve performance. These groups are particularly effective when they are small, because smaller groups (e.g., 10 or fewer people) are better equipped to focus on key organizational objectives related to both strategy and measurement. Data analyzed at this level is a compilation or "rollup" of all the key metrics in the system. These groups decide which measurement areas are important and they modify the high-level measures when required by current business conditions. In short, measures must change as business conditions change—and, most importantly, as customer requirements and expectations change. To ensure high visibility for the measurement system, members of these groups are assigned as "champions" for each of the company's top key measures. These champions are held accountable for ensuring that the measures are appropriate indexes of business performance.

**15.6 PRIORITIES AND FOCUS**   In addition to the practice of creating strategically aligned measures at lower levels of the company, best-practices organizations show other similarities. The measurement system becomes most user-friendly, and the measures themselves become most "actionable," when they are designed, modified, and analyzed at the "local" or subunit level. This local option to develop performance measures allows employees to have buy-in to the measurement approach; it also acts as a mechanism to ensure that employees understand their performance measures and how their work affects the measures. When employees are actively engaged in the development and modification of measures, they become increasingly aware of—and provide greater support for—those measures and guidelines.

**(a) Annual Goal Setting**     Another common best-practices approach to defining measures and measurement systems is annual development of a core set of corporate strategic goals and objectives that create broad, top-level measures (the vital few measures). Historically, one problem that organizations have had with performance measurement and cost management is that they have tried to concentrate on too many measures and objectives at once. Having a vital few performance measures allows companies to concentrate only on the most important business objectives, then to take appropriate action. Top management should assume the task of establishing these vital few measures and communicating them to the organization at large. These broad top measures should cascade down the organization at every level, and in some cases to each entity within that level.

Each lower-level operating unit or entity creates and institutes more focused measures (though all relating to each of the broader measures) that will track its specific contributions to overall strategic objectives.

**(b) Optimum Number of Measures**     Best-practices companies typically have four to eight strategic areas of focus. Each of these areas has long-term goals and objectives. These goals and objectives are translated into a family of measures that will track progress toward the desired outcomes. The number of top-level measures used by best-practices organizations ranges from 9 to more than 40. As a general rule, 8 to 12 key objectives or measures provide optimal results and ample focus. These measures are considered the vital few that senior management needs to make decisions and implement actions for improvement.

Although areas or "families" of measures vary among best-practices companies, depending on their strategic posture or thrust, the goals are always set by executives or senior managers based on the company's overall strategic plan. These strategic goals then become the basis for local measures as the system cascades down through the organization.

For this emerging practice to succeed, corporate entities must establish guidelines for local business units and groups to follow during the creation of measures. A critical element in this process is the identification by senior management of the vital few set of organizational measures during an annual strategic plan. Senior management must come to a consensus on a standard set of key measures that are applicable for all levels and functions within the firm. This process allows for a quick compilation of measures in decentralized firms and ensures that management at all levels works to promote behaviors consistent with the desired strategic direction.

**(c) Linking Metrics Throughout the Organization**     The rollup of data is made possible by using local metrics that can be "inserted" into the numbers of the next-higher-level unit, and so on up the organizational pyramid (a process called rolling up the data). This implies an overall corporate system that allows creativity at the local level yet maintains control at the level of the global, strategically aligned measurement system.

Best practices in performance measurement mean that companies must have clearly defined processes for developing *balanced scorecards* (see Chapter 12) within each related business group. Even if an organization has no local option for measurement (i.e., within departments and business units), there must be a clear linkage established between the company's key measures and those used at lower levels throughout the organization.

**(d) Staying Focused on the "Vital Few" Measures**   As best-practices companies develop performance measurement systems and cascade them down throughout their organization, each level (including the top level) has a tendency to "overmeasure." In many of the cases that were studied by APQC, too many items were being measured, and some of the measurements were too complicated. Naturally, if a measure is too hard to calculate, it has a high probability of being equally difficult to communicate and act on. Also, when measures are hard to understand—or too numerous to comprehend—they intimidate those who are held accountable for meeting the measures.

When overmeasurement occurs, the number of measures can be reduced over time to a manageable few at each level by using two common processes:

1. *Alignment test.* The first method used to reduce or focus measures is to check whether a particular measure is truly aligned with a specific strategic objective. Measures should be challenged at regularly scheduled departmental or "communication" meetings. If analysis and discussion show that a particular measure is not aligned, it should be modified or dropped from the system.
2. *Periodic review.* Another way to reduce the number of metrics to a vital few at each level is to review the results for a particular measure over a period of time. Even when a measure is aligned with a higher-level strategic objective, if analysis of the results fails to say anything or to cause action for improvement, the measure should be dropped.

Actions for improvement are the results of decisions made based on an analysis of the measures. The analyses, decisions, and action planning used to improve a performance measurement system are typically performed within an organization's quality process. The quality function is usually equipped to use standard methodologies for continuous improvement activities and is ultimately held responsible for modifying and refining an organization's systems and capabilities.

**15.7 COMMUNICATION AND EDUCATION**   Performance measurement is so enmeshed in the business practices of best-practices companies that it is difficult to describe communication and education separately from other organizational information exchanges. A measurement system is "culturally manifest" by many formal and informal means. Leading practitioners cite communication and education as being the foremost enablers of any structured measurement or cost-management approach. Company culture plays a large role in defining and selecting the communication tactics that work best for a given organization to articulate the objectives of the measurement system. However, it is possible to identify some common best practices regarding methods used to communicate to and educate employees about performance measurement.

Best practices for communicating the goals and tactics of a performance measurement system include electronic mail, visual aids, face-to-face meetings, education and training opportunities, and databases—to name just a few. Best-practices organizations use these same communication methods to promote acceptance of the measurement approach. How a company applies and implements these various communication vehicles, however, separates best-practices companies from others.

For a measurement system to be effective and to work at optimal levels, the communication channels used must be strong enough to be embraced and understood by employees at all levels and functions of the organization. Note, also, that communication occurs more frequently and more consistently in best-practices companies than in other companies. Once again, mandating that performance measurement be easy to understand promotes clarity and success in communication.

**15.8 FEEDBACK**    Interviews with leading companies reveal another important enabler of a successful performance measurement system that is closely related to communication and education: feedback. Feedback to the performance measurement system may occur formally or informally, but it must allow input by all employees; then, that input must be considered and acted on in a timely way.

Exhibit 15.2 shows the percentages of best-practices organizations (out of 30 surveyed) that use a formal, standard process for providing feedback to their corporate performance measurement systems. Getting feedback from the internal users of a performance measurement system is a crucial part of continuously improving the system. Improving the input of data, its analysis, and the communication of results naturally improves the efficiency and effectiveness of the overall business improvement effort.

Most best-practices companies studied use a formal rather than an informal feedback process for their performance measurement systems. These formal feedback processes range from having an open-door program, in which employees can offer feedback to their immediate supervisors, to including questions about the performance measurement system in annual employee surveys. Informal feedback processes fit into routine departmental or area communication meetings.

Accountability for compiling and communicating feedback about the performance

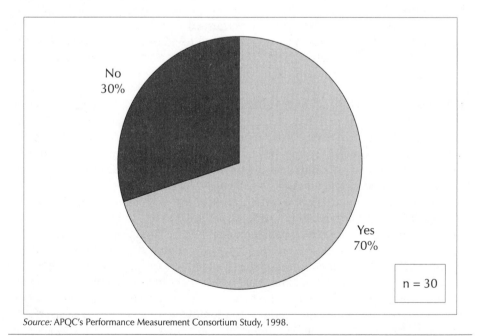

*Source:* APQC's Performance Measurement Consortium Study, 1998.

**Exhbit 15.2    Organizations Employing a Formal Feedback Process for Performance Measurement**

measurement system falls on managers. The manager in a performance measurement system plays the key role of soliciting feedback from employees and ensuring that important ideas for system improvement are communicated to decision makers who can then implement improvements. In addition to this systematic internal review and self-assessment, benchmarking other best-practices companies also enables companies to improve their performance measurement systems.

**15.9 SUPPORT TECHNOLOGY** In this age of fast-paced innovations in technology, performance measurement systems require and receive a great deal of support.

Some companies considered to have best practices in performance measurement have developed homegrown internal systems and databases for storing performance measurement information. Some of these companies have even purchased off-the-shelf systems from outside vendors and modified them to fit their needs. Still others report that their systems evolved over time as technology improved. In all cases, best-practices companies recognize the need to identify systems and technical capabilities that match the specific needs of their respective businesses and customers.

The common element (by consensus among best-practices organizations) is that a system must be simple and easy to use, especially at the initial levels of data gathering and analysis. Early, complicated systems were abandoned by several organizations because they either would not allow fast input and reporting or were too complicated to understand. Best-practices organizations caution in favor of careful benchmarking of systems before purchase and implementation to ensure that the system chosen is compatible with the organization's goals, culture, and structure.

Most organizations connect the electronic measurement and analysis system to an intranet or electronic mail system to increase access and improve communication of performance results. To protect data integrity, all limit access to databases by password protection or other means. In addition, most organizations plan to continuously improve their electronic systems as technology improves.

**15.10 LINKS TO INCENTIVES AND COMPENSATION** Though alignment, leadership, communication, technology, and other enablers are all important components of any successful performance measurement system, none of them can support the system alone. It is the integration of all these factors, along with many others, that leads to a top-notch performance measurement system. Traditional performance measurement and cost-management systems that contained all these important components simply failed to incorporate and integrate them.

Measuring results and tying rewards directly to goals naturally enhance performance. Most best-practices companies tie management compensation to bottom-line financial results. Many have some type of variable compensation, and some offer gainsharing for nonmanagement employees.

Typically, these comprehensive plans base rewards on results from the *entire family* of performance measures at each level of the organization, not simply on the financial aspects. Many best-practices companies insist that financial goals be met before nonfinancial elements are evaluated—in this way, the gainsharing plan pays for itself. Nevertheless, the inclusion of both financial and nonfinancial measures on a balanced scorecard (or family-of-measures table) is critical to achieving the organization's goals. It tells employees that although financial goals are important, there are other things that employees can do—for example, improve customer satisfaction, innovation, and creativity—to improve the organization.

Most leading organizations reward middle and top management with a variable or incentive bonus in addition to base salary and benefits. Traditionally in the United States, these incentives are based on corporate as well as divisional (or business-unit) financial results, and they are paid out annually. Many best-practices organizations also include the entire family of strategically aligned performance measurement results in their management incentive plan.

Some organizations reward a portion of the management incentive for financial results only. The remaining portions reflect personal goals and objectives (agreed on with the manager's immediate supervisor) based on the nonfinancial measures in that manager's immediate sphere of influence.

An additional incentive that best-practices organizations offer is some form of gain-sharing plan for nonmanagement employees. This type of plan encourages all employees, regardless of their rank or position, to become actively involved and engaged in the measurement program.

**15.11 LINKS TO QUALITY AND IMPROVEMENT** Not surprisingly, most best-practices organizations that have adopted performance measurement systems have linked them to other organizational quality and improvement systems. A performance measurement system is thus a numerical scorecard that organizations use to make decisions and plan actions to manage and improve business performance.

In many cases, a performance measurement system blossoms out of an organization's initial efforts to implement a quality or process improvement process. Best-practices organizations typically report direct linkages between their internal quality initiatives and their performance measurement process. Two of the most commonly cited links in best-practices organizations are:

1. To internal self-assessment processes (using criteria such as the Malcolm Baldrige National Quality Award or President's Award or local or state quality awards).
2. To activity-based management processes.

Today, effective performance measurement systems have strong links to all the continuous improvement functions of an organization. Ultimately, the convergence and integration of key functions and processes ensure a dynamic, successful measurement environment that promotes the attainment of strategic goals. These innovative, emerging measurement systems are designed so that senior management can actually measure and ensure that the systems effectively carry out corporate strategy.

The ultimate purpose of the performance measurement system, then, is the compilation and analysis of strategically aligned data from which decision makers and teams can make decisions and implement actions to improve business performance and achieve strategic objectives. When linked this way to a viable quality system, a performance measurement system moves from being simply an indicator of performance to being an enabler of improvement.

Best-practices companies consider the application of information from a performance measurement system, not the system itself, to be the competitive advantage. A performance measurement system complements and provides data to the organization's internal quality initiative and is used as a tool for the success of other quality-related initiatives, such as ISO 9000 certification, activity-based management, and applying for state or national quality awards.

**15.12 LINKS TO STRATEGY**  APQC's research indicates that measurement systems that have been in place for several years quickly become woven into the organizational fabric. They become aligned vertically and horizontally through annual planning and regular, systematic reviews. Each of the partner companies views its performance measurement system as an extension of both its culture and strategic direction. A performance measurement system is the institutionalized scorecard that depicts how well—and whether—the organization is achieving its long-term objectives. The driver of this *alignment* with the strategic goals is top management. The vehicle for ensuring continual alignment is the annual strategic planning process.

**(a) Changes in Strategy**  The annual review of corporate strategies in best-practices companies includes an assessment of the performance measurement system. Any changes in strategic direction will usually dictate a corresponding change in the measurement system. Changes in strategy should cascade down through the entire organization (as well as through the performance measurement system) until the new direction and the progress toward achieving the new goals are measured from the bottom of the organization to the top. Each level of management assumes responsibility for the cascading down of measures.

**(b) Tying Measures to Strategy and Goals**  At each level of an organization, new strategic goals and objectives should be received from the level immediately above it, then used to shape the development of goals and objectives. Measures are developed only after the goals and objectives of each level are revised, thus creating alignment with the overall strategic direction.

Key best practices in developing and implementing performance measures are as follows:

- The performance measurement system is typically a component of a larger initiative within the organization (e.g., total quality management, internal business assessments, or self-directed work teams). These larger initiatives take on many different forms, but all of them usually require training, part of which covers the performance measurement system.
- Every level of management is responsible and accountable for the performance measures used in its individual sphere of influence. Routine departmental or staff meetings stress the importance of the data generated and how the information is used in decision making and in implementing corrective action. The *system itself* is also analyzed in these meetings to ensure that the "right things are being measured the right way."

One best practice in this area is for managers and executives to mandate that the performance measurement system satisfy the goals of the company's business operating system. Each year, leading organizations use an executive group to review performance measurement goals and objectives and to define key measures for the upcoming year. The company uses policy-deployment methodologies to help business units and divisions align their own measurement initiatives with the company's vision, mission, strategy, goals, and tactics. Business-unit and divisional leaders communicate each year's strategic measurement objectives to their employees and instruct them to define measurement goals linked to these major objectives to ensure alignment.

Leaders in performance measurement practices link the annual strategic planning process to changes that occur in a performance measurement program to ensure that measures remain consistent with the organization's vision, mission, strategy, and tactics. They do this because a performance measurement system is essentially a series of interrelated and interdependent segments that cannot exist alone. Actions or changes in any one element or measure affect each of the other elements.

Executives in best-practices companies understand that if they choose to change some component of business strategy, actions need to be taken to improve processes so that they will meet the goals of the strategy. As a result, new measures also need to be determined to assess the effectiveness of the strategy, and new methods need to be established for the reporting and analysis of the new process.

These are the principles that drive a company's ability to effectively and appropriately align its measurement system with its organizational strategy. Regular communication and informal, yet frequent, training are the chief enablers that allow leading organizations to maintain this alignment.

Another trait of best-practices companies is that they use weekly and monthly management review meetings to facilitate the alignment of their corporate measurement system with organizational goals. These meetings encourage sharing and monitoring of key measure results to ensure that the system is appropriately aligned with the company's vision, mission, strategy, and tactics. Also, key performance measures and goals are dictated by and flow from the corporate levels of any organizational entity.

**15.13 SELF-DIRECTED WORK TEAMS**    One particularly innovative method observed in best-practices organizations with respect to implementing a successful performance measurement structure is the use of *self-directed work teams*. Many best-practices companies rely heavily on the involvement of self-directed work teams to facilitate overall company measurement, benchmarking, and quality improvement initiatives.

Self-directed work teams are simply cross-functional groups of employees at all levels of an organization that are charged with ensuring optimal results of the measurement system. These groups meet quite frequently (e.g., weekly or monthly) to discuss quality and performance issues are reflected to the groups in which they operate. They also talk about ways to improve or modify the existing system in an effort to increase its success and effectiveness, and they assume responsibility for recommending changes to the measurement system.

**15.14 INTERNAL BUSINESS ASSESSMENTS**    Another best practice in performance measurement is the process of conducting *internal business assessment*. Internal business assessments are an innovation by companies that have participated in the Malcolm Baldrige National Quality Award program. The Baldrige Award has occurred annually since 1989 and is the culmination of a process whereby leading organizations assess their internal processes against a standardized set of criteria.

In recent years, companies have began to use the comprehensive set of criteria (or some derivative of this criteria) to assess themselves on an annual basis. The results of this assessment help managers identify areas of strengths and weaknesses with respect to both their performance measurement systems and other formal avenues and processes for quality measurement.

**15.15 PERFORMANCE MEASUREMENT BEST PRACTICES IN THE FUTURE**    The evolutionary nature of performance measurement suggests that both the performance measures and the reporting methods used today may change. Success does not occur overnight: The successful implementation of best practices in performance measurement (and in other organizational processes) requires careful, upfront planning and consideration.

Organizations that have become successful in performance measurement and cost management have done so through a series of trial-and-error processes. They know that there are several pitfalls to avoid when attempting to implement best practices for any process or function. The pitfalls include:

- *Ignoring the immediate need for benchmarking and the adoption of best practices.* Too often, companies put off benchmarking and the adoption of best practices because everyone is busy; people think there is simply not enough time or resources available for comparative analyses.

- *"Killing the messenger."* This phenomenon occurs after initial external benchmarking data is obtained and a gap analysis is done by comparing the benchmarking company with best-practices firms. Those who present the information (e.g., the quality department, the planning department, or the executive team) are persecuted and blamed for results when they are not as good as expected. In these situations, the value of benchmarking and best practices is diminished. Employees throughout the organization begin to question the relevance and significance of the process.

- *Limiting reciprocity in external information exchanges.* The idea of disclosing highly sensitive or proprietary information can be difficult for managers to accept. Yet the whole concept of benchmarking and best practices deals with exchanging information and practices to provide a win-win situation for all parties involved. Benchmarking best practices cannot be effective or successful when one or more parties fail to share information in the same quantities or to the same extent as the other parties.

- *Lack of focus for adopting best practices.* The number-one mistake in implementing performance measurement best practices is lack of focus. In early benchmarking efforts, managers believed that adopting best practices meant duplicating anything and everything that the leading organizations did. But this assumption is usually incorrect. Managers and executives must have a clear understanding of the critical business objectives for the firm (again, between 8 and 12), and they should be able to communicate these objectives effectively throughout the organization. Managers should limit their focus and attention to those organizational issues that are of most significance to the business's prosperity. Measuring and tracking insignificant processes is a waste of both time and resources; it does not provide value in the full scheme of benchmarking activities.

Another obstacle to best-practices benchmarking follows the pitfalls just described. A common blunder that leading organizations make is to expect quick results in little or no time. In many situations, companies need results, and they need them immediately to sustain their relative positioning in today's competitive marketplace. However, best-practices implementation requires careful orchestration, focus, and determination. There are no quick and easy shortcuts to best-practices implementation, but once these initiatives are started and deployed, they become a part of the organizational culture and are easier to comply with.

Looking toward the new millennium, organizations of the future will have to calibrate their existing performance measurement systems against other industry and non-industry leaders to maintain a competitive edge and a successful, prosperous enterprise. The firm characteristics observed in best-practices organizations suggest that those groups actively using benchmarking as a tool to investigate leading and best practices, and subsequently implementing these approaches, are ones that will be successful in measuring costs, performance, and other attributes, for years to come. As a result, these firms will experience the reverberating effects and rewards of both financial and organizational growth that occur naturally as best-practices processes mature over time.

# CHAPTER 16

# MANAGING RESEARCH AND DEVELOPMENT PORTFOLIO RISK

**Carey C. Curtis**
**Southern Connecticut State University**

**16.1 INTRODUCTION**   Most financial managers approach investing in research and development (R&D) as a capital budgeting issue. Investments in projects that may result in the next generation of products or services are one of a number of competing ways a company might deploy its limited capital resources. The problem this chapter addresses is that investments in R&D are like other investment alternatives in some ways—but not in others. On the one hand, R&D investments involve estimating cash flows in and out (and the resulting returns) in much the same way as, say, with investments in operating assets. On the other hand, the purpose of R&D investments may be quite different, and the risk and reward parameters may be considerably wider.

Investments in operating assets generally relate to existing product lines, and they are usually designed to generate operating efficiencies. They enhance financial operations mainly through cost savings, though they may also boost sales by expanding capacity. In general, however, most investments in operating assets contemplate generating rates of return at or below market rates. Hence, *hurdle rates* used to assess them tend to fall below 20 percent and take into account only the cost of money, expectations about inflation, and a modest desired return above the sum of those two.

*Product extensions* (e.g., the endless stream of variations from the original Sony Walkman) aim to increase the overall lifetime revenue streams from existing product lines. Similarly, cost-saving process improvements aim to boost the profitability of existing product lines. Thus, these projects are analogous to investments in operating assets, and the risk/return expectations are also similar. But investments in commercializing new technologies are riskier, because there is always the possibility that new products will not prove successful. Consequently, investments in new technologies must be evaluated using different parameters. It is not enough that they generate returns that merely exceed the cost of money, inflation, and normal returns. Rather, they must generate *above-market* returns to compensate for the greater risk. Because they take longer to come to fruition, the chance that they may never do so—and, thus, that the investment will be lost—exceeds the corresponding risks for product extensions or process-improvement projects.

Despite their relative riskiness, projects of this kind are necessary to a company's survival. A continuous stream of new products that generate above-market returns fuels sales growth. Companies that do not grow stagnate and, ultimately, go out of business. R&D is therefore a process of balancing two needs:

1. To support and enhance the profitability of *existing* product lines through timely extensions and process improvements.
2. To replace existing product lines with succeeding generations of new products based on new technologies and at the right time.

Managing R&D is a portfolio management activity, but one that is decidedly different from the process of managing investments in operating assets. To assess an investment in an operating asset, managers generally consider one or more alternatives. They must first determine whether to invest, and then they must determine which alternative to choose (assuming there is more than one).

Most managerial accounting and corporate finance texts do not treat capital budgeting for any kind of project as a portfolio issue. Many, if not most, ignore R&D projects altogether, basing their capital budgeting examples exclusively on operating asset investments.[1] The range of required returns for projects, whether for purposes of discounting the cash flows to their present value or for arriving at a cutoff point based on *internal rate of return* (IRR)—known as the hurdle rate—tends to be in the below-market range (say, 12–16 percent) typical of investments in operating assets. The collective wisdom is *that net present value* (NPV) of cash flows is the best criterion for determining whether to fund a project or to array projects from most to least desirable.

For R&D projects, this approach would be appropriate for product-extension and process-improvement projects, which are analogous to an operating asset investment. For higher risk/return projects, however, using NPV may lead to dysfunctional decisions. Even though the IRRs of these projects may be considerably above the 12 to16 percent range, because of the often lengthy delay (relative to the initial outlay required) before they generate positive cash flows, their NPVs may be considerably lower than those of larger product-extension projects that have lower IRRs but generate positive cash flows earlier. The tendency is therefore to bias the company's R&D portfolio in favor of product-extension or process-improvement projects that have lower risk but also lower returns.

Arguments have emerged in the R&D literature in recent years that different selection criteria are needed for R&D projects because of their different risk/reward trade-offs. Several experts advocate using an option pricing approach for the highest-risk, highest-potential reward projects.[2] The rest of this chapter presents results taken from an R&D management practices database collected since 1993. Because of the focus on R&D as a portfolio of projects that have a wide range of risk and reward parameters, the chapter thus considers alternative approaches to traditional capital budgeting approaches.

**16.2 VALUE OF THE RESEARCH AND DEVELOPMENT PIPELINE**  The major downside risk of using inappropriate criteria to make investment decisions about R&D is that companies spend vast amounts of money each year on the R&D process. The risk is not simply that they may be suboptimizing that huge investment but also that they may be maximizing ill-chosen R&D expenditures. Part of the problem is the way U.S. *generally accepted accounting principles* (GAAP) treats R&D spending.

**(a) Current Accounting Requires Immediate Write-off**  In Financial Accounting Standards (FAS) Statement No. 2, "Accounting for R&D," the Financial Accounting Standards Board (FASB) acknowledges that requiring companies to expense virtually all their spending on R&D is arbitrary.[3] Clearly, some part of R&D spending provides a future benefit, which would ordinarily mean that the expenditures should be capitalized. The difficulty the FASB had was finding an appropriate way to value the R&D pipeline. Not much controversy arose when FAS Statement No. 2 appeared in 1974, nor have serious efforts to overturn it materialized since.

Nonetheless, each year's spending becomes "water over the dam." In effect, there is no mechanism available to keep track of the spending that is taking place currently, along with past R&D spending, to evaluate their combined potential future benefits. Clearly, not all spending results in either a present or a future benefit. By the same token, however, at least some of that spending does provide a present or future benefit; otherwise, companies would not continue investing significant sums in R&D.

**(b) Value of the Research and Development Pipeline Is Lost**  Exhibit 16.1 shows the spending patterns of companies that took part in the first six years of the database on R&D management practices. The 1994 gap resulted from an oversight—not having asked the question, "What percent of sales does your company spend on R&D?," that year. The high point was in 1993, followed by lower spending during the recession years, and a rebound in the later years as the economy recovered.

Each year's survey includes R&D directors from 600 to 900 companies. These companies represent approximately 80 percent of civilian R&D spending in the United States. About 20 percent of these R&D directors respond in a given year to an extensive questionnaire about their R&D practices and other company data, including financial data. The companies are mostly Fortune 500, publicly held, and domestically owned companies, but each year's survey also includes smaller, privately held, and foreign-owned companies. All are either market- or technology-driven manufacturers from nine major industries:

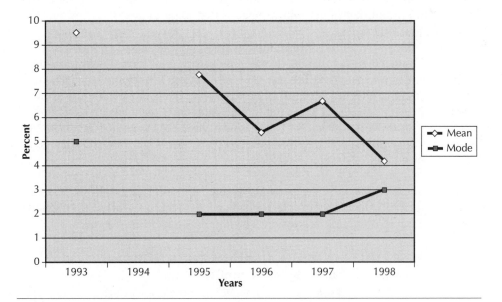

**Exhibit 16.1    R&D Spending as a Percent of Sales: 1993–1998**

| | Industry Category | | |
|---|---|---|---|
| Year | Biotechnology | Pharmaceutical | Consumer Products |
| 1993 | Higher spending | Higher spending | |
| 1994 | N/A—information not collected this year | | |
| 1995 | Higher spending | | |
| 1996 | Higher spending | | |
| 1997 | | | Lower spending |
| 1998 | Higher spending | | |

**Exhibit 16.2  Industry Difference on Spending on R&D Relative to the Average: 1993–1998**

1. Personal care
2. Consumer products
3. Chemical
4. Energy
5. Computer hardware
6. Telecommunications
7. Pharmaceuticals
8. Biotechnology
9. Defense

Note that the mean (average) for the sample is consistently higher than the mode (the most commonly reported value), which suggests that some companies spend substantially more than others.

Exhibit 16.2 bears this out. Biotechnology and pharmaceutical companies spend significantly more than companies in other industries. Not surprisingly, consumer products companies spend less because they rely far less heavily on expensive technologies as a source of a steady supply of new products. Even allowing for this skewing caused by industry differences (and even though companies spent less on R&D during the recession of the early 1990s), R&D investments have been consistently substantial. For example, given an average sales volume of $3.3 billion in 1998, average R&D spending was $139 million.

**(c) Value of the Research and Development Pipeline**  Exhibit 16.3 graphs the results of attempts to quantify the impact of R&D spending for the first six years of the database. The analytical tool is multiple regression. The four dependent variables are:

1. Earnings before interest and taxes (EBIT) as a percentage of sales.
2. Sales from new products as a percentage of total sales.
3. Compounded annual sales growth (CAGR) over the prior five years.
4. A growth effectiveness index (GEI).

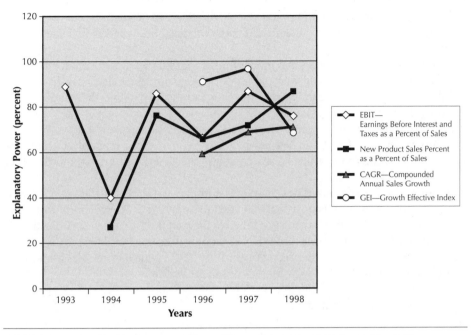

**Exhibit 16.3    Explanatory Power: Financial Performance Models, 1993–1998**

The first two variables have been part of the annual survey from the beginning; the latter two, since 1996.

The GEI is calculated as follows:

(New Product Sales Percentage) (EBIT + R&D Budget as a Percentage of Sales + CAGR)/R&D Budget as a Percentage of Sales

*Example*: $(33\%) \times (20\% + 10\% + 10\%) \div 10\% = 1.32$

An interpretation of this result is as follows: An index greater than 1 indicates that R&D spending is creating value for the company.

The GEI is a variation on the effectiveness index developed by McGrath and Romer: and critiqued by Ellis[4] for not taking into account compounded annual sales growth—and therefore undervaluing the impact of R&D.

Multiple performance measures for R&D are necessary for two reasons. First, EBIT reflects not only current spending but also the realized effects of past spending, which are also reflected in the new product sales percentage. Second, neither captures the future benefits of current spending. They also fail to capture the contribution of R&D to the firm's growth. Both CAGR and the GEI are measures designed to determine this wealth-creation function of R&D investments.

Exhibit 16.3 shows the explanatory power (+/– 5 percent) of the multiple regression models of the four financial performance measures (all years for EBIT and new product sales percentage, but beginning in 1996 for CAGR and GEI)—in other words, the extent to which the R&D management practices in the models explain the variation in the different financial performance measures. Explanatory power greater than 25 percent is considered high, and above 75 percent extremely high. What Exhibit 16.3 suggests is that a company's R&D practices contribute greatly to its financial well-being. Indeed, the impact is much greater than many financial and general managers might think.

Exhibit 16.4 shows averages and modes for the four financial performance measures themselves. Once again, the means and modes differ, sometimes significantly, suggesting skewing caused by some industry or another. Exhibit 16.5 details those industry differences. Specifically, biotechnology and pharmaceutical companies skew the new product sales percentage upward, whereas chemical companies skew it downward. Energy companies skew EBIT and new product sales percent in one year only. Defense and telecommunications companies cause a change in the CAGR pattern to mode less than the mean in 1997.

Exhibit 16.4 further quantifies the positive impact of R&D on the financial well-being of companies. R&D consistently contributes upward of 30 percent of total sales from past spending on R&D (usually defined as the past three to five years), healthy levels of compounded annual sales growth over roughly the same time horizon (five years), and some portion of sustained current operating performance from sales growth and process innovations.

Even though a significant number of companies fall short on the GEI (i.e., the mode is at or below 1), a substantial number of them are achieving consistently high levels on the GEI. Thus, in terms of both the explanatory power of financial performance measures and the average values of those financial measures, R&D spending clearly contributes a great deal to the financial well-being of the firm, again more than general and financial managers realize.

As these results suggest, financial managers need to reconsider the way they perceive the risks and rewards of R&D. The irony is that perhaps 90 percent of the business education for most financial managers is spent teaching tools for managing products after they are launched, whereas only 10 percent or less is devoted to the processes by which products are created and launched.

**16.3 RISK AND RESEARCH AND DEVELOPMENT PROJECTS**  As has already been discussed, financial management treats potential R&D investments like any other capital project. Generally, therefore, decisions are based strictly on NPV, as the managerial accounting and corporate finance textbooks prescribe.

The appropriateness of that approach hinges on the issue of whether the risk and reward parameters are the same for R&D projects as they are for other projects. What financial managers may not realize is that R&D managers use IRR as much as—and possibly even more than—they use NPV. Because the two measures are mathematically similar, and because they are usually highly correlated in the database, the suggestion is that R&D executives use both criteria, perhaps on the same, perhaps on different projects.

**(a) Research on the Use of Net Present Value and Internal Rate of Return**  Besides modeling financial performance outcomes, the research has involved building a *balanced scorecard* for R&D by modeling *speed-to-market* and *customer-satisfaction* outcomes as well as financial performance measures in an effort to determine which R&D management practices contribute best to those outcomes.[5] Among the practices appearing in multiple regression models beginning in 1994 are using NPV and IRR as selection criteria for R&D projects.

Exhibit 16.6 shows that NPV has had mixed impacts (negative with financial performance but positive with speed to market), whereas IRR has (for the most part) had

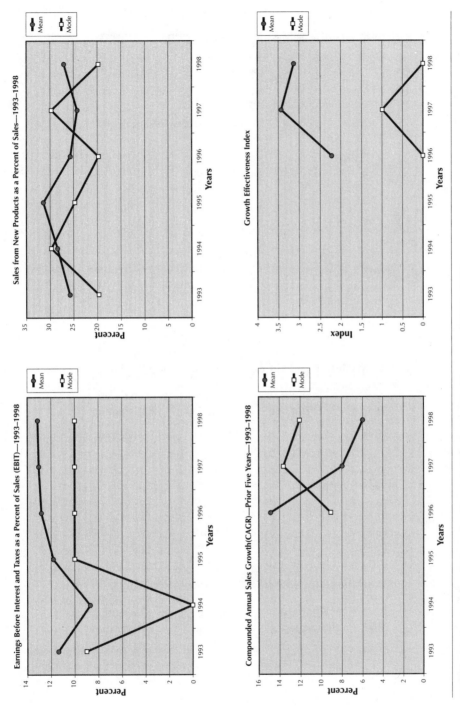

**Exhibit 16.4  Average Values for Financial Performance Measures: 1993–1998**

| Year | Biotechnology | Pharmaceutical | Chemical | Energy | Defense | Telecom-munications |
|------|---------------|----------------|----------|--------|---------|---------------------|
| 1993 | Higher new sales % | Higher new sales % | Lower new sales % | | | |
| 1994 | Higher new sales % | | Lower new sales % | | | |
| 1995 | | | | Higher EBIT and new sales % | | |
| 1996 | Higher new sales % | | Lower new sales % | | | |
| 1997 | | | | | Lower CAGR | Higher CAGR |
| 1998 | Higher new sales % | | Lower new sales % | | | |

**Exhibit 16.5   Industry Differences on Financial Performance Outcomes: 1993–1998**

### NPV Relationships with R&D Outcomes—1994–1998

| Year | Financial Performance | Speed to Market | Customer Satisfaction |
|------|-----------------------|-----------------|-----------------------|
| 1994 | | Positive | Negative |
| 1995 | | | |
| 1996 | | | |
| 1997 | Negative | | |
| 1998 | | Positive | |

### IRR Relationships with R&D Outcomes—1994–1998

| Year | Financial Performance | Speed to Market | Customer Satisfaction |
|------|-----------------------|-----------------|-----------------------|
| 1994 | Positive | | |
| 1995 | | | |
| 1996 | Positive | Positive | |
| 1997 | | | |
| 1998 | Negative | | |

**Exhibit 16.6   NPV and IRR Relationships with R&D Outcomes: 1994–1998**

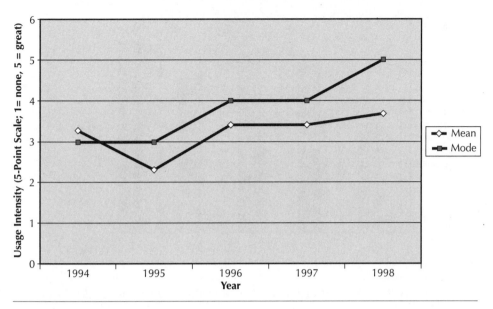

**Exhibit 16.7    Intensity of IRR Usage: 1994–1998**

a positive impact. These results flatly contradict the conventional wisdom that NPV is always a better criterion to use for capital budgeting projects.

Exhibits 16.7, 16.8, and 16.9 use a five-point scale (where 1 = not at all and 5 = extensively) to show the trends in NPV and IRR usage intensity for 1994–1998, both separately (16.7 for NPV and 16.8 for IRR) and compared with each other (16.9). Exhibit 16.10 shows industry differences in the usage of NPV and IRR.

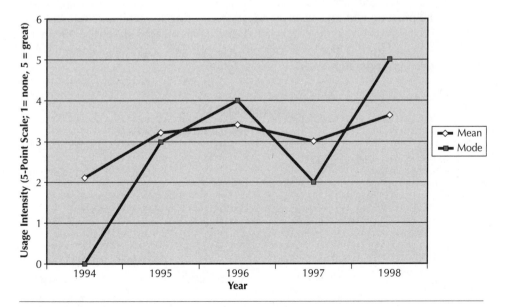

**Exhibit 16.8    Intensity of NPV Usage: 1994–1998**

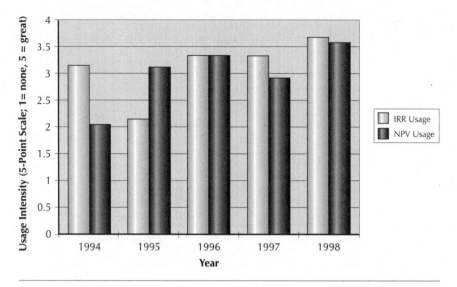

**Exhibit 16.9    Comparative Average IRR and NPV Usage for Project Selection: 1994–1998**

Although IRR still has a slight advantage over NPV at the end of the five-year period displayed in Exhibit 16.9, NPV usage is clearly increasing, and the gap closing. This trend is probably attributable to a climate of increasing scrutiny from general management over the R&D process. R&D managers increasingly need to justify their project selections in terms that both general and financial managers will find comfortable and familiar (i.e., NPV).

**(b) Crossover Effect of Using Net Present Value versus Internal Rate of Return**   But why does this research produce information inconsistent with the accepted wisdom that NPV is the predominant and superior selection criterion for capital investment projects? The conclusion is that the criterion to use depends on the risk/reward parameters for the particular project. For lower-risk projects, NPV gives a rational answer, but for above-market projects, IRR does.

| | INDUSTRY CATEGORY | | | | |
|---|---|---|---|---|---|
| Year | Telecom-munications | Defense | Personal Care | Consumer Products | Biotechnology |
| 1993 | N/A—information not collected | | | | |
| 1994 | | | NONE | | |
| 1995 | | | NONE | | |
| 1996 | | | NONE | | |
| 1997 | IRR used less | | | | |
| 1998 | | NPV used less | NPV used more | NPV used more, IRR used more | IRR used less |

**Exhibit 16.10    Industry Differences in Use of IRR and NPV**

*Example:* Assume a simple case in which the choice is between two projects: a relatively short-term project involving (1) an initial outlay of $5 million followed by cash inflows of $1.5 million for 8 years, versus (2) a relatively long-term project with an initial outlay of $1 million followed by no cash inflows for five years, then by cash inflows of $1,000,000 a year for 10 years. The short-term project has an IRR of 24.95 percent, and the long-term project has an IRR of 27.27 percent.

Exhibit 16.11 maps the NPVs (in thousands of dollars) of the two projects over a span of hurdle rates, the lowest being 5 percent (considerably below the norm for any capital budget) and the highest being 35 percent. The NPVs of both projects over this hurdle-rate range are curvilinear, thus giving rise to two crossover points. The crossover point occurring at about 8 percent is not as important as the other one, because it is below the traditional range of acceptable returns on the capital budgeting project. Between that crossover point and the next we find the lower and upper ranges typically used (i.e., 12–18 percent).

In that range, the shorter-term, lower-IRR project has the higher NPV, so the conventional wisdom of financial and managerial accounting would prevail—quite rightly—in the choice of the shorter-term project. The crossover point at about 22 percent is critical, however. At that point, the shorter-term, lower-IRR project ceases to have a higher NPV than the higher-IRR, longer-term project.

This example illustrates that using the traditional 12 to 18 percent hurdle rates to assess projects having higher IRRs can give the wrong answer if one adheres to the conventional wisdom that NPV is always the superior project selection criterion. Many

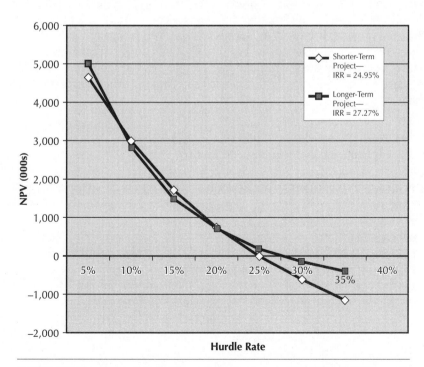

**Exhibit 16.11  NPV of Cash Flows from Projects with Different IRRs and Time Horizons**

R&D projects have IRRs in this above-market hurdle rate range, and it is not unusual for their initial outlays to be modest compared with their shorter-term, less-risky project alternatives.

But financial managers tend to think of capital budgeting as a one-step process, which may be inappropriate for these projects. Breakthrough, technology-based projects may involve a first-stage funding decision, with a "go/no go" decision point programmed into the project.

**(c) Stage Gate Tracking**   Many companies have adopted a disciplined R&D management practice, *stage gate tracking*, particularly for R&D projects.[6] Typical stage gates include:

- Ideation process result: Is it viable technically? Is there a market?
- Design process result: Is it feasible?
- Development process result: Can it be manufactured at a targeted cost?
- Prelaunch process: Can we produce it and market it?

Analysis of the R&D management practices database suggests that using stage gate tracking in moderation has a positive impact on financial performance, speed to market, and customer satisfaction.[7]

Stage gate tracking contributes the ability to manage risk through a resolution process. If the riskiness of a project does not diminish as additional knowledge about its potential commercial success and cash flows emerges, the company abandons the project. This is a critical difference from a "bricks and mortar"-type capital investment process.

Finally, the example suggests that different selection criteria might be appropriate for different projects. Because R&D projects have a wide range of risk and reward parameters, the selection criteria used should reflect this range. In other words, financial managers need to begin to see R&D projects the way R&D managers do—as a portfolio, much like a portfolio of security investments. The keys to successful portfolio management are:

- To diversify risk as much as possible through a balanced portfolio.
- To hedge any risk that one cannot diversify.

**16.4 PORTFOLIO APPROACH TO RESEARCH AND DEVELOPMENT MANAGEMENT**
R&D executives manage a portfolio of projects that have different risk and reward scenarios. As discussed previously, many of those projects—particularly the ones that will spawn the next generation of new products—have IRRs considerably higher than those for traditional "bricks and mortar" capital budgeting projects. R&D managers seek to create a healthy balance in their project portfolios.

From the beginning, research on the R&D management practices database has incorporated Mitchell and Hamilton's three categories of projects for an R&D portfolio:[8]

1. Major new developments, primarily knowledge-building activities, perhaps involving the use of technology new to the company.
2. Minor new developments, or strategic positioning projects that may include segments and product lines beyond those in which the company is currently active.

**3.** Product extensions, or business investment activities closely related to those with which the company is already involved.

Clearly, the greatest risk lies in the first category, but this is a risk that can be diversified, to some extent, by investments in the other two. What cannot be diversified entirely is the downside risk associated with most such projects, which is that the new products will fail. On the other hand, the upside potential of major new products is vast.

What Mitchell and Hamilton and others argue[9] is that an R&D portfolio of projects (but particularly these knowledge-building projects) is analogous to a call option on a marketable security, the value of which varies in ways that are counterintuitive.

The value of an option moves in an opposite direction from the underlying investment; it is most valuable in the beginning when the risk associated with the underlying investment is most unresolved, and it loses its value as the risk of the underlying investment is resolved. The upside potential is highest at the beginning. Another analogy is with a hedge investment, which has to do with managing downside risk. The initial investment in a major, breakthrough project limits the potential loss on the investment in the option to proceed with the project.

Mitchell and Hamilton advocate using an option pricing model (e.g., the well-known Black-Scholes model) to value major new R&D investments rather than NPV. Computer programs now exist to facilitate these complex calculations, and the R&D management community has already begun using this approach to some extent, as Exhibit 16.12 shows, although some companies are obviously doing so with significantly greater intensity than others, because the mean is consistently higher than the mode. No industry differences emerged for use of this project-selection criterion, nor is there any information yet about the types of R&D projects for which managers use option pricing as a selection criterion.

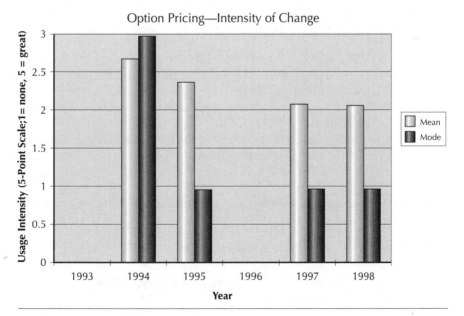

**Exhibit 16.12   Option Pricing Usage and a Project Selection Criterion: 1994–1998**

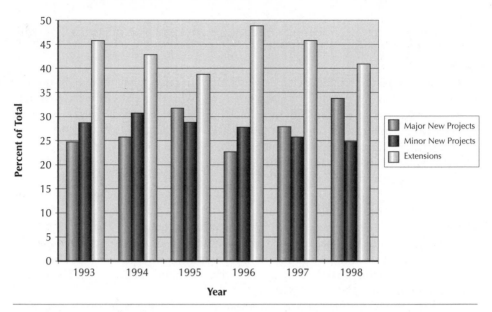

**Exhibit 16.13    Average R&D Project Portfolio Investment Allocation: 1993–1998**

Information from the R&D management practices database suggests that proposals to use project selection criteria other than NPV for major or minor new product development projects are far from academic. Companies invest significant portions of their R&D portfolio dollars in these two categories—more than half, as shown by Exhibit 16.13.

As with previous examples of averages from the database, Exhibit 16.14 shows industry differences among the three categories. At the very least, Exhibit 16.13 demonstrates the need to consider the possibility of expanding the project selection toolbox beyond NPV for the approximately 25 percent of projects invested in major new and approximately 30 percent in minor product development, at least during their early stages.

**16.5 PORTFOLIO VIEW APPLIED TO PROJECT SELECTION CRITERIA**    The discussion of research findings in the previous section leads to a proposal (which continues being explored as the database is developed) to use different project-selection criteria for projects having different risk/reward parameters, particularly in the initial stages when the differences are so pronounced.

Because risk resolution occurs at each stage of the longer-term projects, the second part of the proposal is to change selection criteria as the project moves through each stage to its completion. Exhibit 16.15 summarizes this proposal.

**(a) Where Net Present Value Is Appropriate**    Extension projects are the projects most analogous to bricks-and-mortar capital budgeting projects, for several reasons:

- They generally will not achieve above-market returns.
- Their cash flows are usually nearer term and more easily assessed than major new projects, so NPV estimates for these projects have a credible basis.
- They tend to be one-stage projects.

Relatively few major new projects but many minor new projects pass through all their stage gates. In their final stages, they become more like operating asset capital budget

| | INDUSTRY CATEGORY | | | | | |
|---|---|---|---|---|---|---|
| Year | Pharma-<br>ceuticals | Telecom-<br>munications | Defense | Biotechnology | Chemical | Consumer<br>Products |
| 1993 | More major<br>new | Less minor<br>new | | | | |
| 1994 | | Less minor<br>new | More major<br>new, less minor<br>new | | | |
| 1995 | | | | Less minor<br>new | | |
| 1996 | | | | | Less major new,<br>more minor new,<br>more extensions | |
| 1997 | | | | | Less major<br>new | Less major<br>new |
| 1998 | | | | Less minor<br>new | Less major<br>new | |

| | INDUSTRY CATEGORY | |
|---|---|---|
| Year | Personal<br>Care | Energy |
| 1993 | | |
| 1994 | | |
| 1995 | | |
| 1996 | | |
| 1997 | More<br>extensions | Less major<br>new |
| 1998 | | |

**Exhibit 16.14    Industry Differences—Project Portfolio Investment Allocation: 1993–1998**

projects, so NPV would be an appropriate criterion to use for a decision to proceed or not to proceed.

**(b) Using Internal Rate of Return**    IRR is an appropriate criterion for assessing the desirability of projects involving new applications of technology that a company has al-

| | Project Stage | | | |
|---|---|---|---|---|
| **Project Type** | **Initial<br>Outlay** | **First<br>Stage** | **Later<br>Stage** | **Final<br>Stage** |
| Product extensions | NPV | N/A | N/A | N/A |
| Minor new products | IRR | IRR/NPV | IRR/NPV | NPV |
| Major new products | Option<br>pricing | Option<br>pricing/IRR | IRR | NPV |

**Exhibit 16.15    Proposal for Which Project Selection Criteria to Use for Which Projects and When**

ready used. Because the viability of the technology is established, estimates of cash flows—which are necessary for calculations of both IRR and NPV—are fairly reliable.

The benefit of using IRR is that projects that might have relatively low NPVs (perhaps because cash inflows may not occur for some time, even if the initial outlay is minimal) but high IRRs will still meet the selection criteria. If the cash flow estimates are conservative, the upside potential may be even greater. Similarly, IRR is an appropriate selection criterion to use for major new projects when they pass through the first stage gate and more reliable cash flow estimates become available.

**(c) Use an Option Pricing Approach to Value Major New Projects Initially**   For major new projects (as Mitchell and Hamilton and others propose), the initial decision to invest can be made using an option pricing approach. At the first stage gate, a "go/no go" decision takes place, using either an option pricing model again (if estimates of cash flow are not yet feasible) or IRR (if estimates of cash flow can be made). Finally, NPV might become appropriate as a project nears completion.

**(d) Financial/Management Accounting Implications**   Financial accounting standards require that virtually all R&D investments be treated as current period expenses. Yet analysis of how R&D managers manage their project portfolios suggests that at least some projects should be capitalized. R&D managers have developed working definitions of portfolio "compartments," and a significant portion of the total investment— over 50 percent, according to Exhibit 16.13—is invested in projects that have the potential to generate above-market returns.

Continuing to expense product extensions—which are analogous to investments in marketing campaigns—makes sense, if only because of their relatively short-term nature. Furthermore, the short-term nature of these extension projects is accelerating because of the competitive pressures for speed to market.

**(e) Capitalize Then Expense Minor New and Major New Project Investments**   As information from the R&D management practices database shows, R&D contributes more to the financial well-being of companies than many financial managers realize. Arbitrarily treating investments in longer-term product development projects as a current expense may be short-sighted and may cause the return on those investments to be significantly understated. To the extent that is true, companies may be incurring a higher cost of capital than necessary.

For minor new products using existing technology, companies could capitalize the projects at their NPV and amortize the investments over the life of the project until better estimates of cash flow are available. For major new products using new technology, a reasonable approach would be to capitalize the initial investment using an option pricing model, then to write off the project if it is later abandoned. If the project proceeds, the initial investment would be adjusted to NPV and amortized (as with a minor new product project).

**16.6 SUMMARY**   Many financial managers have little understanding of the new product development process, which is not surprising given the lack of attention paid to the subject in business education. Moreover, a well-established culture of risk aversion prevails among financial managers, which prevents them from fully appreciating the risk/ reward trade-offs (or payoffs) from successful R&D projects, which can lead to products that earn above-market returns for years to come.

To treat all potential investments in R&D the same as other capital projects is short-sighted, and it biases decision making in favor of shorter-term projects that have less potential to contribute to the long-term financial well-being of a firm. Financial managers need to reevaluate their risk tolerances and learn to use some of the sophisticated tools now available for converting high-risk projects from "crap shoots" to calculated risks.

Innovation is the key to a company's future, especially in an increasingly global economy. Financial managers who want to play an active part in that future should thus educate themselves about R&D and the innovation process.

## NOTES

1. D. R. Emery, J. D. Finnerty, and J. D. Stowe, *Principles of Financial Management* (Upper Saddle River, NJ: Prentice Hall, 1998), Ch. 8; R. A. Brealey and S. C. Myers, *Principles of Corporate Finance* (New York: McGraw-Hill, 1996), Ch. 5.

2. P. F. Boer, "Traps, Pitfalls and Snares in the Valuation of Technology," *Research•Technology Management* 41 (September/October 1998): 45–54; T. W. Faulkner, "Applying 'Options Thinking' to R&D Valuation," *Research•Technology Management* 39 (May/June 1996): 50–56; G. R. Mitchell and W. F. Hamilton, "Managing R&D as a Strategic Option," *Research•Technology Management* 31 (May/June 1988): 15–22.

3. Financial Accounting Standards Board, Statement of Financial Accounting Standards No. 2, "Accounting for Research and Development Costs," 1973.

4. M. E. McGrath and M. N. Romeri, "From Experience: The R&D Effectiveness Index: A Metric for Product Development Performance," *Journal of Product Innovation Management* 11 (November 1994): 213–220; L. W. Ellis, *Evaluation of R&D Process: Effectiveness Through Measurements* (Boston and London: Artech House, 1997), 187–187, 227–228.

5. C. C. Curtis and L. W. Ellis, "Balanced Scorecards for New Product Development," *Journal of Cost Management* (Spring 1997): 12–18; C. C. Curtis, "Nonfinancial Performance Measures in New product Development?" *Journal of Cost Management* (Fall 1994): 18–26; C. C. Curtis and L. W. Ellis, "Satisfy Customers, While Speeding R&D and Staying Profitable," *Research•Technology Management* 41 (September/October 1998): 23–27; L. W. Ellis and C. C. Curtis, "Speedy R&D: How Beneficial?" *Research•Technology Management* 38 (July/August 1995): 9–13; L. W. Ellis and C. C. Curtis, "Measuring Customer Satisfaction," *Research•Technology Management* 38 (September/October 1995): 45–48; L. W. Ellis, *Evaluation of R&D Processes: Effectiveness Through Measurements* (Boston and London: Artech House, 1997); R. C. Cooper, "Stage Gate Systems: A New Tool for Managing New Products," *Business Horizons* (May/June 1990): 44–54; L. W. Ellis and R. G. McDonald, "Reforming Management Accounting to Support today's Technology," *Research•Technology Management* 33 (March/April 1990): 30–43.

6. Cooper, op. cit.

7. Curtis and Ellis, 1998, op. cit.

8. Mitchell and Hamilton, op. cit.

9. Others that have agreed with Mitchell and Hamilton include: Boer, op. cit.; Faulkner, op. cit.; Ellis and McDonald, op. cit.

# PART III

# QUALITY

# CHAPTER 17

# QUALITY

## Ross L. Fink
**Bradley University**

**17.1 INTRODUCTION**   This chapter provides an introduction to quality management. The chapter first examines the development of quality management to help readers understand its roots, then it gives various definitions of quality and discusses their relationships with each other.

The quality management philosophies of W. Edwards Deming, Joseph M. Juran, and Philip B. Crosby—three of the pioneers of *total quality management* (TQM)—are investigated, followed by a discussion of the key components of a TQM system.

The chapter concludes by looking at various quality awards (including the Malcolm Baldrige National Quality Award) and ISO 9000 registration.

**17.2 EVOLUTION OF QUALITY MANAGEMENT**   From the earliest times when products were manufactured or services provided, quality has been an important consideration. The ancient Egyptians, for example, evidently used measurements and inspection to ensure that stones were square. The Babylonians were also interested in quality: Item 229 of Hammurabi's Code (around 1750 B.C.) states that, "If a builder build a house for someone, and does not construct it properly, and the house which he built fall in and kill its owner, then that builder shall be put to death."[1]

During the Middle Ages, skilled craftspersons in Europe ensured the quality of items produced. Manufacturing was done on a local level, typically in a home or cottage, with an owner supervising a handful of employees. Each craftsperson served as producer, trainer, and inspector. Quality was built into the products, and workers took great pride in their craft. They ensured the quality of their own work. Also, because they dealt directly with customers, they understood that they had to provide a high-quality product to remain in business. Quality management efforts in this setting were generally informal, and each product was inspected for quality.

The move to factories in the eighteenth and nineteenth centuries brought a change in quality management. No longer could informal systems maintain quality effectively. In the United States, Eli Whitney changed quality management dramatically in the early 1800s when he introduced interchangeable parts to the manufacture of guns for the federal government. Because each part had to fit each rifle of the same type precisely, parts had to be as close to identical as possible. Therefore, conformance to design became a method of operation.

**(a) Scientific Management and Quality Control**   In the early 1900s, the *scientific management movement,* led by Fredrick W. Taylor, changed the way managers ran their companies. Taylor separated planning from execution: Managers were responsible for the plan, workers were responsible for executing it. Inspection was the primary means of maintaining quality during this era.

The 1920s saw the beginning of the quality control era. Bell Systems Laboratories was one of the leaders in this movement. Walter A. Shewhart developed the theory behind the *control chart* and, ultimately, *statistical process control* (SPC), which measures the performance of processes. In 1924, Shewhart wrote a memo that sketched out the first modern control chart.[2] In 1931, Shewhart laid the foundation for the application of SPC.[3]

**(b) Acceptance Sampling and Statistical Quality Control**   At about the same time at the Bell Labs, H. F. Dodge and H. G. Romig developed *acceptance sampling,* a sampling procedure that compares the quality of product batches with predetermined standards. Their work forms the backbone of acceptance sampling, and they became famous for the Dodge-Romig Sampling Inspection Tables.[4] Together, Shewhart, Dodge, and Romig developed the heart of modern statistical quality control, which is still used today.

The onset of World War II brought the first widespread application of statistical quality control. The U.S. military, as a major consumer of U.S. production, became influential with manufacturers. Its initial impact was on the development of a military inspection procedure based on acceptance sampling. Later the military developed the American War Standards Z1.1-1941 "Guide for Quality Control and Control Chart Method of Analyzing Data" and Z1.2-1941 "Control Chart Method of Controlling Quality During Production." These war standards provide the information needed to implement SPC programs in a manufacturing setting. They were very successful in the United States during World War II and helped U.S. manufacturers produce large volumes of high-quality war material.

**(c) Rise of Japanese Quality**   After World War II, U.S. industry entered a golden period. The high-quality products produced by U.S. manufacturers, the shortage of manufacturing capacity elsewhere, and the pent-up demand for consumer goods ultimately led U.S. manufacturers to ignore quality. As a consequence, production became the focus, so quality stagnated.

But Japan did not ignore quality. In an effort to revive its manufacturing base in the 1950s, Japanese manufacturers sponsored lectures on quality by U.S. experts such as W. Edwards Deming and Joseph Juran, who introduced Japanese engineers and managers to the concept of statistical quality control. More important, the Japanese manufacturers, influenced by Deming and Juran, focused on managerial aspects of quality, not just the technical issues. In the United States, quality tended to be the province of specialists; in Japan, quality became everyone's responsibility.

During the 1970s, Japanese manufactured products penetrated many U.S. markets, especially electronics and automobiles. Japanese manufacturers proved that they could produce higher-quality products at lower costs than their U.S. competitors, mainly because of their mastery of quality management and their use of *just-in-time* (JIT) manufacturing techniques. The tremendous improvement in Japanese products made quality paramount to many consumers, who now demanded high-quality products and services as a matter of course.

As a consequence, the 1980s saw renewed interest in quality management in United

States. U.S. manufacturers reexamined the teachings of quality experts such as Deming and Juran. As a result, a movement arose among U.S. manufacturers and in the service sector to develop quality management systems that integrated quality throughout the company and involved the customer in the process. This could be termed the beginning of the TQM era.

**17.3 WHAT IS QUALITY?** To begin the exploration of quality management, *quality* must be defined. The answer to the question, "What is quality?," might seem obvious. After all, everyone who buys or consumes products or services can readily give an evaluation of quality, but defining it is not as simple.

**(a) Fitness for Use** Among the many definitions of quality, one ties quality to *fitness for use,* which means that a product meets the engineering requirements set for it. In other words, the product's quality is high enough to allow it to meet its "intended use." In many cases, this can be thought of as a "degree (or level) of perfection."

A product usually does not have to be perfect, but it must be of a sufficiently high quality to allow it to perform its intended use. Consider impurities in a piece of metal, for example. A certain level of impurities would probably not greatly affect the metal's strength; often, therefore, the impurities would not affect the metal's intended use. But at some point, the impurities *would* affect the physical properties of the metal and make it unfit for certain uses. In most cases, this "fitness for use" definition relies on an engineer, who must determine the "level of perfection" needed for an intended use.

**(b) Design** Another definition of quality is based on design. *Design quality* refers to the design of a product itself. Does the design of the product or service have the potential to satisfy its fitness for use based on its design specifications? Note that differences in specifications for the same intended use signify a difference in quality.

**(c) Conformance** A closely related definition is *quality of conformance* or product quality. This refers to the ability of a process to provide a product or service that conforms to the design specifications. In this case, quality is measured only against design specifications. This definition assumes that the design is correct and meets the intended use of the product.

**(d) Customer Satisfaction** Consumers and marketers like to define quality as the degree to which a product or service meets or exceeds customer expectations. This approach to quality is known as *customer satisfaction.*

Under this approach, customers are satisfied when their perception of actual performance equals or exceeds their expectations regarding a product or service. When their expectations are not met, customers are dissatisfied and actively seek a replacement for the product or service. This model of customer satisfaction is known as a *disconfirmation paradigm.*

**(e) Unified Definition of Quality** Which of these definitions of quality is correct: fitness for use, design quality, product quality, or customer satisfaction? The answer is *all of them.* In fact, they should be merged together to form a unified definition of quality.

Ultimately, customers decide whether a product satisfies their expectations. Thus, the customer satisfaction model seems the most appropriate version of quality. But there is one major problem with this definition. The only effective time to measure customer satisfaction is after the customer has received the product or service—at the output stage. At this point, the only actions available to a company are remedial (e.g., correcting a defective product). Companies should strive to prevent defective items from ever reaching the customer. To do this, quality must be operationalized.

This is where *product quality* or conformance to design enters the picture. Product or service delivery systems need to be able to measure quality as they operate. The yardstick of customer satisfaction cannot be used effectively because of the time delay in receiving information from customers. To receive quality information that helps maintain the quality of a process, companies define quality as product quality or conformance to product design (for people associated with the operational processes). However, this definition is limited by the correctness of the design specifications.

Consequently, quality design is an important input to a product or service delivery system. Without a quality design, it is nearly impossible to produce a high-quality product or service. When looking at the quality design definition, a company should also consider the concepts of fitness for use, "manufacturability" (i.e., the ability to manufacture to the specifications), and customer satisfaction. Without these elements, an effective design cannot be obtained.

Exhibit 17.1 illustrates the relationships between the various quality definitions, the primary people who use those definitions, and the stage of the product delivery system. This exhibit also shows the interrelationship between the quality definitions and the need for information sharing to effectively provide a quality product or service.

As Exhibit 17.1 illustrates, designers rely primarily on the design quality definition. Operations people use product quality. Customers and marketing departments base quality on customer satisfaction, which is the ultimate goal of the company. Good re-

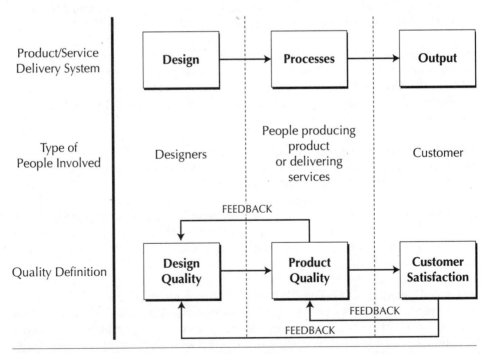

**Exhibit 17.1   Relationship Between Quality Definition, Type of Worker, and Phase of Product Delivery System**

lationships between all these groups ensure that high-quality designs are coupled with high-quality processes to deliver products or services that will produce customer satisfaction.

The next section examines the philosophies of several quality experts, including their definitions of quality.

**17.4 EXPERTS ON QUALITY**   Many people have helped shape our ideas about quality. Along with Shewhart, Dodge, and Romig (who were discussed previously), the following people have had significant influences on quality management:

- *Genichi Taguchi,* who helped develop off-line quality control and the loss function.
- *Kaoru Ishikawa,* who made major contributions to Japan's quality strategy. He was instrumental in the development of quality circles in Japan. To reflect his contributions to quality circles, the American Society of Quality offers the Ishikawa Medal to recognize leadership in the human side of quality. Kaoru Ishikawa also invented the cause-and-effect or fishbone diagram, a tool commonly used by quality circles in Japan.
- *A. V. Feigenbaum,* who laid the foundations for modern quality control and coined the term "total quality control" in his 1951 book: *Quality Control: Principles, Practice, and Administration.*[5]

This section, however, concentrates on the three men who have probably had the most profound impact on quality and the development of TQM:

1. W. Edwards Deming.
2. Joseph M. Juran.
3. Philip B. Crosby.

**(a) W. Edwards Deming**   W. Edwards Deming has probably exerted the most influence on TQM. He was one of the first people to recognize that quality control that is directed only at engineers and factory workers is too limited. Everyone in a company must have responsibility for quality, and the participation of top managers is vital to providing high-quality products and services.

One component of Deming's philosophy is that companies should take a *continuous improvement* approach to quality. This is reflected in the *plan-do-check-act* (PDCA) cycle (see Exhibit 17.2), which was originally called the Shewhart cycle, but the Japanese renamed it the Deming cycle. Exhibit 17.2 illustrates the PDCA cycle.

In the first step of the cycle, the "plan" phase, managers identify and analyze quality problems. Next, the "do" phase requires implementation of changes made in the "plan" phase. The "check" phase involves evaluating data collected during implementation. There should be a good fit between the original goal and the results. If the procedure is successful, it should be standardized and replicated throughout the company as part of the "act" phase. Notice that this leads back to the "plan" phase, which indicates that quality improvement should be continuous.

Most of Deming's philosophy is reflected in his 14 points to quality. Originally, these were published in his book *Out of the Crisis.*[6] The underlying foundations of these 14 points are found in his later book *The New Economics.*[7] The following sections briefly describe his 14 points.[8]

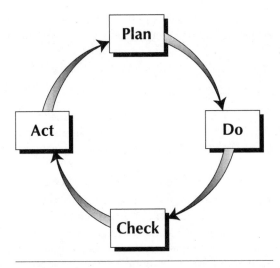

**Exhibit 17.2    Plan-Do-Check-Act (PDCA) Cycle**

1. *Create constancy of purpose about improving products and services to become competitive, stay in business, and provide jobs.* To succeed, companies must develop a vision and plan for providing high-quality products and services in order to remain competitive. But competitiveness for the sake of profitability is not the sole aim: Deming believed that businesses are part of society and exist to serve both customers and employees.

2. *Adopt the new philosophy.* We are in a new economic age. Western managers must awaken to the challenge, learn their responsibilities, and assume leadership for change. The world of management has changed. Management systems built on the scientific management approaches of Fredrick W. Taylor (who used quota-driven production and work measurements) are no longer appropriate. Managers must acknowledge the importance of quality and provide the means for continually improving products and services.

3. *Do not depend on inspection to achieve quality.* Eliminate the need for inspection by building quality into products in the first place: 100 percent inspection does not guarantee quality. Companies cannot afford the cost of not producing products correctly the first time. Moreover, 100 percent inspection has the effect of making quality control the responsibility of the inspector rather than everyone's responsibility.

4. *End the practice of awarding business on the basis of price alone.* Instead, minimize total cost by moving toward a single supplier for any one item and developing long-term relationships of loyalty and trust. Price without consideration of quality has no meaning: Companies should strive for consistency both in quality of purchased parts and in the timing of parts delivery. Deming suggests that "single sourcing" (using one supplier for a specific part) will accomplish this objective.

5. *Constantly improve the system of production and service.* Continuous improvement of quality and productivity is a prerequisite of success and leads to constantly decreasing costs. It is not enough for a company simply to maintain quality. The PDCA cycle depicts this aspect of continuous improvement. By

continually improving and working toward this quality goal, a company can remain competitive.

6. *Institute training on the job.* Any company can purchase equipment, but only employees can give their company a competitive advantage. Therefore, get the maximum from employees. One way to do this is through continual training of the work force, including training on quality. Deming maintains that all employees should understand the problems of variability, the ways to identify problems, and the improvement opportunities.

7. *Institute leadership.* The aim of supervision should be to help people and machines do a better job. Supervision of management needs overhaul as much as supervision of production workers does. For companies to succeed, managers must provide leadership that helps workers achieve the intended results. (See item 12.)

8. *Drive out fear so that everyone may work effectively for the company.* Driving out fear leads to an environment in which continuous improvement can thrive. In a company, fear can take many forms, including fear of reprisal, fear of the unknown, fear of change, and fear of failure. For example, fear of not making a daily quota may prevent workers from suggesting improvements.

9. *Break down barriers between departments.* People in research, design, sales, and production must work as a team to foresee production problems or problems that may be encountered when a product or service is used. Successful companies should have free flow of information between departments, and all departments should work for the company's common goals, not just their own departmental goals. Many companies use concurrent engineering to accomplish this.

10. *Eliminate slogans, exhortations, and targets that ask for zero defects and new levels of productivity from the work force.* Such exhortations only create adversarial relationships, because most causes of low quality and low productivity belong to the system and thus lie beyond the power of the work force. Deming believed that most problems are the result of the system, not the workers. Therefore, urging workers to work harder in an inadequate system only gives rise to frustration and anger toward managers. Managers must take responsibility for the system and strive to improve it.

11. *Eliminate work standards (quotas) on the factory floor and management by objective.* Instead, substitute leadership. Deming claimed that work standards and continuous improvement are totally incompatible. Because work standards are typically set for the average worker, approximately half will make the standard. The other half who do not meet the standard will be disillusioned: They may be fired, or they may quit. Those who can meet the standard will generally not exceed it because of peer pressure. Also eliminate management by objective, management by numbers, and numerical goals: Again, substitute leadership instead. The general problem with most of these approaches is that there is no plan to back up the goal. Any time that such a goal is stated, the question should be, "How will this be achieved?" If there is no plan, these goals are worthless. Managers must lead, not dictate change.

12. *Remove barriers that rob the hourly worker of the right to pride of workmanship.* A supervisor's responsibilities must change from sheer numbers to quality. Hourly workers are often treated as a commodity; they do not know whether they will work the next week. In addition, companies have often used systems

that prevent workers from producing high-quality products. One reason is that quota systems do not consider quality; they primarily concern themselves with quantity. In other situations, the pleas of workers to fix a defective machine go unheard. How, then, can workers take pride in their workmanship?

One way to remove barriers that rob people in management and in engineering of their right to pride of workmanship is to abolish annual merit ratings and management by objective. Many tenets of Western management go counter to Deming's philosophy. One is the emphasis on short-term profitability. Sacrificing the future for improved profitability today does not match a good quality management system. Also, merit ratings and annual reviews rob managers. Merit systems tend to reward individuals who do well in the system; they do not reward improvements made to the system. Moreover, these systems tend to degenerate into short-term counting systems, which, unfortunately, emphasizes short-term thinking. Finally, mobility of managers hurts the company. Again, this encourages short-term thinking, exemplified by the rationalization, "I will only be here for a few years, therefore I must get immediate results. I should not worry about the long-term."

**13.** *Institute a vigorous program of education and self-improvement.* Deming advises everyone that continuous learning is vital to the success of the country. It is not satisfactory to be good; we must continuously improve through education.

**14.** *Put everybody in the company to work to accomplish the transformation.* The transformation is everybody's job: Everyone is responsible for continuously improving quality and productivity. Every process and every job affects quality and productivity. The workers cannot do it by themselves, and neither can managers.

**(b) Joseph M. Juran**   Joseph M. Juran was (along with Deming) one of the first experts to address the managerial as well as the technical side of quality. He and Deming are given much of the credit for improving Japanese manufacturing, especially the quality philosophy adopted by many Japanese companies.

Juran's approach fits well with existing companies. The ideas that Juran is best known for are:

- The involvement of top managers in quality management.
- The Pareto principle.
- Widespread training in quality.
- The definition of quality as "fitness for use."
- The project approach for quality improvement.

*(i) Pareto Principle*   Juran believed that 80 percent of quality defects are controllable by management. Consequently, top managers must be leaders in quality management.

The Pareto principle is a simple but useful tool. It states that 80 percent of the problems are created by 20 percent of the causes. Therefore, it is useful to identify the 20 percent of the causes that cause 80 percent of the problems in order to eliminate them. Doing so will provide the best return on effort. Sometimes people rephrase the principle as separating the "trivial many" from the "vital few." One implementation of this principle is the *Pareto chart,* which has become a standard tool of quality management.

Like Deming, Juran advocated training about quality. However, he especially stressed the importance of training in quality for the top management team. Juran also focused on the "fitness of use" definition of quality. Although he believed that quality means satisfaction for both internal and external customers, he thought that the way to obtain satisfaction was through product features and freedom from deficiencies.

*(ii) Project Approach* Whereas Deming emphasized continuous improvement, Juran advocated a *project approach* to quality improvement. He advocated making specific annual improvements. Managers should select an area with chronic problems, convince others that a breakthrough solution is necessary, analyze alternatives, and select and implement an alternative.

Another major difference between Deming and Juran is that Deming believed that quality was the universal language for a company. Juran, on the other hand, believed that different parts of the company spoke different languages: Workers speak of things, middle managers of things and dollars, and top managers of dollars alone.

Therefore, Juran believed that everything should be converted into the language of dollars. To that end, he advocated the use of quality cost accounting. He was not a believer in quality for the sake of quality. Rather, quality should be justified on a cost basis. Juran also believed that, by focusing on the cost of quality, a company could more readily identify important quality problems.[9]

**(c) Philip Crosby** Unlike Deming and Juran, who addressed both managerial and technical aspects of quality, Crosby focuses on managerial and behavioral processes rather than statistical processes. He stresses managerial thinking rather than a systems approach to quality management. He lets managers determine the finer points of implementing a quality system.

The following two phrases represent Crosby's thoughts on quality:

1. Zero defects.
2. Doing it right the first time.

Crosby's "absolutes of quality management," which form the heart of his philosophy are[10]:

- *Quality means conformance to requirements, not elegance.* Crosby believes that managers must set quality requirements so that everyone knows what is expected and so that misunderstandings cannot occur. Once managers set quality requirements, it can be measured. From then on, quality is strictly defined as conformance to requirements.
- *There is no such thing as a "quality problem."* Quality problems do not originate in the quality department, they are found in the functional departments. Quality departments can measure conformance, report quality findings, and lead quality initiatives, but the responsibility for quality lies in the functional areas.
- *There is no such thing as the "economics of quality"; it is always cheaper to do the job right the first time.* This is Crosby's well-known statement that "quality is free." Crosby believes that it is always cheaper to do it right the first time. The true cost lies in correcting quality problems.
- *The only performance measurement is the cost of quality, which is the cost of nonconformance.* Crosby notes that many companies spend 15 to 20 percent of their

sales dollars on quality costs. This figure should be closer to 2.5 percent, and it should consist primarily of appraisal and prevention costs rather than failure costs. Crosby recommends tracking the cost of nonconformance to bring the manager's attention to the problem.

- *The only performance standard is "zero defects."* The only acceptable goal is zero defects. To accept any other standard is to allow for errors. The "zero defect" approach is a major departure from many quality experts. Deming, for example, believes that the main quality problem is in the system, so how can you hold workers responsible for quality problems when the system causes most problems?

**17.5 KEY COMPONENTS OF TOTAL QUALITY MANAGEMENT**   As the summary of the ideas of quality pioneers in the preceding section shows, there is no one definition of TQM. Nearly every company that has used TQM has changed it to meet its particular situation. This is actually good, but it makes it difficult to provide a definition. However, almost all discussions and explanations of TQM cover four points:

1. People.
2. Process.
3. Customer orientation.
4. Leadership.

**(a) People**   The people component of quality relates to getting the most from employees. The Japanese and their quality circles popularized this aspect of TQM. The question that arose in quality circles was, "Who knows the most about a given machine or process?" The answer is the worker who has been running the machine for years.

Classical scientific management systems did not consider that workers could contribute to improving the system. In Taylor's system, workers simply followed directions. But the Japanese showed that a company wastes a valuable resource when workers are not involved in improving the system. As a result, most TQM systems have some form of employee involvement that taps this wealth of knowledge that workers accumulate over time. The involvement can be simple in form (e.g., quality circle) or it can be more elaborate (e.g., a self-directed work team). This type of approach also ties in with the continuous improvement philosophy common to TQM programs. Everyone should strive to continuously improve themselves and the company.

**(b) Process**   The process component of quality generally deals with monitoring and improving a process. The most common element of this component is the use of SPC or the control chart method to monitor the process. The use of 100 percent inspection is inappropriate. It fosters the attitude that inspection will catch any defective items. It goes against Crosby's "doing it right the first time" philosophy. SPC also places the company in a continuous improvement cycle, thus providing timely feedback of information to prevent quality problems and empower workers.

**(c) Customer Orientation**   Customer orientation is also an important component of quality. The ultimate judge of quality is the customer. Therefore, if customers are not considered throughout the company, the likelihood of producing a product or service that satisfies them is low.

This customer orientation should permeate the company; it is not something that should reside only in the marketing or sales departments. For example, the design department needs to determine customer expectation about the performance of a product as it is being designed. Designers cannot rely only on their engineering expertise for designs.

**(d) Leadership**    Finally, no TQM program can succeed without the support of top management. Managers should make the importance of quality clear and back their talk up with resources and rewards. If top managers do not communicate the importance of quality, no one else in the company will see its importance. However, mere talk is not enough: Top managers must also provide substantive support.

One type of support is financial. TQM programs are not successful overnight—they require time and money to grow and mature. Additional support in the form of training provides employees with the skills necessary to implement the other components of a TQM system. Investment in processes must take place to improve them.

Reward systems must also reflect the TQM system. Those that do not contain a quality component are suspect. If rewards are based only on output with no regard to quality, the TQM system is doomed to failure.

Reward systems should also be tied to a combination of individual, team, and company goals to ensure that the goals of the company—in particular, those relating to quality—will be achieved. The Malcolm Baldrige National Quality Award (discussed in the next section) uses many of the components of TQM systems to evaluate its applicants.

**17.6 MALCOLM BALDRIGE NATIONAL QUALITY AWARD**    The Malcolm Baldrige National Quality Award ("the Baldrige Award") is probably the most prestigious quality award that a U.S. company can earn. It was named for former Secretary of Commerce Malcolm Baldrige, who served as Secretary of Commerce from 1981 to 1987. The Baldrige Award was created by Public Law 100-107 and signed by President Ronald Reagan on August 20, 1987.

The Baldrige Award was established to help improve the quality and productivity of U.S. companies so that they would remain competitive relative to their foreign competitors. Not only does the award recognize excellent companies and their accomplishments, it also requires that winners share information that helped them win the award. Thus, the award encourages other companies to adopt quality practices.

Management of the Baldrige Award is handled by the National Institute of Standards and Technology (NIST), an agency in the Department of Commerce.[11] In addition, the American Society for Quality (ASQ) assists in administering the award program through a contract with NIST.[12]

Since its inception in 1988, the Baldrige Award has been presented to 34 companies. Awards are given in the categories of manufacturing, service, and small business. Two more categories—education and health care—were added in 1999.

**(a) Benefits of the Baldrige Award**    Winners of the Baldrige Award receive a physical award, but they are also allowed to advertise the fact that they have won the award. Winners must also share information about their successful performance strategies with other U.S. companies.

Many companies use the Baldrige Award criteria to evaluate and establish their quality management systems to improve their performance. More than one million copies of the criteria have been requested since 1988.

There are other benefits to applying for the award, even if a company fails to win. All applicants are given a detailed feedback report prepared by at least six experts from the private-sector board of examiners. This review typically contains 300 to 1,000 hours of review time.[13]

Perhaps the most important benefit of quality (as demonstrated by recent winners of the Baldrige Award) is that they have generally had excellent financial performance. A fictitious stock fund composed of publicly traded U.S. companies that won the Baldrige Award from 1988 to 1997 outperformed the Standard and Poor's 500 index fund by more than 200 percent.[14]

**(b) Baldrige Award Criteria**  Although the criteria for the Baldrige Award have changed over the years (and will probably continue to change), the 1999 award contained seven major categories:

1. *Leadership.* How the company's leader guides it, how the company handles its public responsibility, and how the company practices good citizenship.
2. *Strategic planning.* How the company develops and deploys its strategic plan.
3. *Customer and market focus.* How the company determines the requirements and expectations of its customers and markets.
4. *Information analysis.* How the company analyzes and uses data and information for managing key processes, and how it structures and uses its performance management system.
5. *Human resource development and management.* How the company allows its workers to achieve their full potential, and how the workforce is aligned with the company's objectives.
6. *Process management.* How key production and delivery processes are designed, managed, and improved. (This addresses many of the more technical aspects of quality management.)
7. *Business results.* How the company performs and improves in key business areas, including:
   • Customer satisfaction.
   • Financial and marketplace performance.
   • Human resources.
   • Supplier and partner performance.
   • Operations performance.
   • Comparison with competitors.

**17.7 OTHER QUALITY AWARDS**  In addition to the Baldrige Award, there are several similar local and state awards. As of February 1998, there were more than 56 different state and local quality award programs covering more than 42 states.[15]

One notable predecessor to the Baldrige Award is the Deming Prize, which is awarded in Japan. It is named in honor of W. Edwards Deming, the noted U.S. quality consultant, who lectured widely in Japan. The Union of Japanese Scientists and Engineers (JUSE) presents this award annually to individuals or groups who have contributed to the development and dissemination of TQM. It was first awarded in 1951.

Another Japanese quality award is the Ishikawa Prize, which was established in 1970. It is named after Ichiro Ishikawa, the first chairman of the board of directors of JUSE.

This prize (which honors Ishikawa's contribution to quality in Japan) recognizes new methods or new systems for the modernization of management.

Companies that have more than 50 percent of their business in Europe are eligible for the European Quality Award. This award is presented annually to the companies judged to be the best in each category for demonstrated excellence in "the management of quality as their fundamental processes for continuous improvement."[16]

**17.8 ISO 9000 REGISTRATION**    In addition to quality awards, certification or registration to ISO 9000 standards is another measure of a company's quality. ISO 9000 is a series of standards that represent good management practices based on international agreement. The standards are maintained by the International Organization for Standards. There is a common misconception that "ISO" represents the initials of the organization. In fact, the name ISO is taken from the Greek word *iso,* which means *equal.*[17]

Another misnomer is the phrase "ISO certification" or "ISO registration." Neither is correct. ISO 9000 is a set of standards. The organization does not certify or register companies. ISO merely provides the standards. However, through third parties (referred to as "registrars"), a company can be registered or certified to one of the ISO 9000 series of standards. The seal of the registrar is then used to signify that, according to the registrar, the company follows the ISO 9000 standards. Consequently, the reputation of the registrar is an important aspect of registering to the ISO 9000 standards. This approach is what is commonly referred to as "ISO 9000 registration or certification."

**(a) Multiple Standards**    In the 9000 series, there are multiple standards that companies may follow, but the most famous are ISO 9001, 9002, and 9003. The difference between these standards is scope. ISO 9001 is the most comprehensive. It is for companies that do everything from design and development to production, installation, and servicing. ISO 9002 is for companies that do not do design or development; otherwise it is identical to ISO 9001. ISO 9003 is the most limited in scope. It is for companies that primarily use testing and inspection to ensure that their products match the specifications. These companies are not involved in design and development, process control, purchasing, or services.

**(b) Documentation of Procedures**    ISO 9000 concentrates on detailed documentation for procedures, work instructions, and related activities in a company. In other words, it is concerned with the processes and the organization's adherence to the documented procedures. It does not concentrate on the product or quality leadership. Registration to ISO 9000 does not guarantee high quality; it merely indicates that the standards related to the processes have been followed.

Nevertheless, documentation can be beneficial, because it allows departments and customers to examine a company's processes. This, in turn, may lead to more consistency and suggest ways to improve those processes. An additional benefit is that the company will be listed in the ISO directory, which many companies and individuals examine to determine which suppliers they should do business with. Finally, a company can advertise the achievement of certification to the ISO 9000 standards. In other words, it is good business, because it shows a commitment to quality management.

## NOTES

1. http://www.yale.edu/lawweb/avalon/hamframe.htm.

2. *Industrial Quality Control* (July 1947): 23.

3. *Economic Control of Quality of Manufactured Products* (New York: D. Van Nostrand Co., 1931).

4. *Sampling Inspection Table: Single and Double Sampling,* 1st ed. (New York: John Wiley & Sons, 1944).

5. *Quality Control: Principles, Practice, and Administration* (New York: McGraw-Hill, 1951).

6. *Out of the Crisis* (Cambridge, MA: Massachusetts Institute of Technology, Center for Advanced Engineering Study, 1986).

7. *The New Economics,* 2nd ed. (Cambridge, MA: Massachusetts Institute of Technology, Center for Advanced Engineering Study, 1997).

8. http://www.deming.org/deminghtml/wedi.html. Additional information on Deming and his work, writings, and philosophies can be found at the Deming Institute's website, http://www.deming.org.

9. Information on Juran and his work, writings, and philosophies can be found at the Juran Institute website, http://www.juran.com.

10. *Quality Is Free* (New York: McGraw-Hill, 1979). Additional information on Crosby and his work, writings, and philosophies can be found at the website of Philip Crosby Associates II, Inc., http://www.philipcrosby.com.

11. http://www.nist.gov.

12. http://www.asq.org.

13. See http://www.nist.gov/public_affairs/releases/n99-02.htm.

14. Ibid.

15. http://www.quality.nist.gov/97s&ltbl.htm.

16. See http://www.efqm.org.

CHAPTER **18**

# COST OF QUALITY

## Zafar U. Khan
**Eastern Michigan University**

**18.1 INTRODUCTION** According to economic theory, no company in a competitive market can generate excess profits for long: Competition and excess capacity will drive profits down to their normal level. In the current context of global competition, all companies must continually seek ways to develop sustainable competitive advantage.

Generic strategies to develop competitive advantage include *differentiation* or *cost leadership*. For some companies, *quality enhancement* has proved to be a successful method of product differentiation and cost reduction—so much so that it has led Michael Porter (the widely known expert on strategy from the Harvard Business School) to rethink competitive advantage. Porter has recently suggested that in today's competitive business environment, all companies have to be low-cost producers and must also differentiate their product or service from those of competitors.[1] Contrary to conventional wisdom, quality enhancement initiatives have the potential to do both—reduce cost and increase differentiation.

The focus on quality has revolutionized business philosophy and practice since the 1980s. Japanese and U.S. companies that have adopted quality enhancement as a strategic goal have changed the face of competition forever. The quality revolution has moved beyond manufacturing to service industries and other sectors of the economy. With help from such quality gurus as W. Edwards Deming, Joseph M. Juran, and Genichi Taguchi, these companies have assumed the number-one position in several industries. Quality is not just another passing fad; indeed, it is said that a business without quality products or services will not survive in today's global marketplace. The work of Deming and Taguchi, which focuses on reduction of variation to achieve quality manufacturing, has inspired some world-class companies to create these advantages for themselves.

However, this has not been easy for U.S. businesses. Faced with strong competition based on quality from the Japanese in the late 1970s and early 1980s, U.S. managers were slow to respond. In a study of the room air-conditioning industry, for example, Garvin found that Japanese manufacturers had total quality costs of 1.3 percent of sales, whereas U.S. manufacturers averaged from 2.8 to 5.8 percent of sales for rework, scrap, and warranty costs alone.[2]

As late as 1991, U.S. companies trailed the Japanese in quality across a broad range of industries.[3] This led to a loss of market share, reduced profits, and also a loss of jobs for U.S. workers. Robert Cole traces this slow response to institutional forces that impeded the responses of managers to market forces.[4] However, U.S. companies have significantly reduced the quality gap in most industries, thanks to support from quality consultants such as Deming, Juran, and Philip B. Crosby, as well as the efforts of several nonprofit and for-profit institutions, such as GOAL/QPC, the Conference Board, American Society for Quality, SEMATECH, the American Supplier Institute, the Malcolm Baldrige National Quality Award, and the International Organization for Standardization.[5]

In the 1990s, U.S. executives realized that if they were to regain preeminence, they had to give top priority to quality. As a result, many U.S. manufacturers and all the big-three automobile manufacturers instituted and improved their "quality programs." Examples include:

- General Motors's Saturn Project and Mark of Excellence Award.
- Ford's "Quality Is Job Number One" program and Total Quality Excellence Award.
- Daimler-Chrysler's Pentastar Award.

By now, Ford, General Motors, and Daimler-Chrysler have implemented second- and third-generation quality improvement programs. In automobile body quality dimensional control, Daimler-Chrysler's (formerly Chrysler Corporation) ZJ "2 mm Program" is especially noteworthy. Sponsored by the Auto Body Consortium and funded by the National Institute of Standards and Technology (under its Advanced Technology Program), the "2 mm program" has been successfully implemented in several plants run by General Motors and Daimler-Chrysler Corporation.

The popular business press is replete with stories about the success U.S. companies have had at incorporating quality into all areas of their businesses, but it would be a mistake to become complacent. The emphasis on quality must continue, because the competition continues to raise the ante. In the automobile industry, for example, much has been done to improve customers' perceptions about the quality of U.S. cars, but improvements are still needed. A recent customer satisfaction survey for the automobile industry revealed that Lexus leads comparable Ford and General Motors brands by several percentage points.[6]

Japanese manufacturers continue to raise the quality expectations for automobile bodies by reducing variation through their continuous improvement processes. As a demonstration, Toyota ran a series of television advertisements in which a ball rolls along fit lines between body panels of a Lexus to illustrate the precision of the fit and the continuity of slope between the body panels. Later, Nissan ran similar advertisements for the Altima to create similar expectations about body-build quality for all customers—not just luxury car customers. To be competitive, managers of U.S. automobile body-build processes have taken steps to achieve the same precision dramatized in these competitive advertisements. This has become possible only because U.S. managers have discarded their outmoded ideas about quality and embraced a new quality paradigm—to reduce variation.

**18.2 DEVELOPMENTS IN COST-OF-QUALITY MODELS**   Quality is a complex concept involving several attributes.[7] There are many definitions of quality, though most (according to Garvin) of them fall into five categories:

1. Transcendent.
2. Product-based.
3. User-based.
4. Manufacturing-based.
5. Value-based.[8]

The many attributes and definitions of quality are a source of confusion and mis-understanding. Different people view quality differently based on their expectations and their situation in the value chain (design, production, sales, and consumption). Garvin argues that companies need to adopt different definitions of quality—and con-sequently different quality strategies—as their products move from design to market.

For example, *transcendent* definitions (which associate quality with innate excel-lence) may be useful for building and measuring corporate image and brand recogni-tion. Because customer expectations play a major role, *user-based* definitions of qual-ity that focus on customer satisfaction should be used to develop strategies and measure their success across the entire value chain. *Manufacturing-based* definitions that focus on conformance to specifications are, of course, appropriate for assessing the manu-facturing function. There is some evidence that consumers increasingly prefer value-based definitions of quality; the implication is that businesses must provide the highest-quality products at the lowest cost.

Following *total quality management* (TQM), most companies use user-based defini-tions of quality or definitions based on customer satisfaction.[9] Many companies in the forefront of TQM have established "delighting the customer" as a strategic objective. Because this chapter emphasizes *cost of quality* (COQ) for manufacturing operations, the focus is on the manufacturing-based definition of quality—*conformance to design specifications*.

This assumes that businesses use *quality function deployment* (QFD), *target costing*, and *value engineering* practices (which are discussed elsewhere) at the design and devel-opment stages to ensure customer satisfaction. The design specifications generally con-sist of a nominal or target value and tolerance (to accommodate process variation) of some critical parameter or characteristic. The tolerance is often specified as an *upper specification limit* (USL) and a *lower specification limit* (LSL).

**(a) Traditional Quality Concepts**  In the traditional view of quality, products, sub-assemblies, and parts are considered either acceptable (good) or unacceptable (defec-tive). Parts or products whose measurements of the critical parameters fall within the USL and LSL are considered acceptable. Parts or products whose critical measure-ments fall outside the USL or LSL are considered defective and unacceptable, so these parts or products are scrapped or reworked to conform to the specifications.

Under the traditional view of quality, all acceptable parts or products are considered to be of the same quality. No distinction is made between the *level* of quality of parts or products that have measurements equal to the target value (or close to it) and parts or products that have measurements equal to (or close to) the USL or LSL. Thus, this concept of quality leads to a "pass" or "fail" type of sorting of output. Manual in-spection and measurement using custom-made gauges or general-purpose measuring instruments are usually used for sorting good output from bad.

From a COQ perspective, traditional costing methods that follow the traditional model of quality focus only on the cost incurred in the production of the defective or unacceptable parts or products. That is, the production or rework cost (direct material, direct labor, and manufacturing overhead) of the units not meeting quality control standards (specifications) is considered a loss. This loss is further divided into *normal* and *abnormal*. Under this approach, although no formal definition of COQ is presented, the abnormal loss may be considered as such. This is clearly a gross understatement of the total COQ—or, more appropriately, the cost of poor quality.

Many traditional accounting systems only report the abnormal loss as feedback for control and corrective action. The premise is that whereas abnormal loss (i.e., loss due to special causes) is controllable in the short run, normal loss (i.e., loss due to common causes) is an inherent part of the chosen production process, so it cannot be controlled without costly changes in the process or in product design. The implied loss function (see Exhibit 18.1) is a discrete linear function with either zero loss—if the part or product has measurements within the USL and LSL—or full (100 percent) loss (if the product or part has measurements outside the USL or LSL).

Such accounting systems fall short. Instead of helping managers achieve strategic objectives, they are a hindrance. Consequently, several observers have identified accounting systems as one of the major factors contributing to the poor competitive position of U.S. manufacturing during the 1970s and 1980s.

**(b) Contemporary Cost-of-Quality Concepts**   Many contemporary quality cost-systems are based on the works of Joseph M. Juran, William Maser, Philip B. Crosby, and Ar-

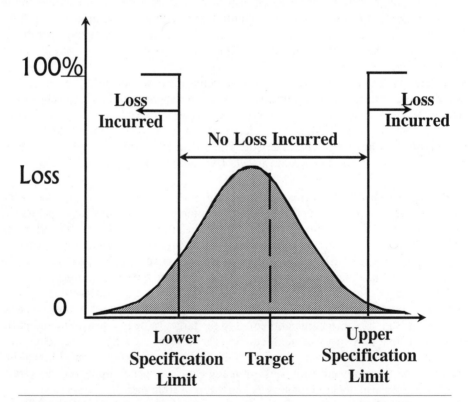

**Exhibit 18.1    Specification-Based Quality Loss Function (for Any Dimensional Characteristic)**

mand V. Feigenbaum. These authors developed the basics of quality cost measurements by classifying quality costs into the categories of *prevention, appraisal,* and *failure*—also called the P-A-F model.[10] Further, prevention and appraisal costs are called *cost of conformance,* whereas failure costs are called *cost of nonconformance* to quality control standards. Exhibit 18.2 illustrates the concept that as voluntary conformance costs increase, involuntary nonconformance costs decrease. The net result is a reduction of total costs.

Just as with "quality," there are many definitions of COQ, which can simply be viewed as the sum of prevention costs, appraisal costs, internal failure costs, and external failure costs. From a conceptual point of view, however, COQ is best viewed as an opportunity to reduce cost and increase customer satisfaction.

Juran defines cost of poor quality as the sum of all costs that would disappear if there were no quality problems. Thus, quality-control efforts should be directed at preventing all quality problems.

*(i) Prevention Costs*    Prevention costs are incurred to ensure that things are done right the first time. These generally include costs of activities:

- Process and product-design reviews.
- In-line process control.
- Analysis and corrective actions to eliminate the root causes of problems.
- Preventive maintenance.
- Training of workers.
- Education of vendors.
- Vendor certification programs.
- Quality assurance programs.

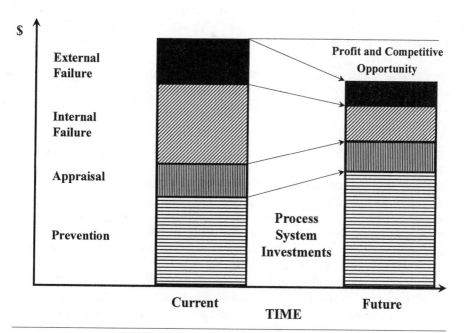

**Exhibit 18.2    Cost of Quality**

Prevention costs should be viewed as an investment. Research indicates that most companies spend too little on prevention activities.[11] This is unfortunate, because prevention packs the biggest bang for the buck. John Gruher, director of manufacturing at Merix Corporation, would rather invest $5 for prevention than $1 in inspection. Expenditure on inspection is a cost, but expenditure on prevention is an investment that pays back many times over.[12]

Preventive quality improvement efforts that were focused on scrap reduction at an international manufacturing company resulted in:

- 50 percent reduction in overhead costs.
- 20 percent reduction in period expenses.
- On-time delivery increase from 80 percent to 93 percent.
- 60 percent increase in work-in-process (WIP) turnover.
- 50 percent increase in raw material turnover.
- 20 percent increase in labor productivity.
- 32 percent increase in revenues.
- $17 million increase in net income.[13]

Another recent analysis at a manufacturing facility of a major automobile manufacturer indicated that for every $0.08 spent on prevention, the company saved $1 in internal failure costs alone.[14] If all downstream cost savings and increase in productivity are included, the true return is much higher.

*(ii) Appraisal Costs* Appraisal costs include amounts spent for inspection, testing, and sampling of inputs, outputs, and WIP. These include expenses for quality inspectors, inspection, and testing equipment, whether products are made in-house or by a vendor. Appraisal costs also include all laboratory costs, inspection setup costs, costs to maintain or calibrate inspection equipment, and associated administrative costs.

For companies facing high external failure costs, appraisal is the main short-term approach for sorting good output from bad in order to prevent bad products from going to customers. For many companies, appraisal costs are a significant part of total quality costs. As discussed later, however, leading companies use technology and innovative management practices to shift their spending for appraisal costs into prevention, where the payoff is much higher.

*(iii) Failure Costs* Failure costs are generally divided into *internal failure costs* and *external failure costs*. Internal failure costs are incurred for either disposal or rectification of defective products before they are shipped to the customer.

All scrap and rework costs are classified as internal failure costs. Most existing accounting systems do a reasonable job of identifying, measuring, and accumulating these costs. In reality, though, these costs are often understated, because standard costs include an allowance for "normal" spoilage, and opportunity costs are not included.

Internal failure costs should also include the cost of downtime, reduced yield, and higher inventory and procurement costs caused by producing defective parts. For most companies, internal failure costs are the highest percentage of the measured quality costs. Further, the impact of successful prevention effort to reduce internal failure costs is probably the easiest to demonstrate.

External failure costs are incurred because of product failure after the product is delivered to the customer. External failure costs generally include:

- Warranty costs.
- Complaint handling.
- Field service.
- Product recall.
- Product liability.
- Loss of sales because of customer dissatisfaction.

Some external failure costs are easily measured and included in existing accounting systems, but others (e.g., lost sales from current and future customers) are difficult to measure and, therefore, are not included. Nonetheless, these costs are often the most significant of all the quality costs. They are referred to as hidden quality costs by Deming, Juran, and Taguchi.

Researchers have developed innovative approaches to estimate external failure costs.[15] These approaches range from using a simple multiplier for measured cost (e.g., two to four times) to surveys of customers and employees to fairly sophisticated mathematical models using the Taguchi loss function. It is important that external failure costs be estimated; otherwise managers are likely to make suboptimal decisions about prevention costs. (As mentioned earlier, there is evidence that most companies spend too little on prevention.)

The advantage of the COQ classification described previously is that it provides a framework for quantifying and minimizing total COQ. Juran's model of optimum quality costs (see Exhibit 18.3), for example, presents a concave total-quality-cost function. As voluntary expenditure on appraisal and prevention increases, the increased conformance (i.e., lower defects rate) leads to lower involuntary failure costs. The minimum total quality cost occurs when the marginal cost of prevention and appraisal equals the marginal cost of failure.

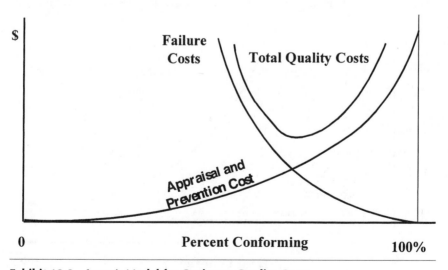

**Exhibit 18.3   Juran's Model for Optimum Quality Costs**

**(c) Problems with Contemporary Cost-of-Quality Concepts**    A careful analysis of Juran's model of COQ reveals several problems. Juran's model (Exhibit 18.3) suggests that the optimal level of quality cost occurs at less than 100 percent conformance. The model depicts an increasingly steep curve for appraisal and prevention costs—an application of classical economic theory concerning the diminishing marginal returns relative to reduction in defective output. As the proportion of defective production is reduced, failure costs decline at a decreasing rate. While the marginal cost of prevention and appraisal increase, the marginal savings from decreasing failure costs decline.

Juran's traditional trade-off model remained unquestioned from its introduction in 1962 until the mid-1980s. Kume and Schneiderman were among the first to question the validity of this trade-off.[16] However, the model still continues to be the basis for the widely held belief that too much quality (perfection) may be uneconomical—that there is an economically acceptable level of quality, and that that level is not 100 percent conformance (or zero defects). This is ironic, because Juran (along with Gryna) modified his model, as shown in Exhibit 18.4, to suggest that minimum quality costs occur at 100 percent conformance.[17]

Although the general nature of the cost curves may appear reasonable, the exact shape of the cost curves has not been empirically determined because of difficulties in measuring many of the costs involved. Both COQ models—Exhibits 18.3 and 18.4—ignore the relationship between prevention and appraisal costs in arriving at the joint prevention and appraisal cost function.

Fargher and Morse argue that the prevention and appraisal cost function cannot be determined by simply adding the prevention and appraisal costs (unless one assumes that this is the minimum cost combination of prevention and appraisal costs at the given level of quality).[18] Managers can decide to invest 100 percent in prevention activities or 100 percent in appraisal activities, but in practice, they choose to invest in some combination of the two. Whether that combination level is optimal is an empirical question that has not been resolved. However, historically there has been more emphasis on appraisal, and the emerging view of quality control argues for more emphasis on prevention.

It is not difficult to understand why companies historically have invested more in ap-

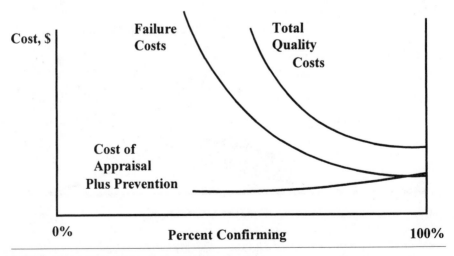

**Exhibit 18.4    Revised Model of Quality Costs**

praisal and less in prevention—it is much easier. Investment in appraisal generally means hiring more inspectors, and buying more equipment, tools, and instruments. However, investment in prevention requires critical analysis to identify the root cause of problems and to find innovative approaches to eliminate them.

Further, it is important to look at appraisal and prevention costs separately, because the two types of costs behave very differently and have different implications for cost control.[19] Appraisal costs based on the old classic inspection approach are largely man-hours of inspection, and they may closely follow the shape of the curve Juran postulated for prevention and appraisal costs. However, two important appraisal developments have dramatically changed appraisal cost behavior. One is technological and the other behavioral.

*(i) Effect of Technological and Behavioral Changes on Appraisal Cost*    Technological advances in automatic gauging, together with other factors such as high labor costs and reliability, have encouraged more and more companies to invest in in-line appraisal or measurement systems. The new gauging devices have made it possible to measure parts more reliably, for more conditions, and at a higher cycle rate than before.[20] For example, new laser-based in-line measurement systems instantaneously detect any changes in body assembly accuracy for every vehicle.[21] Daimler-Chrysler, General Motors, Nissan, and many of their suppliers already use these systems. Similar systems have been developed for use in a wide range of manufacturing businesses.[22]

In the behavioral area, many Japanese and U.S. companies now realize that—however diligent the inspectors—high quality cannot be "inspected in." These companies, following Toyota's lead, are empowering assembly-line employees to be responsible for quality, which virtually eliminates the need for highly paid quality-control inspectors.

Thus, overall costs of appraisal may be significantly less because of the technological and behavioral changes. With 100 percent in-line measurement, these costs are relatively flat—or fixed. Another way to look at this is to consider that once a process is stable (and the technology and behavioral focus on problem solving help achieve early stabilization), the marginal costs of appraisal are very small. As the in-line measurement systems provide data that help identify root causes of problems, there are valid questions about whether the costs of such systems should be considered appraisal or prevention costs.

*(ii) Prevention Cost Behavior*    Most Japanese (and some U.S.) companies have established a system for detecting defects quickly and tracing every problem to its ultimate (root) cause. Once those causes are discovered, steps are taken to ensure that the problem does not recur.[23] This systematic problem-solving system pays significant dividends in the form of reduction in scrap, rework, and warranty costs.[24]

Companies that spend more and more on prevention have found that total quality costs continue to fall, which means that prevention costs have not yet reached the optimal level (i.e., where the marginal increase in prevention cost equals the marginal decrease in failure cost).[25] Further, significant investments in on-line monitoring systems that help prevention efforts may overwhelm the variable component, in which case overall prevention costs are also relatively fixed or flat.

*(iii) Effect of Quality-Based Competition on the Behavior of Internal and External Failure Costs*    It is also useful to look at failure costs separately in terms of internal and external failure costs. Internal failure costs pose few problems in terms of measurement, and

traditional costing systems have measured and reported most of these costs. In the present competitive environment, however, producing high-quality, low-cost products is an important goal. To achieve this goal, companies should increase their focus on preventive activities. When increases occur in prevention costs, internal failure costs should decline sharply, which (in turn) should lower the overall costs of production.

In traditional cost systems, some important external failure costs have largely been ignored. Contemporary COQ systems measure some of the external failure costs, such as warranty costs, product returns, and product liability. Other external failure costs—in particular, contribution lost from customer ill will (due to poor quality) or missed opportunities—have been difficult to measure and, therefore, ignored.

These "hidden" costs become significant in a quality-based competitive environment, and they may be extremely high at conformance levels below 100 percent. That is, a company may rapidly lose market share (and suffer losses) if its products do not match the customers' heightened quality expectations set by the competition. Further, if these costs are not measured or estimated, companies using Juran's traditional COQ trade-off model will underinvest in prevention effort, which exacerbates an already critical situation. The result is a downward spiral of declining market share and profitability.

**(d) Taguchi's Contribution**    Another problem with Juran's COQ model is that it is based on the traditional "pass" or "fail" model of quality. As discussed previously, this approach assigns an equal value for quality to all "good" products or parts, even though one part or product may fall just within the tolerance limit while another may match the target value exactly.

Japanese quality guru Genichi Taguchi has a different view. Taguchi believes that a company gains virtually nothing by shipping a product that barely meets quality-control specifications; he exhorts manufacturers to get "on target" rather than just trying to stay within specifications.[26] The argument is that a product that barely meets specifications is likely to fail in the hands of the customer, which means the possible—and costly—loss of that customer and perhaps several more. Taguchi emphasizes losses incurred after a product is shipped to a customer—external failure costs—as opposed to internal failure costs, which most traditional and contemporary COQ models emphasize.[27]

Taguchi's methods for off-line quality control (e.g., the design of experiments for product and process design) have reportedly found overwhelming success in business. Some major U.S. companies that have adopted Taguchi's methods include Daimler-Chrysler Corporation, Ford Motor Company, ITT, Xerox, Lucent Technologies (formerly Bell Laboratories), United Technologies, 3M Company, and General Motors. Taguchi's ideas about on-line quality control—reducing process variation for overall quality improvement—are also widely discussed in the quality-control literature, but reported practical applications are limited. However, many companies now use the Taguchi quality loss function to estimate the "hidden" quality costs.[28]

**18.3 NEW QUALITY PARADIGM: FOCUS ON VARIATION**    Emerging views of quality and costs of quality are based on the ideas of Deming and Taguchi, which emphasize management of variation. Both Deming and Taguchi believe that variability leads to quality costs and that external failure costs are the most significant—though, unfortunately, they are not measurable in aggregate. But these are the "hidden" costs that management cannot afford to ignore. Deming emphasizes reduction of process variation for quality control; his philosophy is that quality improves as variability decreases.[29]

Efforts to manage variation in all facets of life have gone on for ages. Ancient Egyptians used measurement and prediction to deal with the variation of water in the Nile.[30] Provost and Clifford trace the various concepts used in the past to cope with variation. A simple concept of "fitness for use" served well from about 5000 B.C. to about 1800 A.D. With mass production and the need for interchangeable parts came new challenges and the concept of "specification and tolerance," which is still in use.

In 1924 Walter Shewhart developed the *control chart method* and the concepts of *special causes* and *common causes* of process variation.[31] The method implies that once special causes of variation are removed, a process is stable. Whether the process meets customer requirements is determined by process capability analysis.

Taguchi links improved quality through reduction of variation to costs by his *quality loss function.* Based on experience, Taguchi proposed a quadratic quality loss function as an approximation of the external failure costs. Overall loss is the factory loss (internal failure costs) plus quality loss.[32]

Taguchi's model (see Exhibit 18.5) shows a minimal quality loss when the important characteristics of products or parts equal the target values (i.e., the design intent). The quality loss increases by the square of the deviation of the product's or part's important characteristics from design intent. For example, if the product's important characteristic is two standard deviations away from design intent, the external failure costs (what Taguchi calls *quality loss*) are approximately four times some constant. According to Taguchi and Clausing, this constant is the cost of the effort that the company needs to put in to get back on target.

The focus on reduction of variation provides a methodology and process for improving quality. Acceptance of Taguchi's quality loss function means that the quality of parts, subassemblies, or products decreases—and that cost increases—as their critical dimensions vary from the design intent. Thus, the key to quality improvement—and to lower overall costs—is reducing variability in all stages of the assembly process.[33]

**(a) Implications for Manufacturing**    Both Deming and Taguchi emphasize that even for parts or products that have dimensions (or important characteristics) within the upper and lower specification limits, there are "hidden" quality costs. Deming and Taguchi's

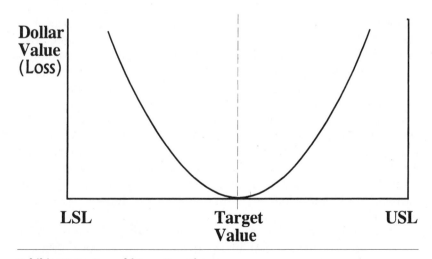

**Exhibit 18.5    Taguchi Loss Function**

ideas have great significance for manufacturing (particularly assembly operations, such as automobile body assembly) in which more than 300 parts are put together on a moving assembly line. When so many parts are randomly selected to be assembled together, even if each individual part is "good" (i.e., its dimensions fall within specifications), the result may be an imperfect product or an inefficient process because of what is called the "tolerance stack-up problem."

The implication of Taguchi's quality loss function is that if managers decide not to incur the voluntary expenses of reducing variation, they will involuntarily incur several times that amount in the form of warranty costs, lost contribution because of customer ill will, and similar costs. Taguchi's concept of variation-based quality loss also applies to different stages of manufacturing, because any stage can be viewed as the customer of the previous stage. (Indeed, experts in TOQ recommend that if the output of one department or stage is the input to another, then the first department should view the second as its customer.)

For example, the "customer" of an auto body shop is the paint shop and final assembly. If there is variation in the output of the body shop, the paint shop and final assembly will incur additional costs (a quality loss) because of rework, adjustments to the process, an inability to automate, and reduced throughput. The only difference is that these losses are called internal failure costs rather than external failure costs. Therefore, variation-reduction efforts should reduce internal failure costs both in the process itself and in downstream processes.

To achieve world-class quality, U.S. manufacturers need to use quality tools such as the *Taguchi methods*. Applying Taguchi methods to the design of products and processes, and to the control of processes by reducing variation, is likely to lead to robust products with a minimum cost to the producer, customer, and society in general.[34] For example, success in the auto-body assembly at Daimler-Chrysler's Jefferson North Assembly Plant (JNAP)—which occurred by an emphasis on reducing variation and centering process means at design intent—demonstrates that the United States can develop the capability to achieve world-class quality in automobile bodies.[35]

**(b) Process Management** To understand the role of in-line measurement systems, cross-functional teams for problem solving, knowledge-based systems for root cause analysis, and continuous quality improvement for reducing variation, one needs to understand the various stages of process development and process management.

For example, Exhibit 18.6 depicts stages of process management applicable to the automobile body-build process, though the exhibit can be used to depict any similar manufacturing or assembly process. What is probably unique about the automobile body-build process is its cyclical nature. The regular introduction of new models results in a periodic repetition of the process-stabilization stages.

The first production stage (shown in the bottom lefthand corner of Exhibit 18.6) is the *start-up stage*. During this stage, many special causes exist for both high deviation and variation (usually outside the specification limits), which lead to poor quality. Exhibit 18.7 shows the role of in-line measurement systems in continuous improvement of body assembly. The in-line measurement system data for the subassemblies and body-as-framed is used to identify the special causes, which are targeted for elimination by cross-functional problem-solving teams.[36]

Once the majority of special causes are removed, the process enters the second production stage, *statistical behavior* (Exhibit 18.6). Here the process exhibits statistical behavior and is generally centered, but its variation is often outside the specification lim-

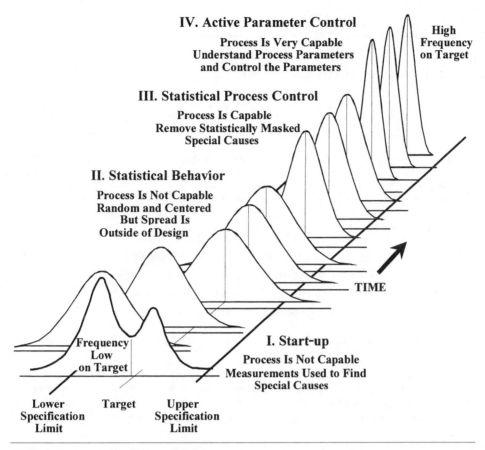

**IV. Active Parameter Control**

Process Is Very Capable
Understand Process Parameters
and Control the Parameters

High
Frequency
on Target

**III. Statistical Process Control**

Process Is Capable
Remove Statistically Masked
Special Causes

**II. Statistical Behavior**

Process Is Not Capable
Random and Centered
But Spread Is
Outside of Design

TIME

Frequency
Low
on Target

**I. Start-up**

Process Is Not Capable
Measurements Used to Find
Special Causes

Lower
Specification
Limit

Target

Upper
Specification
Limit

**Exhibit 18.6    Stages of Process Management**

its. The in-line measurement data are used to change the process to improve statistical variation and establish a high degree of process centering (Exhibit 18.7).

During the *statistical process control* (SPC) stage, the process is capable and in control: The process is usually centered and within specification limits. However, the variation and deviation are usually more than what would be considered "world class." The in-line measurement data are used to improve statistical variation to a world-class level. This is made possible by quickly finding special causes that are normally masked (as random) by traditional, small-sample SPC charts (Exhibit 18.7). This is not to minimize the importance of SPC charts: SPC charts are an important and cost-effective tool for determining whether a process needs adjustment. But to readily determine what adjustments are needed, 100 percent in-line measurement data are becoming essential for modern high-speed assembly lines.[37]

During the final production stage—the *active parameter control* stage—the process is fully understood, so it lends itself to active parameter control. The process is capable and centered, and it has little variation, so it approaches a world-class level (Exhibit 18.6). By this stage, the process control parameters are sufficiently understood so that they can be actively controlled to maintain and (if desired) narrow the variation further (Exhibit 18.7).

The in-line measurement system provides the basis for a "system knowledge base,"

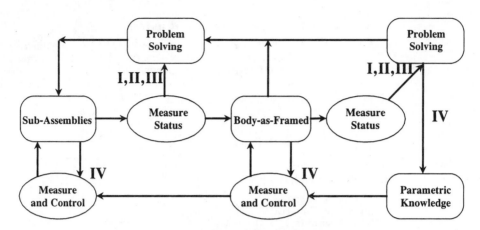

I. Remove Special Causes
II. Obtain Statistical Behaviour
III. Continue to Improve by Removing
Statistically Masked Special Causes
IV. Active Parameter Control—Active Prevention

**Exhibit 18.7    Continuous Improvement of Body Assembly Using In-Line Process Measurement**

which develops from solving problems during the SPC stage and tracking change in real time. This knowledge from the in-line process measurement systems may also be used to develop a preventive maintenance system to avoid future problems.[38]

*(i) Measurement*    Measurement is the key to continuous quality improvement in to-day's automated, high-speed assembly lines. To achieve world-class variation levels and reach the active parameter control stage of process management, companies must have a system for early isolation and analysis of variation problems so they can identify the root cause of problems and take quick corrective action.

For example, Daimler-Chrysler's Jefferson North Assembly Plant recorded body-build continuous quality improvement—and reduced variation from 8.5 mm to below 2 mm—in record time by using laser-based in-line measurement systems and empowered, cross-functional teams.[39] The ability of in-line measurement systems to continuously collect data provides the information necessary to rapidly reduce the time required to achieve world-class variation targets.

To accelerate the pace of variation reduction for continuous quality improvement, use of noncontact in-line optical measurement systems is a must. The common practice of sampling a few units per shift with off-line *mechanical coordinate measurement machines* (MCMM)—or 5 to 10 percent with so-called in-line MCMMs—provides neither timely feedback to contain variation problems nor sufficient data to apply the correlation-based systematic problem-solving methods that researchers have developed.

Assembly processes using MCMMs are likely to stay at the third stage of the process development (see Exhibit 18.6) (i.e., the SPC stage). At this stage (as mentioned earlier), a process may be considered to be in control, but the variation is far from a world-class level. If any progress occurs beyond this stage, it is likely to be slow. The sample measurement data (assuming random sampling) may allow inferences to be made about whether a process is in control or out of control, but it does not provide much help for rapidly detecting changes of variation (or identification of the source of variation) by using systematic methods to analyze the correlation of measurement points.

If Taguchi's loss function is accepted, the implications are clear: There will be high involuntary failure costs (e.g., scrap, rework, and poor automation performance) in downstream processes and customer expectations. To reduce overall failure costs, both in process in question and in downstream processes, quick identification and resolution of variation problems are essential. Modern laser-based optical measurement systems provide this ability to detect and resolve variation problems quickly.

Further, manufacturing facilities today have to cope with shorter model lives, smaller volumes per model, and frequent model changes. Flexible measurement systems become important when quick changeovers are needed because of frequent model changes. A system of laser-based, noncontact measurement devices mounted on robots allows measurements for many different types of models by simply changing the operational data for the robot. It is also sometimes necessary to experiment with different critical points for measurements before arriving at the best configuration. This requires a flexible measurement system that can be quickly changed or reconfigured. Modular construction allows for moving sensors quickly from one critical point to another, or for adding or removing sensors.

This flexibility also helps resolve variation problems that have multiple root causes. When variation occurs because of multiple root causes, it is not always possible to identify or eliminate all the root causes quickly because of incomplete measurement data. In such situations, installation of additional sensors in upstream subassemblies may help significantly to reduce the costs of variation problems from multiple root causes. In one case, failure costs from variation problem were reduced by 96 percent after installing additional sensors in upstream subassemblies to provide useful process measurement data.[40]

*(ii) Cross-Functional Teams for Problem Solving*    For achieving low overall production costs, early detection of variation problems and response time is essential. For example, windshield fractures caught at installation cost $3.60 each to remove and replace, but if the fractures are caught downstream, it costs about 10 times more ($35.70 each) to remove and replace the windshields.[41] Consequently, work teams should be able to quickly identify variation problems, analyze data to determine the root causes, and then take corrective action.[42] In-line measurement system provides this early-detection capability (with minimum failure losses) in high-volume production environments.

Permanent reduction of variation cannot be realized without an understanding of the root causes of variation and a systematic, data-driven, knowledge-based effort to solve problems by identifying and then eliminating them. For example, variation in an automobile body may be attributed to either component variation or variation introduced during the assembly process.[43] Most of the variation problems are caused by problems in product or process design, installation, tooling, maintenance, and supplier components.[44]

Solving variation problems therefore requires a team effort—one that involves product and process design engineers, production operation personnel, maintenance personnel, and suppliers, among others. The integration of a cross-functional team's design and manufacturing process knowledge base with a data-driven analysis is essential for rapid identification of the root causes and corrective action necessary for permanent variation reduction. It also requires the commitment of top managers to an organizational philosophy of continuous improvement. The ultimate objective is to have an error-free assembly process.

*(iii) Knowledge-Based System for Root Cause Analysis*    In recent years, 100 percent in-line measurement systems have been used increasingly in a wide range of manufacturing operations. To take advantage of the tremendous amount of data provided by such systems, researchers have proposed using diagnostic methods, including multivariate techniques such as *principal component analysis*. These techniques have been used successfully to reduce variation in processes.[45] Researchers have enhanced the effectiveness of these statistical tools by integrating knowledge of the product, tooling, and assembly process to provide diagnostic decision-support capabilities; these knowledge-based systems have been used in manufacturing for quite some time now.[46]

Experience with in-line measurement systems makes it possible to detect and resolve certain recurring problems. For example, after examining literally hundreds of process printouts from the laser-based in-line measurement system, Daimler-Chrysler Corporation technicians at the Jefferson North Assembly Plant began to recognize "process signatures" of specific problems.

Knowing about these specific problem "signatures" enables technicians to identify the cause of a variation problem by simply examining the process printout. For example, variation problems caused by loose or broken clamps, or by misaligned weld tips, can be quickly identified by their unique process-variation printouts or problem signatures (see Exhibit 18.8). Quick identification of the cause of a variation problems considerably reduces the time required to resolve the problem. It also significantly reduces the failure costs.[47]

*(iv) Continuous Improvement*    To regain its number-one position, the U.S. manufacturing industry has undergone many changes. One of the most significant of these changes is *continuous quality improvement* (i.e., continual reduction of variation to achieve incremental gains that add up over the long run).

The United States has historically had a significant competitive advantage through innovation, to the extent that some argue that U.S. industry should continue to rely on

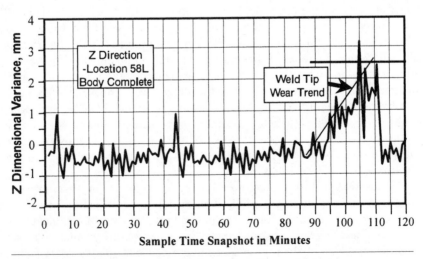

**Exhibit 18.8    Weld Tip Wear Dimensional Variance Signature**

what it does best—innovation. However, U.S. companies realize that innovation and continuous improvement are not mutually exclusive. Sandwiching continuous improvement between innovations can provide an unbeatable combination.

For enhanced quality and low overall production costs, the importance of containing variation problems and eliminating root causes cannot be overemphasized. As discussed earlier, continuous quality improvement results from reducing variation and centering of process means at design intent. To implement continuous process improvement—finding and eliminating root causes of variation problems—a company must detect variation in a timely manner. That is, world-class variation requires:

- In-line measurement in real time to track performance.
- A systematic process of quickly identifying the root causes of problems.
- Taking corrective action to prevent recurrence of variation problems.
- Using empowered, cross-functional teams.

These are the requirements for maximizing continuous improvement in today's automated, high-speed, and complex manufacturing operations.

**(c) Quantification of Variation Reduction Benefits**    Numerous case studies and other reports document the financial benefits that accrue from quality improvement initiatives. Although some of these efforts (and the resulting financial benefits) may have come from focus on variation reduction, published reports that document the benefits of variation reduction are scarce.

One example is Nypro, Inc., a recognized leader in custom injection molding that uses Taguchi methods for both process design and control. Nypro's emphasis on variation reduction and process centering is credited with reducing quality costs by $900,000 a year and with increasing sales by 16 percent, profits by 45 percent, and customers' acceptance of Nypro products without traditional inspection.[48] Another example is Budd Company. David Williams, the president of Budd Company, has credited variation reduction efforts for reducing overall costs at his company.

The documented experience of Daimler-Chrysler Corporation's successful implementation of the "2 mm program" (i.e., reducing total automobile body-assembly variation at the Jefferson North Assembly Plant to less than 2 mm) provides a clear quantification of the tremendous benefits that result from variation reduction. Analysis of the data established clear correlation between costs and variation reduction in the automobile body assembly. The efforts at the Jefferson North Assembly Plant's body shop alone found the following benefits over about two years[49]:

- Moving average scrap rate ($/job) declined by about 71 percent and resulted in an estimated average after-tax savings of about $550,000.
- Moving average labor cost declined by about 73 percent and resulted in an estimated average after-tax savings of about $30 million.
- "Other manufacturing expenses" declined on a cost-per-unit basis by about 50 percent and resulted in estimated average after-tax savings of about $600,000.
- One type of WIP (clones) was reduced from 12 to 4, which resulted in an estimated reduction in investment of about $4,000.
- Launch time was reduced by two weeks, which provided an estimated after-tax contribution of more than $8 million.

- The number of units produced steadily increased by about 26 percent, which provided an estimated after-tax contribution of about $59 million.

A more comprehensive analysis of the implementation of the 2 mm program at five General Motors and Daimler-Chrysler Corporation plants indicated the following direct benefits of reducing total dimensional variation of automobile bodies[50]:

- Decreased production costs.
- Decreased product maintenance costs.
- Improved product quality.
- Reduced time required to launch new products or product models.

Further, macroeconomic analysis performed by CONSAD Research Corporation suggests that once the 2 mm project is implemented at all the General Motors and Daimler-Chrysler Corporation plants, the lower production and maintenance costs alone should save the manufacturers and consumers hundreds of millions of dollars annually. Indirect benefits are projected to increase annual U.S. output by at least $3 billion by the year 2000 and to create thousands of new jobs.

**18.4 SUMMARY**    Research indicates that there are positive links between quality and profitability. High-quality products and services increase market share and sales.[51] Increased quality also leads to lower costs.[52] Higher sales and lower costs mean more profits.[53]

Yet current research shows that many companies do not have a formal COQ system.[54] This is unfortunate, because studies in various industries and businesses show that the cost of poor quality is between 20 percent and 40 percent of total costs, which means that quality problems cost billions of dollars annually.[55] This is a tremendous opportunity. Many businesses could add more to their bottom lines by reducing the costs of poor quality than they could add by doubling their sales.

Traditional cost systems do not measure all of the costs of quality. Most focus on direct costs, which are only a portion of internal failure costs, while significantly underestimating total quality costs. As a result, managers at companies that rely on traditional accounting systems often cannot cost-justify quality-improvement activities.[56] Further, performance measurement systems that evaluate managers only on their reduction of the direct costs of defective products are misguided. Because these performance measurement systems force managers to concentrate on products that have large direct costs, they are likely to make suboptimal decisions. Experience with activity-based costing systems indicates that in the current business environment, a large proportion of product costs are indirect (i.e., support-activity) costs, which are often misallocated by traditional costing systems.[57]

There are problems with both traditional and contemporary concepts of quality and COQ, given new technological developments, ever-increasing quality standards, and cost-based competition. All these factors indicate that any system for achieving high quality with minimum costs cannot be based on outmoded concepts of quality and costing systems.

Furthermore, although customer satisfaction has become a top priority for almost all businesses today, many management control systems for manufacturing overemphasize throughput and short-term cost control (e.g., reducing scrap and rework) within individual departments. These systems based on traditional responsibility accounting lead to goal-congruence and displacement problems. That is, maximizing or minimizing some measure (e.g., quality costs) in individual responsibility centers does not always lead to what is best for the company as a whole. Managers resort to managing the numbers instead of focusing on activities that would lead to higher quality and lower costs.

As a result, many plant managers—who often work with poorly designed products or processes and who are beset with other problems as well—have to resort to shipping products assembled from parts or subassemblies that have high variation. These conditions cause losses in downstream processes and also losses to customers or society. This is obviously inconsistent with the goal of customer satisfaction, and it is also a poor strategy in a globally competitive environment.

Besides embracing the new quality paradigm—reduced variation—businesses should invest in a formal COQ system. Many companies (such as ITT, Xerox, the Federal Reserve Bank of Philadelphia, North American Philips Consumer Electronics Corporation, Westinghouse, MBNA America, Motorola, Daimler-Chrysler, and General Motors) have implemented COQ programs and saved millions of dollars in total quality costs.[58] World-class companies such as Xerox, Westinghouse, and Motorola have reduced quality costs from 30 percent of sales to as low as 2 percent to 3 percent.

Benefits of a formal COQ system include:

- Promotes a companywide focus on quality.
- Puts a monetary value on quality that catches management's attention.
- Helps prioritize quality improvement efforts.
- Emphasizes prevention rather than troubleshooting.
- Quantifies and reports savings from investments in preventive activities, which has a big motivational impact.
- Helps put things in perspective (e.g., helps companies avoid mistakes such as spending $2 per part to improve a $0.25 part).
- Provides data for time-tested discounted cash flow models, which can be used for justifying investments in technology that promote quality.

Other key observations based on recent experience with variation reduction efforts include:

- Building higher-quality products is a successful method of product differentiation in a competitive environment.
- In industries such as the automobile industry where buyers generally purchase upscale, even entry-level products must have the same commitment to quality as luxury models.
- Reduction of variation in all stages of the manufacturing process leads to higher quality and lower overall costs.
- An organization's emphasis on identifying root causes of variation problems and eliminating them is very beneficial.
- Flexible and intensive "in-line noncontact measurement systems" are essential for timely detection and quick resolution of variation problems.
- Early detection by an in-line measurement system and quick response to variation

problems are essential for minimizing costs. Downstream costs of a variation problem may be up to ten times higher than at the station where the problem occurred.

To summarize, focus on variation reduction appears to be the single most important strategic initiative that affects the three key generic success factors: *quality, cost,* and *time*. Two examples further illustrate this point:

1. The 1997 Toyota Camry was the only car in its class that was introduced at a price lower than the price of the 1996 model. The lower price was attributed, in part, to cost savings realized from the redesign of a bumper that had fewer parts. Fewer parts implies lower variation, and lower variation means lower costs. The result: Camry is the best-selling car, having overtaking the Ford Taurus.
2. Quick resolution of variation problems reduces launch time, so products are in the market earlier. The financial success of Daimler-Chrysler's Jeep Grand Cherokee and Ford's Expedition (both of which were brought to market in record time) points out the enormous benefits of bringing products to market early— which occurred, at least in part, because of rapid reduction of variation.[59]

A COQ system is an important and proven element of TQM—one that has had a positive impact on many businesses and has the potential for doing so with many more. A COQ management process should strengthen COQ results by integrating the system across the entire value chain of business functions. Developing and implementing an effective COQ management system across the entire organization would require considerable time and effort and would vary from company to company. However, experience suggests that any plan to achieve world-class status should include the following:

- Executive commitment
- Master plan
  - Establish cross-functional quality improvement teams
  - Conduct training
  - Assess quality status
  - Benchmark
  - Set quality and COQ goals and targets
  - Define and select COQ elements
  - Collect and report data
  - Analyze data
  - Prioritize problems for corrective action
  - Conduct root-cause analysis
  - Implement corrective action
  - Review
- Develop implementation strategy
- Implement master plan
- Review

Many businesses have realized that current cost and managerial accounting practices are not conducive to COQ management; they also fail to promote investment in new technology that would promote quality. The adoption of activity-based costing

(ABC) systems and activity-based management (ABM) are steps in the right direction. An ABC system that measures, accumulates, and reports costs of activities (such as rework or preventive actions) that reflect changes in quality should facilitate quantification of the benefits of quality improvement from variation reduction and technology. Quantification of the benefits of preventive activities and technology that promotes quality should lead to better justification and increased investment.

**(a) Quality, Variation Reduction, and Profits**    Successful variation reduction in the automobile body assembly at Daimler-Chrysler's JNAP and at other General Motors and Daimler-Chrysler plants has led to higher quality and lower costs. The Jeep Grand Cherokee built at JNAP experienced lower warranty claims and lower production costs, and it has enjoyed both strong demand and increased productivity.[60]

The results of the JNAP study show that the variation reduction experience has been a success for Daimler-Chrysler.[61] The Jeep Grand Cherokee built at JNAP is a success with customers and is in great demand. JNAP has successfully reduced total automobile body variation to its original world-class goal of 2 mm. Cross-functional teams focusing on variation problem solving and elimination of root causes achieved this.[62] Exhibit 18.9 presents a model of the impact of reduction in variation on the bottom line.

Reducing variation leads to improved quality. Higher quality has a favorable effect on profits because of reduced costs and increased revenues. Overall costs are reduced because of shortened response to variation problems, lower production costs, lower inventories, lower downstream costs, higher supplier part quality, and lower worker environmental costs. Revenues are increased because of higher throughput and higher satisfaction of both employees and customers.

**(b) Cost Benefits of Variation Reduction**    Even the limited quantification results of variation-reduction efforts at Nypro, Budd Company, JNAP, and other plants at General Motors and Daimler-Chrysler powerfully demonstrate the overwhelming benefits that result from a focus on variation reduction. Analysis done by Diallo, Khan, and Vail at Daimler-Chrysler's JNAP indicate that the benefits of variation reduction far outweigh the costs.[63] Estimates of the net present value of the investment in laser-based in-line measurement system that facilitate variation reduction ranged from $1.5 million to $18 million. Further, every $0.08 spent on corrective action of variation problems reduced internal failure costs by more than $1.00. The conclusion that investment in variation reduction at JNAP is highly profitable is supported by the extended study of five General Motors and Daimler-Chrysler plants conducted by CONSAD Research Corporation.[64]

**(c) General Considerations**    To achieve world-class quality, it is important to train employees about the cost of quality. For quality-improvement efforts to succeed every employee must understand the dollar impact of his actions on the total operations of the business.[65] Deming strongly believed that poor quality does not result from work performed by employees but rather from poorly designed systems and procedures. Companies need to develop COQ reporting systems that identify opportunities for quality improvement and monitor the effectiveness of quality-improvement efforts.

The typical U.S. corporate culture is obsessed with apportioning blame, which must change. If employees who are responsible for gathering and reporting COQ data feel threatened, the system is bound to fail. Management has to realize that errors are natural and sometimes inevitable. The key is to develop robust systems that lead to robust products and processes. The goal of a COQ management system should be to integrate the

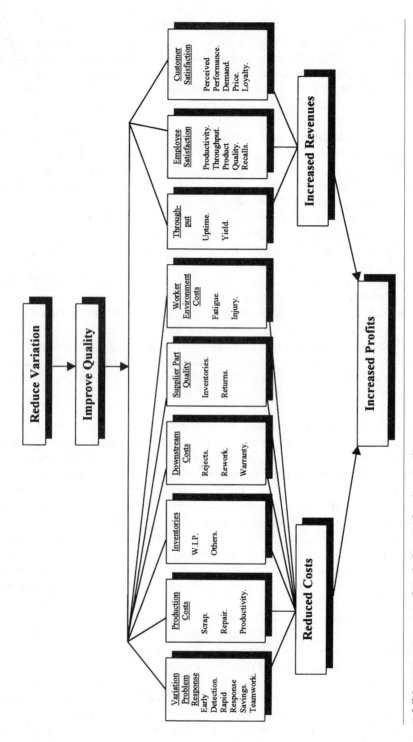

**Exhibit 18.9  Impact of Variation Reduction Profits**

diverse knowledge about products, production processes, tooling, maintenance, suppliers, and statistical quality control techniques of all employees to achieve world-class quality.

*(i) Training* In view of the financial benefits that accrue from a focus on quality, best practices must be implemented across an entire organization. A commitment to total quality is required from everyone. This must be coupled with a systematic training of plant personnel that makes them adhere to the central role of variation reduction in quality manufacturing. (Taguchi's "off-line" methods of quality control applicable to design and development of products also focus on reducing variation.)

The training must demonstrate the importance of technology such as laser-based in-line measurement systems that allow 100 percent sampling in achieving superior levels of prevention activities and process control. Plant personnel must be convinced that no matter how devoted and committed they may be to their work, they can make quality products only by fully utilizing measurement equipment and quickly acting on the information gathered from such equipment.

Each cross-functional team should be proficient in identification of variation problems and root-cause analysis. These include multivariate techniques such as principal component analysis and other tools such as cause-and-effect (or fishbone) diagrams, control charts, Pareto charts, histograms, and brainstorming.

*(ii) Corporate Culture* The necessity for quick action on the plant floor requires a change in corporate culture. Higher management and plant management must empower assembly workers to make decisions regarding quality. Even more important, they must back up those decisions under initial adverse situations. For example, emphasis on variation reduction may at first reduce the plant yield. Assembly workers who used to push products through the line must be convinced that stopping the line to solve quality problems will not be held against them. Thus, yield may have to be deemphasized initially to develop new work approaches and to establish the manufacturing process parameters in every plant equipped with laser-based in-line measurement systems or other technology that promotes quality. Everyone needs to believe that the costs of not meeting customers' expected quality levels could be prohibitive so that they act accordingly.

*(iii) Responsibility* The responsibility for data gathering should be delegated where collection is needed—that is, to those in the plants who are involved with the manufacturing process. This requires making plant workers aware of the importance of quality data. Data forms should be created that meet the data-collection objectives. These forms must remain simple and brief so that assembly workers feel comfortable using them and so that they fill them out consistently.

Responsibility for data gathering must be established at each subassembly level and, ultimately, across the entire value chain. The goal is to determine the cost of all COQ activities using the "prevention-appraisal-failure" framework in a manner that facilitates decision making. Each cross-functional team must document variation problems or cases using a preestablished format that allows for quick cost information.

## NOTES

1. M. E. Porter, Keynote address at the ABC Technologies User Conference, Chicago, August 1998.

2. D. A. Garvin, "What Does Product Quality Really Mean?" *Sloan Management Review* 26 (1984): 25–43.

3. For details, see the special issue: "The Quality Imperative," *Business Week* (1991).

4. R. E. Cole, "Learning From the Quality Movement: What Did and Didn't Happen and Why?" *California Management Review* 41 (1998): 43–73.

5. Among others, see ibid.; S. A. Dellana and M. A. Coffin, "Quality Management Tactics in U.S. Manufacturing: Do They Rival the Japanese?" *Engineering Management Journal* (1996): 27–34; "American Business Survey," *Economist* ( September 16, 1995): 5.

6. Also see E. Updike, "Is Cavalier Japanese for Edsel?" *Business Week,* (June 24, 1996): 39.

7. V. A. Zeithmal, "Consumer Perceptions of Price, Quality, and Value: A Means-End Model and Synthesis of Evidence," *Journal of Marketing* (July 1988): 2.

8. Garvin, op. cit.

9. N. Tamimi and R. Sebastianelli, "How Firms Define and Measure Quality," *Production and Inventory Management Journal* 37 (1996): 34–39.

10. T. L. Albright and H. P. Roth, "The Measurement of Quality Costs: An Alternative Paradigm," *Accounting Horizons* (June 1992): 15–27.

11. K. K. Shah and P. T. FitzRoy, "A Review of Quality Cost Surveys," *Total Quality Management* 9 (1998): 479–486; E. Sandelands, "The Drive Towards Quality," *Work Study* 43 (1994): 23–24.

12. "Cost of Poor Quality," video produced by the Society for Manufacturing Engineers.

13. R. J. Vokurka and R. A. Davis, "Quality Improvement Implementation: A Case Study in Manufacturing Scrap Reduction," *Production and Inventory Management Journal* 37 (1996): 63–68. There are many such case studies. Among other examples, see L. P. Carr and T. Tyson, "Planning Quality Cost Expenditures," *Management Accounting* 74 (1992): 52–56; M. Gupta and V. S. Campbell, "The Cost of Quality," *Production and Inventory Management Journal* 36 (1995): 43–49.

14. A. Diallo, Z. Khan, and C. Vail, "Cost of Quality in the New Manufacturing Environment," *Management Accounting* 77 (1995): 20–25.

15. For example see L. P. Carr, "How Xerox Sustains the Cost of Quality," *Management Accounting* 77 (1995): 26–32; G. Margavio, T. Margavio, and R. Fink, "Managing the Cost of Quality in the Era of Continuous Improvement," *CMA Magazine* 69 (1995): 29–31; M. Kim and W. Liao, "Estimating Hidden Quality Costs with Quality Loss Functions," *Accounting Horizons* 8 (1994): 8–18; L. P. Carr, "Applying Cost of Quality to a Service Business," *Sloan Management Review* 33 (Summer 1992): 72–77; C. D. Heagy, "Determining Optimal Quality Costs by Considering Costs of Lost Sales*," Journal of Cost Management* 5 (1991): 64–73.

16. D. A. Sandoval-Chavez and M. G. Berivides, "Using Opportunity Costs to Determine the Cost of Quality: A Case Study in a Continuous-Process Industry," *The Engineering Economist* 43 (1998): 107–124.

17. J. H. Atkinson, Jr., G. Hohner, B. Mundt, R. B. Troxel, and W. Winchell, *Current Trends in Cost of Quality: Linking the Cost of Quality and Continuous Improvement* (Montvale, NJ: National Association of Accountants, 1991); Carr and Tyson, op. cit., also presents a similar COQ model.

18. N. Fargher and D. Morse, "Quality Costs—Planning the Trade-off Between Prevention and Appraisal Activities," *Journal of Cost Management* 12 (1998): 14–21.

19. Diallo, et al., op. cit.

20. C. A. Griffith, "Advances in Automatic Gaging Techniques," paper (710156) presented at the Automotive Engineering Congress, of the Society of Automotive Engineers, Inc., Detroit, MI, 1971.

21. Y. Sekine, S. Koyama, and H. Imazu, "Nissan's New Production System: Intelligent Body Assembly System," SAE Technical Paper Series, 910816, Society for Automotive Engineers, Inc., 1991, p. 7.

22. S. K. Case and L. E. Prine, "Controlling Manufacturing with Lasers," *Quality* 33 (1994): 50–53; J. G. Salsbury and L. Denes, "Laser Measurements at Cummins Engine," *Quality* 33 (1994): 52–53.

23. J. P. Womack, D. Jones, and D. Roos, *The Machine that Changed the World* (New York: HarperCollins, 1991): 57

24. Z. U. Khan, A. Diallo, and C. F. Vail, "Quality Control and Management of Variation—Assessing Cost Benefits," *International Journal of Strategic Cost Management* (Winter 1999): 37–50.

25. Y. K. Shetty, "Managing Product Quality for Profitability," *SAM Advanced Management Journal* (Autumn 1988): 33–38.

26. G. Taguchi and D. Clausing, "Robust Quality," *Harvard Business Review* (January–February 1990): 65–75.

27. Actually, Taguchi calls it loss to society.

28. There are several published reports in the quality control literature; see note 15 for some examples.

29. W. Edwards Deming, *Out of the Crisis* (Cambridge, MA: Massachusetts Institute of Technology, Center for Advanced Engineering Study, 1991), 335.

30. Will Durant mentioned in L. P. Provost and C. L. Norman, "Variation through the Ages," *Quality Progress* (December 1990): 39–44.

31. Ibid.

32. Taguchi and Clausing, op. cit., p. 68.

33. P. R. Sudhakar, "An Introduction to Quality Improvement Through Taguchi Methods," *Industrial Engineering* 27 (1995): 53–54; G. D. Stocker, "Reducing Variability—Key to Continuous Quality Improvement," *Manufacturing Systems* (March 1990): 32–36.

34. Taguchi and Clausing, op. cit.; E. S. Fine, "Reduce Variation and Save Money," *Quality Progress* 32 (1999): 128; P. R. Sudhakar, op. cit.

35. D. Ceglarek, J. Shi, and Z. Zhou, *Variation Reduction for Body Assembly: Methodologies and Case Study Analysis* (unpublished research report, University of Michigan, 1993), 2.

36. The in-line measurement data are the basis for the correlation-based systematic problem-solving methodology developed by the University of Michigan engineers. See Ceglarek et al., *note 35.* The in-line measurement data could also be used for a simulation-based approach to identifying sources of variation.

37. See D. Ceglarek, J. Shi, and S. M. Wu, "A Knowledge-Based Diagnostic Approach for the Launch of the Auto-Body Assembly Process," *Journal of Engineering for Industry* 116 (1994): 491–500; S. T. S. Bukkapatnam, A. Lakhtakia, and S. R. T. Kumara, "Chaotic Neurons for On-line Quality Control in Manufacturing," *International Journal of Advanced Manufacturing Technology* 13 (1997): 95–100.

38. A. Diallo, Z. U. Khan, and C. F. Vail, *Financial Justification of Quality Related Capital Investment in the Body Shop* (unpublished report, Eastern Michigan University, 1993).

39. See Ceglarek et al., note 35, 3. Also see Sekine et al., op. cit., for use of in-line measurement system at Nissan.

40. Diallo et al., note 38.

41. For details, see cost analysis of case 72 in Bakus et al., *Quantification of Variation Problem Cases.*

42. Womack et al., op. cit., also came to the same conclusion. That is, the Japanese automobile manufacturers' high quality (and low cost) results from identifying and fixing problems. Manufacturing systems that depend on inspection and rework (or scrap) to correct defective output cannot compete with the *lean systems* on quality and costs.

43. C. Wearring and G. Cola, "Identifying Sources of Build Variation Using VSA Audit," *SAE Technical Paper Series* (911644, 1991): 1.

44. Also see Z. Zhou and X. R. Cao, "Optimal Process Control in Stamping Operation," *Quality Engineering* 6 (1994): 621–631.

45. D. Ceglarek and J. Shi, "Case Study: Dimensional Variation Reduction for Automotive Body Assembly," *Manufacturing Review* 8 (1995): 139–145.

46. Ceglarek, Shi, and Wu, note 37, 491.

47. Diallo et al., note 38.

48. B. S. Jones, "SPC to $C_{pk}$ 2," *QUALITY* (December 1989): 25–27.

49. Kahn et al., note 24.

50. CONSAD Research Corporation, *Advanced Technology Program Case Study: The Development of Advanced Technologies and Systems for Controlling Dimensional Variation in Automobile Body Manufacturing* (Gaithersburg, MD: National Institute of Standards and Technology, March 1997).

51. Shetty, op. cit.; Kambize E. Maani, "Does Quality Pay?" *Incentive* (February 1990): 20–26, 133. An anecdotal example is of Toyota's Lexus brand. Within a short time, Lexus has established a reputation as being number one in quality. Lexus now leads Cadillac, Mercedes, BMW, and Lincoln in sales in North America.

52. Khan et al., op. cit.; CONSAD Research Corporation, op. cit.

53. Also see Garvin, op. cit.

54. Atkinson et al., op. cit.; L. M. Sjoblom, "Financial Information and Quality Management—Is There a Role for Accountants," *Accounting Horizons* 12 (1998): 363–373; Shah and FitzRoy, op. cit.

55. A. L. Velocci, Jr., "Cost of Quality An Industry Challenge," *Aviation Week & Space Technology* 149 (1998): 58; J. A. Maycock and T. Shaw, "Quality Costing—The Money in Mistakes," *TQM Magazine* 6 (1994): 20–22; K. E. Schmahl, Y. Dessouky, and D. Rucker, "Measuring the Cost of Quality: A Case Study," *Production and Inventory Management Journal* 38 (1997): 58–64.

56. P. Nandakumar, S. M. Datar, and R. Akella, "Models for Measuring and Accounting for Cost of Conformance Quality," *Management Science* 39 (1993): 1–16; A. Diallo, Z. Khan, and C. Vail, "Measuring the Cost of Investment in Quality Equipment," *Management Accounting* 76 (1994): 32–35.

57. Also see Carr and Tyson, op. cit.; Nandakumar, et al., op. cit.

58. See Gupta and Campbell, op. cit., among others.

59. Ford introduced Expedition in 1996 within a record 36 months at the time. Actually, all the domestic automobile manufacturers are focusing on reducing time to market and have achieved some measure of success. Ford, for example, has reduced time to market to 30 months from 60 months a few years ago. Its current target is to reduce it to 24 months.

60. The weighted average warranty data shows a decline from 16.6 to 12.12 for body panel alignment; the most severe warranty problem. See Diall et al., note 38.

61. JNAP was ranked as one of the top 25 plants in the nation by *Business Week*.

62. Ceglarek, et al., note 35.

63. Diallo et al., note 38.

64. CONSAD Research Corporation, op. cit.

65. P. R. Corradi, "Is a Cost of Quality System for You?" *National Productivity Review* 13, Spring (1994): 257–269.

# CHAPTER 19

# MEASURES OF QUALITY PRODUCT AND QUALITY PROCESS: EMERGING COST-OF-QUALITY MODEL

## Lawrence Carr

**Babson College**

**19.1 INTRODUCTION**   A significant issue surrounding *total quality management* (TQM) is the assessment of program costs and the corresponding benefits to be gained from implementing a total quality system. To make this kind of evaluation requires the development of reliable costs associated with the effects of quality.

The *cost of quality* (COQ) is a well-recognized—although often disputed—tool used to understand the economic consequences of quality. Although definitions of COQ vary, it is generally considered to be the costs—both tangible and intangible—that relate to the quality characteristics of a product or service. Purchasing managers and discerning consumers all want to know the costs related to quality. Contractors are required to provide details of the costs of quality for the products they sell to the government.

Many quality experts recognize the difficulty of associating cost with the benefits of a quality program. They maintain that it is difficult to place a cost figure on quality and that accounting cannot capture the "true" costs of quality. Some fundamental concerns include:

- Quality costs do not readily appear in the accounting journals.
- Large timing delays between quality costs and the related benefits create distortions.
- Accounting rules do not lend themselves to measuring quality
- Numerous cost estimates are needed.
- Some hidden costs never get captured.
- Matching future costs with historical costs is difficult.

These and other arguments have led many to ignore COQ and to advocate the use of direct measures from operations (e.g., *statistical process control*; see Chapter 20)—to measure a TQM program. This chapter explores this controversy and offers guidelines for choosing a measurement system that will fit the characteristics of a company's TQM program and link it to the company's strategy.

Debates over the use of COQ stem from the elusive nature of cost measurement and the lack of a crisp and precise definition of quality. To begin with, quality must itself be defined before costs associated with attaining this characteristic or state of existence can be measured. For some, quality relates to the number of features and attributes of a product. Someone might maintain, for example, that a BMW is a better car than a Nissan because it has more features. Others might make the same observation but base their decision on the reliability of the product, maintaining, for example, that a Chrysler is a better car than a Saab because it needs fewer repairs. There are many such examples, which combine to provide some agreement as to the definition of quality. *Fitness for use* and *conformance to specifications* are the two prime dimensions used to define quality for COQ purposes.[1]

**(a) Fitness for Use**    *Fitness for use* consists of those product attributes that meet a customer's needs and thus provide product satisfaction. Product attributes such as performance, reliability, durability, and aesthetics serve to meet the customer's expectations. *Conformance to specifications* refers to the degree to which a product meets the design specifications or answers the question, "Is the product built to the design?"

For example, a badly made BMW may have high fitness for use, and it might even meet some customers' expectations, but it would still have low quality in terms of conformance. On the other hand, a well-made Nissan may have a lower fitness for use but a high quality of conformance. Quality costs generally represent all costs associated with conformance to specifications or design, or they answer the question, "What are the costs that resulted from not making a product as designed?"

**(b) Conformance to Specifications**    Another approach to quality is conformance based (see also Chapter 17). Crosby describes this as the "conformance requirements" specified by the engineering and product characteristics. Manufacturing is required to conform to the specifications. The closer the adherence to the manufacturing specifications, the higher the quality level. This approach lends itself to objective measures against standards, and the costs associated with conforming to these standards can be calculated. The customer, however, is ignored in these calculations of cost.

**(c) Value Approach**    A third approach to measuring quality is the value approach. This is a customer-based, subjective approach in which the balance between product cost and product value is determined. One can plot a consumer's preferences along the value and cost axes to determine a cost of quality. This value proposition defines the company's competitive position.

It is important that a company clearly reconcile its approach and definition of quality to its competitive strategy. This is essential to the use and measurement of quality and associated costs. In general, companies that use a differentiation strategy will use the fitness-for-use definition of quality, whereas companies that use a low-cost strategy will use a conformance-based definition of quality.

**19.2 TRADITIONAL COST-OF-QUALITY MODEL**    Typically, quality costs are defined as all expenditures associated with ensuring that products conform to specifications. This model does not address the fitness-for-use definition of quality. (This concern and other issues surrounding the use of the traditional COQ model are addressed later in the chapter.) The model states that cost can be divided into two broad categories, each of which has two subcategories:

1. Conformance costs
   - Prevention
   - Appraisal
2. Nonconformance costs
   - Internal failure
   - External failure

The study of the relationship of the COQ categories led to the development of a significant body of literature that offers various models to explain the interrelationship of the COQ categories. Exhibit 19.1 represents the original or classical model. The costs of prevention and appraisal are considered zero with a 100 percent failure rate, but these costs rise as failure rates decrease. The costs of prevention and appraisal rise to infinity as perfection is reached.

This hypothetical model shows that quality costs are high when quality is low. Total quality costs fall as quality improves, though they become infinitely high even before 100 percent quality is attained. According to the model, a company that produces poor-quality (defective) products can greatly reduce failure costs by adding relatively low-cost prevention and appraisal measures. But as prevention and appraisal expenditures continue to rise, the rate of improvement begins to diminish until additional expenditures produce little decrease in failure costs.

The model suggests that an optimal relationship exists between conformance quality costs and nonconformance quality costs. Minimal total quality costs are achieved at the optimal balance of prevention and appraisal expenditures (on the one hand) with internal and external failure costs (on the other hand). Implicit in this model is the trade-off of conformance costs for nonconformance costs to achieve the lowest total

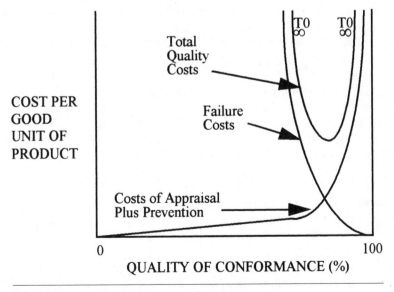

**Exhibit 19.1    Traditional Model of Quality Costs**

quality cost. Also, this model suggests that there is a level beyond which additional prevention and appraisal expenditures will only increase the total quality cost (the law of diminishing returns). Reporting the costs of quality using this model allows managers to monitor the cost trade-off over time.

Implicit in this model of quality costs is the idea that a company with poor quality can greatly reduce the costs associated with detecting and correcting poor quality by adding relatively inexpensive preventive measures. At a certain point, however, additional prevention costs will only increase total quality costs, as shown in Exhibit 19.1. More prevention produces comparatively little decrease in correction costs, which means an overall increase in total quality costs. For example, managers will not achieve the lowest quality cost by increasing appraisal costs to a 100 percent quality-inspection level. This will certainly reduce the external failure costs, but it will also increase the internal failure costs (the cost of scrap and rework). For example, paper manufacturers have discovered this trend and therefore now seek a more balanced approach to reducing the cost of quality.

The key to producing a COQ model such as this is to make sure that the costs of quality are properly captured. Often these costs represent only a portion of an expense line item. For example, training costs are a major element of the cost of prevention. Quality awareness and skills training are covered in both specific quality-improvement sessions and other general training efforts. The issue, then, is how to accurately capture the expenses relating to the cost of prevention? Similar accounting issues occur with other COQ categories. Appraisal and internal failure costs are straightforward; they have distinct cost categories that correspond to a normal chart of accounts. The real problem arises with the cost related to external failure.

**(a) External Failure Cost**   Many external failure costs are part of a company's normal field service and sales activities; they are not designated as separate costs related to quality. How, then, can a company capture the costs (primarily labor time) related to resolving a customer's problem? Sales personnel, customer-service representatives, engineers, and others do not normally differentiate between time devoted to making a sale and time spent resolving a customer's problems.

Many companies estimate these quality costs based on some internal time and cost study. Senior managers often get involved in resolving major customer problems. How are these costs captured? What troubles many critics of this concept is that calculating the hidden costs surrounding those external failures is not reported. Lost opportunities, customer dissatisfaction, and negative customer referrals are certainly costs relating to poor quality. It is important to remember that the cost of quality is, at best, an educated estimate of the costs, not a precise measure. Critics of the COQ model often cite the "soft" numbers as a real concern when using this tool for measurement or evaluation.

**(b) Limitations of the Cost-of-Quality Concept**   The literature is also full of critiques of the COQ model and the use of cost in evaluating the progress of a quality program. The limitations of the COQ concept include the following:

- *COQ measurements do not solve quality problems.* Many question the practical value of using COQ. Maintaining these data does not solve any of the problems that cause the cost of poor quality to exist. The historical nature of accounting data does not tell managers or operations people what needs fixing or what to do to improve quality. For example, Deming does not subscribe to Juran's notion that quality costs can be minimized at some nonzero number (the classic trade-off model above). Both Crosby and Deming believe that the cost of selling defective product is so high that quality costs will be minimized only at 100 percent conformance, or zero defects. Quality managers look for evidence of actions to improve quality. Knowing the costs provides no guidance.

- *Publication of cost figures does not stimulate cost reduction.* Managers quickly point out that decisions and actions are necessary: Changes have to be implemented to affect the costs of quality. Cost numbers provide a reference point, but line managers must still determine the steps necessary to reduce these costs.

- *COQ reports do not indicate specific actions needed.* Managers must decide the cost investments for each of the various categories. Some believe that increased prevention and appraisal costs will lead to a reduction of failure costs. The specific actions are up to the individual manager. Others believe that excess spending in prevention and appraisal will lead to increased total quality costs, because these will not be counterbalanced by a proportionate reduction in failure costs.

- *COQ calculations do not capture all of the cost.* There are implied and hidden costs that make COQ useless. Feigenbaum points out that the COQ calculation ignores indirect and intangible failure costs. Good examples of these costs include[2]:
  —Extra production to compensate for failures.
  —Queuing time in the production process caused by rework.
  —Excessive finished goods inventory to compensate for field failures.
  —Excessive handling costs caused by suboptimal production layouts.

- Garvin had similar concerns and was particularly interested in the involuntary costs that arise whenever customers choose alternative suppliers because of actual or perceived quality deficiencies.[3]

- *Accounting conventions (e.g., rules on capital spending and rules for defining period costs and product costs) render COQ of little use for evaluating a quality program.* COQ looks at spending to improve quality and at the assessment of spending in the various cost categories during a given period of time. Much of the quality spending is capital in nature. When large expenditures for equipment are required, large costs are often also required for up-front training. Investment for the future and depreciation of capital expenditures make accounting assessments of quality difficult.

- *Important costs can easily be omitted from the COQ calculation.* Both Feigenbaum and Garvin expressed concern about the integrity of accounting data collection. They demonstrate that many costs that are not captured actually affect the COQ.

- *There is a time delay between cause and effect, and a COQ report may not capture all the changes in the same period.* Often the effects of quality training and the building of an awareness of quality in an organization are measured in years. Prevention spending in year 1 may only show its effect in year 3, thus overlapping the conventional year-to-year COQ analysis.

- *Quality costs are subject to judgment and estimation, which can cause distortion.* Many of the cost calculations for the categories mentioned previously are the result of judgment calls by both operational personnel and accounting staff. There are often no clear single-account numbers derived from a company's chart of account to capture COQ accounting data.

- *COQ has a tendency to be short term in nature.* Many investments in quality (e.g., for test equipment, process redesigns, or quality awareness training for all employees) are short term. There are large initial costs that yield a stream of benefits over many years. The traditional model does not relate this stream of benefits to the related costs.

From this list, one can see that determining COQ is as much an art as a science. The numbers are inherently "soft" in nature. Not all the costs over time can be captured from the accounting records. Therefore, COQ does provide an indication or general model of how a company spends its quality dollars. Companies know that it takes resources to establish a TQM program, and managers need some feedback about their effectiveness. When COQ data are combined with other operational measures (such as statistical process control trends, yields, defect rates, and customer complaints), a clearer picture of the progress of a quality program is developed so that managers can evaluate its effectiveness.

**19.3 EMERGING COST-OF-QUALITY MODEL**    Limitations of the cost model discussed previously, coupled with the manufacturing and process changes of today's organizations, has led to a slightly different COQ model. As Exhibit 19.2 shows, this model places more emphasis on prevention and appraisal.

Prevention spending is very important in fostering a quality mind-set and instilling a sense of caring in the work force. New technologies have reduced the inherent failure rates of materials and limited the direct labor content of most products. Automation of the manufacturing process and testing routines has changed the shape of the COQ curve.

This revised model looks at the total COQ rather than the unit cost. It suggests that voluntary prevention and appraisal costs are relatively fixed over time rather than di-

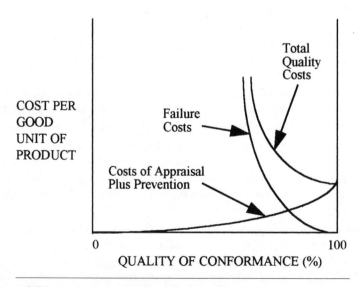

**Exhibit 19.2    Emerging Model of Quality Costs**

rectly proportional to changes in the level of nonconformance, as indicated in the more static traditional model.

The emerging COQ model recognizes that total quality costs include indirect and intangible costs. These costs are probably not minimized at less than 100 percent conformance.[4] Because of the high multiplier effect of perceived quality deficiencies, intangible failure costs may linger even if the actual quality-of-conformance deficiencies are totally eradicated.

Cost minimization is also contentious, because it implies that a specific optimal level exists. In reality, optimization is a moving target, because of technology breakthroughs and competitive pressures.[5] Prevention and appraisal costs are also subject to cost reduction because of experience factors and market competition. The emerging model indicates that some amount of prevention and appraisal must be maintained to keep the earlier quality improvements. This model does not encourage trade-offs.

The concept of loss—rather than nonconformance—better encompasses the total business cost of out-of-pocket, indirect, and intangible failures. Minimizing quality loss acknowledges the multiplier effect of intangible failure costs and recognizes the need to sustain the quality improvement effort beyond the minimization point of out-of-pocket costs.

**19.4 OTHER METHODS TO MEASURE THE COST OF QUALITY**  As the previous sections discuss, there are many problems associated with producing accurate COQ numbers. Managers expect to show performance in accounting terms. The emerging practices recognize the difficulty and theoretical nature of seeking an optimal COQ by making the trade-offs between conformance and nonconformance quality costs. The classic model shown in Exhibit 19.1 gives a reasonable general model, but it does not reflect how these costs behave. A business must still know the level of its costs of poor quality. Managers want to compare the costs in various areas before quality programs are introduced to correct deficiencies. They would like to use accounting data to measure the COQ.

Several well-documented studies outline innovative techniques used by companies such as IBM, Xerox, Tennant, Ford, Westinghouse, Pacific Bell, and others.[6] These companies employ COQ calculations as an integral part of their quality programs. They are flexible in their definitions of quality costs, comfortable about making cost estimations, and practical in the way they present the information. In general, the accounting department takes an active role and assists the company in calculating the economic effect of poor quality.

**(a) Experience at Tennant Company**  Hale, Hoelscher, and Kowal implicitly refute the traditional model by recommending a different proportional distribution as the target for the quality cost categories.[7] They describe how the Tennant Company has significantly improved product quality and reduced total quality costs. Specifically, Tennant's total COQ decreased from 17 percent of sales in 1980 to 7.9 percent by 1986 and to 2.5 percent of sales in 1988. Average annual sales growth of 11 percent accounted for some, but not all, of the cost reduction. The proportional distribution of costs changed among the quality cost categories over the eight-year period. Failure costs decreased from 50 percent in 1980 to 15 percent in 1988, whereas prevention costs increased from 15 percent to 50 percent during the same period.

Clearly, Tennant does not endorse a model that depicts the location of optimal quality-cost expenditures at the intersection of voluntary and involuntary costs. Nor does the company target cost minimization if this occurs at less than 100 percent confor-mance. According to a Tennant executive, no one really knows where the minimum COQ is: "There may be a theoretical answer to that issue, but not a practical answer. I feel that message is out-of-date and belongs in the same category as engineers who still use slide rules."

Despite the fact that only 15 percent of total quality costs are now represented by out-of-pocket failures, Tennant Company continues to incur additional voluntary quality-cost expenditures. The company believes that backsliding will occur unless a steadfast commitment to quality improvement is maintained. Regarding their com-pany's ongoing commitment, Hale, Hoelscher, and Kowal write[8]: "The quest for qual-ity never ends. A company can make progress, and even reach the point where it has no quality problems. But unless quality improvement is a continual activity, all the progress that has been made will be lost."

**(b) Policy Conflict at Texas Instruments**    An example of the policy conflict regarding the reduction of quality cost versus the reduction of failure rates is the Texas Instru-ment (TI) Materials and Controls Group case.[9] The division instituted a COQ program in response to a corporate program, "Total Quality Thrust." At the division level, COQ was designed to highlight the high COQ and to demonstrate the impact on overall cor-porate profits.

TI used the Juran COQ model; the company emphasized the most efficient trade-off between cost and quality levels. The COQ program immediately got the attention of di-vision managers because COQ data was integrated with the regular financial reporting system. However, managers expressed reservations about the "soft" numbers used to es-timate external failure costs; they were bothered by how hard it was to take proper ac-tion based on the COQ data. Specifically, the COQ reports did not suggest any specific action that managers should take and thus did not offer a solution to a quality prob-lem. The cause and effect of specific quality actions and costs could not be accurately determined. In this case, COQ data may have served as a motivator, but its limits as a performance measure were evident.

TI continues to track COQ data and to report this information internally. However, the vice president of people and asset effectiveness understands the "softness" and the incomplete nature of the cost data. Consequently, TI has now gone to "hard" SPC numbers to manage quality in its materials and control group. The company has ceased improving quality on some processes because it is not considered economically feasible given the existing process equipment.

**(c) Role of Cost-of-Quality at Xerox**    Xerox Corporation, the winner of the 1989 Baldrige award for quality, strongly advocates total quality, and COQ plays a major role in its quality program. Xerox has modified the traditional COQ model by incor-porating lost opportunity cost and the benchmarking process. Quality management considers prevention and appraisal costs as fixed over the short run. These costs are simply considered necessary for obtaining conformance and conducting business. Managers view internal and external failure costs as COQ opportunities.

In the U.S. marketing division alone, 11 COQ opportunities, totaling $250 million, were identified for project management action. The cost of nonconformance (for proj-ects such as excessive spare parts usage, sales personnel turnover, and maintenance strategy) were estimated. The division created empowered, multifunctional teams to re-duce the cost of nonconformance. In 1989, a $53 million cost savings for the 11 projects was achieved, which correlated with the division's income statement. The thrust of this program was not a trade-off of prevention and appraisal costs for failure costs, as the traditional COQ model suggests, but rather a project management process that seeks to continually reduce the cost of nonconformance.

**(d) Caveats for Using Cost of Quality**   Several caveats should be noted about using COQ. Descriptions of these warnings include:

- *Direct trade-offs between conformance and nonconformance expenditures are economically difficult to measure.* Accounting justifications require subjective estimates and an underlying belief that a trade-off does exist. This approach will not help when evaluating the effectiveness of the expenditures.
- *The optimal level of the trade-off is a theoretical point that is probably not at the 50/50 intersection point.* It is nearly impossible to know when this point has been exceeded. Continuous process improvement and the reduction of quality cost expenditures make the theoretical optimum a moving target and therefore impractical.
- *Zero-defects programs—also known as "six sigma" programs—require significant expenditures and capital investment.* Improved quality takes time and may be realized in terms of higher customer satisfaction rather than increased short-term profits. These programs often have a greater impact on market share than on improved accounting returns.
- *Accounting data may not accurately capture or distinguish between the various cost categories.* As a result, incorrect expense analysis may lead to inappropriate policy recommendations.

As this chapter has discussed, managers often use initial calculations of COQ to generate excitement for a quality program. They can create a perceived need for quality because COQ puts an economic value on quality. It measures the cost factors related to the quality issues facing an enterprise. However, many companies abandon the use of COQ after they establish their quality programs. Managers replace the "soft" COQ numbers with "hard" operational numbers (e.g., statistical process control data) for use as a measurement of quality. Various nonfinancial quality measurement systems serve as the guide for attaining a certain level of TQM. The push for continuous improvement or attainment of a specific quality-defect level—such as six sigma—limits the use of COQ for companies that pursue these quality plans. Many argue that COQ fails to provide insight for solving quality problems.

**19.5 SUSTAINING COST OF QUALITY: THE XEROX STORY**   Despite the limitations of COQ, companies continue to find value in the concept. As the previous section discusses, Xerox applied the COQ principles to its U.S. sales and marketing group (which is referred to as U.S. Customer Operations, or USCO) and realized a savings of $53 million in the first year. The improvements were relatively painless and did not involve layoffs or drastic cost cutting. Many line managers, initially skeptical of COQ, began to appreciate the value of this tool. Could they sustain the benefits of this successful COQ program?

Over the subsequent four years, Xerox achieved a $200 million savings in quality costs. The company overcame severe business pressures and organizational distractions. These diversions alone would have been sufficient to dilute any COQ effort; however, the program prospered.

COQ is an integral part of Xerox's "Leadership Through Quality" program, which defines quality as 100 percent customer satisfaction. With the funding and support of the division's chief financial officer, USCO created a separate COQ reporting system. This system used COQ data as a tool and guide for selecting and organizing quality improvement projects. The COQ savings improvement over a four-year period is shown in the following table:

| Year | Savings |
|------|---------|
| 1989 | $53 million |
| 1990 | $77 million |
| 1991 | $60 million |
| 1992 | $20 million |

This impressive example of sustained improvement in COQ is a benchmark for the corporation.

USCO continues to use COQ with multifunctional, empowered teams to call attention to cost-savings opportunities. The division focuses on the business process to identify mechanisms that are not working well or appear inefficient. The first assessment in 1989 of the total potential COQ was $1.05 billion. Further analysis revealed a realistic potential savings of $253 million. The major difference was that USCO concentrated only on the business processes it fully controlled. USCO does not manufacture the product in question and more than 50 percent of the total potential COQ relates to products made by a separate division. These opportunities for quality cost savings did not require significant cash investment and were totally controlled by USCO. The initial COQ projects represented the glaring problems in the company.

**(a) Changes in the Cost-of-Quality Program**    During the five COQ program years, the list of major projects for COQ process improvement changed. The division completed 4 of the 11 initial projects in the first two years. Team members identified new projects through open brainstorming sessions and added these to the list.

Concurrently, the other project teams continued to work on reducing the COQ and found a continuing stream of quality savings in their business processes. They sought a targeted savings based on process improvements, or they used benchmarking to identify an attainable level of performance. In all cases, they used estimates in cost-savings calculations and provided only annual project assessments.

The COQ projects fit the Xerox quality culture: The division faced continued pressure to reduce costs and respond to intensive competitive pressure. The personal energy and actions of the program managers ensured that project teams met regularly and identified cost-savings opportunities. They sponsored brainstorming sessions for new COQ ideas and encouraged the involvement of middle management. It was difficult to overcome the managers' prime focus on their current crises or their normal financial and operational performance measures, because these areas were a major part of their personal evaluation.

The finance quality manager inspired the search for new opportunities for quality cost savings. Many of the successful COQ projects had matured, and the program produced excellent results. The COQ opportunities rewarded the company with significant initial savings. But turnover in the project teams hampered the momentum. This, coupled with the less frequent and less formal project meetings, led to sporadic identification of new COQ projects. There was clearly a need for renewed enthusiasm for the program.

**(b) Starting a Successful Cost-of-Quality Project**    To understand the Xerox COQ program, one may look at the details of one of the company's more successful COQ projects. The Excess/Cancel COQ project was one of the company's initial 11 COQ projects. The project focused on the excessive annual replacement-parts write-off. The team met once a week. Its members included the parts and supplies controller, the manager of nonequipment inventory, the manager of parts planning, and several inventory analysts. The annual accounting provision (expense) for excess and obsolete spare parts was over $22 million, or 7.3 percent of receipts. By any measure, this cost was enormous.

**(c) Tools and Techniques**    Using the TQM "Problem Solving Process," a Xerox quality tool, the team met weekly to identify what actions were necessary to reduce the annual accounting provision. The structured process consisted of six steps:

1. Identification—select the problem.
2. Analyze the problem.
3. Generate potential solutions.
4. Select and plan solutions.
5. Implement solutions.
6. Evaluate solutions.

The team benchmarked other companies and other Xerox operations to authenticate the desired state and to frame the size of the problem. The team felt that a target of 2.1 percent of receipts was the level the company needed to achieve for "world class" status. That left a gap of 5.2 percent of receipt—or a COQ opportunity of $16 million. (Note that Xerox uses COQ and "quality opportunity cost" interchangeably.)

The team then focused on identifying the causes of the excess. Using another Xerox quality tool, the "fishbone" diagram (Exhibit 19.3), the team analyzed the root causes of the problem.

The problems and solutions they identified were:

- Excess inventory at field sites caused planners to order more parts because they were too far down the chain to have control over the inventory. There was no system for effective inventory use and no disciplined inventory control process. The solution was to establish a comprehensive field inventory management system.
- The spare-parts failure rate was too high based on the stated engineering specifications. The solution was to change the spare-parts management process by making engineering responsible for the failure rates. Engineering was also financially responsible for the excesses created by the incorrect failure rates. This encouraged "getting it right the first time," which was a cornerstone of the Xerox quality program.
- There was no product end-of-life strategy. Product planners did not communicate with the parts planners. The solution was to establish a communication network between product and parts planners. This brought about better parts ordering as

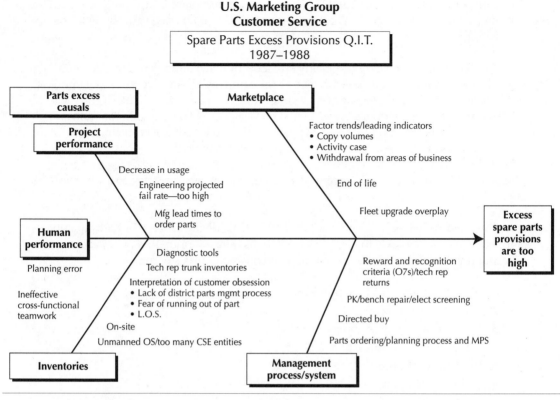

**Exhibit 19.3    "Fishbone" Diagram**

well as a centralized logistical system for parts to support the old equipment remaining in the field.

- The parts planners set parts activity trends using product leading indicators and product trend factors for parts and products. The solution included the data from repair activity and customer-service engineering, which contained specific parts usage. They updated the revised consolidated parts planning database monthly for the planners' review.

The cross-functional team used an array of quality tools that Xerox adopted to study the problem. Team members took several steps:

- They initiated a number of needed process changes.
- They improved the data collection and analysis system.
- They changed some organizational accountability to match responsibilities.

Although the cost of implementation was minimal, the potential savings were substantial—$5.5 million in 1988. The results pleased the team, those involved with the parts program, and internal customers at Xerox (the vice presidents of service, logistics and distribution, and finance).

**(d) Cost-of-Quality Project in Subsequent Years**    The COQ Excess/Cancel Parts team continued to operate in later years. The team felt that additional implementation efforts

U.S. Customer Operations
Western Hemisphere Logistics and Distribution
Cost of Quality

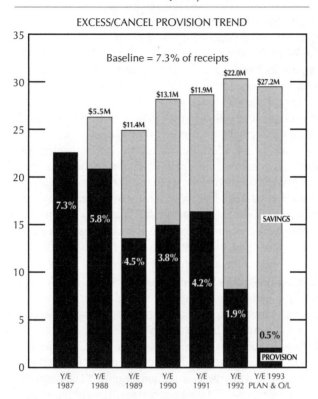

EXCESS/CANCEL PROVISION TREND

Key message: Cumulative savings of $91.1M in E/C provision
1998 through 1993
(Based on continuing at the 7.3% of receipts level)

**Exhibit 19.4    Cumulative Savings from the COQ
Excess/Cancel Parts Team**

were necessary to fully realize the solutions identified. In addition, further refinement of the solutions would move the operation closer to the benchmark target of 2.1 percent. As Exhibit 19.4 shows, the team continued to work on the process and made additional recommendations for change. The team exceeded the benchmark after five years and is currently operating at a theoretical level of 0.5 percent of receipts.

As the team members became more comfortable with each other, and as they became more familiar with the problem, they were able to challenge the parts logistical system creatively. The meetings became less formal, and each member enlisted the assistance of colleagues to solve problems. The project results overcame the high turnover of team members. The new people, who were all familiar with the Xerox quality process, recognized the accomplishments of the project and the team's enthusiasm. They also understood the level of importance given to it by managers. The team's other projects operated in a similar manner—with structured meetings, team empowerment, and extensive use of various quality tools.

The team had no rigid project protocol. Projects could be cross-functional or part of a single function. The goal was to solve the division's business problems and achieve a cost savings.

Over the five-year history, the three finance quality managers were challenged with the problem of sustaining the energy and excitement levels of the program. Many managers lost interest when process costs improved or benchmark levels were attained. During the third year of the program, Xerox announced a major corporate reorganization that required extensive changes at USCO. Managers gave the financial group one year to change the recordkeeping and adjust the various measurement systems. This was a major undertaking and a real distraction.

Yet the COQ program remained, and although its priority in the company was greatly reduced, positive results continued. USCO senior managers realized that the COQ program needed an injection of new energy. Brainstorming sessions by departments and by business process groups produced some good ideas, but the savings were small. Major cost-saving opportunities were not forthcoming. Both the division CFO and general manager encouraged the search for a way to reduce waste in the organization and to improve the division's performance. The COQ process was one of the tools used to identify opportunities and initiate positive changes. It was a proven system that used accepted metrics to value potential cost-saving opportunities.

**(e) Extending the Cost-of-Quality Project to District Sales**   While the new COQ project search continues, managers are working more closely with the field sales and sales support of the 65 district offices. It is a natural extension to move the successful COQ program from the central headquarters to the field.

Expenses of the sales districts were increasing, and many managers suspected that nonconformance costs were contributing to this negative trend. As Sandra Schiffman, the manager of quality and customer satisfaction said: "The districts will buy into the program. We have shown Xerox COQ is not a measurement hammer, but rather a good process improvement tool."[10]

Part of Xerox's COQ strategy for the 1990s was a commitment to quarterly COQ reporting for the sales districts. The company examined *lost opportunity* (synonymous with COQ) due to quality from three areas:

1. Revenue—lost sales due to quality.
2. Process—costs due to business process inadequacies.
3. Expense—costs due to wasteful or excessive business expenses.

Xerox based the calculations on estimates and available accounting data. Internal benchmarks in the three areas served as the comparison to determine the COQ or lost opportunity.

Under the *continuous improvement* approach (*kaizen* in Japanese), the performance of the top 10 sales districts set the internal benchmark for improvement. The company conducted a gap analysis for each opportunity area and provided assistance to the sales districts as needed. The graphic display of quarterly performance motivated district performance and provided credible internal comparisons. The internal benchmark created a custom and accepted reference point for the Xerox field sales operations. People in sales now recognized the costs of not meeting—or of exceeding—customer requirements.

As Sandra Schiffman reports: "The district COQ program may have the wrong label (COQ) with their use of a revised set of quality cost definitions. The well-organized data, however is a tool to help managers identify areas that can improve revenue or reduce costs. We will continue to support the program."[11] The COQ program provided an instrument to help the empowered sales districts attain success.

**(f) Effects of the Implementation Method**   The unique implementation method of Xerox's COQ program sustained the stream of positive results. The COQ program is consistent with the well-established divisional and corporate quality culture. The quality process is second nature for the managers. The various quality tools—such as fishbone diagrams, the problem-solving process, and especially the mind-set of continuous improvement—establish an atmosphere for reducing COQ. The company does not use COQ as a measurement "hammer" or for individual performance evaluation. Instead, Xerox evaluates managers on their knowledge and support of the "Leadership Through Quality" program, of which COQ is an element. Achieving specific cost-savings targets is not the responsibility of a specific manager or of any one group. There is a process "owner," however, who benefits from an empowered, cross-functional team that performs COQ as a collateral assignment.

Xerox uses its COQ program exclusively for identifying opportunities and setting priorities. It is an enabler. Managers realized that there would be few identified cost-savings opportunities if people were held individually accountable and measured for a specific achievement level. No one wants to be penalized for identifying a cost-savings opportunity. Early in the program, managers considered using COQ as an additional performance measurement, but they quickly rejected the idea. The extensive use of estimates and one-time annual reporting were not conducive to measuring people's individual performance. Anyway, the existing traditional financial performance measurement system (which is based on budgets) works well.

The divisional financial organization made extensive use of estimates when calculating COQ. This required considerable change, because the various controllers are accountants who are, by nature and training, precise and want an audit trail of documented evidence. As Sandra Schiffman remarks: "This was the most difficult adjustment for us. Only after we saw managers were using the cost information as a guide to set priorities rather than an absolute measure did we become comfortable with using estimates." Managers have accepted and are comfortable with the COQ metrics.

Xerox makes the definition and use of quality costs part of the business operation. As the business processes changed or as the organization was restructured, the definitions and uses of COQ also changed. There remained, however, the universal measure of 100 percent customer satisfaction. Both internal and external benchmarks serve as a reference for calculating the opportunity cost—or COQ—for achieving the desired operational level. COQ is a dynamic concept that provides a useful economic metric of the overall business process improvement. It gives a broad indication of progress.

Other critical elements of the COQ process were project team empowerment and the extensive training conducted throughout the organization. The USCO financial organization conducted a half-day COQ training session for its 65,000 employees during the first year of the program. The training made line managers comfortable with the COQ data. With full explanation, users saw COQ as a valued management tool. The absence of accounting rules, the use of estimates, and Pareto analysis techniques made COQ user-friendly.

The most important sustaining factor is the strong support from top management.

The chief financial officer, Phil Fishbach, is often called "Mr. Cost of Quality." He is vigorous in his support of the program. His organization has assumed leadership of the program and committed significant financial and human resources to achieving results. The finance organization also ensures that estimated numbers used are supportable and honest.

**(g) Future of the Cost-of-Quality Program**    The recent modest COQ results and the difficulty of identifying the projects that may prove valuable in the future create a real challenge. Benchmarking and continuous improvement are part of the culture at Xerox, and COQ provides a good measure of achievement. The less frequent COQ team meetings, the fact that COQ is not used to evaluate performance, and the lack of COQ knowledge among new employees threaten the program.

As the program matures, estimated costs can start to exceed gains, or the cost-savings opportunities can exceed the customer requirements. Identifying opportunities for early breakthroughs becomes more demanding, and finding new project champions is also becoming more difficult. Distractions and other projects contribute to the loss of discipline in assessing COQ opportunities.

**19.6 LESSONS FROM XEROX**    The Xerox COQ program is difficult to replicate. The quality culture and corporate value system provide the atmosphere for COQ to flourish. Sustaining COQ takes a great deal of energy and support from senior managers. It requires a friendly atmosphere and a sound quality culture in which the quality process becomes second nature and quality tools are abundant.

Managers need to be comfortable with the use of estimates, and they must trust the judgment of the financial managers. Most important, a sustained program must avoid the temptation of using COQ as an individual or departmental performance measure. The results of process change take time before they produce economic results. COQ projects have lives of their own and do not always fit into a single functional area.

The Xerox COQ program may have a cost label, but in reality at USCO, it is the way they conduct business. It is part of the managers' fiber and fits nicely into the companywide quality culture. The company eliminates the mystique of cost measurements because the COQ system provides the division with an excellent way to confirm continuous improvement. It also allows managers to set COQ targets and establish priorities for continuous improvement. The manufacturing operational data and SPC information do not fit into a sales and marketing organization. COQ helps corroborate this service division's performance. It is the Xerox way of doing business.

Xerox plucked the low-hanging COQ fruit during the first five years of its program. It will require greater energy and resources to address the remaining opportunities. The future of the program will certainly be more difficult and will require the full support of senior managers. But, given the continuous improvement culture, one would expect to see further positive results.

**19.7 ACCOUNTING SUPPORT OF TOTAL QUALITY MANAGEMENT**    A controller or accountant can take one of four possible approaches when evaluating the cost implications of a TQM Program:

1. *Use COQ as part of the regular reporting and control process.* The traditional or emerging COQ model can be used with quality costs collected by cost categories.

Most companies do not seek an optimal cost point. Rather, they assess total quality costs and match the cost with the changes in quality as a result of the various TQM efforts.

2. *Focus the accounting and control efforts on nonconformance (internal and external failure) costs reduction.* Xerox and Tennant Corporation are good examples of companies that concentrate on nonconformance costs. The conformance costs are a natural part of the TQM program and can be considered a fixed cost of quality. Economic gains come from changing processes to reduce failure costs.

3. *Support the operation by focusing on specific nonfinancial "hard" SPC numbers to monitor the progress of TQM.* In essence, the company has chosen to ignore COQ and rely on operational data as the real measure of success. Statistical process control, yield rates, waste amounts, and defect percentages provide managers with data to measure the progress of a TQM program. It is assumed that these data correlate well with improved economic performance.

4. *Do not use COQ.* Instead, aid the company with a focus on the general, overall nonfinancial measures of conformance—such as six sigma—to monitor the progress of TQM. IBM and Motorola are strong proponents of this approach. These nonfinancial measures drive the company to achieve a specific level of quality performance and make the necessary investment to achieve the target.

These four avenues of involvement for the accountant in the TQM program vary greatly in the level of activity. Using COQ in options 1 and 2 offers the best course for active participation in the TQM process.

**19.8 OTHER MEASURES OF TOTAL QUALITY MANAGEMENT**    Managers continue to seek innovative and creative means to demonstrate the value of TQM. These measures help direct activities and resources to solve problems. They also serve as a means of reporting progress to higher levels of the organization. The measures, which normally focus on important issues facing the company, provide valuable feedback for performance improvement. They can be part of the regular TQM or financial reporting scheme, or they may be used as a separate reporting process. The following sections give examples of some of the creative measurement schemes.

**(a) Lost Opportunity Cost**    Many companies recognize the large hidden cost of losing customers, because quality problems cause customer dissatisfaction. Xerox and others refer to this as "lost opportunity cost." They have developed measurement systems to measure the expected business loss caused by customers who do not order or who significantly reduce their business with the company. A computer company refers to this as "defection analysis" and places a value on the stream of lost revenue. This loss is part of the cost of poor quality.

Other companies employ outside consultants to conduct customer surveys to rank the company's performance. In the automobile industry, the J. D. Powers customer quality survey is used as the standard of performance excellence. IBM has its consultant survey over 100,000 internal and external customers per quarter to determine quality levels of service. To get the customer perspective of quality (i.e., meeting expectations), companies are relying increasingly on external surveys to provide reliable data for analysis.

**(b) Half-Life Model**    Analog Devices employs a half-life model for evaluating TQM progress. Art Schneiderman, the originator of the program, observes that any defect level subjected to a legitimate quality improvement process decreases at a constant rate. When plotted on semilog paper against time, it falls on a straight line. He developed a model (based on extensive data) that shows that for each type of defect, the defect level drops 50 percent over a specific level of time. For example, if the initial defect level was 10 percent and the defect half-life was six months, then after the first six months, the defect level would fall to 5 percent, after the next six months the defect level would fall to 2.5 percent, and so on.

Analog Devices adopted the half-life system as an integral part of its divisional performance scorecard to balance the strictly financial point of view. The company measured such items as:

- On-time delivery.
- Outgoing defect level.
- Lead time.
- Manufacturing cycle time.
- Process defect level.
- Yield.
- Time to market.

The managers found this data very useful in measuring the movement in continuous improvement or *kaizen*. This measurement device serves the company well.

**(c) Common Characteristics**    The new, innovative measures of quality normally have three things in common:

1. The use of time.
2. A willingness to use outside data sources.
3. Flexibility regarding the sources and mixture of data.

Traditional accounting records do not capture the dynamics of most organizations or the complexity of their processes. Operational data alone do not give managers the economic consequence of their decisions. To gain a complete view of the impact of TQM, a holistic approach involving all the stakeholders is necessary. Thus, companies are putting more reliance on the quality assessment of the customer. Operating managers want measures that make sense, provide valuable feedback, and fit the nature of the business being assessed. The mix is based on what is appropriate.

**(d) Balanced Scorecard Approach**    Companies are rapidly learning that measuring performance using financial measures alone can distort performance and mislead managers. Many companies are turning to the *balanced scorecard* approach. They incorporate measures from accounting, operations, human resources, customers, and other stakeholders to arrive at a more integrative and holistic measure of performance. This trend also apples to measuring the impact of a TQM program, which is natural because TQM is designed to influence the total organization. The Xerox COQ measurement system outlined earlier is a good example of a balanced scorecard. Analog Devices,

| TQM Element | Financial Measure | Nonfinancial Measue |
|---|---|---|
| Customer satisfaction | External failure cost<br>Field service expense | Customer satisfaction survey results<br>On-time delivery<br>Number of customer complaints |
| Internal performance | Appraisal cost<br>Internal failure cost<br>Prevention cost | Defect rates<br>Yields<br>Lead times<br>Idle capacity<br>Unscheduled machine downtime |

**Exhibit 19.5    Balanced Scorecard Measures of TQM**

while placing a heavy emphasis on the operational numbers, sought to balance the strict financial measures of quality. Exhibit 19.5 demonstrates how this can work.

The use of operational measures for TQM provides the flexibility to adjust the company's measurement system to a quality emphasis. For example, possible measures for a Taguchi ("design quality in") process would be the number of parts in a product, the percentage of common versus unique parts, or the number of suppliers required.

**19.9 IMPLEMENTATION**    There is no set or lockstep process for implementing a TQM measurement or COQ program. They are not stand-alone systems. The measurement program must be fully integrated into the TQM process.

The first implementation step is to gain the complete support of senior managers and the active participation of the financial manager. Remember, the key to measurements is providing reliable data for process feedback. This allows managers to assess the progress of the TQM process and to make changes as appropriate. The senior managers will monitor the information, and the financial manager is key in developing the appropriate costs.

The second stage of implementation is to obtain the cross-functional involvement of the TQM team. Clearly, the financial and accounting personnel are critical for cost calculations. Input from various people in manufacturing and marketing are important for developing a set of operational metrics that will capture the effect of TQM.

Other caveats key to implementation are:

- Use reliable estimates. Precise measures may be too costly to obtain.
- Use TQM measures for process indication. Avoid the temptation to use the measures for performance evaluation.
- Use a team approach to determine the parameters of the measures.
- Understand that the rhythm of the reports can vary from daily to yearly. It takes time for TQM to make a measurable difference. Most companies opt for the longer reporting time of quarterly or annually.
- Accept training as key to understanding the meaning of the measures.
- Make the measures should be by natural business unit, such as a subsidiary, a specific plant, or an independent division. Keep the measures within the TQM operation.
- Set realistic expectations.
- Be flexible and change with the shift in TQM focus.

**19.10 SUMMARY**   As a company's TQM program develops, the approach to COQ reporting can take one of the following four approaches:

1.  Use COQ analysis as a regular management reporting and control tool.
    *   Used by Ford in the 1980s.
    *   Consistent with Juran.
    *   Used by TI until 1990.
2.  Focus on reducing the price of nonconformance, including opportunity losses.
    *   Assumes that conformance costs (in Crosby's terminology) will continue at a high level and will be managed by budgets and continuous improvement programs.
    *   If spending on conformance remains consistently high, the reporting focus can switch to nonconformance costs, with specific inclusion of the opportunity cost of bad quality. The goal is the steady reduction of nonconformance costs to zero.
    *   This approach is adopted by many companies committed to TQM, including Xerox, Westinghouse, and Tennant Company.
3.  Focus on nonfinancial production information to monitor TQM progress with an emphasis on *input* measures and SPC.
    *   Deemphasizes formal COQ reports.
    *   Used by TI (materials and control group) and Daishowa Paper (Japan).
4.  Focus on nonfinancial production information to monitor TQM progress with an emphasis on *output* measures of conformance.
    *   Deemphasizes formal COQ reports.
    *   Used by Motorola, IBM, and Analog Devices.
    *   Is customer-focused.

Assessing the economic impact of TQM can take many forms. The classic COQ model provides a reference point for understanding the theoretical behavior of these quality costs. The emerging model reflects the modern view of the behavior of quality costs with a continuous investment in prevention. The difficulty with using these measures is the practicality of gathering the cost data and the accuracy of the accounting information. Many companies recognize these difficulties and ignore any measures of COQ. However, various stakeholders persist in asking how much TQM costs—and, in particular, whether it is worth the substantial costs involved.

Significant value is gained by being able to state the impact of a TQM program in financial terms. This requires active participation by the accounting group—and their creativity and flexibility. Each system should be designed specifically for an individual company. The operational forces that drive quality costs are unique for each company.

Finally, COQ is not a stand-alone measure; it is best used in conjunction with other TQM measures. It is not designed to be an absolute measure or to be used as a "hammer." It is an indicator of progress or lack of progress, because it provides a general reference level about spending, and it can verify the economic impact of quality.

## NOTES

1.  J. M. Juran and F. M. Gryna, *Quality Planning and Analysis* (New York: McGraw-Hill, 1980).
2.  A. V. Feigenbaum, *Total Quality Control,* 3rd ed. (New York: McGraw-Hill, 1983).

3. D. A. Garvin, *Managing Quality: The Strategic and Competitive Edge* (New York: The Free Press, 1988).

4. A. M. Schneiderman, "Optimal Quality Costs and Zero Defects: Are They Contradictory Concepts?" *Quality Progress* (November 1986): 28–31.

5. W. J. Morse, H. P. Roth, and K. M. Poston, *Measuring, Planning, and Controlling Quality Costs* (Montvale, NJ: National Association of Accountants, 1987).

6. L. Carr and T. Tyson, "Planning Quality/Cost Expenditures," *Management Accounting* (October 1992): 52–56.

7. R. L. Hale, D. R. Hoelscher, and E. Kowal, *Quest for Quality* (Minneapolis: Tennant Company, 1987).

8. Ibid., 53.

9. Ittner, Harvard Business School Press, 1989.

10. L. Carr, "Cost of Quality: Making It Work," *Journal of Cost Management* (Spring 1995): 61–65.

11. Ibid.

## SUGGESTED READINGS

American Society for Quality Control. *Accounting for Quality Costs*. Milwaukee, WI: ASQC, 1991.

Carr, L. P. "Applying Cost of Quality to a Service Business." *Sloan Management Review* (Summer 1992): 72–79.

Carr, L. P. and L. Ponemon. "Managers, Perceptions About Quality Costs." *Journal of Cost Management* (Spring 1992): 65–71.

Carr, L. and T. Tyson. "Planning Quality/Cost Expenditures," *Management Accounting* (October 1992): 52–56.

Deming, W. E. *Quality, Productivity, and Competitive Position*. Cambridge, MA: MIT Center for Advanced Engineering, 1982.

Feigenbaum, A. V. "The Challenge of Total Quality Control." *Industrial Quality Control* (May 1957):17–23.

Feigenbaum, A. V. *Total Quality Control*. 3rd ed. New York: McGraw-Hill, 1983.

Freeman, H. L. "How to Put Quality Costs to Work." *12th Metropolitan Section All Day Conference* (September 1960).

Garvin, D. A. "Competing on the Eight Dimensions of Quality." *Harvard Business Review* (November–December, 1987): 101–109.

Garvin, D. A. *Managing Quality: The Strategic and Competitive Edge*. New York: The Free Press, 1988.

Hale, R. L., D. R. Hoelscher, and E. Kowal. *Quest for Quality*. Minneapolis: Tennant Company, 1987.

Juran, J. M. and F. M. Gryna, (1980). *Quality Planning and Analysis*. New York: McGraw-Hill, 1980.

Masser, W. J. "The Quality Manager and Quality Costs." *Industrial Quality Control* (October 1957): 5–8.

Moore, W. J., H. P. Roth, and K. M. Poston. *Measuring, Planning, and Controlling Quality Costs*. Montvale, NJ: National Association of Accountants, 1987.

Schneiderman, A. M. "Optimal Quality Costs and Zero Defects: Are They Contradictory Concepts?" *Quality Progress* (November 1986): 28–31.

CHAPTER **20**

# STATISTICAL PROCESS CONTROL

## Harold P. Roth
### The University of Tennessee, Knoxville

**20.1 INTRODUCTION**   Controlling the quality of processes, services, and products is a critical management function for all businesses, but especially for businesses that must compete in a global economy. To help businesses control quality, the cost-management literature identifies many techniques that managers can use. These techniques include:

- Identifying quality measures (e.g., number of defects or number of customer complaints).
- Measuring quality costs.
- Eliminating non–value-adding activities (e.g., rework).
- Using diagrams (e.g., fishbone charts) to understand the source of quality problems.

A statistical technique that can be used in conjunction with many of these quality management tools is *statistical process control* (SPC). Usually SPC is implemented using *control chart* methodology. This chapter provides an introduction to SPC, shows how control charts can be developed, and demonstrates how they can be used to help improve quality and manage costs.

**20.2 HISTORY OF CONTROL CHARTS**   Control charts are based on the discipline of statistics that "is especially concerned with the study of variability represented in sets of numbers. . . ."[1] The development of the field of statistics provided techniques for measuring variability and for evaluating the stability of processes over time. These techniques are the basic tools used in SPC.

The application of statistical concepts to quality problems was developed by a group of statisticians and engineers working at Western Electric's Bell Telephone Laboratories in the 1920s. The group was led by Walter A. Shewhart. One of the techniques developed by this group was the "Shewhart chart," which is the principal method of SPC.

Control charts are critical to studying and understanding many quality problems. Because they are appropriate to many different situations, managers and accountants need to understand the basics underlying control charts and how the knowledge gained from a chart can be used to improve quality and manage costs.

**20.3 BASICS OF STATISTICAL PROCESS CONTROL**   SPC is based on the idea that variation exists in all repetitive activities and processes. This variation may be random, or it may be caused by special events.

If variation is random, the activity or process is operating efficiently: It is operating in an in-control state. Variation caused by special events, however, is not random: It indicates that there is a problem in the process or activity. Therefore, nonrandom variation indicates an out-of-control process or activity. SPC is a technique for identifying when variation is random and when it is caused by special (or "assignable") causes.

**(a) Random Variation**   *Random variation* exists in all types of repetitive activities. It generally has characteristics that differ from those of nonrandom variation. Characteristics of random variation include[2]:

- The variation may have many individual causes.
- Any one cause results in only a small amount of variation.
- When many causes act simultaneously, the total amount of variation may be significant.
- The variation cannot be eliminated without changing the process.

**(b) Nonrandom Variation**   Characteristics of *nonrandom variation* include[3]:

- The variation usually has several causes.
- Any one cause may or may not account for a large amount of variation.
- Causes of the variation are often easy to identify.
- Depending on the specific cause, eliminating the cause may or may not be economically feasible.

An understanding of the difference between random and nonrandom variation is essential to improving quality. When all variation is random, processes and quality can be improved only by changing the process. But when variation is due to nonrandom events, quality can be improved by finding and eliminating the cause of the nonrandom variation.

**20.4 CONTROL CHARTS**   SPC is implemented using control charts. A control chart is a graph on which measurements of a characteristic are plotted. The chart shows the variation of the characteristic over time; it also shows the amount of variation to be expected when the process is stable. A characteristic shown on a control chart may be an *attribute* characteristic or a *variable* characteristic.

**(a) Attributes**   Attributes refer to measurements used to classify a product or service into one of two or more categories. Examples of these categories include:

- Acceptable or defective.
- Number of blemishes per unit.
- Percent defective.

The measurement is usually based on counts of a quality characteristic. The counts are usually measured from a sample of observations (rather, that is, than measuring all the units in the population).

**(b) Variables**    Control charts for *variables* show measurements of physical characteristics such as:

- Weight
- Length
- Density
- Thickness

These measurements are made on a continuous scale using scales, micrometers, X rays, or the like. They, too, are usually based on samples.

When control charts are used for variables characteristics, two different control charts are required. One chart graphs the measurement itself (or the average of a sample); the other chart shows the variability of the measures within each sample.

**(c) Form of Control Charts**    To evaluate whether the attribute or variable is from a stable process, control charts show a plot of the measurements, a central line, and two control limits. Exhibit 20.1 shows the general form of a control chart.

The central line on a control chart is generally computed as the average (i.e., arithmetic mean) of the attribute or variable, though other measures (e.g., the median) can be used. Control limits show bounds on how much variability is attributed to random causes. As long as the plotted values fall within the control limits and form a random pattern around the central line, the process is assumed to be operating in a stable, in-

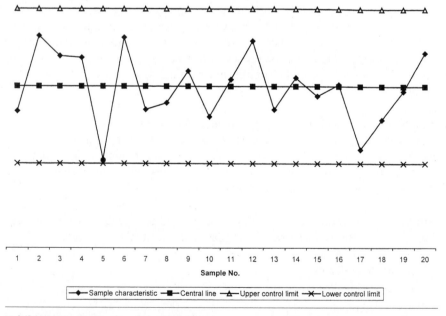

**Exhibit 20.1    Example of Control Chart**

control state. However, when observations fall above an *upper control limit* (UCL) or below a *lower control limit* (LCL), the process is said to be out of control.

When a data point shows an out-of-control situation, an investigation of the process is needed to determine the reason for the out-of-control observation. The reason is referred to as an *assignable* or *special cause* to indicate that it is not due to random fluctuations in the data or to common causes.

**(d) Types of Control Charts** Different types of control charts are appropriate, depending on the attribute or variable measured and the statistical distribution underlying the data. Exhibit 20.2 lists common types of control charts.

As Exhibit 20.2 shows, there are four types of control charts for attributes: p, np, c, and u. The p and np charts are used when quality is measured using counts or percentages of defective units. The np chart should be used when the defective units are counted and the lot size is constant. The p chart should be used when defects are measured as a percentage or fraction of the total. With p charts, the lot size may be constant, or it may vary across lots.

The c and u control charts are used when the number of defects or blemishes is counted for each item. In other words, the count is for the number of blemishes rather than the number of defective units. If the area in which blemishes are counted is constant across samples, the c chart should be used. If the area in which blemishes are counted is not constant, the u chart should be used.

When values rather than counts are recorded, control charts for variables are needed. The $\overline{X}$ (pronounced "X-bar") chart is a graph of the average of the measurements from a sample. It is a control chart that shows the location of the distribution of the measured variable. The R chart is a graph of the ranges of the samples. R is measured as the difference between the highest and lowest values in a sample. It is a measure of the variability in the measured characteristic.

The variability in the characteristic may also be measured using a standard deviation, or s chart. The standard deviation is a common measure of the variability in a set of data. It is calculated as the square root of the variance.

When control charts for variables are used, both the location (X-bar) and the variability (R or s) charts should be evaluated. The R or s chart should be evaluated first to ensure that the process is in control with respect to variability. If it is not, then the underlying distribution is not stable, and the X-bar chart will not be valid. If the R chart

**Control Charts for Attributes:**

| Type | Description |
| --- | --- |
| p | Fraction or percent nonconforming |
| np | Number of nonformities |
| c | Number of blemishes per unit |
| u | Average number of blemishes per unit |

**Control Charts for Variables:**

| Type | Description |
| --- | --- |
| X-bar | Average chart |
| R | Range chart |
| s | Standard deviation chart |

**Exhibit 20.2  Types of Control Charts**

shows that the process is stable, the X-bar chart can be evaluated to determine if the underlying distribution has a stable location.

In addition to the types of control charts identified in Exhibit 20.2, there are also other types, such as moving-average charts, cumulative-sum charts, and multivariate charts. Moving-average and cumulative-sum (CUSUM) charts are useful for detecting small shifts in the mean of a variable.[4] Multivariate control charts monitor several variables at the same time and show when the relationships among variables change.[5] A discussion of each of these types of charts is beyond the scope of this chapter; further information can be found in books and articles dealing with SPC.

**(e) Statistical Distributions Underlying Charts**    Each of the control charts identified in Exhibit 20.2 is based on an underlying statistical distribution. For attribute charts, the p and np charts are based on the binomial model. The binomial model is relevant when each item must be classified as either possessing or not possessing the attribute. For example, a manufactured part may be classified as either conforming or not conforming to product specifications. The binomial model applies to this situation because units are classified into one of two categories. The control chart could show either the number conforming or the number not conforming.

The c and u charts for attributes are based on the Poisson distribution. This model is used when the following four conditions apply[6]:

1. The counts are of discrete events.
2. The discrete events occur within some well-defined region of the product or of time.
3. The events occur independently of each other.
4. The events are rare compared to what would occur if everything went wrong. If these "worst case" events are at least 10 times greater than actual occurrences, the events are considered to be rare.

The control charts for variables (i.e., X-bar, R, and s charts) are based on the normal distribution. This distribution is the bell-shaped curve, where 50 percent of the values are above the mean and 50 percent are below the mean. Variability of a normal distribution is generally measured using the variance or the standard deviation.

**20.5 STARTING CONTROL CHARTS**    Before control charts can be used for maintaining control over processes and products, data must be collected and preliminary control charts developed. The first step in developing control charts is to determine the characteristic to be measured. Once the specific attribute or variable characteristic is identified, the number of observations to include in each sample (often the "subgroup") must be selected. The number of items in each sample affects the calculation of the control limits.

Various factors are considered in determining the size of the subgroup:

Shewhart suggested four as the ideal subgroup size. In the industrial use of the control chart, five seems to be the most common size. Because the essential idea of the control chart is to select subgroups in a way that gives minimum opportunity for variation within a subgroup, it is desirable that subgroups be as small as possible. On the other hand, a size of four is better than three or two on statistical grounds. The distribution of $\bar{X}$ is nearly normal for subgroups of four or more even though the samples are taken from a nonnormal universe; this factor is helpful in the interpretation of control chart limits.[7]

After the decisions concerning the specific characteristic and the number of units to include in each sample are made, samples are drawn from the process and the characteristic is measured. After a number of samples are taken, these measurements are used to develop the central line and the control limits. The number of samples needed to develop preliminary control charts generally represents a trade-off between the desire to be able to use the control chart quickly and a desire for reliable control limits. Usually, data for at least 20 subgroups are collected before control limits are calculated.

**(a) Establishing Control Limits**   After data for each subgroup are available, the appropriate measurement for each subgroup is plotted on the control chart, then the control limits are determined. For example, if the attribute is defects, the number of defective units found in each subgroup is plotted. If a variable characteristic is measured, the value of the variable is plotted.

Control limits are generally set at three *sigmas* from the central line. A sigma is simply a measure of the scale of the data. It is comparable to a standard deviation. For a homogeneous set of data, over 99 percent of the measurements will be located within a distance of three sigma units on either side of the mean.[8] Thus, when a process is operating in a stable manner, the probability is very low that data points will fall outside the three-sigma control limits.

**(b) Interpreting Control Charts**   Control charts provide two signals that may indicate an out-of-control or unstable process. One signal is provided when a plotted point falls outside the control limits. The other signal occurs when there is a *run in the data.*

A run refers to a number of consecutive points above or below the central line. Various rules have been developed to indicate when runs in the data are statistically significant. One rule is that a problem exists when eight or more successive points fall on the same side of the central line. Other run tests relate the number of values in a run to the number of sigma units where they fall.

Wheeler and Chambers have summarized the decision rules for detecting nonrandom variability.[9] Specifically, lack of control is indicated whenever:

- A single point falls outside the three-sigma control limits.
- At least two out of three successive values fall on the same side of—and more than two sigma units away from—the central line.
- At least four out of five successive values fall on the same side of—and more than one sigma unit away from—the central line.
- At least eight successive values fall on the same side of the central line.

When the data points fall randomly around the central line and no points fall outside the control limits, the process is said to be *in control*, which means that the control chart provides no signal indicating that the process is unstable.

If the preliminary control chart shows points falling outside the control limits, those points should be investigated to determine an assignable cause and whether it is likely that the cause can be eliminated. If the cause can be eliminated, the subgroup that showed the lack of control should be eliminated and new control limits calculated.

**(c) Continuing the Charts**   After the central line and the control limits have been determined using data from the preliminary subgroups, the control charts should be used to evaluate the stability of the process on an ongoing, real-time basis. This evaluation requires taking additional samples from the process, then plotting the attribute or variable characteristic on the chart. If the process is stable, the plotted point should fall within the control limits and runs should not occur. If a point falls outside the control limits, the process should be investigated to determine why. In other words, an assignable cause needs to be determined.

Periodically, data that are collected after the initial periods should be used to recalculate the central line and the control limits. If their values differ from those made in the preliminary calculations, the control charts should be changed to reflect the new values.

**20.6 EXAMPLE OF CHART FOR ATTRIBUTES**   To illustrate a control chart for attributes, consider an example in which samples of gaskets for truck windows are inspected each day. The sample size is constant at 400 units daily. Inspectors record the number of bad gaskets in the sample of 400, then these records are used to develop the control charts. Exhibit 20.3 shows the results for 20 days of inspections.

Exhibit 20.3 shows the number of items that are nonconforming in each subgroup of 400. Because each unit must be classified into one of two categories—acceptable or nonconforming—the control chart limits should be based on the binomial distribution. Because the size of each subgroup (400) is constant, the data may be plotted on an np chart or a p chart. The formulas for calculating the central line and the UCL and LCL on an np chart are as follows:

| Day Sample No. | Number of Gaskets |
|:---:|:---:|
| 1 | 10 |
| 2 | 13 |
| 3 | 14 |
| 4 | 9 |
| 5 | 11 |
| 6 | 12 |
| 7 | 12 |
| 8 | 14 |
| 9 | 11 |
| 10 | 15 |
| 11 | 10 |
| 12 | 9 |
| 13 | 11 |
| 14 | 14 |
| 15 | 14 |
| 16 | 15 |
| 17 | 12 |
| 18 | 11 |
| 19 | 10 |
| 20 | 13 |

**Exhibit 20.3    Number of Bad or Nonconforming Gaskets**

Central line value $= n\overline{p}$

UCL: $UCL_{np} = n\overline{p} + 3\sqrt{n\overline{p}(1 - \overline{p})}$

LCL: $LCL_{np} = n\overline{p} + 3\sqrt{n\overline{p}(1 - \overline{p})}$

where:

$$\overline{p} = \frac{\text{Total number nonconforming in subgroups}}{\text{Total number of items in subgroups}}, \text{ and}$$

$n =$ Number of items in subgroups.

For the data in Exhibit 20.3, the calculations are as follows:

$$\overline{p} = 240/(20 * 400) = 240/(8,000) = 0.03$$

$$n\overline{p} = 400 * 0.03 = 12$$

$$UCL_{np} = 12 + 3\sqrt{400 * 0.03 * (1 - 0.03)} = 22.23$$

$$LCL_{np} = 12 - 3\sqrt{400 * 0.03 * (1 - 0.03)} = 1.76$$

Exhibit 20.4 shows the np chart for the data in Exhibit 20.3. As the chart shows, all the plotted points fall within the control limits, and there are no runs in the data. Because the control chart provides no signal of special or assignable causes of variation in the number of bad gaskets, the process in said to be in control.

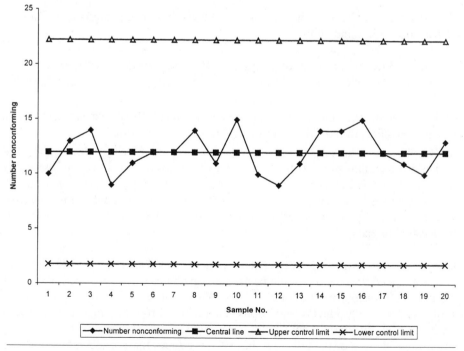

**Exhibit 20.4  np Chart for Attributes**

**(a) Interpreting the np Chart**    The data on the np chart in Exhibit 20.4 show that, on average, 3 percent (12 ÷ 400) of the gaskets do not meet quality standards and are classified as nonconforming. However, the chart shows that the process is operating in a stable manner, because all the points fall within the control limits. Thus, all the variation in the process is due to common causes, and no assignable causes are apparent.

**(b) Cost Implications**    Although the process is stable, managers should recognize that there are costs associated with the nonconforming items. Examples of costs associated with the nonconforming items include:

- Production costs.
- Inspection costs.
- Failure costs.

Production costs (such as materials and labor) are incurred in manufacturing the nonconforming items, and inspection costs are incurred in detecting the nonconformities. In addition, if less than 100 percent of the production units are inspected, some nonconforming units are being sent to customers. Thus, there are external failure costs from customers who are unhappy with the quality of the gaskets.

To use the information in the np chart to manage costs, managers must first recognize that production, inspection, and failure costs exist. Then they can decide what approach they want to take to manage costs. For example, if they want to reduce the failure costs caused by nonconforming items, they could increase the number of units inspected. This approach, however, will increase inspection costs. Another approach would be to improve the process to reduce the number of products that are nonconforming.

Reducing the number of nonconforming products should help improve profitability in at least three ways, including:

- It will reduce the total costs of production. Because fewer units will need to be produced, the total costs of materials and other manufacturing resources will be reduced.
- It will reduce the amount of lost customer goodwill. Because customers will be more satisfied, they will likely buy more gaskets in the future.
- It will provide capacity for more throughput of good units by reducing the number of nonconformities. If the failure rate can be lowered to 1 percent, the ability to produce good units will be increased by 2 percent of the capacity of the plant. If capacity is 10,000 gaskets per day, the reduction in the nonconforming rate from 3 percent to 1 percent will allow for additional production of 200 units a day, or 1,000 units each week.

**20.7 ANOTHER EXAMPLE OF A CONTROL CHART FOR ATTRIBUTES**    As Exhibit 20.2 shows, c and u control charts should be used for attributes when units are classified by the number of nonconformities or blemishes. When a product is complex (e.g., an automobile) or when a product is continuous in nature (e.g., rolls of paper stock), it is impractical to classify a unit as conforming or nonconforming based on whether it contains a single blemish or imperfection. For such products, the c or u chart can be used to determine whether the number of blemishes on an area is due to random variation or whether the number is due to special causes.

Both c and u charts are based on the Poisson distribution. A c chart should be used when the space or area where the blemishes are counted is constant for each sample. If the area changes from sample to sample, the u chart should be used.

To illustrate the development of a c chart, consider the data in Exhibit 20.5 for the number of blemishes on the finished surface of manufactured entertainment centers. Ten units are inspected each day, and the number of blemishes is counted. Exhibit 20.5 shows the results for 20 samples.

The central line on a c chart is equal to the average c. The formula is as follows:

$$\bar{c} = \frac{\text{Total number of blemishes in samples}}{\text{Number of samples}}$$

Formula for the control limits on a c chart are:

$$UCL_c = \bar{c} + 3\sqrt{\bar{c}}$$

$$LCL_c = \bar{c} - 3\sqrt{\bar{c}}$$

**(10 units inspected each day)**

| Day | Number of Blemishes |
|:---:|:---:|
| 1 | 22 |
| 2 | 18 |
| 3 | 17 |
| 4 | 14 |
| 5 | 18 |
| 6 | 11 |
| 7 | 17 |
| 8 | 12 |
| 9 | 9 |
| 10 | 14 |
| 11 | 16 |
| 12 | 17 |
| 13 | 12 |
| 14 | 11 |
| 15 | 16 |
| 16 | 10 |
| 17 | 8 |
| 18 | 14 |
| 19 | 18 |
| 20 | 17 |

**Exhibit 20.5   Number of Blemishes**

For the data in Exhibit 20.5, the values are:

$$\bar{c} = 291 \div 20 = 14.5$$

$$UCL_c = 14.5 + 3\sqrt{14.5} = 25.9$$

$$LCL_c = 14.5 - 3\sqrt{14.5} = 3.1$$

Exhibit 20.6 is a c chart for these data.

**(a) Interpreting the c Chart**    As Exhibit 20.6 shows, the finished entertainment centers have an average of 14.5 blemishes in each sample of 10 units. The chart also shows that all of the data points fall randomly around the central line, and there are no runs in the data. Thus, all the variability between samples is due to random causes.

If the number of blemishes is too high, managers need to study the finishing process

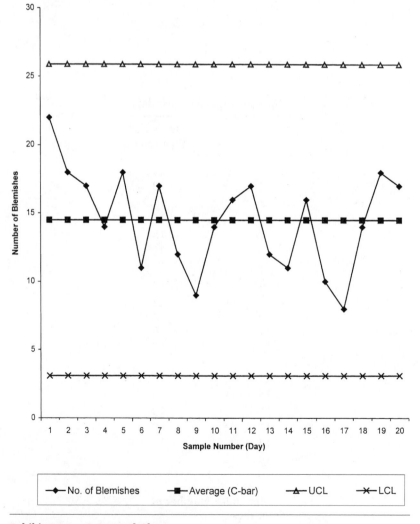

**Exhibit 20.6    C Control Chart**

to determine how it should be changed. Perhaps new air filters are needed to prevent dust particles from affecting the finish, or perhaps a different type of finish should be used.

**(b) Cost Implications**    To determine whether the process should be changed to reduce the number of blemishes, managers need to consider the cost-benefit trade-off. If the blemishes do not affect the marketability of the product now or in the future, the benefits of changing are probably worth less than the costs of changing. In this situation, managers would probably decide to continue the process without changes. However, if the expected benefits of a better finish exceed the costs of changing the process, then a change should be made.

Whether products have imperfections and blemishes or nonconformities (as discussed previously), manufacturing costs are similar. Reducing the number of blemishes may reduce rework and failure costs, which should improve profits. The c and u control charts should help managers understand how the process is behaving and why there may be quality costs incurred even when the process is stable and all variability is due to random causes.

**20.8 EXAMPLE OF CONTROL CHART FOR VARIABLES**    To illustrate an X-bar chart and an R chart, consider a process where vegetable oil is packaged in bottles that are marked as containing 48 ounces of oil. To establish a control chart for the quantity of oil in each bottle, samples of five bottles each are taken periodically from the production process so that their contents can be measured. Exhibit 20.7 shows the number of ounces of oil in each bottle in 20 samples.

Because the data in Exhibit 20.7 represent measurements on a continuous scale, they should be analyzed using control charts for variables (i.e., X-bar and R charts). An R chart shows the variability within the samples, whereas an X-bar chart shows the mean for each sample. Values for R and X-bar for each sample are shown in the last two columns of Exhibit 20.7.

The range values in Exhibit 20.7 are the differences between the highest and lowest values in each sample. For sample 1, the highest value is 48.66, and the lowest value is 47.79, so the range for this subgroup is 0.87 (48.66 − 47.79). The average of the Rs, R-bar, is the central line on the R chart. For these data, R-bar equals 0.80. The UCL and LCL are calculated using the following formulas:

$$\text{UCL for R:} \quad \text{UCL}_R = D_4 \overline{R}$$

$$\text{LCL for R:} \quad \text{UCL}_R = D_3 \overline{R}$$

Values for factors $D_4$ and $D_3$ depend on the number of observations in each subgroup. Exhibit 20.8 shows the factor values for subgroups to size 10.

As shown in Exhibit 20.8, when the subgroup consists of five observations, there is no value of $D_3$ because the lower limit on a three-sigma chart would be less than zero. The value for $D_4$ is 2.114. Thus, the UCL for R is:

$$\text{UCL}_R = 2.114 * 0.80 = 1.69$$

Exhibit 20.9 is an R chart for the data in Exhibit 20.7. Because all points fall within the control limits and there are no runs in the data, the process is stable with respect to variability.

| Sample | Observation | | | | | | |
|---|---|---|---|---|---|---|---|
| No. | 1 | 2 | 3 | 4 | 5 | Range | Average |
| 1 | 48.22 | 48.03 | 47.79 | 48.66 | 47.88 | 0.87 | 48.12 |
| 2 | 48.51 | 48.53 | 48.46 | 48.59 | 48.77 | 0.31 | 48.57 |
| 3 | 48.20 | 48.25 | 48.58 | 48.33 | 48.87 | 0.67 | 48.45 |
| 4 | 48.09 | 49.29 | 48.75 | 48.36 | 47.70 | 1.59 | 48.44 |
| 5 | 47.94 | 48.03 | 48.65 | 48.22 | 47.83 | 0.82 | 48.13 |
| 6 | 48.89 | 48.30 | 48.23 | 48.34 | 49.03 | 0.80 | 48.56 |
| 7 | 48.80 | 48.10 | 48.41 | 48.13 | 48.19 | 0.70 | 48.33 |
| 8 | 48.88 | 47.88 | 48.18 | 47.96 | 48.93 | 1.05 | 48.37 |
| 9 | 48.40 | 48.88 | 48.80 | 48.08 | 48.64 | 0.80 | 48.56 |
| 10 | 48.33 | 48.13 | 48.45 | 47.78 | 48.25 | 0.67 | 48.19 |
| 11 | 48.61 | 48.46 | 48.42 | 48.52 | 48.04 | 0.57 | 48.41 |
| 12 | 48.86 | 48.26 | 49.15 | 48.48 | 48.45 | 0.89 | 48.64 |
| 13 | 48.98 | 49.12 | 48.26 | 48.18 | 48.12 | 1.00 | 48.53 |
| 14 | 48.10 | 48.45 | 48.97 | 48.51 | 48.07 | 0.90 | 48.42 |
| 15 | 47.95 | 48.02 | 48.52 | 48.41 | 48.14 | 0.57 | 48.21 |
| 16 | 48.22 | 48.95 | 48.10 | 48.96 | 48.17 | 0.86 | 48.48 |
| 17 | 48.22 | 48.29 | 47.82 | 48.08 | 48.05 | 0.47 | 48.09 |
| 18 | 48.01 | 48.12 | 48.30 | 48.31 | 48.13 | 0.30 | 48.17 |
| 19 | 48.45 | 48.34 | 47.67 | 48.49 | 48.23 | 0.82 | 48.24 |
| 20 | 48.20 | 47.87 | 49.24 | 48.90 | 48.15 | 1.37 | 48.47 |
| Average | | | | | | 0.80 | 48.37 |

Exhibit 20.7   Samples of Weights of Oil in Bottles

| Number of Observations in subgroup | Factor for X-bar chart $A_2$ | Lower control limit for R $D_3$ | Upper control limit for R $D_4$ |
|---|---|---|---|
| 2 | 1.880 | — | 3.268 |
| 3 | 1.023 | — | 2.574 |
| 4 | 0.729 | — | 2.282 |
| 5 | 0.577 | — | 2.114 |
| 6 | 0.483 | — | 2.004 |
| 7 | 0.419 | 0.076 | 1.924 |
| 8 | 0.373 | 0.136 | 1.864 |
| 9 | 0.337 | 0.184 | 1.816 |
| 10 | 0.308 | 0.223 | 1.777 |

Exhibit 20.8   Factors for Determining Three-Sigma Control Limits. *Source:* Adapted from Donald J. Wheeler and David S. Chambers, *Understanding Statistical Process Control* (2nd ed.) (Knoxville, TN: SPC Press, 1992).

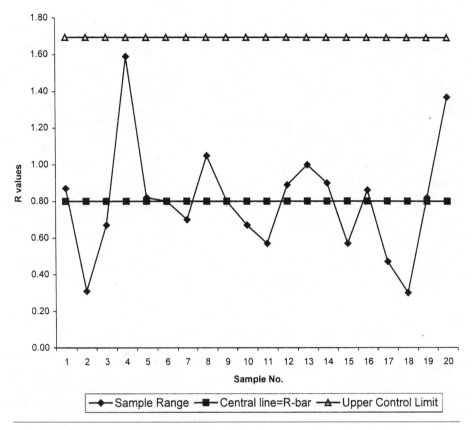

**Exhibit 20.9   Range Control Chart**

The X-bar chart shows the averages of the subgroups. These averages are shown in Exhibit 20.7. The average for the first sample in Exhibit 20.7 is calculated as follows:

$$(48.22 + 48.03 + 47.79 + 48.66 + 47.88)/5 = 48.12$$

The grand average of the sample averages, $\overline{\overline{X}}$ (pronounced "X-double bar" or "X-barbar") is 48.37. The UCL and the LCL are based on the following formulas:

$$\text{UCL for X-bar:}\quad \text{UCL}_{\overline{X}} = \overline{\overline{X}} + A_2\overline{R}$$

$$\text{UCL for X-bar:}\quad \text{UCL}_{\overline{X}} = \overline{\overline{X}} - A_2\overline{R}$$

The value of $A_2$ is found in Exhibit 20.8. When the subgroup size is five, $A_2$ is equal to 0.577. Thus, the control limits are:

$$\text{UCL}_{\overline{X}} = 48.37 + (0.577 * 0.80) = 48.37 + 0.47 = 48.83$$

$$\text{LCL}_{\overline{X}} = 48.37 - (0.577 * 0.80) = 48.37 - 0.47 = 47.91$$

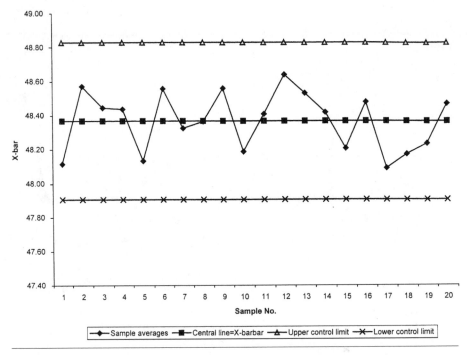

**Exhibit 20.10    Control Chart for Averages**

Exhibit 20.10 is an X-bar chart for the data in Exhibit 20.7. As shown on the chart, all the points fall within the control limits. Also, there are no runs in the data that would indicate a shift in the process mean.

**(a) Using R and X-bar Charts**    In this example, the control charts for variables show how the process of bottling vegetable oil is behaving. As Exhibits 20.9 and 20.10 show, the process is in control, with an average of 48.37 ounces per bottle and an average R of 0.80. Further samples can be taken in real time and plotted on the charts to see whether the process continues to operate in a stable state.

The information provided by these control charts should help managers understand how the process is behaving. The first observation is that there is quite a bit of variability in the amount of oil in the bottles: The difference between the UCL and the LCL is 0.92 ounces (48.83 – 47.91). If managers want a more consistent fill rate, the process needs to be changed. Because the process is operating in control, there are no special or assignable causes for the variability; it is due to common causes. A possible solution would be to buy new bottling equipment, which might reduce the variability of the amount of oil put into the bottles. A reduction in variability would result in more consistency in the amount of oil per bottle.

The X-bar chart shows that the average quantity contained in a bottle exceeds the 48-ounces target value. However, the process is in control with respect to the volume, so there is no assignable or special cause for the excess fill. Again, the process would have to be modified or changed if managers wanted to reduce the fill volume.

**(b) Costs When Actual Quantities Exceed Target**    Managers need to recognize that there are costs incurred when the average fill volume exceeds the target. On average, each bottle contains 0.37 ounces more than target. If production is 1,000 bottles a day, the excess of the actual quantity over the target quantity would be 370 ounces daily or 1,850 ounces a week. The excess quantity causes production costs to be higher than expected if the budgeted costs are based on 48 ounces of oil in each bottle.

In addition to higher costs of production, the excess oil will cause higher shipping costs and, possibly, more repairs and higher maintenance costs if the excess fill causes excess wear on the bottling and packaging equipment. These costs are not normally classified as quality costs, but here they are clearly identified with a quality problem. SPC charts should help managers understand why these costs are incurred and what has to be done to reduce them.

**20.9 STATISTICAL PROCESS CONTROL CHARTS ON SPREADSHEETS**    Although specialized software can be used to develop and maintain control charts, they can also be developed using spreadsheet software. Spreadsheets such as Lotus 123® and Excel® provide the ability to calculate the central line and control limits with ease. The spreadsheets also have graphing capabilities, so it is relatively easy to prepare the actual control chart.

To develop SPC charts using spreadsheets, the values for the observations must be entered in cells. If the subgroup size is five, five adjacent columns should be used to enter the data for each subgroup. If the data are for a variable characteristic (e.g., weight or density), the next two columns can be used to calculate the average and the range for the subgroup. The columns would be similar to those shown in Exhibit 20.7.

| Row/column labels | A | B,...,F | G | H | I | J |
|---|---|---|---|---|---|---|
| 1 | Sample No. | | R | R-bar | UCL R | LCL R |
| 2 | 1 | | 0.87 | 0.80 | 1.69 | 0 |
| 3 | 2 | | 0.31 | 0.80 | 1.69 | 0 |
| 4 | 3 | | 0.67 | 0.80 | 1.69 | 0 |
| 5 | 4 | | 1.59 | 0.80 | 1.69 | 0 |
| 6 | 5 | | 0.82 | 0.80 | 1.69 | 0 |
| 7 | 6 | | 0.80 | 0.80 | 1.69 | 0 |
| 8 | 7 | | 0.70 | 0.80 | 1.69 | 0 |
| 9 | 8 | | 1.05 | 0.80 | 1.69 | 0 |
| 10 | 9 | | 0.80 | 0.80 | 1.69 | 0 |
| 11 | 10 | | 0.67 | 0.80 | 1.69 | 0 |
| 12 | 11 | | 0.57 | 0.80 | 1.69 | 0 |
| 13 | 12 | | 0.89 | 0.80 | 1.69 | 0 |
| 14 | 13 | | 1.00 | 0.80 | 1.69 | 0 |
| 15 | 14 | | 0.90 | 0.80 | 1.69 | 0 |
| 16 | 15 | | 0.57 | 0.80 | 1.69 | 0 |
| 17 | 16 | | 0.86 | 0.80 | 1.69 | 0 |
| 18 | 17 | | 0.47 | 0.80 | 1.69 | 0 |
| 19 | 18 | | 0.30 | 0.80 | 1.69 | 0 |
| 20 | 19 | | 0.82 | 0.80 | 1.69 | 0 |
| 21 | 20 | | 1.37 | 0.80 | 1.69 | 0 |
| | | | 0.80 | | | |

**Exhibit 20.11    Data Needed for Graphing R-Chart in Excel**

To illustrate the steps involved in graphing a control chart in Excel, an R chart will be used as an example. The R values for each subgroup are those shown in Exhibit 20.7.

To plot the central line and the control limits in Excel, a column for each line must be added to the spreadsheet. The cells in the central line column for each subgroup should show the average of the Rs (i.e., R-bar). The cells in the UCL column should contain a formula calculating the UCL. Each cell will contain the same formula, because the UCL is a straight line. Because the number of units in the subgroup in this illustration equals five, there is no real LCL; that is, there is no value for $D_3$ in Exhibit 20.8. However, if one wants to plot the LCL at zero, simply enter the formula for the LCL in the cells and give factor $D_3$ a value of zero. Each cell in the column should show the value of zero, and these value can be plotted as the LCL. Exhibit 20.11 shows the data columns needed for the R chart.

After the spreadsheet data are developed, the graph is prepared using the (XY) scatter plot function under the Chart Wizard menu. Identify the appropriate columns where the data are located and the graph will be similar to the one shown in Exhibit 20.9. Complete instructions for using Excel to develop control charts are provided by Steven M. Zimmerman and Marjorie L. Icenogle.[10]

## NOTES

1. C. P. Quesenberry, *SPC Methods for Quality Improvement* (New York: John Wiley & Sons, Inc. 1997), 2.

2. L. S. Aft, *Fundamentals of Industrial Quality Control* (Reading, MA: Addison-Wesley, 1986), 139.

3. Ibid., p. 140.

4. Quesenberry, op. cit., 266.

5. T. L. Albright and H. P. Roth, "Controlling Quality on a Multidimensional Level," *Journal of Cost Management* 7 (Spring 1993): 29–38.

6. D. J. Wheeler and D. S. Chambers, *Understanding Statistical Process Control*, 2nd ed. (Knoxville, TN: SPC Press, 1992), 272.

7. E. L. Grant and R. S. Leavenworth, *Statistical Quality Control* (5th ed.) (New York: McGraw-Hill Book, 1980), 120.

8. Wheeler and Chambers, op. cit., 6.

9. Ibid., 96.

10. Steven M. Zimmerman and Marjorie L. Icenogle, *Statistical Quality Control Using Excel®* (Milwaukee, WI: ASQ Quality Press, 1999).

# CHAPTER 21

# Process Capability

## Ross L. Fink
**Bradley University**

**21.1 INTRODUCTION**  Determining process capability implies answering one apparently simple question: "Is the process capable of producing the desired quality?" The answer to this question is not so simple. What does it mean for a process to be capable? And how do we measure quality? Another issue is time. Does the process have the *potential* to produce the product at the desired quality or is it *currently* producing at the desired quality? This chapter provides an introduction to process capability. It examines some of the basic concepts of process capability, process capability ratios and their application, and Motorola's "Six Sigma Quality."

**(a) Statistical Control**  The first step in determining process capability is to bring the process into a state of statistical control. This is accomplished by the use of control charts, such as the X-bar and R chart.

Being in a state of statistical control does not, by itself, guarantee high quality. Specifically, control charts remove assignable or special-cause variability from the process while leaving the common cause (or random variability) of the process. Common-cause variability cannot be removed from the process without changing the process. Another way of looking at a process that contains only common-cause variability is that the process has been stabilized. In other words, the variability ($\sigma^2$) and mean ($\mu$) of the quality characteristics are stable over time, based on the use of control charts. It is generally argued that process stability must be achieved before the true quality of a process can be measured. After all, if quality is changing (unstable), can an accurate measure of the process's quality be made?

Therefore, once a process is in statistical control, a determination must be made about the quality of the process. Comparing the quality of parts that leave a process with the specified quality accomplishes this. However, quality must be operationalized. This is generally done by establishing specifications for the various quality characteristics of the part or product.

**(b) Upper and Lower Specification Limits**  The most common type of specification is one that has a *target value* (referred to as "T" in formulas) and a *tolerance*, or range within which the characteristic is considered acceptable. This results in the establishment of an *upper specification limit* (USL) and a *lower specification limit* (LSL). As long as a part has a dimension that is between the USL and LSL, it is considered to be of acceptable quality. The ideal value would be at the target value or specification nominal. Although this chapter focuses on this basic two-sided specification, the analysis that follows can easily be converted to a one-side specification.

Therefore, to answer the question of process capability, a company must determine whether the natural variability of its process will fit between the specifications of the part. This can be accomplished using a variety of different methods, but the most common is to use a process capability ratio, such as $C_p$ and $C_{pk}$.

**21.2 PROCESS CAPABILITY RATIO ($C_p$)**    First one must decide what is acceptable quality, given the specifications. Note that design engineers normally determine specifications through product drawings. They use their experience and knowledge to establish the appropriate specifications. In some cases, they conduct experiments to determine the best specifications. It is a difficult process to take the more or less intangible requirements of customers and turn them into definitive specifications. However, this must be done to operationalize quality. Once the specifications are known, a process must produce parts in accordance with them.

To conceptualize the relationship of a part's quality to the specifications, assume that the quality characteristic to be considered follows a normal distribution. Most professionals are satisfied if the majority of the spread or shape of the quality characteristic can be placed between the USL and LSL. For the normal distribution, plus or minus three standard deviations from the process mean is generally used, because this represents 99.73 percent of the items. Stated differently, only .27 percent of the items fall outside of the USL and LSL. Exhibit 21.1 illustrates this point.

**(a) Upper and Lower Natural Tolerance Limits**    Plus three standard deviations from the process mean is referred to as the *upper natural tolerance limits* (UNTL), and minus three standard deviations from the process mean is referred to as the *lower natural tolerance limits* (LNTL) of the process. If the specification limits are outside these natural tolerance limits, the process is generally thought to be producing items of an acceptable quality.

To facilitate this analysis, a simple procedure is needed to determine whether the spread of the process will fit between the specifications. One of the most common methods is to calculate the *process capability ratio* ($C_p$):

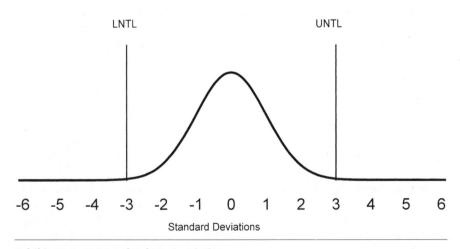

**Exhibit 21.1    Natural Tolerance Limits**

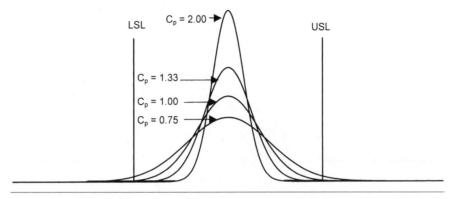

**Exhibit 21.2    Various $C_p$ Values in Relationship to Specifications**

$$C_p = \frac{USL - LSL}{6\sigma},$$

where $\sigma$ is the standard deviation of the process. If the specifications are at exactly plus or minus three standard deviations ($\pm 3\sigma$), the $C_p$ ratio is equal to 1.00 ($C_p$ = USL – LSL/$6\sigma$ = ((+3$\sigma$) – (–3$\sigma$))$6\sigma$ = 1.00). Increasing the value of $C_p$ will improve the quality of the items leaving the process.

To illustrate this concept, Exhibit 21.2 graphically depicts various values of $C_p$ in relationship to the specification limits. Further, Exhibit 21.3 shows the probability that an item will have its quality characteristic within the specification limits for selected $C_p$ values.

**(b) Minimum Acceptable Quality**    A $C_p$ of 1.00 is generally considered the absolute minimum acceptable quality. It is only acceptable when the process mean ($\mu$) is at the target or specification nominal value. In other words, $\mu$ = T.

However, if there is any drift of the process mean away from the target value, the quality will be unacceptable. Therefore, most organizations place a slight level of safety for their value of $C_p$ and set the minimum value as 1.33.[1] This allows for a drift in the process mean of one standard deviation from the target value.

| $C_p$ | With No Shift in Process Mean | | With One-Sigma Shift in Process Mean | |
| --- | --- | --- | --- | --- |
| | Probability of Being Within Specifications | Probability of Being Outside Specifications | Probability of Being Within Specifications | Probability of Being Outside Specifications |
| 0.50 | 0.866385542 | 0.133614458 | 0.685252788 | 0.314747212 |
| 1.00 | 0.997300066 | 0.002699934 | 0.977218252 | 0.022781748 |
| 1.33 | 0.999936628 | 0.000063372 | 0.998649746 | 0.001350254 |
| 1.50 | 0.999993198 | 0.000006802 | 0.999767308 | 0.000232692 |
| 2.00 | 0.999999998 | 0.000000002 | 0.999999713 | 0.000000287 |

*Note:* The probabilities are based on a normal distribution of the quality measurement

**Exhibit 21.3    Probability of Being Within Specification**

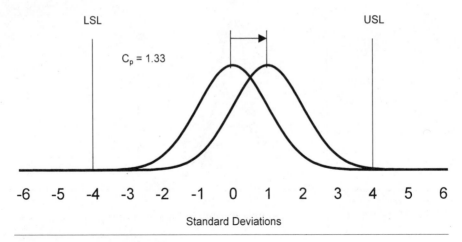

**Exhibit 21.4    One-Sigma Shift**

For example, a process with a $C_p$ value of 1.33 and a shift in the process mean of one standard deviation from the target value still has about the same probability of being within the specification limit as does a part with a perfectly centered process and a $C_p$ value of 1.00. Exhibit 21.4 illustrates a one-sigma shift in the process mean in relationship to the specification limits.

**21.3 CONSIDERING THE PROCESS MEAN ($C_{pk}$)**    But Exhibit 21.4 illustrates one problem associated with the use of the $C_p$ ratio: It does not consider where the process mean is located. As a consequence, the spread of the quality characteristic could be totally outside the specification limits yet still have an acceptable $C_p$ value.

The $C_{pk}$ ratio addresses this problem by including the process center in its calculation. Specifically, the $C_{pk}$ ratio splits the $C_p$ ratio in half and adjusts each half to account for the relationship between the target value (specification nominal) and the process center. It is calculated as follows:

$$C_{pk} = \min\left\{\frac{USL - \overline{\overline{X}}}{3\sigma}, \frac{\overline{\overline{X}} - LSL}{3\sigma}\right\},$$

where $\overline{\overline{X}}$ is the process center obtained from the $\overline{X}$ chart.

When the process is perfectly centered (the process center equals the target value), $C_p$ equals $C_{pk}$. As the process center moves from the target value, $C_p$ does not change. However, $C_{pk}$ will decrease the farther the process center moves away from the target value. It is possible to have a $C_{pk}$ of zero or negative. Either of these cases would imply that the process center is outside one of the specifications: This represents extremely poor quality, because more than 50 percent of the items would likely be defective. It is a situation that should rarely—if ever—occur.

Generally, the cutoff values for $C_{pk}$ are similar to the cutoff values used for the $C_p$ ratio. However, because the $C_{pk}$ ratio adjusts for the process center, a minimum value of 1.00 can be used. Most organizations still stay with a minimum cutoff value of 1.33 for $C_{pk}$. Exhibit 21.5 illustrates the impact of various shifts in the process mean on the values of $C_{pk}$ and the probability of parts being within the specifications.

| No Shift | | | | Shift of 0.5 Sigma | | | |
|---|---|---|---|---|---|---|---|
| $C_p$ | $C_{pk}$ | Probability of Being Within Specifications | Probability of Being Outside Specifications | $C_p$ | $C_{pk}$ | Probability of Being Within Specifications | Probability of Being Outside Specifications |
| 0.50 | 0.50 | 0.866385542 | 0.133614458 | 0.50 | 0.33 | 0.818594678 | 0.181405322 |
| 1.00 | 1.00 | 0.997300066 | 0.002699934 | 1.00 | 0.83 | 0.993557647 | 0.006442353 |
| 1.33 | 1.33 | 0.999936628 | 0.000063372 | 1.33 | 1.17 | 0.999763926 | 0.000236074 |
| 1.50 | 1.50 | 0.999993198 | 0.000006802 | 1.50 | 1.33 | 0.999968027 | 0.000031973 |
| 2.00 | 2.00 | 0.999999998 | 0.000000002 | 2.00 | 1.83 | 0.999999981 | 0.000000019 |
| Shift of 1.0 Sigma | | | | Shift of 1.5 Sigma | | | |
| 0.50 | 0.17 | 0.685252788 | 0.314747212 | 0.50 | 0.00 | 0.498650033 | 0.501349967 |
| 1.00 | 0.67 | 0.977218252 | 0.022781748 | 1.00 | 0.50 | 0.933189370 | 0.066810630 |
| 1.33 | 1.00 | 0.998649746 | 0.001350254 | 1.33 | 0.83 | 0.993790301 | 0.006209699 |
| 1.50 | 1.17 | 0.999767308 | 0.000232692 | 1.50 | 1.00 | 0.998650032 | 0.001349968 |
| 2.00 | 1.67 | 0.999999713 | 0.000000287 | 2.00 | 1.50 | 0.999996599 | 0.000003401 |

Note: Assumes normal distribution for quality characteristic

Exhibit 21.5    Probability of Being Within Specification for Various $C_p$ and $C_{pk}$ Values

**21.4 POTENTIAL VERSUS CURRENT QUALITY**    Choosing which of these two ratios—$C_p$ or $C_{pk}$—to use presents an interesting question. At first glance, it appears that $C_{pk}$ is a far superior ratio and should thus be used at all times. Yet each ratio contains valuable information. That information is similar in many ways, but the ratios differ in how they treat the process mean. An interesting way to look at the difference in these two ratios follows:

- The $C_p$ ratio tends to measures potential quality.
- $C_{pk}$ is a better measure of actual or current quality.

If the value of $C_{pk}$ is unacceptable, there are three ways to change it:

1. Reduce the standard deviation.
2. Center the process.
3. Change the specifications.

Ideally, however, the specifications have been set at an appropriate level, so changing the specification should not be an issue. If the specifications have been set arbitrarily, an experiment should be performed to determine their correct value.

Of the first two ways to change $C_{pk}$, adjusting the process center is easier than reducing the standard deviation of the process. Changing the standard deviation of the process implies that the process itself must be changed. This can be accomplished in many ways (e.g., through new equipment, better tooling, better raw materials, or increased operator training). Changing the process center generally involves adjusting the process rather than changing it, which is generally a much easier and less costly approach. Therefore, the preferred approach is to adjust the process center closer to the target value.

**(a) Potential Quality**    $C_p$ is a useful measure to tell whether a process can "potentially" be made to fit within the specification limits by adjusting the center of the process. In other words, it is a good measure of potential quality.

Originally, process capability studies were developed for this specific purpose. They answered the question, "Which machine or process should be used to produce a new part?" In other words, they represent a selection process—how to pick the appropriate process to produce the part—rather than a measure of today's quality. In this situation, the *potential* quality of the process is considered, not its current quality. Consequently, $C_p$ is an appropriate measure in this situation.

**(b) Current Quality**    However, many organizations have expanded their use of process capability ratios to include day-to-day monitoring of quality. In many cases, they require this information from their suppliers. In this situation, the $C_{pk}$ ratio will provide a more accurate view of current quality and would thus be a preferable measure. However, because the calculations of $C_p$ and $C_{pk}$ are similar, it is relatively easy to calculate both ratios. Indeed, doing so may be desirable, because the ratios convey different information.

**(c) Unacceptable $C_p$ and $C_{pk}$ Values**    When $C_p$ falls below an organization's established cutoff values, the traditional response is to change the process to improve the $C_p$ ratio. Changing the process implies that a substantial change must be made. This could include using a different machine, different materials, different tooling, and different operators or providing additional training for operators. In most cases, deciding how to change the process will require some effort and also consume time.

What should be done when there is not enough time to change the process and improve the $C_p$ ratio to an acceptable level? In the short run, the only viable answer is to use the process whose $C_p$ ratio is unacceptable. But in order to ensure quality, 100 percent inspection must be used to "inspect quality into the process." Anything less means that defective products will be shipped to the customer.

In the long run, 100 percent inspection is generally considered a poor quality management practice. The organization should still strive to improve the process so that quality reaches an acceptable level and 100 percent inspection of the process can cease.

When the $C_{pk}$ ratio falls to an unacceptable level, it may be possible to improve quality in a timely manner by adjusting the process center to more closely match the specification's target value. This is only possible if the $C_p$ ratio possesses an acceptable value. If $C_p$ is unacceptable, adjusting the process center will not increase $C_{pk}$ to an acceptable level, and 100 percent inspection should be used for the short run.

**21.5 CALCULATING SIGMA**    One piece of information that is necessary for both the $C_p$ and $C_{pk}$ ratios is the standard deviation ($\hat{\sigma}$). Determining the value of the standard deviation appears straightforward. However, there are various ways to estimate its value. The first inclination is to use all the measurements collected to calculate the estimate of the population standard deviation by using the established formula:

$$\hat{\sigma} = \sqrt{\frac{\sum (X - \overline{X})}{n - 1}},$$

where X is the quality measurement, $\overline{X}$ is the mean, and n is the sample size of all observations.

A better estimator of the population standard deviation is:

$$\hat{\sigma} = \frac{\overline{R}}{d_2},$$

where $\overline{R}$ is the mean sample range from the control chart (the center line of the R-chart), and $d_2$ is a constant based on sample size found in Exhibit 21.6. This procedure provides a better estimate of the population standard deviation than the first method, which collects the total sample over a relatively long period of time.

If the process mean were to drift slightly over time—but the process remained in statistical control—the first method would tend to overestimate the population standard deviation. The latter procedure uses the *sample range,* where the data used to calculate each sample range are taken at approximately the same time. Therefore, even if the process mean does drift slightly, the drift does not affect the sample ranges. Consequently, this produces a more accurate estimate of the population standard deviation.

**(a) Motorola's Six Sigma Quality**    One adaptation of process capability, Motorola's Six Sigma Quality, has received a great deal of publicity and praise. The basis of this program can be stated in terms of process capability ratios. Specifically, Motorola requires that the quality characteristic be plus or minus six standard deviations in relationship to the specifications, allowing for a 1.5-sigma drift of the process center from the specification nominal value.[2] This can be interpreted to be a $C_p$ of 2.0, with a $C_{pk}$ of 1.5.

| n, sample size | $d_2$ |
|:---:|:---:|
| 2 | 1.128 |
| 3 | 1.693 |
| 4 | 2.059 |
| 5 | 2.326 |
| 6 | 2.534 |
| 7 | 2.704 |
| 8 | 2.847 |
| 9 | 2.970 |
| 10 | 3.078 |
| 11 | 3.173 |
| 12 | 3.258 |
| 13 | 3.336 |
| 14 | 3.407 |
| 15 | 3.472 |
| 16 | 3.532 |
| 17 | 3.588 |
| 18 | 3.640 |
| 19 | 3.689 |
| 20 | 3.735 |

**Exhibit 21.6    Constant to Calculate Standard Deviation**

| No Shift | | | | Shift of 0.5 Sigma | | | |
|---|---|---|---|---|---|---|---|
| $C_p$ | $C_{pk}$ | Probability of Being Within Specifications | Defective Parts Per Million (PPM) | $C_p$ | $C_{pk}$ | Probability of Being Within Specifications | Defective Parts Per Million (PPM) |
| 0.50 | 0.50 | 0.866385542 | 133614.46 | 0.50 | 0.33 | 0.818594678 | 181405.32 |
| 1.00 | 1.00 | 0.997300066 | 2699.93 | 1.00 | 0.83 | 0.993557647 | 6442.35 |
| 1.33 | 1.33 | 0.999936628 | 63.37 | 1.33 | 1.17 | 0.999763926 | 236.07 |
| 1.50 | 1.50 | 0.999993198 | 6.80 | 1.50 | 1.33 | 0.999968027 | 31.97 |
| 2.00 | 2.00 | 0.999999998 | 0.00 | 2.00 | 1.83 | 0.999999981 | 0.02 |
| Shift of 1.0 Sigma | | | | Shift of 1.5 Sigma | | | |
| 0.50 | 0.17 | 0.685252788 | 314747.21 | 0.50 | 0.00 | 0.498650033 | 501349.97 |
| 1.00 | 0.67 | 0.977218252 | 22781.75 | 1.00 | 0.50 | 0.933189370 | 66810.63 |
| 1.33 | 1.00 | 0.998649746 | 1350.25 | 1.33 | 0.83 | 0.993790301 | 6209.70 |
| 1.50 | 1.17 | 0.999767308 | 232.69 | 1.50 | 1.00 | 0.998650032 | 1349.97 |
| 2.00 | 1.67 | 0.999999713 | 0.29 | 2.00 | 1.50 | 0.999996599 | 3.40 |

*Note:* Assumes normal distribution for quality characteristic

**Exhibit 21.7    PPM for Various $C_p$ and $C_{pk}$ Values**

Motorola has also popularized another measure that expresses quality in terms of defective *parts per million* (PPM), which is a measure that is easier to understand than $C_p$ or $C_{pk}$. Assuming that the quality characteristic is normally distributed, the process produces 3.4 PPM defective for a $C_p$ of 2.0 and a $C_{pk}$ of 1.5. To further illustrate this concept, Exhibit 21.7 shows the PPM defective for various combinations of $C_p$ and $C_{pk}$.

Motorola's Six Sigma Quality is substantially higher than the normal cutoff values used for $C_p$ and $C_{pk}$. The standard cutoff values of $C_p = 1.33$ and $C_{pk} = 1.00$ correspond to 1,350.3 PPM defective. Motorola's change in cutoff values means an improvement in quality by a factor of close to 400. Obviously, if an organization can maintain this level of quality, it will be at a competitive advantage (in terms of quality, at least). But is this high level of quality so important that an organization should use it as the goal?

**(b) Multiple Quality Characteristics**    Part of the answer to this question is that if there were only one quality characteristic that determined the quality of a finished part or product, such a high level of quality would not be necessary. However, most products have multiple quality characteristics that determine the quality of the finished part or product. If all these quality characteristics must be of satisfactory quality simultaneously, the number of defective finished parts or products will increase substantially.

With a $C_p$ and $C_{pk}$ of 1.33, the number of defective PPM would be:

- 63.37 with 1 quality characteristic.
- 126.74 with 2 quality characteristics.
- 316.82 with 5 quality characteristics.
- 6,317.37 with 100 quality characteristics.

Considering that each part will have multiple quality characteristics and that there are hundreds or thousands of parts in a given product, even the lowest of these quality

| Number of Quality Characteristics in Part | Probability of Not Being Defective C$_p$ = C$_{pk}$ = 1.33 | PPM Defective | Motorola's Six Sigma Probability of Not Being Defective C$_p$ = 2.00, C$_{pk}$ = 1.50 | PPM Defective |
|---|---|---|---|---|
| 1 | 0.999936628 | 63.37 | 0.999996599 | 3.40 |
| 2 | 0.999873260 | 126.74 | 0.999993198 | 6.80 |
| 3 | 0.999809896 | 190.10 | 0.999989798 | 10.20 |
| 4 | 0.999746536 | 253.46 | 0.999986397 | 13.60 |
| 5 | 0.999683180 | 316.82 | 0.999982996 | 17.00 |
| 10 | 0.999366460 | 633.54 | 0.999965992 | 34.01 |
| 20 | 0.998733321 | 1266.68 | 0.999931986 | 68.01 |
| 50 | 0.996836311 | 3163.69 | 0.999829974 | 170.03 |
| 100 | 0.993682631 | 6317.37 | 0.999659977 | 340.02 |
| 500 | 0.968809735 | 31190.27 | 0.998301040 | 1698.96 |
| 1,000 | 0.938592302 | 61407.70 | 0.996604967 | 3395.03 |

**Exhibit 21.8    PPM Defective Based on Number of Quality Characteristics**

levels might prove unacceptable. Therefore, a higher level of quality, such as Motorola's Six Sigma, could very well be preferable. Exhibit 21.8 illustrates a variety of PPM defective for C$_p$ and C$_{pk}$ of 1.33, versus Motorola's Six Sigma Quality (C$_p$ = 2.00 and C$_{pk}$ = 1.50). The exhibit also includes the number of quality characteristics in a part or product.

**21.6 FACTORS THAT AFFECT C$_p$ AND C$_{pk}$ CUTOFF VALUES**    In addition to Motorola's cutoff values, standard cutoff values used for process capability ratios may be changed—typically raised—based on circumstances such as:

- The nonnormality of the quality characteristics.
- The cost of a part or product failure.
- The likelihood that the process will go out of control.

**(a) Nonnormality**    Cutoff values are typically based on the assumption that the quality characteristic is normally distributed. For many parts, this is a reasonable assumption. As long as the quality characteristic is reasonably close to the normal distribution, the standard cutoff values can be used. However, the more nonnormal the distribution, the greater the likelihood that defective parts will be produced.

Must the use of process capability ratios cease when the quality characteristic is nonnormally distributed? The answer is no. Usually the cutoff values of C$_p$ and C$_{pk}$ are increased to compensate for the nonnormality of the quality characteristics. The more nonnormal the distribution, the higher the cutoff values for the process capability ratios. The process capability ratios can still be used because the standard deviation of the process continues to provide useful information about the likelihood of being within a certain range.

Several formulas can be used to provide insight to this problem. One is *Tchebychev's Inequality*, which tells the probability that a variable will be plus or minus $k$ standard deviations from its mean, regardless of the distribution of the variable. Specifically, the probability of being plus or minus $k$ standard deviations from the mean is $1/k^2$. When applied in real-life situations, this inequality is generally too conservative and greatly overestimates the probability of being outside of the range. Use of Tchebychev's Inequality would suggest that tolerances should be set at approximately plus or minus 10 standard deviations, or a $C_p$ of 3.33.

A variation of this inequality is the Camp-Meidel version of Tchebychev's Inequality. This version applies to any distribution that is unimodal, which means that the distribution is monotonically decreasing from its one mode. In this case, the probability of being plus or minus $k$ standard deviations from its mean is $1/(2.25k^2)$.

Basically, Tchebychev's inequality is a worst-case scenario. Exhibit 21.9 demonstrates the impact of relaxing the normality assumption—using the Tchebychev's Inequality and the Camp-Meidel variation—and shows the difference between the normality assumption and the two inequalities.

**(b) Cost of Failure**   Besides a nonnormal distribution, another reason to raise cutoff values occurs when the cost of failure is substantially higher than normal. This could include either internal or external failure costs. One possible reason for an unusually high failure cost is that a part or product presents a safety issue—(e.g., if failure of the part or product might cause injury to a user). If so, the part simply must not fail. One way to reduce the chance that a part will fail is to raise the cutoff value, which reduces the chance of a defective part or of a part that falls outside the specification limits. The higher the cost of failure (whether internal or external), the higher the cutoff value used.

Another problem with the use of cutoff values for $C_p$ and $C_{pk}$ is that they present the concept of meeting a minimum level of quality. As long as the $C_p$ and $C_{pk}$ values are over the established cutoff values, the process is acceptable. However, is there any incentive to increase beyond these minimum values? One way around this problem is to adopt an economic approach to establishing process capability. In this situation, a determination can be made about the value of improving the process capability. The cost of making the improvement can be compared to the value of the improvement.

One method uses the *Taguchi loss function* to represent the value of the improvement; generally, the costs of the improvement are fairly well defined. At this point, traditional capital budgeting techniques, such as *net present value,* can be applied to answer whether the improvement in quality represented by the Taguchi loss function offsets the cost of the improvement.[3]

**(c) Going Out of Statistical Control**   Another consideration in setting process capability cutoff values is the frequency at which the process goes out of statistical control. Processes that are extremely stable can successfully operate at the minimum cutoff levels. However, processes that regularly go out of statistical control may need to have a higher cutoff values established for them.

The more frequently a process goes out of control, the higher the cutoff value needed. In addition, the size of the shift in the process mean or the size of the increase in process standard deviation will have an impact on the increase required in cutoff values when a process goes out of control.

**21.7 SUMMARY**   Once processes have been stabilized through the use of such *statistical process control* procedures as control charts (see Chapter 20), the quality leaving the processes must be compared to the operational definition of quality—the specifications. There are many ways of doing this comparison, but the most common is to calculate one or more process capability ratios, such as $C_p$ or $C_{pk}$. If these ratios are above

**With No Shift in Process Mean**

| Normal Distribution | | | | |
|---|---|---|---|---|
| $C_p$ | $C_{pk}$ | Probability of Being Within Specifications | Probability of Being Outside Specifications | Parts Per Million Defective (PPM) |
| 0.50 | 0.50 | 0.866385542 | 0.133614458 | 133614.46 |
| 1.00 | 1.00 | 0.997300066 | 0.002699934 | 2699.93 |
| 1.33 | 1.33 | 0.999936628 | 0.000063372 | 63.37 |
| 1.50 | 1.50 | 0.999993198 | 0.000006802 | 6.80 |
| 2.00 | 2.00 | 0.999999998 | 0.000000002 | 0.00 |

| Camp-Meidel Version of Tchebychev's | | | | |
|---|---|---|---|---|
| $C_p$ | $C_{pk}$ | Probability of Being Within Specifications | Probability of Being Outside Specifications | Parts Per Million Defective (PPM) |
| 0.50 | 0.50 | 0.802469136 | 0.197530864 | 197530.86 |
| 1.00 | 1.00 | 0.950617284 | 0.049382716 | 49382.72 |
| 1.33 | 1.33 | 0.972222222 | 0.027777778 | 27777.78 |
| 1.50 | 1.50 | 0.978052126 | 0.021947874 | 21947.87 |
| 2.00 | 2.00 | 0.987654321 | 0.012345679 | 12345.68 |

| Tchebychev's Inequality | | | | |
|---|---|---|---|---|
| $C_p$ | $C_{pk}$ | Probability of Being Within Specifications | Probability of Being Outside Specifications | Parts Per Million Defective (PPM) |
| 0.50 | 0.50 | 0.555555556 | 0.444444444 | 444444.44 |
| 1.00 | 1.00 | 0.888888889 | 0.111111111 | 111111.11 |
| 1.33 | 1.33 | 0.937500000 | 0.062500000 | 62500.00 |
| 1.50 | 1.50 | 0.950617284 | 0.049382716 | 49382.72 |
| 2.00 | 2.00 | 0.972222222 | 0.027777778 | 27777.78 |

**Exhibit 21.9    Impact of Nonnormality on PPM Defective**

an established cutoff value (which is generally set at $C_p$ or $C_{pk}$ > 1.33), the process is considered to be producing products of acceptable quality.

However, Motorola has led the way—through its Six Sigma Quality program—to set the standard substantially higher than the traditional cutoff values. They use cutoff values of $C_p$ = 2.00 and $C_{pk}$ = 1.50. This level corresponds to 3.4 PPM defective. The term "PPM" is used by Motorola to provide a more meaningful number to measure the quality of the process. Motorola believes that the standard cutoff values do not represent an acceptable level of quality. This becomes more evident when one considers the following:

• Each part has multiple quality characteristics.
• There are hundreds—or even thousands—of parts in a product.
• All the parts must work correctly for a product to function as planned.

In addition to the belief of Motorola—and many other companies—that cutoff values should be set higher, they are frequently increased for other reasons. These reasons include:

- Parts with high failure costs.
- Nonnormality of the quality characteristics.
- The likelihood that the process will go out of statistical control.

In conclusion, process capability ratios serve a vital function because they allow companies to compare the natural tolerance of a process to the specifications developed during the design of the product. Despite their limitations, process capability ratios can answer the vital question about whether a process can produce the desired quality.

## NOTES

1.  J. M. Juran, F. M. Gryna, and R. S. Bingham, *Quality Control Handbook* (New York: Mc-Graw-Hill, 1979).

2.  J. J. Harry, *The Nature of Six Sigma Quality* (Schaumburg, IL: Motorola University Press, 1997).

3.  For more information on this approach, see R. L. Fink, G. W. Margavio, and T M. Margavio, "Evaluating Capital Investments in Quality Improvement," *Journal of Cost Management* (Spring 1994): 57–62.

# PART IV

# ACTIVITY-BASED MANAGEMENT

# CHAPTER 22

# ACTIVITY-BASED COSTING AND ACTIVITY-BASED MANAGEMENT: AN INTRODUCTION

## John B. MacArthur
### University of North Florida

**22.1 EVOLUTIONARY DEVELOPMENT OF ACTIVITY-BASED COSTING** Activity-based costing (ABC) became popular in the 1980s when manufacturing companies needed more accurate assignment of indirect costs. Factors prompting the development of more refined costing systems such as ABC include:

- Growing overhead costs because of increasingly automated production.
- Decreasing costs of information processing because of continual improvements in, and increasing applications of, information technology.
- Increasing market competition, which necessitated more accurate product costs.
- Increasing product diversity to secure economies of scope and increased market share.[1]

Deere & Company (Deere) was a pioneer in the development of ABC and coined both the name and the acronym for a new costing method that its cost accountants developed in the mid-1980s. Like other companies with many products, Deere found that its traditional cost system overcosted high-volume products and undercosted low-volume products. For example, the gear and special products division of Deere lost a bid to produce high-volume component parts because the bid price was based on the overcosted products and was therefore uncompetitive. Not surprisingly, however, this division was successful on bids to produce its low-volume component parts, because they were undercosted.[2]

**22.2 INDIRECT COSTS** The problem of over- or undercosting products (cross-subsidization[3]) is caused by allocating manufacturing overhead costs using unit-level or volume-level overhead allocation, or cost assignment, bases (e.g., direct labor cost or machine hours) when a significant proportion of the overhead costs are not affected by changes in production volume. This problem is particularly acute in companies such as Deere that market multiple products and services that consume overhead resources in different proportions.

Service organizations experience cross-subsidization problems, too. For example, in banking institutions, profitable customers subsidize unprofitable customers when pricing schedules do not reflect the full cost of serving individual customers. First Tennessee National Corporation used ABC concepts to help identify and correct the cross-subsidization problem with its certificate of deposits (CDs). The regional bank's success with its CDs later led to an ABC project that helped to correct the cross-subsidies in the commercial loans processed by its bank loan officers.[4]

The following presents a simple example to illustrate the cross-subsidization problem caused by different production volumes and the ABC solution.

**(a) Over- or Undercosting Caused by Variations in Production Volume**    Exhibit 22.1 shows a simple example of a company that has three products. The company uses a traditional cost system with a plantwide overhead application rate based on direct labor hours. The direct costs of the three products are identical, but the batch sizes vary. Product $A$ is a low-volume product, product $B$ is a medium-volume product, and product $C$ is a high-volume product. For the period shown, the plant's overhead budget was $500,000 and direct labor hours were predicted to be 100,000. The predetermined overhead application rate was thus $5 ($500,000/100,000) per direct labor hour.

The company bid on a contract for 10 units of product $A$, 100 units of product $B$, and 1,000 units of product $C$. The bid price was 200 percent of the total product cost, as shown on the bottom row of Exhibit 22.1.

|  | Product A | Product B | Product C |
|---|---|---|---|
| Units produced | 10 | 100 | 1,000 |
| Direct labor hours (DLHs) per unit | 5 | 100 | 1,000 |
| Direct materials cost per unit | $5 | $5 | $5 |
| Direct labor cost per unit | $5 | $5 | $5 |
| Overhead cost per unit (driver: DLHs)[a] | $5 | $5 | $5 |
| Total product cost per unit | $15 | $15 | $15 |
| Total product cost (TPC) | $150 | $1,500 | $15,000 |
| Bid price (TPC × 200%) | $300 | $3,000 | $30,000 |

[a] $5 × 1 direct labor hour

**Exhibit 22.1    Over- or Undercosted Products Caused by Variations in Production Volume: Traditional Overhead Cost Assignment Model—An Example**

The company was awarded the contract for product *A*, and a competitor won the contract for the other two products. The company was concerned that it was frequently losing bids on highly desirable, high-volume contracts such as product *C*, while it was more successful on less desirable, low-volume contracts (like product *A*).

Suspecting a cost assignment problem, the controller conducted a quick *activity analysis. The CAM-I Glossary of Activity-Based Management* defines activity analysis as:

> The identification and description of activities in an organization. Activity analysis involves determining what activities are done within the department, how many people perform the activities, how much time they spend performing the activities, what resources are required to perform the activities, what operational data best reflect the performance of the activities, and of what value is the activity to the organization. Activity analysis is accomplished using interviews, questionnaires, and by observation and review of physical records of work.[5]

Based on the activity analysis, the controller determined that about $300,000 of the budgeted overhead was related to unit-level activities (e.g., electric power) and about $200,000 was related to batch-level activities (e.g., material handling). For simplicity, the predominant batch-level activity for the company is assumed to be machine setups.

The traditional cost system applied the batch-level activities portion of the budgeted overhead at the rate of $2 ($200,000/100,000) per direct labor hour. Therefore, the high-volume product *C* was assigned $2,000 ($2 × 1,000) of batch-level cost, which is 100 times the $20 ($2 × 10) of batch-level cost assigned to the low-volume product and 10 times the $200 ($2 × 100) of batch-level cost assigned to the medium-volume product. Although shop-floor managers determined that all three products consumed about the same amount of the batch-level resources, the traditional costing system did not reflect it. For example, the setup time was about one hour for each of the company's products and was independent of the different volume levels. For comparison purposes, the controller decided to recast the bid prices using this activity information.

"Direct labor hours" was determined to be a suitable cost driver to assign the cost of unit-level activities, but "setup hours" was selected as a more appropriate cost driver of the batch-level activities. The setup hours for the period were estimated to be 4,000. The predetermined application rate was $3 ($300,000/100,000) per direct labor hour for the unit-level activities and $50 ($200,000/4,000) per setup hour for batch-level activities. The batch-level cost for each product is $50 ($50 × 1 setup hour). Exhibit 22.2 shows the revised product costs and bid prices using the simple ABC approach.

The bottom row of Exhibit 22.2 shows the difference between the cost-plus bid price using ABC compared with the traditional cost approach shown in Exhibit 22.1. Based on the ABC information, product *A* was undercosted by $30 and hence underpriced by $60 (16.7 percent), which resulted in a competitive and successful bid. Products B and C, however, were overcosted by $150 and $1,950 and thus overpriced by $300 (11.1 percent) and $3,900 (14.9 percent), respectively. Because the bids on products *B* and *C* were uncompetitive, they were unsuccessful. Clearly, therefore, an inadequate costing system can lead to unfortunate economic consequences.

The competitor that had made the successful bids on products B and C may have had a more sophisticated costing system than the unsuccessful company. Alternatively, the competitor company may have had fewer volume variations between products so that its traditional cost system provided less distorted costs as the basis for its cost-plus bids.

|                                          | Product A | Product B | Product C |
|------------------------------------------|-----------|-----------|-----------|
| Units produced                           | 10        | 100       | 1,000     |
| Direct labor hours (DLHs) per unit       | 10        | 100       | 1,000     |
| Setup hours per batch                    | 10        | 10        | 10        |
| Direct materials cost per unit           | $5.00     | $5.00     | $5.00     |
| Direct labor cost per unit               | $5.00     | $5.00     | $5.00     |
| Unit-level overhead cost per unit (driver: DLHs)[a] | $3.00 | $3.00 | $3.00 |
| Batch-level overhead cost per unit (driver: setup hours) | $5.00[b] | $0.50[c] | $0.05[d] |
| Total product cost per unit              | $18.00    | $13.50    | $13.05    |
| Total product cost (TPC)                 | $180.00   | $1,350.00 | $13,050.00 |
| ABC bid price (TPC × 200%)               | $360.00   | $2,700.00 | $26,100.00 |
| Traditional costing bid price (exhibit 22.1) | $300.00 | $3,000.00 | $30,000.00 |
| ABC minus traditional costing bid price (difference as a percentage of ABC bid price) | +$60.00 (+16.7)[e] | – $300.00 (–11.1)[f] | –$3,900.00 (–14.9)[g] |

[a] $3 × 1 direct labor hour.
[b] $50/10 units.
[c] $50/100 units.
[d] $50/1000 units.
[e] ($60/$360) × 100.
[f] (–$300/$2,700) × 100.
[g] (–$3,900/$26,100) × 100.

**Exhibit 22.2   Over- or Undercosted Products Caused by Variations in Production Volume: ABC Overhead Cost Assignment Model— An Example**

**(b) Product Diversity Can Cause Over- or Undercosting**   In addition to volume differences, products and services can be over- or undercosted if they consume organizational resources in differing proportions. Extending the previous example, the manufacture of product $D$ may involve the use of an expensive machine, and it may benefit from an extensive advertising campaign. Product $E$ does not use this expensive machine or benefit from an extensive advertising campaign. However, the traditional cost system, with a plantwide overhead rate, applied depreciation on the expensive machine to all products based on direct labor hours.

As is typical, the traditional costing system did not specifically apply marketing costs to the products, but all nonmanufacturing costs, plus the profit margin, were covered by the uniform 200 percent markup. Therefore, the different consumption of the advertising resources by products $D$ and $E$ was unrecognized.

**(c) Activity-Based Costing and Cost Assignment**   An ABC system should be designed to apply the costs of the various indirect manufacturing, marketing, and other activities to products and services in proportion to the extent that they utilize the organization's resources. The degree of accuracy in cost assignment provided by a particular ABC system involves cost-benefit considerations, which are further discussed in section 22.7.

**22.3 NON–VALUE-ADDED ACTIVITIES**   The original reason for implementing ABC systems was to correct over- or undercosting through more accurate assignment of indirect costs as illustrated previously. Later, the identification and costing of non–value-added (NVA) activities emerged as an important additional benefit.[6]

An NVA activity represents work that is not valued by the external or internal customer. NVA activities do not improve the quality or function of a product or service, but they can adversely affect costs and prices. Moving materials and machine setup for a production run are examples of NVA activities. NVA activities are found in both the private and public sectors. For example, in the Internal Revenue Service, rerouting documents and the wait or delay time in completing a case are examples of NVA activities in the "installment agreements" area.[7]

The preparation of tax returns and other compliance work by organizations do not directly benefit the customers of their products and services, but because they are required by law, they are not considered NVA activities.[8]

Extending the simple example shown previously, the cost of setups for the budget period was estimated to be $180,000 of the $200,000 batch-level costs. Given that the time to set up machines was estimated to be 4,000 hours, the average cost is $45 ($180,000/4,000) per setup hour. Managers can use this quantified information to judge whether the time and cost of setups are excessive. Managers may be able to obtain comparative benchmark information, and they can also compare setup activity information over time using trend analysis. Such information can instigate efforts to eliminate or reduce NVA activities.

**(a) Caveat**   Even if an activity is classified as NVA, it is not necessarily completely nonessential. For example, given the current state of technological development in a particular field, it may be impossible to reduce setup time to zero. The unavoidable portion of setup time is thus necessary to produce the product and therefore is not currently valueless. The definition of an NVA activity by the Consortium for Advanced Manufacturing-International (CAM-I) recognizes this point: "An activity that is judged to be *or contain* non-essential actions that do not contribute to customer value or the organization's needs."[9] Of course, future technological developments to automate the particular production process (e.g., flexible manufacturing systems) may reduce potential setup times to negligible levels.

Similarly, a so-called value-added (VA) activity may contain nonessential components that could be classified as NVA. Unnecessary materials costs and production time caused by excessive components in a product design and, in a service context, excessive mileage and time devoted to a taxi ride because the driver did not take the quickest route, are two examples of VA activities that contain NVA aspects.

CAM-I stresses the need for businesses to identify the difference between activities that are:

- Not required at all and can thus be eliminated (e.g., a duplication of effort).
- Ineffectively accomplished and can thus be reduced or redesigned (e.g., because of outdated policies or procedures).
- Required to sustain the organization and therefore cannot be reduced or eliminated (e.g., provide plant security).[10]

**(b) Behavioral Implications**   There are important behavioral aspects associated with classifying work as NVA. Managers and employees who perform NVA activities, such as machine setups, are likely to feel unappreciated and threatened by the description of their work as NVA.[11] The NVA designation may be interpreted as indicating imminent job layoffs. Also, employees whose jobs are classified as NVA may experience job dissatisfaction and low morale because of the perception that their activities are of little value to an organization. Increased worker turnover may result, and organizations could lose their best, most marketable managers and employees who perform NVA tasks.

Possible ways to avoid or mitigate behavioral problems include:

- Use of a less emotionally loaded term (e.g., "nonproduction activities").
- Participation by lower-level managers and employees in the design of ABC systems and in job redesign.
- Full disclosure of current and future employment plans to managers and employees.
- Creation of value-added work for displaced managers and employees.

**22.4 PROCESS IMPROVEMENTS**   By definition, ABC focuses on costing activities. The initial intent was to improve the assignment of costs to products and services. Later, the identification of activities and their cost drivers was recognized as valuable for organizations that were trying to continuously improve *processes* and not just activities within departments. For example, material handling is likely to cross departmental boundaries. One of the cost drivers of material handling (a NVA activity) is the distance traveled between operations. The reduction of such distances—say, through machine reconfigurations—should help reduce material handling costs. The cost assignment (vertical) view and process (horizontal) view is pictorially represented in a CAM-I exhibit reproduced as Exhibit 22.3.

A process is defined by CAM-I as: "A series of activities that are linked to perform a specific objective."[12] Improving processes rather than individual activities within

**COST ASSIGNMENT VIEW**

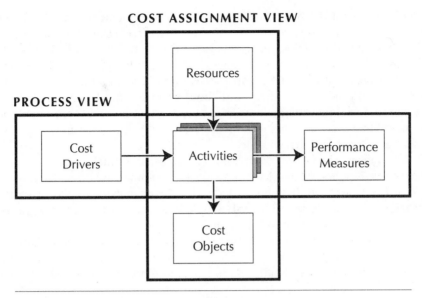

**Exhibit 22.3    CAM-I Basic ABC Model.** *Source:* From *The CAM-I Glossary of Activity-Based Management,* Edited by Norm Raffish and Peter B. B. Turney, (Arlington: CAM-I, 1991).

processes or organizational units helps avoid suboptimization problems. For example, if quality inspection activities are cut back to reduce costs in one department (without offsetting quality improvements to the product or service), departments further on in the process may have to increase their activities to investigate and correct quality problems. These correction activities may cost far more than the upstream cost savings.

Process value analysis (PVA) has been developed to complement ABC in cost management endeavors. PVA is defined as "a methodology for reducing costs and improving processes by identifying resource consumption within a process and the underlying root causes of cost (i.e., cost drivers)."[13] Activity analysis, which calculates "*business process costs* . . . the costs of sets of activities which cross departmental boundaries,"[14] is analogous to the PVA/ABC methodology. PVA is a systematic way to identify VA and NVA activities. PVA was used by the IRS in conjunction with *activity-based management* (ABM) in the development of a cost management information system.[15] (ABM is discussed in the next section.)

PVA supports ABC by seeking to improve the identification of activity cost pools, the causal factors of activities ("operational cost drivers"), VA and NVA activities, and the most appropriate activity drivers (or stage-two cost drivers) for assigning activity costs to products and services.[16]

PVA steps include:

- Prepare flow charts to document the activities in the processes of organizations.
- Define activities as VA or NVA.
- Identify the cost drivers, the causal factors of each activity.
- Identify improvement possibilities based on PVA and ABC information.[17]

**22.5 ACTIVITY-BASED MANAGEMENT**    A natural development from the success of ABC as a costing tool is to manage costs at the activity level using an ABM model. For example, it makes sense to budget activity costs using activity-based budgeting[18] when actual costs are costed and reported by activities in an ABC system. Also, the continuous improvement aspect of PVA is part of the ABM effort to manage activities and activity costs. ABM adds a dynamic, continuous improvement dimension to the more static ABC model. Interestingly, it has been observed that Japanese accountants began exploring activity-based techniques in the early 1990s following movement in the United States toward the ABM model.[19]

CAM-I defines ABM as: "A discipline that focuses on the management of activities as the route to improving the value received by the customer and the profit achieved by providing this value. This discipline includes cost driver analysis, activity analysis, and performance measurement. Activity-Based Management draws on Activity-Based Costing as its major source of information."[20]

Exhibit 22.4 pictorially represents this ABM model in a chart developed for CAM-I. In commenting on this model, one of its co-developers stated, "ABC supplies the information, and ABM uses this information in various analyses designed to yield continuous improvement."[21]

**(a) Cost Driver Analysis**    The factors that cause activities to be performed need to be identified in order to manage activity costs. Cost driver analysis identifies these causal factors.

For example, a cost driver analysis study might determine that slow processing of customer invoices results largely from lack of training of the customer invoice associates. This lack of training is thus a cost driver of the customer invoice processing activity. It is one of the factors causing this activity to take place (in this case, inefficiently). Managers have to address this cost driver to correct the root cause of the slow processing problem. To accomplish this task, managers might decide that an internal training

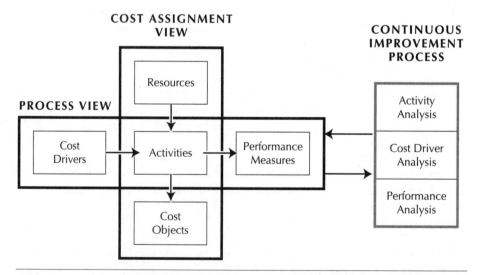

**Exhibit 22.4    Activity-Based Management Model.** *Source:* **From *The CAM-I Glossary of Activity-Based Management,* Edited by Norm Raffish and Peter B. B. Turney, (Arlington: CAM-I, 1991).**

program for customer invoice associates should be designed and implemented to increase the speed of customer invoice processing.

The time saving from the improved training may lead to a reduction in the number of customer invoice associates and, thus, to lower costs for the "customer invoice processing" activity. Of course, real salary cost savings occur only if the number of jobs in the organization actually decreases (e.g., through attrition) or if displaced customer invoice associates are redeployed to VA activities, thus canceling the need to hire new employees from outside. The tangible cost savings and intangible benefits from the customer invoice processing improvements should be compared with both the tangible and intangible costs of the new training program in a cost-benefit analysis.

The hypothetical customer invoice processing example shows that the identification and analysis of cost drivers (causal factors) is a necessary first step toward improving the cost-effectiveness of activities and cost management through ABM.

**(b) Activity Analysis**   Activity analysis, defined in section 22.2(a), identifies the activities of an organization and the activity centers (or activity cost pools) that should be used in an ABC system. Activity analysis also identifies VA and NVA activities. The degree to which activities are grouped together into activity centers depends on the costs and benefits of the alternatives. The number of activity centers is likely to change over time as organizational needs for activity information evolve.

For example, only a few activity centers may be used in an initial ABC pilot study. As managers become more accustomed to the initial ABC system and find the output useful, they may request a more detailed and refined ABC model.

**(c) Performance Analysis**   Performance analysis involves the identification of appropriate measures to report the performance of activity centers or other organizational units, consistent with each unit's goals and objectives. Performance analysis aims to identify the best ways to measure the performance of factors that are important to organizations in order to stimulate continuous improvement.

Extending the hypothetical customer invoice processing example, assume that timely processing of customer invoices is one of the activity center's goals. A performance analysis study identified the *number of customer invoices processed per hour* as the most appropriate performance measure to monitor timeliness in processing customer invoices. A subsequent benchmarking study revealed the relatively slow processing of customer invoices in the organization's customer invoices activity center and led to the cost driver analysis study discussed previously.

**22.6 STRATEGIC AND TACTICAL APPLICATIONS OF ACTIVITY-BASED MANAGEMENT/ ACTIVITY-BASED COSTING**   ABM/ABC (hereafter, ABC) provides activity information primarily to help managers make strategic, long-term decisions.[22] For example, ABC information should be valuable input for strategic decisions such as long-term pricing decisions, whether to add or delete a product line, and capacity management decisions (i.e., by measuring the costs of organizational resources used and unused).[23] ABC measurements correspond to the economists' long-term average cost curve rather than the short-term average cost curve.

Applications of ABC to support tactical, short-term decision making include the assignment of the actual costs of resources to activities, using resource drivers, for comparison with annual operating activity-based budgets. This facilitates variance analysis and short-term control decisions. Another tactical application is the assignment of the costs of activities to products, using activity drivers, for inventory valuation purposes, which helps organizations prepare their annual financial statements to calculate short-term profits.

**(a) ABC Complements Variable Costing and Throughput Accounting**   ABC complements strictly short-term models such as variable costing and throughput accounting—the accounting model associated with the *theory of constraints* or *synchronous manufacturing*.[24] ABC models typically assign to products and services all short-term variable indirect costs and fixed indirect costs (or long-term variable costs) that can be sensibly assigned using appropriate cost drivers. For example, some selling costs may be attributable to particular products or services (e.g., advertising), whereas others may not (e.g., the sales vice president's remuneration). Of course, for external financial reporting purposes, all manufacturing costs have to be assigned to products whether or not an appropriate cost driver exists. But for internal decision-making purposes, cost assignments should be based on cost-benefit considerations.

Variable costing assigns only short-term variable costs to products and services and calculates the contribution (sales – variable costs) toward the longer-term fixed costs. This model is useful for short-term decisions such as whether to accept a special order when spare capacity exists.

The basic throughput accounting (or super-variable costing[25]) model deducts direct materials costs from sales revenue to calculate the throughput margin. Apart from inventory costs (which include property, plant, and equipment), all other costs are classified as operating expenses. Operating expenses include direct labor costs and variable overhead that would be included with direct materials costs in the conventional variable costing model. To aid product mix decisions that maximize profits, the throughput per unit of scarce resource can be calculated, which is clearly a short-term decision model.

Proponents of throughput accounting do not generally support allocating operating expenses to products and services, even using ABC. They are concerned that cost allocations contribute to local optimization versus global optimization within organizations, which impedes competitiveness. Others argue, however, that the long-term focus of ABC complements rather than conflicts with the short-term focus of throughput accounting and that the information from both models is valuable when used properly for decision-making purposes.[26]

At least one company, Bertch Cabinet Manufacturing., Inc., decided to abandon ABC in favor of throughput accounting. The company obtained sufficient benefits from an ABC pilot study, and management decided that:

- Further developments of ABC would be too time-consuming and expensive.
- ABC information could not be provided on a timely enough basis for many marketing decisions.
- It was not cost-effective to make frequent updates to a complex ABC system to support the company's frequently changing manufacturing technology and processes.
- Throughput accounting was compatible with the company's new synchronous manufacturing system.[27]

**(b) ABC Overlaps with Just-in-Time Manufacturing and Contrasts with Backflush Costing**[28]   ABC is a costing methodology, whereas just-in-time (JIT) is an approach to improve manufacturing and purchasing activities, but they have features in common. For example, both ABC and JIT:

- Aim to help organizations compete more effectively and efficiently in the global marketplace.
- Analyze activities to help reduce and remove NVA activities (though the primary reason for performing activity analysis in an ABC system is to better assign indirect costs to products and services).
- Help improve costing accuracy. This occurs in JIT by plant reorganizations that reduce indirect costs by ascribing such costs directly to work cells, which are dedicated to particular product lines. It occurs in ABC systems by more accurately assigning indirect costs to products and services.

However, the costing system commonly associated with JIT manufacturing and purchasing, *backflush* costing, differs from ABC. Backflush costing is designed to be much simpler than even traditional costing systems. Because of the lower inventory levels and dedicated work cells under JIT systems, sophisticated ABC systems may not be cost-effective for some organizations that adopt JIT. However, using ABC for purposes that do not overlap with JIT (e.g., marketing cost analysis) may provide benefits that justify the information processing costs of an ABC system in a JIT organization.[29] It may also be cost-beneficial for these organizations to replace costly perpetual inventory systems with less expensive periodic inventory models.

**22.7 ABC COMPLEXITY**    ABC is more complex than a traditional costing system, but the degree of complexity varies on an organization-by-organization basis. The number of activity cost pools and cost drivers varies according to the detail required from the ABC system, which should be determined on a cost-benefit basis.

For example, plant managers in Deere tended to prefer more activity cost pools and cost drivers than did their counterparts in Fisher Controls (Fisher), based on cost-benefit considerations in both companies. In Deere, the number of plant activities and cost drivers typically ranged from 20 to 60 and 10 to 15, respectively. Fisher restricted the complexity of its ABC model to minimize the resources needed to reprogram the company's existing cost system. However, Fisher later bought ABC software for future developments of ABC. For example, Fisher planned to expand the scope of ABC to cover nonmanufacturing activities in administration, marketing, and so on. The introduction of ABC software and the planned expansion to cost nonmanufacturing activities within Fisher illustrate the evolutionary nature of ABC developments over time. ABC is not a static process, and the level of costing detail and scope should change to meet the evolving needs of users, subject to cost-benefit considerations.[30]

**(a) Imposed Versus Participatory Development of ABC Systems**    The type and complexity of ABC systems adopted by organizations can be imposed by top management or selected by unit managers in a participatory process. There is an imposed-participatory continuum, with various degrees of top-down and bottom-up involvement possible. Exhibit 22.5 depicts this imposed-participatory continuum.

In decentralized companies such as Deere and Fisher, the degree of participation by plant managers compared with a mandate from above should be heavily weighted toward the participation end of the continuum. In fact, this is how ABC was developed

| Imposed | Participation |
|---|---|
| **IMPOSED-PARTICIPATION CONTINUUM** | D&R[a] |

---

[a] This is an assumed location on the imposed-participation continuum for Deere & Company (D) and Fisher Controls (F), for illustration purposes.

---

**Exhibit 22.5    Imposed-Participation Continuum**

in both companies, with the use of interdisciplinary ABC development teams. This leads to the implementation of ABC systems that plant managers want. The high level of participation by Deere and Fisher plant managers is illustrated in Exhibit 22.5 by the assumed, representative location of Deere (D) and Fisher (F) at the participation end of the continuum.

The likely advantages of an imposed corporate ABC system for plants include use of a proven model with systems problems already resolved, quicker implementation, and lower ABC development costs. However, plant managers may resist using the output of an imposed ABC system. The likely advantages of an ABC system developed with the participation of the plant managers include implementation of a model that has "buy-in" from plant managers, production of ABC information that will probably be used by the plant managers, and the addition of an extra ABC model that can be considered for use by other plants in the organization.

To gain some of the benefits of an imposed ABC system without acceptance problems at the plant level, a corporate model can be developed that can be modified to meet the needs of individual plants. Deere generally adopted this approach, though two plants still elected to build their own ABC systems rather than modify the corporate model.

**(b) Cost-Benefit Approach**   More complex, more detailed cost systems provide more accurate cost assignments and cost information for decision making, but only at a greater cost to organizations. The critical question is whether the benefits of cost improvements exceed the costs. Both tangible and intangible benefits and costs need to be taken into account.

For example, activity analysis reveals NVA activities, and ABC assigns a tangible dollar amount to them. This should prompt managers to seek tangible cost savings through the reduction and possible elimination of NVA activities. But real (rather than paper) cost savings will accrue to organizations from the reduction of NVA activities only if the released resources are either used more productively or eliminated. An intangible cost of reducing NVA activities might be reduced morale of the work force caused by layoffs.

**22.8 FINAL THOUGHTS**   ABC is nearly two decades old and has evolved into a widely used costing model that is useful for strategic and tactical decision making at the national and international level, such as in the United States, Europe, and Japan. Also, ABC provides helpful information for manufacturing and nonmanufacturing organizations. However, some companies have found the ABC model more useful than others, and the early euphoria has passed. It is not the answer to *all* the global competitive problems of industry, though it is a potentially useful tool.

The conceptual understanding of ABC has been refined by developments such as the recognition of hierarchical activity levels. These levels include unit-level activities (e.g., machining), batch-level activities (e.g., material handling), product-level activities (e.g., product-specific advertising), and facility-level activities (e.g., security monitoring). A major contribution of ABC is the underlying, commonsense costing of activities, which even nonaccountants can appreciate and understand. This facilitates meaningful dialogue between accountants, engineers, manufacturing personnel, and others.

## NOTES

1.  For a discussion of the cost design factors (measurement costs, competition level, and the extent of product diversity), see R. Cooper and R. S. Kaplan, *The Design of Cost Management Systems* (Englewood Cliffs, NJ: Prentice-Hall, 1991), 4–5.

2.  The source of the material discussed in this paragraph is R. S. Kaplan, "John Deere Component Works (A)," *Harvard Business School Case Series 9-187-107* (Rev. November 1987). For further details on the ABC system of Deere & Company, see R. S. Kaplan, "John Deere Component Works (B)," *Harvard Business School Case Series 9-187-108* (Rev. November 1987), and J. B. MacArthur, "Activity-Based Costing: How Many Cost Drivers Do You Want?" *Journal of Cost Management* (Fall 1992), 37–41.

3.  Called "product-cost cross-subsidization" in C. T. Horngren, G. Foster, and S. M. Datar, *Cost Accounting: A Managerial Emphasis,* 9th ed. (Upper Saddle River, NJ: Prentice-Hall, 1997), 103.

4.  The example on banks is taken from R. B. Sweeney and J. W. Mays, "ABM Lifts Banks Bottom Line," *Management Accounting* (March 1997), 20–22, 24–26.

5.  *The CAM-I Glossary of Activity-Based Management*, ed. N. Raffish and P. B. B. Turney (Arlington, TX: CAM-I, 1991), 1.

6.  See J. B. MacArthur, "The ABC/JIT Costing Continuum," *Journal of Cost Management* (Winter 1992), 61.

7.  See J. B. MacArthur, "Cost Management at the IRS," *Management Accounting* (November 1996), 44–45.

8.  P. B. B. Turney, "Activity-Based Management: ABM Puts ABC Information to Work," *Management Accounting* (January 1992), 22.

9.  First sentence of the definition of an NVA activity (emphasis added), in *The CAM-I Glossary of Activity-Based Management*, op. cit., 8.

10.  Ibid., 16 (with some modifications).

11.  For example, M. E. Beischel, "Improving Production With Process Value Analysis: The Foundation for Activity Based Costing," *Journal of Accountancy* (September 1990), 55, reported: "In working with clients, our firm has constant battles over designating finished goods storage as NVA. The warehouse manager does not wish to be labeled, along with his or her entire department, as NVA."

12.  *The CAM-I Glossary of Activity-Based Management*, op. cit., 9. The CAM-I definition of "process" continues: "For example, the assembly of a television set or the paying of a bill or claim would contain several linked activities."

13.  M. R. Ostrenga and F. R. Probst, "Process Value Analysis: The Missing Link in Cost Management," *Journal of Cost Management* (Fall 1992), 4.

14.  R. Booth, "Activity Analysis and Cost Leadership," *Management Accounting* (UK) (June 1992), 32 (emphasis in original as part of a subheading).

15.  See J. B. MacArthur, "Cost Management at the IRS," *Management Accounting,* (November 1996), 44–46. The IRS calls ABM Activity-Based Cost Management (ABCM). Also, the U.S. Postal Service has adopted ABC and ABM; see Institute of Management Accountants Management Accounting Committee, *Practices and Techniques: Tools and Techniques for Implementing ABC/ABM*, Statements on Management Accounting, Statement Number 4EE (Montvale, NJ: Institute of Management Accountants, November 1998), 1.

16. See M. R. Ostrenga and F. R. Probst, "Process Value Analysis: The Missing Link in Cost Management," *Journal of Cost Management* (Fall 1992), 4–13.

17. These bulleted points summarize the first three steps and last step identified in Beischel, op. cit., 53–55, 57. Steps 4 through 6 included in this article include costing aspects that may involve ABC.

18. See J. Brimson and R. Fraser, "The Key Features of ABB," *Management Accounting* (UK) (January 1991), 42–43, and M. Morrow and T. Connolly, "The Emergence of Activity-Based Budgeting," *Management Accounting* (UK) (February 1991), 38–39, 41.

19. M. Sakurai, "What You Can Learn from Cost Management Practices in Japan—Target Costing and Activity-Based Costing," Unpublished paper presented at the University of North Florida (Tokyo, Japan: Senshu University, February 19, 1999).

20. *The CAM-I Glossary of Activity-Based Management*, op. cit., 3.

21. P. B. B. Turney, op. cit., 20. Turney discussed and gave examples of cost driver analysis, activity analysis, and performance analysis throughout his article (pp. 20–25). These terms are defined in *The CAM-I Glossary of Activity-Based Management*, op. cit.

22. R. N. Anthony and V. Govindarajan, *Management Control Systems*, 9th ed. (Irwin/McGraw-Hill, 1998), 323, states: "ABC is a strategic planning tool." Also, S. Dub, "ABM at Lawson: Beyond the Technology," *Management Accounting* (March 1997), 35, stated: "Although the dollar value of cost savings and productivity is an important result of implementing ABM, the true value of ABM will be the availability of activity-level information that will support the strategic decision-making process."

23. For further discussion of ABC and capacity usage, see R. Cooper and R. S. Kaplan, "Activity-Based Systems: Measuring the Costs of Resource Usage," *Accounting Horizons* (September 1992), 1–13.

24. For example, see: E. M. Goldratt, *What Is This Thing Called Theory of Constraints and How Should it Be Implemented?* (Croton-on-Hudson, NY: North River Press, 1990); E. M. Goldratt, *Sifting Information out of the Data Ocean: The Haystack Syndrome* (Croton-on-Hudson, NY: North River Press, 1990); M. Umble and M. L. Srikanth, *Synchronous Manufacturing: Principles for World Class Excellence* (Cincinnati, OH: South-Western Publishing, 1990).

25. See C. T. Horngren, G. Foster, and S. M. Datar, *Cost Accounting: A Managerial Emphasis*, 9th ed. (Upper Saddle River, NJ: Prentice-Hall, 1997), 308.

26. For example, see J. B. MacArthur, "Theory of Constraints and Activity-Based Costing: Friends or Foes?" *Journal of Cost Management* (Summer 1993), 50–56, and R. Kee, "Integrating ABC and the Theory of Constraints to Evaluate Outsourcing Decisions," *Journal of Cost Management* (January/February 1998), 26–36.

27. J. B. MacArthur, "From Activity-Based Costing to Throughput Accounting," *Management Accounting* (April 1996), 30, 34, 36–38.

28. This section is primarily based on J. B. MacArthur, note 6, 61–63.

29. For example, see R. J. Lewis, "Activity-Based Costing for Marketing," *Management Accounting* (November 1991), 33–38; D. R. Hansen and M. M. Mowen, *Management Accounting*, 4th ed. (Cincinnati, OH: South-Western College, 1997), 136–137.

30. This paragraph and the next section are largely based on J. B. MacArthur, note 2.

# CHAPTER 23

# IMPLEMENTING ACTIVITY-BASED MANAGEMENT

**John A. Miller**

COMPX

**23.1 INTRODUCTION**   This chapter provides an overview of the implementation requirements for *activity-based management* (ABM). The chapter explains what is necessary to plan for pilot projects or for full ABM implementation. It discusses various models and outlines a four-step program in detail. The four-step model, a foundation of ABM implementation, includes planning, activity analysis, activity/product costing, and documentation. It can be applied to small units (e.g., specific departments) or to an entire enterprise.

**23.2 WHAT ACTIVITY-BASED MANAGEMENT IMPLEMENTATION REQUIRES**   A fully implemented ABM information system accumulates and reports activity-based information on a periodic basis for an entire organization. For a successful program, several things must happen:

- Business processes and activities must be defined throughout the organization.
- Systems and procedures must be in place to collect both actual activity data and budgeted activity data.
- Product or service cost and activity information must be provided in a format and within a time frame that is useful and relevant for decision making and for tracking operational performance.
- Finally, a fully implemented ABM information system must have activity information for important activities documented in an activity dictionary.

The level of activity information typical of a completed installation is best illustrated with an example of an activity that might be included in an activity dictionary. The example of the "maintain payroll master file" activity is common to many organizations and deals with the maintenance of employee information (e.g., salary level, marital status, and dependents) needed for payroll and regulatory reporting requirements. Exhibit 23.1 outlines activity information that might be contained in the activity dictionary for this example. As illustrated, the level of activity knowledge, information, and understanding includes a clear description of the activity and its associated tasks, costs, outputs, output measures, cost drivers, performance measures, and other

| ACTIVITY DICTIONARY | |
| --- | --- |
| **Activity** | Maintain payroll master file |
| **Business process** | Administration of payroll/human resources |
| **Activity number** | 113 |
| **Activity description** | Maintain current status of all employee master files |
| **Activity tasks** | Receive changes, enter changes, edit changes, and run file |
| **Annual activity cost** | $306.00 |
| **Activity output** | Updated payroll master file |
| **Activity output measure** | Number of employee files maintained |
| **Annual activity output** | Updated payroll master file for average of 6,600 employees |
| **Cost per unit of output** | $46.36 per employee per year |
| **Customer/user of activity** | Employee, government agencies |
| **Value-added/non–value-added** | Value added |
| **Performance measurements** | Quality: First-pass yield on changes |
| | Cycle time: Employee change request to updated file |
| | Productivity: Cost per employee file updated or number of files dated per day |
| **Cost drivers** | Employee turnover |
| | Frequency of changes or updates |
| | Changes in federal laws |

**Exhibit 23.1    Maintain Payroll Master File**

attributes. A completed ABM implementation would have this level of knowledge for all activities tracked by the system.

**(a) Amount of Reporting Detail**    Exhibit 23.1 can also be used to make an important point about ABM implementations, which is that the amount of detail required depends on the information used. In general, more detail and specificity about activities are required for process-improvement applications than for product- or service-cost applications.

In Exhibit 23.1, for example, activities were specified to the detail and level required to drive and support a process improvement initiative for a payroll department. This might be one of several activities defined for the payroll department and reflects the detail that might be required to manage and control the activities of the department. Had the purpose of the ABM application been product or service costing—where the objective is to trace costs to products or services—the entire payroll department might have been defined much more broadly as one activity: "pay employees."

**(b) Time Frame for Implementation**    In a very large organization, a complete ABM installation could take three to five years to complete, whereas in a small company the effort might be accomplished in six months. The total work effort required is a function of several factors. The first factor is the size of the organization; larger organizations require more time for ABM installations. A second major factor is the starting point. Some organizations have never defined the significant processes and activities of their organization, whereas others may have already prepared process flow charts for all significant areas of operation. Starting from scratch is a significant undertaking. Additional factors include the degree of accuracy and detail required, the frequency of reporting, and the diversity of management needs. ABM implementations that require highly detailed and precise reporting on a monthly basis will require greater installation efforts than those systems that require less precision and frequency of reporting.

**(c) Steps Required for Activity-Based Management Implementation**   Regardless of how ABM information will be used by an organization, the scope of the effort, or the organization's size, the general implementation steps are about the same. ABM implementations require the following steps:

- Activities must be specified and defined.
- Activity outputs and measures must be determined.
- Judgments about activity value must be made.
- Activity performance measures must be established.
- Costs must be traced to activities, and then from activities to the products or services that consume them.
- Efforts to develop and install the ongoing activity-based information system must be completed.

**23.3 BACKGROUND ON ACTIVITY-BASED MANAGEMENT**   By the late 1990s, thousands of implementations of activity-based costing (ABC) or ABM had been undertaken throughout the world. The sale of commercial ABM software systems has mushroomed over the past 10 to 15 years. Nonetheless, although many organizations have implemented ABM, relative to the use of traditional cost management systems, activity- and process-based management information systems are still in their infancy.

The earliest ABM initiatives were driven by forward-thinking companies willing to experiment and apply the theory and conceptual framework of ABM to the real world. Most of these organizations began by experimenting with small pilot implementation efforts that included the activities of one department, several departments, a plant, a facility, or a companywide business process. Where the objective was product cost, the focus was on manufacturing overhead.

Until recently, few organizations have undertaken ABM implementations with the intent of covering the entire organization, because a major overhaul of management information systems is expensive and time-consuming. Managers want assurance that the resulting information will be useful to them. In addition, undertaking an implementation for a large organization all at once could seem overwhelming and risky.

**23.4 COMMON APPROACH TO IMPLEMENTATION**   The common approach to initial or pilot implementations for many companies is to use a five- to seven-person cross-functional team that will work from three to six months to implement ABM principles, techniques, and methods for some part of the organization. The team is composed of internal people (dedicating from 25 to 100 percent of their time), external consultants, or both.

**(a) Typical Pilot Program**    In a typical pilot installation, team members draw up an implementation plan that covers the steps and requirements of activity analysis and activity or product costing. Data are gathered through interviews and "crunched" off-line in commercial ABM software or homegrown spreadsheets. A final report containing key findings, observations, recommendations, and next steps is then issued to signal the end of the initial pilot phase. The report's appendix should contain costing assumptions, detailed reports, and activity information.

Report recommendations are generally of two types. The first type suggests taking whatever actions were identified to improve the performance of the organization. The second type of recommendation outlines the next steps required to continue the implementation of ABM systems and methods. These next steps might involve either taking on additional parts of the organization or refining and improving the data-collection and reporting methods developed in the pilot (or both).

**(b) Strengths of Pilot Approach**    Successful pilot efforts lead to additional implementation phases. The knowledge and experience gained from pilot efforts are used to leverage resources and to speed implementation as larger and larger chunks of the organization are included in subsequent phases. This is a practical approach to getting started. It is senseless to undertake a large-scale ABM implementation without first having assurance that the resulting information will be useful.

A pilot approach is also practical for another reason. Early implementers of ABM have been willing to share approaches, methodologies, and practices used to conduct pilot ABM installations. The results of some of the earliest implementations directed toward product cost are well-known and published. "John Deere Component Works" is covered in a Harvard Business School case study issued in 1989–1990. "Siemens Electric Motor Works" and the "Ingersoll Milling Machine Company" case studies are other published Harvard Business School case studies. Case studies now appear on a regular basis, both in finance trade publications and also in publications directed toward the engineering, manufacturing, sales, and quality functions of an organization.

**(c) Drawbacks of Pilot Approach**    Pilot projects are a practical way to get started, but their primary weakness is that they often fail to identify and leave behind efficient systems, procedures, and methods to collect and report activity-based information on an ongoing basis. Without timely, relevant, and ongoing reporting of activity information, an implementation will fail. Another weakness with the pilot approach is that it fails to access and identify the needs of the entire organization and to prepare an overall implementation plan for the organization taken as a whole. Pilot efforts to experiment with ABM do not require a companywide perspective. As a result, pockets of ABM knowledge may become independent and isolated.

To achieve its full potential an ABM information system must be integrated with mainstream information systems and the organization's cultures and values. As most organizations have learned, a more holistic approach to implementation is required.

**23.5 RECOMMENDED IMPLEMENTATION APPROACH**    The use, application, and benefits of ABM are well-documented and widely published. For most organizations this information, supplemented by analysis, should provide an adequate base deciding whether to implement a broad-based ABM system or to experiment with a pilot effort. When experimenting, use the common approach discussed earlier. When the goal is to implement an ABM system, a more intense commitment to implementation is required.

**(a) Commitment Required**    Significant commitments are required to achieve a full-blown ABM system. These commitments involve greater commitments of resources than those typically associated with improving an existing system. This difference can be explained in terms of the change in management mind-set from managing cost to managing activities. In addition, implementing ABM requires a willingness to pursue a strategy for improving the activities of the business. Without efforts to improve, resources devoted to implementation are wasted.

A total approach to the ABM implementation includes the following three steps:

1.  Do an overall assessment, and prepare an overall implementation plan.
2.  Divide and conquer, using a building-block approach. First, divide the organization into manageable segments. Then implement each segment in phases, using the four-step model shown in Exhibit 23.2 as the basic building block. The steps in the model cover the detailed planning, analysis, data gathering, cost tracing, and documentation necessary to implement an ABM system successfully. The model represents the basic implementation steps and can be applied to all significant portions of the business. (It can even be used to conduct a pilot implementation.)
3.  Develop a cost-effective, ongoing data collection and reporting system.

**(b) Overall Assessment and Implementation Plan**    Implementing a new ABM information system requires considerable effort and planning. As for any significant project undertaking, goals must be established, overall requirements must be specified, work must be planned, resources must be identified and earmarked, responsibilities must be assigned, and priorities must be set. An assessment is designed to gather information necessary to prepare and document the overall implementation plan. The result is a preliminary understanding of the requirements, resources, and time lines necessary to fully implement the ABM system.

| DATA GATHERING AND ANALYSIS | | | |
|---|---|---|---|
| **Planning** | **Activity Analysis** | **Activity/Product Costing** | **Documenting Results** |
| Purpose | Specific activities and business processes | Select or develop software | Prepare report |
| Objectives | | | Make recommendations |
| Scope | | Specify resource drivers | |
| Time | Outputs and output measures | | Assign action |
| | | Specify activity drivers | Refine data |
| Resources | Value-added analysis | | |
| Expectations | | Trace costs | Identify next steps |
| | Identify cost drivers | | Track improvement results |
| Team development | | Develop costing model | |
| | Activity performance | | |

**Exhibit 23.2    Four-Step ABM Implementation Model**

An assessment provides:

- *Business process relationship map:* Documentation and relationship of key business processes.
- *Preliminary list of key and significant activities:* Identification, on a preliminary basis, of major activities, including possible performance measures and potential cost drivers.
- Preliminary costing of activities and business processes.
- Estimates of non–value-added activities and costs.
- Linkage of business processes and activities to the organization's strategic plan.
- Applicability of ABC product or service costing.
- Availability of data and information required for the installation.
- Existing systems capabilities and the ability of those systems to integrate with activity information.
- Primary uses of activity-based information.
- Available resources and implementation requirements.
- Recommendations for implementation, steps to be taken, and a time line.

Typically, assessments take two to six weeks to complete and are performed by consulting firms that specialize in ABM installations. Most organizations will find it difficult to conduct assessments internally because they lack the necessary experience and expertise. The assessment provides a better understanding of the needs and requirements before internal resources are committed. It also tends to put the entire organization in perspective; that is, the whole can be broken down into manageable parts. Finally, an assessment also enables management to set priorities and select those initial areas for implementation where efforts will yield the greatest value.

**(c) Four-Step Building Blocks**   The general steps involved in an ABM implementation can be expressed in a number of different ways and performed in different sequences. Six-, eight-, and twelve-step implementation models have also been developed. However, each model includes steps that involve planning: activity analysis, activity/product costing, and documenting results, as shown in Exhibit 23.2. Choosing a model is a matter of personal preference and a matter of adapting general models to specific situations. Most models yield similar end results.

The primary difference in the ABM models is in the area of responsibility for action the vision of how ABM fits the organization. Some view ABM as a management information system only, in which responsibility for action occurs when the information is provided to the decision makers and those responsible for the processes, activities, products, and services of the organization. In other words, ABM is a tool to support improvement initiatives and to improve decision making. Others view ABM as a methodology for improvement, in which ABM implementation steps assume a greater level of responsibility for implementing actions, decisions, and changes.

This chapter takes the view that ABM is an information system designed to improve decision making and to drive and support continuous improvement efforts, whether the initiative is total quality management (TQM), business process reengineering (BPR), just-in-time (JIT) manufacturing, or benchmarking.

In essence, this is the middle ground between the two viewpoints. ABM information must do more than just support decision making and improvement initiatives. It must drive decision making and improvement. It is not a replacement for existing initiatives such as TQM, BPR, JIT manufacturing, or benchmarking. It is an information system that puts teeth into these improvement initiatives by establishing accountability, measuring results, and setting priorities.

The activity-based implementation model selected for use in this chapter was simplified to cover the tasks and work required in the area of planning, activity analysis, activity/product costing, documenting results, and data gathering and analysis, as shown in Exhibit 23.2. (The process of data gathering and analysis is ongoing and is an integral part of each step.) The individual tasks involved in planning, activity analysis, activity/product costing, and documenting results are shown under their respective area in the model.

Because the four-step model represents the basic building block of the ABM implementation, it can be applied on a small scale to a specific area of the organization, such as a department, function, or application. It can also be applied on a larger scale to an entire plant, a business unit, or a facility—and simultaneously to several plants, facilities, departments, or functions. In application, the model is applied over and over until all significant segments of the business have been covered. A summary of each model area follows.

*(i) Planning*    The four-step model includes detailed planning to define the purpose, objectives, and expectations for each specific ABM building block. A significant part of this planning includes developing a detailed project plan (complete with time line and assigned responsibilities), defining the resources required, and selecting specific people to do the work. It also documents the methods that will be used to collect data. Although planning consumes only a small part of the effort (5–15 percent), it has a significant bearing on the outcome.

*(ii) Activity Analysis*    Activity analysis is the heart of an ABM implementation. Specifying activities and processes, identifying cost drivers, documenting outputs and output measures, analyzing activities from a value-added perspective, and developing performance measures all represent major undertakings. Activity analysis can consume as much as 50 to 55 percent of implementation resources.

*(iii) Activity/Product Costing*    Activity/product costing is the most mechanical part of the four-step model. It means documenting the cost-tracing methodology and base assumptions. A large part of the work required by this step involves the development or use of a software system to export, import, and accept data necessary to calculate activity and product or service cost. The software system selected or developed as part of this step is often used for the ongoing reporting of activity information.

Unless there are significant systems issues or problems, no more than 25 to 30 percent of the project's resources should be devoted to this step. For organizations that offer thousands and thousands of products or services and require detailed product or service cost information, a significantly higher percentage of project resources would be required to accomplish this area of work.

*(iv) Document Results*    The final step of the four-step implementation model involves documenting the work completed, including results, recommendations, and conclusions. This step is exceedingly important but often neglected. To be successful, an ABM

project should induce management to act based on the knowledge gained. Decisions regarding next steps are required. To be useful, information about actions to be taken and recommended next steps must be documented. A minimum of 10 percent of the project effort should be devoted to documenting results.

*(v) Data Gathering and Analysis*   Data gathering and analysis are an integral part of each of the four steps reviewed. Planning involves gathering information and data to document the purpose, expectations, and objectives of the implementation effort. Data gathering also plays a significant role in the activity analysis. Most of the information required by this step must be gathered from the existing knowledge base in the organization. To complete the activity/product costing step, information about the consumption of resources and activities must be collected and analyzed. Finally, information and data must be analyzed as the basis for the recommendations, conclusions, and next steps contained in the documented report. Data gathering and analysis can represent about 33 to 50 percent of the effort involved in each of the four steps.

**(d) Developing a Cost-Effective Data Collection and Reporting System**   The final part of the recommended total approach to an ABM implementation is developing an effective, cost-efficient, ongoing data collection and reporting system. The four-step implementation model is designed to provide information about the activities of the organization at a particular point in time. To be useful, activity information must be collected and reported on a continuous basis.

There are two stages to implementing an ongoing ABM information and reporting system. Stage 1 involves establishing the base set of procedures, systems, and methods for ongoing collection of data. Stage 2 relates to ongoing system maintenance requirements.

*(i) Implementing Procedures, Systems, and Methods (Stage 1)*   During stage 1, procedures, systems, and methods needed for ongoing reporting are implemented. This often involves creating procedures to collect data for the first time, as well as redirecting information and other data from existing sources. Stage 1 is a true hands-on period in the organization. It requires extensive use of information services personnel. Data formats and due dates must be established, and the quality requirements expected of data entering the system must be standardized.

*(ii) Maintaining the Activity-Based Management System (Stage 2)*   Like any information system, the ABM information system must be maintained on an ongoing basis. Activities change over time. New activities are added. Improvement initiatives should eliminate non–value-added activities. Activity performance measures will improve and change over time. New products and services will be added; others will be discontinued. The system must be updated to reflect these changes.

**23.6 COMPARISON WITH OTHER IMPLEMENTATION MODELS**   Many organizations have recommended approaches and steps for implementing ABC and ABM. For several of these organizations, recommended steps are shown and compared with the four-step model previously presented.

**(a) American Productivity & Quality Center**   The American Productivity & Quality Center (APQC),which is based in Houston, Texas, is a nonprofit organization estab-

| Steps | Planning | Activity Analysis | Activity/ Product Costing | Document Results | Data Gathering |
|---|---|---|---|---|---|
| 1. Emphasize management commitment | ✗ | | | ✗ | ✗ |
| 2. Define activities | | ✗ | | | ✗ |
| 3. Determine time period for costing | | | ✗ | | ✗ |
| 4. Trace cost to activities | | | ✗ | | ✗ |
| 5. Determine value/non–value-added | | ✗ | | | ✗ |
| 6. Define activity outputs/measures | | ✗ | | | ✗ |
| 7. Identify cost drivers | | ✗ | | | ✗ |
| 8. Calculate product/service cost | | | ✗ | | ✗ |

**Exhibit 23.3    APQC Implementation Model**

lished in 1977 to work with people in organizations to improve productivity, quality, and quality of work life by the following methods:

- Providing educational, advisory, and information services of exceptional value.
- Researching new methods of improvements on both domestic and international fronts and broadly disseminating these findings.

Exhibit 23.3 illustrates the APQC model.

Step 1 of this model emphasizes upfront planning, including the agreement, in advance, that actions will be taken on the basis of knowledge gained. Step 2, which calls for the specification of business processes and activities, emphasizes the need to reach consensus on key and significant activities early in the implementation. Step 3 is relatively short and involves a decision about the period of time under which activities will be costed. Activities could be costed for a month, a quarter, a year, or any other period. In addition, the costing could be done on actual expenditures or on budget amounts. Step 4 involves tracing costs to the activities specified in step 2. Step 5 involves the analysis of activities and judgments about whether the activities add value from a customer's (internal or external) perspective. Step 6 involves the identification of activity outputs and activity performance measures for each key and significant activity. Step 7 involves the identification and measurement of cost drivers. Finally, step 8 involves tracing activity costs to products, services or other cost objects, which consume the activities.

**(b) Amercian Management Association**    The American Management Association (AMA) is widely recognized for its training capabilities, offering hundreds of courses annually in 29 specific areas of interest. Since 1989, the AMA has offered ABM training in its accounting and controls area of interest. The material used by the AMA was developed by ICMS, Inc., and reflects the philosophies of Tom Pryor and Jim Brimson, each of whom headed the cost management task force of the Consortium for Advanced Manufacturing-International (CAM-I). Exhibit 23.4 outlines the AMA steps to implementation.

Step 1 is comprehensive and intended to establish a picture of the significant activities as they are currently performed in the organization. This step involves defining activities and identifying cost drivers, performance measures, activity outputs, and

| Steps | Planning | Activity Analysis | Activity/ Product Cost | Document Results | Data Gathering |
|---|---|---|---|---|---|
| 1. Understand significant activities | ✗ | ✗ | ✗ | | ✗ |
| 2. Determine activities that need to be changed | | ✗ | | | ✗ |
| 3. Improve activities | | | | ✗ | ✗ |
| 4. Sustain improvement through organizational culture and management systems | ✗ | | | ✗ | ✗ |

**Exhibit 23.4    American Management Association Implementation Model**

non–value-added activities. Step 2 is primarily analysis to identify high-priority activities for improvement. Step 3 relates to synchronizing activities within a business process, eliminating wasteful activities, simplifying and improving methods, reducing workload, and matching service levels to customer requirements. Step 4 is designed to sustain improvement by changing the organizational structure, culture, and management information systems through the use of activity-based budgeting, planning, and reporting of activity-based information.

This implementation model emphasizes process improvement, and to a large degree, it positions ABM as a methodology for improvement. The individual model steps track a common approach to process improvement advocated by many management improvement experts:

- Determine the "as is" (understand significant activities).
- Determine the "should be" (determine activities that need to be changed).
- Change the process (improve activities).
- Measure the result (sustain improvement).

**(c) ABC Technologies, Inc.**    Oregon-based ABC Technologies, Inc., is a leading provider of ABM software. Its recommended implementation steps, which are based on building a computer model, emphasize activity analysis and activity/product costing. Exhibit 23.5 shows the first four steps. The "planning and documenting results" aspects of an ABM implementation are not covered in this material.

Step 1 encompasses most of the work required by the activity analysis. Step 2 involves the identification and documentation of the methods used to assign, or trace,

| Steps | Planning | Activity Analysis | Activity/ Product Cost | Document Results | Data Gathering |
|---|---|---|---|---|---|
| 1. Identify resources, activities, and cost objects | | ✗ | | | ✗ |
| 2. Define cost assignment paths and specify drivers | | ✗ | ✗ | | ✗ |
| 3. Enter data | | | ✗ | | |
| 4. Calculate costs | | | ✗ | | |

**Exhibit 23.5    ABC Technologies, Inc., Implementation Model**

| Steps | Planning | Activity Analysis | Activity/ Product Cost | Document Results | Data Gathering |
|---|---|---|---|---|---|
| 1. Define the problem or scope | X | | | | X |
| 2. Identify the activities involved and their drivers | | X | | | X |
| 3. Lay out the schematic | | | X | | X |
| 4. Collect related data and rules | | X | X | | X |
| 5. Build the model | | | X | | X |
| 6. Validate the model with historical data | | | X | | X |
| 7. Interpret the new information | | X | | | X |
| 8. Play scenarios and make recommendations | | | | X | X |

**Exhibit 23.6    Institute of Management Accountants Implementation Model**

costs to activities and cost objects. Step 3 involves entering the data required by the model. The final step, performed by the computer, calculates both the cost of activities and the cost objects.

**(d) Institute of Management Accountants**    Developed by Derek J. Sandison and Paul A. Sharman, the Institute of Management Accountants' eight-step model is based on developing an ABC system and emphasizes the system and reporting aspects of an ABM implementation. (See Exhibit 23.6.)

Step 1 is directed toward the business issues to be resolved and toward setting priorities for objectives. Step 2 involves determining what activities are important and what drives the activity. Step 3 is used to symbolically document operational flow. The result of step 3 is a schematic of the network of activities representing the defined problem. This schematic is the foundation of model documentation. Step 4 involves the use of existing reports (both operational and financial), expert knowledge from department supervisors, existing standards, or best guesses. Step 5 involves combining the schematic and the collected data and rules to create a computer model using modeling software. Step 6 calls for the validation of both operational and financial information. Step 7 is analytical in nature; its intent is to understand what the activity-based information means to the organization. Finally, step 8 involves "what if" analysis and makes specific recommendations for improvements.

**23.7 SUMMARY**    Most early ABM implementations were pilot efforts directed to parts of an organization. They were designed to validate theory and to test the principles, applications, methods, and procedures in the real world. Evidence was required to show that these new ABM systems were better than traditional cost and management information systems. Pilot efforts, which were often underplanned and underfunded, got the ball rolling but failed to address the overall requirements of the organization and to leave behind the necessary systems, procedures, and reporting required to integrate ABM into the organization.

Judging by the significant increases in both the number and the scope of implementations since the early 1990s, the evidence indicates that organizations have found ABM information valuable. Many organizations have now begun to aggressively replace traditional information systems with process- or activity-based systems. Pilot efforts are required less frequently, but when they are, the scope of effort is more aggressive. Large-scale ABM projects demand a more committed approach to implementation that requires:

- Perform an overall assessment, and prepare an overall implementation plan.
- Use the four-step implementation model as the basic building block, then implement it in phases.
- Put in a cost-effective data collection and reporting system.

# CHAPTER 24

# ACTIVITY-BASED MANAGEMENT IN SERVICE ORGANIZATIONS

## John Antos
**Value Creation Group**
## James A. Brimson
**IPM**

**24.1 INTRODUCTION**   The purpose of this chapter is to:

- Contrast the differences between traditional costing and activity-based service costing for service organizations.
- Describe the conventional approach to service cost, including its limitations.
- Describe an activity management approach to service cost, including an in-depth discussion of cost elements that are traceable.
- Discuss special considerations such as the frequency of service cost calculation, setup costs, bottleneck costs, and work orders

**24.2 CONSUMPTION OF RESOURCES**   In activity management, resources are consumed to perform activities. Services, in turn, consume activities and supplies. An activity service cost system assigns supplies and all traceable and assignable activities to services based on the usage of each activity.

Activity management represents a major change from traditional cost accounting. The primary differences include:

- The emphasis is on decreasing the cost of the service and support activities while improving quality. The cost of providing the service is often a secondary cost objective.
- Direct labor is charged to the activity or business process rather than directly to the service. This approach eliminates the need to voucher the labor to services except in cases in which the accuracy is suspect because of the variability and magnitude of the estimated labor content.
- A *cost pool* is a collection of related costs. An *activity pool* is a collection of related activities and their cost.

- Activity usage is based on the amount of activity or business-process volume consumed by a service. Activity or business-process volume is the number of activity or business process output units the service requires.
- Direct tracing of activities or business processes to services reduces the amount of overhead that must be allocated.
- Direct tracing of activities to services occurs without regard to whether the costs in question are direct or indirect costs. The cost is directly traced or assigned as long as a cause-and-effect relationship can be established between the activity and the service. Traceable costs such as marketing, accounting, administration, and other support costs are directly charged to services. This approach results in a focus on total cost, not just direct costs of the service operations.
- *Service cost* includes the total cost to design, produce, distribute and provide customer service. Many life-cycle costs, which have traditionally been expensed, should instead be traced to the service and distributed over its life. Life-cycle cost provides management an understanding of long-term profitability and makes possible the quantification of the cost impact of alternative business processes and levels of service.
- The impact of changes in the volume of activities or business processes on service cost is determined.
- Nonfinancial performance measures are aligned with strategy to judge service and business process performance.

Activity management benefits an organization because it:

- Provides more accurate service costs.
- Makes opportunities for cost reduction and performance improvement more visible.

Competition increases the need for more accurate service costs because it usually means that an organization cannot pass on its inefficiencies through higher prices.

Accurate and detailed information on the actual cost of the activities that make up a service is vital in vendor selection, make-or-buy decisions, design-to-cost, and similar decisions. In terms of increasing competitiveness, being able to identify opportunities to reduce waste, pare costs, and improve performance may be even more important than knowing service cost.

**24.3 USES OF SERVICE COST**    An accurate determination of service cost is important because decisions that organizations make require data on service costs. To be relevant, the reported service cost must mirror the service operations.

Service-cost information is required in various forms and at different levels of detail to meet various objectives, which include:

- Estimating the cost of new services and special one-time services.
- Determining profitability for expansion or abandonment of different service segments, such as service lines, market segments, distribution channels, or customers to be served.
- Calculating the margins associated with individual services.
- Facilitating make-or-buy decisions.

- Assisting in the investment analysis process.
- Valuing inventory and calculating the cost of goods sold for external financial reporting purposes (e.g., retail stores).
- Assisting in offshore sourcing decisions (e.g., the following activities all take place in Ireland: Massachusetts Mutual Life Insurance processes U.S. claims; Wright Investors Service organizes databases; Quarterdeck's, a computer software company, provides technical support; Cigna processes U.S. medical claims; and Mc-Graw-Hill maintains worldwide circulation files).

**24.4 TRADITIONAL APPROACH TO SERVICE COST**   The service-cost model implemented in most organizations identifies three major elements in the cost of a service:

1. *Direct supplies.* The acquisition cost of all supplies that can reasonably be traced to the service.
2. *Direct labor.* The wages of all labor that can be associated directly with a service in an economically feasible manner.
3. *Service or administrative overhead.* All costs other than direct labor and direct supplies associated with the activities that constitute a service. Service overhead is traditionally considered an indirect cost and cannot be traced directly to specific services. An overhead application rate is used to assign a reasonable portion of overhead costs to services. The essence of overhead allocation is the top-down application of costs from a cost center to all services produced during the period.

Exhibit 24.1 outlines the basic flow of costs in a traditional cost accounting system. Exhibit 24.2 illustrates this approach and shows two services with equal volume.

**(a) Step 1**   Labor and supplies are assigned directly to each service whenever feasible. Costs of direct labor and supplies are easily attached to services. Charges for

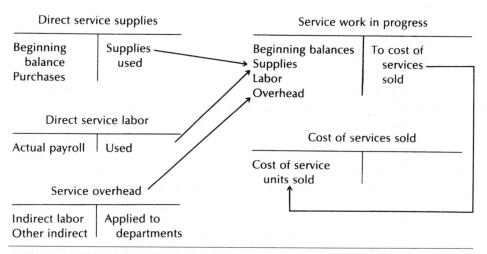

**Exhibit 24.1   Flow of Costs in a Traditional Cost Accounting System.** *Source: Activity-Based Management for Service Industries, Government Entities & Nonprofit Organizations,* **by James A. Brimson and John Antos. Copyright © 1998 by John Wiley & Sons, Inc. Reprinted by permission of John Wiley & Sons, Inc.**

|  | Services | | |
| --- | --- | --- | --- |
|  | A | B | Total |
| Annual cost (in $1,000s) | $ | $ | $ |
| Direct labor |  |  |  |
| Direct labor wages | 3,000 | 1,000 | 4,000 |
| Direct supplies |  |  |  |
| Direct supplies | 3,000 | 3,000 | 6,000 |
| Purchased items | 500 | 500 | 1,000 |
| Total supplies/purchased | 3,500 | 3,500 | 7,000 |

**Exhibit 24.2    Costs in a Traditional Cost Accounting System.** *Source: Activity-Based Management for Service Industries, Government Entities & Nonprofit Organizations, by James A. Brimson and John Antos. Copyright © 1998 by John Wiley & Sons, Inc. Reprinted by permission of John Wiley & Sons, Inc.*

supplies are posted from requisitions for supplies and direct labor charges from time tickets.

**(b) Step 2**    All remaining costs are considered overhead and applied to services on a predetermined basis. Overhead is typically applied to services according to an overhead rate computed by dividing overhead costs by a rate base such as direct labor hours, direct labor cost, supplies, total cost input, sales, or computer hours. An overhead application rate expresses a relationship of service overhead to a factor of service operations that can be traced directly to services. Service overhead is assigned to services in proportion to this factor.

The following procedures are used to apply overhead to services:

- *Determine costs to be included in overhead.* Service overhead often includes all costs other than direct labor, direct supplies, and *selling, general, and administrative* (SG&A) costs.
- *Determine the period of benefit.* Two rules of thumb for determining whether a cost should be capitalized are as follows:
  1. Costs that benefit current services should be expensed.
  2. If the future benefit is uncertain, the costs should be expensed.

The decision to capitalize or expense a cost depends on whether the venture is expected to be successful and whether the future earnings are expected to be sufficient to match the known expenses. Expenditures that benefit multiple periods should be capitalized and charged to future periods as the benefits from the expenditure are consumed. Alternatively, the expenditures can be charged to future periods based on estimates of the portion of the asset applicable to the current period.

Exhibit 24.3 shows an example of a service overhead budget.

- *Determine level of overhead control.* Cost centers represent the smallest area of responsibility for which costs are accumulated. Cost centers (e.g., accounts payable) are often subsets of departments (e.g., accounting) and departments are often subset of functions (e.g., finance).
- *Select an allocation base and calculate an overhead rate.* An overhead rate expresses the relationship of service overhead to the selected allocation base. The implicit

| Cost Category | $ |
|---|---:|
| Fringe benefits | 4,000 |
| Indirect labor wages | 2,000 |
| Indirect labor supplies | 1,000 |
| Supplies management | 1,000 |
| Utilities | 750 |
| Overtime premium of direct labor | 500 |
| Local administration and accounting | 400 |
| Depreciation—service operation equipment | 300 |
| Shift premium | 300 |
| Local MIS | 250 |
| Quality assurance | 100 |
| Office management | 275 |
| Local personnel/human resources | 200 |
| Scrap supplies | 200 |
| Property taxes | 150 |
| Rework labor | 150 |
| Service equipment supplies | 100 |
| Special supplies/labor | 200 |
| Engineering | 400 |
| Research & development | 1,000 |
| Supervisory salary | 225 |
| Purchasing | 50 |
| Payroll department | 200 |
| Security | 225 |
| Depreciation building | 100 |
| Insurance property | 25 |
| Insurance liability | 30 |
| Invoicing | 15 |
| Miscellaneous | 100 |
| Total overhead | 14,245 |

**Exhibit 24.3    Sample Services Overhead Budget.** *Source: Activity-Based Management for Service Industries, Government Entities & Nonprofit Organizations,* by James A. Brimson and John Antos. Copyright © 1998 by John Wiley & Sons, Inc. Reprinted by permission of John Wiley & Sons, Inc.

assumption when overhead is charged to services according to sales, direct labor, or total direct costs, for example, is that the overhead cost component varies in proportion to these costs. The procedure of calculating an overhead rate also assumes that *budgeted* overhead is a good approximation of *actual* overhead. As long as the actual total overhead cost and base rate approximate the forecasted volumes, the under- or overabsorption of overhead cost is minimal.

Accounting practice does not dictate criteria for choosing an allocation base: Organizations have significant latitude in their choice. Use of direct labor as an allocation basis, for example, is based on the assumption that a strong relationship exists between

| Annual cost ($1,000s) | Service | | Total |
| --- | --- | --- | --- |
| | A | B | |
| Service overhead | $10,680 | $3,565 | $14,245 |

Exhibit 24.4   Computation of Overhead Rate. *Source: Activity-Based Management for Service Industries, Government Entities & Nonprofit Organizations,* by James A. Brimson and John Antos. Copyright © 1998 by John Wiley & Sons, Inc. Reprinted by permission of John Wiley & Sons, Inc.

the amount of direct labor used to create a service and the overhead costs consumed. Services that require more direct labor generally require more indirect labor (e.g., supervision and timekeeping costs), more wear and tear on equipment (e.g., computer depreciation), and also greater use of utilities, accounting, management information systems, and human resource departments.

Exhibit 24.4 illustrates how an overhead rate is computed and gives the results of the overhead application.

**(c) Step 3** SG&A costs are often not part of service costs; they benefit the entire enterprise, so they are often not assigned to individual services. Selling costs are expenses incurred in marketing a service. They include:

- Salespersons' salaries, commissions, and travel and entertainment expenses.
- Advertising.
- Sales department salaries and expenses.
- Samples.

General and administrative costs include the cost of managing or directing an enterprise, which encompasses management, public relations, and legal services. Generally accepted accounting principles require that these costs be expensed in the same period in which they are incurred. They are usually shown separately in a profit-and-loss statement. In a "funds balance statement" used by nonprofits and governments, they may also be broken out separately. Nonprofits have fundraising expenses, which are the equivalent of sales and marketing expenses in for-profit organizations. The government generally does not have selling expenses. Exceptions include the U.S. Postal Service's costs to market its overnight mail service or the Bureau of Engraving's costs to market its postal stamp printing capabilities.

Exhibit 24.5 shows examples of SG&A expenses and the cost breakdown that results from applying the traditional cost accounting model.

**24.5 SHORTCOMINGS OF THE TRADITIONAL SERVICE-COST MODEL** The traditional service-cost model distorts the cost of providing a service for several reasons:

- Service overhead costs are allocated rather than traced to services.
- The overhead component of service cost has generally grown faster than direct costs. As overhead becomes a larger percentage of service cost, the distortion in the total service cost inherent in the allocation process increases.

| Expense Category | $ (in 1,000s) |
|---|---|
| Executives | 750 |
| Administration and accounting | 400 |
| Sales and marketing | 300 |
| Interest expense | 100 |
| Total SG&A | 1,550 |

| | Services | | |
|---|---|---|---|
| | A | B | Total |
| Annual Cost (in $1,000s) | $ | $ | $ |
| Direct labor wages | 3,000 | 1,000 | 4,000 |
| Direct supplies | 3,500 | 3,500 | 7,000 |
| Direct service overhead | 10,680 | 3,565 | 14,245 |
| Total direct service cost | 17,180 | 8,065 | 25,245 |
| SG&A | | | 1,550 |
| Total cost | | | 26,795 |

**Exhibit 24.5    SG&A Expenses and Cost Breakdown in Traditional Cost Accounting Model.** *Source: Activity-Based Management for Service Industries, Government Entities & Nonprofit Organizations,* by James A. Brimson and John Antos. Copyright © 1998 by John Wiley & Sons, Inc. Reprinted by permission of John Wiley & Sons, Inc.

- Generally accepted accounting principles often dictate or influence cost accounting practices. One of these principles—the conservatism principle—is inconsistent with accurate service cost determination in two important ways:
  1. Conservatism requires that reported cost be based on precise and easily verifiable data, whereas management often needs costs that are based on forecasts and plans.
  2. Conservatism encourages organizations to expense many costs that should be capitalized. This practice distorts life-cycle costs.
- Many activities included in SG&A are traceable to specific services.

Each of these issues is discussed in more depth in the remainder of this section.

**(a) Service Overhead Costs Are Allocated Rather Than Traced to Services**    Service overhead includes all costs other than direct service labor and direct supplies associated with a specific service. (Examples of direct labor include police officers or phone installers riding in their vehicles. The direct supplies would include gasoline and oil for the vehicles, and wire and switches for the phone installers.) Overhead is allocated from cost centers to services according to an overhead application rate. Whether a cost is allocated or traced depends on whether a cause-and-effect relationship is established.

For example, a common method of allocating purchasing costs to services is to include these costs in "supplies overhead," then to charge supplies overhead to services on the basis of supplies cost. These costs might be allocated if no direct cause-and-

## Cost Center: Purchasing Department

| Account | Description | Actual $ | Budget $ | Variance $ |
|---------|-------------|---------|---------|-----------|
| 0009 | Salaries | 80,150 | 83,000 | 2,850 |
| 0010 | Wages, hourly | 124,360 | 110,000 | (14,360) |
| 0201 | Benefits, salaried | 21,812 | 22,600 | 788 |
| 0202 | Benefits, hourly | 37,688 | 32,600 | (5,088) |
| 0352 | Travel | 62,515 | 70,500 | 7,985 |
| 0366 | Facilities | 32,000 | 32,000 | 0 |
| 0380 | Supplies | 1,394 | 1,500 | 106 |
| 0463 | Training | 20,240 | 30,000 | 9,760 |
| | Total | 380,159 | 382,200 | 2,041 |

**Exhibit 24.6    Example of Cost Assignment Using Responsibility Accounting.**
*Source: Activity-Based Management for Service Industries, Government Entities & Nonprofit Organizations,* by James A. Brimson and John Antos. Copyright © 1998 by John Wiley & Sons, Inc. Reprinted by permission of John Wiley & Sons, Inc.

effect relationship can be established between purchasing costs and individual services. Therefore, a surrogate basis for spreading supplies cost is used.

However, purchasing costs might be traced to services by identifying the cause-and-effect relationship between purchasing activities and services. Consider the activity of ordering supplies. The number of purchase orders (the output of the activity of ordering supplies) might be traced to services based on the number of purchase orders consumed. The number of purchase orders necessary to acquire the supplies for any particular service can be precisely specified: That is, a cause-and-effect relationship can be established, so the cost of ordering supplies can be directly traced to services rather than allocated. For example, if the purchasing department processed 6,000 purchase orders during the year and it costs $600,000 to issue purchase orders, then it costs the organization $100 ($600,000/6,000) to issue a purchase order. If a complex service submits 25 purchase orders during the year, then $2,500 (25 purchase orders at $100 per purchase order) is traceable to the service.

Under *responsibility accounting*, costs are assigned to managers of each organizational unit responsible for a set of related but unique activities. These costs are homogeneous with respect to function, but each activity has its own unique cost-behavior pattern. The composite cost is, therefore, a mixture of several cost behaviors. For example, consider a purchasing department such as that shown in Exhibit 24.6.

The purchasing department activities are to plan procurement, select and evaluate vendors, negotiate contracts, order supplies, and coordinate vendors. The resources consumed in each activity, the cost-behavior pattern, and cost drivers for each activity are unique. Consider first the resources consumed in each activity as shown in Exhibit 24.7.

The department spends $161,492 or 42 percent ($161,492/$380,159) of the total department cost on the "order supplies" activity and $29,150 or 8 percent ($29,150/$380,159) of the total cost on planning procurement.

Next consider the cost behavior patterns and the activity measures of the activities. "Select/evaluate" vendors, for example, varies with the number of new vendors; "order supplies," on the other hand, varies with the number of purchase orders or purchase order lines.

| Activity Description | Actual $ | Budget $ | Variance $ |
|---|---|---|---|
| Plan procurement | 29,150 | 30,000 | 850 |
| Select/evaluate vendors | 43,360 | 45,200 | 1,840 |
| Negotiate contracts | 45,632 | 50,000 | 4,368 |
| Order supplies | 161,492 | 150,000 | (11,492) |
| Coordinate vendors | 100,525 | 107,000 | 6,475 |
| Total | 380,159 | 382,200 | 2,041 |

**Exhibit 24.7    Resources Consumed by Activity.** *Source: Activity-Based Management for Service Industries, Government Entities & Nonprofit Organizations,* by James A. Brimson and John Antos. Copyright © 1998 by John Wiley & Sons, Inc. Reprinted by permission of John Wiley & Sons, Inc.

Finally, consider the cost drivers. The principal cost drivers for negotiating contracts include vendor policy (e.g., multiple vendors or a sole source) and degree of service standardization. The principal cost drivers for order supplies include order size, purchasing policy, stocking policy (e.g., just-in-time manufacturing or supplier stocking), and degree of service standardization.

Traditional cost systems obscure unique activities by capturing cost at the cost element level (e.g., supplies or travel) rather than by activities. This systematically distorts the cost of individual services by including a mixture of activities with different cost-behavior patterns. For example, knowing that the purchasing department spends $124,360 on hourly wages provides no insight into how the wages are employed. To obtain that information, costs must be allocated to services.

When costs are allocated, a service containing more direct labor hours (or total direct costs or sales) than another service is assumed to incur proportionately more indirect cost. But, volume-related allocations reliably distribute overhead costs to services *only* if overhead varies directly with volume output.

By grouping cost elements (e.g., supplies or travel) into unique activities, costs can be traced through the activities that make up a service rather than allocated. Costs are traceable if a cause-and-effect relationship is established between the activity and service operations. Costs are allocated differently if no cause-and-effect relationship is established.

Consider the development of a process plan for a new service. The number of hours expended by service engineering to develop a plan on how a service will be delivered is directly attributable to that service. Failure to trace costs to services and business processes causes organizations to resort to allocating costs arbitrarily with a resulting cost distortion.

### (b) Overhead Component of Service Cost Has Generally Grown Faster Than Direct Cost

Today, indirect cost has become a significant component of the cost of most services. In the past, when overhead costs were nominal and direct labor and direct supplies were the predominant cost components, the distortion caused by improper selection of an overhead allocation method was minimal. The concept of materiality dominated.

The rapid increase in overhead costs lies at the heart of this distortion, which was originally created by using direct labor as the basis for allocating service overhead. Direct labor as a percentage of total service cost has generally decreased, while overhead costs have risen. As organizations have increasingly incorporated information systems

|  | Service A $ | Service B $ | Total $ |
|---|---|---|---|
| Labor (24 hours at $10) | 40  (4 hours) | 200 (20 hours) | 240 |
| Supplies | 300 | 300 | 600 |
| Technology (12 hours at $20) | 200 (10 hours) | 40  (2 hours) | 240 |
| Other overhead | 385 | 385 | 770 |
| Total | 925 | 925 | 1,850 |

**Exhibit 24.8    Service Cost Allocated Based on Supplies.** *Source: Activity-Based Management for Service Industries, Government Entities & Nonprofit Organizations,* by James A. Brimson and John Antos. Copyright © 1998 by John Wiley & Sons, Inc. Reprinted by permission of John Wiley & Sons, Inc.

and automation into the service enterprise, overhead (rather than labor or supplies) has grown at the fastest pace. Traditional systems consider service overhead as fixed in the short and medium run, yet in reality it has been the most dynamic.

Because overhead is a significant component of service cost, the choice of allocation methods has a major impact on service cost. Consider a service organization that is evaluating labor hours and equipment hours as a basis for allocating overhead. Depending on which of the two methods is selected, a substantial difference in the amount of cost applied to the service would result. Exhibit 24.8 assumes the first case, in which "other overhead" is split based on supplies.

To illustrate the importance of choosing an appropriate basis of allocation, first compute a service cost using direct labor. An overhead rate is computed as follows:

$$\text{Direct-labor overhead rate} = \frac{\text{Total cost} - \text{Direct labor and supplies}}{\text{Total direct labor cost}}$$

$$= \frac{(\$925 + 925 - 40 - 200 - 300 - 300)}{(40 + 200)}$$

$$= \frac{\$1,010}{\$240} = 421\%$$

The accounting system calculates a service cost by the direct-labor-based overhead rate as shown in Exhibit 24.9.

|  | Service A $ | Service B $ | Total $ |
|---|---|---|---|
| Direct labor (24 hours at $10) | 40 | 200 | 240 |
| Supplies | 300 | 300 | 600 |
| Technology & other overhead (421% × 40, 200) | 168 | 842 | 1,010 |
| Total | 508 | 1342 | 1,850 |

**Exhibit 24.9    Service Cost Allocated Based on Direct Labor.** *Source: Activity-Based Management for Service Industries, Government Entities & Nonprofit Organizations,* by James A. Brimson and John Antos. Copyright © 1998 by John Wiley & Sons, Inc. Reprinted by permission of John Wiley & Sons, Inc.

|  | Service A $ | Service B $ | Total $ |
|---|---|---|---|
| Direct labor (24 hours at $10) | 40 | 200 | 240 |
| Supplies | 300 | 300 | 600 |
| Technology & other overhead (@ $84.17/hour) | 842 (10 hours) | 168 (2 hours) | 1,010 |
| Total | 1,182 | 668 | 1,850 |

Exhibit 24.10  Service Cost Allocated Based on Service Equipment. *Source: Activity-Based Management for Service Industries, Government Entities & Nonprofit Organizations,* by James A. Brimson and John Antos. Copyright © 1998 by John Wiley & Sons, Inc. Reprinted by permission of John Wiley & Sons, Inc.

Next, consider computing a service cost by using service-equipment hours:

$$\text{Service equipment overhead rate} = \frac{\text{Total cost} - \text{Direct labor and supplies}}{\text{Total equipment hours}}$$

$$= \frac{\$1,010}{12 \text{ hours}} = \$84.17 \text{ per hour}$$

The accounting system calculates a service cost by the service-equipment-based overhead rate as shown in Exhibit 24.10. This example illustrates how selection of an allocation basis dramatically affects cost when overhead becomes a significant proportion of total cost.

For illustrative purposes, assume that the average difference between allocation methods is 40 percent. If the overhead component of total cost is 10 percent, the 40 percent discrepancy in the choice of overhead methods results in only a 4 percent difference in total cost (40 percent × 10 percent). But, if overhead constitutes 40 percent of total service cost, a difference of 16 percent in total cost (40 percent × 40 percent) results. As overhead costs increase in magnitude, the importance of selecting allocation methods increases.

**(c) Generally Accepted Accounting Principles Often Dictate or Influence Cost Accounting Practices**    This section discusses how the conservatism principle affects cost accounting practices.

*(i) Conservatism Requires That Reported Cost Be Based on Precise and Easily Verifiable Data*    To accurately match overhead costs to services requires precise knowledge of future business conditions, including service volumes. Such precise knowledge of the future is impossible. As a result, the matching of overhead cost to services must be based on estimates, which are inherently imprecise. An ingrained fear of making decisions based on imprecise data causes organizations to resort to using allocation bases that are easily verifiable but irrelevant.

To illustrate this point, consider that the prevailing practice in U.S. industry is to use direct-labor-based allocations and straight-line depreciation in spite of the fact that these practices no longer reflect reality. The reason they are popular is that both direct-labor-based allocation and straight-line depreciation use data that are easily verified and understandable. However, the reported cost is not relevant to decision making because the assumptions underlying the approaches are flawed.

It is important to base cost decisions on relevant information even if the data are based on imprecise estimates. Estimates derived from realistic cost behavior patterns provide an excellent basis for making routine decisions and controlling service operations. Consider equipment-hour-based depreciation. The organization must estimate the number of hours of usage for the equipment per year and in total for the life of the equipment. Clearly, this type of estimating is much less precise than merely estimating the number of years the machine will be used, then recovering the cost in equal increments over the machine's useful life.

However, consider the actual cost-behavior patterns of equipment. First, rarely is usage of the equipment steady throughout its life. As the service demands fluctuate, so will equipment usage. A depreciation method not based on equipment hours charges too much depreciation during periods of low demand and, conversely, too little during periods of high demand.

Second, the only direct relationship between equipment cost and services is in equipment hours. This relationship is analogous to that of direct labor and services. The amount of time a piece of equipment takes to process specific services varies by service. An organization is forced to use surrogates such as labor hours or supply cost, which rarely reflect how much of an equipment's cost is consumed to produce services.

*(ii) Conservatism Encourages Organizations to Expense Many Costs That Should Be Capitalized*    Organizations expense costs of activities that benefit future periods because this course of action is conservative, it minimizes taxable income, and it maximizes cash flow. If start-up costs are capitalized and the service, or investment, is abandoned or unprofitable, an organization must write off the asset. Some believe that an organization is financially healthier if it expenses costs that are potentially risky.

There are several problems with expensing instead of capitalizing the cost of activities that benefit future periods. First, any potentially traceable costs that are treated as an expense in the current period (rather than matched to services) create service cost distortion.

Cost distortion occurs for one of two reasons:

1. *The magnitude of cost is large.* When one considers the many research, design, and marketing activities necessary to commercialize a service or implement an investment, one realizes the costs involved. They are needed if an enterprise is to remain in business in the long run. Governments and nonprofits may also have a variety of capital investments that allow them to provide a service (e.g., buildings, police cars, computers, firefighting equipment, garbage trucks, prisons, hospitals, therapy equipment, and classrooms).

2. *The expenditure pattern is uneven.* The distribution of activities between those that benefit the current or future periods varies based on factors such as management policy and budgetary considerations.

Expensing confuses the issue of matching and risk. The goal of matching is to infer how costs attach to services. Risk is a function of the probability of achieving the desired results. Risk is directly related to anticipated variability of estimates.

The issues of risk and matching are separate and distinct. No matter what the degree of risk, the identification of how costs attach to services is unchanged. Risk should be managed through a rigorous review of all activities from start-up to retirement as events unfold in relation to the original plan. Risk should not be managed by the choice of accounting methods.

Also, service life cycles are decreasing. Shorter service life cycles increase the need to understand the total service cost over its entire life cycle to determine profitability. Reduced life cycles mean organizations have less available time to respond to changes in market demand and to recover service development costs.

**(d) Many Activities Included in SG&A Are Traceable to Specific Services**    Consider advertising as a cost that can be traced to specific services. General advertising benefits all services and is not traceable to individual services. Specific advertising about a service, however, is traceable to the individual service. Although there may be a spin-off effect to other services, the primary goal of specific advertising is to increase the sales of the service being advertised. Failure to trace costs misrepresents the profitability of the services. Similarly, sales commissions are often service dependent and thus traceable to specific services. Again, failure to trace these costs distorts service cost.

**24.6 IMPLICATIONS OF SERVICE-COST DISTORTION**    The distortion of service costs caused by flawed allocation schemes leads to cross-subsidization of services. When distorted cost information is used to guide marketing strategies, it encourages managers to provide many low-volume services. In many cases, total profit margins decline and companies perceive difficulty in competing with focused competitors (e.g., Japanese banks in the late 1980s).

Service variety and complexity increase cost distortion. Several factors have contributed to the growth of overhead in recent decades. The primary ones include:

- Customer demands.
- Increased diversity, or scope, of output (not increased volume, or scale, of output).
- Increased use of technology.
- Increased regulations.

Thus, traditional cost accounting systems tend to overcost high-volume services—not the ones that cause most growth in overhead—and undercost the low-volume services that are chiefly responsible for the overhead growth.

Many overhead costs are driven by diversity of volume, services, business processes, and customers. This diversity increases the complexity of the service operations. Activities such as "moving supplies," "scheduling," and "setups" tend to grow with the number of services in the service line and the support required in complex service environments. If an office produces only one service with no options, the scheduling function is simple: Complexities (and the requirement for additional scheduling personnel and overhead) occur only because of the variety of services, sizes, colors, customers, and options provided.

Consider the overhead costs for the Internal Revenue Service. There are forms and laws for sole proprietors, partnerships, C corporations, S corporations, limited liability corporations, foreign corporations, resident aliens, individuals, trusts, estates, and so forth. The vast multitude of forms and laws drive the number of employees and people the IRS must employ.

The conventional methodology of allocating the cost of overhead activities related to service variety and complexity using a volume-related allocation base distorts service cost. Think of the complexity of running a hospital. There are infectious diseases, bone and heart problems, gunshot wounds, psychosomatic illnesses, and so forth. Some problems can be cured with a bandage, but some need 16 hours of surgery and cost hundreds of thousands of dollars.

**24.7 ACTIVITY SERVICE COST**    Activity management is based on the principle that activities (or business processes) consume resources, then services consume activities (or business processes) and supplies. Service costing is enhanced by more specific tracing of support costs that have traditionally been lumped into overhead and allocated to all services. Activity service cost is derived by identifying the supplies and activities (or business processes) necessary to produce a service, then determining the quantity of activity (or business process) for each service. Service cost is determined by summing the costs of all traceable activities or business processes.

Consider the service of assisting the birth of a child at a hospital. The procedures specify the following activities:

- Admit mother.
- Prepare mother for labor room.
- Check dilation, inform doctor, and assist with labor.
- Bring mother and father to delivery room.
- Deliver child.
- Check baby, tag and weigh baby.
- Transport baby to nursery.
- Transport mother to recovery room.

When the cost of each activity required to help with the birth of a baby has been determined, the service cost can be computed. The cost of the "deliver child" activity, for example, consists of the cost of direct labor (e.g., wages), depreciation for the delivery equipment, and the supplies consumed in the delivery process. Labor, supplies, and equipment are all specified by the procedure manual.

The cost factors of service operations are easily associated with each activity; the cost of the service process is directly computed from the amount of supplies and labor time the "deliver child" activity consumes. The service cost for the delivery is the sum of the cost of the various activities.

However, to concentrate exclusively on these prime service costs excludes many of the following activities that are required to support the production of a service:

- The service must be designed.
- The labor, equipment, facilities, and supplies must be procured.
- The service process must be scheduled and controlled (e.g., the number of staff needed on hand for deliveries today).

- Performance must be reported to internal parties (the mother and father, the doctor's committee, patient accounting, and candy stripers) and external parties (e.g., the state government, the county, and the insurance company).
- A myriad of other support activities must be accomplished (janitorial, supply room, maintenance, bookkeeping, grounds and facilities). Each of these activities consumes resources and is a prerequisite for service operations (e.g., delivering a child).

Support activities have traditionally been included in overhead and allocated to services on a direct basis, such as direct labor, equipment usage (e.g., time spent in the delivery room), supplies, or sales. Activity accounting requires that support activities be traced to services. Consider the activity of designing a service (e.g., how to perform a hip transplant, how to sell cold beer on a hot day in August, how to remove snow from a highway, or how to conduct a fundraiser). A service cannot be produced without being designed. The "design service" activity is easily identifiable with a specific service; one need not lump design costs into overhead, then allocate the costs to all services. Failure to trace support costs distorts service cost.

To further illustrate the importance of tracing activities to services, consider the major activities of a typical department that controls supplies:

- Handle incoming supplies (e.g., bombs in military).
- Handle in-process supplies (e.g., blood brought to operating room).
- Handle outgoing supplies (e.g., food or drinks served on a plane or train).
- Store supplies (e.g., cleaning supplies for real estate management organization).
- Store work-in-process (e.g., operating room supply kits that hospitals prepare).
- Store finished services (e.g., donated gifts).
- Manage department.
- Train department.

The "handle supplies" activity is controlled differently from the activity "store supplies." The costs of handling supplies attach to the services being moved. Services might or might not be stored, depending on the procedures. (Red Adair might not store dynamite to extinguish oil well fires, but banks might store new account kits, and fundraisers might store information kits.) Only services that require storage should be charged with the cost of storing supplies. To include "store supplies" costs in overhead and arbitrarily allocate them to all services penalizes services that do not use storage.

Activity cost is the sum of the natural expense categories (e.g., wages) and interorganizational activities (e.g., hire employees). Exhibit 24.11 illustrates the process involved in determining activity service cost.

Activity management systems compute a service cost by tracing all service-related activities to services on the basis of the services' usage of each activity. For example, quality costs would be assigned where the quality effort is expended. Real estate taxes and utilities would be assigned based on occupied square footage. A service cost thus becomes a summation of the cost of all traceable activities to design, produce, and distribute a service. Activities represent the capabilities of a service enterprise. Service production uses varying amounts of those capabilities. A service consumes activities

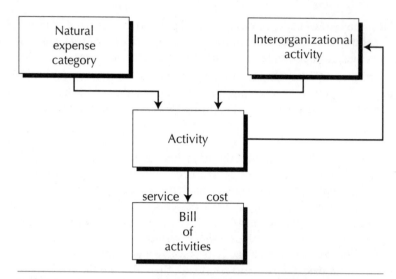

**Exhibit 24.11   Process of Determining Activity Cost.** *Source: Activity-Based Management for Service Industries, Government Entities & Nonprofit Organizations,* **by James A. Brimson and John Antos. Copyright © 1998 by John Wiley & Sons, Inc. Reprinted by permission of John Wiley & Sons, Inc.**

during its life cycle—activities such as "research market," "design service," "plan marketing and sales," "produce service," "deliver service," and "provide customer service." For example, one state-of-the-art service may require significant market research and design activities (e.g., architectural plans for a symphony hall). Another commodity-type service would require fewer of these activities (e.g., plans for a toll booth).

Many support functions, such as service supervision and quality control, involve service-related activities. The percentage of time spent on activities can be determined from interviews with managers and service workers and traced according to the number of transactions. When the interview has not identified specific measures for activities, a general measure such as the number of service hours per service is used.

Administrative support activities cannot be directly related to specific services or equipment. These activities relate to the people managed or supported. Activities of managers and secretaries have many administrative aspects that are nontraceable directly to services and must be assigned to primary activities which are traced to services.

An activity management system better mirrors service operations and therefore distorts service cost less than traditional costing for the following reasons:

- Activities represent the lowest level of homogeneous cost.
- There are multiple bases of assignment inherent in the selection of activity measures.
- Activities facilitate the linking of related activities (into business processes), which transcend organizational boundaries. Business processes can then be assigned en masse to the originating cause.
- Most variances are caused by the activity rather than by the service.
- Life-cycle costing permits better matching of time periods.

- Traditionally, there were two major classifications of service cost—direct service cost and SG&A. In activity management, there can be others, such as orders, customers, services, projects, contracts, or channels of distribution.
- It is possible to trace service-related costs, including SG&A.
- Accurate activity costs depend only minimally on an organization's existing organizational structure and level of detail captured within the accounting system.

**24.8 ACTIVITY SERVICE-COST APPROACH**   Once activities are costed, they can be combined to form a *bill of activities* (BOA) for the various services an organization provides. This BOA will render a more accurate service cost than traditional systems.

**(a) Service Bill of Activities**   The traceability of service costs can be improved by identifying all significant activities triggered by the decision to provide a service. Activities make up the business process "Create service." One approach is to specify this process in terms of a BOA based on the sequence of activities to provide this service. The BOA includes all organizational activities, both support and direct service, required to provide a service.

The BOA approach provides management with the capability of defining the quantity and cost of activities within a service, across service families, or within the entire enterprise.

*(i) Bill of Activities*   A bill of activity is created in two steps:

- *Step 1.* Determine costed BOA for organizational processes. Key business processes that are consumed in a service are costed in total rather than listed individually.
- *Step 2.* Determine a costed BOA for each service.

*(ii) Service Design Process*   The source for determining the service operation activities of a service cost is the service design, which specifies how a service is provided. Typical information available on most designs includes:

- Procedures.
- Department performing procedures.
- Setup hours.
- Labor grade for direct labor.
- Direct labor hours per unit of service.
- Equipment type.
- Equipment hours (e.g., connect time on computer terminal).
- Service operations lead time for move, queue, setup, and runtime for a typical service.

It is essential that the design procedures represent the way an order actually moves through an office or facility and the service operation processes. If it does not, the wrong activities will be charged against the service. When an alternate procedure is used, the BOA for the order should reflect the alternate procedure.

A service cost BOA represents all the activities necessary to provide a service. (See, for example, Exhibit 24.12.) The BOA represents all activities over the entire life cycle.

| Activity | Activity Measure | Activity Quantity | Activity Unit Cost $ | Life-Cycle Cost ($) for 5,000 Loans | Activity Cost | Subtotal |
|---|---|---|---|---|---|---|
| *Life-Cycle Costs* | | | | | | |
| Design loan | Designs | 1 | 5,000 | 5,000 | 1.00 ($5,000/5,000 loans) | |
| Design procedures | Procedures | 5 | 200 | 1,000 | .20 ($1,000/5,000 loans) | |
| Acquire supplies | Supplies | 1 | 50 | 50 | .01 (50/5,000 loans) | |
| Subtotal of life-cycle costs | | | | | 1.21 | |
| Take applications | Applications | 1 | 150 | | 150.00 | |
| Order credit survey, appraisal | # reports | 3 | 30 | | 90.00 | |
| Review documents | Reviews | 1 | 70 | | 70.00 | |
| Review by loan committee | Applications | 1 | 200 | | 200.00 | |
| Prepare loan documents | Pages | 30 | 5 | | 150.00 | |
| Disburse funds | Disbursements | 1 | 100 | | 100.00 | 760.00 |
| Total continuing operating cost | | | | | | $761.21 |
| Total cost of reports | | | | | | $150.00 |
| Total life cycle, operations, and report cost process | | | | | | $911.21 |

**Exhibit 24.12 Service Design Showing How and in What Order a Service Is Provided. *Source: Activity-Based Management for Service Industries, Government Entities & Nonprofit Organizations,* by James A. Brimson and John Antos. Copyright © 1998 by John Wiley & Sons, Inc. Reprinted by permission of John Wiley & Sons, Inc.**

| Activity | Life-Cycle Cost | Cost per Unit |
|---|:---:|:---:|
| Design service | ✗ | ✗ |
| Design service procedures | ✗ | ✗ |
| Plan for quality | ✗ | ✗ |
| Store supplies | | ✗ |
| Move supplies | | |
| Set up | | ✗ |
| Perform procedure 1 | | ✗ |
| Perform procedure 2 | | ✗ |
| Deliver | | ✗ |
| Provide customer service | ✗ | ✗ |
| Support in field | ✗ | ✗ |

**Exhibit 24.13    Typical Bill of Activities.** *Source: Activity-Based Management for Service Industries, Government Entities & Nonprofit Organizations,* **by James A. Brimson and John Antos. Copyright © 1998 by John Wiley & Sons, Inc. Reprinted by permission of John Wiley & Sons, Inc.**

Activities that are independent of a service order are charged on a per-unit basis over the planned volume of the service. Exhibit 24.13 shows A typical BOA.

The primary costs that comprise a service cost include supplies, direct labor, technology (e.g., depreciation), quality, design, development, research and development, supplies handling, marketing and advertising, service support, customer technical support, and finished services distribution.

**(b) Supplies Cost**    Supplies costs are derived from the budget or a *bill of supplies* (BOS). A BOS is any document that defines the service from the design point of view by listing supplies for each portion of the service (e.g., supplies necessary to install a burglar alarm). The BOS structure pertains to the way the service is structured and to the supplies needed at the outset and in each state of completion. Thus, the BOS specifies the composition of a service as well as the process stages in that service's production. It defines service structure in terms of levels of service, each of which represents a step in the production of the service. Exhibit 24.14 shows a graphic representation of a BOS.

A BOS is the key source of supplies cost used to compute a service cost. Several ac-

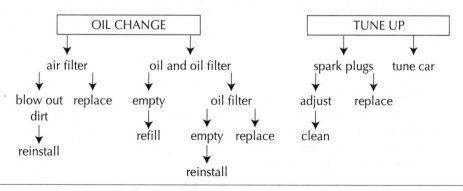

**Exhibit 24.14    Graph of Bill of Supplies**

tivity service cost systems incorporate a BOS into the service cost roll-up, whereas others interface with the BOS and extract supplies cost in total. In determining a service cost, three features of the BOS are important:

1. A given supply item may either be purchased or produced internally. The cost of purchased supplies consists of the purchase price and all traceable costs of bringing the supplies to the activity that consumes it. The cost of a service component consists of all traceable costs to provide the component (e.g., a portion of the insurance policy; the eye test, written test, and driving test for driver's license renewal; and fuel for vehicles).

2. A given service can exist in its own right as a uniquely identified unit (supplies, component part, minimum coverage in an insurance policy, oil change) or as an item of another package (oil, air and oil filter change, grease job). In either case, the activities to provide the component are identical. However, if the service unit is stored, the component cost will be higher due to storage costs (e.g., cleaning and storing winter coats).

3. The BOS establishes the service item lead times (e.g., when promotional displays or bombs must arrive). This information is used for performance measurement.

**(c) Direct Labor Costs**   In a pure activity management system, labor costs are charged to the service operation activities and not to the individual services. The approach is based on the observation that laborers perform activities, then services consume activities. Labor cost is one component of activity cost.

Labor costs are assigned to services according to the amount of the activity consumed by the service specified in the BOA. For example, the cost of reports required for a mortgage (e.g., credit, appraisal, and survey reports) is charged to the service according to the number of reports specified in the service BOA for a mortgage. Based on the wage rates and number of people assigned to an activity, a cost-per-activity measure is derived. For example, the labor associated with workers obtaining credit reports is charged to the loan underwriting activity. Knowing the total number of credit reports allows an organization to compute a cost per credit report or cost per loan.

There are several reasons for charging costs directly to activities rather than services. First, labor variances are more often the result of process variances than of any aspect of the service. Changing loan demand, operator experience, and training variations result in operator efficiencies and inefficiencies. These factors cause variances related to an activity rather than to the service. Second, labor reporting is greatly simplified, because there is no need to voucher labor to services.

There are exceptions, however, when some labor-related costs require special time reporting. The primary situations include:

- *Estimates of direct labor are imprecise.* It may be difficult to precisely estimate labor hours for one-time services.

- *Labor may be transferred between activities.* Determine whether labor is being shifted between cost centers based on the complexity of the service (e.g., roofers helping carpenters in real estate construction and community service personnel assisting fundraising personnel).

- *Contractual requirements may apply to labor reporting.* Defense department regulations, Federal Acquisition Regulations, and Cost Accounting Standards Board requirements often require specific direct labor reports (e.g., computer science or EDS).

- *Floating labor may complicate reporting.* Determine whether additional laborers are hired to fill in for absent workers. Proper service costing requires accountability for the use of these workers.

Process variances for an activity are computed by comparing the labor hours earned during a time period with the actual hours expended. The earned hours are derived by summing the total hours specified in the BOA for all services using the activity during the specified time period.

Continued significant variations between actual and earned hours might indicate that the service BOA must be reviewed. Those responsible for service profitability, such as the service manager or service line manager, should identify instances of above- or below-normal activity. Those responsible for the activity or business process, such as the service operation manager, should identify instances of variation in activity. Earned hours can be periodically validated by industrial engineering studies and random checks of actual time spent on services compared to earned time.

**(d) Technology Costs**   The costs of technology are traced to services on the basis of the usage of the activity as reflected in the activity measure (e.g., computer time, transportation equipment hours, scanning time, typesetting time, filming time, etc.).

**(e) Quality Costs**   Activities associated with quality are classified into four categories:

1. *Prevention:*
   - Plan quality (e.g., plan organization quality activities).
   - Design and develop quality measurement and control equipment (e.g., check flow meters for a gas station).
   - Calibrate equipment (e.g., set dispenser to control amount of liquor in a drink).
   - Train associates (e.g., train for statistical process control).
   - Administer quality assurance program.
   - Audit system (e.g., audit quality training system).
   - Develop quality improvement projects.

2. *Appraisal:*
   - Conduct laboratory acceptance testing (e.g., implement corporate testing of food in fast-food restaurant chain).
   - Inspect and test (e.g., test trained soldiers).
   - Inspect and test setup (e.g., set up cash register test).
   - Inspect in-process (not by inspectors but by process workers).
   - Audit service quality (e.g., audit hotel properties).
   - Review inspection test results before acceptance.
   - Evaluate at customers' sites (e.g., evaluate new software).
   - Review data from inspection and test reports.

3. *Internal failure* (directly charged to the department that incurs the cost, but classified as a quality activity):
   - Handle scrap (e.g., discard burnt food).
   - Rework service (e.g., redo insurance policy with errors).

- Troubleshoot service (e.g., troubleshoot new software).
- Analyze defects and failures (e.g., errors in public law).
- Reinspect and retest (e.g., review rejected audit report).
- Provide for lost service production due to faulty vendor supplies (e.g., retail store receives merchandise that does not meet its needs).
- Provide for lost service production due to own supplies (e.g., computer system crash causes defective contracts or wills).

4. *External failures* (a suggested activity measure might be the number of returns from the field for poor quality; the source of information includes internal quality reports, vendor quality reports, and shipping reports):
    - Administer complaints.
    - Manage reliability: The engineering activity of tracking and analyzing customer returns to determine the causes of quality problems (e.g., analyze returned software).
    - Provide customer service.
    - Handle liability (e.g., defend or settle lawsuits).
    - Process service returns (e.g., accept return of TV that still does not work).
    - Process service recalls (e.g., carry out recall of pacemakers).
    - Provide service replacement (e.g., replace service or cancel charge for meal or hotel).
    - Correct marketing errors (e.g., reprint promotion that has printing errors).

Additional service-related costs include:

- *Administer warranty or service contracts.* The cost of warranty and service contract administration should be traced to the services according to the distribution of time and cost incurred in this activity. In addition, warranty service costs should certainly be an element of the cost-of-quality report.
- *Provide customer service in field.* Field customer-service activities include installations and repairs performed by field service personnel. These costs should be charged to the specific service repaired. The regional supervisor's cost and the cost of maintaining field service offices should be factored into the activity rates used for charging the cost of these activities to segments. Repair work represents a cost of quality (e.g., repairing the same street twice within a month or commissioning several studies for the same road expansion).
- *Perform in-house repair.* In-house repair activities include installations and repairs performed by maintenance. These costs should be charged to the specific service repaired. The supervisor's cost and the cost of maintaining the repair office should be factored into the activity rates used for charging the cost of these activities to services. Repair work represents a cost of quality.

**(f) Service Design Costs**   Costs related to developing new or enhanced services are charged directly to specific services or service lines. Design costs are charged to specific projects or service lines using the estimated number of designs, design hours, or a project-tracking system. Project-tracking systems may be manual time collection systems, or they may automatically extract information from the computer project-tracking system. Sources of information include payroll records and design and quality control reports. The costs of outside services, testing, and supplies are directly charged to specific services through accounts payable.

Service design changes or documentation control activities originate from design enhancement of services. Usually they are triggered by a customer or by the marketing department through a *design change order* (DCO) and include control and administration of the following types of documentation:

- Marketing manuals.
- Service manuals and specifications.
- Installation manuals.
- Bills of supplies.
- Process or service operation procedures.

The cost of these design change activities should be traced to services according to the number of DCOs a service line generates. However, when these activities are performed for a new service under development, the costs should be directly assigned to the service on the basis of design hours.

**(g) Service Development Costs**    Activities associated with service development include:

- Plan process and procedures.
- Modify process and procedures.
- Program service.

Service development activities represent a life-cycle cost that should be associated with the service operation process.

**(h) Research and Development Costs**    Activities associated with research and development include:

- Conduct basic research (e.g., develop a new type of insurance policy).
- Research service process (e.g., how to cook hamburgers that have less cholesterol).
- Develop a new service (e.g., McDonalds' Happy Meal for children).
- Develop new service procedures (e.g., how to perform plastic surgery on an outpatient basis).

Basic research and service process research should be charged to organizationwide, nontraceable overhead or applied to development projects as a secondary activity, depending on the organization's policy.

**(i) Supplies and Work-in-Progress Handling Costs**    Costs associated with supplies include:

- Supplies, medicine, fuel in storage.
- Associated recordkeeping. The costs are traced to the supplies-handling activity. Each service BOA would include a supplies-handling activity based on the service procedures involved.

Costs associated with work-in-progress handling include:

* Mortgages or insurance applications awaiting additional information.
* Moving patients in a hospital.

**(j) Marketing and Advertising Costs** Activities associated with marketing and advertising include:

* *Manage corporate sales.* This includes the costs of the vice president of sales and other personnel who administer the sales organization and all associated support costs, such as occupancy cost. Sales reporting is also included in this function. The costs of managing corporate sales could be treated as a secondary activity within the sales department and assigned to the primary selling activities.
* *Administer sales.* The personnel assigned to this activity support the field sales offices by performing order-entry and customer-service activities. These costs are assigned to the activities performed and later traced to services or orders.
* *Support sales in field.* The total cost of each region's field sales efforts should be considered directly traceable to services and/or customers in each region.
* *Administer major accounts.* The personnel assigned to this activity support selected major customers. The cost of the activity should be charged to the services supported and to those major customers.
* *Manage service lines.* The cost of managers dedicated to the support and management of individual service lines should be charged to the services supported. These activities include:
  —*Research market.* Activities related to organizationwide market research are treated as secondary activities and allocated to the department's primary activities. Research efforts for specific service lines should be charged to the service line through general ledger project numbers.
  —*Market at trade shows.* The cost of trade shows for individual service lines should be charged to the service line through general ledger project numbers. If numerous service lines are exhibited at a show, the activity cost is allocated to the various services lines.
  —*Advertise service.* The costs of service-specific newspaper or regional publication advertisements should be assigned directly to services. Advertisements for numerous services or organizationwide advertisements are treated as nontraceable SG&A costs. In either case, these costs are assigned to territories through a general ledger project number.
  —*Provide sales literature.* The costs of brochures or literature developed for a single service are assigned to the service. Sales literature of a more general nature is treated as a nontraceable SG&A cost or as a secondary cost for service specific literature.
  —*Administer department.* Administrative costs are treated as a secondary activity and assigned to the department's primary activities.

**(k) Service Operations Support Costs** Depending on the complexity of the service, significantly different service operations support activities can arise. Some service operation support activities that can be assigned to services include:

- Schedule service operations (e.g., schedule pilots, clerks, drivers, and military personnel required).
- Control service operation (e.g., verify that dump sites have enough capacity for this week's garbage collections).

Service operation support activities are traceable to orders or customers and do not vary according to order quantity. Thus, small-lot-size orders require a proportionally larger service operation support cost per unit than do orders of large-lot sizes.

**(l) Customer Technical Support Costs**   In-house technical support people handle a variety of questions from end users and sales representatives. They also deal with customer returns. Their costs are directly traceable to service lines on the basis of the number of return authorizations generated for each. When the analysis is unable to trace costs to the specific service or service lines supported, these costs are considered a common organization cost. However, in service life-cycle costing, all costs of this activity can be charged to specific services.

**(m) Finished Services and Distribution Costs**   Activities associated with finished services and distribution include:

- Store finished services (e.g., store collected garbage or cars towed by the police).
- Ship service (e.g., deliver promotional items bought by a customer).
- Package service (e.g., choose a type of seminar notebook).
- Provide field support (e.g., give computer technical support).
- Supply spare parts (e.g., provide spare computer or truck parts).
- Maintain equipment (e.g., inspect and repair postal trucks, tanks, or computers).
- Coordinate dealerships or franchises (e.g., coordinate hotel or fast-food chains).

These costs should be directly traceable to services or service lines through service BOAs.

To illustrate the significance of tracing costs, consider the impact of tracing the costs in Exhibit 24.15 and the new reported service cost that is calculated in Exhibit 24.16.

**24.9 SPECIAL SITUATIONS**   A number of situations require special consideration. These include service cost frequency, service setup costs, bottlenecks, profit velocity, and work orders.

**(a) Service-Cost Calculation Frequency**   A BOA separates the quantity of an activity from the cost of the activity. A BOA specifies the sequence and quantity of activities. The cost of an activity is separately computed by the activity management system. This approach simplifies the standard-setting process, because the BOA need only be modified if a change occurs in the activity or process. Changes to the cost elements of service operations do not require a modification to the BOA.

**(b) Service Setup Costs**   The conventional practice of preparing service operations in lots (e.g., operating room kits) in advance of current demand is intended to spread setup and ordering costs over a larger number of service units—and, as a consequence,

## Traceable Labor

| | Annual Cost ($1,000s) |
|---|---|
| Direct labor and fringe benefits | 4,500 |
| Setup of service | 600 |
| Rework | 300 |
| Overtime premium | 250 |
| Training | 150 |
| Shift premium | 125 |
| Workman's compensation | 75 |
| Miscellaneous | 50 |
| Subtotal | 6,050 |

## Traceable Supplies

| | ($1,000s) |
|---|---|
| Supplies | 6,000 |
| Purchased items | 1,000 |
| Incoming shipping charges | 575 |
| Subtotal | 7,575 |

## Other Traceable Costs

| | ($1,000s) |
|---|---|
| Supplies labor | 2,500 |
| Supplies storage | 800 |
| Quality assurance | 900 |
| Service operation utilities | 500 |
| Depreciation on service equipment | 1,150 |
| Scrap | 200 |
| Service designers | 600 |
| Industrial engineering | 225 |
| Service-specific advertising | 320 |
| Operations control | 400 |
| Subtotal | 7,595 |

## Nontraceable Costs

| | ($1,000s) |
|---|---|
| Office supervision and management | 275 |
| Building utilities | 280 |
| Office security | 75 |
| Information systems | 925 |
| Building taxes and insurance | 175 |
| Depreciation on lobby/parking lot | 100 |
| Miscellaneous supplies | 600 |
| Other purchasing | 50 |
| Other capital carrying costs | 50 |
| Miscellaneous | 800 |
| Subtotal | 3,330 |

## SG&A

| | ($1,000s) |
|---|---|
| Basic research & development | 550 |
| Administration | 350 |
| Marketing | 250 |
| Corporate human resources | 840 |
| Corporate information systems | 750 |
| Accounting | 425 |
| Subtotal | 3,165 |
| Total cost | 27,715 |

**Exhibit 24.15 Traceable Costs.** *Source: Activity-Based Management for Service Industries, Government Entities & Nonprofit Organizations*, by James A. Brimson and John Antos. Copyright © 1998 by John Wiley & Sons, Inc. Reprinted by permission of John Wiley & Sons, Inc.

| | Services | | |
|---|---|---|---|
| | A $ | B $ | Total $ |
| Direct labor | | | |
| Direct labor wages | 4,695 | 1,565 | 6,260 |
| Direct supplies | 3,909 | 3,909 | 7,818 |
| Direct technology | 464 | 2,000 | 2,464 |
| Quality | 600 | 360 | 960 |
| Research and development | 1,000 | 2,033 | 3,033 |
| Service work in process | 100 | 41 | 141 |
| Marketing and advertising | 70 | 71 | 141 |
| Service operation support | 626 | 400 | 1,026 |
| Finished services and distribution | 250 | 336 | 586 |
| Nontraceable overhead | 1,847 | 1,565 | 3,412 |
| Total service costs | 13,561 | 12,280 | 25,841 |
| SG&A | | | 1,874 |
| Total cost | | | 27,715 |

**Exhibit 24.16   Revised Reported Service Cost.** *Source: Activity-Based Management for Service Industries, Government Entities & Nonprofit Organizations,* by James A. Brimson and John Antos. Copyright © 1998 by John Wiley & Sons, Inc. Reprinted by permission of John Wiley & Sons, Inc.

to reduce the total annual costs. For example, making food in large batches can be more economical, because ingredients can be ordered and prepared in quantity. However, lean thinking requires minimizing setup time and cost so services can economically be created in batches of one.

*Setup* involves preparing a service process for operation for the first time. Setup is dependent on the service operation schedule, the service complexity, and the service operation technology. If a process must be set up from scratch, a fixed amount of effort will be required. However, if the preceding process was set up for a service item within the same family of service items, a simple changeover (rather than an entire setup) may be all that is required. A *changeover* is a partial setup in which not all procedures are required.

For example, a changeover for a printing press might require changing all guides for different sizes and print stock thicknesses. To change the color requires extensive effort and a full setup. Only minor effort is required, however, to change from one paper thickness to another paper thickness, as long as the color remains the same. This is a changeover. In the post office's system of sorting mail, there is frequently a major setup effort for different envelope thicknesses but only a minor effort to change from one envelope size to another size (within certain parameters).

The cost of a setup could be insignificant (e.g., serving one type of mixed drink versus another type of mixed drink) or significant (e.g., reconfiguring a plane for cargo at night versus reconfiguring it for passengers during the day). An obvious cost is the time it takes an operator to set up the equipment to create the next service. Less obvious costs include the cost of paperwork associated with each setup, the cost of personnel sitting idle during the setup, and, in some cases, the scrap loss on the initial service run (e.g., in a convenience store, changing from cola ice cones to lemon-lime ice cones requires that the line be flushed with lemon-lime to remove the cola taste). When operators are inexperienced, moreover, a learning curve occurs before the process works at standard efficiency. Finally, when equipment is operating at full capacity, the service operating time lost during each setup increases cost.

**(c) Bottleneck Costs**    Service operation bottlenecks are generally considered temporary blockages to increased output; they may occur anywhere in the service operation process. The stationary bottleneck is easy to identify because work-in-progress accumulates behind it (e.g., mortgage applications waiting for credit reports, surveys, and appraisals or insurance policies waiting to be reviewed by underwriting). Its cause is usually also clear—long waits for vendor services, equipment has broken down, key workers are absent, or demand has outstripped the capacity of the process.

More subtle are bottlenecks that shift from one part of the organization or business process to another or that have no clear cause; work builds up in different places at different times. Perhaps bottlenecks result from flaws in quality caused inadvertently by one or more workers who are trying to keep pace with operational demands that should not have been placed on them. Bottlenecks may also be caused by missing service items (e.g., different missing supplies during construction of a building), new service startup, or changes in the mix of services through the organization (e.g., less demand for building permits but greater demand for bankruptcy filings). In such cases, the remedies are less clear-cut.

Bottlenecks are often a chronic management dilemma of job shops (e.g., individually structured business loans) and batch-flow processes (e.g., government-fare ticket processing by airlines). In a batch flow ( job shop), process capacity usage is volatile, because the process is indeterminate. For example, changing volume or introducing a new service changes the service mix and might place excessive demands on a single department (e.g., a new special education department at a school).

The only way to decide how to remedy a bottleneck is to analyze the costs associated with each option. One must compare the incremental costs incurred by each alternative, because those are the only costs that differ between the options being considered.

The following example evaluates a service setup-time reduction. It highlights some of the problems encountered when studying the cost impact of bottlenecks. Suppose that two types of equipment (e.g., computers), $A$ and $B$, support the same service operation activity. The time necessary for equipment $A$ to change from producing one service to producing another averages about 10 minutes, whereas the setup time for equipment $B$ is one hour. An engineering study indicates that the setup time of equipment $A$ could be reduced by half at a cost of $50,000; equipment $B$'s setup time could also be cut in half at a cost of $5,000.

Superficially, equipment $B$ seems to pay off better in terms of time reduction per investment cost. This approach focuses on the work center at which the setup reduction occurs by examining the cost savings in work center service inventory and direct labor costs. However, this myopic view ignores the impact of the setup reduction on subsequent operations and services.

When the effects of a setup time reduction are evaluated for the entire service operation system, the economics of the decision can alter dramatically. If, for example, equipment $A$ is set up 25 times a day, it can produce 1,000 units per day with its current changeover times. If equipment $B$ is set up 4 times a day, it can produce 1,500 units per day. As a consequence, the output of the service operation line is limited to the 1,000 units per day that equipment $A$ can produce.

Few benefits would be gained by reducing the setup time on equipment $B$, because the output of the line would still be 1,000 units per day, and no additional revenue would be generated. A small labor savings will result, but unless this savings reduces the number of employees or their time is redeployed to alternative activities, no cost savings are realized. In most cases, there are minimal benefits—at best—to reducing setup time on equipment that is not creating a bottleneck.

But two substantial benefits can be realized by reducing the setup time on equipment $A$. First, the time saved increases organizational capacity, because equipment $A$ essentially sets the output of the organization. Alternatively, the additional time can be used to reduce the service operation lot sizes, thus increasing flexibility. Or it can be used to expand the range of services to the line, both of which increase the effective variety of the organization output.

Benefits of a setup-time reduction should be examined in terms of capacity. If the setup time of equipment $A$ is reduced to 5 minutes, the output of the equipment activity will increase by 125 minutes [(10 – 5 minutes) × 25 setups] per day; the 2 extra hours of activity capacity are worth a substantial sum of money. More throughput also decreases the overhead costs per unit. Seen another way, gains in capacity can offset reduced batch sizes, which in turn reduce work-in-progress service inventory, increase response time, and improve customer service.

The cost management systems used in most organizations are practically useless for this type of bottleneck decision. Estimating the benefits of reduced changeover time requires information other than the cost of equipment and the hours saved. What is needed is an estimate of the value of increased capacity, variety, and flow times. Tracing the impact of the reduction to activities will better quantify the impact of the decision.

Focusing on the work center may lead to an overestimation of the savings in setup-time reduction for equipment $B$ and an underestimation of the benefits of a setup-time reduction for equipment $A$. Systemwide information is required for appropriate analysis. Such information must assess the effect of setup-time reduction at a specific work center on the entire service operation process as well as the effect of such a reduction on service quality.

**(d) Profit Velocity**    Profit velocity is the ratio of service profit to lead time.

$$\text{Profit velocity} = \text{Profit/lead time}$$

Profit velocity is based on the observation that organizational profitability is a function of both the absolute profitability of a service and the number of services that can be produced during any given period. To illustrate profit velocity, consider the two services in Exhibit 24.17.

| Service | Profit $ | Lead Time (days) |
|---|---|---|
| A | 50 | 5 |
| B | 35 | 2 |

**Exhibit 24.17    Profit Velocity for Services A and B. Source: Activity-Based Management for Service Industries, Government Entities & Nonprofit Organizations, by James A. Brimson and John Antos. Copyright © 1998 by John Wiley & Sons, Inc. Reprinted by permission of John Wiley & Sons, Inc.**

Conventional cost accounting would proclaim service $A$ more profitable than service $B$—which is correct in absolute terms. The profit velocity of the two services presents a different conclusion. The profit velocity for service $A$ is $10 ($50/5 days) per service operations day, whereas for service $B$ it is $17.50 ($35/2 days) per service operations day. Assuming sufficient demand for service $B$, the organization would be most profitable selling service $B$ rather than service $A$. The organization may thus choose to redirect its marketing effort to emphasize service $B$.

**(e) Work Orders**  Work orders should not be used for standard services—or for nonstandard services when the estimate is deemed sufficient. Work orders should be used when estimates might be considered suspect.

**24.10 ACTIVITY SERVICE-COST EXAMPLE**  The steps in calculating an activity service cost are similar to those for calculating an activity cost. However, when calculating an activity service cost, allocate secondary activities to the primary activities *before* calculating the activity cost per unit of activity. The key steps for calculating activity service cost are listed here and displayed in Exhibits 24.18 through 24.25.

| Accounting Department | $ |
|---|---|
| Labor | 500,000 |
| Travel | 100,000 |
| Management information systems | 100,000 |
| Others | 100,000 |
| Total | 800,000 |

**Exhibit 24.18   Step 1: Extract Accounting Department Cost from General Ledger.** *Source: Activity-Based Management for Service Industries, Government Entities & Nonprofit Organizations,* **by James A. Brimson and John Antos. Copyright © 1998 by John Wiley & Sons, Inc. Reprinted by permission of John Wiley & Sons, Inc.**

☑ Pay invoices
☑ Process receivables
☑ Prepare financial reports
☑ Pay employees
☑ Provide managerial reports
☑ Manage employees
☑ Train employees
☑ Other

**Exhibit 24.19   Step 2: Determine the Activities of the Accounting Department.** *Source: Activity-Based Management for Service Industries, Government Entities & Nonprofit Organizations,* **by James A. Brimson and John Antos. Copyright © 1998 by John Wiley & Sons, Inc. Reprinted by permission of John Wiley & Sons, Inc.**

| Accounting Department | % | Primary/Secondary |
|---|---|---|
| Pay invoices | 20 | Primary |
| Process receivables | 20 | Primary |
| Prepare financial reports | 15 | Primary |
| Pay employees | 15 | Primary |
| Provide managerial reports | 10 | Primary |
| Primary subtotal | 80 | |
| Manage employees | 5 | Secondary |
| Train employees | 5 | Secondary |
| Other | 10 | Secondary |
| Total | 100% | |

**Exhibit 24.20    Step 3: Define percentage of Time Expended on Each Activity.** *Source: Activity-Based Management for Service Industries, Government Entities & Nonprofit Organizations,* by James A. Brimson and John Antos. Copyright © 1998 by John Wiley & Sons, Inc. Reprinted by permission of John Wiley & Sons, Inc.

- *Step 1.* Select cost base.
- *Step 2.* Determine activities.
- *Step 3.* Define percentage of time per activity.
- *Step 4.* Trace cost to activities.
- *Step 5.* Assign secondary activities to primary activities.
- *Step 6.* Determine total cost for each activity.
- *Step 7.* Calculate cost per unit of activity output.
- *Step 8.* Create a BOA.

The following assumptions are used for the BOA in Exhibit 24.25:

- Assume one invoice per 100 loans; therefore, the quantity is .01.
- Assume that each loan is collected monthly over 10 years; therefore, the quantity is 120 months.

| Accounting Department | Labor $ | Travel $ | MIS $ | Other | Total |
|---|---|---|---|---|---|
| Pay invoices | 100,000 | | 30,000 | | 130,000 |
| Process receivables | 100,000 | 10,000 | 30,000 | | 140,000 |
| Prepare financial reports | 75,000 | 20,000 | 10,000 | | 105,000 |
| Pay employees | 75,000 | | 20,000 | | 95,000 |
| Provide managerial reports | 50,000 | | 10,000 | | 60,000 |
| Manage employees | 25,000 | 40,000 | | | 65,000 |
| Train employees | 25,000 | 30,000 | | | 55,000 |
| Other | 50,000 | | | 100,000 | 150,000 |
| Total | 500,000 | 100,000 | 100,000 | 100,000 | 800,000 |

**Exhibit 24.21    Step 4: Trace Cost to the Specific Activities Using the Total Department Method for the Labor.** *Source: Activity-Based Management for Service Industries, Government Entities & Nonprofit Organizations,* by James A. Brimson and John Antos. Copyright © 1998 by John Wiley & Sons, Inc. Reprinted by permission of John Wiley & Sons, Inc.

| Accounting Department | Secondary Costs $ | | Primary Activity %/Total Primary % | Secondary Costs Allocated $ |
|---|---|---|---|---|
| Pay invoices | 270,000 | × | (20%/80%) | 67,500 |
| Process receivables | 270,000 | × | (20%/80%) | 67,500 |
| Prepare financial reports | 270,000 | × | (15%/80%) | 50,600 |
| Pay employees | 270,000 | × | (15%/80%) | 50,600 |
| Provide managerial reports | 270,000 | × | (10%/80%) | 33,800 |
| Manage employees | | | | |
| Train employees | | | | |
| Other | | | | |
| Total | | | | 270,000 |

Exhibit 24.22   Step 5: Assign Secondary Costs to Primary Activities Using Primary Activity Labor Time as the Basis of Assigning Secondary Cost. *Source: Activity-Based Management for Service Industries, Government Entities & Nonprofit Organizations,* by James A. Brimson and John Antos. Copyright © 1998 by John Wiley & Sons, Inc. Reprinted by permission of John Wiley & Sons, Inc.

| Accounting Department | Labor | Travel $ | MIS $ | Secondary Assignment | Total $ |
|---|---|---|---|---|---|
| Pay invoices | 100,000 | | 30,000 | 67,500 | 197,500 |
| Process receivables | 100,000 | 10,000 | 30,000 | 67,500 | 207,500 |
| Prepare financial reports | 75,000 | 20,000 | 10,000 | 50,600 | 155,600 |
| Pay employees | 75,000 | | 20,000 | 50,600 | 145,600 |
| Provide managerial reports | 50,000 | | 10,000 | 33,800 | 93,800 |
| Manage employees | | | | | |
| Train employees | | | | | |
| Other | | | | | |
| Total | 400,000 | 30,000 | 100,000 | 270,000 | 800,000 |

Exhibit 24.23   Step 6: Determine Total Cost for Each Activity. *Source: Activity-Based Management for Service Industries, Government Entities & Nonprofit Organizations,* by James A. Brimson and John Antos. Copyright © 1998 by John Wiley & Sons, Inc. Reprinted by permission of John Wiley & Sons, Inc.

| Accounting Department | Total $ | Measure (Units) | Measure | Cost/ Unit $ |
|---|---|---|---|---|
| Pay invoices | 197,500 | 13,000 | invoices | 15.192 |
| Process receivables | 207,500 | 20,000 | collections | 10.375 |
| Prepare financial reports | 155,600 | 12 | reports | 12,966.67 |
| Pay employees | 145,600 | 5,000 | checks | 29.12 |
| Provide managerial reports | 93,800 | 60 | reports | 1,563.33 |
| Manage employees | | | | |
| Train employees | | | | |
| Other | | | | |
| Total | 800,000 | | | |

Exhibit 24.24   Step 7: Calculate Cost per Unit of Activity Output. *Source: Activity-Based Management for Service Industries, Government Entities & Nonprofit Organizations,* by James A. Brimson and John Antos. Copyright © 1998 by John Wiley & Sons, Inc. Reprinted by permission of John Wiley & Sons, Inc.

| Activity | Activity Measure | Activity Quantity | Activity Cost $ | Life-Cycle Cost ($) for 5,000 Loans | Current Unit Cost | Subtotal |
|---|---|---|---|---|---|---|
| *Life Cycle Costs* | | | | | | |
| Design loan | Designs | 1 | 5,000 | 5,000 | 1.00 ($5000/5000 loans) | |
| Design procedures | Procedures | 5 | 200 | 1,000 | .20 ($1000/5000 loans) | |
| Acquire supplies | Supplies | 1 | 50 | 50 | .01 ($50/5000 loan) | |
| Subtotal life-cycle costs | | | | | 1.21 | |
| *Continuous Operating Costs* | | | | | | |
| Take applications | Applications | 1 | 150 | | 150.00 | |
| Order credit survey, appraisal | Reports | 3 | 30 | | 90.00 | |
| Review documents | Reviews | 1 | 70 | | 70.00 | |
| Review by loan committee | Applications | 1 | 200 | | 200.00 | |
| Prepare loan documents | Pages | 30 | 5 | | 150.00 | |
| Disburse funds | Disbursements | 1 | 100 | | 100.00 | 760.00 |
| Subtotal continuing operating costs | | | | | | 761.21 |
| Total cost of reports | | | | | | 150.00 |
| Subtotal life-cycle, operating, and report costs | | | | | | $911.21 |
| Accounting department | | | | | | |
| Pay invoices (a) | | .01 | | | .15 | |
| Process receivables (b) | | 120 | 15.19 | | | |
| Prepare financial reports (c) | | | 10.38 | 1,245.60 | | |
| Pay employees (d) | | | | | | |
| Provide managerial reports (e) | | 120 | .78 | | 93.56 | |
| Accounting department subtotal | | | | | | 1,339.31 |
| Other departments | | | | | | 320.00 |
| Total bill of activity cost for loans | | | | | | 2,570.52 |

**Exhibit 24.25  Step 8: Create Bill of Activities.** *Source: Activity-Based Management for Service Industries, Government Entities & Nonprofit Organizations,* by James A. Brimson and John Antos. Copyright © 1998 by John Wiley & Sons, Inc. Reprinted by permission of John Wiley & Sons, Inc.

- Assume that external reports are not traceable to services already charged to other activity costs.
- Assume each managerial report has approximately 2,000 loans. The average loan is for 120 months; the quantity is 120 months. The monthly cost per loan for managerial reports is $1,563.33/average of 2,000 loans per month equals $.78/loan.

**24.11 SUMMARY**    An activity-based service cost is derived by tracing the usage of all activities required to build a service. Thus, an activity service cost becomes a summation of the cost of all traceable activities to design the service, procure supplies, and produce and distribute the service.

Activity management directly relates activities to the services that consume them. This is in contrast to conventional cost accounting systems, which spread overhead costs among services based on some allocation base that does not necessarily mirror their actual consumption. Activity service costing is enhanced by more specific tracing of support costs, which have traditionally been lumped into overhead and allocated to all services.

# CHAPTER 25

# ACTIVITY-BASED BUDGETING*

## James A. Brimson
IPM, Inc.
## John Antos
Value Creation Group, Inc.

**25.1 INTRODUCTION**   The purposes of this chapter are to discuss problems with traditional budgeting, define activity-based budgeting (ABB), and discuss the ABB process.

A budget is a financial expression of a plan. Traditional budgeting focuses on planning resources for an organizational unit. Each year, managers look at history and any significant changes and create an annual budget. The budgeting process starts with the senior executive's announcing budget goals. These may consist of revenue and profit goals as well as goals for new services.

Many managers respond by looking at last year's numbers and increasing their budget for the year based on inflation and/or the amount of the increase in revenues (see Exhibit 25.1). For example, if revenues increase 10 percent, the various department managers might increase the budgets for their departments by 10 percent.

The problem with this approach is that last year's inefficiencies are incorporated into this year's budget. Often, little attention is paid to improvements in each department. Finally, little incentive is incorporated into the budgeting process for continuous improvement. Changing workload for each department often is not considered.

Senior managers, during budgeting, often make arbitrary cuts across the board. A potentially negative consequence is that the better-managed departments may have already cut the majority of waste and now may have to cut into necessary resources. Instead, other, less efficient departments should make more radical reductions to bring them to the same level of efficiency as the better-managed departments.

Budgets in this environment often become wrestling matches in which those who are the best presenters are given larger budgets. The theory goes that the best at presenting the reasons for the larger budget deserves the larger budget.

Once the budget is agreed on, it is often cast in concrete for the year.

---

*This material has been adapted from James A. Brimson and John Antos, *Activity-Based Management for Service Industries, Government Entities, and Not-for-Profit Organizations* (New York: John Wiley & Sons, 1994).

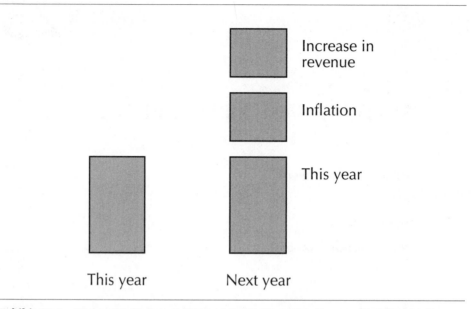

Exhibit 25.1    Manager's Response to Next Year's Forecast. *Source: Handbook of Budgeting, Fourth Edition,* Robert Rachlin (ed.), Copyright © 1999 by John Wiley & Sons, Inc. Reprinted by permission of John Wiley & Sons, Inc.

**25.2 TRADITIONAL BUDGETING DOES NOT SUPPORT EXCELLENCE**    First, the budgeting process should highlight cost reduction and the elimination of wasteful activities and tasks. Traditional budgeting does not make visible what the organization does. Instead, managers look at their history of spending and simply increase last year's budget and/or actuals based on inflation and/or increases in revenue.

Second, budgeting should be a formal mechanism for reducing workload to the minimal level to support enterprise objectives. Excess workload due to poor structuring of activities and business process drives up cost and does not improve customer satisfaction. The budgeting process itself should give insight into how to reduce workload and how to set workload reduction goals.

Third, budgeting should consider all costs as variable; yet budgeting often formalizes the laissez-faire attitude toward occupancy and equipment costs. Most are familiar with the concept of fixed and variable costs. The problem with this classification is a psychological one. The term "fixed costs" seems to imply that these costs cannot be eliminated because they are fixed. Yet we all know that buildings and equipment can be put to alternative use, sold, demolished, or leased. Many assets are often dedicated to specific activities. By making these assets more flexible, the total capital base of an enterprise can be lowered. Even property taxes and property insurance can be reduced. A budget based on variable and fixed costs often focuses attention on the variable costs and implies that the fixed costs are not controllable.

A better classification would be utilized and unutilized capacity. This classification simply shows that some assets are being used and some are not. It does not present the psychological barrier to change that the term "fixed costs" does. Unutilized capacity can be saved for future growth, eliminated, used for other purposes, or consolidated with another division.

An important goal of budgeting should be to improve each process on a continuous basis. Traditional budgeting, as it is commonly practiced, seems to focus on simply repeating history. Activity budgeting sets improvement targets by activity/business process. Thus, this approach is something everyone can understand and use to work toward improvement. However, traditional budgeting sets goals such as "reduce costs" by a specific percentage, without giving employees insights on how to achieve those targets.

Activity budgeting works to synchronize activities and thus improve business processes. Traditional budgeting may take the approach of "every department for itself." Managers pay lip service to coordinating between departments; however, managers will almost certainly respond in a way that will maximize their own department's performance. The inevitable consequence is to lower the performance of the organization as a whole.

Activity budgeting sets business-process improvement goals, which requires the joint efforts of employees from a variety of departments. Because the goal is to improve the business process, old barriers between departments begin to crumble.

Traditional budgeting does not formally consider external and internal suppliers and customers. However, activity budgeting requires asking the internal and external suppliers and customers to describe their needs and their respective workload requirements.

Too often, the focus in traditional budgeting is to control the result. For example, consider the organization that closes its financial books in 4 to 15 days. Each month managers focus on information that is 34 to 45 days old.

It makes more sense to control the *process* rather than to try to control the *result* through financial statements. The Japanese have unsophisticated accounting systems compared to U.S. companies of a similar size. If the secret was a more sophisticated accounting system, U.S. companies should be superior. Yet that is not necessarily the case.

Activity budgeting and activity management focus on controlling the process. Only by controlling the process can results improve.

In a similar vein, traditional budgeting tends to focus on the effects rather than the causes. For example, it often requires a long time to hire new employees or introduce a new service. In reality, organizations should focus on the causes of these long lead times. In Japan, managers come to meetings asking their peers for suggestions to solve their problems. In the United States, our individualistic attitudes often make managers consider a request for help as a sign of weakness. Managers therefore make up excuses to explain the reasons they were over budget, rather than concentrating their efforts on how to improve operations.

Because activity budgeting focuses on the root cause of problems, everyone can work to identify how to reduce or eliminate them. Only by eliminating the "root cause" of the problem can the cost be permanently eliminated.

Activity budgeting requires that customers be asked for their requirements. Only by asking the customer can an organization understand whether it has properly applied resources to meet the customer's needs (e.g., do the patrons of the U.S. Postal Service want two- to three-day delivery, or do they want consistent delivery within some stated time period?). By asking the customer, the workload connected with the activities necessary to please the customer can better be determined.

Activity budgeting focuses on output, not on input. It focuses on what work is done, how the work is performed, and how much work is done. The required resources are only a consequence of the activities. The problem with traditional budgeting is that it lacks ownership. Even if the department manager "owns" the budget, seldom do the individual employees in that department own the budget. Activity budgeting asks each person to look at the activities he or she performs and to set performance targets for those activities in the context of customer requirements and organizational objectives.

Activity budgeting allows people to be empowered to manage their activities properly. If something is wrong, if there is a better way to perform the activity or business process, or if a quality issue arises, the employee(s) who performs the activity or business process should make the necessary improvements or corrections without requiring management approval. (This assumes that the employee is not changing the service or the quality provided to the customer, and is improving the service or business process at a lower cost.)

Senior management needs to remember that people will not work themselves out of a job. People will contribute ideas to improve operations only if they understand that improvement in value-added activities allows the transfer of resource to growth-enabling activities.

Under activity budgeting, mistakes are acceptable, but repetition of mistakes is unacceptable. An executive told Sam Walton of a $10 million mistake and submitted his resignation. Walton told the executive he could not resign because the company had just spent $10 million training him. People need to know they can make mistakes, but they must learn from those mistakes and not repeat them.

Activity budgeting uses a common language—the language of the activities or business processes that everyone is performing. Traditional budgeting uses terms with which only the accountants are familiar. This Tower of Babel makes communication more difficult and encourages specialization at the expense of cooperation.

Activity budgeting looks for consistency of the output. This means that the activity should be performed in a consistent way over time. Continuous improvement must be encouraged, but the activity should only be performed in accordance with current best practice. Success depends on finding the best possible way to perform an activity or business process and consistently looking for ways to improve it while performing the activity/business process in a consistent manner.

Activity budgeting requires setting activity or business process targets as the minimum level of performance rather than the absolute level. These activity or business-process targets should identify the minimum level of performance necessary to support organizational objectives. Managers should not try to exceed these minimum levels. Instead, they should look at ways to reduce waste and non–value-added portions of various activities.

**25.3 ACTIVITY-BASED BUDGETING DEFINITIONS**    *Activity-based budgeting* is the process of planning and controlling the expected activities of the organization to derive a cost-effective budget that meets forecast workload and agreed strategic goals.

Activity-based budgeting is a quantitative expression of the expected activities of the organization, reflecting management forecast of workload and financial and nonfinancial requirements to meet agreed strategic goals and planned changes to improve performance.

The three key elements of ABB include:

1. Type of work to be done.
2. Quantity of work to be done.
3. Cost of work to be done.

**(a) Principles of Activity-Based Budgeting**   Activity-based budgeting must reflect what is done, that is, the activities or business processes, not cost elements. Resources required (cost elements) must be derived from the expected activities or business processes and workload. *Workload* is simply the number of units of an activity that are required. For example, in the human resource department, the workload for the activity "hire employees" might be to hire 25 employees. The cost elements to perform that activity might be the wages and benefits of the recruiter, travel, advertising, testing, supplies, and occupancy costs for the space occupied by the recruiter and for interviewing. If a hiring freeze occurs, the workload for this activity would be zero.

Budgets must be based on the future workload in order to meet:

- Customer requirements
- Organizational/departmental goals and strategies
- New/changed services and service mix
- Changes in business processes
- Improvements in efficiency and effectiveness
- Quality, flexibility, and cycle-time goals
- Changes in service levels

The final budget must reflect the changes in resource cost levels and foreign exchange fluctuations. However, it is better to initially budget using constant cost and foreign exchange rates to facilitate comparisons and then to add inflation and foreign exchange adjustments at the conclusion of the budgeting process.

As part of the activity budgeting process, it is important to highlight continuous improvement. Each department should identify the activities or business processes to be improved, the amount of improvement, and how it plans to achieve its improvement targets.

**(b) Requirements for Successful Activity-Based Budgeting**   The organization must be committed to excellence. If the organization does not have this commitment, resources will be wasted on data-analysis activities that will never be implemented. Changing is not easy. It is easier to study the problem than to make the difficult decisions required to improve.

**(c) Process Management Approach**   The organization must use a process management approach to improvement. This requires defining each activity as part of a repeatable, robust business process that can be continuously improved and the variability removed. Activities defined in this way can use various techniques to decrease time, improve quality, and reduce the cost of those activities.

Process management is crucial to excellence because high levels of performance are possible only when activities are done to best practices, the unused capacity is minimal, the best practices are continually made better, and the activities are executed perfectly. Activity definitions must support process management. Activities must be in the form of verb plus a noun. There must be a physical output. Two-stage definitions of drivers are usually not adequate. For example, the activity "pay employee" is compatible with process management. To define an activity as "supplies handling" and the output measure as the "number of service production runs" would not be compatible activity definitions. Two-stage activity definitions might be used in assigning costs to a service, but it does not help in improving operations. A better way to define this sample activity would be "move supplies," with the output measure defined as the "number of moves."

One of the first steps that an activity manager may have to take is to review activity definitions to make sure that they are compatible with a process approach.

**(d) Culture Encourages Sustaining Benefits**    The organizational culture should encourage sustaining benefits. These benefits should not be something that lasts for only a short while, after which everyone goes back to the old way. These benefits should change the way the people in the organization think and act. Often this means changing the way the employees are compensated, so that they share in the productivity improvement.

Organizations must overcome the cultural barriers shown in Exhibit 25.2. Next to these barriers are actions the organization must take in order to overcome these cultural barriers.

**(e) Commitment to Excellence**    Many organizations take a short-term approach to improving operations. Costs are easy to control—simply stop spending money. This approach is similar to a crash diet. The problem with crash diets is that the dieter usually regains what he or she lost and often gains even more weight. If an organization is committed to excellence, its goal is to change the way it does business. This is similar to changing eating habits. For example, organizations must start compensating people based on business-process performance rather than the traditional actual versus budget of cost elements that most organizations have historically used. Business process performance must be tied to the balanced scorecard and strategy.

**25.4 ACTIVITY-BASED BUDGETING PROCESS**    The ABB process begins with the customer. The organization must determine who the customer is and what the customer wants. It must look to its competitors. Competition consists of both direct competitors and alternate services that might compete with the organization's services.

The organization must develop a strategy to meet customer needs. A restaurant must decide whether to be a five-star restaurant, with crystal and linen tablecloths, or to provide good food in a clean environment with less sophisticated decor but with good value to the customer.

Next, the organization should forecast workload. Management and sales determine what sales levels will be, and managers need to estimate their workloads as a result of these sales levels. Often, the sales forecast includes new services and new markets, as well as any changes in strategy.

Planning guidelines must be articulated to each manager to establish the specific activity-level targets within a business process context. Eventually, every activity manager should have targets for improving his or her respective value-added activities and eliminating non–value-added activities. This improvement must tie into strategy.

Next, interdepartmental projects should be identified. Because these projects will affect the workload, as well as the activities in several departments, they must be coordinated and done prior to each manager improving his or her own activities.

At this point in the budgeting process, specific activity-level projects can be identified. These are projects to improve operations at the individual activity level. However, improvement should always be within organizational objectives, a business-process context, and the balanced scorecard.

Activity-based investment analysis consists of defining improvement projects, eval-

| Cultural Barriers | Actions |
|---|---|
| • Departmental structure often interferes with departments interacting, in order to minimize total enterprise cost. | • Change information systems so the organization can see total cost of business processes rather than just the costs in a specific department. |
| • Policies and procedures provide guidelines for employee behavior. These were often set up to ensure consistency and to make it easy for employees to handle specific situations. | • Empower employees to handle various situations to ensure customer satisfaction. Use policies to set general guidelines and train, support, and empower employees to satisfy the customer. |
| • Suggestion programs usually require the approval of management to implement change. This slows the change process. | • Suggestion programs are only for changes to the service or for capital requests. Have employees make changes to efficiency without management approval. |
| • Measurement systems tend to focus on the department level. | • Abolish micromanagement. Give managers and employees the tools, authority, and responsibility to do their jobs. Make them responsible for outputs and a budget level of resources to do their work. |
| • Specialization assumes that lowest cost is achievable through economies of scale. | • Today flexibility is critical. Cross-train people for a variety of tasks. First, as slack or heavy periods occur, have employees help out in other departments. Second, ensure that employees understand how what they do affects other departments, and how what other departments do affects them. |

**Exhibit 25.2    Cultural Barriers. *Source: Handbook of Budgeting, Fourth Edition,* Robert Rachlin (ed.), Copyright © 1999 by John Wiley & Sons, Inc. Reprinted by permission of John Wiley & Sons, Inc.**

uating those projects, and then using committees to select projects that will meet the organization's goals and meet customers' needs.

The final step is to determine the activities and workload for the coming year.

**25.5 LINKING STRATEGY AND BUDGETING**   One of the problems with traditional budgeting is that a clear link between the enterprise's strategy and budgeting often does not exist. Therefore, operating managers do not know how to incorporate strategy into their budgets.

**(a) Principles of Strategic Management**   A variety of seminars and books are available on the subject of strategic management. This chapter does not discuss those techniques but simply assumes that a strategic plan exists. The role of senior management is to set performance targets based on the strategic plans. The performance targets might be for sales, number of new services and/or markets, cycle time, cost, quality, or customer-service levels. The role of the activity manager is to achieve or exceed those targets.

Strategic objectives and performance targets must be translated into activity-level targets. Activity managers must ensure that service requirements are a direct derivative of customer needs.

The translation process starts with customer requirements and an analysis of competitive strategies. Then strategic objectives are set. The price for services allowable by the market are determined and time, quality, and cost targets are determined. Then these targets are translated into activity-level targets.

There are several important strategic management tools to assist with this process. The key ones include:

- Customer surveys
- Core competency analysis
- Benchmarking
- Quality function deployment
- Reverse engineering

**(b) Customer Surveys**   One of the first steps in the strategic management process is to perform a customer survey. The customer survey can be done in person, by telephone, or by direct mail. The survey asks a variety of questions, but the focus is on the factors that are important to the customer, a ranking of those factors by the customer, and, finally, the customer's perception of the organization's performance regarding those factors.

Based on this survey, the organization needs to start with the factors most important to the customer and determine whether it is satisfying the customer on those factors of performance. Activity or business process and investment preference must be given to those activities or business processes that the customer feels are most important. Especially when satisfaction levels are not satisfactory to the customer, the organization needs to change, improve, or increase resources and effectiveness of those activities or business processes.

For example, if an organization determines that it needs to allow nurses to spend more time with patients and less time doing paperwork, it could create an activity budget in the following way:

For the activity "complete medical charts":

| Total Cost | Salaries | Depreciation | Supplies | Phone | Occupancy |
|---|---|---|---|---|---|
| $24,410 | 22,000 | 400 | 900 | 150 | 960 |

The assumptions are that a person would be hired to "complete medical charts." The employee's salary and benefits would be $22,000 per year. Depreciation on his or her desk and computer would be $400. Supplies connected with filling out the charts are estimated to be $900. Because this person would be communicating with other departments, a phone would be necessary for interhospital calls. The fully loaded cost of hospital space (including depreciation, heat, electricity, building maintenance, and janitorial cost based on the number of square feet occupied) equals $960.

Hiring this person will enable 10 nurses to spend 10% of their time comforting, informing, and answering questions for patients. A nurse earns $36,000 annually, including benefits.

For the activity "communicate with patients":

| Total Cost | Salaries | Depreciation | Supplies | Phone | Occupancy |
|---|---|---|---|---|---|
| $46,320 | 36,000 | 1,000 | 2,000 | 320 | 7,000 |

The following assumptions were made. Annual salaries and benefits for 10 nurses at $36,000 per nurse equals $360,000. Because they will spend 10 percent of their time on this activity, the salary portion of this activity cost equals $36,000. There would be some depreciation on the desk for the portion of time performing this activity. Some educational literature would be given to the patients, which would total approximately $2,000. Nurses would need a phone line for tracking down answers to patient questions, and a reasonable percentage of the total phone cost was estimated at $320. Because the nurses spent some time sitting at a desk for this activity, 10 percent of their total occupancy costs was apportioned, which amounted to $7,000.

Now senior management can look at the customer survey and performance as it relates to nurses communicating and comforting patients—a high-priority item in the eyes of the customer. Then they can determine whether it is worth spending a total of $70,730 ($24,410 plus $46,320) to improve customer satisfaction in this area.

**(c) Core Competency Analysis** An organization starts by asking what activities or business processes are critical to its industry. These activities or business processes become the *core competencies* of that industry. Then the organizations can ask themselves which activities or business processes they perform well. They need to compare themselves with external benchmarks and determine where there is a core competency gap. Then the organizations can set budget targets in terms of cost, quality, and time.

| Industry | Core Competency |
|---|---|
| Banking | Accuracy, fast turnaround, full service |
| Insurance | Low rates, knowledgeable representatives, fast claims handling |
| Hospitals | Friendly nurses, full service, high success rate |
| Airlines | On-time, convenient departures, reasonable fares |
| Fast food | Quality, service, cleanliness |
| Internal Revenue Service (IRS) | Rules that are easy to comply with, fairness, easy access |
| Fund raisers | Good cause, large percentage of funds directly to cause |

An auto dealer decided that a core competency of the repair shop was to provide quality repairs the first time. A further analysis revealed an opportunity to improve performance by conducting auto repair training seminars for the mechanics. Four seminars for 20 mechanics who earn $14 per hour were planned. Each seminar was to be five hours long with $500 in training supplies. A consultant will charge $3,000 per training session. For the activity "train mechanics":

| Total Cost | Salaries | Supplies | Phone | Consultant |
|---|---|---|---|---|
| $18,100 | 5,600 | 500 | 0 | 12,000 |

**(d) Benchmarking**   The benchmarking process compares performance to other organizations, either internally or externally. Benchmarks may measure the following:

- Activities
- Business processes
- Time
- New service introduction
- Customer service
- Quality
- Cost

Comparisons should be made, where possible, across divisions, with competitors, and with the best organizations in the world. For example, one telephone company can process a request for new phone service within 43 seconds. This is a speed few other organizations can duplicate and would serve as a great benchmark for the activity "process new customers' credit requests."

One association felt it was important to answer the phone after only two rings. This would be a high-quality service to the members and would avoid lost sales of books and seminars because people tired of waiting for someone to answer the phone. The association's operators were currently answering the phone on the third or fourth ring. It decided to increase the number of telephone operators by three. Telephone operators could be hired for $18,000 per year. They would need a desk, a personal computer (PC), a phone, and supplies for order taking. Fully loaded occupancy costs were running $10 per square foot. Each operator would need 64 square feet of space.

For the activity "answer phones":

| Total cost | Salaries | Depreciation | Supplies | Phone | Occupancy |
|---|---|---|---|---|---|
| $60,120 | 54,000 | 2,000 | 1,200 | 1,000 | 1,920 |

**(e) Activity Function Deployment**   Activity function deployment (AFD) is a concept similar to quality function deployment (QFD), which originated in the quality field, and is applicable to activity budgeting. In AFD, the organization compares the customers' requirements with the activities or business processes necessary to meet those requirements. For each activity or business process, a comparison is also made with the competition to determine how the organization is doing against the competition. Also, a correlation is made between activities to show which activities have a strong positive or strong negative correlation with meeting customer requirements. Some activities will have no correlation with each other. Finally, a correlation is made between various activities and customer requirements. Thus, the organization can determine which activities are critical to greatest customer satisfaction. Customer requirements are ranked as part of this analysis.

Although a complete explanation of this technique can be found in a number of quality books and seminars, a simple example is discussed here. An airline is looking to increase market share by better satisfying its customers. Using AFD, the airline determines that quick turnaround time is important in order to have on-time departures. One way to improve in this area is to have two jetbridges to load passengers instead of only one. There are two activities—"move jetbridge" and "maintain jetbridge"—connected with this second jetbridge.

The airline determines that 10 percent of a ticketing agent's time is needed to handle this second jetbridge. A ticketing agent earns $32,000 per year. Two hundred ticketing agents will be affected. This means that salaries with benefits dedicated to the activity "move jetbridge" would be $640,000 (200 × 10% × $32,000). An additional 100 jetbridges would have to be purchased, at the rate of $10,000 per jetbridge. Therefore, the depreciation on $1 million (100 × $10,000) using a five-year life would be $200,000 per year. The annual cost of maintenance labor is $100,000 on these jetbridges and is $50,000 on maintenance parts. Occupancy costs are $20,000 for the maintenance space needed for these jetbridges.

For the activities "move jetbridge" and "maintain jetbridge":

| Activity | Activity Cost | Salaries | Depreciation | Parts | Occupancy |
| --- | --- | --- | --- | --- | --- |
| Move jetbridge | 640,000 | 640,000 | | | |
| Maintain jetbridge | 370,000 | 100,000 | 200,000 | 50,000 | 20,000 |
| Total cost | 1,010,000 | 740,000 | 200,000 | 50,000 | 20,000 |

**(f) Reverse Engineering**    Reverse engineering involves studying a competitor's services. At first glance, one would think that reverse engineering is a concept that applies only to products. However, applying reverse engineering to a service and seeing how competitors perform the service is a useful tool.

For example, consider a company that has a regulatory affairs department that must file with the Food and Drug Administration (FDA) to get regulatory approval. The company's managers studied the competitor's process of filing for regulatory approval. The objective was to determine how to perform the process more effectively.

Using reverse engineering principles, they started by asking the customer, in this case the FDA, the testing requirements in order to get this new product approved. Then, based on the FDA's comments, they improved how they designed their products and their testing procedures in order to get approval more quickly.

For "improve the FDA approval process," the managers determined the following activity costs: Regulatory personnel with salaries of $50,000 will spend 10 percent of their time on this project. They will have travel costs amounting to $3,000. Supplies are expected to be $600. A seminar on this topic will cost $1,700. A 10 percent share of office occupancy cost is running $2,000 per year.

For the activity "improve FDA approval process":

| Total Cost | Salaries | Travel | Supplies | Seminar | Occupancy |
|---|---|---|---|---|---|
| $12,300 | 5,000 | 3,000 | 600 | 1,700 | 2,000 |

**25.6 TRANSLATE STRATEGY TO ACTIVITIES**   Strategy must be translated to an activity level to identify necessary changes. An example of a translating procedure follows:

| Steps | Example |
|---|---|
| Define mission statement with enterprise goals | Dominate the market and diversify where advantage can be applied |
| Establish critical success factors | Grow market share: increase new service sales as percent of total sales |
| Establish service targets | Increase market share: Service 1 by 7%; Service 2 by 8%; discontinue Service 3 |
| Establish service-level targets | Service 1: increase sales 5%; decrease cost 8%; deliver in 2 hours |

**(a) Identify Activity Targets by Bill of Activities**   The next step is to identify activity targets for each service.

For example, the mission might be to dominate the consumer loan business in Dallas; the critical success factor might be to grow market share; the service target might be to grow auto loan revenue by 7 percent; and the service level targets might be to increase auto loan sales by 5 percent and decrease cost by 8 percent.

**Bill of Activities**

| Activity Description | Cost/ Output ($) | Units of Output | Costs of Service ($) | Target Activity Reduction (%) | Target Activity Reduction ($) | Target Cost of Service ($) |
|---|---|---|---|---|---|---|
| Take application | 100 | 1 | 100 | <5> | <5> | 95 |
| Order reports | 50 | 3 | 150 | <10> | <15> | 135 |
| Review loans | 200 | 1 | 200 | <7> | <14> | 186 |
| Complete paperwork | 25 | 4 | 100 | <30> | <30> | 70 |
| Disburse funds | 250 | 1 | 250 | | | 250 |
| Totals | | | 800 | <8> | <64> | 736 |

This table shows that the employees have established cost reduction targets for four of the five activities. The total reduction of $64 is an 8 percent reduction from last year's bill of activities cost.

Once these strategic management tools are employed, cost, time, and quality targets can be set by the employees for each activity. Following is an example of cost, time, and quality targets.

**(b) Strategic Management Tools and Targets**

| Tool | Activity | Cost | Time | Quality |
|------|----------|------|------|---------|
| Customer survey | Communicate with patients | C: 46,320 T: 40,000 | C: 10 minutes T: 30 minutes | C: 80% satisfaction T: 90% satisfaction |
| Core competency | Train mechanics | C: 18,100 T: 22,000 | C: 20 hours T: 24 hours | C: 9% redos T: 5% redos |
| Benchmarking | Answer phone | C: 60,120 T: | C: 4 rings T: 2 rings | C: T: |
| AFD | Move and maintain jetbridge | C: 1,010,000 T: 900,000 | C: 45 minutes T: 30 minutes | C: 85% on time T: 90% on time |
| Reverse engineering | Obtain FDA approval | C: 12,300 T: 10,000 | C: 5 years T: 2 years | C: 75% approval T: 80% approval |

C = current; T = target.

**(c) Match Resource to Goals**    Next, match resources to goals. Goals should be set to be achievable. Resources should be oriented toward goals. Identify improvements to business processes as well as activities.

**25.7 DETERMINE WORKLOAD**    There are three major steps in determining activity or business process workload:

1. Forecast service-determined activities or business processes.
2. Forecast non–service-related activities or business processes.
3. Forecast special projects.

**(a) Workload of Service-Determined Activities or Business Processes**    The first step in forecasting total organization workload is to forecast workload for service-determined activities:

- Identify activities for new services.
- Identify planned changes to services.
- Create/update a bill of activities for each service line.
- Forecast services by service lines rather than individual services, in most cases.
- Explode bill of activities to determine activity quantity for each service line.

**(b) Explode Bill of Activities**    To explode a bill of activities, simply list each service line and the forecasted quantity of that service line. List the units of each activity used by each service line. Then, multiply units of service times the units of each activity to calculate the activity quantity volume by service. Then, sum the total activity quantities.

| Service | Units of Service | Bill of Activity Units required for Each Service | Activity Quantities |
|---|---|---|---|
| Mortgages | 5,000 | Order report 3 | 15,000 |
| Auto loans | 1,800 | Order report 1 | 1,800 |
| Personal loans | 1,000 | Order report 1 | 1,000 |
| | | Total reports | 17,800 |

**(c) Workload for Non–Service-Related Activities**    The second step is to forecast work load of non–service-related activities. Non–service-related activities are those performed by support departments such as management information systems, human resources, security, and accounting.

| Activity Class | Activity measures |
|---|---|
| General management | Number of employees |
| Financial reporting | Number of financial reports |
| Corporate advertising | Number of TV advertisements |
| | Number of promotions |
| Marketing | Number of trade shows |
| | Number of market surveys |
| Research | Number of new services |
| Facilities | Number of square feet |

**(d) Workload for Special Projects**    The third step is to forecast workload for special projects. Examples of special projects include:

- Install activity-based management.
- Install activity-based budgeting.
- Install new computer system.
- Expand office.

Then, the organization needs to set up a calendar for each special project, with the activities and tasks listed by time period.

**25.8 ACTIVITY-BASED BUDGETING CALENDAR**

| | | | | | | |
|---|---|---|---|---|---|---|
| Brief senior management | * | | | | | |
| Select team | ** | | | | | |
| Select departments/services | | ** | | | | |
| Review activity definitions | | | **** | | | |
| Review strategic plan | | | | **** | | |
| Explode bill of activities | | | | | **** | |
| Start improvement projects | | | | | | *** |

Each * equals a week

**25.9 CREATE PLANNING GUIDELINES**    An organization should identify activity or business-process-level projects with the goal of continuous improvement. Look at the budgeted workload and divide it into mandatory, discretionary, and optional units for each activity or business process. This split helps to decide what portion of value-added activities to eliminate. For example, an organization might determine that it needs only one quote to purchase supplies. The workload to obtain quotes is the minimum mandatory work. Discretionary work occurs when the purchasing agent believes a lower price is obtainable through two quotes. For optional work, the agent feels better by getting three or four quotes, some of which are from noncertified vendors.

**25.10 IDENTIFY INTERDEPARTMENTAL PROJECTS**    The organization should look at its business processes to eliminate duplicate activities and synchronize the remaining ones. Consider the following business process to "procure supplies."

**(a) Activity-Based Budget for Procuring Supplies**

| Activity | | Labor | Technology | Facility | Utilities | Supplies | Travel | Other | Total |
|---|---|---|---|---|---|---|---|---|---|
| LY | PQ | 89,088 | | 7,827 | 1,293 | 1,075 | 4,000 | 162 | 103,445 |
| TY | | | | | | | | | |
| LY | IP | 101,479 | | 8,915 | 1,472 | 1,225 | 4,000 | 175 | 117,266 |
| TY | | | | | | | | | |
| LY | AP | 108,404 | 190,299 | 9,524 | 1,573 | 1,308 | 4,000 | 187 | 315,295 |
| TY | | | | | | | | | |
| LY | SS | 29,211 | | 2,568 | 424 | 353 | 5,562 | 50 | 38,168 |
| TY | | | | | | | | | |
| LY | MA | 65,545 | | 5,871 | 938 | 578 | 200 | 111 | 73,243 |
| TY | | | | | | | | | |

PQ = prepare quotes; IP = issue purchase order; AP = administer PO; SS = source supplies; MA = manage area; LY = last year; TY = this year.

After reviewing last year's total costs for each activity, the next step is to calculate last year's unit cost for each activity. For example, the activity "prepare quotes" cost $103,445. Last year, 2,000 quotes were prepared. By dividing annual quotes into total cost, the unit cost for this activity is $51.72 per quote.

| Activities | Workload Measures | Volume | Total Cost ($) | Unit Cost ($) | Target Cost ($) |
|---|---|---|---|---|---|
| Prepare quotes | Quotes | 2,000 | 103,445 | 51.72 | 50.00 |
| Issue purchase order (PO) | PO | 5,679 | 117,265 | 20.65 | 19.65 |
| Administer PO | PO | 5,679 | 315,295 | 55.52 | 53.00 |
| Source supplies | New suppliers | 100 | 38,167 | 381.68 | 375.00 |
| Manage area | Staff | 28 | 72,243 | 2,580 | 2,200 |

**(b) Activity-Based Budgeting Example of Target Cost**    The organization has set a target of $50 per quote. This is a reduction of $1.72 from last year's cost of $51.72 per quote. The improvement process for 2,000 quotes at $1.72 per quote results in a savings of $3,440. Managers feel that they can reduce supplies by $440 by keeping more information on the computer and less on paper. Travel could be reduced $1,000 by having more vendors come to the organization's offices. Because quotes will be kept on the computer, there will be a reduction in the filing activity, saving $2,000 for part-time employee wages and benefits.

**(c) Creative Thinking Approaches**    Continuous improvement requires innovative approaches to streamlining the way an activity is done. Although creativity is a very personal trait, studies have shown that certain environments and methods are better suited to drawing out creative ideas. Some of the more effective methods are:

- Challenging assumptions about:
  —People.
  —Supplies.
  —Business processes.
  —Location.
  —Capital.
  —Automation.
  —Activities.
- Viewing activities or business processes based on new assumptions.
- Perceiving patterns from other:
  —Division.
  —Offices.
  —Services.
  —Departments.
- Making connections with other organizations.
- Establishing networks between suppliers, suppliers' suppliers, you, customers, and end users.
- Exploiting failures (e.g., the glue for Post-It notes was too weak).
- Performing activity or business process backward and from the middle.
- Using idea triggers (e.g., a new idea for each of Baskin & Robbins 31 flavors).
- Creating superheroes.
- Imagining you are the service, activity, or business process.

**(d) Brainstorming**    Brainstorming techniques are fairly common today. They consist of:

- Suspending judgment until all ideas are on the table.
- Emphasizing quantity of ideas without worrying about quality.
- Stimulating a freewheeling session, with wild ideas encouraged.
- Involving people from throughout the organization.
- Reminding people that wild ideas often will fertilize the thinking process.

**(e) Storyboarding**  Storyboarding is a creativity tool that consists of using colored index cards to show business processes, activities, and tasks. The first step is to define the department mission statement. For a hotel, the department mission for the maids might be "to keep rooms clean in order to delight customers at a minimum cost."

| Activities | Stock Cart | Clean Rooms | Empty Carts |
|---|---|---|---|
| T | Stack towels | Empty trash | Dispose garbage |
| A | Stack linens | Change bedsheets | Separate linens/towels |
| S | Stack toiletries | Clean bathroom | Store cart/vacuum |
| K | Stack stationery | Restock toiletries | |
| S | Stack cleaning supplies | Replace towels | |
| | | Dust room | |
| | | Vacuum room | |
| | | Refill stationery | |

**(f) Value Management**  Value management is an organized way of thinking. It is an objective appraisal of functions performed by services and procedures. The focus is on necessary functions for the lowest cost. It increases reliability and productivity. Costs are decreased. Value management challenges everything an organization does.

It starts by gathering information such as:

- The purpose and use of each service.
- The operating and performance issues.
- The physical and environmental requirements.

For example, fresh fish must be kept cold. Jewelry must be kept in a secure environment. What types of support requirements are there? What problems exist? Which and how many liaison personnel are required? What are the economic issues?

These requirements are translated into required function of the service. Begin by determining the worth of each portion of the service. Then calculate the value improvement potential. What part of the service does the customer want? Which parts add cost? Which part is the customer willing to pay for?

Begin using creativity. Ask the customers to value different features. Ask suppliers for ideas. Use cross-functional teams and brainstorming. Use reverse engineering techniques and look at the competitor's services. Benchmark in other industries. Find the best customer service, warehousing, and order-fulfillment organization. Eliminate part of the service. How can the organization create more commonality of services and support services as well as common reports and forms?

Evaluate whether it would be better to buy a portion of the service from outside (e.g., catering/training/maintenance for airlines; check processing and MIS for banks; body work for car dealers; janitorial, engineering, waste collection for cities) or to perform those services and support services in-house. Analyze customer trade-off of cost and features. Calculate value versus cost to produce various portions of the service. Eliminate functions, procedures, and reports. Simplify procedures, business processes, and functions. Use alternate supplies, specifications, and methods. Shorten the service operation cycle with cross-training of departments.

**(g) Task-Level Analysis**   Sometimes it is useful to analyze the tasks of an activity to determine the improvement potential. For example, the activity "pay vendor invoice" has the following tasks:

| Task | Total | Non–Value-Added | Value-Added | Best Practice |
|------|-------|-----------------|-------------|---------------|
| Receive PO | .50 | .50 | | |
| Locate receiver (R) | .50 | .50 | | |
| Get vendor invoice (I) | .50 | .50 | | |
| Match PO, R, I | 2.00 | 2.00 | | |
| Enter data | 4.50 | | 4.50 | 2.00 |
| Determine errors | 2.50 | 2.50 | | |
| Expedite payment | 1.25 | 1.25 | | |
| Make payment: computer | 3.00 | | 3.00 | 2.75 |
| Make payment: manual | 1.00 | 1.00 | | |
| Document file | 3.00 | 1.50 | 1.50 | 1.25 |
| Total | 18.75 | 9.75 | 9.00 | 6.00 |

**25.11 IMPROVEMENT PROCESS**   The improvement process starts with creative thinking to determine solutions. An investment proposal is then prepared. Management selects the projects that have the highest priority in meeting customer needs. The solution is implemented and incorporated into the activity budget

**(a) Ranking Budget Requests**   After all the budget requests have been made, they are ranked. One convenient way to rank them is through a rating system in which management looks at the budget requests in comparison with the customer needs. Another useful tool is to classify them according to whether they support the current level of service or whether they are at the minimum or intermediate. "Current" implies that this is the cost of activities as they are presently performed. "Minimum" implies that this is the minimum level of service for an activity. "Intermediate" implies that this is not a final solution.

**(b) Impact of Projects**   Then the organization should look at the impact of these projects in terms of the change in workload, but also in terms of the changes in activity or business process cost.

**25.12 FINALIZING THE BUDGET**   Budget proposals are created for the most promising projects. They should be reviewed and the highest-priority projects selected. An implementation plan should be conceived. An activity impact report should be generated to include its cost impact, assuming no inflation or foreign currency issues. This allows for comparisons with previous activity or business-process performance. Finally, inflation and foreign currency should be incorporated into the budget.

**(a) Budget Review Panels**   Budget review panels should consist of cross-functional teams whose purpose is to question and review the budget. A review panel might consist of the directors, such support departments as human resources, administration, quality, finance, and operations.

**(b) Budgeting Options**    An organization has two options for activity budgeting. First, budget and report by activities. Second, budget by activities and convert the activity budget into a traditional cost element budget. In this second approach, the organization plans on an activity or business process basis. Managers would use activity costs per unit to determine cost elements. Then they would summarize by cost elements. This second approach is only temporary until the organization better understands how to manage by activities, and usually lasts for only a year.

**(c) Steps in Implementing**

| Activities/Tasks | Months | | | |
|---|---|---|---|---|
| | 1 | 2 | 3 | 4 |
| Train and educate | ** | | | |
| Perform strategic analysis | **** | | | |
| Forecast workload | ****** | | | |
| Establish planning guidelines | **** | | | |
| Propose interdepartmental | **** | | | |
| Propose activity improvement | ******** | | | |
| Select improvement options | ******* | | | |
| Finalize budget | *** | | | |

Each * equals one week.

**(d) Initial Project**    A steering group of three to five members should be created. A series of panels with five to six members from different departments should be created to discuss cross-departmental issues. Each budgeting unit should have a budgeting manager, who could be someone other than the department manager. There would be 10 to 20 budgeting units per in-house coordinator or per consultant.

**25.13 PERFORMANCE REPORTING**    The most effective reports are those that do not have to be made. Therefore, introduce proactive control rather than reactive cost monitoring wherever possible. Activity-based budgeting encourages this approach.

Emphasis should be made to control the process so that output is consistent. Also, make sure resources can be shifted when workload varies—workload seldom stays the same throughout the year. Plan and budget for using those slack times to improve the organization.

**(a) Data Capture**    There are three methods for data capture within an ongoing system. First, there are *dedicated resources.* Set up cost centers and define workload measures at the activity or business-process level. Second, there are *shared resources,* in which an organization does time reporting by activity. Third, use a *surrogate* in which actual outputs are used at a standard activity cost. Actual costs would be compared to total department earned cost in this approach. Total actual cost could also be compared to best-practices earned value.

## (b) Activity-Based Budget Report

| Department Total | | | Activity Analysis | | | |
|---|---|---|---|---|---|---|
| Expense | Budget ($) | Actual ($) | Issue Purchase Order | Certify Vendor | Expedite Order | Other |
| Wages | 180,000 | 180,000 | | | | |
| Supplies | 40,000 | 38,000 | | | | |
| Space | 30,000 | 30,000 | | | | |
| Equipment | 18,000 | 18,000 | | | | |
| Travel | 22,000 | 20,000 | | | | |
| Other | 10,000 | 8,000 | | | | |
| Total | 200,000 | 194,000 | | | | |

| Output measure | Total | Number of Purchase Orders | Number of Certifications | Number of Orders | |
|---|---|---|---|---|---|
| Charge rate | | $50 | $2,000 | $10 | $9,000 |
| Budgeted volume | | 3,000 | 20 | 100 | 1 |
| Budgeted value | 200,000 | $150,000 | $40,000 | $1,000 | $9,000 |
| Actual volume | | 2,700 | 18 | 90 | 1 |
| Earned value* | 181,000 | $135,000 | $36,000 | $900 | $9,000 |
| Earned-value variance | 13,000 | | | | |

*Charge rate times actual volume.

In this example, the organization budgeted the activity "issue purchase orders" at $50 per purchase order. It budgeted 3,000 purchase orders. This yielded a budgeted value for the "issue purchase order" activity of $150,000. The same activity budgeting process was followed for the remaining activities, including an "other" or miscellaneous category of activities. This yielded a total activity budget for this department of $200,000, which was backflushed into expense categories.

The actual expenses for the period were $194,000. Compared to the original budget of $200,000, this looks very good. However, when the earned value is calculated, the department is shown to have an earned value variance of $13,000. Earned value is calculated for each activity by multiplying the actual volume for each activity by that activity's charge rate. For the "issue purchase order" activity, the actual volume of 2,700 purchase orders when multiplied by the charge rate of $50 yields $135,000. The same calculation is made for all activities and the answers added for each department. This earned value total of $181,000 is compared to actual expenses of $194,000 to yield an earned value variance of a negative $13,000. This is a different picture than simply comparing actual ($194,000) with budget ($200,000), which yielded a favorable variance of $6,000. Managers can now use this as a planning tool as well as a means to operate the organization more efficiently.

(c) **Business-Process Reporting**   In business-process reporting, activity cost could be shown for each department, as well as for each business process that delivers a service. This is an exercise for organizations that are more advanced in ABB techniques.

**25.14 SUMMARY**    ABB gives managers the tools they need to make better decisions about running their organization. This budgeting technique spends most of the time on improvement rather than filling out forms, which is often the case with traditional budgeting. This technique gives managers a method to improve activities as well as business processes.

## SOURCES AND SUGGESTED REFERENCES

Antos, John J., "Activity-Based Management for Service, Not-for-Profit, and Government Organizations," *Journal of Cost Management,* vol. 6, no. 2, 1992.

Brimson, James A., and John J. Antos, *Activity-Based Management.* New York: John Wiley & Sons, 1994.

Brimson, James A., *Activity Accounting.* New York: John Wiley & Sons, 1991.

Brimson, James A., *Activity-Based Investment Management.* New York: American Management Association, 1989.

Brimson, James A., and John J. Antos, *Driving Value Using Activity-Based Budgeting.* New York: John Wiley & Sons, 1999.

# CHAPTER 26

# ACTIVITY-BASED COSTING SOFTWARE SELECTION

## Don Hansen
## David Murphy
**Oklahoma State University**

*It must be considered that there is nothing more difficult to carry out, nor more doubtful of success, nor more dangerous to handle than to initiate a new order of things. For the reformer has enemies in all those who profit by the old order, and only lukewarm defenders by all those who could profit by the new order. The lukewarmness arises partly from fear of their adversaries who have the laws in their favor, and partly from the incredulity of mankind who do not truly believe in anything new until they have had actual experience with it.*—Machiavelli, *The Prince*

**26.1 INTRODUCTION**  There seems to be a natural tendency, in almost all systems projects, to begin the project by selecting hardware and software based on preliminary and superficial understandings of information needs and processing requirements. The result of these implementations often is the modification of organizational structures and processes so that they mesh with the data structures and processing logic of the purchased systems. These modifications are driven by the software choice and not by strategic objectives of the organization, and it thus becomes difficult, if not impossible, to use the new information system as a tool to provide a competitive advantage. A better approach is to recognize that the selection and purchase of activity-based costing (ABC) software is just one step in a larger systems acquisitions process. Thus, ABC software acquisition should be integrated with this more general systems acquisitions process. Any discussion of ABC software selection should be placed within this context.

   This general acquisition process is defined by three phases, summarized in Exhibit 26.1. The process begins with systems planning. Systems planning ensures that the implementation of an ABC system (and its software) supports the organization's goals and objectives. The systems planning phase is followed by requirements definition. Requirements definition provides a complete and detailed listing of system specifications so that the software that best satisfies the indicated needs can be selected. The third phase, system selection, entails preparing and evaluating a request for proposal (RFP). An RFP is a formal document used in competitive bidding procedures to specify the functional requirements for a proposed system. In the case of ABC software, the RFP lists the software requirements and provides space for software vendors to enter their

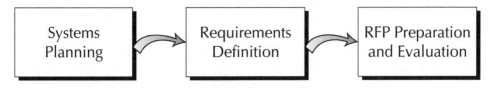

**Exhibit 26.1   Systems Acquisition Process**

prices, service agreements, and other terms. This systems selection process (which is a subset of the formal systems development life cycle) is appropriate for ABC projects provided that the new system will not replace an existing ABC system and that the organization has decided to purchase rather than build the new system.

**26.2 SYSTEMS PLANNING PHASE**   New systems are often the result of perceived internal needs rather than the product of a conscious strategic decision. In selecting and implementing an ABC system, an organization should consider such factors as:

- The objectives and direction established in the organization's long-range strategic plan.
- The organization's current and desired competitive position.
- The organization's business processes and product mix.
- The organization's ability to implement, learn, and use new information.

The objective of systems planning is to define systems development priorities and an implementation plan, thus ensuring that the system development activities are consistent with—and support—the organization's desired strategic position. Exhibit 26.2 shows the interrelationships between organizational and information systems planning and design.

As shown in Exhibit 26.2, all aspects of information systems (IS) planning should be driven by the organization's strategic plan.[1] First, the mission and strategy of the organization are specified. Next, goals and objectives related to IS are derived from the organization's strategy. The IS goals and objectives are then linked to other organizational goals and objectives.

An organization's information system cannot be used to help establish a competitive advantage if IS goals and objectives do not derive from the organization's strategy and are not explicitly linked to the remaining corporate goals and objectives. Furthermore, IS development activities are unlikely to receive the requisite support from top-management unless the IS activities are adequately planned and they support key strategic objectives.

A systems project to select and implement an ABC system is more likely to succeed if the corporation has defined specific strategic objectives relating to customers, processes, and shareholders.

Suppose, for example, a bank has decided to increase revenues by selling new financial service products to targeted customers. Timely access to accurate information about customers (e.g., Is this customer a member of the targeted segment?) and services (e.g., Which financial services fit this customer?) is essential for achieving the strategic objective of increasing revenues.

Information needs—primarily for decision making, monitoring, and control pur-

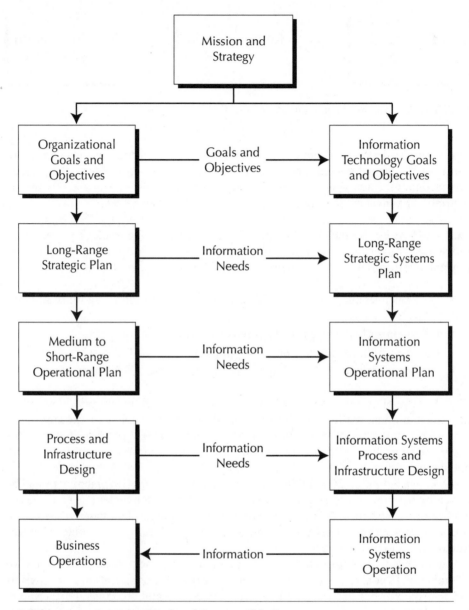

**Exhibit 26.2 Organizational and Systems Planning**

poses—are derived from the subsequent steps in the planning process. Organizational information needs are used to specify IS requirements and priorities. Finally, IS operations provide the information needed to support management decision-making processes.

**(a) Systems Planning Process** Exhibit 26.3 summarizes the steps in the IS planning process. A company first identifies its present position with respect to IS technology and its desired future goal state, then develops a plan to move toward the goal state as it follows the process steps identified in Exhibit 26.3.

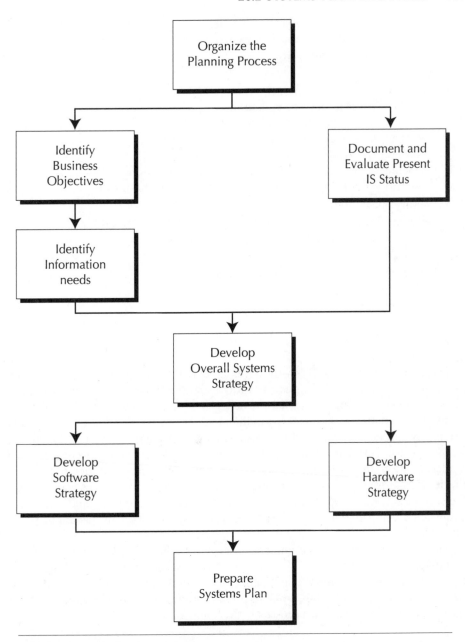

**Exhibit 26.3   IS Planning Process**

The critical activities in the project organization step include:

- Establishing an IS steering committee.
- Developing a project mission directive.
- Defining the project goals and objectives.
- Developing a project work program.
- Identifying project team members.

The identification of business objectives and the corresponding information needs can take place simultaneously with the documentation and evaluation of the present IS status. Key activities in these steps are:

- Identify business objectives:
  —Evaluate present scope of operations.
  —Review long-range strategic plan.
  —Review medium and short-range operational plans.
  —Review existing systems plans.
  —Document business objectives and systems implications.
  —Identify criteria for establishing systems development priorities.
- Identify information needs:
  —Review documented business objectives and system implications.
  —Interview management and user personnel.
  —Summarize functional requirements.
- Document and evaluate present IS status:
  —Document present IS.
  —Evaluate system operations and capacity.
  —Evaluate present technical capabilities.
  —Evaluate overall adequacy of present systems.

In the next step in the process—the development of an overall systems strategy—the planning team compares the status quo with the desired IS state and develops a "what" plan (i.e., a plan that identifies what the new systems environment should look like in terms of information technology capabilities and resources). The "how" of the plan is defined by specific software and hardware strategies or plans (which take technology trends into account) that identify specific systems to be implemented, the order of their implementation, the preferred methods of software development or acquisition, and the desired hardware platform for future operations. The overall systems plan as well as the specific software and hardware plans are then packaged, in the final step, into a strategic systems plan that should be reviewed and approved by management before the plan is implemented.

The decision to acquire and implement an ABC system should result from such a planning process. If it does not, there is a risk that ABC in general—including the specific ABC system selected—will fail to improve decision making and the organization's performance significantly. ABC systems present several new decision opportunities in the planning process that are discussed in the following section.

**(b) Activity-Based Costing Planning Considerations**    Three important planning considerations need to be explored:

1. The degree of ABC system integration.
2. ABC system interfaces.
3. Reconciliation of ABC with the general ledger.

Decisions relating to these issues are critical, because they cross system boundaries and affect other systems in addition to the ABC system.

*(i) System Integration*   Enterprise resource planning (ERP) software implementations have focused attention on the development and use of integrated systems—that is, systems that run *all* the operations of a company and provide access to real-time data from the various functional areas of a company.

Major ERP companies (including SAP, Oracle, and PeopleSoft) have entered the ABC software market recently by deciding to develop or acquire significant ABC modules for their ERP products.[2] SAP, for example, has acquired an equity interest in ABC Technologies (a market leader in ABC software), Oracle has purchased Activa (ABC software originally developed by Price Waterhouse LLP), and PeopleSoft has teamed up with KPMG to develop its ABC module. One reason for this interest, according to Shaw, is that the market for analytic applications is a major growth market: It is projected to grow from about $1 billion in 1997 to more than $2.6 billion in 2001.[3] ABC supposedly is the hottest analytic application expected for the next several years. Validating the emergence of ABC as a major accounting measurement system is one benefit of this ERP interest. A second benefit is the attention that ABC will now receive from higher-level management. Yet some concerns have been expressed that deserve mention.

For one, ERP software applications are functionally oriented and emphasize the use of real-time data to improve the efficiency of organizational units and processes. Thus, ERP software has been developed to support an organization's operational learning and control system. ABC systems, by contrast, were developed to help managers to improve their assessment of customer and product profitability and to identify opportunities for process improvement.[4] It also identifies other significant differences between operational control systems and ABC systems.

An operational control system (such as ERP software applications) is designed to provide managers with entity-based performance information. Performance information focuses on *responsibility centers* such as human resources, purchasing, and maintenance. Operational control is based on an *actual* costing system. Because performance efficiency is at issue, costs must be measured with a high degree of precision. Finally, an operational control system requires frequent updating: To support continuous improvement, timely, accurate, and detailed information is needed.

The scope of ABC systems is much broader than the organizational-unit perspective provided by an operational control system. ABC provides information about the entire value chain: suppliers, internal processes, and customers. Standard activity rates are computed based on the practical activity capacity; then costs are assigned by multiplying these standard rates by *actual* usage. Thus, the costs assigned to products, customers, and other cost objects are not the actual costs incurred (unless the actual activity usage happens to correspond to the practical capacity). Furthermore, because ABC is concerned with how much work can be done by an activity given a specific amount of resources (rather than how much work is actually done), only periodic updating is required. For example, activity rates have to be adjusted only when a permanent change in activity capacity or efficiency occurs.

Given that the purposes, scope, cost definitions, and other attributes of an ABC system differ so radically from those of an operational control system, it is entirely appropriate to view an ABC system as something that is separate and distinct from an operational control system. Everyone involved should recognize and accept the dual nature of cost systems and the need for two cost systems (i.e., different systems for different purposes), thus avoiding turf battles and other problems associated with the perception of system "duplication."

Although operational control systems and ABC systems are two distinct systems, the two systems should interface to exchange vital information. For example, Cooper and Kaplan note that the two systems should exchange information about efficiency, sustained operational improvements, and capacity usage.[5] In addition, the development of *activity-based budgeting* can strengthen the ties between the two systems.

Shaw classifies ABC software as *analytic application software*, which indicates that it should function independently of an organization's core transactions yet, at the same time, be *dependent* on the data resident in the ERP system (an operational control system).[6] Furthermore, ABC software should be able to send results *back to* the operational control system. For example, activity-based product costs calculated by an ABC system should act as input for pricing proposals obtained from the operational control system.

Thus, integration of ABC and operational control systems takes on a limited meaning. The outcome is *partial integration*, but it provides a level of integration that is vital for the two systems to exist in harmony. Two choices are available for an ABC system to achieve the targeted integration:

1. Use software from an integrated solution provider that has an ABC module (e.g., SAP or Oracle).
2. Select ABC software that has sufficient linking and importing capabilities to establish the necessary bridge between the operational and ABC systems.

This integration, if it takes place, should be planned during the systems planning phase. If the integration is not planned then, it will probably never take place (or the "integration" will take place only manually).

*(ii) Activity-Based Costing System Interfaces*    Before beginning the ABC system design and acquisition process, a company should identify the desired interfaces that should exist between existing and planned IS. For example, output from an ABC system may be used as input into *decision support systems* (DSS) used for cost estimating, product pricing, or planning and budgeting. Output from an ABC system may also be used as input for more traditional transaction processing systems (e.g., customer order quotation systems or logistics planning systems) and to more advanced systems, such as *executive information systems* (EIS) or *on-line analytical programs* (OLAP). An ABC system may complement the use of productivity tools as well, such as process modelers, business process flowchart generators, and activity schedulers. The synergies that develop from building interfaces between an ABC system and other systems can only be harnessed if the related systems are identified and the linkages are planned.

*(iii) General Ledger Reconciliation*    Traditional accounting systems are transaction oriented. Transaction data are captured, processed, and converted into journal entries; then the financial effects of the transactions are eventually posted to the general ledger. Data from the general ledger, in turn, are used to generate financial reports.

ABC systems, on the other hand, are process or activity oriented. ABC also can be used to calculate cost of goods sold and to value inventory. ABC cost assignments, however, follow managerial guidelines, which may differ from *generally accepted accounting principles* (GAAP). Thus, two different cost-and-profitability outcomes are produced. One of the two systems must be chosen for evaluating and rewarding performance. Theoretically, at least, the ABC system is the better choice, because it translates the general ledger into information useful for end users.[7] It makes more sense to base performance evaluation on information that is used and understood. Therefore, if ABC is used for evaluating and rewarding performance, reconciliation and adjustments will be required for the financial statements based on ABC to conform to GAAP.

**26.3 REQUIREMENTS DEFINITION PHASE**    The requirements definition phase is arguably the most critical phase in an ABC project. Problems with information systems result from errors and misunderstandings that may occur in any phase of the project. Exhibit 26.4 summarizes Finkelstein's reported distributions of error sources and correction effort.[8]

Requirements definition is the least technical of all of the phases in the systems development process, yet it is the phase in which most errors originate and which require the most effort to correct. Incomplete and incorrect requirements definitions lead to the selection, modification, and installation of suboptimal systems.

The objective of the requirements definition phase is to define *what* the ABC system will do, but not *how* it will accomplish those tasks. Consequently, the goal of this phase is to develop functional—not technical—system specifications. These specifications will be used in the following phase to develop a formal *request for quotation* (RFQ). Exhibit 26.5 identifies the major steps in this phase.

**(a) Organize the Requirements Definition Phase**    Phase organization is the first step in the requirements definition phase. The composition of systems project teams changes from phase to phase, because different skills and expertise are required in each phase. To maintain a sense of continuity in the project, new team members should review the project history so that they understand and accept the decisions made before they became part of the new team. During phase organization, the project manager (with input from the team members) should revise the project work program. The work program identifies the tasks to be completed, the responsible team member, the working papers and other documentation to be prepared, and the deadline. The work program is the primary project management tool used by the project manager to ensure that the project is completed on schedule. Functional requirements definition can begin once the phase has been organized.

**(b) Define Functional Requirements**    Defining in detail *what* the ABC system will do is necessary so that a functional request for proposals can be prepared. The activities in-

| Error Source | Percentage of Errors | Pecentage of Error Correction Effort |
|---|---|---|
| Requirements definition | 56% | 82% |
| System design | 27% | 13% |
| Programming | 7% | 1% |
| Other | 10% | 4% |

**Exhibit 26.4    Error Sources and Correction Effort.** *Source:* C. Finkelstein, *An Introduction to Information Engineering: From Strategic Planning to Information Systems* (Reading, MA: Addison-Wesley, 1989).

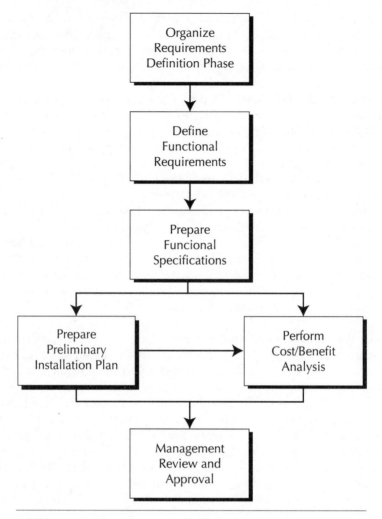

**Exhibit 26.5    Requirements Definition Phase**

cluded in this step include the identification of system-specific functional requirements, information needs, performance, security, control and audit objectives, and output and input design and processing requirements.

*(i) Identify Functional Requirements*    As noted in Exhibit 26.4, most of the errors or problems in systems originate in this phase of a project, so it is critical that the project team carefully consider the needs of the organization. The project team in this phase needs to specify the characteristics of the ABC system. Key issues to be addressed include the identification of:

- Objectives of the ABC system.
- Primary users.
- Activity identification (type and number of activities to be used).
- Resource types.

- Required number of activity layers for cost assignment.
- The need for reciprocal activity costing.
- Activity and resource drivers.
- Cost objects and their levels.
- Bill of activities.
- Sources of data and methodologies for data extraction.

The objective of an ABC system is to provide strategic cost information about the underlying economics of a business. It does so by providing cost assignments that are based on cause-and-effect, demand-driven consumption patterns. By providing more accurate information, managers can identify opportunities for improvement and better manage a firm's resources. Early in the design phase it is also important to identify the intended primary users of the ABC system. These individuals should be expected to provide necessary input for the specification of *functional design parameters*. If an ABC system encompasses the entire value chain, users of ABC will be found in all functional areas, including research and development, purchasing, manufacturing, sales, and customer services.

Before selecting an ABC system, it is necessary to specify the *systems parameters* so that the most appropriate software solution can be selected. Interviews with key employees are a common way to identify activities. Once identified, resource costs are assigned to the individual activities using *resource drivers* or to cost objects by *direct tracing* (e.g., direct materials, a resource cost, is assigned to products by direct tracing). The cost of activities is then assigned to other activities or to cost objects using *activity drivers*.

ABC software consequently must have at least three distinct levels or *modules*: resources, activities, and cost objects. Modules are structures that allow a user to enter, manipulate, and view data. For example, an activity module contains activities, a resource module contains resource expense accounts, and a cost object module contains cost objects.

ABC software should also provide the ability to assign costs both within and between modules. Cost assignments are based on the drivers and the quantities consumed by the object receiving the costs. Drivers are the factors that define the cost assignments. The particular cost assignment paths allowed by ABC software should be carefully considered. For example, *secondary* or *support* activities are consumed by other activities or by an intermediate cost object (e.g., purchased components). *Primary* activities are consumed by final cost objects (e.g., product or customers). The costs of secondary activities must be assigned to the activities that consume them.

Therefore, questions such as the following need to be answered:

- Does the ABC software allow the assignment of one activity to another?
- What if the activity is being consumed by an activity that, in turn, is consumed by another activity?
- How many layers of activity consumption are needed, and which software packages satisfy this requirement?
- What if reciprocal relationships exist among secondary or support activities?
- If reciprocal relationships are viewed as significant, does the software allow reciprocal cost assignments?

As a final example, consider data entry. The resource module requires entry of resource cost data—data that come from the general ledger. Does the ABC software have an interface that allows these data to be imported, or must they be entered manually?

*(ii) Identify Information Needs*    Information needs derived from the system objectives and the primary system users are used to define system output requirements. Information needs are usually defined by first identifying the critical decisions made by the key users of the system, then identifying the information needed to support those decisions.

An ABC system is of little use if it cannot provide the information required by the key users of the system. For example, a company's environmental cost manager may wish to identify all environmental activities so that environmental costs can be assigned to products and processes. Knowing the environmental product costs may be essential to reducing costs by changing product design or product mix. Similarly, a purchasing manager may wish to have all costs caused by suppliers traced to individual suppliers so that better supplier-selection decisions can be made. If this information is passed on to individual suppliers, it may also help improve supplier performance.

*(iii) Identify Performance, Security, Control, and Audit Objectives*    Consideration must be given to the environment in which a system will operate, the importance of the information generated by the system, and the number of system users. These parameters will help identify the need for specific performance, security, control, and audit objectives.

For example, if a system is expected to operate in an environment in which physical security is difficult to maintain, logical access control (e.g., password protection) may be important. If the system is going to operate in a network with multiple users, password protection will be important and should also be supplemented by maintenance of a system log to report user accesses and actions. Performance requirements such as maximum acceptable response time may be established if the system is mission critical and if the information generated will support real-time decision making.

*(iv) Design Output and Input*    When an information system is developed, it is common to design system outputs before specifying inputs. Users are interested in the information that they will receive from the system but generally less interested in the input required to generate the needed output. Once information needs and performance, security, control, and audit objectives have been specified, it is possible to package the required information into screens and reports. Generic, but common, reports generated by ABC systems include:

- Activity reports:
  - —Bill of activities.
  - —Resource consumption by activity.
  - —Activity capacity usage.
- Cost and profitability reports:
  - —Profitability by dimension (e.g., product, customer, or channel).
  - —Cost by dimension (e.g., products, suppliers, or customers).
  - —Value-added and non–value-added costs.
  - —Non–value-added cost reports.
  - —Environmental cost reports.
  - —Quality cost reports.

- Control reports:
  —Table data listing.
  —Error-tracking reports.
  —Input/output control reports.

Once the required outputs are identified, it is possible to specify the inputs needed to generate the desired outputs, along with the sources of those inputs. Future system maintenance is facilitated if information about resources and cost drivers can be obtained from the existing information systems. Production managers and line personnel tend not to support additional data collection activities.[9] In addition, a report by Ness and Cucuzza indicates that the ability to provide all the operational data required by an ABC system from existing information systems with additional data collection efforts is a critical success factor for an ABC implementation.[10] This information will be used either to verify that all required input data can be obtained from existing productions systems or to determine that additional data collection processes and systems will need to be designed and implemented.

*(v) Processing Requirements*    A project team must think about the ways in which the ABC system will be used to identify specific processing requirements. One of the first issues to be addressed is the potential need for reciprocal costing. Exhibit 26.6 summarizes the processing features of a sample of ABC software packages.

Reciprocal costing is important for some organizations (especially service organizations) that maintain complex support activities in their value chain. Reciprocal allocation allows costs from one support activity to be allocated to another while costs from the second activity—which also provides support activities to the first—are allocated as well. For example, some information service activities and their associated costs may need to be allocated to the accounting function, even though the accounting function also provides services (and thus, associated allocatable costs) to the information systems function. Not all ABC systems support reciprocal allocation before selecting an ABC package, so it is important to determine whether this feature is needed.

An analysis of reporting and decision-making requirements will help determine the most appropriate system architecture. Two common ABC system architectures are *bill-of-material* and *process-assignment architectures.*

Resources are assigned from activities to products and services in the bill-of-materials approach. This approach facilitates analysis from cost objects (back through activity drivers) to unique activities and then back from activities (through resource drivers) to resources or accounts. Resources are assigned from activities to processes and finally to cost objects in the process-assignment architecture.

The bill-of-materials approach provides for more reporting flexibility and transparency, whereas the process-assignment approach facilitates data collection and process modeling—but at the cost of detail that may be required for operational analysis. Critical decisions must be made about the needs for (and importance of) reporting flexibility and transparency, ease of data collection, and process modeling because of the benefit trade-offs that arise between the two architectures.

Some ABC systems generate *data cubes.* A data cube is a multidimensional hierarchy of aggregate values in which values higher in the hierarchy are aggregations of the values found lower in the hierarchy. With this hierarchical organization, users can easily navigate between high- and low-precision views of the same aggregate data. The

| Product | ABECAS | ABECAS C/S | Activity Analyzer | CostControl 4.0 |
|---|---|---|---|---|
| Company | Argos Software | Argos Software | Lead Software | QPR Software |
| Platforms | DOS | Windows 95<br>Windows 98<br>Windows NT | Windows 95<br>Windows 98<br>Windows NT | Windows 95<br>Windows 98<br>Windows NT |
| Networks supported | Novel<br>Windows NT | Novel<br>Windows NT | Banyan<br>Novel<br>Windows NT | Windows NT |
| System database | C-Tree | Interbase<br>Microsoft SQL 7.0<br>Oracle | Foxpro | Access 95<br>Access 97<br>Borland Paradox<br>Informix<br>Oracle<br>Sybase |
| Open database | No | No | No | No |
| Quantitative limit | No | No | No | No |
| Language | ARGOL | Delphi | Visual FoxPro 5.0 | Borland Delphi |
| Code availability | No | No | No | No |
| Disk requirement | 400 Mb | 400 Mb | 50 Mb | 10 Mb |
| Memory requirement | 64 Mb | 64 Mb | 32 Mb | 32 Mb |
| Password protection | Yes | Yes | Yes | Yes |
| Multiuser licensing | Yes | Yes | Yes | Yes |
| Cost Allocation | R-A-C | R-A-C | R-A-C | R-A-C<br>R-C |
| Functional modeling | Yes | Yes | Yes | Yes |
| ABC model | Bill-of-activity | Bill-of-activity | Bill-of-activity | Bill-of-activity<br>Process<br>assignment |
| Reciprocal costing | N/A | N/A | Yes | Yes |
| Data cubes | N/A | N/A | Yes | No |
| Interfaces | N/A | Spreadsheet<br>interfaces are<br>planned | Access<br>Cognos Powerplay<br>Excel<br>FoxPro<br>Lotus<br><br>All ODBC<br>compliant DSS<br>tools | Access<br>Cognos Powerplay<br>Excel<br>FoxPro<br>Lotus<br>ProcessGuide<br>QPR Scorecard<br>QPR<br>Quattro Pro |
| Data export | ASCII format | Yes | Yes | No |
| Profit analysis | Yes | Yes | Yes | Yes |
| Price | N/A | N/A | $7,500 - $25,000 | $9,995 |
| Contact | argos@<br>argosoftware.com | argos@<br>argosoftware.com | leadsoftware@<br>compuserve.com | jonathan.nye@<br>aprsoftware.com |
| Company | Modus Operandi | Sapling Corp. | ABC Technologies | Prodacapo AB |
| Platforms | Windows 3.1<br>Windows 95<br>Windows 98<br>Windows NT | Windows 95<br>Windows NT | Windows 3.1 or<br>later<br>Windows NT | Windows 3.1<br>Windows 95<br>Windows 98<br>Windows NT |
| Networks supported | N/A | Banyan<br>Novel<br>Windows NT<br>Unix | Banyan<br>Novel<br>Windows NT | Novel<br>Windows NT |

**Exhibit 26.6  Characteristics of a Sample of ABC Systems**

| Product | is/Modeler 4.00 | NetProphet | Oros | PRODACAPO S1 |
|---|---|---|---|---|
| System database | Proprietary | Access 95<br>Access 97<br>Oracle<br>Peoplesoft<br>OLAP compliant | ODBC compliant databases | Access 2.0 |
| Open database | No | Yes | N/A | Yes |
| Quantitative limit | No | No | No | 250 activities/dept<br>20,000 cost pool records |
| Language | C++ | N/A | C/C++ | Visual Basic |
| Code availability | No | N/A | N/A | No |
| Disk requirement | 2.75 MB | N/A | Server: 140 MB<br>Client: 14 MB | 100 MB |
| Memory requirement | 16 MB | N/A | 8 MB<br>16 MB recommended | 32 MB |
| Password protection | No | Yes | N/A | Yes |
| Multiuser licensing | Yes | Yes | N/A | Yes |
| Cost allocation | R-A-C<br>R-C | R-A-C | Multidimensional cost object allocation | R-A-C |
| Functional modeling | Yes | Yes | Yes | Yes |
| ABC model | Bill-of-activity | Process assignment | N/A | Bill-of-activity<br>Process assignment |
| Reciprocal costing | No | Yes | N/A | N/A |
| Data cubes | No | Yes | N/A | Yes (late spring 1999) |
| Interfaces | Excel | Access<br>Excel<br>Cognos Powerplay<br>Forest and Trees | Text file import<br>ODBC drivers | Access<br>Cognos Powerplay<br>Excel |
| Data export | No | Yes | N/A | No |
| Profit analysis | Yes | Yes | Yes | Yes |
| Price | $1,895/license | $7,500 - $67,850 | N/A | N/A |
| Contact | mwolf@<br>modusoperandi.com | ledmonds@<br>sapling.com | N/A | Prodacapo Support<br>support@<br>prodacapo.com |

*Note:* All data were provided by the respective vendors and was not independently confirmed.

*Key:* **N/A** = Not answered

    **Open database** = A database environment in which users can formulate their own inquiries and access the database directly.

    **Quantitative limit** = A limit on the number of activities, cost pools, or cost drivers that the system can maintain.

    **Code availability** = The ability of the purchaser to access and modify program code.

    **Cost allocation**

        R-A-C = Resource-Activity-Cost Object

        R-C = Resource to Cost Object

    **Functional modeling** = The ability of a system to trace allocated resource costs to functional entities such as cost centers, employees, and customers.

    **ABC model** = The model approach that the package uses to allocate costs.

    **Data export** = The ability of a system to export data to an external system through either a custom-designed link package or through the use of an open database environment.

    **Profit analysis** = The ability of the system to provide multidimensional profitability analysis (e.g., cost reporting by product, customer, and distribution channel).

**Exhibit 26.6    Continued**

hierarchical organization supports *drill-down*, an operation that increases the level of detail of the aggregate data being viewed, and *roll-up*, which decreases that level of detail.

For example, suppose a manager is using a data cube to look at monthly sales for a particular product line and notices that sales in January were low. The manager might drill down to look at monthly sales by model within the product line or roll up to a higher level of aggregation to look at sales for all product lines combined.

Many companies have begun to use OLAP and the ability of the ABC system to interface with OLAP software, as noted earlier, may be an important processing feature. All OLAP share the common attribute of multidimensionality (the ability to analyze data using several views: customer profitability, product profitability, activity cost, etc.), and even some non-OLAP products also exhibit this attribute. OLAP products in addition exhibit the characteristics of sharing rapid information and multidimensional information analysis. Rapid analysis usually means that the system usually responds to an inquiry within 1 second, though a few applications require more than 20 seconds.

Information analysis implies that a system can perform any application and user-relevant logical or statistical analysis using the multidimensional shared database. Because the data are shared, an OLAP system must implement all the security requirements for confidentiality (possibly down to the cell level) and, if multiple write access is needed, provide concurrent update locking at an appropriate level. Finally, OLAP systems provide a multidimensional conceptual view of the data, like that provided by data cubes. Clearly, if a company is using or contemplating the use of OLAP software, the ability to export data from the ABC system to the OLAP database (or to give the OLAP software access to the ABC system's database) becomes an important processing feature.

The ability to interface with office productivity tools (e.g., spreadsheet and word processing packages), decision support systems, and accounting systems (e.g., the general ledger) is another important processing feature. Some packages interface directly with specific applications (see Exhibit 26.6 for a summary); others provide such an interface through *open database connectivity* (ODBC) drivers.

ODBC is a core component of Microsoft Windows Open Services Architecture and is based on the *call level interface* specification of the SQL Access Group. This interface has emerged as the industry standard for data access for both Windows-based and Macintosh-based applications. ODBC provides an interface that permits data access in a heterogeneous environment of relational and nonrelational database management systems. Thus, it provides an open, vendor-neutral way of accessing data stored in a variety of proprietary personal computer, minicomputer, and mainframe databases. With ODBC, application developers can allow an application to concurrently access, view, and modify data from multiple, diverse databases. ODBC offers powerful capabilities that support client/server on-line transaction processing and DSS applications, including system table transparency, full transaction support, scrollable cursors, asynchronous calling, array fetch and update, a flexible connection model, and stored procedures for "static" SQL performance.

The ability to directly access data in an ABC system's database to facilitate the execution of ad hoc inquiries or to generate special reports not provided by the software is an important and powerful feature. However, as shown in Exhibit 26.6, not all ABC systems support an open database architecture. Some vendors, such as PROMODEL Corporation, do provide a proprietary query language so that users can formulate their own ad hoc inquiries.

**(c) Prepare Functional Specifications**    The results of a functional needs analysis are summarized in a functional specifications report. This report should be reviewed and approved by user representatives and management, because it serves as the basis for the preparation of a request for proposals.

**(d) Prepare Preliminary Installation Plan**    Assuming that management decides to continue the process of acquiring an ABC system, management should receive a cost-benefit report that summarizes all the costs and benefits associated with the proposed system. The preparation of the preliminary installation plan is necessary so that the related project costs can be estimated and also to ensure that no critical steps in the installation process are omitted.

*(i) Identify Installation Steps*    The first step in preparing an installation plan is to identify the steps in the process.

The following list identifies common steps in this process:

- Development of user procedures:
  —Develop security and control procedures.
  —Develop data generation and input procedures.
  —Prepare a user manual.
  —Prepare a training manual.
- Preparation of a conversion plan:
  —Develop conversion procedures.
  —Develop test plan and procedures.
- Site preparation:
  —Prepare a physical site preparation.
  —Prepare network configuration and physical installation.

*(ii) Establish Personnel Requirements*    One of the critical outcomes of installation planning is the identification of those who will interact with the new system. These individuals include the system users, people who will generate and prepare system input, and people who will receive and use the resulting outputs. Other key individuals include those who will be responsible for system maintenance, user training, the help desk, documentation maintenance, the data dictionary, and the process model maintenance. The time allocation of these individuals to the project should be estimated so that the cost of their efforts can be used for the cost-benefit report.

*(iii) Develop Conversion Approach*    The conversion approach selected for system implementation will depend (at least in part) on whether the new ABC system will be used as a *replacement* for an existing system or simply an enhancement to existing systems.

If the new ABC system will replace an existing system, the project team must decide between parallel and direct conversions. In parallel conversions the old system and the ABC system operate in parallel for a while to ensure that the new system works properly. In direct conversions, use of the old system is discontinued and the new system is placed into production. The second alternative is more risky but usually also less costly. If the new ABC system will be used to enhance current systems, a direct conversion is likely to be most appropriate. The project team must (after selecting the conversion approach) estimate the cost of the conversion effort so that it can be included in the cost-benefit report.

*(iv) Develop Installation Work Plan*    Once an installation effort has been planned, the project team should develop an in-depth work plan that identifies the specific steps in the installation process with individual task assignments and completion time estimates. This information will be used to control the installation phase once the software has been selected and purchased.

**(e) Perform Cost-Benefit Analysis**    A cost-benefit analysis should be prepared and documented so that management can make an informed decision about acquiring the ABC system. Costs that should be included in the cost-benefit analysis include:

- Estimated acquisition cost.
- Estimated installation cost.
- Estimated operating costs.

It is much easier to estimate system costs than it is to quantify the benefits that the new system will provide. Nevertheless, an attempt should be made to quantify the value of the new ABC system in terms of operating efficiencies—for example, the elimination of non–value-added activities that results from process modeling and cost management—as well as the value of better information. In addition, the cost-benefit analysis should identify and discuss the intangible (unmeasurable) benefits of the new system.

The results of the cost-benefit study are summarized in an economic feasibility report that is forwarded to management with the functional system specifications. These two documents provide management the information required to make an informed decision about system selection.

**26.4 SYSTEMS SELECTION PHASE**    The objective of the system selection phase is to select the ABC software package that best meets the company's information and processing needs. Exhibit 26.7 summarizes the activities included in this phase. Some of these activities are discussed in detail in the next sections.

**(a) Establish Software and Hardware Direction**    Once the functional specifications for the system are defined and documented, the project team should initiate a make-or-buy decision. A company with sufficient technical expertise may decide that its processing needs are sufficiently unique to warrant in-house development of an ABC system. In-house development (the "make" alternative) should lead to a software package that exactly meets the organization's information and processing. This approach provides optimal flexibility, but it also has its drawbacks. First, the software development cost cannot be allocated over a number of customers, so it must be borne entirely by the developing company. Second, the "make" approach promises a package that is tailored to the specific needs of the company, but there is no guarantee that the system will work as planned—or even that it will work. Hence, the "make" approach is usually viewed as both more costly and more risky than the "buy" approach. It should be used only when information and processing requirements are so unique that the "buy" approach is not feasible.

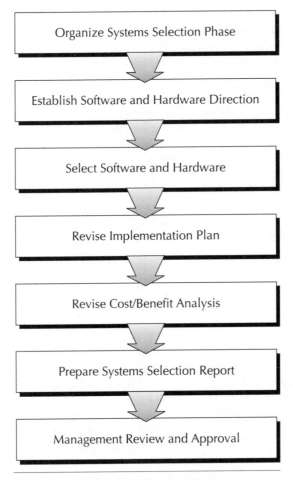

**Exhibit 26.7    Systems Selection Phase**

The alternative to the "make" approach is to purchase an ABC package that has been developed by a software firm. This approach is usually less costly and presents a lower level of risk. However, the purchased software may not meet all of the information and processing needs of the company. A company faces two alternatives when this occurs. One alternative is to change its internal processes so that they are consistent with those assumed by the software. The other alternative is to modify the purchased software so that it more closely meets the company's own identified needs. This approach may be implemented if:

- The purchasing company has the required technical expertise.
- The software vendor will sell the system source code.

If either of these two prerequisites are not met, the purchaser may explore the possibility of contracting with the vendor to make the necessary modifications in the software. We assume from here on, however, that ABC software (with or without modification) will be purchased from a vendor, not developed in-house.

Once a company decides on a software direction, it can select hardware. Again, there are two common alternatives. The company may install the software on existing hardware, or it may acquire new hardware. If the decision is made to acquire new hardware, no decisions should be made until the software is selected, because there is a risk that the new hardware will be inconsistent with the hardware requirements of the purchased software.

**(b) Select Software and Hardware**    The first step in both software and hardware selection is the preparation of an RFP. This is followed by the identification of qualified vendors, the evaluation of vendor proposals, the selection of a specific system, and negotiation of a purchase or licensing contract.

*(i) Prepare Request for Proposal*    An RFP is a formal document that specifies functional system requirements. The alternative to an RFP is an RFQ, which is a technical design document. An RFP specifies *what* the ABC system should do, whereas an RFQ specifies both *what* the system should do and *how* it should do it. An RFQ usually includes technical systems documentation, such as screen and report layout diagrams, database definitions, and the specification of processing logic. The primary advantages of RFPs are that they take advantage of the potential vendor's technical capabilities and knowledge of its software. An RFP is also relatively easy to prepare. Appendix A summarizes the contents of an RFP.

An RFP is normally accompanied by a cover letter that notifies prospective vendors that the company is requesting proposals for a specific information system. The cover letter should also specify critical dates, such as the proposal due date and the expected system installation date. Finally, the cover letter should identify the person whom the potential vendor may contact about the RFP.

The first section of the RFP, as shown in Appendix A, provides background information about the company. This information is provided to help the potential vendors understand the scope and complexity of the organization and the required information system. This section of the RFP includes a short history and description of the organization, an overview of relevant existing systems, and a summary of problems and needs to be addressed by the proposed system.

The second section of the RFP usually includes a statement of the objectives and scope of proposed system, a narrative description of the proposed system, and a functional requirements questionnaire.

The functional requirements questionnaire is the most critical part of the RFP. It lists, in questionnaire format, the features and functions that the new system must perform. The prospective vendors indicate whether their proposed system complies with and meets the specified functional requirements (and also how). The questionnaire may request information about the vendor's history, background, clients, training, and maintenance programs. It may also ask information about the performance, reliability, and security of the system.

The cost summary section of the RFP asks the vendor to specify the costs of its proposed information system—not only initial system acquisition cost but also any recurring costs, such as update fees and system maintenance costs. The vendor should also be asked to identify the cost of items (e.g., documentation) that may be purchased separately or for which there may be a unit purchase cost.

It is important to specify how RFPs will be evaluated. A common technique is to divide system functions into mandatory and optional categories. Systems that do not comply with all the mandatory functions and features are eliminated from consideration. The functions and features in the optional category are subjectively weighted in terms of relative importance, then degree of compliance with those optional features is used to rank-order all systems not eliminated earlier. Appendix A includes a list of additional factors that may be used to evaluate proposals.

*(ii) Identify Qualified Vendors*    The next step in the process is to identify vendors that may be able to provide software that meets the identified needs. Industry publications and the Internet are good sources of information for vendor identification. Care should be taken, however, to identify vendors that have a good track record and will be available over the long run to provide software support and updates.

There are few barriers to entry in the software industry, so software vendors seem to come and go. One website, prepared in 1995, lists 16 different ABC packages. Only five of the packages appear available (in early 1999).

Appendix B provides summaries of a small sample of ABC packages, those included in Exhibit 26.6, to provide an idea of the capabilities of different packages and vendors.

*(iii) Evaluate Proposal*    Proposal evaluation usually begins about four to six weeks after an RFP is issued. This provides prospective vendors sufficient time to respond to the RFP. A selection review committee should quickly review all of the proposals and eliminate those proposals that do not conform to the minimum system requirements. For example, if reciprocal cost is a mandatory feature, any systems that do not support reciprocal costing would be eliminated. Similarly, RFPs whose cost greatly exceeds the acquisition budget may also be eliminated at this time.

Proposals that remain in consideration then undergo a detailed evaluation to consider optional features. The objective of this evaluation is to identify a small number of systems, usually two or three, for testing and evaluation. This final evaluation may involve reference calls, site visits to companies that have installed the software, and the use of benchmark data to compare system performance, ease of use, and information usability.

*(iv) Negotiate Contract*    Once a final system is selected, the company begins contract negotiations with the vendor. The objectives of contract negotiation are to:

- Identify and define buyer expectations in order to avoid future misunderstandings.
- Define the available remedies should the vendor fail to comply with the contract.
- Protect the buyer against unexpected events, such as the bankruptcy of the vendor (it is common to stipulate, for example, that, in the case of bankruptcy or other dissolution, the vendor will provide copies of all technical system documentation and source code to the buyer at no additional cost).
- Provide for the best possible terms for the buyer.

The following guidelines should be followed by the buyer's negotiating team:

- Seek the advice of an attorney who specializes in computer contract law.
- Do not accept the vendor's standard contract. (Standard contracts are usually one-sided, disclaim all responsibility for performance and support, and are designed to protect the vendor not the buyer.)

- Negotiate with a representative who has the authority to bind the vendor to the negotiated contract.
- Do not accept oral promises; put everything in writing.
- Negotiate in good faith and do not make unreasonable demands.

**(c) Revise Implementation Plan**    After a contract for the purchase of software (and, potentially, also hardware) is signed, the project team can identify a realistic system installation date. Also, identification of a specific software package may make changes to the implementation plan necessary. The project team should therefore review the implementation plan and make any adjustments necessary to activities, activity sequences, and activity start and completion dates.

**(d) Revise the Cost-Benefit Analysis**    The cost-benefit analysis previously prepared used an estimate of system acquisition and installation costs, so it should be revised to show actual system acquisition costs and a better estimate of implementation costs (i.e., one based on the revised implementation plan).

**(e) Prepare System Selection Report**    A system selection report is a formal report to management that summarizes the activities performed during a project. The report should include the following sections:

- Management summary.
- A copy of the formal RFP.
- A list of vendors from whom RFPs were solicited and which ones replied.
- A summary of the evaluation of RFPs and justification of the selected system.
- A copy of the negotiated contract.
- A copy of the revised implementation plan.
- A copy of the revised cost-benefit analysis.

**(f) Management Review and Approval**    Management should review the report and either approve the acquisition and installation of the selected software or reject the software selection. (If the latter, management should provide further guidance.)

**26.5 SUMMARY**    Selecting an ABC system and the software to be used requires a thorough and structured approach consisting of three phases:

1. Systems planning.
2. Requirements definition.
3. Systems selection (RFP preparation and evaluation).

The planning phase is important because it ensures that the selection of an ABC system and software will support the achievement of the organization's strategic objectives. It also identifies the important conceptual issues, such as the degree of integration needed and the need for critical interface with other software applications. Requirements definition details the functions desired for an ABC system. This phase is critical and must be carefully developed: Most problems and errors with an ABC system can be traced to incomplete or incorrect requirements specifications. The final phase selects the software package that best meets the company's information and processing needs. Software selection is an important decision, but its value to the company depends on how well the information and processing needs are specified.

## NOTES

1. R. S. Kaplan and D. P. Norton, *The Balanced Scorecard* (Boston, MA: Harvard Business School Press, 1996).
2. R. Shaw, "ABC and ERP: Partners at Last?" *Management Accounting* (November 1998): 56–58.
3. Ibid.: 57.
4. R. Cooper and R. Kaplan, "The Promise and Peril of Integrated Cost Systems," *Harvard Business Review* (July–August 1998): 109–119.
5. Ibid.: 112–113.
6. Shaw, op. cit.: 57.
7. G. Cokins, "If Activity-Based Costing is The Answer, What is the Question?" *IIE Solutions* (August 1997): 38–42.
8. C. Finkelstein, *An Introduction to Information Engineering: From Strategic Planning to Information Systems* (Reading, MA: Addison-Wesley, 1989).
9. K. Krumwiede and H. Roth, "Implementing Information Technology Innovations: The Activity-Based Costing Example," *S. A. M. Advanced Management Journal* (Autumn 1997): 4–12.
10. Ibid.

## SUGGESTED READINGS

Cooper, R. and R. Kaplan. "The Promise and Peril of Integrated Cost Systems." *Harvard Business Review* (July–August, 1998): 109–119.

Cokins, G. "If Activity-Based Costing Is the Answer, What Is the Question?" *IIE Solutions* (August 1997) 38–42.

Finkelstein, C. *An Introduction to Information Engineering: From Strategic Planning to Information Systems*. Reading, MA: Addison-Wesley, 1989.

Kaplan, R. S. and D. P. Norton. *The Balanced Scorecard*. Boston, MA: Harvard Business School Press, 1996.

Krumwiede, K. and H. Roth, "Implementing Information Technology Innovations: The activity-based costing example." *S. A. M. Advanced Management Journal* (Autumn 1997): 4–12.

Lead Software, Inc., web site www.leadsoftware.com, accessed March 8, 1999.

Modus Operandi, Inc., web site at www.ismodeler.com, accessed March 8, 1999.

Ness, J. and T. Cucuzza. "Tapping the Full Potential of ABC." *Harvard Business Review* (July–August 1995): 130–138.

Prodacapo AB, web site at www.prodacapo.com, accessed March 8, 1999.

QPR Software Inc., web site www.qprsoftware.com, accessed March 8, 1999.

Shaw, R. "ABC and ERP: Partners at Last?" *Management Accounting* (November, 1998): 56–58.

## APPENDIX A    REQUEST FOR PROPOSAL

1. Executive summary
2. Background information
    a. History and description of the organization
    b. Overview of relevant existing systems

    c. Summary of problems and needs
3. Functional description of proposed system
    a. Objectives and scope of proposed system
    b. Narrative description of proposed system
    c. Functional requirements questionnaire
        i. Outputs
        ii. Files and databases (including expected data volume)
        iii. Processes
        iv. Networking and data communication requirements
    d. Support requirements
        i. Implementation
        ii. Training
        iii. Documentation
        iv. Source code
        v. Maintenance (software and hardware)
    e. Systems cost summary
4. Required vendor information
    a. Vendor evaluation criteria
        i. Time in business
        ii. Financial stability (financial statements for past five years)
        iii. Product experience
            • Number of similar installations
            • Version proposed
    b. References
        i. System reliability and dependability
        ii. Vendor reliability and dependability
        iii. Documentation quality
        iv. Support quality
        v. System quality
        vi. Training quality
5. Instructions to vendors
    a. Proposed format
    b. Proposal due date
    c. Evaluation criteria
        i. Was all data needed to evaluate the proposal included in the proposal?
        ii. Is the proposal clear and unambiguous?
        iii. Is the costed proposal within the established budget?
        iv. Does the proposed system meet the mandatory functional requirements?
        v. How well does the system meet the desirable functional requirements?
        vi. Will software modification be required so that the system meets specified functional requirements?
        vii. Does the system contain adequate controls?
        viii. Does the system contain an adequate audit trail?
        ix. Is the system well documented?
        x. Is the system user-friendly?
        xi. How many other organizations are using the configured system?
        xii. Are current users satisfied with the vendor (e.g., support, training, and documentation quality)?
6. Vendor contact information

# APPENDIX B    SUMMARY OF SELECTED ACTIVITY-BASED COSTING PACKAGES

**Activity Analyzer™**
According to Lead Software, Inc. (1999), the new version of Activity Analyzer was developed using object technology from Microsoft's Visual Developer Studio. Key features of the software include:

- The use of object-oriented programming in the development of the software
- 32-bit architecture for Windows 95/NT
- Drag-and-drop assignments
- Customizable browse grids
- On-line editing of screen field titles for screen customization
- User security access controlled by project
- Department and function
- Fast processing speeds for large and complex models
- Recursive cost reallocation from mutually supporting activities
- Multidimensional cost objects
- Multilevel manufacturing bill of material
- Flexible import/export utilities
- Open access to data with any ODBC-compliant software tool
- Data extract into an Excel file with Microsoft Query
- Over 150 standard reports
- Integrated query/report writer outputs to a report or Excel

**Cost Control 4.0™**
According to the vendor, QPR Software Inc. (1999), CostControl provides a comprehensive picture on how resources are being spent by linking costs to each individual customer, product, service or activity. CostControl creates activity-based business models that help a company understand its real cost structure and identify how the business really works. CostControl has a standard Windows user interface that is easy to learn and use. In addition, the process model and reports can be tailored to meet specific and data can be imported and exported directly to and from existing information systems and charts and graphs can be exported to any Windows-compatible program.

**is/Modeler™**
This process-modeling tool was developed by Modus Operandi (1999). It is designed to identify sequencing, costs, dependencies, and to prepare management reports. It features an intuitive interface and a wide range of tools and palettes and can be used for activity-based costing, process analysis, business process reengineering, continuous process improvement, total quality management, requirements communications, creation of training systems, and force sizing. It employs drawing tools, relational database tables, spreadsheet computation capabilities, and a graphical interface to diagram exactly what's going on in your operations.

is/Modeler helps business managers easily determine costs at the activity level: The business user determines the appropriate level of detail, models the activity steps in a process, and enters cost drivers, rates and volumes and is/Modeler then calculates costs across activities.

### NetProphet™

Sapling Corporation's software tool creates activity-based management models. These models help solve cost-management problems by simultaneously addressing financial and operational issues. NetProphet models can be used for activity-based costing or products, processes and services and also to prepare more accurate budgets, coordinate benchmarking initiatives, plan rationalization strategies, perform job costing, and assess options for improving productivity and reducing costs. The package provides for scenario playing, so it is possible to model changes and view possible outcomes. The package also supports international operations through foreign currency exchange rate conversion.

### Oros 99 Core and Oros Expansion

These are ABC Technologies integrated activity-based operational management software tools. Oros 99 Core contains the software necessary to build and maintain ABC models, integrate them into existing accounting systems, generate reports, and conduct analyses. The Oros Expansion Pack seamlessly plugs into Oros 99 to extend the package beyond the pilot stage and can be used with ABC Technologies client server technology and also perform activity-based budgeting.

### PRODACAP S1™

The Prodacapo concept (1999) includes mapping activities performed in the departments into processes using the existing organization structure chart. Costs from the existing accounting system are traced to activities via resources to the products and the customers that are consuming the activities. Product and customer profitability can be calculated simultaneously in PRODACAPO.

*Note:* Product descriptions were provided by vendors and their contents have not been verified.

# PART V

# MANAGEMENT TRENDS AND TECHNIQUES

# CHAPTER 27

# REENGINEERING

## David K. Carr
## Ann Hopkins
**PricewaterhouseCoopers**

**27.1 INTRODUCTION**  The term "reengineering" refers to the process of making radical changes in major processes to greatly increase their performance. It is also called business process reengineering or business process redesign (both abbreviated as BPR). Since the late 1980s, many organizations have had to reengineer some of their most important business processes to stay competitive. Reasons for reengineering include new technology, fundamental discoveries in science, and the emergence of a truly global marketplace.

**(a) Disagreements about Reengineering**  Despite the substantial experience that organizations have had with reengineering, major misconceptions abound. First, there is no consensus on just what reengineering means. Some people call any large change project "reengineering": They see reengineering as, for example, a means to implement a new computer system, to reorganize, to downsize, or to enhance operations to meet internal requirements.

But, at its best, reengineering has to do with achieving results that are beneficial for—but external to—an organization. These results include decisions customers make to purchase a product or service at a price favorable to the producer, actions by companies to reduce environmental pollution, or efforts organizations make to improve society in some way. New computer systems or restructuring may be part of a solution to gain those external results, but to start a reengineering project by assuming that they are *the* solution weakens the power of reengineering to create the desired change.

Some critics scoff that reengineering is merely a repackaging of earlier systems and industrial engineering methods. Granted that effective reengineering does use older methods along with newer ones, the genius of the approach is how the separate parts are aimed, integrated, and deployed. In this way, reengineering is much like the concept of the core processes that are often its primary focus. *Functions* and *processes* (which are discussed later) are arrangements of components that cut across functional boundaries, operate in several dimensions (e.g., process, technological, human, organizational, or cultural dimensions), and are closely connected with other processes in an organization.

**(b) Functions and Processes**    An enterprise is made up of core and support processes. Core processes are the processes by which an enterprise transforms its inputs into outputs to satisfy customer needs. Typical examples are order fulfillment, product realization, and new product development. Core processes cut right across the functions of an enterprise, including planning, engineering, sales, production, product delivery, and customer service.

**(c) Support Processes**    Support processes are internal to the enterprise and provide the administrative and organizational infrastructure to support the core processes. Typical examples are management of human resources, financial services, and information services.

**(d) Essential Ingredients of Reengineering**    Our experience working with hundreds of reengineering clients shows many ingredients essential to this complex approach to major change. These include:

- A multidimensional approach that considers (at a minimum) the following dimensions of change: process, technology, human, cultural, and organizational.
- A structured framework around which to build reengineering tasks and techniques.
- Teamwork among leaders, managers, reengineering teams, and facilitators or consultants.
- Effective management of human, cultural, and organizational change.
- Consideration of the organization's strategy.
- Sound business planning.
- Performance goals that compel those who do the reengineering to look for high-performance solutions.
- Listening to the voice of the customer when establishing performance goals.
- Minimizing the time and resources spent understanding the current situation.
- Understanding how to choose the right approach.

**27.2 EVOLUTION OF REENGINEERING**    Reengineering has been called a revolutionary approach to improvement, but this "revolution" is, in fact, evolutionary. A look at the brief history of reengineering reveals both the reasoning behind it and the causes of problems that arise when it is applied.

**(a) Two-Dimensional Reengineering**    By 1990, many organizations realized that earlier approaches to achieving major improvements in operations had shortcomings. Chief among these approaches were:

- *Information systems.* Automating operations through the use of new information systems.
- *Functional focus.* Improvement initiatives that focused on functions.

Reengineering was well received when it first emerged in the late 1980s because it integrated systems engineering and process redesign. What is more, it could deal with core processes across functional boundaries.

**(b) Information Systems**    Starting in the 1960s, many companies installed increasingly sophisticated information systems, but they often failed to make changes in their work processes concurrently. Often this meant that the new systems simply replicated existing manual processes. As a result, companies ended up "paving the cow paths" of inefficient, outmoded work methods—in other words, they simply gained the capability to do the wrong things faster.

Some organizations did reconfigure their work processes as they installed new systems, but often the changes were made by systems engineers who had little or no input from the managers and operators who would later have to use the reconfigured processes. Failure to blend systems and process knowledge during the design phase produced suboptimal systems and processes, resistance by users, and sometimes both.

Other reengineering practitioners advocated redesigning processes first, then developing information systems to fit these new operations. However, advanced business systems packages for manufacturing (such as materials requirement planning, or MRP, and manufacturing resource planning, or MRP II) and enterprise resource planning (ERP) require that an organization change at least some of its major processes to fit the requirements of the new systems.

A few reengineers had the right idea from the start: Effective reengineering requires that the design of systems and processes be parallel (or concurrent) activities. In this way, process designs respond to the transformational capabilities of technology, but the design teams (unlike systems engineers working alone) also understand the requirements of process operations. Today, concurrent design is an accepted doctrine in reengineering (later we discuss how it happens under the topic of "reengineering teams"—see section 27.5(b)). Yet, because concurrent design is accepted doctrine, all reengineering consultants claim to do it. Prudent organizations will carefully evaluate a consultant's approach to concurrent design.

**(c) Functional Focus**    One of the greatest problems reengineering has overcome is that of taking a functional approach to improvement. Despite the visual isolation of functions on an organizational chart (departments, branches, offices, and etc.), the work of core processes actually flows through them. This work stream, when depicted on flow charts and process maps, is a process view of how an enterprise is configured. For reengineering, the stream is more accurate than boxes on an organizational chart in showing how work is done.

Major downfalls in functionally focused changes include:

- *Improvements in one area are offset by declines in others.* When improvement initiatives are functionally focused, they cannot take critical interrelationships among processes into account. Most functional improvements are carried out by middle managers in an office or department, who concentrate on improving processes within their boundaries without considering how these improvements might affect processes outside their boundaries. For example, it would be relatively easy to improve productivity in a purchasing department by requiring that other parts of the organization take on tasks previously done by the department. However, this may be a suboptimal solution if productivity of the organization as a whole deteriorates because of the extra work. To avoid this problem, the organization should focus the improvement program on the senior executives who can address problems that cross functional boundaries.

- *Some process improvements contribute little to meeting strategic goals.* First things first: Core processes that are critical to success must be improved before other processes. Support processes such as human resources (HR) management are important, but they lack intrinsic value, especially as perceived by customers. They derive their value from how they facilitate and improve the operation of core processes. A wise organization makes HR changes after it takes care of pressing needs to redesign core processes, and it makes these changes support core processes.

**(d) Supply Chain Management**  Even when reengineering efforts are cross-functional, they often fail to consider that some core processes cut across almost every activity in an enterprise—within a company and across the activities of suppliers and customers. This enterprise view of processes gave rise to the concept of *supply chain management,* which may require reengineering of core processes that start well before and end well after a company's boundaries. For example, Federal Express supplies its large-volume customers with personal computers, software, and modems in their offices to address and track packages picked up by FedEx agents. These customers, although they are outside FedEx's organizational boundaries, are key to the delivery process work flow before, during, and after FedEx delivers.

In summary, in the early years of reengineering, most organizations welcomed it because it integrated process redesign and information systems engineering. Reengineering permitted major improvements to happen across functional—and sometimes even organizational—boundaries. However, many organizations quickly found that reengineering approaches with just these two dimensions of change promised more than they could deliver.

**27.3 MULTIDIMENSIONAL REENGINEERING**  Many organizations had difficulties with their reengineering projects, largely because of resistance to change by employees and managers. Employees concluded that BPR stood for "big personnel reductions" rather than "business process reengineering," because reengineering often occurred along with downsizing. Indeed, what some organizations sometimes called reengineering really was little more than downsizing; few or no changes occurred to existing processes and systems. Reengineering was also widely perceived as something that was imposed on most managers and employees, as opposed to being an approach in which they could participate and come to trust.

**(a) Dimensions of Change**  Even the best concurrent design work in reengineering is incapable of overcoming these problems, if only the process and technology dimensions to change are considered. There are three other dimensions:

1. *Human.* The focus of the human dimension is process operators, managers, customers, and suppliers. This dimension includes how people accept a new way of working, its effect on their lives, and their capabilities to operate under the new way, including skills, rewards, attitude, and motivation.
2. *Organizational.* The focus of the organizational dimension is structure, infrastructure, and management. It takes into account how an organization is structured to accommodate new ways of operating, including authority levels, lines of communication, and basic infrastructure.

3. *Cultural.* The focus of the cultural dimension includes both formal and informal norms, values, and beliefs held by personnel. It takes into account how an organization's culture fosters or hinders changes in the other dimensions.

There may be other dimensions as well, depending on the nature of an organization and its line of business. For example, government organizations must sometimes consider the political dimension of major changes to their way of doing business. The point is that an organization has to recognize and address all the dimensions of change it will encounter during reengineering.

**(b) Change Management**    By recognizing the human, organizational, and cultural dimensions of change, reengineers opened the door to the application *change management,* which is the planned management of these aspects of major transitions, as is discussed later (see also Chapter 8).

Integrating the reengineering of all dimensions is best done by working on them concurrently. More advanced reengineering approaches do this with frameworks that have different streams of activities for each dimension yet also have an integration mechanism to ensure that they are tied together (this is discussed later in the chapter). Also, the advanced methods make heavy use of cross-functional and multidisciplinary teams throughout the reengineering process.

In summary, reengineering was developed to address major changes in the operations of organizations. Because these changes occur in several dimensions, effective reengineering focuses on aspects of the organization that go beyond processes and technology. What does an advanced reengineering project look like? The next section reviews its framework.

**27.4 A FRAMEWORK FOR REENGINEERING**    When people talk about a methodology for advanced reengineering, they usually mean a structured framework or way of organizing and scheduling activities that flow across all dimensions of change. The framework approach makes it easier for people involved in a project to understand and communicate by breaking the effort up into manageable pieces and by providing a common language with which to discuss reengineering.

**(a) Process-Driven Change**    PricewaterhouseCoopers' reengineering framework is called *process-driven change* (PDC). It depicts in matrix form the stages of reengineering and the streams of activities that address the various dimensions of change. Exhibit 27.1 shows the matrix layout, while Exhibit 27.2 and 27.3 show its vertical and horizontal components.

Exhibit 27.2 shows the six stages of reengineering. Note that these six stages could be "sliced and diced" into more or fewer categories, which is fine. What matters is to address all the work shown in the exhibit. Not doing so is to risk failure (or, at the least, suboptimal results).

Within each stage, there are four separate tracks of activities (shown in Exhibit 27.3). A fifth set of activities related to change management underlies the other four. These activities start by analyzing the effect of changes made in organizations on personnel, customers, and suppliers. Through communication, demonstrations, inclusion on reengineering teams, and other techniques, those effected become more willing to adopt and adapt to the new ways of working.

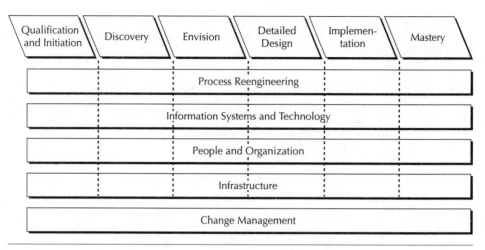

Exhibit 27.1   Process-Driven Change: A Framework for Reengineering

| PDC Stage | Description |
|---|---|
| **1. Qualification and initiation** | Ensure that the right approach is configured. The stage is complete when a high-level milestone plan for the project has been developed. |
| **2. Discovery** | Review the current situation and identify the problems, challenges, and issues that must be addressed, as well as any ideas for change. |
| **3. Envision** | There are three parts to "envision": 1. Develop a vision of what the organization plans to achieve. 2. Investigate high-level alternative solutions and understand how they interact. 3. Select a high-level solution. |
| **4. Detailed design** | Prepare a blueprint for redesigned processes, including details about new ways of working, organizational structure, infrastructure, and technology. |
| **5. Implementation** | Implement changes so that they become imbedded in the enterprise. |
| **6. Mastery** | Sustain the change and introduce continuous improvement. |

Exhibit 27.2   Stages of Process-Driven Change (PDC)

| PDC Track | Description |
|---|---|
| A. Process reengineering | Redesigning processes (i.e., the way work is done). |
| B. Information systems and technology | Installing or changing information systems or applying new types of information technology. |
| C. People and organization | Developing new capabilities, roles, and responsibilities among human resources, management styles, rewards, and work group structures. |
| D. Infrastructure | Identifying and solving issues related to hardware support, constraints in use of space, maintenance, equipment use, economies of scale, transport economics, and so on. |
| E. Change management | Managing the human, cultural, and organizational aspects of change. |

**Exhibit 27.3    Tracks of Process-Driven Change (PDC)**

**(b) Developing the Framework**    We recommend that organizations start with an established framework, then modify it to reflect specific requirements and internal preferences for tools, language, and so on. Starting with a few external examples of frameworks (versus designing one from scratch) helps avoid two problems:

1. *Missing stages or tasks.* If internal managers design the framework, they may "slide past" critical stages or tasks—either because they do not consider them important or because they fail to consider them at all.
2. *Frameworks not tailored to the organization.* Reengineering frameworks developed by external consultants or found on books about reengineering tend to have been applied in many organizations, so they reflect that experience.

**27.5 WHO DOES REENGINEERING?**    Given a framework for reengineering, who does the work? We divide those who do reengineering into four groups: leaders, reengineering teams, process managers, and facilitators/consultants.

**(a) Leaders**    To avoid suboptimal decision making by functional managers, major process change has to be led by an organization's top executives. By establishing a broad vision for the outcome, a company's top executives guide the design and implementation of a reengineering effort.

Only top leaders command both the resources and respect required to drive process changes and to sustain organizational support through difficult periods. Input from top executives is especially important during the early stages of reengineering, when assessments are made that lead to establishing critical success factors, performance goals, and the high-level planning of new operations. Throughout a reengineering project, executives are central figures in communicating the need to change to those who are affected by it. In reengineering projects undertaken by joint ventures or similar partnerships of more than one company or organization, top leaders are often the only participants who are capable of reaching consensus on cross-organizational issues.

So far, this discussion of leadership has focused on the role of an organization's (or a partnership's) senior management team. But a major reengineering project also needs a top executive leader who will "own" it—that is, take overall responsibility and accountability for the effort. For core processes, this is usually a line executive; for support processes it may be the head of the functional department that is most affected by the project.

**(b) Reengineering Teams**    Reengineering uses a team-based approach to change, because using a good framework requires the involvement of so many disciplines and affects so many parts of an organization that no one person, however expert that person may be, can adequately address all issues.

Typically, the reengineering framework selected will indicate the types of teams required. In PDC, there would be a team for each of the four tracks listed and also a team for change management. To avoid problems, delays, and rework later on, the work of the various teams is carried out concurrently or in parallel as they move through the stages of the framework. However, frequent communication and planning are required to make concurrent work successful. Therefore, team leaders should meet periodically to discuss the problems and progress of their teams. Meeting together, team leaders serve the same purpose as "integrators," the individuals or groups who, in other approaches to complex project management, harmonize the work of several other groups. Under a concurrent approach to reengineering, team leaders do this job themselves, which avoids extra costs and delays of using old-style integrators. Primarily, the team leaders work together to achieve consensus on their decisions. However, some final decisions have to be made by the executive responsible for the reengineering project.

Reengineering teams should include technical experts in process redesign, information systems, and change management. It is equally important to include managers and key personnel who will operate the new process. Because these managers and key personnel will have insights and ideas that the experts will overlook, their participation is a signal to the entire organization that everyone's concerns and issues are being considered.

To ensure success, reengineering teams must draw on the best and the brightest managers and staff across a range of functions. They should be dedicated full time to the reengineering effort, because making major change is much more than a collateral duty. For example, when the U.S. Postal Service reengineered the training process for its 750,000 employees, six key managers worked on the redesign full time and offsite for several months.

In some cases it will be important to include customers, suppliers, and other stakeholders on the reengineering teams (or, at least, to seek their input when doing assessments and design tasks). This is particularly critical when they are going to be involved in operating a process that is being reengineered.

What must be avoided at all costs is to have some individual or a group of specialists go off independently—that is, without obtaining input from other participants in the reengineering effort—to design some critical component of a new process or its information system. Even if they develop a component that optimizes the whole process, this group will have lost the opportunity to gain support for their ideas by involving others in the planning. Such lack of support may become an obstacle to implementation.

**(c) Process Managers**  Another potential obstacle to implementation can arise if line managers are excluded from the reengineering effort. If this happens, line managers will likely resist change.

Note that the term "line managers" (as it is used here) refers to senior and middle managers who work in and around a process. They contribute the main resources to the project (i.e., not only team members, but probably part of the budget as well) and (in the end) they work to implement the solutions. For these managers to support a project, they have to be briefed about plans, progress, problems, and results throughout the initiative. Their opinions should also be valued and used so that they will feel represented and part of the reengineering process.

In short, the involvement of line management is critical. If a reengineering process stalls, it is probably because of resistance on the part of line managers.

**(d) Facilitators and Consultants**  Reengineering is a team effort, so it requires excellent team dynamics. But reengineering teams composed exclusively of an organization's own employees usually lack experience with the framework and tools of reengineering. This is why many organizations use facilitators and consultants to coach reengineering teams in group dynamics and to help the teams conduct their meetings. Facilitators and consultants provide the tools, techniques, training, and expert-level reality checks on conclusions and direction as the effort progresses.

Organizations can use internal facilitators and consultants, provided they have been trained and are experienced in the requisite specialties. Some large organizations that have reengineered many processes over time establish a cadre of internal facilitators and consultants, augmenting them with outside assistance when needed. Other organizations rely on outside facilitators and consultants from the start.

We believe that the best practice is to start with outside facilitators and consultants and then (over the course of several reengineering projects) have the outsiders train internal facilitators and consultants for future efforts. This gives an organization a longer-lasting internal capability to carry out major change projects. To ensure that this happens, an organization needs to evaluate the skills of outsiders based (at least partially) on their ability to transfer knowledge to internal personnel.

**27.6 PEOPLE DIMENSIONS: REENGINEERING AS CHANGE MANAGEMENT**  As the previous section discusses, part of the reason for using teams and involving top leaders and line managers in reengineering is to get them to invest their time and thought into the reengineering process. Having done this, they are more likely to accept the solutions that result.

But what do they need—indeed, what does everyone in an enterprise need—to cause them to open up to new ways of doing business? The following discussions attempt to shed some light on this question.

**(a) Compelling Need**  In a comprehensive approach to change management (see Chapter 8) the first step would be to identify and articulate a *compelling need* for major change. A compelling need may be a "burning platform" or a "sunlit uplands" issue. The platform metaphor suggests that an issue is a bit like standing on a burning oil platform in the middle of the ocean: The choice is to jump off the platform into a new, risky situation, or to stay put—and die. The cost of maintaining the status quo in such a situation is prohibitively high, due (perhaps) to pressures from competitors or disaffection on the part of customers. A "burning platform" issue is a mixed blessing: Although it indicates serious problems, the problems are recognizable and most people, once they understand them, will agree on the need to change.

The metaphor "sunlight uplands" refers to the higher aspirations of a company that is already doing well—so well that its employees may be complacent. "Sunlit uplands" issues are driven by business strategies that seek to avoid burning platforms by actively taking advantage of opportunities. Here, for example, a market leader who wants to stay in front of the competition must make major changes in anticipation of evolving markets, technologies, and other external business drivers. People may be less likely to agree on the need to change when the status quo seems fine, so that sunlit uplands issues require extra attention to articulating and communicating the need to change.

**(b) Communication**    Communication about a reengineering initiative should begin the moment it is conceived by an organization's top leaders. This can be problematic, however, because early communications can lead to rumors about job loss, downsizing, or problems with new technologies. Uncontrolled communication could then continue throughout the project and, ultimately, be a major obstacle to successful implementation.

Therefore, planned communication is the most important tool for obtaining buy-in from everyone affected by or concerned with a reengineering initiative. The communication needs to be two-way, with feedback from those concerned about change to those who are creating it. The communication should also let people know the answers to questions such as "How will this affect me?" and "What's in it for me?"

It is impossible to communicate too much about a reengineering project, and—above all else—it is important to be honest. For major projects that will affect many people, it is a good idea to assign someone full time to coordinating communications about the changes.

**(c) Readiness for Change**    Another area to explore is the readiness of an organization to undergo major changes, including whether its culture will support those changes. There are several ways to do this, such as through employee surveys about corporate culture, focus groups of workers, and interviews with key personnel. Understanding this information from inside the organization helps in determining whether new processes need to be designed to fit the culture of the organization or whether the culture will have to change to support new ways of working.

For example, a potential redesign of a process might require employees to think and act independently in the future when they are used to working "by the book" and under close supervision. If so, the prevailing command-and-control culture may have to change to foster independence.

Another important cultural issue relates to access to information. To most managers, information is something to be closely guarded because it gives them power. A reengineered process may require spreading information to people throughout an organization. If so, this new openness must be planned for and rewarded.

**(d) Organizational Issues and Change Management**    Some change management activities are obvious, such as providing training in new ways of working to process operators. Others are subtler, such as changing how people are compensated and rewarded for their work.

If a new process requires teamwork among several functions but performance is evaluated based on optimizing each function (or each individual's productivity), then expect suboptimization. New rewards systems will need to stress teamwork and the performance of an entire core process.

Other important organizational issues include:

- How people inside and outside an organization will communicate.
- The ease of making continuous improvements to operations.
- How an organization measures process performance.

Each of these organizational issues has a powerful effect on the behavior of individuals, and each must be addressed before or during the reengineering process.

**27.7 DECIDING TO REENGINEER**   Reengineering is an expensive proposition—and, thus, similar to a capital investment. If only because it costs a lot of money, a decision to reengineer should be made at a strategic level. The investment has to be justified by making a convincing business case that links to business strategy.

**(a) Relation to Strategy**   Reengineering is not strategy. Some top executives mistakenly believe, however, that reengineering is a strategic response to virtually any problem. If, for example, prices for a particular product family are falling because of a long-term trend toward reduced demand, and if the end of this trend is beyond the company's planning horizon, then reengineering to lower costs and preserve profits would be folly. Instead, it would be far smarter simply to get out of the business entirely.

Yet reengineering can and should be a strategic tool. Ideally, all reengineering efforts should be connected to business, market, and organizational strategies, goals, and objectives. By this we mean that a reengineering project can show the linkage between its objectives and an organization's written strategic plans. Failure to make this link certainly lowers its priorities.

For example, if a company's strategic goal is to become a "one-stop shop" for all of a customer's needs in a certain area, then reengineering projects that aim at creating single point-of-purchase systems for serving customers could properly be called strategic and top priority. Unless cost is an issue that is addressed in corporate strategic plans, reengineering proposals that simply lower costs are lower priority.

Unfortunately, corporate strategy is rarely detailed enough to identify a specific process for reengineering. Strategic plans are better at indicating the broad priorities, goals, and objectives of an organization. (They may also indicate what is unimportant simply by failing to mention some issues or strategies.) And, unfortunately, the strategic plans of some organizations are mere paper documents meant to fulfill some external requirement; they simply gather dust on bookshelves.

Absent clearly defined strategic targets, what can reengineers do? They can begin by asking the most fundamental strategic questions about an organization:

- What business are we in?
- What does success look like?

- How successful do we want to be?
- How will we know when we are successful?

It is fairly safe to assume that everyone with a major role in a reengineering effort—leaders, team members, and even customers—knows the answers to these questions. The problem, quite often, is that everyone has a different answer.

Good facilitators can help. Going through a group exercise to reach consensus on the answers before undertaking a reengineering project is enormously helpful for everyone involved. From that point forward, everyone will be better able to determine *as a group* what is important, the levels of performance desired, how to measure the gap between current and desired levels, and what processes will be involved in success. It helps, of course, if success is defined in terms of external results.

**(b) Business Cases**    In the past, reengineering projects have been slow to get under way and have sometimes dragged on for years. In this era of rapid change, such slow change is unacceptable.

In the PDC framework, the initial stage of reengineering ("Qualification and Initiation") involves quickly developing key issues, project scope, project objectives, and a vision of future operations. Why be quick about these activities? To begin with, although understanding the current state of affairs is important, it does nothing to add value in the eyes of customers and stakeholders. Therefore, do the minimum analysis needed to build a convincing business case for change.

A business case shows a vision of how an organization will operate in the future, the reasons for changes, the potential results, and the level of time and effort required to carry out a reengineering project. Information for the business case should reflect external results and issues. This may involve:

- Reviewing existing documentation.
- Initial benchmarking of the performance of competitors and organizations that do similar operations.
- Discussions with key customers, suppliers, stakeholders, and business partners.

Information for a business case should also reflect internal issues, so discuss them with managers and key personnel, especially any problems they foresee with existing processes, systems, and infrastructure. Yet another area to explore is the readiness of the organization to undergo major changes (see section 27.6).

**27.8 STRETCH PERFORMANCE GOALS**    Reengineering will be about dramatic change only if an organization sets stretch goals for reengineering. Such goals should be double-, triple-, or even quadruple-digit performance increases in one or a few areas.

For example, electronic commerce ("e-commerce") can change the cycle time for processing a customer order from weeks to minutes, starting from when a customer logs on to the Internet. But if a company were to set a goal of reducing customer response time by only 10 percent, managers might never even think of e-commerce. Instead, they would look only for marginal improvements—or decide simply to "manage harder." If, by contrast, the company sets a 1,000 percent reduction goal, managers will *have* to think about the full capabilities of e-commerce.

When do goals become ridiculous? If other industries with similar operations (though not necessarily similar products) or similar problems fail to come close to the desired performance levels, then perhaps the stretch goal is too much of a stretch. The only way to find this out is to benchmark the performance of world-class organizations thought to have superior processes. Absent diligent benchmarking, any claim that a performance level is out of reach is suspect.

Benchmarking also has other benefits. First, a thorough examination of high-performance processes provides valuable ideas to use in a reengineering project. Second, seeing is believing: If skeptics visit an outside organization to see a high-performance process in operation, they are more likely to support its adoption.

**(a) Voice of the Customer**    Of all these initial activities leading to a business case, the most important one is to listen to the voice of the customer. Understanding what customers want—both now and in the future—is the most effective means of ensuring an external focus.

For this purpose, "the customer" should be defined at first as the external users of an organization's outputs. A customer survey, focus groups, or interviews should include questions about the customer's requirements for the supplied good or service, in terms of its cost, delivery, reliability, and after-sales service and support.

Whenever possible, customers should be asked to rank-order competitors against the attributes. In this way, an organization's leaders can see what the customer base perceives as being important and where the strengths and weaknesses of existing processes are located.

**(b) Limitations to Listening to Customers**    It can be dangerous to rely solely on customer input to determine the aims of a reengineering project. Customer expectations are linked to the here and now, not the future. Therefore, it is important to ask customers about their views of (and plans for) the future, then to probe their responses and get them out of a "business as usual" mode of thinking.

It is just as important to review forecasts for markets, technologies, demographics, and other factors. Customers may not realize how these factors will influence their expectations in the future. Just a few years ago, for example, people thought that telex, fax, and telephone were the fastest way to transact business, though e-commerce has now become a requirement in many industries. Because technology advances so rapidly, anticipating where customers will be by the time a reengineering project is complete is critical to success.

**(c) Understanding the Status Quo**    After a company understands what customers want both now and in the future, they should avoid spending too much time trying to understand why existing processes fail to deliver on customer expectations. A thorough examination of the status quo can take months yet yield far fewer ideas for radical redesign than would arise if the time were spent instead on benchmarking or creative thinking. It is sufficient to understand the following about existing processes:

- *Gaps between current and desired levels of performance.* If the gap is moderate (e.g., 10–20 percent), then approaches other than reengineering may be sufficient to close it.
- *Work flows at a high to middle level.* A detailed mapping of all processes involved may be unnecessary, because many will simply disappear. However, it is important

to identify all the people involved in the processes targeted, because some people may need to be retrained or reassigned to other work.

* *Operational relationships among processes targeted for reengineering and other processes.* This includes the internal-supplier and customer processes that provide raw materials or work-in-progress to targeted processes; it also includes any support processes necessary for their sound functioning. Some of these processes may need to go through minor changes to support the reengineered processes. In some cases, they, too, will disappear (e.g., quality-control functions will not be needed for Six Sigma processes).

It is also critical to understand the parts of existing process that will remain after reengineering, because some invariably do; no reengineering project completely eliminates the status quo.

**(d) Blank Slates Versus Open Concepts**    Some reengineering advocates say that starting with a blank slate or "greenfield" approach is the best way to develop radical new concepts for operations. These are the reengineers who want to "blow up" existing processes and replace them with something totally new. This is rarely possible, but they have the right idea: Dismiss current assumptions and go for something new.

The problem is that most reengineers dismiss only their assumptions about internal operations. The greatest internal assumption of all, however, is that an organization truly understands the external results it must achieve—which is often not the case. More than anything else, starting with a clear, accurate understanding of external results promotes development of a *conceptual* blank slate so that a company will be unencumbered by old ways of thinking about business.

A focus on external results also opens people up to desired outcomes that are created outside the boundaries of their organization in processes that they do not directly control. For example, when the U.S. Patent and Trademark Office (PTO) reengineered its certification process, it was working on an operation in which a new order passed through three intermediaries on its way to the PTO and four intermediaries on the way back to the end user. Changing how these intermediaries handled the orders was critical to the success of the reengineering project.[1]

Other benefits of focusing on external results include the setting of reengineering performance targets in terms of what customers or stakeholders value most, rather than targets being limited by what functional managers value most. Their process designs can be configured to fit into customer processes instead of being limited by the need to suit internal noncore processes. Thus, an external focus becomes the unifying principal for the reengineering of processes both inside and outside the boundaries of an organization.

**(e) Choosing the Process Approach**    What specific approach should be used in reengineering a process? One set of considerations is:

* The amount of process improvement needed to meet requirements.
* The degree of risk an organization is willing to assume.
* How quickly improvement must occur.
* The resources available for reengineering.
* The readiness of an organization's people to undertake major change.

**Least Time**

**Most Time**

Preempt or eliminate non–value-added activities
Outsource or insource
Leverage suppliers or customers
Minimize handoffs
Convert serial processing to parallel processing
Restructure the organization
Change the physical layout
Automate manual processes
Improve effectiveness of existing technology
Utilize alternative technologies

**Least Risk**

**Most Risk**

**Exhibit 27.4    Time and Risk in Reengineering.**

- Political considerations, such as international cooperation.
- Management policy that requires following specific improvement approaches (e.g., lean manufacturing or Six Sigma).
- The degree of comfort that an organization has with different approaches.

Time and degree of risk must also be considered. Exhibit 27.4 shows 10 approaches used in reengineering and other major change initiatives. These 10 approaches are ranked, in general, according to the time required and the risk involved to implement them.

If an organization is concerned primarily with reducing costs or if the amount of improvement needed in a core process is relatively small, then preempting or eliminating non–value-added activities may be the best approach. Tools and techniques to use might include process mapping, activity-based management (or a similar approach), and industrial engineering or value analysis. Installing alternative technologies is the riskiest and most long-term approach and requires in-depth information-technology support, including partnerships with technology vendors. Enterprise resource planning solutions fall into this category.

It is also important to understand that reengineering poses both technical and organizational risks. The technical risks include the risk that a new process will fail to perform as planned, or that a process for implementing solutions will disrupt normal business. These risks can be mitigated through careful research, design, and project management. Usually the organizational risk is resistance from managers and employees, which can be prevented (or substantially reduced) through sound change management. When resistance does occur, however, an organization's leaders often have to take strong, personal action to communicate the need for change to both managers and workers.

**(f) Detailed Design**    Teams engaged in redesigning processes should start out with a few design parameters, such as the management policies listed previously. Other parameters might include a mandate to provide easy information access to everyone in an enterprise, to minimize supervision, to outsource noncritical activities when doing so is cost effective, and so on. These parameters are likely to be part of a general transformation within an organization, not specific to a reengineering project.

Informed by the parameters—and knowledge of external results, benchmarking, and other research—reengineering teams can then creatively develop new process ideas. The teams may engage in activities designed to free their imaginations and develop new approaches, such as challenging assumptions, "blue skying," brainstorming, and asking "what if" questions.

Only when all ideas are out on the table should teams begin to analyze the feasibility and value of the ideas. Swatting down ideas as they arise—or initially favoring some specific solution—is a sure way to kill creativity. If an organization opts for a solution imbedded in a commercially available business software system (such as ERP), there may be less room for creativity. Even so, it is important to consider all the possibilities. Electronic meeting software or groupware can contribute to creativity and encourage the free exchange of ideas.

The next step for a reengineering team is to evaluate the ideas, narrowing them down to a few that will be tested in depth. This testing can occur through modeling and simulation to investigate different configurations under various assumptions; computerized simulation software speeds this process. This is followed by financial and technical analysis (including cost-benefit analysis) to weed out all but one or two alternatives. The final decision for a solution is made by top management.

Redesign teams usually discover a number of "quick fixes" during this part of the reengineering process. These are minor changes that can be made without waiting until the end of a project; the changes typically do not require altering information systems. It is a good idea to implement these minor changes immediately. Besides improving operations in the near term, the changes can be a first demonstration of the value of reengineering, and they can help prepare people for larger changes in the future. Other types of demonstrations, such as pilot projects, serve the same purpose.

**(g) Implementation and Mastery**    One of the best things an organization can do when implementing reengineering solutions is to involve the people who will operate them. This gives them an investment in the new way, which enhances their acceptance of it.

Mastery of a new process means that the operators both understand and can continuously improve it. Thus, it is critical that they have the three essential components of mastery:

1. Training in the new way.
2. Performance measures to keep them informed of process effectiveness and external results.
3. The skills, authority, and responsibility to continuously improve operations.

## NOTE

1. *Report of the U.S. Patent and Trademark Office Certification Division Reengineering Project As-is Analysis,* Price Waterhouse (November 27, 1996).

# CHAPTER 28

# THEORY OF CONSTRAINTS

## Robert J. Campbell
**Miami University**

**28.1 INTRODUCTION**   One strategy to manage operations successfully includes:

- Select or design the right product mix for the targeted customer base and business processes.
- Acquire raw materials on a timely and cost-effective basis.
- Convert those raw materials into quality products in the manufacturing process.
- Distribute those products to customers in a timely and efficient manner.

The key to profitability is to balance the flow of products to customers—known as *throughput*—with the business-process and departmental capacities that are created and maintained to design, market, manufacture, and distribute these products. This chapter discusses how companies can help balance that flow to ensure profitability.

**28.2 MEASURE OF THROUGHPUT**   Throughput should generate a positive margin or markup over the cost of raw materials. Quality products that match customer demand influence selling prices and volume. *Total revenues* (prices multiplied by volume) reflect the customer value the company creates. If the company delivers sufficiently high customer value, there will be a significant markup over the cost of raw materials to cover the costs of capacity and still provide a profit. If the company does not deliver enough value to justify continued operations, revenues may barely recover the cost of raw materials.

**(a) Calculating Throughput**   The *theory of constraints* (TOC) uses throughput ("T" in formulas) to establish how much positive margin, or markup, over raw material costs a company has earned through its sale of products to customers. Specifically:

$$T = \text{Revenues} - \text{Cost of Raw Materials}$$

Assume, for example, that a manufacturing company has a product mix consisting of five products. The throughput for each product and for the company as a whole may be determined as follows:

| Product Line | Revenues | Materials | Throughput |
|---|---|---|---|
| A | $1,000,000 | $ 650,000 | $350,000 |
| B | 2,400,000 | 1,850,000 | 550,000 |
| C | 2,800,000 | 1,450,000 | 1,350,000 |
| D | 1,750,000 | 1,000,000 | 750,000 |
| E | 500,000 | 300,000 | 200,000 |
| Total | $8,450,000 | $5,250,000 | $3,200,000 |

**(b) Direct and Variable Costs**   Note that throughput recognizes only direct materials (and packaging) as truly direct and variable costs in the short run. As managers increase or decrease the production volume of selected products, the organization must automatically increase or decrease purchases of raw materials to maintain inventories and supply sufficient materials to produce the units required.

This is in direct contrast to staffing levels and capital investments, which change only as a result of management's analysis of departmental capacities and deliberate decisions to change capacity. The costs of personnel, tools, supplies, technology, and space are assumed to be fixed, in the short run, with respect to decision making and volume changes. Variable selling costs, such as promotions and commissions, are deducted from gross revenues to obtain net revenues—the value used in measuring throughput.

**(c) Capacity and Resources Used**   Whether or not a company achieves an adequate profit is a function of the amount and cost of capacity that is used to create customer value. The business processes of research and design, marketing, materials acquisition, manufacturing, distribution, and customer service are represented by resources and resource costs. These resources are the people employed by the company to perform various tasks and functions (plus the tools and technology that they use in their work). Other resources used to create customer value include work space, supplies, and utilities.

Each business process is needed to create customer value. It is not enough to design and manufacture products: A company must also market or distribute them in order to complete the link of the value chain to the customer.

Whether these business processes are performed in-house or outsourced, the resources to support the business processes need to be provided. The question is whether the amount of capacity provided and the associated costs of resources are appropriate or matched with the throughput the company creates. Inefficient use of the capacity of the various business processes can mean low or nonexistent profits.

**28.3 OPERATING EXPENSES**   Capacity costs reflect the resources committed to the various business processes. Assume, for example, that a company has typical in-house business processes (e.g., research and development, or R&D; marketing; materials acquisition; manufacturing; and distribution). Further, each of these business processes incurs the following types of expenses each year:

- Employee wages.
- Tools.
- Equipment depreciation.

- Supplies and utilities.
- Space or building costs.

The table provides assumed resource cost values to support and maintain capacity in the various business processes of this hypothetical company:

| Business Processes | Capacity Cost |
| --- | --- |
| R&D | $250,000 |
| Marketing | 600,000 |
| Materials acquisition | 500,000 |
| Manufacturing | 1,200,000 |
| Distribution | 400,000 |
| Total cost | $2,950,000 |

The total of all business process resource costs ($2.95 million in this example) is known as *operating expenses* (OE) in the language of the TOC. These are the annual costs of maintaining planned organizational capacity. Before the beginning of each year, the company makes capacity decisions about staffing and capital investment.

The capacity of each business process is established as part of an overall integrated business plan and an assessment of organizational capacity needs. Manufacturing and distribution capacity are dependent on sales forecasts and availability of capital. Marketing capacity is influenced by an assessment of the market potential given the company's product mix and the capacities of manufacturing and distribution. Excess capacities may be funded in some (or many) of the business processes to handle unexpected business fluctuations and peak periods of activity demand.

In general, the TOC approach to cost measurement assumes that these operating expenses are fixed, at least in the short run. Therefore, allocation of these "fixed" costs to products is usually discouraged by TOC advocates because "it implies that changing product volumes will result in changed costs."[1]

However, a complete disregard of operating expenses (i.e., ignoring the fact that a company has to recover all of its operating expenses in order to be profitable, at least in the long run) can be dangerous. One expert describes a manufacturing company that used throughput analysis to make substantial price reductions that were later matched by competitors. The result was a lowering of market prices and a loss in profits.[2] (To address this issue, section 28.7 discusses the recognition of operating expenses in product profitability analyses.)

**28.4 MEASURING PROFITABILITY**    The annual or periodic profitability of a company is measured under the TOC by the following equation:

$$\text{Profit (P)} = T - OE$$

$$\text{where } T = \text{Throughput; and}$$

$$OE = \text{Operating expenses}$$

To continue the example begun earlier, the profit of $250,000 for the year is calculated by subtracting the operating expenses of $2.95 million from the total throughput of $3.2 million. Based on a sales volume of $8.45 million, this appears to be a low return on sales—about 3 percent. Poor or mediocre financial performance suggests several fundamental problems:

- The features, functions, and quality of the company's products or services do not provide sufficient customer value to generate revenues adequate to recover the cost of the capacities of the various business processes.
- The constraining capacity is underutilized or mismatched with the company's current customer or product mix.
- The company has long-term excess capacity in many or all of the business processes.

Solutions to the first problem may require redesigning existing products or introducing new products. Improving short-term capacity utilization may require finding a better product or customer mix. Long-term capacity management requires the identification of the company's critical capacity areas and implementation of appropriate changes in capacity to maximize cash flow and profitability.

The TOC can be used to analyze the impact of decisions that are intended to make throughput or profit improvements and solve one or more of the three problem areas identified above. As the next section discusses, a series of five steps in the TOC literature describe how to manage a company's capacity effectively.[3]

**28.5 FIVE STEPS**   The TOC as a management tool can be explained by considering five steps:

1. Identify the system's constraints.
2. Decide how to exploit the system's constraints.
3. Subordinate everything else to the constraints.
4. Elevate the system's constraints.
5. Repeat the process if the constraint is broken.

The following sections discuss these steps and describe how they are evaluated using the TOC approach.

**(a) Identify the System's Constraints**   A company's ability to generate sales and volume will always be limited by constraints, which may be either internal or external to the company. The first step is to identify what the constraint is and where it exists. Given random fluctuations in demand and operations, there may be several resources that are either constraining or potentially constraining internally if they are not managed properly.[4]

Significant manufacturing technology that has limited flexibility may represent a constraining bottleneck on product throughput. Similarly, complicated procedures and policies necessitated by the use of many vendors may limit the ability of a company's purchasing function to support higher production volumes or changes in customer and product mixes. These policies and procedures may therefore cause the purchasing function to be a potential constraint or bottleneck.

**(b) Exploit the System's Constraints** An existing constraint may be used more effectively by exploring the short-term impact of various customer and product mixes on capacity. Mix options that are available in the short run represent different ways of using the full capacity of the bottleneck resource without making changes in the capacity itself. The linkage of these various options to profit improvement is made by determining what mix (or mixes) generates the greatest throughput from existing capacity.

What each product or customer provides in terms of "throughput per constraint hour potential of products and customers" should be evaluated. Managers should focus their efforts on increasing the volume and percentage of those product mixes providing the highest throughput per constraint hour.

A strategy of promoting the growth of certain products will, of course, be limited by sales demand for the products. Shifts in mix may require selective reductions in selling prices or additional outlays for promotion and advertising. These price and cost changes will change (reduce) the throughput potential of targeted products. The key objective remains—to find ways to significantly increase the organization's total throughput in both the long and short run.

**(c) Subordinate Everything to the Constraints** Nonconstraining business processes must be subordinated to the bottleneck or constrained resource. If the bottleneck is in manufacturing, then materials acquisition, marketing, and distribution processes are considered subordinate. Consequently, decision making related to determining the best product and customer mix should be based solely on optimizing the use of production capacity. The impact of changing mixes on marketing and distribution, for example, must be ignored, based on the following arguments:

- These nonconstraining processes have sufficient idle capacity to handle a variety of customer and product mixes.
- Most resource costs for these nonconstraining processes are fixed over the relevant decision time period—the short run. Changes in idle capacity do not change the company's total resource costs unless managers act to change the capacities of the business processes in question.
- Availability of idle capacity means that sufficient resources have been made available for "less than efficient" use of that resource in order to provide flexibility to accommodate business fluctuations and peak periods. Only the bottleneck resource needs to be scheduled to maintain maximum efficiency and effectiveness.

However, when managers consider significant changes in product mix, they create the potential for significant changes in demand for marketing and distribution activities. This change in activity demand may exceed the capacity of one of the business processes, thus introducing a new constraint. In that event, sufficient pressure may exist to warrant expanding capacities—particularly capacities represented by people—in the nonconstrained processes to support the new mix.

The TOC approach does not provide a cost estimate of these potential capacity increases. Rather, all capacity is assumed to be unchangeable in the short run. But ignoring capacity issues in marketing and distribution may lead to quality and service problems if the demands made on those activities are significant. Therefore, although focusing decision making only on the current bottleneck may provide short-term gains in throughput and profitability, it can also have undesirable consequences in the long run.

**(d) Elevate the System's Constraints**    When a bottleneck is an internal constraint, an organization cannot satisfy all external demand for its products or services. The fourth step identified by the TOC philosophy is to "elevate the constraint."

Assume, for example, that a constraint exists in manufacturing. *Elevating the constraint* means finding ways to break or relieve the constraint. This could involve one of two approaches:

1. Invest in new equipment or technology to increase the total available operating time for the constraint.
2. Increase the productivity of the bottleneck by eliminating non–value-adding activities and reducing cycle time in the bottleneck.

Assume, for example, that products going through the bottleneck manufacturing department previously required an extensive setup that caused a cycle time of 50 hours for an average batch. Then a change is made in setup procedures, which results in a reduction of setup time by 6 hours per batch, so cycle time is reduced to an average of 44 hours per batch. Because of this change, the company can process more batches through the bottleneck and thus generate more throughput per year. If sufficient non–value-added time can be eliminated, the machine center may no longer be considered a critical constraint.

Investment in technology to expand capacity is a capital budgeting decision and should be based on long-term sales potential. However, the expectation is that the increase in throughput will more than offset the increase in operating expenses. Capital budgeting proposals should include projections of changes in T and OE over the economic life of the project. The present value of the incremental cash inflows represented by the proposed change in T should be greater than the present value of the incremental outflows associated with changes in OE [T > OE]. For example, TOC can be used to evaluate proposals to expand capacity in the bottleneck. The investment cost in new equipment and added employees should be less than the resulting increase in cash flows from serving new customers or markets that previous capacity limitations did not allow.

Alternatively, reducing product cycle time in the bottleneck to boost output from existing capacity can be a short-run strategy that should free up non–value-added time for redeployment on other products or projects where it can boost throughput. The benefits of reduced cycle time can occur over a period of years; net present value analysis (NPV) is appropriate if there are significant initial investment costs.

**28.6 EXPLOITING A SYSTEM'S CONSTRAINTS**    The second of the five TOC steps—to exploit the system's constraints—recommends that managers pay significant attention to how the constraining resource is used. Step three—to subordinate the nonconstraining resources—recommends that analyses to determine appropriate product or customer mix decisions should not take into account capacity measures of the nonconstraining resource. These nonconstraining resources are assumed to have idle capacity that will not be eliminated—but only vary in amount—when different product mixes are considered. Consequently, capacities containing idle time can be ignored for the purposes of short-term decisions about product mix and volume.

**(a) Accounting for Throughput**    Accounting for a company's throughput provides an overview of how well the company can use its constrained capacity with respect to the output (or throughput) potential from various product mixes that have to flow through that constrained capacity. As discussed previously, managers need to be able to evaluate whether the company's product and customer mix is the right match for its existing capacity. The following paragraphs provide a discussion of accounting for throughput and product profitability measurement.

Accounting measurements of throughput can provide managers valuable insights about where the company is not generating adequate throughput from its capacity, given opportunities in the market. The company's measure of throughput is a summary of the individual throughput available from customers in the company's customer mix or product lines in the company's product mix. Throughput is recognized only when goods and services are actually sold to outside customers: Production that is added to inventory levels has no value in the TOC philosophy.

During the current year or in the short run, a company's ability to generate throughput is limited by a lack of sales demand (an external constraint) or by constrained resources in one or more of the business processes (an internal constraint). The following sections provide an expanded discussion of constraints and related financial analysis.

**(b) External Constraints**    A lack of sales demand is an *external constraint*. In this case, the quality, design, and function of the company's products do not attract enough customers willing to pay adequate prices. This may require product redesign or changes in the company's product mix. Alternatively, the company may need to change its marketing strategy or how it communicates what it offers customers.

Cost analysis should compare the following:

- Investments necessary to change the value perceived by customers.
- The annual throughput dollars that could be generated by such changes.

For example, assume that a product redesign proposal would incur the following upfront investment costs:

| Investment Cost: | |
| --- | --- |
| Engineering | $25,000 |
| Manufacturing planning | 15,000 |
| New tooling | 50,000 |
| Purchasing planning | 10,000 |
| Total investment | $100,000 |

The investment cost would be a one-time increase in operating expenses. The planning costs are included under the assumption that these costs are out-of-pocket expenses rather than an allocation of managers' time. (If the project were undertaken using idle management and engineering time, the change in operating expenses with respect to the planning costs would be zero.)

The contribution of this project is in the potential increase in annual throughput. Assume for example that annual sales volume is expected to increase by 40%, from 10,000 units to 14,000 units, and the selling price will be increased by $4.00 per unit. Direct material costs will increase by $1.50 per unit. These changes provide a net change in throughput per unit of $2.50 ($4.00 less $1.50).

| | Old Design | New Design | Changes |
|---|---|---|---|
| Price per unit | $55.00 | $59.00 | + $ 4.00 |
| Direct materials | 30.00 | 31.50 | (1.50) |
| Throughput per unit | $25.00 | $27.50 | + $ 2.50 |
| @ Volume in units | 10,000 | 14,000 | + 4,000 |
| = Total value of T | $250,000 | $385,000 | $135,000 |

The benefit of the product redesign is an increase in throughput of $135,000 per year, assuming a constant sales-volume increase. Under the TOC, no other operating costs are considered, because the company has not made a decision (for the short run, at least) to change or expand capacity, other than to add new tooling.

No additional employees are expected to be hired and trained to facilitate the production of the new design. Rather, it is assumed that manufacture of the redesigned product will use existing idle capacity in the manufacturing and distribution processes. If, however, the idle internal capacity proves insufficient and the total increase in demand cannot be accommodated, managers will have to consider capacity rationing.

**(c) Net Present Value Analysis with External Constraints**    A net present value (NPV) analysis can be conducted by estimating the useful economic life of the redesign. A decision to invest in product redesign is not a one-year decision: The impact on sales over a period of years should be considered.

Assume that the product redesign has a useful life of three years. If so, a concern might be raised about the TOC view on short-term capacity. In the manufacturing process, the redesign need not change capacity because it was intended to make the use of existing capacity more efficient. But higher sales volume may put capacity pressures on marketing and distribution. If so, payroll in those areas may increase over time to support the new volume. If payroll increases $70,000 in these processes, the annual benefit of the redesign would be the additional throughput ($135,000) less the additional operating expenses ($70,000), or a net increase in profits of $65,000.

The present value (PV) of the future cash flows from increased throughput less increased operating expenses can be compared with the upfront investment costs. This will determine whether the redesign provides a satisfactory return and a positive NPV. Assuming a hurdle rate of 15 percent per year, the PV factor for three years would be 2.2832. The NPV calculation would be as follows:

| | |
|---|---|
| Annual benefit | $65,000 |
| PV factor (3 years) | × 2.2832 |
| Discounted cash inflows | $148,408 |
| Initial investment | ($100,000) |
| NPV | $ 48,408 |

In this example, the product redesign would provide a return well in excess of the hurdle rate of 15 percent, so managers should proceed with the project, assuming the sales and pricing projections are considered realistic and reliable.

**(d) Internal Constraints**    An *internal constraint* means that, for the next planning year, inadequate capacity exists in one or more business processes. In this case, a company cannot produce and deliver all the products in the next year that customers may demand. As this is a short-term viewpoint, it is assumed that capacity decisions (e.g., about personnel, technology, and space) have already been made. The company has already made the decision that, in the short run, the amount of unmet demand is an acceptable alternative to the cost of investment needed to expand capacity. Currently scarce capacity will thus need to be rationed and dedicated to those products that provide the highest throughput per scarce resource.

Assume that a company's manufacturing process is the limiting factor or scarce resource. Typically the scarce resource is represented by a major investment in capital equipment—often in the manufacturing area. The measure of the bottleneck in manufacturing capacity is annual available machine hours in the fabrication department, which will be labeled "Department Y" in a later example. The number of constraining machine hours is assumed to be 4,000 machine hours annually.

**(e) Apportioning Bottleneck Resources to Products or Customers**    In the example that follows, manufacturing capacity is common to all products—in other words, each product is produced on a common set of machines. When this is the case, bottleneck hours must be wisely apportioned among competing products and customers.

In cell manufacturing (i.e., when a single product is made in one cell), "capacity rationing" refers to the allocation of scarce resources among potential customers for that product. The throughput value from different customers can vary according to the characteristics of the customers. One customer, for example, might order small batch sizes, which means that fewer units are produced from a single setup. When cycle times take into account batch-level time drivers such as setups and inspection, small batch sizes are seen to consume more constraint time per unit than do large batch sizes. Similarly, another customer might have high tolerances, which would probably mean that the machine would have to be run slower to accommodate the higher demands on inspection. Again, therefore, the result would be fewer units per constraint hour.

To take best advantage of excess demand for products, the company's product mix should favor those products that provide the greatest throughput per scarce resource; in this case, machine hours. For example, assume that a company manufactures two products, $A$ and $B$. The manufacturing process has three departments, $X$, $Y$, and $Z$, and each product passes through each of the three departments. The bottleneck exists in Department $Y$, where product $A$ uses 0.2 machine hours per unit and product $B$ uses 0.6 machine hours per unit. The unit cycle times are based on the average batch cycle times divided by the average batch size. For example, the batch cycle time for product $A$ in Department $Y$ is 200 minutes and the average batch size is 1,000 units. Thus the average time per unit is 0.2 (200 minutes divided by 1,000 units per batch).

Determination of batch cycle time for product $A$ is provided in the following table. Note that the batch cycle time is the cumulative total of sequential activity times, adjusted for the simultaneous performance of multiple activities. The needed batch cycle time is the total time in bottleneck hours that a product batch ties up the constraint. Note that some activities are batch-related and some unit-related. Therefore, cycle time per unit must be based first on calculating the batch cycle time, then dividing by the batch volume in units.

### Batch Cycle Time in the Bottleneck Department
### Product A Batches

| Activity | Batch Activity Time | Cumulative Batch Cycle Time |
|---|---|---|
| Set up machines | 3 hours | 5 hours |
| Feed raw materials | 2 hours | included |
| Machine running time | 5 hours | 8 hours |
| Unload work in process (WIP) | 2 hours | 1 hour extra |
| Inspect WIP | 3 hours | 3 hours |
| Move WIP from machine | 2 hours | 1 hour extra |
| Total machine hours per batch | | 18 hours |
| Average batch size for product A | | 90 |
| Average bottleneck time per unit of product A | | 0.2 |

In the table that follows, the unit throughputs for A and B are provided. Product A's throughput is $60 per unit, and product B's throughput is $150 per unit. Potential demand in units is multiplied by average machine hours per unit in Department Y, the constraint. Total machine hours needed to meet demand is 6,000 machine hours.

| | | | | Constraint | | |
|---|---|---|---|---|---|---|
| Product | Price | Raw Materials | Throughput per Unit | Potential Demand | Machine Hours/Unit | Machine Hours |
| A | $100 | $ 40 | $60 | 15,000 units | 0.2 | 3,000 |
| B | $300 | $150 | $150 | 5,000 units | 0.6 | 3,000 |
| | | | | | | 6,000 |

The company is unable to meet demand in the short run because of inadequate production capacity. Total machine hours needed to meet annual demand are 6,000, but there are only 4,000 machine hours currently available (based on the company's prior capacity decisions). Because available capacity and demand are known during the planning stage, the company can decide to influence or change its product mix for the coming year through a marketing strategy of promotions, advertising, and bonus or commission structure. The question is, Which product should be promoted the most heavily? If the company knew which product would provide a higher throughput per machine hour, prioritizing that product would generate the highest overall throughput for the company. Multiplying the 4,000 constraint hours times the highest throughput per machine hour will obtain the most dollars of throughput.

To rank the two products, calculate how many dollars of throughput are provided for a single machine hour. This ranking is provided below:

| Product | Price | Raw Materials | Throughput per Unit | Machine Hours/Unit | Throughput per Machine Hour |
|---------|-------|---------------|---------------------|--------------------|-----------------------------|
| A | $100 | $ 40 | $60 | 0.2 | $300 |
| B | $300 | $150 | $150 | 0.6 | $250 |

Product *A* has the higher throughput of $30 per machine hour and should be prioritized. Product *B*, which has a higher throughput per unit ($150 compared with $60 for product *A*), requires more constraint time per unit. Thus, the company can only produce one-third as many units as product *B* does in one constraint hour. In one constraint hour, the company can produce five units of *A*, which earns $300 (5 units × $60 of throughput per unit). In contrast, the company can produce one and two-thirds units of *B*, which generates throughput of $250 per constraint hour (5/3 units @ $150 T per unit).

**(f) Calculating Potential Throughput**    The potential throughput of the optimal product mix, assuming sufficient sales demand, is as follows:

| Product | Throughput per Unit | Planned Output | Throughput | Machine Hours/Unit | Total Needed Machine Hours |
|---------|---------------------|----------------|------------|--------------------|----------------------------|
| A | $ 60 | 15,000 units | $900,000 | 0.2 | 3,000 |
| B | $150 | ? | ? | 0.6 | 1,000 (plug) 4,000 (capacity) |

The throughput potential for *A* is the potential demand of 15,000 units times the throughput per machine hour of $60, or $900,000. The remaining capacity—1,000 machine hours (i.e., the capacity of 4,000 hours minus 3,000 hours dedicated to product *A*)—is then available to make units of product *B*. This remaining 1,000 hours can make up to 1,666 units of *B*. The throughput potential for *B* would be 1,666 units times $150 per unit, or $249,900. The total throughput for the company would be $1.149 million ($900,000 + $249,900).

**28.7 THROUGHPUT AND FULL-COST ALLOCATION**    Each product line that a company offers should contribute to the coverage of OE. In total, the combined product lines should recover all operating expenses before the company can be considered profitable. Total profit, P, is measured by the formula, $P = T - OE$. Note that OE represents the cost of capacity commonly available to support all product lines. Changes in product mix or product-line volume in the short run are assumed not to change operating expenses. Personnel and technology costs are planned and budgeted for—and therefore assumed to be unchangeable—in the short run. Operating expenses are not directly related to any one product line or customer. Assignment of a portion of operating expenses to any one product line represents an arbitrary allocation; no causal relationship between the allocated cost and product line volume is assumed to exist.

**(a) Allocating Operating Expenses to a Product Line**    The allocation of operating expenses to any one product line should follow this simple rule: Deduction of an allocated share of operating expenses from the throughput of each one of a company's several product lines should not alter the product profitability ranking that was based on throughput per scarce resource. A decision maker who is considering product mix or pricing decisions should have equal or improved information after deducting for allocated operating expenses. There should not be a multiple product-profitability ranking that could confuse decision makers about which products are more (or less) profitable and how managers should make better use of constrained resources.

Returning to the previous example, assume that the company has two products, *A* and *B*. The traditional allocation method (based on total direct labor dollars) applied factory overhead at the rate of $30 per direct-labor hour. Assuming that product *A* uses 0.8 labor hours per unit, the overhead charge would be $24 per unit for this product. Assuming that product *B* uses 1 direct-labor hour per unit, the overhead charge would be $30 per unit.

If the product profitability analysis deducted the allocated overhead from throughput, the profit per unit would be $36 for product *A* (i.e., $60 throughput per unit – the $24 per unit of allocated overhead). Similarly, the overhead allocated to product *B* is $30, so the net profit per unit would be $120 (i.e., $150 throughput per unit – $30 of allocated overhead). The result is a picture of product *B* that shows significantly more profit per unit than product *A*. Even with a revision of product profitability that takes into account the use of bottleneck time, product *B* still looks better. The implication for a manager who reads such data is that scarce manufacturing capacity should be directed to expanding the output of product *B*.

| | | | Constraint | | | |
| | | | | | | Profit per |
| | Throughput | Per Unit | Traditional | Profit | Machine | Constrain |
| Product | Per Unit | Labor Hours | Overhead | Per Unit | Hours/Unit | Hour |
| --- | --- | --- | --- | --- | --- | --- |
| *A* | $60 | 0.8 | $24 | $36 | 0.2 | $180 |
| *B* | $150 | 1.0 | $30 | $120 | 0.6 | $200 |

The product ranking shown in the chart indicates that product *B* provides the higher profitability per constraint hour after deducting for operating expenses. The product ranking based on throughput per constraint hour was presented earlier. Product *A* had the highest throughput per constraint hour of $300, whereas product *B* had a lower throughput per constraint hour of $250.

Which is the better product? Which product makes better use of constrained hours? The answer is the same as it was before allocation. Product *A* generates more dollars of cash flow from the use of constrained hours. The arbitrary allocation of common capacity using an overhead rate of $30 per direct-labor dollars provides no useful information; in fact, it provides confusing, contradictory signals. There is no direct, causal relationship between total overhead dollars and the use of direct labor in the manufacture of products *A* and *B*. Factory overhead is only one part of operating expenses: The arbitrary allocation of R&D, marketing, distribution, and other costs could further distort the product profitability ranking.

**(b) Allocating Operating Expenses Based on Scarce Resources**   One approach to allocating operating expenses that does not distort product profitability ranking is to allocate based on the scarce resource—in this case, constrained machine hours. Because decision makers must determine a product mix that makes the best use of the constrained resource, one way of looking at the constraint is to consider it a valuable asset that must be "leased or rented" to the highest bidder.

Assuming operating expenses of $800,000 a year that support 4,000 constrained machine hours of output, a break-even "rental fee" for use of machine hours would be as follows:

$$\text{Cost of constrained machine hours} = \$800,000/4,000 \text{ machine hours}$$

$$= \$200 \text{ per machine hour}$$

Profitable product lines will generate throughput per constrained hour that exceeds the cost of $200 that is currently required to support a constrained machine hour. The $200 represents the resource costs, or operating expenses, invested in the total system of business processes. It reflects the cost of both the constrained capacity and the subordinated, nonconstrained capacities.

Both products $A$ and $B$ have sufficient throughput per constraint hour to recover their fair share of operating expenses or resource costs that were invested to provide the system's capacity. The net amount of the operating expenses charge of $200 per constraint hour is the *throughput margin:*

| Product | Throughput per Hour | Charge per Constraint Hour | Throughput Margin |
| --- | --- | --- | --- |
| A | $300 | $200 | $100 |
| B | $250 | $200 | $50 |

If a third product, $C$, provided a throughput of only $150 per constraint hour, it would not recover the fair share of the investment in OE made to support the total system capacity. Should the product be dropped? Not necessarily. The OE are a short-term fixed cost of capacity that would not necessarily be reduced in the current year by dropping product $C$. A better strategy would be to find other products or projects that do generate enough throughput to recover their share of operating expenses plus profit.

Assuming that the company wishes to earn a target profit of $400,000 before taxes for the year, the analysis above could be enhanced by calculating a minimum charge for bottleneck capacity usage that provides for recovery of all operating expenses and also the targeted profit. The total amount to recover is $1.2 million ($800,000 operating expenses plus the $400,000 target profit). The above charge would then be determined as follows:

$$\text{OE and target profit} = \$1,200,000/4,000 \text{ machine hours}$$

$$= \$300 \text{ per machine hour}$$

If the current pricing of product lines generates an average throughput of at least $300 per constraint hour, the company will be able to achieve its target profit. Of the $300-per-constraint-hour value, $100 represents the additional throughput earned to meet the target profit.

In the example, product *A* provides a throughput per constraint hour of $300. This product provides just enough throughput to keep the company on track to earn its target profit. However, product *B* has a throughput value of $250 per constraint hour, so it does not provide all of the target profit per constraint hour.

For the company to meet its profit target, the selling prices might have to be raised on one or both products to achieve an average throughput per constraint hour of $300. Alternatively, the company could reduce capacity costs in nonconstraining departments. This would lower average operating expenses sufficiently so that $100 per constraint hour could be dedicated to generating the targeted profits.

**28.8 PRODUCT-LINE INCOME STATEMENTS**  The allocation of operating expenses based on an internally constrained resource can be shown in greater detail. The following product-line income statement is based on the original example of a five-product manufacturing company having a full range of business processes; it uses the total operating expenses displayed earlier. However, only the first two products (*A* and *B*) are highlighted:

### Product-Line Income Statement for the Year Ended 12/31/XXXX

| Product Line Throughput: | Product A | Product B | Total |
| --- | --- | --- | --- |
| Net revenues | $1,000,000 | $2,400,000 | $8,450,000 |
| Less: Materials | 650,000 | 1,850,000 | 5,250,000 |
| Throughput | $350,000 | $550,000 | $3,200,000 |
| Constraint usage (%) | 10% | 35% | 100% |
| Less: Operating Expense | | | |
| R&D | $25,000 | $87,500 | $250,000 |
| Marketing | 60,000 | 210,000 | 600,000 |
| Materials acquisition | 50,000 | 175,000 | 500,000 |
| Manufacturing | 120,000 | 420,000 | 1,200,000 |
| Distribution | 40,000 | 140,000 | 400,000 |
| Subtotal | $295,000 | $1,032,500 | $2,950,000 |
| Product line income before taxes | $55,000 | $(482,500) | $250,000 |

The product-line income statement identifies—for each product line—the percentage of the constrained resource consumed. Here, for example, the constrained resource is found in the machining department of the manufacturing process. The constraint is measured by machine hours and estimated to be 4,000 machine hours per year. Product *A* uses 400 machine hours during the year, or 10 percent of the total, whereas product line *B* uses 1,400 machine hours, or 35 percent of the total.

**(a) Allocation of Cost Pools Based on the Constrained Resource**  The cost pool associated with each business process is allocated to the products based on their consumption of the constraint. Thus, 10 percent of the marketing cost pool was assigned to product *A* and 35 percent to product *B*. This allocation is justified on the grounds that the short-term costs—in terms of people, tools, technology, and space—of each business process are fixed and committed during the capacity-planning phase. In the short run, these costs will not be changed by any decisions or changes in the product mix. Therefore, the purpose of the allocation is to identify which products recover their fair shares of total operating expenses, given their use of the scarce resource.

Product-line $B$ is easily identified in the income statement as a product that is making poor use of the scarce resource. Its throughput for the product line is very low in relation to its 35 percent use share of the bottleneck. The $1,032,500 charge for operating expenses simply reflects its high use of the bottleneck.

Improvements in profitability for product-line $B$ depend on whether managers can make several changes. For one, the customer value of product $B$ needs to be increased to raise the throughput per unit. Another approach would be to reduce the bottleneck capacity utilization of the product relative to its sales volume, which would reduce the share of operating expenses that the product is expected to recover. A third approach would be to look for other products or projects to use the bottleneck machine hours currently devoted to product-line $B$. These alternative uses may generate more total throughput and enable the company to recover all of its fixed operating expenses.

**(b) No Changes Assumed in Resource Costs**    Care must be taken in interpreting product-line income statements based on throughput. For example, managers may be aware that product-line $A$ is a fairly new product that requires extensive marketing support. This marketing effort is not reflected in the 10 percent rate of bottleneck-resource usage. Assume that 20 percent of the efforts of the marketing process are devoted to product $A$. Dropping the product would release 20 percent of marketing time to work on other projects.

What must be kept in mind is that the throughput product-line income statement represents the current—and short-term (i.e., one year or less)—time period. In the short run, other products cannot be introduced: The total resources of the marketing process (including people) are fixed. No changes in employment or of the investment in marketing are assumed for the next year. Therefore, there is no causal linkage between product mix and the costs of marketing resources. Whereas the marketing time and effort spent on a specific product line may be altered in the short run, the total marketing costs will *not* change in the short run.

A throughput product-line income statement is a short-term planning tool for product mix and pricing decisions. The information can indicate whether the company should consider replacements for one or more of its current products. The information should not be used for any longer-term business process capacity changes; it should *not* be used to predict how resource costs would change in the long run if new products are introduced or old products dropped. In the long run, managers can and will adjust business process capacities as needed, and these adjustments will change total operating expenses. The throughput model, however, assumes no changes in resource costs.

**28.9 RELAXING THE THROUGHPUT MODEL**    The throughput model assumes that all business process resource costs are fixed and unchangeable. This is based on selecting a relatively short decision time period—one year or less. During this short time period, all staffing and investment decisions are assumed to have been made and are unchangeable.

As the time period is extended, however, certain capacity decisions can be revisited, particularly those that deal with employee staffing decisions. Over a longer time period, capacities in departments may be expanded or contracted. This is particularly true when those capacities are really defined in terms of the number of people employed in that department.

Assume, for example, that the purchasing department employs 10 purchasing agents and 15 clerical staff this year. Management has decided to maintain the purchasing department's capacity by having that many employees. Capacity of the department may be measured in terms of the number of purchase orders issued, the number of vendor contracts signed, or the number of vendors managed. During the current year, this capacity allows enough slack to handle peak workloads, and no staffing changes are anticipated. Over a longer time period, however, changes in product mix, the parts used in the products, and vendor policies all may affect the department's workload to such an extent that one or more employees may have to be hired or laid off. Changes in departmental capacity and the cost of resources may change in purchasing, but not in the bottleneck resources.

**(a) Adapting the Model to Changes in Resource Costs**    Decisions to change the product mix and volumes can lead to changes in operating expenses that can be predicted on a department-by-department basis. Suggested mix changes can have predictable effects, which may lead to changes in employee head count and payroll costs.

If the decision is made to promote a product mix that calls for more product *A* and less product *B*, the new product mix may be feasible and may conform to the limitations of the machining bottleneck. However, the change in mix and volumes may require more employees in marketing to handle necessary customer education and relations. Therefore, the throughput model may be more useful if it can be adapted to reflect the causal relationships between various product activity drivers and resource costs in selected business processes that exist over longer periods.

One fundamental point to recognize is that TOC tends to recognize internal constraints in departments or processes that are primarily driven by technology and major capital investments. These sources of bottlenecks are based on long-range investment decisions; they change infrequently because of the large investment involved. For example, a million-dollar investment in a plastic extruding machine may establish a constraint in a plastics plant. Additional such investments will be made only after conducting extensive and long-range strategic analysis, a cash-flow analysis, and a new sales forecast.

**(b) Internal Constraints Determined by Technology, Not People**    Internal constraints rarely involve departments or areas in which the work is primarily paced or driven by people. This is because the company can hire and train additional employees when needed to relieve potential bottlenecks caused by shortages of qualified personnel. People-based bottlenecks, where they exist, tend to be "wandering," because they occur when experienced personnel are added or leave the organization.

The use of wandering, unstable constraints in an accounting system would introduce data credibility questions when, in a short period of time, the ranking of products changes dramatically because of changing bottlenecks. Therefore, a more stable, technology-based bottleneck is needed as the foundation for a throughput accounting system.

The basic throughput model allocated all business process and department costs based on constraint usage. This was justified as long as it was assumed that no causal relationships exist between costs and product volume. But because causal relationships between employee payroll costs and cost drivers over a relevant time period do exist for certain departments, the following discussion describes how the basic throughput model can be that adapted by blending the best ideas from the TOC and activity-based costing (ABC).

The TOC is best applied to those departments whose capacity is unlikely to change during a time period relevant to product mix and volume decisions. Such departments generally will be those in which the work procedures and output are determined by a significant investment in technology. These departments can be classified as *machine-intensive.*

ABC can best be applied in those departments in which work procedures and output are linked to the number of people employed in the department. These departments can be classified as *people-intensive.* Departments within business processes need to be classified on two factors:

1. Is the department constraining or nonconstraining?
2. Is the department people-intensive or technology-intensive?

The following section discusses in detail classifications of departments as either people-intensive or machine-intensive[5]

**(c) People-Intensive Departments**    A manufacturing company usually has many departments that have significant numbers of employees who perform tasks, make judgments, and follow procedures. The time and effort to do each task may vary with the requirements of the product or customer. The work of these employees is subject to activity identification and analysis. There are strong linkages between:

- The volume of activities and the need for specific numbers of employees.
- Changes in customer and product mixes and the overall demand for activities.

Such departments may be labeled people-intensive. People-intensive departments are distinguished by three characteristics:

1. Adaptable or redeployable resources.
2. Employee-paced work flows.
3. Resource costs that consist primarily of employee wages and benefits.

For these departments, people are the primary asset. These employees perform a variety of tasks linked to the activities of the department. As tasks and activities change, these employees generally are capable of being retrained for other tasks. They may also be reassigned or let go if work levels change.

While departments such as scheduling, purchasing, raw material stores, and shipping are usually considered a fixed capacity in the short run, their capacity may be changed by managers. As activity levels significantly increase, the need for more people becomes apparent. Managers may chose to solve the problem by hiring and training new workers. The time frame for hiring decisions—while not really short term because of fringe benefits and severance-costs considerations—are considerably shorter than the time frames required for decisions to expand technological capacity through capital investments in a production department. Staffing decisions and changes in staffing levels are part of the annual capacity-planning process in many companies.

**(d) Terminating or Redeploying Employees**    The demand for services provided by some support departments diminishes over time, so some activities are performed less frequently. If these activities are performed primarily by people, managers may chose to reduce departmental capacity by terminating employees or redeploying them to other departments and tasks. Training costs would certainly be incurred for redeployments. For example, several years ago a steel service center replaced its overhead crane system of material handling with automated conveyors. The unneeded crane operators were redeployed to manufacturing and trained as machine operators. These added employees in production supported an overall increase in product volume.

The changeable nature of capacities in people-intensive departments points out a limitation of the TOC. Decisions that go beyond the very short run and that have an impact over the next year or two may well involve changing capacities in people-intensive areas. Cost information that identifies the impact of changing activity levels—and, thus, managed changes in resource costs—can and should be included in the throughput product-line income statement.

For example, assume that the purchasing department has a cost pool of $200,000 and the principal activity driver is the number of purchase orders. Assume also that the purchasing department employs 10 purchasing agents, who provide a capacity to issue 10,000 purchase orders per year. The ABC charge rate for the purchasing cost pool is as follows:

$$\text{ABC rate (purchasing)} = \$200,000/10,000 \text{ purchase orders}$$

$$= \$20 \text{ per purchase order}$$

For the ABC rate to be meaningful, it must represent a causal relationship between the cost pool and the activity driver. A causal relationship means that changes in activity levels will, over time, cause managers to adjust capacity in the department or activity. Capacity adjustment, in turn, means that managers are willing to change resource costs by changing employment levels in the department. Thus, pricing or decisions that will increase the number of purchase orders issued by 2,000 (20 percent) will require some change in purchasing capacity. Perhaps two additional purchasing agents will have to be hired. The ABC rate represents the cost of creating and maintaining capacity; the cost of anticipated capacity changes can be predicted by using the ABC rate. To estimate the cost of additional capacity to handle the increased workload in purchasing, the following estimate can be made:

$$\text{Cost of adding capacity} = 2,000 \text{ purchase order increase} \times \$20 \text{ per purchase order}$$

$$= \$40,000 \text{ additional cost}$$

This estimate would be reasonable if the cost pool were from a people-intensive department where the primary costs were wages and benefits. Thus, the ABC rate would reflect the costs of maintaining certain employee head counts in relation to the workload. If the workload changes significantly, managers should expect to have to change the employee head count as well.

These predictive causal relationships should be provided in the throughput product-line income statement. For example, if product $A$ uses a unique set of materials that are purchased through 500 purchase orders a year, it should carry a purchasing cost as follows:

Purchasing cost for product $A$ = 500 purchase orders @ $20 per PO = $10,000 a year

The assumption is that if product $A$ were dropped or its volume altered such that a significant decline occurred in the total number of purchase orders issued, managers would need to adjust capacity, which would likely lead to cost reductions in the purchasing cost pool. This type of information should be made available for people-intensive departments in the product-line income statement.

**(e) Machine-Intensive Departments**    Certain departments are characterized by significant investments in technology. This technology may be in the form of automated or semiautomated machines that cannot be easily adapted to different tasks or methods. They may represent repetitive tasking or production steps. A plastic extruding machine, for example, may be adjusted to place more or less plastic into molds, but it is impossible to change the basics of how the machine works.

Machine-intensive departments are primarily found in production departments such as machining or fabricating departments. Characteristics of machine-intensive departments include:

- Machine-paced work flows.
- Depreciation-oriented resource costs.
- Employees who are often assigned to work crews whose size is dictated by machine characteristics and whose tasks depend on the existing machine technology.

Capacity in machine-paced departments is typically measured by the number of productive hours that the machine can be operated during shifts worked. For example, an extruding machine might be in operation about 85 percent of a company's one eight-hour shift. Note that some downtime for maintenance and adjustments is expected. If the one shift works an average of 22 days a month, the machine capacity is 85 percent × 22 days × 8 hours per day = 150 hours a month.

This capacity of 150 hours per month is unchangeable in the short run—and even in the intermediate run unless significant new investments are made in equipment or equipment enhancements. With respect to product or customer mix decisions, managers should not consider the resource costs of the machine but only how to make the best use of the constrained resource hours available from the machine.

The resource costs of these machine-intensive departments are not relevant to short-term decision making, whether the machine or department is a constraining or nonconstraining resource. These costs should be allocated through the constrained-resource time measure when preparing a throughput product-line income statement. In the near term (or even in a couple of years), idle capacity in nonconstraining, machine-intensive departments may continue to expand or contract as changes in product mix are made. However, the upper limits of each department's capacity will not be violated (except by short-term overtime), and product mix and volume decisions will have to recognize limited time resources in each department.

Breaking these machine-intensive departments into activities and assigning a share of departmental resource costs to each activity provides no meaningful information. For example, in an ABC system, a charge of $250 per setup may be calculated. However, this is not really a direct cost, because no causal relationship exists between the resource cost pool and the activity driver.

The cost pool would include wages for the setup crew and machine costs. Assume that product and customer-mix decisions change the number of setups next year. The impact of increasing the number of setups is limited to reallocating available machine time, because there is no change in resource costs. Assume that the number of setups increases from 100 to 120 next year. If each setup requires an average of 4 hours, then 20 additional setups ties up 80 machine hours. If there is idle time on the machine, nothing is lost. If the machine is a bottleneck, then 80 machine hours are taken away from production, so throughput is lost. But the total setup costs for the crew and machine (part of operating expenses) would not change.

The next section provides a brief case study of an actual manufacturing company. It features a customer profitability model based on throughput that recognizes the differences between machine-intensive and people-intensive departments.

**(f) Designing a Customer Profitability Model**    A project was undertaken at a midwestern manufacturer of electronics components to develop a customer profitability model. The pilot study was limited to a single plant that produced four different products that were used to support or house electric or cable transmission lines in commercial buildings. The products may be encased in cement floors or suspended from ceilings, depending on the application and the product.

Several departments—such as busway, wireway, and cable tray—could be considered manufacturing cells dedicated to the production of individual product lines. Each cell contained an actual or potential bottleneck because of the high demand for each of the plant's four products. However, because managers could decide to shift the mix of styles and product variations in each product line, cell capacity was allocated to various segments of each product line during peak demand periods. Therefore, the cost of cell capacity was allocated to individual customer orders based on how much of the bottleneck resource was used order. A customer order for two different product lines would receive a separate charge for each product line.

In another manufacturing department, the blanking (i.e., steel-coil cutting) machine performed activities common to all four product lines. The demand on this common machine was such that it also was a potential bottleneck. At certain times during the year, therefore, the blanking machine had to have its capacity allocated among the four product lines.

The project identified which departments were people-intensive, and ABC was applied to these departments. The major departments and the annual resource dollars budgeted at the electronics plant are listed in Exhibit 28.1.[6]

Each department is categorized as either machine-intensive or people-intensive. The machine-intensive departments were all producing departments. The costs of common resources were assigned to product lines based on the amount (or time) of the bottleneck resources used by the product line in question. This is in accordance with the TOC methodology.

For example, resource costs associated with operating the busway cell are charged to customers based on their usage of the cell's bottleneck. Managers identified the cell's bottleneck as a specific, expensive piece of equipment called a "roll-form machine." Each item produced in the department used this machine. Assuming that the annual operating expenses of the busway cell total $792,500, a capacity charge rate can be calculated based on the available machine time on the roll-form machine. Based on the work shift schedule, the machine was estimated to provide 240,000 productive minutes a year. The capacity usage charge for the busway cell is therefore:

| Department | Budget | Classification |
|---|---|---|
| Information services | $207,600 | People-intensive |
| Engineering | 283,000 | People-intensive |
| Customer service | 390,300 | People-intensive |
| Quality control | 172,500 | People-intensive |
| Product management | 276,800 | People-intensive |
| Purchasing | 262,400 | People-intensive |
| Receiving and stores | 204,800 | People-intensive |
| Shipping | 212,600 | People-intensive |
| Blanking machine | 480,000 | Machine-intensive |
| Busway cell | 792,500 | Machine-intensive |
| Wireway cell | 449,100 | Machine-intensive |
| Cable-tray cell | 437,750 | Machine-intensive |
| Pain Line | 365,450 | Machine-intensive |
| Personnel | 179,300 | People-intensive |
| Accounting | 189,900 | People-intensive |
| Outside sales | 204,800 | People-intensive |
| | $5,108,800 | |

**Exhibit 28.1    Classification of Departments**

$$\text{Capacity charge} = \$792,500/240,000 \text{ minutes}$$

$$= \$3.30 \text{ per roll-form machine minute}$$

The user charge for a customer order is based on the cumulative roll-form machine time used. This is the sum of the times required by a customer batch for various activities, such as setups, material input, machine runtime, and unloading of finished items. Assume that an order uses 100 minutes on the roll-form machine. The cell costs assigned to the order are as follows:

$$\text{Busway order cost} = 100 \text{ minutes @ } \$3.30 \text{ per minute} = \$330$$

The support departments were generally identified as people-intensive departments. A manageable set of activities was identified for each department. The next step allocated the department's line-item expenses into activity cost pools and identified activity drivers assumed to have a strong causal relationship with the cost pool.

Based on the selected drivers, activity charge rates can be determined for the year. As an example, examine the customer service department. The resource costs incurred by the department are assumed to total $390,300 for the year. A series of interviews was conducted with employees, then the following list of activities was created from those interviews:

- Preparation of customer bids.
- Receipt of customer orders (called "shippers").
- Correction to customer order.
- Scheduling of standard products.

| Activities | Activity Drivers | Cost Pool | Driver # | ABC Rates |
|---|---|---|---|---|
| Bid preparation | No. of bid requests | $116,500 | 1,470 | $79.25 |
| Receive shipper | No. of shipper sets | 53,700 | 4,088 | $13.14 |
| Correct shipper | No. of shipper errors | 53,400 | 9,275 | $5.76 |
| Schedule standard items | No. of standard item ordered | 31,400 | 8,774 | $3.58 |
| Schedule custom items | No. of custom items ordered | 73,900 | 8,113 | $9.11 |
| Follow-up on shipping | No. of shipments | 61,400 | 3,909 | $15.71 |
| | | $390,300 | | |

**Exhibit 28.2    Activities in the Customer-Service Department**

- Scheduling of custom products (called "specials").
- Follow-up to orders.

Based on employee-reported time spent on each of the various activities, the departmental resource costs would be assigned to activities. Exhibit 28.2 provides hypothetical cost assignment to activities.

Note that the activity labeled "schedule special (custom) items" has a cost pool of $73,900 and a selected activity driver count of 8,113, which is the cumulative number of unique specials contained in all of the various customer orders. The ABC rate is calculated to be $9.11 per special per customer order. Assuming that a customer order requests three different custom or special products, the ABC charge to the order for the activity of scheduling specials would be as follows: Customer order cost = 3 specials @ $9.11 per special = $27.33. Each customer order would accumulate activity costs in people-intensive departments based on the consumption of activities.

**(g) Customer Profitability Analysis**    Exhibit 28.3 provides an example of a customer profitability statement.

This customer has requested a number of busway cell products. Customer revenues are netted against material costs to provide a throughput value of $3,100. The next deduction is for the use of production capacity in the machine-intensive departments with bottlenecks. A charge is made for both the blanking machine and the busway cell. The netting of bottleneck capacity charges against throughput provides the throughput margin, which is $2,110 in the example.

The next deduction is for activity usage in the people-intensive departments. On the customer profitability statement proper, deductions are shown for the departments as a whole. For example, the customer-service department activity charges total $304 for the order. Activity details can be provided as supplemental schedules. Details for customer service charges on individual activities are provided at the bottom on the statement. The netting of activity costs and throughput margin produces a measure of customer contribution, which is shown to be $785 for the order.

Finally, there is an allocated charge for corporate overhead. In simpler TOC applications with one bottleneck, corporate overhead could be included in the cost pool for total operating expenses. In this example, however, there are multiple bottlenecks—one in busway and one in the blanking machine department.

| | | | |
|---|---|---:|---:|
| Revenues | | | $8,000 |
| Less: Material costs | | | 4,900 |
| Throughput | | | $3,100 |
| Less: Machine-intensive constraint costs | | | |
| Blanking machine | | $330 | |
| Busway Cell | | 660 | 990 |
| Throughput Margin | | | $2,110 |
| Less: People-intensive activity costs by department | | | |
| Engineering | | $174 | |
| Customer services* | | 304 | |
| Product management | | 184 | |
| Purchasing | | 175 | |
| Shipping | | 294 | |
| Outside sales | | 194 | |
| Subtotal | | | 1,325 |
| Customer contribution | | | $785 |
| Less: Allocated corporate overhead | | | 100 |
| Customer profitability | | | $685 |

*customer service details

| Activities | Driver Count | ABC Rate | ABC Cost |
|---|---|---|---|
| Bid preparation | 2 | $79.25 | $158.50 |
| Receive shipper | 1 | $13.14 | 13.14 |
| Correct shipper | 8 | $5.76 | 46.08 |
| Schedule standard items | 5 | $3.58 | 17.90 |
| Schedule custom items | 4 | $9.11 | 36.44 |
| Follow-up shipping | 2 | $15.71 | 31.42 |
| | | | $303.48 |

**Exhibit 28.3    Wilson Company Customer Profitability Statement**

Multiple bottlenecks create an allocation dilemma. With two or more bottlenecks, there are multiple bottleneck cost pools and bottleneck capacity charge rates. How can corporate overhead be logically allocated to the two bottleneck cost pools? Given this dilemma, managers usually allocate corporate overhead directly to the customer orders based on a simple allocation base, such as sales dollars (i.e., based on the "ability to bear" criterion).

In the example, the customer earns $685 for the company. As a percentage of revenue, this is only 8.6 percent. If the company expects to average 12 percent of sales on orders for this product, managers may wish to take action on this product line. Assuming that pricing is standard for this product across all customers, several conclusions can be drawn. The product line may be underpriced with respect to the amount of bottleneck capacity required for this batch size, or this customer may have other characteristics that demand a higher level of activity frequency in one or more of the business processes.

The TOC information in the customer report can focus attention on how much of the company's bottleneck capacity is being used by this customer. Perhaps some changes in customer order characteristics (e.g., increasing the order or batch size) can reduce the average use of bottleneck capacity for each unit produced.

The ABC information can be used to analyze the high- and low-activity cost consumption by the customer. There may be excessive activity usage caused by customer ordering characteristics, such as incomplete information or rush ordering. The customer might be able to lower ABC costs in the future by altering ordering behavior. By reducing TOC and ABC costs, the customer may be rewarded with lower prices in the future. The company can still maintain its profit margins and gain loyal, satisfied customers as well.

**28.10 SUMMARY**    Business firms often keep an eye on short-term profitability, and they often expect important business decisions to have an impact even in the short run. But this is often impossible because of capacities that cannot be changed in the short run. The TOC is a valuable management philosophy that can point to better ways to manage existing capacity for greater profits.

In the short run, managers can have a significant impact on a very important measure: throughput. Throughput is a performance measure that calculates the margin or cash flow generated by sales revenues by deducting the only truly direct and variable cost, raw materials.

The TOC assumes that every company has limitations on its ability to generate cash flow from throughput. These limitations are known as constraints or bottlenecks, and they can exist internally or externally. Internal constraints are bottlenecks in one or more business process—generally in manufacturing, which is characterized by machine-intensive departments.

When a company has multiple products or a mix of customers having different demands and characteristics, the company may have to ration its scarce capacity among competing products or customers if the bottleneck is internal. Products can be rank-ordered by throughput per constraint measure to determine which products are the most profitable. Throughput per constraint measure (e.g., machine hours) indicates how much value is derived by allocating scarce resource time to a particular product. The product with the highest throughput per constraint measure is assumed to be the best, given adequate sales demand.

The TOC also addresses capacity management, which is a key to total profitability. There are five steps in TOC capacity management:

1. Identification of the bottleneck.
2. Exploitation of the bottleneck.
3. Subordination of nonconstraining resources.
4. Relieving the bottleneck.
5. Repeating the first four steps.

Exploiting the bottleneck means finding the best mix of products and customers to maximize throughput. Subordinating nonconstraining resources means not considering their costs in making short-term decisions about mix and volume. Relieving the bottleneck means expanding capacity in the bottleneck through additional technology investment or by making existing capacity more productive by reducing batch cycle times for various products. Accounting for TOC and its related decisions involves determining the impact of decisions and proposals on total throughput, operating expenses, and profits.

# NOTES

1. S. Demmy and J. Talbott, "Improve Internal Reporting with ABC and TOC," *Management Accounting* (November 1998): 18–24.

2. E. Noreen, D. Smith, and J. T. Mackey, *The Theory of Constraints and Its Implications for Management Accounting* (Great Barrington, MA: North River Press, 1995), 24.

3. E. Goldratt and J. Cox, *The Goal* (Croton-on-Hudson, NY: North River Press, 1986); E. Goldratt, *The Haystack Syndrome* (Croton-on-Hudson, NY: North River Press, 1990), 58–63.

4. J. S. Holmen, "ABC vs. TOC: It's a Matter of Time," *Management Accounting* (January 1995): 37–40.

5. R. Campbell, P. Brewer, and T. Mallie, "Designing an Information System Using Activity-Based Costing and the Theory of Constraints," *Journal of Cost Management* (January–February 1997): 17–18.

6. Ibid., 20.

# CHAPTER 29

# GOAL SETTING THROUGH VALUE ANALYSIS

## Frank O. Sunderland
## Jeanine Wilmot
**The Spectrum Management Group, Inc.**

**29.1 INTRODUCTION**   At the heart of the business model is the idea that a supply chain, an organization, a business process, and even an employee must "add value" to survive. Statements such as "We are in business to deliver value to our customers" and "We are in business to deliver economic value to our owners" are typical pronouncements from executive suites everywhere; often they are followed by statements concerning value delivered to employees and communities. These pronouncements become the foundation of mission statements, which are often mounted on the wall—a trophy for all to see.

But drafting a mission statement is the easy part. Linking the creation of value to local goals within an organization, then taking synchronized action to create value is the hard part. Value is multidimensional: Creating value is a complex, interactive process that can happen by chance—or by plan.

Debates often occur over definitions of "value" and the priorities that guide actions to create value. After all, a company might deliver lots of value to its customers simply by giving away products or service—thus bankrupting the company in the process. A company can also pursue cost-reduction strategies that produce short-term profits but employee burnout in the longer term.

Improving the rate of value creation requires guiding an organization to a delicate balance involving trade-offs and priorities. Many senior executives have more than one horror story to tell about the effects of getting this balance wrong. Few credit strong performance improvements or the attainment of "world class" status to getting it right. Strategies that focus on creating value for any one stakeholder without considering the impact on value creation for the others can lead to disaster for the company as a whole. At the same time, when a company is successful, a silver-bullet program is more often cited as the reason for success than a balanced stategy that benefited all stakeholders.

The trouble is that everyone talks about value but few organizations define value, set goals, or measure results in terms of value.

And, like beauty, value is in the eyes of the beholder. So when managers look at their own businesses from the perspective of value, they begin to understand how outsiders view the value their company creates. This can be a difficult but illuminating experience.

Besides, just who is the "beholder?" There are many to choose from, and each has a unique perspective on value. Although the key stakeholders and their relative priorities vary from company to company, the goal-setting methodology presented in this chapter is substantially the same for all organizations.

The scope of this chapter is limited, by necessity, to value as perceived by two of the more important stakeholders in most businesses: customers and owners. Employee value (an extremely important topic and the subject of numerous books, articles, and workshops) is addressed only briefly.

In brief, this chapter looks at various enterprises, how they work, and how they perform from a value perspective. The chapter shows how to build a framework and how to structure value-based performance into an organization to support continuous improvement. The overarching objective of the chapter is to help align an entire organization so that it can manage the trade-offs between customers, owners, and employees, thus creating fundamental "*value.*"

**29.2 BILL OF VALUE**    A *bill of materials* (BOM) is an organizational tool widely used in many businesses today. BOMs provide people with a formal, written identification of the components required to make a product or service that a company provides. For example, a BOM for a magic marker might specify that to make one marker you need one casing, one cap, one label, and three ounces of ink, to name only some of the components. This BOM drives and coordinates activities and decisions throughout the organization in an effort to make a consistent product with all the correct parts.

But what about value? Does an organization have a *bill of value* (BOV) that itemizes the value it creates and how much of each component is needed to create this value? A formal structure is essential—one that will align all actions and help people avoid wasting time, energy, and materials on elements that are not part of the BOV.

If the goal is to create more value, then a company should begin by defining the value to be created—to orchestrate a common vision of what that value is made from and how it will be created for the benefit of all the stakeholders. Without this knowledge, an organization can spend a great deal of time creating conflict that can result in only one thing—nothing of value.

**(a) Value from the Customer's Perspective**    History has shown—and sales executives will agree—that if a product or service provides value to a customer, the customer will barter for it with money, time, commitment, or other things that the seller values.

Ask a good marketing and sales organization to calculate the value it provides to customers, and it will most likely describe the many ways that it brings value to customers. Marketing and sales organizations do this every day and at every sales opportunity.

But ask financial managers how to calculate the value of a product, and they are likely to equate value with cost. Likewise, an operations manager might feel quite comfortable with the idea that a business unit adds value by spending money to convert materials from a raw to a finished state. Indeed materials are "valued" more as finished product than as raw materials on the balance sheet. This view implies that value is created by creating inventory.

But a sales executive would argue that the value a company creates for a customer is not based on what the company spends or on the assets it uses to create that value. Customers perceive value relative to other choices they have. From a customer's perspective, simply putting a product into a warehouse does not generate value. Rather, value arises only when customers receive and benefit from a product or service. If anything, customers value speed and reliable delivery, not the mere fact that inventory is on the producer's shelf. (An organization creates customer value at the "pull" of the customer, not the "push" of production.)

Looking at it from a customer's perspective, however, sales dollars are a simple, convenient indicator of the relative overall value received by customers of a value chain. Customers vote for value with their wallets. The customer value that any one business unit in a value chain adds can be measured simply as sales minus purchases—nothing more, nothing less.

It is easy to equate customer value with supply-chain sales, but it is not so easy to identify the elements that *create* the value a customer buys from some business unit that is part of a value chain. A goal of increasing sales by 10 percent by growing market share rings hollow without an identification of what element of value will change in the eyes of customers and motivate them to buy 10 percent more. And it is at this second level in the BOV that simplicity turns into complexity for managers. The elements of value are slippery and not easy to pin down with numbers.

Womack and Jones, in their book *Lean Thinking,* define value this way: "Value—A capability provided to a customer at the right time at an appropriate price as defined in each case by the customer."[1]

**(b) A Case Study: Beanie Babies**    But the definition above may be only part of the picture, as illustrated by the recent craze for Beanie Babies—the small stuffed animals made by Ty.

Consider the case of Jessica, an eight-year-old girl, who saves her allowance for six weeks and buys Chirp, the Beanie Baby robin, at a local card shop for $6. Later she discovers from a Beanie Baby collector website that, according to an estimate by the manufacturer, Chirp has a collector's value of $60. "Chirp is worth a lot of money. Maybe I can get $30 for it and buy a lot more Beanie Babies with the money," Jessica thinks to herself. She tries to sell Chirp to her friend Sue for $30 (half price in Jessica's opinion), but Sue knows she can still get Chirp for $6 at the local store. Sue also has her heart set on Sammy the seal (she loves Sammy's colors), which is also at the store, but she cannot buy both. So Sue tells Jessica that she plans to buy Sammy next week when she gets her next allowance.

In this simple example from everyday life there are three different opinions of Chirp's value: the manufacturer's (Ty's), the "enterprise's" (Jessica), and the customer's (Sue). Sue considers the value of Chirp compared with Sammy and decides to spend her money on Sammy, because she believes that Sammy will provide her greater value.

This value can be attributed in several ways:

- To the product itself.
- To the intangible value created by a good marketing strategy by Ty.
- To the limited availability of the product.
- To the customer's own needs.

It comes as no surprise that Jessica's parents had trouble explaining to Jessica that Sue—and not she or Ty—decides Chirp's true value.

The next week, just after Sue gets her allowance, Jessica tries again to sell Chirp to Sue but for $10 this time. Sue changes her mind and buys Chirp rather than Sammy. Sue values Jessica's friendship, and at $10, she decides she really did not want to walk all the way to the store after all.

In the end, Jessica added value to Chirp—$4—the amount Sue was willing to pay, given the value she received. A simple BOV in this example might be that the value received was made from a dash of friendship, one Chirp, a splash of availability, and a pinch of timing. This idea of value and its components is messy—especially when the buyer has a choice and emotion is involved. But even a simple BOV serves as a framework for Jessica to duplicate her success in creating value with another customer.

**(c) Intangible Value**  Buyers have choices, and they allocate their money according to their own needs and the value proposition they perceive. These choices often involve emotion, personal relationships, or politics as much as the typical components of value, such as form, fit, function, quality, availability, service, or price. Intangible value—such as friendship or brand name—can often outweigh tangible value. And the effect of good marketing can multiply this perceived value.

A company can try to convince customers that they will get a good value based on the costs incurred in making the product. But customers weigh what is of value to them, then decide whether the price represents a good deal or a bad deal. Exhibit 29.1 illustrates this comparison. And, as in the story about Chirp the Beanie Baby, the customer's fuzzy math is what counts.

**(d) Major Elements of Value**  The second level in a BOV contains the major elements that customers consider essential. The number of elements must be limited to a handful, because that is all a typical buyer can keep track of when calculating the value a company provides and comparing it to the value competitors offer. (Section 29.5 discusses how to identify the critical elements of value and how to determine the amount of each element the business needs to provide in a BOV.)

A perception of value can be created by advertising, then destroyed by a retail sales clerk who steers a customer to a competitor's product—perhaps because it provides a better sales commission. A perception of value can be long-lasting (e.g., when a company decides to relocate operations to a customer's hometown because of tax incentives) or short-lived (as at a fast-food restaurant). It can be illogical—for example, when a candy bar shrinks though the price stays the same. It can even be unexpected, as when the owner of a high-end furniture store tells the manufacturer not to deliver a dresser to a customer quickly because the customer envisions a toiling craftsperson who requires a long time to make a quality piece of furniture.

**(e) Value Propositions**  Indeed, in the brave new world of electronic commerce, the trend is for customers to state a price they are willing to pay for a product, then wait to see what value proposition a company will provide. In customers' minds, the price they are willing to pay a company depends on the value proposition offered by the competition. And—in the case of the consumer—the competition includes all other value chains from all other segments of the economy.

The perceptions that customers have of the value they receive can be greatly influenced by the image created through marketing. This difference in perspective becomes uncomfortable for executives when they realize that the information companies use to establish traditional goals, set budgets, and judge performance are often based on financial numbers that are greatly influenced by the volumes produced rather than the

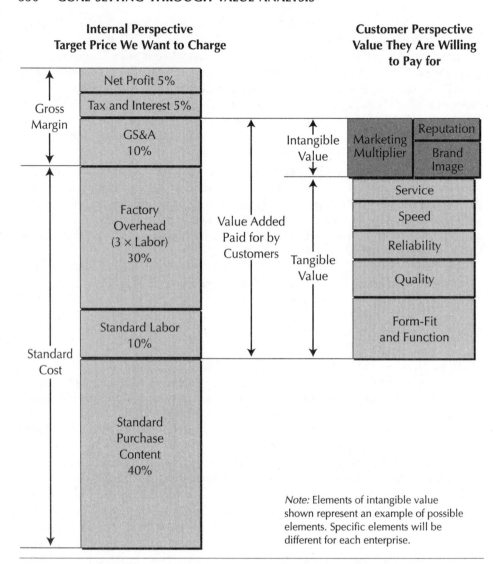

**Exhibit 29.1    Elements of Relative Value for Customer Compared to Elements of Target Price**

volumes sold or the actual cash spent. Costs are simply absorbed into inventory, which is traditionally thought of as an asset of value.

When creating a BOV for a customer, think backward by starting with the customer. Turn assumptions upside down to challenge traditional thinking. Make the entire value chain aware of the customer's BOV.

When calculating the value delivered to customers and establishing value-based goals, use external sales dollars. Do not use internal standard cost calculations, because they do not add up. Also, do not ignore the many intangible elements that affect sales dollars.

**(f) Value from the Owner's Perspective**    Customers are very demanding. To stay in business, a business unit has to meet these demands. (Just ask any PC maker, retailer, or supplier to a big-three auto maker.) Yet shareholders are also very demanding. A company has to generate a fair value for shareholders who have invested in the company. Otherwise, the shareholders will redirect their time and capital to investment opportunities that yield more value over time.

In Statement on Management Accounting (SMA) Number 4AA,[2] the Institute of Management Accountants defines shareholder value as follows:

> From the economist's viewpoint, value is created when management generates revenues over and above the economic costs to generate these revenues. Costs come from four sources: 1) employee wages and benefits; 2) material, supplies, and economic depreciation of physical assets; 3) taxes; and 4) the opportunity cost of using the capital.
>
> Under this value-based view, value is only created when revenues exceed all costs including a capital charge. This value accrues mostly to shareholders because they are the residual owners of the firm.

Although the definition of value added for the shareholder is different from the definition of value added for the customer, they are undeniably linked. Customers will only pay so much for the value they perceive (see Exhibit 29.1). Managers must generate shareholder value from this customer value, as Exhibit 29.2 illustrates. And, like customer value, shareholder value has its own intangible components, as the exhibit suggests.

**(g) Calculating Shareholder Value**    Beyond this point, the calculation of shareholder value gets bogged down in accounting theory. Clinton and Chen[3] provide a thorough analysis of the pros and cons of using various approaches, such as Stern Stewart's *economic value added* (EVA)™ or the Boston Consulting Group's *cash flow return on investment*. Their article attempts to correlate different value-based performance measures with stock value. It concludes that cash-based measures of shareholder value creation provide the best correlation with stock price.

But these techniques for calculating shareholder value often turn simplicity into complexity. The numbers are ground through the accounting mill, which strives for accuracy to the penny. Unfortunately, little shareholder value is generated when a management team gets so wrapped up in calculations or in the management of financial statements that they lose sight of the following simple fact. The creation of shareholder value—whatever the calculation—is ultimately based on the creation of customer value less the checks that are written in the process and an opportunity cost for the invested capital.

**(h) XYZ Example**    To illustrate, consider the case of XYZ Co., founded in the early 1900s, which is well regarded in its industry. XYZ is a large manufacturer of highly engineered, multi-million-dollar machinery used in petrochemical plants. The company also has a significant spare-parts business and a much smaller refurbishment business.

A major business strategy typically employed in XYZ's industry is to sell machines at "a loss" in order to "make a profit" on high-margin spare parts in future years. Spare-part sales generally start four to five years after the installation of a machine, and machines typically need to be replaced or refurbished after 20 to 25 years of service.

The market is very competitive—too many manufacturers chase too few projects. Profitability in the spare-parts business has also eroded as an increasing number of "pirates" copy the most lucrative spares and sell them at prices significantly below those charged by XYZ.

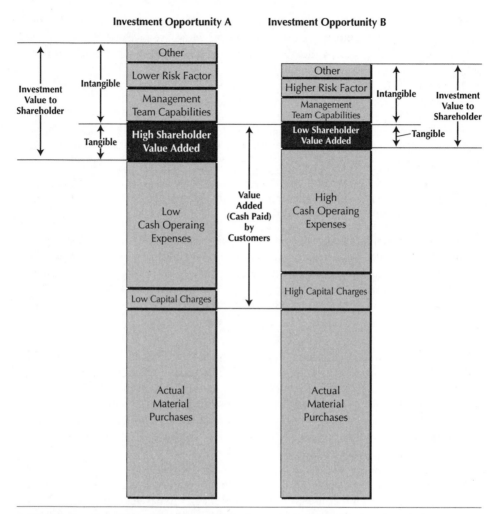

**Exhibit 29.2    Example of Elements of Relative Investment Value for Shareholders Given Same Value Added for Customers**

XYZ Co. was bought by a major German industrial corporation about five years, 2,000 employees, $60 million in losses, and two presidents ago. When XYZ Co. signs a contract for a machine, it must set up a loss reserve (under German accounting standards) to cover the anticipated loss in a year and a half when the machine is shipped. Unlike U.S. accounting standards, the German standards require that the loss reserve cover fully absorbed overhead. Consequently, an increase in sales leads directly to short-term losses, whereas a decrease in sales leads to short-term profits, because more existing loss reserves are freed up than new ones added.

Recently the German parent corporation brought in Bill, a new president, from a competitor. Bill was charged with the job of turning the company around, so he put a plan in place that called for the company to sell significantly fewer machines over the following three years. Shrinking sales translates into profits on the income statement because of favorable reductions to the loss reserve. The plan was to outsource the manufacture of many parts to save on production costs and also to reduce direct labor costs.

Indirect labor and the general administration head count were to be downsized across the board to drop XYZ's break-even point. In the long run, Bill's plan called for an attempt to rebuild lost market share. Based on these plans, actions, and resulting cost standards, XYZ's chief financial officer (CFO) put together financial projections that showed that the company would earn healthy profits within two years.

Unfortunately, managers failed to evaluate their plans or set their goals in terms of cash value for shareholders. After the restructuring, XYZ Co. will reach a new stable spending level that, outside of purchases, will not vary much with volume. It is also in excess of the value-added projections for the customers. On a cash basis, significant losses in shareholder value will continue into the foreseeable future. This is a different picture of the economic value provided to the owners—given the investments they have made and risks they will incur—than the one presented by the president and CFO to their board of directors.

Real tangible value for the shareholder is measured the old-fashioned way—in cash. It is just like the simple cigar-box accounting a child might use when selling lemonade on the street corner—cash in minus cash out. The resulting size of the money pile in the cigar box minus an opportunity cost of investing it somewhere else is a true indicator of the additional value received for the effort and investment put into the business.

The managers of XYZ Co. were so tied up in the management of the short-term financial picture that they lost sight of the opportunity to produce tremendous value for their customers and, as a result, financial value to their owners. Although the rate of construction of new projects plummeted over the last decade, the population of aging machines remains very large. The fundamental value that XYZ can provide its customers is to refurbish aging machines and concurrently upgrade them with new technology. The net result is more value to the customer at a lower cost than a new machine. The net result to XYZ Co. is a lower sales number but a very positive value added for the owners.

In today's global economy, customers are only willing to pay for the value received, given the other choices they have. A company has to plot a strategy to create economic value for owners from the value that they add for their customers. A company has to measure productivity in terms of the value they add for customers per dollar spent and per dollar invested: This is all customers are willing to pay for and all that the shareholders will benefit from.

Keep the calculations simple—do them in cash.

**(i) Value from the Employee's Perspective**  As mentioned at the beginning of this chapter, the creation of value for employees of an organization is an issue that is as important as customer and owner value. This is especially true in segments of the country and economy where quality employees are in short supply. However, employee value is beyond the scope of this chapter. Suffice it to say that employees are usually far less frustrated and receive far more value from an organization that is working in harmony toward a common goal than one that is torn by conflicting values.

**29.3 CONFLICTING VALUES**  Companies that have visionary leaders—leaders who can share their vision, set clear priorities for their organization, and inspire results—are the envy of their competitors. These organizations know where they are going, why, and how. The vision and drive of their leaders provide a framework for both formal and informal strategic planning throughout the organization.

More frequently, companies rely on a bottom-up strategic planning process to plot a safe passage through turbulent competitive waters. The strategic plans for the business, however, often become a compilation of the plans for each of the major functional organizations. Too little effort is made to add structure or to set priorities.

Each functional plan may be very worthwhile by itself, but, taken together, they simply do not add up to bottom-line results. Traditional performance goals encourage political gridlock, which limits cross-functional planning for the good of the entire company.

**(a) Marketing and Sales Focus on the Top Line**   It is obvious that marketing and sales executives have been hard at work promoting value for customers. Their efforts have led to the following:

- Market survey groups (both internal and external).
- Shrinking product life cycles (as product enhancements are introduced).
- The proliferation of new products (as product development revs into high gear).
- The trend toward "mass customization."
- The use of revenue-management concepts to enhance all of the above.
- The growth of e-commerce (your new website).

All too often, these worthy initiatives push the capabilities of inflexible plants and equipment beyond their limits because of attempts to respond cost-effectively. All too often, constraints to flow prevent improvements from reaching the customer.

**(b) Example: John's Retail Stores**   Consider the case of John, who owns a chain of retail stores. He allocates his floor space to manufacturers based on the sales contribution of their products per square foot. That, at least, is John's policy: In reality, "good old boy" relationships with sales representatives influence how much space they get.

The Buymything Co. is one of his suppliers. Buymything is a relatively small company in its industry that prides itself on being a design leader in the product it sells. Every year it adds to the products it sells with new and updated styles—at no small cost (in terms of design and engineering) to Buymything. In fact, Buymything is proud of the fact that it spends 8 percent of sales on new product development. (This includes the cost of disruptions caused to production facilities during development and initial production runs. It also includes writedowns for obsolete inventory.) Consequently, the company's catalog has expanded substantially over the years.

With the same floor space, John sells about the same number of units each year but of a greater variety because of the increasing list of features and options customers can choose from. Gross sales are up marginally, but Buymything's wholesale prices are up even more. Consequently, John has not given the company any more floor space. In fact, he is thinking seriously about reducing the allocation. John cannot understand why Buymything replaces perfectly good designs each year when they still have another year or two of life left in them. Sales of the product line in total are growing slowly, while sales of any one stock keeping unit (SKU) are going down. Customers just do not value a new product any more than the product it replaced.

Buymything's volume is constrained to a large extent by the amount and location of retail floor space its products receive. The strategy of increasing the number of product offerings and of providing more features and options for customers has resulted in the same unit volumes spread over more products. Although greater selection is offered, it has not justified higher prices. Buymything, having made new product design a priority, has not invested enough in capital equipment and training to make its production facilities more flexible. As a result, costs have gone up. In addition, John's buyers order product from Buymything monthly. Only now the monthly quantities for any specific SKU are half what they used to be. Even so, John's inventory of finished goods is growing overall because he is trying to stock the line but never seems to be able to guess right on the specific features a customer actually wants to buy.

Buymything's efforts proved counterproductive. Marketing assumed that the constraint was a lack of new products, when the real constraint was lack of floor space. Much waste but little value was created for stakeholders, so there was frustration all around.

**(c) Operations Focused on the Middle Line: Cost of Goods Sold**   Over the last decade, manufacturing executives have expended much effort pursuing internal strategies to improve value from the perspective of operations. Managers have tried to design costs out of products and value into products through techniques such as the following:

- *Quality functional deployment* and value engineering.
- *Total quality management* to improve quality levels.
- *Lean manufacturing* to remove *muda* (Japanese for non–value-adding waste).
- Automation to reduce labor expenses.
- Relocation of facilities to developing countries around the world.

But although these strategies are all pure and noble, the smoke of battle masks the reality of execution, because the results often do not help the bottom line.

Initiatives are often taken in defiance of traditional performance metrics ("remember, quality is free") or in defiance of logic (e.g., filling warehouses with products that do not sell, even though they are made very efficiently to get the best unit cost).

Too often, the manufacturing cells that were set up in a *kaizen* blitz last quarter are idle this quarter because the product mix has shifted. Much overtime is run at the end of the month to make the production budget. Orders are pulled in from the next reporting period and shipped, while strong pricing incentives are offered to induce customers to take product early. Quality standards are a casualty in the rush to make the numbers. Cost-reduction efforts are launched for specific products without asking customers what they value. And, in fact, these cost-reduction efforts may just shift costs to another product line.

Initiatives are often taken at the expense of a company's knowledge pool (such as when an organization is de-layered). They can be at the expense of the company's future. Examples are 10 percent (or some other percentage) across-the-board cost reductions mandated from the top, which completely disrupt months of effort to implement a new, long-term manufacturing strategy.

Efficiency, utilization, unit costs, and even revenues per employee look better than ever, but your competitors are thankful for your efforts.

**(d) Dilemma in Operations**   Ted, the vice president of operations at Buymything, looks bruised and battered after his monthly performance review. His operations just cannot seem to make the right product now that the product line has expanded so much. And the new designs with all the curved surfaces are overloading his computer numerical control cells.

As usual, sales is more than happy to point the finger in his direction. "We can't sell more product because Ted can't produce it on time. We need more finished product in the warehouse so we have something to sell." To which Ted counters, "give me a decent SKU forecast for a change, and we can get it out. We will also be more efficient, because we will be able to smooth the production schedule to reduce our average manpower requirements and not have to expedite as much." Everyone knows the drill.

After months of jousting, the president finally authorizes a multi-million-dollar expenditure for sophisticated forecasting software to help the sales organization come up with reliable forecasts of sales for the next 12 weeks. According to their new materials requirement planning (MRP) II system, Ted's group needs this lead time to purchase raw materials, make parts, and assemble product in time to make delivery for the forecasted demand. With the new forecast loaded, Ted and his team are ready to go. The forecast—smoothed and lot-sized into a master schedule—even adds up to Ted's production budget. Now they will finally be able to make the right product. The trouble is that customers do not read forecasts.

Purchase orders are launched 12 weeks before customers are expected to buy the product. Orders for manufactured parts are launched into operations six weeks before forecasted sales. Meanwhile, a never-ending effort is put into expediting and reprioritizing both purchase orders and manufacturing orders because daily sales volume and mix do not match average forecasted demand.

Because it was understaffed and overworked as the result of a headcount reduction, purchasing did not have time to cancel unneeded materials when actual sales fell short of forecasted demand on many items. But they did have time to place new orders to cover unexpected demands. As a result, raw material inventory grew. Customers did not seem to notice the "frozen window" that manufacturing tried to enforce. Consequently, production orders were released to manufacturing to make the products forecasted but not sold.

Expediting takes over to try to push the product that does sell through the increasingly clogged operation. When parts fall behind schedule, there is not enough manpower to catch up, so components are late for assembly. In assembly, the push for utilization forces workers to assemble whatever they can get their hands on—which includes stealing common parts not meant for the product being assembled. At the end of the month, operations goes into autopilot and works overtime to make the production budget any way they can. By this time, production is up and operations is making its "hours," but the value stream has turned into a trickle. Customers cancel orders in frustration. Inventory climbs. Value is lost by all.

Operations believed that the constraint they faced was a lack of knowledge about what consumers would buy months in the future. The real constraints were related to staffing and performance measures. Operations were disconnected from customer demand by the forecast.

**(e) Conflicting Values Lead to Mixed Results**    Few organizations set clear performance goals or measure their performance in terms of the value they add for stakeholders. Fewer still are able to tie it all together with their business strategies and communicate it down through their organizations to focus efforts on creating the most value with the least effort, at the least expense, and with the least capital invested. Too many still rely on the tired concept that local efficiency and utilization are the driving forces behind financial performance, believing that the only way to improve value is to be the low-cost producer. The word from the top is "add value," while the bottom of the organization only hears "cut costs." The latter view is often reinforced by the bonus structure. And what about the employee in the middle? The result is frustration in the executive office all the way down to the front-line employees.

The business system produces value for a number of stakeholders. But the organization's decisions are driven by financial performance goals and related measures on a more local, functional basis. A plethora of local measures may tell managers they are doing a great job even though the company is slowly tearing itself apart. As Exhibit 29.3 illustrates, the people in an organization may not all be marching in the same direction toward the same goals and with the same priorities.

What goals should an organization be heading toward that will provide the best overall value for the stakeholders? How far should that goal be from the current reality, and why? How can a company put a framework in place that will guide a fair trade-off between competing interests? How do you get an organization heading in the same direction so that the efforts expended are synergistic rather than conflicting? The following sections provide some ideas on how to answer these questions.

**29.4 CREATE A VISION OF THE VALUE STREAM**  The value-based goal-setting discussed in the remainder of this chapter is an integral part of a continuous improvement process driven by cross-functional teams. Exhibit 29.4 shows the key elements of this continuous improvement process.

The improvement cycle begins at the strategic level of the business with the development of a common vision of the value stream. It continues with the identification of

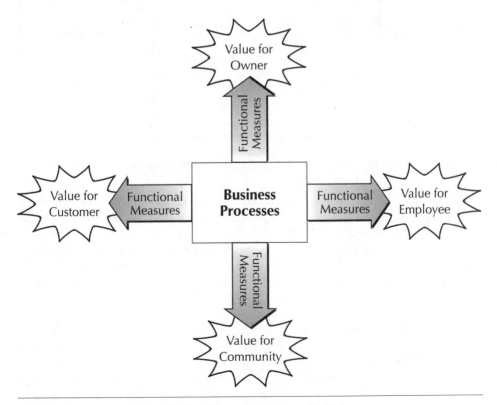

**Exhibit 29.3    Organizational Direction as Seen by an Outsider**

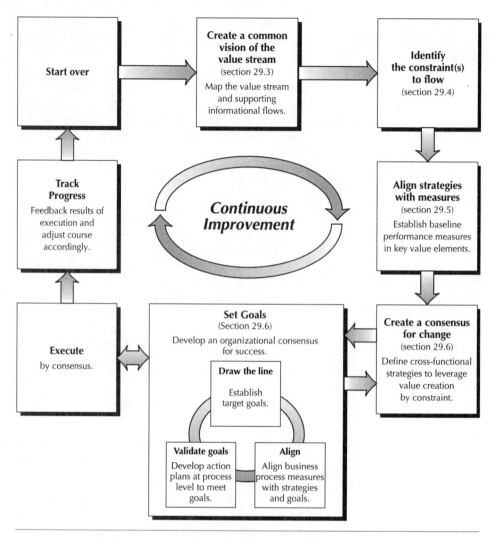

**Exhibit 29.4   Value-Based Goal Setting as Part of a Continuous Improvement Process**

*constraints to flow,* then aligns a value-based measures framework with strategies that leverage the constraints. General strategies and initial goals are refined at the operations level of the business. If groundwork is done on a team basis, the probability that the organization will attack its focused goals on a united front as a high-performance team improves dramatically. As the demonstrated performance level of the organization rises and goals are met, the process starts over again at the beginning with a new "as-is."

**(a) Mapping Value Streams**   Constraints control the flow rate of every value stream and its tributaries. The performance of unconstrained resources that support the value stream is greatly influenced by where they are relative to the constraint. Consequently, the value goals established and the calculations made about the worth of reaching these goals for the stakeholders must be set in relation to the critical constraints in the value stream. This concept is described next.

The Value Chain: a series of dependent resources

| Steel Mill | Rolling Mill | Slitting Mill | Stamping Plant | Assembly Plant | Distributor | Retailer |

**Value Stream**—a flow of material/infromation being transformed by the value chain.

Customers

**Exhibit 29.5  Example of a Value Stream Flowing Through a String of Dependent Value-Chain Resources**

At the heart of the value creation process is a *value chain* (see Chapter 2). The value chain is a string of dependent resources through which the value stream flows to transform raw materials and information into value for the customer. Exhibit 29.5 shows an example of a simple value chain and value stream. Something in this string of resources will limit the rate of flow of the value stream; otherwise, the flow volume would be infinite. The constraint to flow is the leverage point where a small change can have a dramatic impact—positive or negative—on the performance of the whole system.

**(b) Extent of Value Streams**  A value stream in its entirety spans both geography and time—from the birth of a product or service idea to the death of an aging product line. This is true for custom-made products or services (e.g., an oil refinery) and mass-produced products or services (e.g., boxes of cereal).

Today a value stream can span the globe as materials are converted into products and services that are consumed. For example, oil can be pumped in Argentina, turned into fiber and fabric in China, cut in Thailand, sewn in Korea, packaged in Mexico, and sold in Peoria as a family tent. Or it can be a local stream—for example, apples in a pick-your-own orchard that local customers buy. It can be a complex stream that involves many different companies in interdependent tributary networks that feed huge rivers. The value chain network that feeds the massive Boeing 747 assembly plants, for example, is tremendously complex.

"Raw materials" that are fed into the beginning of a value stream can be data in today's business world, sick patients who want to become well patients, or iron ore that will make a car.

In reality, the most important part of a company's value stream may be limited in scope—from the point in the tributaries where multiple suppliers compete actively for the company's business to the highest consumption point that recognizes the company's name. For some vertically integrated enterprises (such as a major oil company), it may be the whole picture—from oil in the ground to gas in the tank. For others (such as makers of standard electronic components), it may involve only one direct supplier (one up the chain) and one direct customer (one down the chain).

Because identifying and understanding a value chain may seem like a mind-numbing exercise if it is done in detail, a value chain must be kept simple and understandable. The key is a top-down, big-picture perspective, such as the one shown in Exhibit 29.5. This simple map will be used to understand the influence constraints have on the establishment of performance goals and improvement strategies for a value stream.

**29.5 IDENTIFY THE CONSTRAINT TO FLOW**   "The degree to which any system can perform is ultimately determined by the set of constraints that govern the system. Practically speaking, *any specific area, aspect, or process that limits the business' performance from a customer, competitive or profit point of view is a constraint.*"[4]

To improve the productivity and profitability of a firm, managers must focus on the constraints that limit the performance of the system. Fortunately, this is not a battle that must be fought on many fronts. In most firms, only a small number of constraints significantly limit current performance. Experience and the insight gained from the analogy of a chain confirm that the number of weak links in an organization is not large. In a dynamic manufacturing system, however—especially one in which appropriate improvements are continuously being implemented—the constraints are likely to change over time.

The importance of knowing an organization's constraints, then managing them properly, cannot be overemphasized. The significance of constraints can be stated most bluntly by highlighting the consequences of not managing constraints properly: "Failure to properly manage constraints will cause the performance of the organization to be lower than the limit set by the constraints. The organization will perform below its capability."[5]

**(a) Balanced Resource Capacities**   The idea of identifying a constraint to the flow of value involves, by definition, a search for something that should exist everywhere in the value chain if traditional management methods are successful. Traditionally, a business system provides the best value if each resource is working at full capacity: High utilization yields the best unit costs. Consequently, much management effort is usually directed toward reaching a goal of "balanced capacities" to minimize cost. This can be seen in the "line balancing" done in an assembly department to minimize the number of underutilized assemblers within a plant and in the head count control enforced across entire divisions to minimize underutilized labor and supervision.

Despite the best efforts of managers to design or force balanced resource capacities on a value stream, the reality is that it never works out that way. Balanced systems quickly come undone. Take, for example, a manufacturing cell that is "kaizened" into place quickly so that it will run with very little excess labor. But then the product mix changes, which causes a continuing need for overtime or an underutilized cell.

Or consider the scenario in which a company builds a plant to supply components to division $X$ only to find a sister (and larger) division siphoning off capacity and leaving division $X$'s needs unmet. It is not unusual for a manufacturing department to be operating at a smooth pace until the end of the accounting period, when people work overtime and are moved around in an effort to meet or beat budgets.

Customers are a frequent cause of unbalanced systems. Customers never seem to cooperate by consuming exactly the same products in exactly the same mix for a week at a time, let alone a month or a quarter—except when it is to their own advantage. Something always happens to unbalance the system. In fact, it is unusual to encounter a value stream that flows through a string of resources that have truly "balanced capacities." Some element in the resource string almost always limits value creation.

**(b) Customers as Constraints to Value Flow**   Since Latin America, Eastern Europe, China, and the rest of the Pacific Rim have opened up to the world, supply has gotten ahead of demand in many sectors of the economy. The global automobile business has often been characterized this way, and growth of the trade deficit bears it out. Indeed,

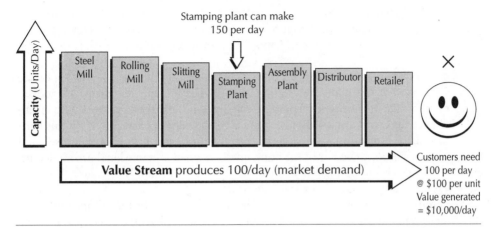

**Exhibit 29.6    Example of a Value Stream Flowing Through a String of Dependent Value-Chain Resources Where the Market Limits the Volume of Flow**

it has become a buyer's market in many parts of the economy where supply exceeds demand.

This situation is exacerbated when consumer dollars are attracted to a value proposition made by products and services (or investment opportunities) in entirely different segments of the economy. Demand for one product or service goes down, while demand for a competing value stream goes up. For example, many families have used their discretionary income to purchase PCs rather than new furniture for their home. Others have found greater value at a casino or through a state lottery than at a doctor's office or hospital.

In a buyer's market, the customer is king. The marketplace (as shown in Exhibit 29.6) limits the value that is created. Customers purchase 100 units a day at $100 a unit, so $10,000 a day in value is created, even if the supply chain has enough capacity to produce much more.

**(c) Value Creation Occurs Only When Customers Buy**    Consider the case of Al, who was the owner of a manufacturing company that made spindleback wood chairs that were finished in several natural stains. His factory could produce 5,000 chairs a month. Al had a counter next to his desk in the corporate office to keep track of daily production. Each chair off the line made a clicking sound, and each click meant $20 in the bank. Running near capacity and with high utilization made Al happy, because this meant that he was making money. He even offered incentives for months in which new production records were set. Al's managers were hard at work figuring out how to increase productivity so that the company could make even more chairs and more money.

One day a designer in Montana who was employed by an insignificant competitor from Canada showed her new chair creation to a group of her friends. They loved the combination of painted surfaces contrasted with natural wood surfaces. They loved the worn look of country age that was a character of the finish. In fact, her friends loved her chair so much that her client—the Canadian manufacturer—brought it to market quickly and caught a design wave that had been developing that year for the country look.

Al saw these chairs in a store that offered his product, but he scoffed at the idea of a two-tone chair. Ignoring input from his retail customers, Al spurred his plant on to higher output to reduce unit costs even more, thus providing even more value to his customers.

As demand for his chairs dropped below 3,000 a month, the throttle was kept wide open. Efficiency of the plant was setting records. His income statement still looked good, even though inventory was climbing rapidly as he absorbed overhead into inventory. He knew he could always sell his chairs after the market recovered from this periodic downturn. His inventory was an investment in the future, he told both himself and his managers. He continued until the bank finally reigned him in when he exceeded his credit line while accumulating (very efficiently!) a six-month supply of chairs. Al's company was eventually acquired at a steep discount.

The product value perceived by the customer turned out to be more important than the inventory value perceived by Al. Producing product efficiently—in excess of market demand and in a buyer's market—leads to no value for the customer, just excess inventory somewhere in the system. That inventory does not represent an increase in value for anyone. In fact, it leads to a *loss of value* for everyone. Al's cash was spent to build inventory, but customers perceived a better value proposition elsewhere. Employee value suffered when production was slashed to bring inventories in line with demand. Moral: *Value is not created until the customer buys the product.*

Al's productivity measures (i.e., utilization, efficiency, and chairs per employee) sent a false signal, because they were based on production, not consumption. If Al had measured the real productivity of his business (i.e., in terms of the value added for which his customers were willing to pay) he would have seen early on that he was in trouble. For one thing, his value added was declining because his sales were declining and because he was overbuying materials to keep production high (value added = sales – purchases). Inventory productivity (value added per dollar of inventory employed) was declining because the value added that his company provided for the inventory held was declining sharply. Labor productivity (value added per dollar spent on labor) was also declining sharply. All of which provided an unheeded early warning of trouble.

**(d) Focusing on the Voice of the Customer**    The case of Dave, who rose through the ranks to become a plant engineer and, eventually, the president of a major paper manufacturer, provides another example. As president, Dave made sure that his company spared no expense to build the "Rolls Royce" of pulp mills on a huge scale. He wanted to make absolutely the best-quality paper at the best cost per ton to provide the best value to his customers.

The trouble was that Dave's competition built the "Chevy" of pulp mills and produced paper at a quality level that met—but did not surpass—customer specifications, and at a lower cost per ton. Dave was forced to dramatically lower the price per ton he charged to keep the plants operating at capacity. EVA™ took a nosedive, along with the company's stock price. Employees were let go when a number of mills were closed. Customers dictated the value produced for everyone in the system.

When the marketplace is the constraint, a focus on the voice of the customer is the lever. Both Al's and Dave's efforts to improve productivity were ineffective because they were not focused on the constraint. The result of the best of intentions and much hard work was a loss of value for customers and of economic value for the owners.

**(e) Physical Resources as Constraints to Value Flow**    Some lucky businesses operate as part of a seller's market, as shown in Exhibit 29.7. In this example the stamping plant has a daily capacity of 100 units, so it cannot keep up with the customer demand of 150 units a day. The stamping resource controls the amount of value—$10,000 per day—created by the value stream. Businesses that operate as part of a seller's market cannot (or do not choose to) produce enough to meet market demand. Some resource exists that limits value creation. This resource is a leverage point for such businesses.

Consider, for example, the case of Sue, who is a very successful regional sales associate for a first-tier electronics supplier to the auto industry. Over the years, Sue's dedication and ability to work with the company's large accounts had raised sales and led to her promotion to a senior vice president and officer of the company. The company produced a high-tech sensor that is a critical component of automobiles. The proprietary manufacturing process used to make the product employs a sophisticated, high-volume processing line that only a few competitors can match. Sue's company pumps out as much product as it can to meet the demands of the big-three auto makers. It is providing good value to both customers and shareholders.

One day Sue receives a call from the buyer at her largest account. A new supplier partnership program is being implemented that involves converting first-tier suppliers to a just-in-time (JIT) product flow. A consultant is to be provided (at no cost) to show the company how to put a JIT system in place, assuming the company cannot do it on its own. To drive production, the company's JIT system will be linked to the customers' assembly plants through an electronic data interchange of real-time assembly-schedule information. As a reward for participation in this voluntary supplier partnership program, Sue's company will be allowed to keep its business and share the benefits. Ironically, "sharing the benefits" is clearly defined as a 10 percent price cut.

After the JIT system is implemented, orders start flooding in. Whereas the company used to get one order per month for large quantities of many different sensors, it began to receive daily orders for small quantities. As a result, production plummeted while orders for delivery became late. The production process was not designed or built to handle the frequency of line changeovers required by the new system.

Run rates (including setup times) for the customer's product settled in at 66 percent of the run rate for comparable products being made for the other auto companies. At

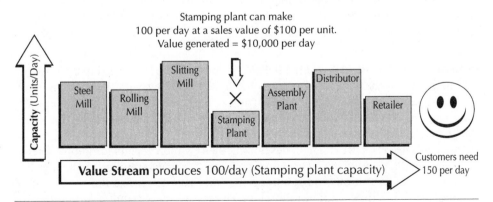

**Exhibit 29.7    Example of a Value Stream Flowing Through Dependent Value-Chain Resources Where a Resource Limits the Volume of Flow**

the same time, the price paid was 10 percent less. Lacking an adequate supply of sensors from Sue's company and unable to secure them elsewhere, the automobile company was forced to reduce its own assembly plant's scheduled production.

A good value situation for the stakeholders turned into a nasty situation for all. Everyone had ignored the fact that an hour of time lost on the constraint translates directly into an hour of sales (value) lost to the consumer and an hour of profits lost to the shareholder. The drive for a 10 percent savings on a $10 part had resulted in the loss of sales of $25,000 sports utility vehicles.

Labor is an often-overlooked resource constraint in a booming economy for three reasons:

1. Unemployment rates often dip to the low single digits.
2. Companies are hard pressed not to increase wages to attract more labor.
3. Traditional management policies dictate that head count be kept at the bare minimum in an attempt to balance capacities for maximum utilization.

**(f) Constraints Dictate "True North"**    Wherever a constraint lies in a value stream, it determines the value added to the system for all the stakeholders. Performance goals cannot be set realistically without an understanding of where constraints are, how they affect flow, and how they can be better managed to produce value.

Although preceding sections of this chapter focused on markets and physical resources as constraints, constraints to the flow of value can also take many other forms. For example, constraints relating to raw materials, policies, bonus programs, government regulations, environmental concerns, or safety may significantly limit the flow of a value stream.

In addition, many products shipped to customers today are hybrids composed of not just a physical item but also information or a knowledge transfer. Significant constraints to processing the necessary information or performing a knowledge transfer may exist that are more limiting to the creation of value than the physical constraints to the flow of material. And sometimes the most obvious constraints are the hardest to find.

Does the management team share a clear picture of the value stream? Do the team members agree where and what the major constraints to flow are in the value stream? If this constraint is removed, is it clear that the business will see a significant performance improvement? These issues are examined next.

**29.6 ALIGN STRATEGIES WITH MEASURES**    To be realistic, goals need to be based on the capabilities of the value stream, the constraints to the flow, and the possibilities of change. To be effective in setting goals and improving performance toward these goals, each manager of a cross-functional team needs to share the same vision of the value stream: how it works, how it performs, and why.

Managers need to participate in developing their own blueprints for improvement. To be driven as a team, managers need a framework for understanding the linkage between strategies, execution, and results so that they can determine the true value of reaching their objectives—not just for their own areas of responsibility, but for the organization as a whole.

Exhibit 29.8 illustrates the structure of a value-based performance framework that aligns an organization for focused action. Major elements of this framework include:

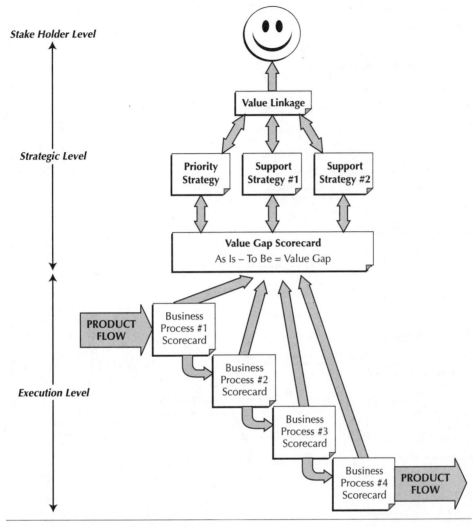

**Exhibit 29.8    Illustration of How a Value-Based Performance Framework Is Structured Through the Organization**

- A value linkage component that links prioritized strategies to the value produced for the stakeholders.
- A value gap scorecard that links strategies to operational initiatives at the execution level.
- Business-process scorecards that guide everyday decision making that affects the product flow in line with improvement strategies and goals established.

**(a) Link Strategies to Value Creation**    Exhibit 29.9 illustrates important elements of a financial framework to link strategies to value. *Stakeholder value* is the first level in a BOV. This includes concepts of a *value-added flow* for customers (sales minus purchases) and *economic value flow* for owners (cash generated less capital charges), which is built on a foundation of the best *employment value* for the people that make up the enterprise.

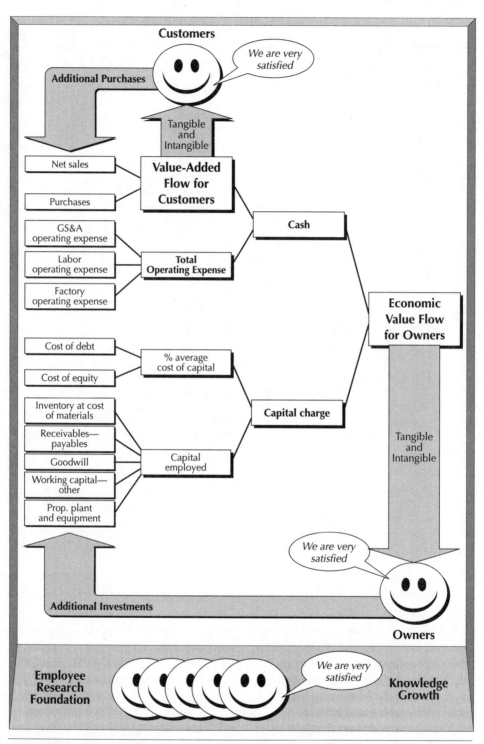

**Exhibit 29.9 Elements of a Financial Framework to Link Strategy with Value Flow.**
*Source:* M. Srikanth and S. Robertson, *Measurements for Effective Decision Making* (Spectrum Publishing Co., 1995), 59.

Strategy must be attached to this framework. These strategic initiatives become the second level in a BOV. For example, the management team at Fastrack Inc. has identified that the market is the major constraint to the flow of the company's value stream. Consequently, Fastrack has established three major strategic initiatives that will eventually break this constraint, if they are executed successfully. These initiatives represent the "flags" around which the management team will rally the organization and coordinate the direction in which they will move for maximum impact. In the example, these three initiatives are:

1. *Implement flow management in operations to facilitate a fast and reliable flow of products.* Managers have determined that unreliable delivery performance causes an increasing loss of business. Unreliable delivery occurs because Fastrack's value-stream management methods are obsolete and need overhauling. In addition, Fastrack does not take advantage of the capabilities of newly installed enterprise resource planning systems.

2. *Become the supplier of choice to the customer and noncustomer base by publicizing improved performance beyond competitors' capabilities.* The overhaul needs to be accomplished before marketing promotes Fastrack's improvements in the field to win more full-margin business. Customers are rightly skeptical of claims about improvements, so changing customers' opinions could take time. As results are seen, they need to be leveraged to obtain more business.

3. *Rightsize the business without negatively affecting growth in the value flow.* Fastrack recognizes that overall productivity has been declining because excess resource capacity has grown—a situation that will require rightsizing. Fastrack does not want to overadjust capacity prematurely and further jeopardize delivery performance to its customers. When it does adjust capacity, it wants to do so carefully rather than precipitously.

The management team has linked these initiatives to the value flow framework shown in Exhibit 29.10 so that the team members can share their vision with the rest of the organization. The team wants to take actions that will increase value for customers while reducing operating expenses and the capital employed (or at least prevent expenses from going up as fast as value added). In this way, it will be clear that enterprise productivity—the result of generating more value with less spending and less capital—will improve.

**(b) Value Gap Scorecard**    Strategic initiatives are backed up with a limited number of specific objectives ("improved speed") and related goals ("three-day delivery") that are necessary to accomplish the initiative. These objectives become the components of the third level of a BOV.

Exhibit 29.11 illustrates a value gap scorecard that links initiatives to objectives and specific performance improvement goals. It summarizes the anticipated impact on economic value—*the value gap*—for the owners of success in changing from baseline performance to the performance levels specified by the goals.

**(c) Provide Business-Process Scorecard**    Strategic objectives are backed up with aligned measures for major business-process teams, as shown in Exhibit 29.12. This becomes the fourth level in a BOV. Each business-process team is responsible for identi-

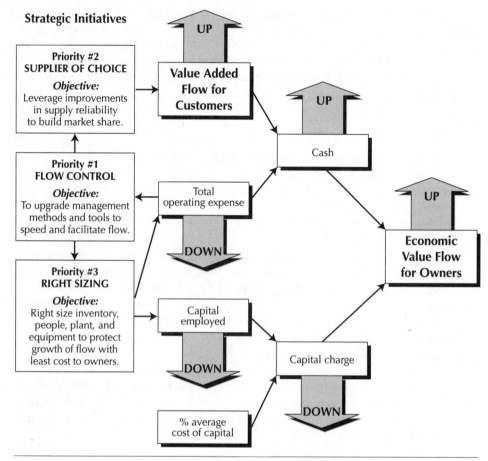

**Exhibit 29.10   Example of Linkage Between Strategic Initiatives and Value Flow**

fying the actions it will take to improve performance in its area to meet the strategic objective goals within the required time period.

Each team is also responsible for identifying a limited set of performance measures that will track the team's progress toward the specific goals. Results for each performance measure should be posted, and senior managers should provide feedback about progress toward meeting the goals.

This framework provides managers organizational structure, feedback, and control mechanisms to get an entire organization moving toward strategic goals. It will help an organization construct a BOV.

**29.7  "WE CAN DO IT" MIND-SET**   As in the previous section, the management team has developed a process map of the value stream and identified the major constraints to value flow. A framework has also been identified to link strategies and align actions for results throughout the organization. Now new strategies must be identified (or existing strategies refined) and goals established that focus on maximizing value, given the constraints of the system. This is a repetitive process. Plant a stake in the ground and get started—expect to refine the size and location of the stake as assumptions are challenged and the business-process teams become engaged in the goal-setting process.

| Strategic Initiative | Objectives | Baseline Performance | Value Gap—Strategic Goals | | | | Performance Gap Operational Goals |
|---|---|---|---|---|---|---|---|
| | | | Measure | 1999 Baseline | 2000 | 2001 | |
| Supplier of choice | Increase share of widget market | Market share = 5% <br> Growth = .5% per year | Sales <br> − Purchases <br> = Value Added | — | — | — | Market share > 8% <br> Growth = +1% per year |
| Flow control | Be fast <br> Be reliable <br> Use least inventory <br> Release jobs on time | 12 day response time <br> 75% delivery reliability <br> Value Added/Inv. < 5 <br> 3 days late for release | − OE <br><br> − Capital charges <br> = EVA | — <br> — <br> — <br> — | — <br> — <br> — <br> — | — <br> — <br> — <br> — | 3 day response time <br> 95% delivery reliability <br> Value Added/ Inv. >10 <br> <1 day late for release |
| Rightsize | Exceed quality specs <br> Be on time <br> Be lean | PPM Defects = 10,000 <br> Late production = 6 days <br> Value Added/OE (Labor) = 5 <br> Value Added/OE (Plant & Equip) = 2 | VA/OE <br><br> VA/CE | — <br> — <br> — | — <br> — <br> — | — <br> — <br> — | PPM defects = 900 <br> Late production = 10 days <br> Value Added/OE (Labor) = 5 <br> Value Added/OE (Plant & Equip) = 2 |

**Exhibit 29.11   Example of a Strategic Improvement Plan Summary: Calculation of Value Gap and Establishment of Improvement Goals**

## Value Stream Business Processes Team

| Strategic Objective | New Product Development | Marketing Process | Sales Process | Order Fulfillment Process | Flow Control Process | Material Conversion Process | Strategic Objective Performance |
|---|---|---|---|---|---|---|---|
| Be Fast | 1.<br>2.<br>3. | 1.<br>2.<br>3. | 1.<br>2.<br>3. | 1.<br>2.<br>3. | 1.<br>2.<br>3. | 1.<br>2.<br>3. | ☺ ☺ ☺ |
| Be Reliable | 1.<br>2.<br>3. | 1.<br>2.<br>3. | 1.<br>2.<br>3. | 1.<br>2.<br>3. | 1.<br>2.<br>3. | 1.<br>2.<br>3. | ☺ ☺ ☺ |
| Minimize Inventory | 1.<br>2.<br>3. | 1.<br>2.<br>3. | 1.<br>2.<br>3. | 1.<br>2.<br>3. | 1.<br>2.<br>3. | 1.<br>2.<br>3. | ☺ ☺ ☺ |
| On Time Job Release | 1.<br>2.<br>3. | 1.<br>2.<br>3. | 1.<br>2.<br>3. | 1.<br>2.<br>3. | 1.<br>2.<br>3. | 1.<br>2.<br>3. | ☺ ☺ ☺ |
| Exceed Quality Specs | 1.<br>2.<br>3. | 1.<br>2.<br>3. | 1.<br>2.<br>3. | 1.<br>2.<br>3. | 1.<br>2.<br>3. | 1.<br>2.<br>3. | ☺ ☺ ☺ |
| Be On Time | 1.<br>2.<br>3. | 1.<br>2.<br>3. | 1.<br>2.<br>3. | 1.<br>2.<br>3. | 1.<br>2.<br>3. | 1.<br>2.<br>3. | ☺ ☺ ☺ |
| Be Lean | 1.<br>2.<br>3. | 1.<br>2.<br>3. | 1.<br>2.<br>3. | 1.<br>2.<br>3. | 1.<br>2.<br>3. | 1.<br>2.<br>3. | ☺ ☺ ☺ |
| **Team Performance** | ☺ ☺ ☺ | ☺ ☺ ☺ | ☺ ☺ ☺ | ☺ ☺ ☺ | ☺ ☺ ☺ | ☺ ☺ ☺ | |

Enter 3 most critical performance measures linked to each strategic objective for each process.

**Exhibit 29.12  Example of a Structured and Balanced Measures Set Aligned with Strategic Objectives**

Although each company will follow a different path (the details of which are outside the scope of this chapter), several common themes and approaches are presented here. The objective is to create a common vision for change within an organization and a consensus on (and commitment to) reaching stretch goals that are attainable.

**(a) Goal Setting When the Customer Is the Constraint**    In a buyer's market, significantly more capacity exists in the value stream than the market will demand in the foreseeable future. This is easy to see when all resources are only working one shift or when labor utilization is very low. A choice exists between downsizing (to cut costs and assets) or aggressively going after the value that could be generated with the excess capacity without major capital expenditures. But to do this requires taking share from competitors by improving the value proposition to customers.

Two strategies—short-term revenue management and long-term fundamental improvement—are described here, along with the implications for the goals that are set.

*(i) Short-Term Revenue Management*    Excess capacity can provide the opportunity for pricing flexibility in the marketplace and significant bottom-line value, as the following example demonstrates.

The FOS Co. has 20 percent excess capacity in labor and equipment. The management team is in the process of selecting an appropriate improvement strategy and related goals. The team will choose between the following two options:

1. A cost-reduction strategy (a 20 percent reduction in head count).
2. A revenue-management strategy (providing new customers a 10 percent price break on new business to gain higher market share).

The *head-count reduction option* scenario follows. Exhibit 29.13 depicts the company's existing cost structure and typical goals that might be established to improve profit margins. The cost structure of the company consists of 60 percent raw materials, 10 percent direct labor, and 30 percent overhead, with a gross margin of $15 (as shown). Based on the head-count reduction plan, a goal has been established to improve margin by 18 percent to $17.70. Managers are happy with this plan to significantly improve performance, and they perceive relatively little risk, because this is a tried-and-true strategy.

But significant risk does exist if this action goes too far and causes resources in the value chain to become constraints. Many dependent production resources require people to set them up, run them, and maintain them. When labor is cut back, the capacity of physical resources is also cut back, because value flow processes cannot produce product without people. When delays happen at one resource in the string of dependent resources—and they will happen—the delays will propagate down the line and result in both late deliveries and smaller volumes than anticipated. This is especially true in operations in which labor flexibility has not been developed.

Customers will not be happy, and the company may end up expediting in overtime. Much of the company's "savings" from the reduction in head count will be lost in the push to get product out by the end of the month. Many hidden costs will be incurred and, as a result, the margin goals may not be met.

Going too far and creating a labor constraint does not seem to make the most sense, considering that labor has shrunk to only 10 percent of the value of sales—not to mention the repercussions on the creation of employee value by the company. Therefore, la-

| | Reduce Labor 20% | | | | |
|---|---|---|---|---|---|
| | **Baseline** | | **To Be Goals** | | |
| | **$** | **% of Cost** | **$** | **% of Cost** | |
| Sales | $150.0 | | $150.0 | | |
| Raw material | 81.0 | 60% | 81.0 | 61% | |
| Value-added | $69.0 | | $69.0 | | |
| Direct labor | **$13.5** | 10% | **$10.8** | 8% | (20% decrease) |
| Overhead | 40.5 | 30% | 40.5 | 31% | |
| Total (operations) | $54.0 | 100% | $51.3 | 100% | |
| Gross margin | **$15.0** | 10% | **$17.7** | 12% | |

UP 18%

**Exhibit 29.13   Example of Financial Goals Established When Labor Reduction Strategy Is Employed**

bor reduction is not the target of opportunity it once was. If anything, tight manning policies can force labor to become the constraint in the value stream, thus jeopardizing customer satisfaction and value creation for customers.

The *revenue-enhancement option* follows. Exhibit 29.14 shows the same cost structure as in the previous example. This time, however, goals have been established based on a revenue-management strategy. A new market segment has been identified, or the company has targeted a specific competitor's customers. A short-term, 10 percent price reduction has been offered to this segment, and, as a result, unit sales have risen 20 percent while total sales dollars have risen by 15 percent. Raw material costs increased by 20 percent (the same as unit sales), but direct labor costs remain the same, because there was excess capacity in terms of both labor and overhead. Based on the numbers shown, managers have set a goal of improving performance by 42 percent—more than twice the improvement of the previous cost-reduction strategy.

Is there risk in this revenue-management strategy? Yes, and it is not to be ignored. A company should not adopt a general strategy of predatory pricing but, rather, a focused market strategy that results in selling excess capacity to the highest bidder. For market segmentation to be effective and profitable for the company, however, the strategy must be transparent to the primary market. A price war could start if the market is attacked improperly. The company could risk losing its most important, full-margin customers.

To reduce the risk, the company must differentiate its offering in one way or another to create a distinctly different perception of the product. The airline industry has done this well. Tickets are sold to business people at a higher price, but they are refundable, and people can change them at the last minute. Leisure travelers, on the other hand, may get the same seats at significantly reduced fares (based on availability up until the plane leaves the gate), but the tickets are nonrefundable and are available only for specific dates and times. There is no flexibility.

The strategy chosen should aim at achieving maximum value by taking full advantage of nonconstrained resources. The market potential for the "differentiated" prod-

**Reduce Price 10% on New Sales**

| | $ | % of Cost | | OE | % of | |
|---|---|---|---|---|---|---|
| Sales | $150.0 | | | $172.5 | | (15% increase) |
| Raw material | 81.0 | 60% | ↑ | 97.2 | 64% | (20% increase) |
| Value-added | $69.0 | | | $75.3 | | |
| Direct labor | **$13.5** | 10% | | **$13.5** | 9% | |
| Overhead | 40.5 | 30% | | 40.5 | 27% | |
| Total (operations) | $54.0 | 100% | | $54.0 | 100% | |
| Gross margin | **$15.0** | 10% | | **$21.3** | 12% | |

UP 42%

**Exhibit 29.14    Example of Financial Goals Established When Revenue Management Strategy Is Employed**

uct needs to be determined and the resulting opportunity for value creation estimated. Performance goals and gaps need to be calculated and posted to the scorecard accordingly.

*(ii) Long-Term Fundamental Improvements*    Short-term pricing decisions, as illustrated previously, are easy for competitors to imitate. In fact, many a price war has evolved over a poorly executed revenue-enhancement initiative. Fundamental improvements, on the other hand, are much more difficult for competitors to imitate and—even if they try—take much time.

Toyota, for example, has hosted visits to its facilities by representatives of many companies, including competitors, interested in learning about the Toyota production system. Toyota recognizes that the time (a decade) and effort level (total commitment) necessary for another company to adopt its management culture and management methods effectively is a significant hurdle—one that few short-term-minded companies can overcome. Toyota also recognizes that traditional financial measures used in the United States hamper the deployment of the quality initiatives necessary for Toyota's management strategy to work effectively. Toyota has therefore had a big head start and never intended to sit still. Its goal was to continuously improve so that it could always stay ahead of the competition.

Srikanth and Robertson[6] make a strong case that a long-term improvement program for a buyer's market relies on knowledge and focus—knowledge of what is important for the customer and a focus on improving what is important for the customer. Other efforts may not produce nearly the same value for any of the stakeholders. At the same time, managers cannot go overboard, because the generation of economic value for owners will decline if they do.

Srikanth and Robertson also point out that improving the value proposition for customers in terms other than price takes time and effort. To start with, managers may or may not have a good feel for business performance from the perspective of the customer. Internal performance measures may be misleading.

There are many ways a company can paint a performance picture from its own perspective that differs drastically from what customers see. For example, a company's internal delivery performance may show a 95 percent on-time delivery record when customers see only a 50 percent on-time delivery record. This can easily occur if, for example, the company measures its performance according to the "week promised"—even though customers want deliveries throughout the week on the "day promised".

If a company gets this long-term focus wrong, its managers waste a lot of time, energy, and money tilting at windmills. If a company gets it right, its managers can generate enough growth to move the company into a seller's market condition—one in which it becomes the supplier of choice.

Srikanth and Robertson suggest that a starting point is the identification of the top six or seven *current* competitive elements that the company's customers use to determine value. This list represents significant components of a company's BOV. This BOV should preferably be prioritized in the sequence that constitutes most value in the customers' eyes. There are many ways to do this, including:

- *Listen to the voice of the customer.* Customers may already be signaling what they expect through their supplier-ranking initiatives. Many customers today indicate their expectations about performance through their regular ranking surveys. These should be evaluated and the issues identified.

- *Learn from failure.* Analyzing lost opportunities and lost customers helps clarify customer preferences. Critical information is obtained from evaluating these lost sales, because they may indicate cases in which the company has failed to keep pace with changing demands and expectations.

- *Ask for guidance.* Both customers and noncustomers can be asked for their opinions. Noncustomers may base their purchasing decisions on different value criteria, which could be an opportunity to differentiate service offerings. There are various techniques for surveying and interviewing customers to collect this information. Either external consultants (who can provide an unbiased view) or the company's own employees can conduct these efforts.

Exhibit 29.15 provides an example of priorities established by one company after it surveyed both customers and noncustomers. It shows that quality is the number-one issue in the company's marketplace, even more so than product customization. (Many commodity markets have priorities similar to the ones shown.)

These surveys need to be conducted regularly to ensure that current preferences are identified, because competitive elements tend to be dynamic. The competitive element that gave an edge in the past may not be relevant today.

An *internal benchmark* and *trend charts* need to be established once competitive elements are identified. This assures the organization that it is seeing its own performance in the same way that its customers see it.

The survey presented in Exhibit 29.15 suggests that market segments that could be characterized as "price shoppers" might be exploited. This market segment is relatively insensitive to other issues: They shop for the best bargain or best purchase price variance. Other segments have different priorities. Exhibit 29.16 presents the results of a follow-up survey, which indicates that the company is positioned to provide more value than necessary to one group of customers and less value than required to the second. This has obvious implications for sales strategy and improvement strategy.

| | Competitive Elements Used to Determine Value | | | | | |
|---|---|---|---|---|---|---|
| | Product Capability | Response Speed | Delivery Reliability | Quality | Price | Overall Reputation |
| Customer 1 | 4 | 3 | 2 | 1 | 5 | 6 |
| Customer 2 | 5 | 1 | 3 | 2 | 4 | 6 |
| Customer 3 | 4 | 3 | 2 | 1 | 5 | 6 |
| Customer 4 | 5 | 2 | 4 | 3 | 1 | 6 |
| Potential Customer | 2 | 6 | 5 | 4 | 1 | 3 |
| Overall Rank | 4 | 3 | 3.2 | 2.2 | 3.2 | 5.4 |

Customers have been asked to rank their preferences among the various competitive elements.
1 = Most important to 6 = Least important

**Exhibit 29.15   Example of Customer Value Priorities: Forced Ranking by Customers with Lowest Number the Most Important**

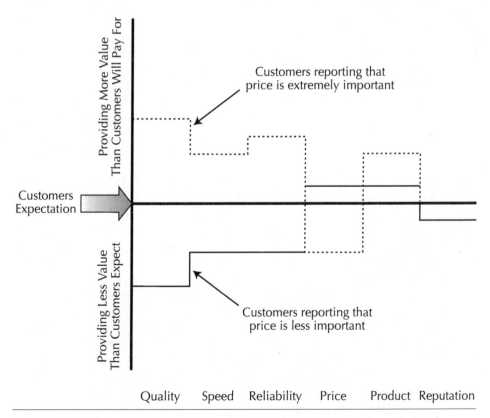

**Exhibit 29.16   Example of Calibration of Your Performance to Customer's Needs**

The company may have a well-known reputation for quality and delivery, in which case it may be able to price its product accordingly. Given excess capacity and a significant opportunity to sell to a medium- or low-price market niche, the company may still forgo the opportunity if it wishes to maintain "high-end brand image." (It may, however, discover private branding as a market for its excess capacity.)

A different picture may emerge from the competitive perspective. Exhibit 29.17 presents the results of a competitive survey in which customers were polled and asked to force-rank a selection of competitors to indicate how well each competitor met their needs in each top decision criterion. The survey illustrates that the company in the example is well ahead of the competition in terms of quality but significantly behind in terms of both delivery speed and reliability. Customers desire better quality, but the company is already the best in this category, so major investments to improve quality may not provide the same value to customers as improvements in speed and reliability would. Therefore, the survey identifies a focus for fundamental improvement for the company.

These targets become specific performance goals for the company. They provide a value deal to customers that puts the company ahead of its competitors. It thus achieves the "supplier-of-choice" status needed in the marketplace at existing price levels. Competitive surveys indicate the quantity of each competitive element a company needs in its BOV to become the supplier of choice.

For example, the FOS Co. has to exceed the customers' expectations in both speed and reliability of delivery. It must also show improvement in quality. The following represent specific goals:

- Improve benchmark delivery performance from a 12-day response time to a 3-day response.
- Improve reliability from 75 percent on-time delivery on the day promised to 98 percent.
- Improve quality from the baseline of 10,000 parts per million (ppm) to 900 ppm.

Now a goal of a 10 percent improvement in volume rings true. A commitment by sales to higher volumes is much less risky when these goals are backed up by a focused plan that details the market share that will be taken, from which competitors it will be taken, and also how it will be taken. Market commitment is backed up with available supply-chain capacity—capacity is not the constraint.

The score must be tallied for the value-creating strategies chosen. Calculate the value of the performance gap and post it to the scorecard. Estimate the potential for additional sales volume (assuming the previously discussed criteria can be met); also estimate the resulting opportunity for value creation.

There may be a significant lag time from the establishment of a fundamental improvement strategy that is focused on competitive elements and the value generated from additional sales. For example, a newly engineered product may take one year to hit the market after product development and market testing occur. Value generated from the sales of this product (which may still only be in the development stage) will only be realized after the first year, and the full potential of the sales may only be felt later. This is significant to note, because certain expenses may increase as a result of the marketing effort required for developmental of the product, though they may also decrease after the new product is introduced.

## Buyer's Top 6 Decision Criteria

| | Market Share | Quality | Speed | Reliability | Product Features | Reputation | Overall Value | | Price |
|---|---|---|---|---|---|---|---|---|---|
| **Weighting** | | 1 | 1.2 | 1.3 | 1.4 | 1.5 | | | |
| Competitor #1 | 2% | 2 | 1 | 3 | 3 | 4 | 15.5 | | 6 |
| Competitor #2 | 3% | 4 | 5 | 2 | 5 | 3 | 22.3 | | 5 |
| Competitor #3 | 10% | 3 | 2 | 1 | 4 | 1 | 17.7 | | 2 |
| Competitor #4 | 4% | 5 | 3 | 6 | 6 | 5 | 20.925.5 | | 3 |
| Competitor #5 | 4% | 6 | 6 | 4 | 1 | 6 | 18.1 | | 1 |
| Your value stream | 5% | 1 | (4) | (5) | 2 | 2 | | | 4 |

**Exhibit 29.17   Example of a Ranking of Competitive Value Propositions of a Specific Market Segment.** *Source:* **M. Srikanth and S. Robertson,** *Measurements for Effective Decision Making* **(Spectrum Publishing Co., 1995), 59.**

Other initiatives, such as total quality management or business-process redesign, also span a number of years. These programs are not easy to copy, and they take significant time to implement. To succeed, they often require substantial change in a company's culture. That is precisely why these long-term improvement strategies are such a powerful competitive weapon.

*(iii) RightSizing Without Constraining the Flow*    In a buyer's market, customers set the standard for the value proposition they expect and the capabilities of competitors dictate what they get. The ability of managers to control product flows in this environment dictates the value added a company generates for customers. At a given price, a company that provides less value to the marketplace than the competition (however value is defined for the company's market) loses market share, whereas a company that provides more value gains share.

At the same time, a company has to provide a *financial value flow* to shareholders. This means that shareholders must get a fair return for their investment; otherwise, they will invest their money elsewhere. A company that oversizes the value stream, provides a performance level that customers do not value, or manages the value stream without an eye toward demand gets what it deserves: The customer will not pay for waste in the system.

Rightsizing implies having just the right amount of all the resources necessary to provide both the uninterrupted value flow customers are willing to pay for and the economic value flow owners expect. It is the job of managers to provide and manage both the resources and the flow of product that consumes these resources.

Nothing illustrates the issues involved in this trade-off better than the day-to-day tug-of-war that goes on in the attempt to rightsize labor and inventory. Customers rarely purchase the same volume or mix of product from one week to the next. With "lean" finished-goods inventories and order backlogs that measure in days rather than weeks or months, many companies do not have a cushion in front of their value chain to filter out the effect variation in demand has on operations. This simple fact (combined with a buyer's market condition) has a significant influence on improvement goals.

As Exhibit 29.18 shows, the FOS Co. has 150 production employees that support its value stream. Over the previous quarter, however, only an average of 100 employees were required based on the standard labor content of actual weekly sales. Labor utilization (at 66 percent) looked bad, but with excess labor available delivery performance looked good (at close to 100 percent delivered on the day required by the customer). FOS Co. provided value to the customer, but it also incurred the extra cost associated with the excess labor.

Managers have the following choices:

- Reduce prices to get more volume.
- Increase production and build inventory to earn more hours.
- Downsize the company.

Given that FOS makes a customized product that is engineered into the customer's product, cutting prices will not result in quick volume improvements. (Typically there is a 12-month lag time between the times FOS is awarded a contract and it delivers the first order of parts.) In addition, building finished-goods inventory is not an option, despite the favorable impact that "overabsorption" can have on the financial statement. (Each customer order specifies a number of custom configurations for the model being ordered, so forecasting future demand by SKU is not possible.)

The edict came down to operations: Reduce the head count. Managers saw that only 100 people were required (based on average demand and standard labor rates), so plans were put in place to reduce manpower levels accordingly. As the headlines announced to the investment community, "FOS Co. has announced a restructuring program today that will result in the reduction of one-third of its employees and a related charge to earnings of. . . ." Spending immediately went down, and the management team declared victory.

Customers, however, saw a different picture. FOS had been a reliable supplier, but it became unreliable. As Exhibit 29.18 illustrates, customer weekly demands on capacity exceeded the capacity available in 6 out of the 12 weeks in the quarter. With less labor available, all the orders cannot be completed in the week required. Consequently, they are carried over to the next week and become late for delivery.

When customers do not get their product on time, they demand that FOS Co. build an inventory of finished goods that can be shipped when ordered. And no, the customers are not willing to pay more for the product: A 100 percent fill rate within one week of order is the service level customers expect. As a result, FOS Co. starts on a downward spiral of hidden costs, because it has to run overtime to make enough additional volume to set up finished-goods inventory; it also must add a warehouse and invest in additional materials.

An outside observer may ask the simple question, "Why doesn't FOS Co. simply pull in the work from next week to the current week if next week's orders are heavy?" The simple answer is that it may or may not have this capability: It depends on how well the company can predict the next week's demand by specific SKU without having the actual orders in hand and how flexible its labor force is.

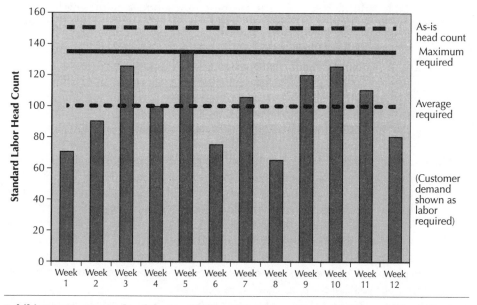

**Exhibit 29.18    Example of the Variability of Customer Demand Measured by Labor Required**

Managers went too far. They had turned a nonconstrained resource into a major constraint to flow. Had they reduced manpower to the level needed for a historically high week (week 5), the customer would not have noticed any difference in performance. Managers might have even made the decision that reducing manpower levels to those required in week 3 and week 10 was worth the risk that 1 week out of 12 they might not be able to deliver on time.

Although the short-term financial feedback from FOS Co.'s cost-reduction strategy may have been positive, the long-term feedback from customers was not, so sales continued to slide. Given the lag time between lack of performance and the decisions customers made to switch to a competitor, managers did not connect their actions to the result—lost business. A second round of downsizing appeared necessary.

It is outside the scope of this chapter to describe the various improvement strategies that managers may employ to manage their value streams while continuously reducing the non–value-added waste in a system. Examples of these strategies include *business-process reengineering, lean manufacturing, synchronous manufacturing, concurrent engineering,* and *total quality management,* to name a few. Nor is it in the scope of this chapter to identify the strategies used to design value into a product with less waste, reduce costs for a specific manufacturing process, or eliminate an unnecessary purchase.

However, an important point to note is that in a buyer's market, knowledge and focus are critical. A company will set strategies and establish goals that put the delivery of value for all stakeholders at risk unless the whole organization understands:

- The nature of the value that it delivers to customers.
- The fact that it only has to provide a value that is noticeably ahead of that provided by the competition.
- The fact that it must protect that value as its number-one priority.

**(b) Goal Setting When a Resource Is the Constraint**    In the enviable situation in which the constraint to value flow is an internal resource, the leverage point is within the organization, so the company has far more control over value creation. Critical questions arise:

- How does one generate the most value from a constraint resource?
- What are the internal drivers for improved value creation?
- How does the entire value chain support these objectives?
- What needs to be measured in order to generate the appropriate behavior?

The value framework will indicate the linkages between the strategic initiatives available to the company and assist in the calculation of the projected value creation

The company needs to know how much constraint time is worth to the stakeholders. The organization then needs to understand that value and how a focus on the constraint is a lever to increasing that value. Efforts need to be made to ensure that the time of the constrained resource is not being misallocated. Additional efforts need to be made to ensure that the time spent produces the best value yield per unit of time for the stakeholders. Performance of the constrained resource then needs to be monitored closely, and performance goals need to be established accordingly.

Efforts to improve in other areas of the value chain, while also worthy, must be done in subordination to the focus on the constraint.

*(i) Tell the Organization the Value of Constraint Time*    Consider, for example, JW Co., which recently launched a new product. The product line represents a leap in technology and styling that competitors cannot duplicate. As a result, orders are flooding in faster than anyone had ever dreamed—and also faster than operations can deliver. Although plans are in the works to build a new plant to supplement capacity, it will take 12 to18 months to come on stream.

Managers have identified that the major constraint to the value stream is a component plant in Division 1. The assembly plant cannot get enough subassemblies from this component plant and also cannot outsource the subassemblies. A management team has mapped the value stream for this particular product line in the plant and has also identified that subassemblies are held up for lack of components made on a computer numeric control (CNC) machine that is part of a lean manufacturing cell.

The company sells two products in the new product line—product *A* and product *B*—that require subassemblies from the plant. Each subassembly requires several component parts that run on the custom CNC machine. Additional parts are also made on this machine for other, more established product lines. Basic information the management team has about these products is shown in the table:

|                                  | Product *A* | Product *B* |
| -------------------------------- | ----------- | ----------- |
| Sales price                      | $400        | $330        |
| Material costs                   | $130        | $120        |
| Value added                      | $270        | $210        |
| Truly variable expense per unit  | $40         | $32         |
| Contribution per unit to cash    | $230        | $178        |
| Weekly volume                    | 90          | 90          |

From this information, the managers calculated that sales of these two products contribute about $43,000 per week in value added for customers and $36,000 per week in cash to the business (before fixed expenses). They also realize that another unit of sales cannot be made without the parts from the CNC machine. The CNC machine—the bottleneck—controls the value created for the stakeholders.

Given that the CNC machine is staffed to operate seven days a week on three shifts, the team has calculated that the time of this resource is worth $214 an hour to the company. The team has ignored the value of $45 an hour (assigned by accounting and based on labor and overhead) because team members consider it irrelevant.

A *process improvement team* (PIT) has been assigned the task of increasing production volume for the new product line before competitors can get into the market and challenge the company's position of market leadership.

*(ii) Focus Local Teams on Reducing Wasted Time*    Time of constrained resources can be wasted in many ways. One root cause often relates to the fact that managers and employees are not aware of the importance of the resource or of the value of its time. Supervisors think that an hour that the CNC is shut down costs the company only $45—no big deal compared to $214 (the value added per hour, as calculated previously).

By focusing on the constraint, the PIT team uncovered the following possibilities for misallocation of constraint time:

- Production is shut down for morning and afternoon breaks and for lunch. Over the course of a week, therefore, 15 to 20 percent of the time available is wasted.
- The resource is used to produce parts needed to fill sales orders for products *A* and *B*, but a significant amount of time is misallocated to make other products for inventory. Making inventory is not consistent with making value flow at the pull of customers. Local efficiency may look good, but enterprise efficiency—as measured in value added per unit of actual spending and per unit of capital employed—will look bad.
- Upstream, unconstrained processes experience delays and starve the constrained resource for work. Other upstream departments work the schedule to make their own departments as efficient as possible, but—by doing so—they fail to produce parts needed by the constraint resource. A time buffer in front of the constraint would prevent this. Schedules for upstream resources synchronized with the schedule for the constraint are thus essential.
- Preventive maintenance has not been done, so the constrained resource grinds to a halt regularly and unexpectedly. Because the undermaintained equipment cannot hold to tolerance, significant scrap results. By focusing on unit costs, the department's managers have chosen not to spend money required for normal maintenance. This is especially painful when the PIT realizes that all the spending is just a reallocation of existing fixed costs from the maintenance department (now called a profit center) to the constraint department.
- Batch sizes are too small, so unnecessary production time is lost to setup time. The JIT batch sizes have shrunk too far.
- Parts and materials delivered to the constraint have not been inspected. Consequently, the constraint has to work with defective material that gets scrapped down stream.

With focus, the PIT uncovered many opportunities for improvement. These opportunities support setting goals that look ambitious, but the team knows that they are all low-hanging fruit. There is a consensus for change built around the knowledge that "we can do this."

*(iii) Challenge Policy*   Internal policies and procedures in many companies have evolved over a long period. Many are outdated, but they persist, thus haunting performance and preventing managers from making wise decisions that would contribute value for stakeholders, especially decisions that relate to constraints to flow.

The constraint is straining at the seams, yet there is some old equipment sitting in the back of the warehouse unused. The old equipment can manufacture some of the items now loaded on the constraint, but it is not as efficient as the equipment now used at the constraint. The constraint can produce parts twice as fast as the old equipment, and with half the labor.

The PIT suggested dusting off the old equipment and offloading the parts. But manufacturing engineering resisted this idea, because doing so would violate cost-reduction goals. The production department also resisted, because it would get hit with negative labor variances. Accounting objected because unit costs would go up. It is easy to overlook the fact that this option would generate another 50 units of sales per week of the product that customers are screaming for, and there would be little additional operating expense for the company. This is value lost forever.

The PIT has found that product shipments to customers are done once a week to save shipping costs. They also discovered that the value of shipping every day is a shorter cash-to-cash cycle for the company, and a reduction in the inventory that customers need to hold on-site between deliveries more than outweighs the savings in shipping costs. Once the product has made it through the most constrained resource, it is sold goods that customers will pay for it as soon as they can get their hands on it.

*(iv) Go for Value Yield per Unit of Constraint*    Product mix becomes an important issue in establishing goals when several products require different amounts of time on the same constrained resource. The time of that resource is valuable to the company—the total value added for the product sold—and the cash the company generates is greatly influenced by the decision about which constrained products to promote through the sales force.

Relying on traditional gross margin to set priorities may be dangerous. It might mean paying high commissions for selling a product that provides the worst value-added yield and low commissions for selling a product with the best value-added yield, as shown later.

Exhibit 29.19 shows how JW Co. uses *traditional priorities.* It provides an example of five products that JW Co. offers as part of its new product introduction and shows a calculation of each product's gross margin. If sales commissions are based on a percentage of gross margin and the sales force can sell more product than the company can make, the company will naturally attempt to sell higher-margin product whenever possible. Products *A* and *B* would become a logical focus. Indeed, this is what JW Co. is selling now, even though it could sell the other products in the line.

Exhibit 29.20 illustrates (through the use of *constraint-driven priorities*) the true financial impact this decision has on JW Co. All five products have multiple parts made on the customized CNC machine—the constrained resource of the value stream. All other products have been offloaded back to older processes to make as much time as possible available to this line. As a result, this resource is available 140 hours per week. Each product requires a different amount of time on this machine for a combination of parts, as shown in Exhibit 29.20. A calculation has been made of the truly variable costs per unit for these products, how much contribution would be available to cover fixed costs, and how much contribution there would be per minute of CNC time for the product.

As Exhibit 29.20 shows, JW Co. can make much more money promoting the sale of products *E* and *D* rather than *A* and *B.* In fact, the value of time of the constrained resource is not the $214 per hour based on selling product *A* and *B* but $375 per hour based on selling a 50-50 mix of products *E* and *D*—two products that were at the bottom of the margin list.

Setting improvement goals for a value stream can be a risky business if the management team acts in ignorance of the constraints to value flow. On the other hand, knowledge and focus can help a management team develop integrated strategies that will provide significant and fundamental improvement that competitors cannot easily duplicate.

Setting value-based goals is an iterative process between the development of a proposed strategy and the unbiased reality check necessary from the perspective of the most constrained resource in the value stream. It is a team sport for the good of the enterprise, not an individual sport for the good of a single organizational component of the value stream.

| Product Sales Priority | Sales Price | Raw Material Cost | Labor Cost | Burden | COGS | Gross Margin | % Margin |
|---|---|---|---|---|---|---|---|
| A | $400 | $130 | $40 | $80 | $250 | $150 | *38%* |
| B | $330 | $120 | $32 | $64 | $216 | $114 | 35% |
| C | $300 | $120 | $30 | $60 | $210 | $90 | 30% |
| D | $280 | $170 | $18 | $36 | $224 | $56 | 20% |
| E | $240 | $130 | $20 | $40 | $190 | $50 | 21% |

**Exhibit 29.19   Example of Product Mix Priorities: Based on Standard Margin**

**Constrained Equipment**
Customized CNC machine
Available 140 hours per week

| Product Sales Priority | Sales Price | Raw Material Cost | Labor Cost | Total Truly Variable Costs | Contribution | Constraint Minutes Per Unit | Contribution Per Constraint Minute | Maximum Units Per Week | Maximum Contribution Per Week |
|---|---|---|---|---|---|---|---|---|---|
| *E* | $240 | $130 | $20 | $150 | $90 | 10 | $9.00 | 840 | *$75,600* |
| D | $280 | $170 | $18 | $188 | $92 | 15 | $6.13 | 560 | $51,520 |
| A | $400 | $130 | $40 | $170 | $230 | 50 | $4.60 | 168 | $38,640 |
| B | $330 | $120 | $32 | $152 | $178 | 45 | $3.96 | 187 | $33,227 |
| C | $300 | $120 | $30 | $150 | $150 | 50 | $3.00 | 168 | $25,200 |

**Exhibit 29.20 Example of Product Mix Priority: Based on (Contribution after Variable Costs) per Minute of Constrained Time When an Equipment Resource Is the Constraint**

Update the value gap scorecard to reflect the strategies and priorities identified by the management team. Calculate the value generated for stakeholders when performance is improved from "as-is" to the value-based goals. Establish a consensus among the management team that this represents a doable plan and a framework for the company to operate within that is best for the business overall. Attack goals by consensus— with the entire organization focused and aligned for success.

**29.8 SUMMARY**    Goal setting through value analysis will identify realistic goals that are aligned with the strategic objectives of maximizing value for the stakeholders. Through developing and refining strategies, a senior management team will be challenging and changing policies and procedures for the organization while they establish challenging goals that recognize the reality of constraints. A new framework for improvement will be provided for execution. Members of the senior management team will all share the same vision of what the company can be and what strategies are needed to get it to the goals they established.

First, share this vision and challenging goal down throughout the organization. Turn strategies into action plans that managers feel confident they can execute successfully to reach their goals. It does not make sense if the goals are conflicting between individuals, teams, departments, or business units. Create a coherence of thought among all levels and across all functions of the company. Focus the organization for maximum competitive impact.

Second, construct a BOV for the stakeholders so that time and effort are not wasted on things that provide no value. Share the vision of how the business can prosper by building that value, and also share the specific improvement goal necessary for each component of value. Link value-based goals to team and individual goals and action plans so that everyone knows how their individual actions contribute to building value for stakeholders. Eliminate the "mixed signals" of traditional performance measures, or actions will remain in conflict.

Third, institute a set of measures in line with these goals and objectives—a balanced set of measures focused on value so that progress can be monitored and feedback given on how well teams and individuals are meeting their objectives and executing their own action plans. Exhibit 29.12 illustrates a table for the development of a focused and balanced set of measures by process. Have the process teams develop detailed change plans that will support the effort or give feedback about newly discovered constraints. Validate improvement plans across the various processes and in light of the constraints to assure that worthy changes made in one business process will not be offset by changes made in other business processes.

Fourth, give feedback about performance to the organization.

The process will continue in an endless cycle, with each cycle generating a greater level of value creation. Do not allow inertia to set in; otherwise, the business will stagnate or a competitor will fill the empty space in the market. The last step is the first step: Start back at the beginning.

## NOTES

1. J. P. Womack and D. T. Jones, *Lean Thinking* (New York: Simon & Schuster, 1996), page 311.
2. Measuring and Managing Shareholder Value Creation, March 31, 1997.

3. B. D. Clinton and S. Chen, "Do New Performance Measures Measure Up?" *Management Accounting* (October 1998).

4. M. L. Srikanth and M. Umble, *Synchronous Management,* vol. 1 of *Profit-Based Manufacturing for the 21st Century* (Guilford, CT: Spectrum Publishing Company, 1997).

5. *Ibid.* page 119 (also)

6. M. Srikanth and S. Robertson, *Measurements for Effective Decision Making* (Guilford, CT: The Spectrum Publishing Co., 1995).

# CHAPTER 30

# CONTINUOUS IMPROVEMENT

## William Maguire
## Martin Putterill
### The University of Auckland

**30.1 INTRODUCTION**   As organizations begin operating in the new century, thoughtful financial managers will be wondering how to better serve the collective interests of their stakeholders in coming years. This chapter is built on the belief that turbulent conditions in the future will demand special effort to ensure business success and survival. To cope with these challenging conditions, financial managers will need strong technical skills, an appreciation of operational and strategic management, and appropriate attitudes for facilitating and promoting performance.

Performance is about achieving targets—doing better than before but also doing better than others. Innovation enables a company to get ahead, but the leaps that innovation can achieve are not enough to maintain a lead without continuous improvement.

Given the priority of satisfying or exceeding customer demands, continuous improvement has been defined as "the relentless pursuit of improvement in the delivery of value to the customer."[1] This requires sustained effort: "Continual improvement in production science is the ultimate measure of world-class manufacturers. They push at the margins of their expertise, trying on every front to be better than before. They strive to be dynamic, learning organizations."[2]

Continuous improvement is a management philosophy that the Japanese call *kaizen*. Managers and other employees of a company must internalize *kaizen* and commit themselves to it. Although continuous improvement is now a well-known concept in management circles, it is not easy to find practical guidance to help financial managers apply the concept. Therefore, this chapter explains the fundamental ideas and practices of *kaizen*, including how to facilitate the continuous improvement process.

**30.2 PHASES OF THE BUSINESS CYCLE**   The duties of most top financial managers include decision support and the establishment of a database that can provide planning and control information throughout an enterprise. A second span of responsibility requires financial managers to have significant technical skills, foresight, and the ability to translate investment plans into financial terms. Third, whereas new activities and investments play a large part in the life of an organization, an equally large set of responsibilities for financial executives usually relates to existing investments and operations. Someone capable of discharging these three responsibilities effectively is indispensable to an organization intent on pursuing continuous improvement.

**(a) Turbulent Business Environments** Turbulence imposes abnormal pressure to perform in any one of three possible phases of the business cycle:

1. Success.
2. Downturn.
3. Strategy building.

Many companies in the United States and elsewhere, having enjoyed a long period of sustained growth since the 1980s, have been in the *success phase*. In this phase, even if growth in the overall economy continues, individual enterprises have to intensify their efforts to meet growing internal and external expectations.

The *downturn phase* is usually a time of "deconstruction" and "downsizing," and frequently of knee-jerk intervention by management.

Innovation in technology and processes is ongoing and a recognized feature of most business agendas. Though the overall flow of new ideas and products into the market may seem linear, from time to time individual companies are intensely preoccupied with strategic choices. This can be called the *strategy-building phase,* which overlaps both the success and downturn phases.

During the next decade, financial managers will face many challenges, not the least of which will be to identify the onset of a new phase and how long each phase is likely to endure. This analysis would be even more difficult if financial management responses differed from one phase to the next. Conversely, the work life of financial managers would be considerably easier provided they could apply a single approach effectively in all three phases.

Managers who are responsible for sustaining business momentum and balance are likely to be concerned with the following issues:

- Finding better ways to deliver customer (or consumer) satisfaction through the quality of the goods and services they provide.
- Pursuing the elimination or reduction of waste.
- Fostering coordination supported by relevant information and a balance of activities within the organization.
- Providing leadership that engenders commitment and creativity.
- Ensuring the planned, controlled flow of funds required to support the organization.

Each of these concerns plays a part in lifting the fortunes of the enterprise, and collectively they suggest that continuous improvement is important not only in the success phase but in the downturn and strategy-building phases as well. Whereas the strategy-building phase occurs infrequently and concurrently with either of the other phases, the concerns just listed are equally relevant.

**(b) Competitive Pressures** Business around the world is being conducted at a faster pace because of markets that are almost instantaneously linked. Shorter product life cycles accelerate obsolescence, which threatens companies trying to maintain a technological lead. Competitive pressures lead to new ways of doing things, which may lead to the reconfiguration of a company's value chain. When information technology is (as one observer writes) "harnessed to its full potential (that is, in conjunction with the associated software, databases, and telecommunications), the digital computer permits vast leveraging of knowledge-work."[3] Given the complex causes and effects, it is nevertheless clear that the impact of computers is significant and far-reaching. Not only is the finance industry trading day and night around the world, but manufacturing plants are moving toward operations that last 24 hours a day, often because of the growing reliance on robotics.

Under normal conditions in the past, financial managers could often afford to be reactive; they could take actions that nested comfortably within their routine planning and control duties. But when a business moves into a turbulent business environment, demands for information and analysis become imperative and more challenging. At these times of heightened complexity, financial managers face three fundamental questions:

1. How can the finance function become an active contributor to decision-making in the search for corporate success?
2. What organizational rearrangement will improve the quality and timing of decision-support information?
3. Are analytical techniques and skills up to the standard required to support continuous improvement?

A positive attitude toward continuous improvement is a significant component of efforts to deal with turbulence. This state is characterized by striving for better outcomes through a sustained process of "learning from learning." Financial executives in the future must also have a keenly developed sense of strategic direction. A positive attitude on their part implies a sharp reorientation from past to future, and willingness to foster approaches that challenge the status quo across the spectrum of business processes. Sections 30.3, 30.4, and 30.5 develop the strategy and continuous improvement themes, whereas section 30.6 suggests the reshaping of organizational structures in a manner appropriate for continuous improvement.

There are dangers that misuse of analytical techniques or inappropriate reliance on formal reports may lead to suboptimal outcomes. Section 30.7 outlines decision-support methods and techniques, then discusses some of the decision-making approaches currently in use. That section also analyzes the extent to which these methods and techniques are compatible with strategic continuous improvement.

Financial executives who have a positive attitude toward continuous improvement can effectively promote companywide efforts to improve performance. Indeed, the financial function must take an active part in fostering continuous improvement, particularly in the area of *advanced manufacturing techniques* and related investments (which includes computer-aided design, materials resource planning systems, automated materials handling systems, robotics, computer-controlled machines, flexible manufacturing systems, and electronic data interchange). These techniques have in common a high level of dependence on information and technology, and all add significant complexity to decision making.

**30.3 EXTERNAL TRENDS**   Deregulation in the marketplace and rapid technological advances present both opportunities and challenges in a global economy that is characterized by demanding consumers and high expectations. Well-established and previously successful companies must compete under a new set of rules or else see their competitive positions eroded. There are many opportunities for enterprising companies that can rapidly transform consumer specifications and innovative ideas into new goods and services. Although having a large resource base makes this transformation easier, smaller companies using similar concepts can also succeed if managers can channel their energy through robust strategies and flexible responses.

Awareness of the evolving social and economic environment in which an organization operates is central to the development of strategic positioning in the marketplace. One characteristic of a positive attitude to continuous improvement is willingness to scan the environment for new opportunities and directions and also for new methods and materials. Short-term objectives are, in turn, a flexible expression of strategic aims and managerial response to more immediate changes in the environment. The capacity to identify and interpret business trends is important in all phases of the business cycle, and although general management takes the lead, financial managers need to develop this capacity if they are to act as effective business partners.

Organizations are open systems that interact with their environments and with other systems. Strategy draws from this interaction. Skill in analyzing the environment lies in accurately identifying the nature of prominent systems, important variables, and key trends in those variables. Before forming strategy, many companies conduct "SWOT" analysis to examine the company's *strengths, weaknesses, opportunities,* and *threats.* Management can then concentrate on building strengths and eliminating weaknesses to take advantage of opportunities and to defend against threats.

Since the 1980s, some experts on strategy have tended to focus on the external aspect of strategy analysis. Porter's "five forces" framework, for example, assists in analyzing the environment;[4] management then develops strategies that will make the best use of this environment. Others have taken a resource-based view of strategy, under which management identifies the company's resources and seeks to use these to the best advantage.[5] These approaches are not mutually exclusive. Their use in combination approximates the SWOT approach mentioned previously, though they bring additional powerful concepts and techniques.

Porter's framework comprises the prominent systems in a company's environment, namely, customers, suppliers, rivals, providers of substitutes, and potential entrants to the industry. Among the key trends are continuing deregulation, global market development, and information explosion, all of which have a deep impact on the way in which companies conduct business and make profits.

Environmental appraisals reveal trends that companies must address if they are to survive and prosper. Among others, external forces that have the greatest potential impact are:

- Innovations in manufacturing technology and business systems.
- Accelerating capabilities in telecommunications and data transfer.
- Changing attitudes to workers and work structures.
- Demands for new products and services of higher quality.
- Constraints on resource utilization and waste disposal.

These forces share several characteristics. First, they are evolutionary; from a seminal idea or development, each body of knowledge compounds through time. Second, though much of this knowledge is amassed for private advantage, a great deal emerges into the public domain. Universities, journals, conferences, and public libraries offer free or low-cost access to information to any organization committed to maintaining its knowledge base. The explosion of information from database services and the Internet in recent years has made it much easier to keep abreast of business developments. Third, their use is discretionary.

Consequently, a company can control its degree of exposure to the changing landscape, through medium- and short-term budgetary appropriations for information gathering, attending conferences, and the like. Regardless of an individual organization's decisions to participate, the external resource base will grow until new insights supplant the idea from which it sprang, or society at large no longer supports the public institutions upon which this knowledge transfer depends.

**(a) Innovations in Manufacturing Technology and Business Systems**    The pace of technological innovation and associated business information processes has been accelerating as new ideas form the platform for advances in later years. Over time, some technologies and methods move ahead, thus becoming platforms for additional development, whereas other processes are superseded.

Delays in the diffusion process and a tendency to cling to old ways increases the probability that the leading edge of change will become rather ragged, particularly when (as now) the rate of change is exponential rather than linear.

**(b) Accelerating Capabilities in Telecommunication and Data Transfers**    Convergence of computer-based technology has resulted in a remarkable level of global connectivity. This allows companies not only to move alphanumerical information safely and quickly anywhere in the world but also to exchange graphical material (i.e. drawings, plans, and pictures) at will. These services speed up the cycle of business interchanges, giving commercial benefits to those companies that can synthesize the communication technologies and business operations.

**(c) Changing Attitudes to Workers and Work Structures**    Higher degrees of automation and robotics, coupled with restructuring within business units, are factors promoting a shift in the relationship between the number of employees and a company's output. Downsizing continues to be a feature of most Western economies, and this tendency is likely to persist in coming decades.

Among prime issues to consider are delegation of responsibility in highly automated workplaces, performance appraisal and rewards, and questions about employees' commitment (e.g., their willingness to remain in employment and to be productive). In advanced manufacturing centers, expectations of numeracy and computer literacy will be greater (e.g. every employee may be provided with a personal computer as an aid to productivity). In settings such as these, cycle time will be shorter, so traditional arrangements for supervision are likely to be counterproductive. People will need to be able to make decisions on the spot, and management will encourage them to anticipate problems.

Essential strategic and tactical actions include retraining for existing staff and better selection, training, and monitoring of future employees. External sources of knowledge will be essential for busy executives who must deal with these issues.

**(d) New Products and Services, Higher Quality, and Greater Productivity**    The global trading environment is much more complex than intraregional activities. For example:

- Target pricing increases the complexity of new products that have components from many sources and are intended for diverse markets.
- Flexible manufacturing (based on an extensive list of options) demands an ongoing marketing review and supervision.
- Companies that are attempting to maintain a global competitive position require regular appraisal of prices in diverse markets.

Effective external monitoring to support manufacturing efforts involves keeping abreast of international prices, currency parities, trade tariffs, and importing regulations. International competition is intense: Quality requirements (based on design and conformance) play a central role in getting new business, just as consistency and service are essential to maintaining customer support.

Productivity indicators relating to industry groups can give a company important external confirmation about its performance reputation. These indicators may appear in research reports as relative performance or as market ratings.

**(e) Constraints on Resource Utilization and Waste Disposal**    Rapid globalization, a rash of mergers, and the emergence of public concern about the environment (including genetically modified foods) foreshadow further significant changes in manufacturing as never before. Explicit consideration will have to be given to externalities, whether the issue is the use of scarce materials or the impact on indigenous people of incursions such as timber cutting.

At the other end of the production process, companies can attract hostility as a consequence of careless waste disposal. Though waste disposal was once taken lightly, it will be a key concern for strategists in the future. Once the focus is on resource utilization and waste control, there are opportunities to save money, improve efficiency, and gain the regard of the community. This calls for a precise understanding of expectations about national and international resource and waste-management requirements.

The external processes described previously simultaneously offer threats and opportunities. Companies that ignore them may fall irretrievably behind their competitors, whereas those that seize the opportunities may be able to enhance and transform their businesses. Indeed, knowledge about each of these processes is expanding continuously, so that each represents resources available for the exploitation of opportunities. It follows that financial managers should be monitoring the development of these resources, and tapping them where appropriate. To some extent, industry organizations have played a role in this. More recently, strategic alliances and benchmarking have facilitated direct acquisition of this accumulated external knowledge.

For strategy to work, practices within an organization must be up to the demands of that strategy. A company that aims to challenge turbulence in the environment must have the appropriate organizational culture, people, and skills. The financial function is an essential part of this personnel and skill set. The section that follows focuses on the organization itself, including the ways in which financial managers can adopt continuous improvement and make it part of their management practices.

**30.4 CONTINUOUS IMPROVEMENT INITIATIVES**    Organizations may ordinarily deal with the decision-support situations illustrated in Exhibit 30.1 when they arise. However, those that have adopted a strategic continuous improvement philosophy are active. They scan regularly to identify:

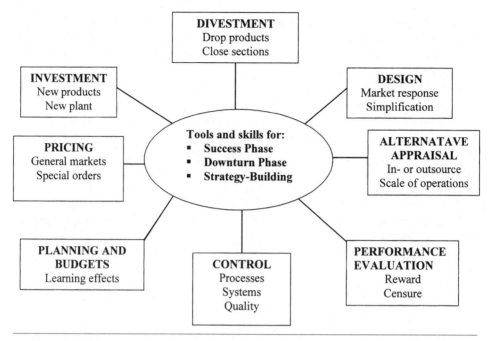

**Exhibit 30.1    Analysis and Decision Support Information for Continuous Improvement**

- Activities or processes for improvement (improvement target).
- How improvements can be achieved (improvement path).
- What it is feasible to change now (improvement action now).

Exhibit 30.2 illustrates this focused effort in six key areas. Although individual companies are expected to select areas according to their business segments and stages of development, key initiatives for most companies are:

1. Harmonize work environment.
2. Restructure operational systems.
3. Align product range.
4. Enhance quality.
5. Innovate technology.
6. Adapt decision-support systems.

Other initiatives that organizations could be expected to pursue may concern scale of enterprise, level of technological advancement, and balance between people and machines. More subtle elements in the process of shaping and controlling each enterprise are organizational structure and associated information flows, as well as patterns of rewards and sanction.

Visits the authors have made to companies in different countries point out forces at work and responses to changing circumstances, especially by companies having a base in engineering and good reputations for innovation in manufacturing. In particular, advanced manufacturing practices and companywide integration of computer technology are features of these organizations.

|  | (i) | (ii) | (iii) |
|---|:---:|:---:|:---:|
| 1. Maximize work environment | ✓ | ✓ | ✓ |
| 2. Restructure systems | ✓ | ✓ | ✓ |
| 3. Review product range | ✓ | ✓ | ✓ |
| 4. Enhance quality | ✓ | ✓ | ✓ |
| 5. Invest technology | ✓ | ✓ | ✓ |
| 6. Adapt management accounting | ✓ | ✓ | ✓ |

*Note:*
(i) improvement target
(ii) improvement path
(iii) improvement action now

**Exhibit 30.2   Key Areas for Continuous Improvement Tools and Skills**

The range of advanced manufacturing uses includes building electric motors, computer products, cutting tools, houses, aluminum products, and household appliances. The activities at each site strongly reflect unique management attitudes to strategic and short-term objectives. Significant differences in the balance between people and machines are apparent; in some plants, the level of integration of computers with the manufacturing process is high, whereas in others it is rudimentary.

Technological leadership is clearly a key strategic objective, almost an obsession with some, and part of a wider strategic concern for others. The period over which a business has survived shows up as a relevant factor in many instances, as do the level of export orientation, concern for quality, and use of appropriate technology. One appliance manufacturer's actions during the previous decade reflect cycles of change during which it introduced new levels of automation and occasions on which it revised its internal organizational form. In most cases, there was an impression of ongoing management commitment to pursuing improvement through shorter-term objectives linked to strategy.

Further visits about a year later reveal a process of fine-tuning at these sites, expressed in actions such as:

- Revising or replacing computer systems.
- Reassessing plant and equipment performance.
- Replacing plant or equipment for which the original specifications are inappropriate.
- Giving attention to staff and organizational development.
- Reviewing and adjusting quality throughout the value chain, both upstream and downstream.

These actions, taken in different sectors, are similar to the continuous improvement initiatives included in Exhibit 30.2.

A single pass through the initiatives shown in Exhibit 30.2 is insufficient for compa-

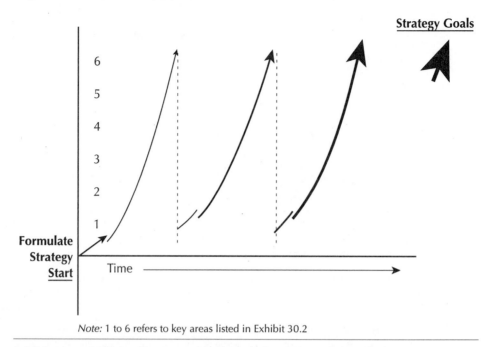

*Note:* 1 to 6 refers to key areas listed in Exhibit 30.2

**Exhibit 30.3    Learning from Learning: A "Spiral" Representation of Strategic Continuous Improvement**

nies that are seeking to prosper by establishing creative, learning-oriented, waste-free, and resilient organizations. Financial managers must apply careful thought and judgment to translate Exhibit 30.2 into practice. Further, for these initiatives to be effective, managers representing different functions (marketing, production, etc.) must have similar attitudes toward continuous improvement. This should apply in cases in which continuous improvement is an organizationwide philosophy. The growing tendency of technologies to converge also demands greater interdisciplinary cooperation and integration of actions.

Balanced, incremental improvement is a process of "learning from learning" (see Exhibit 30.3), which relies on iterative assessment. Although the ascending order (1 to 6) in each iteration is a logical progression, the imperatives of a particular situation may demand that this sequence be disturbed. An essential component of learning from learning is that the organization should sustain and encourage curiosity and associated creativity. Such qualities are unlikely to flourish in organizations in which rules, fixed standards, or strict agency constructs prevail.

Exhibit 30.4 consolidates Exhibits 30.1, 30.2, and 30.3 with environmental tracking of information and developments to present a view of active financial management in a continuous improvement environment. To shift from conventional practice to continuous improvement (and then to maintain it) demands companywide commitment, a measurement basis, and a searching review of organizational arrangements.

**30.5 MEASURING AND EVALUATING CONTINUOUS IMPROVEMENT**    Measured progress provides a basis for evaluation, and evaluation guides action. For many years, most companies have measured their business performance in financial terms,

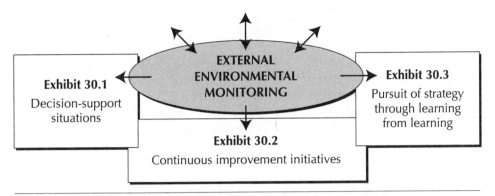

**Exhibit 30.4    Overview of Active Financial Management in a Continuous Improvement Environment**

with the emphasis on variables such as sales, profits, and cash flows. Companies such as Du Pont, General Motors, and General Electric (GE) became well-known for their elaborate systems for financial performance and control. Although financial performance is vital for any business, preoccupation with financial variables takes care only of variables of interest to shareholders, to the detriment of other important stakeholders.

Intensification of competition demands more attention to customers, which calls for direct measures. A detrimental change in processes that begins to shed customers does not necessarily show up in financial performance until much later, when remedial action is likely to cost more than it would otherwise. Direct measures can also provide information that financial measures do not capture and, in any event, provide it much earlier than do financial results. Financial measures are lagging indicators that do not present a rounded view of performance.

**(a) Balanced Scorecard**    The *balanced scorecard* remedies excessive reliance on financial measures by presenting four perspectives:

1. Financial.
2. Internal business.
3. Customer.
4. Innovation and learning perspectives.[6]

Ray Stata, chairman of Analog Devices, felt that his company had been placing too much emphasis on financial measures. In adopting a balanced scorecard, he deliberately deemphasized the financial perspective and encouraged employees to pay more attention to the other three, which had previously received relatively little attention.[7]

Although the scorecard provides balance, it is not sufficient to promote improved performance. It is essential that a company's strategic vision link strongly with measures used on the scorecard and that decision makers compare those measures with reference points such as past trends and targets. Most important is that the comparison should be with best-in-class performances rather than with industry averages. Whereas industry averages clearly do not inspire industry leadership, benchmarking targets the "best in class." Further, benchmarking facilitates the examination of the best performance of a particular function, which may be outside the industry under examination.

**(b) Organizational Learning**    In his quest for improved performance at Analog Devices, Stata emphasizes the importance of organizational learning—hence the emphasis on quality-improvement rates. When plotted, the rate of improvement is nonlinear, which makes interpretation and comparison difficult. By plotting improvement rates on a logarithmic scale (where time is represented on the horizontal axis), decision makers can read these graphs to establish the number of months representing a half-life. This graphical representation is easy to interpret and allows comparison across divisions

The diagram in Exhibit 30.5 shows the delivery performance of three divisions. The target for late deliveries is 5 percent of total deliveries. With the achievement of the target as the criterion by which performance is judged, Division C is the best performer, because it has consistently performed better than the target. Division A is second, because it has improved its performance to within the target range. Division B performs worst because it has not once achieved the 5 percent target.

A continuous improvement philosophy would encourage a different objective—that is, to work toward eliminating *all* late deliveries through organizational learning. In quality management terms, this means perfect quality or a defect rate of zero.

Exhibit 30.6 presents the results of the three divisions in a way that highlights this altered emphasis. Division B clearly has the highest rate of improvement, or the shortest half-life. Division A shows some improvement, but Division C, which previously appeared to be the best performer, shows no improvement. Reporting half-lives is a powerful way of presenting improvement rates, thus stimulating appropriate action.

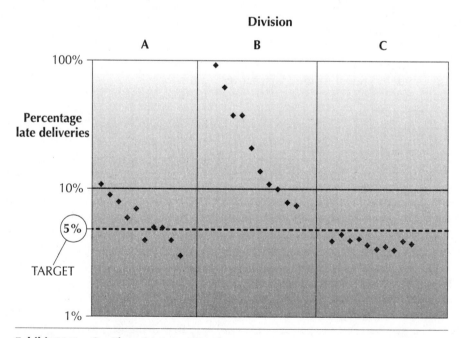

**Exhibit 30.5    On-Time Customer Service**

**(c) Constraints on Improvement**    Conventional organizations and ways of managing are likely to impose constraints on improvement. The solid line in Exhibit 30.6 represents an estimate of the half-life, while the scatter plots reflect performance achieved. The estimate is based on experience or by referring to empirical results for a similar activity.[8] The plots approximate the line, and improvement is progressing according to the estimate. A drift to the right suggests a constraint—perhaps a delivery fleet that requires maintenance or replacement. Once remedied, the constraint falls away, so improvement should resume at the previous rate. Departmental barriers could also cause a drift to the right. Workers on a process may have reached the limit of their own efforts, so further improvement may be possible only with the cooperation of other departments.

The continuous improvement culture ensures that cooperation and good communication are natural features of an organization. Employee empowerment is clearly consistent with this culture. When workers have authority to devise and implement improvements on their own initiative, there is less reason to expect a drift to the right. Given a corporate culture of continuous improvement, a plant is available when needed, and cooperation occurs as a matter of course (i.e., without being sought).

At a higher level in the organization, a lack of balance among the key areas described in section 30.4 may impose a constraint. A rapid rate of development in advanced manufacturing techniques (AMT) may benefit a company, whereas inadequate accompanying decision-support systems may limit or annul these benefits, as may a failure to align the company's product line with what its customers demand.

Some of the capabilities associated with the key initiatives are quantifiable. For example, an estimate of the practical capacity of AMT may indicate when to increase it to avoid imbalance. In other instances, decision makers need to rely on subjective assessments.

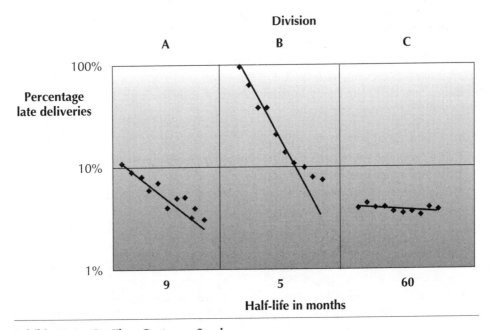

**Exhibit 30.6    On-Time Customer Service**

**30.6 RESHAPING ORGANIZATIONAL STRUCTURE**    If management adopts and fosters strategic continuous improvement, it should ensure that the company's structure is compatible with continuous improvement,[9] because structure can either facilitate or hinder continuous improvement. The most meaningful way to reinforce this point is by examining one of the six initiatives shown in section 30.4—for example, innovating technology.

As section 30.2 mentions, AMT is a family of technologies that includes computer-aided design, materials resource planning systems, automated materials handling systems, robotics, computer-controlled machines, flexible manufacturing systems, and electronic data interchange. As companies seek to meet competitive challenges, they often invest in diverse forms of equipment, systems, and organizational arrangements, and frequently in a piecemeal fashion.

Investment in AMT takes the form of a continuum, with hardware, equipment, and software at one end, and increasing concentration of information technology and attention to process toward the other, tending ultimately to *computer-integrated manufacturing* (CIM). CIM is the term given to state-of-the-art manufacturing practices, a synthesis of activities strategically undertaken to deal with fast-growing commercial and social complexity, which is made possible by information technology.

As an illustration of the AMT continuum, management may acquire robotics in the belief that it will improve performance, or they may redesign a factory and its processes by installing robotics as part of an improvement strategy. From another perspective, the introduction of AMT presents the opportunity to stay in business (e.g., by using AMT to meet quality standards) or to gain competitive advantage (e.g., by exploiting strategic opportunities arising from use of AMT). Companies that have invested in AMT in a reactive, piecemeal manner may be able to convert this to strategic advantage by consolidating these early investments and moving toward CIM.

At the same time, the integrated nature of CIM places heavy demands on an organization, because practices and ways of working must change substantially to facilitate the new system. Michael Hammer's exhortation "don't automate, obliterate!" succinctly conveys the need to think through the demands of AMT and CIM before proceeding with major decisions.[10] Companies should reshape their organizational arrangements as they progress to CIM.

If management brings about the conditions for continuous improvement specified in section 30.3, the organization is likely to[11]:

- Monitor its environment continually.
- Have achieved (or be working toward) a learning organization.
- Foster creative employee attitudes.
- Have decision guidelines for capital investments that are consistent with the company's strategy and its focus on continuous improvement.
- Ensure that integration throughout the value chain is a major criterion to be met by an AMT acquisition program.
- Use benchmarking to appraise performance relative to best in class and to sharpen the strategic direction.
- Provide training for all operators who will use the new equipment and systems.
- Use teams as a key feature of all phases of AMT acquisitions.
- Devolve responsibility for financial analysis to the teams rather than concentrating it in the finance function.

In moving toward a continuous improvement culture, a company needs to reshape its structure to stimulate and support that culture. First, a flat organizational structure is compatible with effective communication and employee empowerment. Exhibit 30.7 shows the four components of the reshaped structure for AMT investment:

1. Support of top management.
2. Project evaluation teams.
3. Project implementation teams.
4. A strategy development team.

The following sections discuss each of these components of a reshaped structure for AMT investment (see Exhibit 30.7).

**(a) Support of Top Management**    In a continuous improvement culture, management stimulates creativity, empowers employees, provides leadership, and establishes a framework for providing resources. Leadership extends to showing the way for strategy formation and displaying commitment to new initiatives.

Countless case studies have shown that this commitment is crucial. Lip service is not enough; top managers must not only be committed, they must be seen to be committed. One effective way to do this is by being present at key gatherings, actively participating in them, and supporting these initiatives in both word and deed. Jack Welch put this kind of personal energy into developing GE's statement of core values, a process in which hundreds of managers participated, and into his projection of GE's values and strategy while he was shaping the group's transformation.[12]

In addition to the commitment of top management, various other factors are prerequisites for the success of new initiatives, such as having a project "champion," teamwork, and the involvement of those most affected by the changes. A champion is a high-profile person who has the support of top management, can devote time to the project,

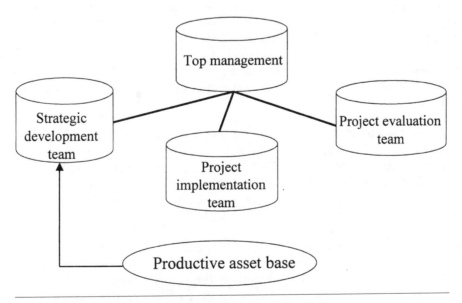

**Exhibit 30.7    Reshaped Organizational Structure for AMT**

is closely involved, and motivates people to devote the effort required to maintain momentum. Because a successful project depends ultimately on acceptance by those who will be part of the intended outcome, their involvement is critical, from inception to completion of the implementation, and beyond.

In a similar vein, a successful team should represent the primary functions involved with inputs and outputs. The number of team members required to achieve the requisite breadth depends on the size of the company, the nature of its business, the way in which it is organized, and the proposed investment. Effective communication, education, and training are all part of this process.

**(b) Project Evaluation Team**    Members of the project evaluation team bring a strategic view to their work, and they should be receptive to all opportunities. The nature of the work calls for technical competence but also accounting literacy. (The strategic development team, which is discussed later, is a major source of project proposals for evaluation.)

The project evaluation team uses a variety of techniques for project evaluation, including payback, return on investment and discounted cash flow (DCF). No matter how sophisticated the method or how elegant the model, hidden and otherwise inconsequential weaknesses may become critical in a particular application. For example, several aspects of using DCF require careful attention, such as the accurate identification of cash flows, including contingent requirements (e.g., training, selection of corporate or project-based hurdle rates, a realistic estimate of the discount rate, and recognizing the "moving baseline," i.e., the market-share consequences of a decision not to invest.[13])

A project evaluation team may also need to analyze risk further. With many investments—particularly investments in AMT—qualitative factors are critical. The simultaneous use of multiple techniques cannot correct all flaws or shortcomings, but different measures from different perspectives may alert decision makers to imperfections of certain models and promote a holistic approach to decision making.

With the development of AMT and progress toward CIM, an increasing interdependence occurs among the various systems and equipment in a plant. Not only does technological development lead to increased efficiency, improved quality, and superior ways of doing things but it can also stimulate strategic development, involving changes in the nature of products, services, or the corporate mission itself. The DCF model is not designed to capture either the interconnectedness or the strategic implications of AMT.

**(c) Project Implementation Team**    Because a project implementation team guides the implementation of an AMT project, it should include representatives from product design, engineering, and production. This cross-functional representation promotes communication and prevents the familiar "over the wall" mentality. Moreover, a membership that extends beyond these three functions can improve a team's ability to assess downstream implications of AMT.

**(d) Strategic Development Team**    A team should also monitor a company's strategic development. This is done by examining the performance of not only new projects but existing projects as well. Although absolute performance measures are a starting point, effective monitoring should concentrate on relative performance by examining trends over time, by comparing performance against targets, and by benchmarking. Monitoring triggers ideas for both investment and divestment; the team refers these ideas to the project evaluation team. Membership in the strategic development team is more broadly based than the memberships of the evaluation or implementation teams, although the need for detailed technical knowledge is less pressing than it is for the other two teams.

This team also takes responsibility for post-implementation audits, although some companies may prefer to form a separate team for this purpose. Although "post-audits" of projects have been recommended for years, few companies seem to perform them. Once a project has been implemented, managers and employees tend to move on to the next pressing problem. But monitoring is critical to strategic continuous improvement, because feedback on previous initiatives is a rich source for organizational learning.

Although the recommended organizational arrangements in this section focus on AMT issues, they also apply (adapted where necessary) to other continuous improvement initiatives, such as harmonizing work environments, restructuring systems, reviewing product range, enhancing quality, and adapting decision-support systems.

Managers in a large organization with plentiful resources find it easier to shape these arrangements than those in a smaller organization. However, the essence of these suggestions is more important than the specific detail. The detail differs not only according to size but also according to the nature of the business and the stage of a company's strategic development.

The number of teams is a case in point. If management attempts to form three teams for each of the six areas, the availability of employees and the feasibility of meeting may be problematical. Subject to the specific circumstances, it may be feasible to merge some of these teams so that, for example, one implementation team takes care of more than one area.

**30.7 HOW CURRENT PRACTICES SHAPE UP**    Although many leading-edge companies have adopted the conditions and techniques appropriate for continuous improvement, many others have decision-support and decision-making procedures that are not conducive to continuous improvement. The practices and techniques reviewed next provide a sample. But no matter how sophisticated the technique, it can do only what it is designed to do. The proper use of these techniques depends on the user's ability to apply them appropriately within an organizational culture that encourages decision makers to think beyond the numbers.

**(a) Project Evaluation**    Accounting rate of return, payback, and DCF are among the available financial techniques for project evaluation. Major advantages of DCF are that it avoids accounting distortions and recognizes the time value of money. A DCF model that is soundly constructed is technically capable of capturing the economics of a decision.

Sound construction and careful application of a DCF model requires determining cash flows and estimating the cost of capital. This applies, in particular, when plant investments are stand-alone items and can be justified on the basis of labor-cost reductions. However, careful decision makers have always checked their decisions with "reasonableness tests" (e.g., by computing multiple measures, including the accounting rate of return and payback method). Notwithstanding their limitations, these other measures may provide fresh or complementary perspectives. Further, these decision makers broaden their view of a decision by identifying and examining qualitative factors.

In practice, decision makers may favor one particular method. For example, some large U.S. companies used the payback method exclusively to evaluate new investment in South Africa because of the perceived political risk. Academics and others have argued for the superiority of DCF for years, and some surveys of corporate controllers reveal that most companies, at least in the United States, use DCF for investment decisions. This emphasis on DCF may have led some companies to rely exclusively on it.

**(b) Costing**    The distinction between direct and indirect costs is central to traditional job, process, and product costing. These systems trace direct costs to the cost object, then allocate indirect cost to the cost object, usually by means of a single allocation base.

Although some organizations use two or more allocation bases, they are usually related to volume (i.e., they are unit-level allocation bases). The cost system at John Deere Component Works (before activity-based costing was used) is a well-known example.[14]

A single allocation base cannot capture costs accurately if the cost objects consume resources differently. Although the use of multiple unit-based allocation bases may improve accuracy by capturing some differences in consumption patterns, the improvement is limited because unit-level bases cannot capture the costs of batch-level or product-sustaining activities accurately. The increased automation of manufacturing plants has led to higher levels of indirect costs, which accentuates the need to adopt a more sophisticated approach to cost determination.

**(c) Activity-Based Systems**    A well-designed activity-based costing system reflects resource consumption patterns more accurately than does a traditional cost system for organizations with a high level of indirect costs and diverse processes and products. Activity-based systems model resource consumption rather than spending. Consequently, familiar fixed-variable distinctions are irrelevant when working with this model.

A cost that appears fixed in conventional terms is variable in activity-based terms. This is appropriate when taking a strategic view of operations, involving a medium- to long-term focus. It is not appropriate for short-term decisions or for short-term performance measurement.

**(d) Capacity Costing**    When a significant proportion of a company's total costs is committed, the use of estimated or budgeted production volume as the denominator can lead to the "death spiral" in times of weakening demand. As demand weakens, management cuts back on production, which leads to even higher unit costs. If costs are the basis for prices, a company can price itself out of the market and out of business.

Managers can avoid this problem by selecting practical capacity for the denominator in unit-cost determination. If an organization uses activity-based systems, selection of the appropriate denominator is important for every major activity with the potential for unused capacity.

**(e) Budgeting and Budgetary Control**    A budget can be defined as the identification and allocation of resources necessary to carry out the mission of an organization effectively and efficiently. Although budgets comprise both planning and control elements, they are primarily control devices.

In some organizations, preparation of a budget consumes significant time and energy on the part of line managers and the finance function alike. For the finance function, it may dominate much of the year's work. Not all budgets encountered in practice are mission enablers; indeed, the budgeting process may hinder more than it helps. Budgets may constrict programs, inhibit the exercise of discretion, promote game playing, and divert attention from vital concerns of the business.

Recent developments in cost management have deemphasized the role of rigid budgets. In many cases, companies have discontinued standard and variance reporting in favor of approaches that work toward (and with) continuous improvement and organizational learning. Tools such as zero-based budgeting and activity-based budgeting are designed to improve the effectiveness of budgeting, but history has shown that technical superiority does not guarantee superior performance. These systems do not help unless their implementation harmonizes with employee empowerment and organizational learning. Some companies have abolished their traditional budgeting systems and are instead using other planning systems and performance reports, such as the balanced scorecard.[15]

**(f) Standard Cost Systems**    Standard cost systems have been a central pillar of management control systems for some 50 years. Standard costs are predetermined rather than historical, and they generally represent full production cost. A variance shows the difference between a standard cost and actual costs, and it provides a basis for corrective action. Employees and their supervisors are expected to take this corrective action with a view toward eliminating the variances.

Standard costing and variance reporting systems have been criticized in recent years because standards are usually narrowly conceived. Although standards are predetermined, they are computed in terms of prevailing production conditions and physical constraints. This is not compatible with continuous improvement, which is concerned with breaking through constraints and with the rate of improvement rather than with the achievement of constrained targets. Further, variance reporting focuses narrowly on individual factors of production; it does not reflect interaction between them.

Although variance reporting may sometimes promote adherence to these narrowly defined targets, it is unlikely to encourage workers to exercise discretion in pursuit of creativity or innovation. The extent to which standards encourage or motivate has been the subject of considerable debate; loose standards may make things too easy for the workers, whereas demanding standards could either stimulate them or crush motivation.

Unless managers take deliberate steps to ensure otherwise, a standard cost environment encourages a situation in which managers determine the best way to do things and workers are expected to act accordingly. Variance reports can also be confusing to those who are not well acquainted with accounting. Anecdotal evidence suggests that operational supervisors and workers often find variance reports difficult or impossible to understand and interpret.

Another important point is whether workers participate in setting standards. Although researchers have studied these issues, the results are not clear-cut. Whatever the verdict, standard costing systems may not be up to the challenge of a turbulent environment. Manufacturing activities involve fewer employees than previously, and those that remain are in a man-machine partnership that is less amenable to the kind of control for which standard costing systems were designed. Further, standard costing systems focus on individuals rather than teams.

**(g) Performance Measurement**    A company that "manages by the numbers" can evaluate performance using an extensive array of financial measures. But financial measures provide a limited view of performance, so nonfinancial performance measures have gained increasing prominence in recent years. Although the balanced scorecard is a device for arranging these measures, it can be effective only if it is rooted firmly in the corporate vision and linked to strategy.

**(h) Hierarchical Organization Structure**    A hierarchical organizational form generally persists in large, centralized organizations that feature formalized rules and procedures. However, elaborate hierarchies tend to inhibit the ability of members of a company to anticipate or respond to environmental changes. In addition, the long lines of command and many layers of management hinder speed and clarity of communication. A hierarchical organizational structure also frequently has the effect of locking efforts into "functional silos," which is incompatible with the idea of learning organizations.

**(i) Focus on Human Resources**    Managers have adopted relatively sophisticated evaluation measures to ensure the best use of capital, presumably because they recognize that it is a scarce resource. Unfortunately, commensurate treatment of human resources is not widely evident. Many managers appear to adopt the role of commanders; if they do not actually decide how to do things, they are perceived as doing so, and subordinates act accordingly. Management's attention and performance evaluations tend to center on individuals rather than teams. Standard costing and variance reporting are consistent with this view of the world. These controls appear to emphasize policing rather than potential, whereas employee empowerment is aimed at unlocking that potential.

**(j) One-Dimensional Decision Making**    The term "one-dimensional decision making" refers to the practice of decision makers who represent only one or two functions yet who make decisions involving multiple functions.

Although it is important to be aware of the strengths and weaknesses of the techniques considered in this section, their appropriate use is of equal or greater importance. The users' skills and experience are vital to ensuring their effective use. There are also many overarching features that are capable of enhancing or inhibiting their use in a turbulent environment. Although this section does not provide a comprehensive review of current practices, it does highlight some of the methods and techniques that are widely used. Clearly, many conventional tools are not compatible with continuous improvement and organizational learning, so they should be changed or replaced.

**30.8 SUMMARY**    Any organization's road to improvement starts with an audit of its current status—that is, its culture, its people, its decision-making techniques, and its organizational structure. The next step is to take action toward the following state:

- *Culture.* The learning organization is guided by a continuous improvement philosophy, with empowered employees sharing in decision making.
- *Peoples' attitudes and skills.* People are forward- and outward-looking. This applies equally to the chief financial officer and finance function personnel, who are business partners, not "backroom workers."
- *Decision-making techniques.* The techniques used facilitate rather than obstruct continuous improvement efforts. Reports are widely understandable to support employee empowerment.

- *Organization structure.* A flat, team-based organization structure facilitates continuous improvement.
- *Balanced continuous improvement process.* Continuous improvement progresses in such a way that key capabilities remain in balance.

## NOTES

1. P. B. B. Turney and B. Anderson, "Accounting for Continuous Improvement," *Sloan Management Review* (Winter 1989): 37–47, 38.

2. R. H. Hayes and R. Jaikumar, "Manufacturing's Crisis: New Technologies, Obsolete Organizations," *Harvard Business Review* (September–October 1988): 77–85, 85.

3. R. K. Elliot, "The Third Wave Breaks on the Shores of Accounting," *Accounting Horizons* 6 (June 1992): 61–85.

4. M. Porter, *Competitive Advantage* (New York: Free Press, 1985).

5. C. K. Prahalad and G. Hamel, "The Core Competence of the Corporation," *Harvard Business Review* (May–June 1990): 79–91.

6. R. S. Kaplan and D. P. Norton, "The Balanced Scorecard: Measures That Drive Performance," *Harvard Business Review* (January–February 1992): 71–79.

7. R. Stata, "Organizational Learning—The Key to Management Innovation," *Sloan Management Review* (Spring 1989): 63–74.

8. A. M. Schneiderman, "Setting Quality Goals," *Quality Progress* (April 1988): 51–57.

9. A. D. Chandler, *Strategy and Structure* (New York: Anchor Books Doubleday, 1962).

10. M. Hammer, "Reengineering Work: Don't Automate, Obliterate," *Harvard Business Review* (July-August 1990): 104–112.

11. M. Putterill, W. Maguire, and A. S Sohal, "Advanced Manufacturing Technology Investment: Criteria for Organizational Choice and Appraisal," *Integrated Manufacturing Systems* 7 (1996): 12–24.

12. N. M. Tichy and S. Sherman, *Control Your Destiny or Someone Else Will* (Hammersmith London: HarperCollins, 1996).

13. R. A. Howell and S. R. Soucy, "Capital Investment in the New Manufacturing Environment," *Management Accounting* (November 1987): 26–32.

14. R. S. Kaplan and A. March, "John Deere Component Works (A)," Harvard Business School case no. 187-107.

15. P. Bunce, R. Fraser, and L. Woodcock, "Advanced Budgeting: A Journey to Advanced Management Systems," *Management Accounting Research* 6(3) (September 1995): 253–265.

# CHAPTER 31

# LEAN MANUFACTURING

## Suresh S. Kalagnanam
University of Saskatchewan
## Ganesh Vaidyanathan
Brandon University

**31.1 INTRODUCTION**   The business environment today is characterized by intense global competition. Companies compete on the basis of not only price but also quality, product flexibility, and response time. As a result, companies must focus on ways to increase customer satisfaction while also earning a reasonable return.

Moreover, markets are continually changing, which leads to what some call *agile competition.*[1] Companies must thus be prepared to respond to new demands and threats. These competitive pressures have made companies focus increasingly on the manufacturing function and consider manufacturing an area of strategic importance and a source of competitive advantage. Consequently, many companies are now adopting new manufacturing philosophies, such as *lean manufacturing,* and shifting away from traditional mass production.

Viewed from the narrow perspective of manufacturing and the shop floor, the principles of lean manufacturing are the same as those of *just-in-time* (JIT) manufacturing. The phrase "lean manufacturing," however, better conveys the fundamental principle underlying JIT—namely, reduction and elimination of waste.

Contrary to what some people believe, the focus of lean principles (and of JIT) is not simply the elimination of inventories. Indeed, inventory reduction is both a tool and a consequence of applying the techniques of lean management; it is not an objective. To avoid misunderstandings of this nature, the recent literature has adopted the phrases "lean production" and "lean manufacturing" to refer to the principles, techniques, and philosophy originally called JIT.[2]

Therefore, lean manufacturing can be defined as a production system whose characteristics include:

- Production is initiated only when a signal indicating a need for the product is received—not before.
- The time between the receipt of an order and the delivery of the order is greatly shortened, because waste is eliminated.

- A defect-free product or service that is produced according to the customer's specifications.

A lean manufacturing system is thus a *reactive* system: It starts up in response to the signal of need. It is a *responsible* system: It does not produce output that is not needed. It is a *responsive* system: It fulfills the demand for a product *quickly* and ensures that the customer is satisfied. It is an *efficient* system: Production occurs with minimal waste.

A lean manufacturing approach is also a management philosophy. Its tenets—namely, to carry out work only when needed, in the amount needed, quickly, and without waste—apply to any activity or process. But lean manufacturing is not limited to manufacturing subsystems or processes. Indeed, the principles of lean manufacturing *must* be applied to every activity and process; they should not be applied in isolation (e.g., to manufacturing alone).

This chapter presents the characteristics of lean manufacturing and discusses the support mechanisms required. It covers both the management accounting and the control implications of adopting lean manufacturing. The discussion is confined at first to facets most closely allied with the manufacturing process. The scope then expands to consider the implications for other processes and activities within the company. The chapter also discusses how the principles of lean manufacturing are evolving to extend beyond a company's internal value chain to affect a product's external value chain.

In what follows, it is important that readers keep in mind the distinction between objectives (on the one hand) and the methods and practices that are used to achieve the objectives (on the other). The *objectives* of a lean manufacturing system are as stated previously: To respond to customer needs only when signaled, and to do so quickly and efficiently. The *techniques* or *practices* of lean manufacturing are methods that are applied by the manufacturing system to achieve the objectives. These practices and techniques must further be distinguished from the steps and methods needed to create and sustain the supporting infrastructure and to make an *obese* system *lean.* These are *enabling* practices. The chapter is organized with these distinctions in mind.

The next section covers the characteristics of lean manufacturing systems. Section 31.3 discusses the enabling systems that must be in place for the techniques of lean production to be effective. Section 31.4 studies the implications of the practice of lean manufacturing on marketing and distribution. The implications of lean principles on management accounting and control are presented in section 31.5. The chapter concludes in section 31.6 with an examination of the broader implications of adopting the principles of lean manufacturing for competition and strategy.

**31.2 CHARACTERISTICS OF LEAN MANUFACTURING SYSTEMS**    The characteristics of a lean manufacturing system can be described in terms of the activities, techniques, and practices that occur in the system. The architecture of a manufacturing system includes "its hardware, its material and information flows, the rules and procedures used to coordinate them, and the managerial philosophy that underlies them all."[3] Exhibit 31.1 displays two examples of obese systems and their lean counterparts.[4]

*Obese* systems are batch-and-push production systems in which material is pushed through the various stages of production. At each stage, the work that is completed is inventoried and also checked (e.g., obese B). In these systems, the tendency for each

## Obese (A)

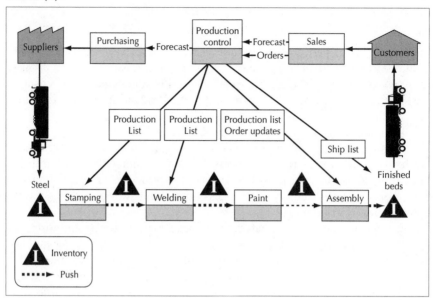

## Lean (A)

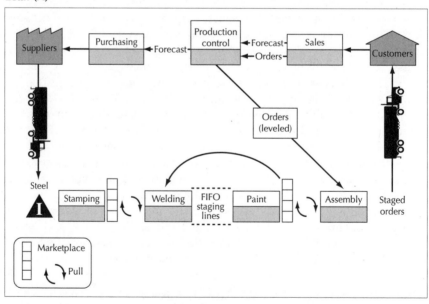

Exhibit 31.1   Examples of Obese and Lean Systems (A & B). *Source:* Jeffrey Liker, *Becoming Lean: Inside Stories of U.S. Manufacturers.* Copyright © 1997 by Productivity Press, a division of Kraus Organization Limited, P.O. Box 13390, Portland, OR 97213-0390, (800) 394-6868. Reprinted by permission.

**Obese (B)**

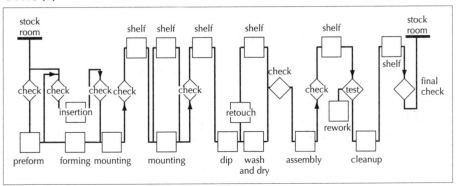

**Lean (B)**

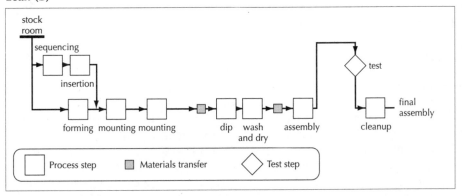

**Exhibit 31.1    Continued.** *Source:* **Reprinted by permission of The Free Press, a Division of Simon and Schuster, Inc., from** *Dynamic Manufacturing: Creating the Learning Organization* **by Robert H. Hayes, Steven C. Wheelwright, and Kim B. Clark. Copyright © 1988 by The Free Press.**

processing stage is to work independently (i.e., without regard to what is required at adjacent stages).

For example, in obese system A, each processing stage receives its requirement from production control separately: the stages operate as "isolated islands" and produce in batches.[5] In contrast, in the corresponding lean system (A), the production is "pulled" from assembly to which production control dispatches the leveled production requirements. This *final assembly schedule* (FAS) is the only schedule for the entire system. In this system, production at a given station occurs in response to requirements sent to it from adjacent downstream processes, all of which are pulled by the FAS at the mouth of the system.

**(a) No Batching**    In a lean system, a customer order does not wait to be bundled with other orders and "batched" for later production so that economies of scale in production can be exploited. (That is what happens in an obese system.) There is no need for batching in a lean system, because it is oriented to producing small lot sizes—and those only on demand. A lean system strives for the ideal of "one piece flow" through the system.

Small-lot production is facilitated by quick changeover procedures and setup times at the various processing stages. Flexible manufacturing techniques and setup-reduction techniques, such as *single minute exchange of dies* (SMED), are employed to accomplish this. Closer ties are forged with suppliers through long-term contracts, and the number of suppliers is reduced drastically. Personnel who are involved directly in the action are entrusted with the responsibility for placing supply orders, as dictated by current needs.

Traditionally, such decisions were delegated to a purchasing department isolated from (and blind to) the needs of the production process. Criteria for ordering are not to maximize economies from quantity discounts (although they can be important in some cases). Instead, supplies are pulled into the system only as dictated by the needs of production. This allows the worker in charge to order material and supplies more frequently and in smaller lot sizes. The tactic generally employed is to zero in on the relevant costs (e.g., ordering and shipping costs) to achieve reductions in lot sizes and setup times. Outsourced parts and components are delivered by suppliers directly to the location of the processing stage on the shop floor.

**(b) Continuous Material Flow**    Another feature of obese systems is that the material flow is discontinuous. The flow is interrupted by the *work in process* (WIP) inventories, where the output of one processing stage waits to be moved to the next stage. Lean systems, by contrast, display far more integration of processing stages. There is tight coupling between the processing stages and no unnecessary branching of the material flows into inventories, inspection stations, rework areas, and so on.

This connectivity and material flow is the most striking aspect of lean production systems. Operations at each processing stage are synchronized with those of adjacent stages to achieve a balanced rate of throughput over the entire system. The consequence of such close connectivity and synchronization is that no WIP inventories are needed. The production is triggered (pulled) from the mouth of the system in response to a customer order. To fulfill the customer order quickly, an order is immediately released into the system. Each processing stage responds by carrying out its activity only after it receives a signal to do so from the adjacent upstream process. Control of the starts and stops in a lean system is accomplished through the use of visual signaling devices (e.g., color-coded cards or empty containers), also known as *kanban*. Only what is needed is produced, and that only when needed.

**(c) Elimination of Transactions**    Both obese systems are also characterized by many more transactions than their lean versions, where several transactions have either been eliminated (e.g., interstage inventories and checks in system B) or streamlined (e.g., the transmittal of production orders in system A).

Typically, the distance traversed by the material in obese systems is longer than the distance covered in their lean counterparts. This is due mainly to extensive branching and loose connectivity between processing stages in obese systems. In lean systems, material does not flow very far before it is worked on.

**(d) Lean Architecture**    The lean architecture just described may be viewed as an evolutionary incarnation of traditional product-focused production. Product-focused production systems were suitable only for mass production of products that were well into the maturity stages of their life cycle, by which time their design and features are standardized.

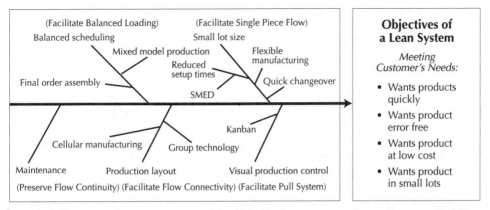

*Note:* This is the core manufacturing system. Interrelationships with other processes are illustrated in a separate exhibit.

**Exhibit 31.2   Lean Manufacturing System**

Lean systems illustrate the application of the principles of dedicated production systems to the manufacture of a wide variety of products in various lot sizes without batching or queuing. The connectivity of process flows that helps lean systems do this is brought about by such techniques as group technology, cellular manufacturing, and *mixed model production* (MMP).

The norm in lean systems is *total productive maintenance,* which protects a system's integrity. Equipment is maintained to ensure flawless operation. Operators are cross-trained so that they can be assigned to a variety of tasks, which enables the system to ride out perturbations caused by unforeseen absences. Exhibit 31.2 illustrates the core manufacturing process in a lean setting.

A final observation can be made about the architecture of lean systems as displayed in Exhibit 31.2. It might seem that there is a lack of concern for quality (in the "small q" sense) of the output, given the absence of inspection stations and rework areas. However, nothing can be further from the truth.

The concern for quality in lean systems is all-pervasive. It cannot be otherwise. Any interruption to the flow in a lean system is a threat to achievement of the system's objectives. Poor quality can delay the completion of an order by slowing down work, increasing costs, and causing customer dissatisfaction. This is an offshoot of the close integration of processing functions in a lean system, which increases the dependency of a processing stage on its adjacent upstream neighbor to deliver defect-free work. To ensure the continuity of the flow of work through the system, every processing stage must produce defect-free output. That means that every procedure, technique, method, practice, tool, and person is introduced into the process only after being carefully designed or trained to prevent defective output from ever being produced.

In summary, a lean manufacturing system is a production system whose architecture is oriented toward the manufacture of a particular product or a family of products. The architecture is characterized by tight connectivity between processing stages, which are sequenced to facilitate the smooth flow of materials and components.

Operations at various processing stages are set up, synchronized, and balanced to enable fast throughput of production over the entire system without errors or defects. Production occurs in small lots, and it is facilitated by quick changeover procedures and reduced setup times. Production is triggered only after an order is received, and it is controlled through the use of visual signaling devices. Each station produces only the quantity required, and only when required. The integrity of the system is assured by a total maintenance policy and by a team of cross-trained workers.

**31.3 HOW DOES LEAN MANUFACTURING ACHIEVE THE OBJECTIVES?**    The preceding section outlined *what* a lean manufacturing system is—its purpose and characteristics, and what it does. This section begins an analysis of lean systems. Given the premise that it is *desirable* for manufacturing systems to be lean, how can a system be made lean? The mechanism through which the characteristics and practices outlined above are introduced into a manufacturing system is the relentless and continual elimination of waste from the processes that are part of the manufacturing system.

**(a) Elimination of Waste**    Waste (*muda* in Japanese) is any human activity that absorbs resources but does not create value.[6] Note that waste in a process consumes time. Therefore, some have argued that the elimination of waste is synonymous with the reduction of the time to carry out activities.[7] Exhibit 31.3 lists the seven types of waste and the "seven Ms" that make up a process.

The elimination of waste—in all its forms—and the application of lean techniques make a production process "lean." To purge waste, however, it must first be identified. One technique for identifying waste is *process value analysis* (PVA), which is a systematic approach for understanding processes by focusing on activities.[8] In doing so, PVA "relates activities to the events, circumstances, or conditions that create or 'drive' the need for the activity and the resource consumed."[9] PVA helps separate the value-added activities from those that do not add value—the non–value-added activities. A value-added activity is defined as one that contributes to creating or building customer value or satisfies an organizational need.[10] All non–value-added activities are considered to be waste.

**(b) Root-Cause Analysis**    Another technique to identify and eliminate waste is the familiar "root-cause analysis" from *total quality management* (TQM). Each process and the activities that are part of it are mapped and all facets of the activities are relentlessly questioned. The questioning involves asking "Why?" at least five times, beginning with the problem, then moving on to each underlying problem or situation. This is the "5 whys" procedure of problem analysis. Identifying the root cause of a problem corresponds with identifying waste. In lean manufacturing, the root of all problems can ultimately be traced to some kind of waste.

Costantino describes an example of problem identification in a small wood-processing company. The main theme was a bottleneck at the resawing operation, which was responsible for cutting rough wood into boards. The main complaint was "[t]he resaw can't cut wood fast enough."[11]

The root-cause detection procedure first identified the general problem, which was too much stop time in the process. The stop time for each activity in the process was next identified. One activity, changing the saw blade, was singled out for deeper analysis. This activity, which was then decomposed into its elements, included 16 separate actions.

The "5 whys" procedure was then applied to each action to determine the underlying problem. For example, by investigating the causes of the length of stop time for the action of accessing the saw blade, it was determined that the blade was not easily accessible (why 1), because it involved a worker to climb up the ladder (why 2), because the blades were stored on the roof of the office (why 3), because there was no other place

| The Seven Wastes | The Seven Ms of a Process |
| --- | --- |
| *Overproduction:* Producing more than is needed before it is needed. | *Manpower:* Human resources |
| *Waiting:* Any non–work time waiting for tools, supplies, parts, machine setup, etc. | *Methods:* Product and process design and operationg procedures |
| *Conveyance:* Wasted effort to transport materials, parts, components, finished product into or out of storage or between processes. | *Machines:* Tools and equipment used in processes |
| *Processing:* Providing higher quality than is necessary, extra operations, improper procedures, etc. | *Maintenance:* System and procedures including training for providing care for process components |
| *Inventory:* Maintaining excess inventory of raw materials, work-in-process, and finished goods. | *Management:* Policy work rules and environment |
| *Motion:* Any wasted motion to pick up parts or stack parts or moving to a work-station, etc. | *Measurement:* Techniques and tools used to gather process performance data |
| *Correction:* Repair or rework. | *Materials:* Raw materials, components, anything requiring processing |

**Exhibit 31.3    Seven Types of Waste and Seven Ms.** *Source: Becoming Lean: Inside Stories of US Manufacturers,* ed. J. Liker. Copyright © 1997 by Productivity Press, a division of Kraus Organization Limited, P.O. Box 13390; Portland, OR 97213-0390, (800) 394-6868. Reprinted with permission. And R. Schonberger and E. Knod, Jr., *Operations Management: Customer Focused Principles* (New York: Irwin/McGraw-Hill, 1997). Reprinted with permission of The McGraw-Hill Companies.

to store the saws. This last "why" resulted in the identification of the root cause for the poor accessibility of the blade saw.

**(c) Infrastructure Systems for Lean Manufacturing**    Elimination of waste leads to simplification. Activities and processes become simpler and transparent to everyone. But simplification cannot be achieved in the production subsystems in isolation. Once again, connectivity is involved.

The chain begins with the customer, whose needs are analyzed carefully (market analysis). These needs are translated into design specifications so that the final product matches what the customer needs (rather than what the producer thinks the customer needs). This can be achieved through *quality function deployment* (QFD), which is a systematic process to translate a customer's quality requirements (demanded quality) into operational specifications that can be used at the production operator level within the company.[12]

*Overengineering* a product in any way is waste. Overengineering could mean any of the following:

- Providing features not requested by the customer.
- Using materials that might prolong the life of the product beyond when it will be needed by the customer.
- Designing a product so complex that it is difficult to produce.

A product must be designed and engineered to satisfy the customer yet also be simple to manufacture and recycle (design for disassembly). Right from the outset, the design should facilitate the error-free production of defect-free products.

*Process* designers should interact with *product* design teams to determine the design of the production process. The steps necessary to manufacture the product can be mapped and put through the "5 whys" questioning. The goal is to make every procedure as simple as possible and to streamline by eliminating unnecessary steps. Ideally, the processing steps and actions required will make it impossible for production errors to occur. This is "failsafing," or (in Japanese) *pokayoke.* The result is that connectivity and flow are protected by eliminating the need for a product to wait between processing steps.

**(d) Interrelationships Across Functions and Processes**    These interrelations across functions—or better yet, across processes—and the dependency of the total system on these relationships are dogma for companies that embrace the principles of lean manufacturing. Logically, for a lean manufacturing system to perform, it must be part of an overall system in which every component system is geared to help the company achieve the overarching goal of customer satisfaction. In other words, without the support of a complementary organizational infrastructure, installing a lean manufacturing system at the core of the company is doomed to fail. A vision of the architecture of such infrastructure systems is shown in Exhibit 31.4.

**(e) Role of the Work Force**    The "bricks and mortar" of a lean manufacturing system are people, or human resources. Whether one considers the system as a whole, the infrastructure point of view, or the core manufacturing point of view, people are the key to achieving success and sustaining it. A lean system places unique demands on the people responsible for carrying out the activities and, thus, achieving the lean objectives. To put it succinctly, a lean system requires a "dedicated and flexible work force (including management personnel) working with their heads as well as their hands."[13] But what does this mean?

A lean system requires a work force that will embrace the basic principles of lean management—waste identification and elimination from everywhere in the company. The work force must be committed to this concept and must dedicate itself to achieving it. Why? Consider the trauma of an obese system making the transition to a lean system. People are asked to identify waste and suggest solutions for eliminating it. This will, in all likelihood, involve elimination of jobs. Will people willingly participate in a process that might lead to the elimination of their own jobs and careers?

Womack and Jones suggest that a 75 percent reduction in human effort can result when an obese system becomes lean, with little or no capital investment, and that a 50 percent reduction in human effort is possible from converting a conventional production system to a leaner system through elimination of indirect activities, rework, and line imbalances.[14] They also advise that a company must take decisive actions quickly when it has more people than it needs for the lean activities. It will be better off if the company quickly reduces its work force instead of engaging in a slow and torturous cut-

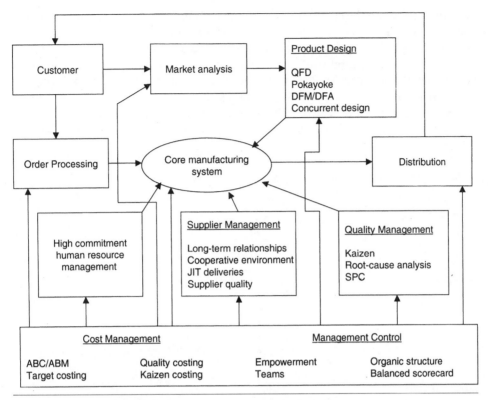

**Exhibit 31.4    Interrelationships in a Lean Manufacturing System**

back of personnel. Having gone to the ideal level, the company must first promise that no future job losses will occur because of the introduction of lean techniques, then it must adhere to that promise. Clearly, without the dedication and commitment from employees, lean will be labeled "mean," so improvements will be hard—if not impossible—to sustain.

**(f) Flexibility and Different Responsibilities**    A "flexible" work force means that people can move across jobs with little effort and are willing to accept varying degrees of responsibility. Workers who have done several jobs inside a process are more likely to have a holistic view of the part they play in the transformation (value-creating) function of the process in which they participate. Such workers will appreciate the chain-of-customers perspective of TQM. This is crucial to the objective of doing error-free work: "I can do a better job if I receive error-free work from my supplier, and my customer can do a better job if I provide error-free work."

Clearly, for a company to succeed at waste identification and elimination, it must involve the people who are closest to the process. If a quick turnaround is to be achieved, a complex, bureaucratic procedure to eliminate waste cannot be used. Instead a "lean" procedure must be implemented. This will involve (first and foremost) giving employees the right to voice their opinions and take appropriate actions to protect the objectives of the lean production system. It is typical for employees who work in lean systems to have the authority to stop a production line whenever they notice waste and to suggest and implement a solution. To do this, people must be allowed to "use their heads."

Such demands on the people who work in lean systems have led to the application of many of the *human resources management* (HRM) practices listed in Exhibit 31.5 in support of managing lean systems. Together, these practices make up what Baron and Kreps have labeled "high commitment human resource management."[15] High-commitment HRM is necessary in companies that embrace the principles of lean manufacturing.

Baron and Kreps identify four key processes on which to focus in order to connect high-commitment HR practices to the objective of achieving a dedicated and flexible work force that carries out and sustains the principles of lean manufacturing. These key processes are:

1. Recruitment
2. Training
3. Enabling
4. Motivation

| Practice | Description |
| --- | --- |
| *Employee guarantees* | Once ideal number of workers has been achieved, do not discharge personnel except for cause |
| *Egalitarianism in word and deed* | Deemphasize rank and status differentials among personnel |
| *Selfmanaging teams and team production* | Emphasize teamwork and empower teams to make decisions and selfmanage |
| *Job enlargement and enrichment* | Increase scope and variety of duties and responsibilities |
| *Premium compensation* | Introduce efficiency wages and superior benefits |
| *Incentive compensation* | Tie to team, unit, and firmwide performance |
| *Extensive socialization and training* | Educate, orient, and communicate principles of lean thinking; cross-train extensively |
| *Extensive job rotations* | Apply cross-trained workers; promote holistic thinking and the principle of "chain of customers" |
| *Open information* | Achieve transparency in all activities; eliminate secrecy |
| *Open channels of communication* | Encourage personnel from all levels to help identify and eliminate or reduce waste |
| *Promote strong lean-based organizational culture* | Tie to an overarching lean objective (zero defects; total customer satisfaction; "quality is Job #1...") |
| *Enlarged recruitment function* | Screen potential employees extensively for compatibility with organizational philosophy to ensure cultural fit |
| *Minimize "agency relationships"* | Emphasize ownership, symbolic and financial, over "hired-gun" mentality |

**Exhibit 31.5   Human Resource Practices. *Source:* J. Baron and D. Kreps, *Strategic Human Resources.* © 1999, John Wiley & Sons. Adapted by permission of John Wiley & Sons, Inc.**

To summarize, the principal components of the supporting infrastructure for lean manufacturing are:

- Product design
- Work force
- Organizational characteristics
- Quality management

**(g) Quality**   Quality management has not been covered explicitly so far because TQM principles (in the "Big Q" sense) are a superset of the principles of lean manufacturing. In essence, the principles of TQM permeate all facets of a lean production system and dictate the need for (and the form of) the supportive infrastructure just described.

Lean manufacturing can be viewed as an approach that has resulted from efforts to put in practice the principles of TQM. On a companywide basis, the principles of lean manufacturing, when applied to transformation (value-creating) processes in nonmanufacturing domains, become the principles of lean thinking. Companies that are lean everywhere—lean in manufacturing and in all internal domains—become lean enterprises.

Companies can try to adopt TQM without embracing the concept of lean transformation, but doing so will not maximize the benefits of TQM. The road to becoming lean is the most direct route to getting the most of TQM. The reverse does not hold, however. Trying to become a lean company without TQM will lead to failure. TQM provides the necessary supportive underpinnings for lean transformation.

**31.4 FROM LEAN MANUFACTURING TO LEAN THINKING: THE VALUE CHAIN**   The preceding section made the case that a supportive infrastructure is necessary to successfully apply the principles of lean thinking in manufacturing. As Exhibit 31.6 shows, the other links in the organization's internal value chain lie outside the manufacturing domain:

- Research and development
- Product development
- Marketing
- Distribution
- Service

There are also several support functions:

- Procurement
- Technology development
- Human resource management
- Company infrastructure (administration, accounting or finance, and information systems)

The previous discussion has already highlighted the role played by several of these links in the chain to facilitate the application of lean manufacturing, especially product development and design, procurement (supplier and supply-chain analysis), and HRM.

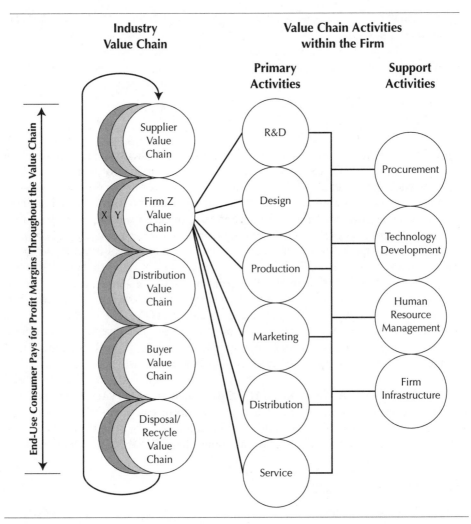

**Exhibit 31.6    External and Internal Value Chains. *Source:* From *Value-Chain Analysis for Assessing Competitive Advantage,* Management Accounting Guideline #41 (Society of Management Accountants of Canada, 1996). Reprinted with permission of CMA Canada.**

The role of marketing and distribution is no less important. This section dwells briefly on the role of marketing and distribution in lean companies and poses an important question that applies to all nonmanufacturing domains of the company: How can these domains play their roles "leanly"? And is it necessary that the role be played this way? In other words, "How can distribution and marketing and product development be made lean? And should they be?"

**(a) Distribution in Lean Companies**    In obese systems, distribution is where everything ends up. Obesity can be measured in terms of finished goods inventories, inventory turns, and so on.

When obese systems fail, the chain of events can look like this:

- Customers do not get the right product.
- Customers have to endure lengthy waits to get the product.
- The product is defective and requires rework.
- The process repeats.

Obese systems operate on a replenishment philosophy and take pride in off-the-shelf service. But that is exactly the problem: Items are stocked according to the convenience of batch production schedules without regard to usage. When this practice is "stacked" across the supply chain, the cumulative lead time customers face to obtain product becomes inordinately lengthy.

Stalk and Hout consider a simple example that involves a factory, warehouses at the factory, and distributor and retailer levels of the distribution channel.[16] In that system, the cycle time for a product to wend its way from production to delivery is 19 weeks. All internal planning must conform to this 19-week cycle time. The length of the cycle implies that the system will be incapable of quick response to any perturbations in the forecasts. Even more significant is that desired changes will take 19 weeks to take effect.

Womack and Jones, describing the Toyota distribution system as it existed in the mid-1960s, note that the system required 58 days of lead time.[17] In terms of waste that is created by the use of fixed-lot sizes up and down through the product's bill of materials, the effect on the total system is like that of a *tsunami* (Japanese for "tidal wave"). A large wave of artificial demand moves through the system, totally unrelated to the actual demand at the mouth of the system. The result is extensive inventories of all kinds.[18]

The drivers of such practices in obese systems typically include:

- Shipping costs.
- Long distances between the factory and distribution centers.
- Long distances between distribution centers and usage centers.
- Adversarial relations with suppliers.
- Bulk quantity discounts.
- Incentives promoting false economies (e.g., do not send out delivery trucks half-empty; do not send in an order for half a truckload).
- Warehouse layout that focuses on efficiency of storage instead of efficiency of storage *and retrieval.*

Ironically, obese distribution systems, in an effort to exploit economies of scale and minimize costs, must also implement an expediting system to bypass the routine *obese* procedures for filling orders.

In lean systems, distribution is where everything begins: The product is there to be delivered because the customer requested it. This is the pull system. Such systems operate on the requirements philosophy: That is, make the product only if there is a need, and get the requested product to the customer quickly.

But what is "distribution" in lean systems? Traditionally, the production process has been isolated from both inbound logistics (getting supplies) and outbound logistics (getting the product into the hands of the customer). In lean systems, distribution is not an isolated or even a distinct process. Rather, distribution is the "whole ball game." It encompasses the entirety of processes shown in Exhibit 31.4. This follows from the view that, in lean systems, the production process responds to pull from the customer, which requires close connectivity between suppliers, the production process, and customers. Thus, viewing distribution through the narrowly focused lens of logistics does not convey the richness of the implications for lean systems.

It is a mistake to think of lean systems as being inventory*less* everywhere. Certainly, inventory is *muda*. But no system can be truly empty of inventory when it operates in steady state on a "rolling horizon" basis. In lean systems, parts and supplies necessary for product support and service are not made in large batches according to "economic lot sizes" to minimize holding and ordering costs.

Consider a company that has a factory, a national distribution center, several regional distribution centers, and numerous usage centers that interact with the end user. The usage centers are encouraged to order daily to replenish materials. This allows the centers to stock a broader variety of parts yet carry fewer of each item. The ordering from usage centers pulls the material from the regional distribution centers, which (in turn) pull from the national distribution center, which then pulls from the factory.[19]

Warehouses are laid out to facilitate quick and accurate picking. The storage and layout are established to take into account frequency of movement and size. Slow-moving parts are stored away from the parts that are "active." As orders from usage centers aggregate at regional and then at the national centers, the organization's information processing system groups the orders by bin location at the appropriate picking location (national or regional). The picking requirements are then allocated to various pickers to achieve a balanced picking load in terms of the cycle time for each picker.

The process of managing at this detailed level is parallel to managing on the shop floor. The entire toolbox—ranging from visual control devices to transparency of operations—can be bought to bear. The ideal is to achieve seamless "cross-docking," where parts are unloaded from one transport and loaded to another and never see the inside of the warehouse. With the aid of modern tools such as *electronic data interchange* (EDI), it is becoming easier for retailers to stay in constant touch with their suppliers. The movement of product out of the retailers is completely transparent to the supplier, which can monitor the transactions on a real-time basis and react accordingly.

In summary, distribution in lean systems must also be lean. In many lean systems, distribution may not even be a separate function; instead, it is woven into the fabric of the total system. Lean practices can be introduced through the familiar waste-identification and elimination cycle described earlier (see section 31.3(a)). The earlier discussion about infrastructure systems (see section 31.3(c)) is also relevant. A company must involve its suppliers and its personnel in the process.

**(b) Marketing in Lean Companies**    Because the overarching objective of lean companies is to satisfy customers, the role of marketing is extremely important. As Exhibit 31.4 shows, marketing is the interface between a company and its customers.

For a pull system to work properly, a company must know what the customer wants. This is where many of the traditional marketing activities relating to intelligence gathering about the customer and the market become relevant.[20] These include researching such bread-and-butter questions as:

- How do we listen and learn about the key requirements and drivers of purchase decisions for current, former, and potential customers?

- How do we determine or predict key features of the product or service and their relative value to customers?
- How do we use this information to get closer to our customers?

Lean companies are equally interested in customer retention and winning new customers. To this end, companies must work at building relationships with their customers. They must ensure that customers can obtain assistance and information and also provide feedback or complaints. Here, the role of marketing becomes blurred with the TQM practices that lean companies normally have in place to stay in constant touch with their customers and suppliers.

Marketing also has a role in *demand smoothing*.[21] "Smoothed" demand facilitates level production schedules, which are crucial for maintaining flow inside a manufacturing system. Demand smoothing can be achieved through special promotions or pricing policies.[22] Finally, as already discussed, customer input (answers to the questions just raised above) is important in product design and development.

Here again, the line between marketing and TQM becomes blurry, because TQM practices such as QFD are meant to facilitate the flow of information about (and accurate mapping of) customers' wants into the company's capabilities in development and production. Despite the fact that a casual reader of the literature on lean thinking might form the mistaken impression that marketing is absent from lean companies— because it is rarely discussed in functional terms—the customer is always paramount, and much of the functional role of marketing is subsumed by TQM practices. Indeed, as Karmarkar points out, from a seller's viewpoint, JIT is a marketing requirement.[23]

Earlier sections described the features of a lean manufacturing system and also discussed how obese systems can be transformed to lean systems. Lean manufacturing systems require a supportive infrastructure that is also lean to function effectively.

The following section describes how lean companies are managed. The main question is, "How can a company's internal organization—including its information gathering, decision making, and control systems—introduce, execute, and sustain the practices of lean manufacturing?"

**31.5 MANAGEMENT ACCOUNTING AND LEAN MANUFACTURING**   Why should the management accounting system of a company be different in a lean manufacturing environment? Lean manufacturing systems provide value to the customer (i.e., the right product at the right time and at the right price) by focusing simultaneously on the dimensions of quality, time, and cost. Quality consists of understanding customers' requirements, translating them into design specifications, and producing them correctly. Time addresses the issues of flexibility and responsiveness to customers. Finally, cost is a measure of the efficiency or productivity of the processes in a company's internal value chain.

Traditional management accounting systems (e.g., standard costing and variance analysis) do not provide information that allows decision makers to assess performance on all of the three dimensions (quality, time, and cost). Unlike a mass-production system, which emphasizes internal efficiencies in narrow functional units, a lean manufacturing system is process-focused and concentrates on decisions across the entire internal value chain of a company.[24]

Moreover, the relentless pursuit of continuous improvement requires a different set

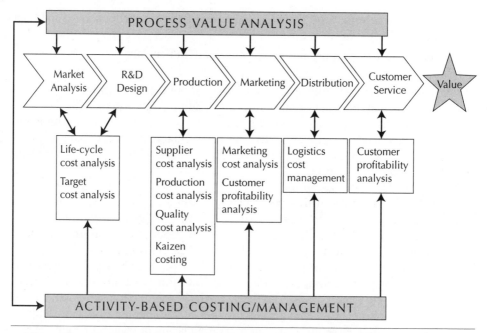

**Exhibit 31.7    Cost Management in a Lean Manufacturing Environment**

---

of accounting information compared with a situation where the focus is on just meeting the standards. In particular, management accounting must take a "holistic" approach rather than focusing on costs and measurements in narrow functional domains. Exhibit 31.7 provides a framework that offers such a holistic approach for effective cost management in a lean manufacturing environment.

An important theme of the framework is PVA, which is aimed at improving the processes in a company's internal value chain. The framework also suggests that the existence of *activity-based costing* (ABC) facilitates PVA (see Chapters 22 to 26). In addition, the framework identifies several cost-management techniques that can be used at the different stages of a company's internal value chain. Note that many of the cost analysis or management methods listed in Exhibit 31.7 require a cross-functional team approach if the analysis and results are to be meaningful. Linking the cost-management methods to a particular process in the value chain merely indicates that these methods would most likely be used while those processes are being carried out.

Cost management in a lean manufacturing system must also be supplemented by a performance measurement system that develops leading and lagging indicators that pertain to organizational capabilities, business-process efficiency, and outcomes. This information can be used to assess how well individual components of the value chain function and whether the intended outcomes are indeed achieved.

**(a) Cost Management in a Lean Manufacturing Environment**    Cost management is extremely important for all processes along the internal value chain. A company's objective should be to reduce overall costs of the *entire* value chain rather than narrowly cutting costs in individual processes, which might create undesirable ripple effects in other processes along the value chain. As Exhibit 31.7 suggests, several techniques are available for this purpose. A brief discussion of these techniques follows.

*(i) Market Analysis, Research and Development, and Design*  The importance of market analysis, research and development (R&D), and design in a lean manufacturing environment cannot be emphasized enough. Trying to develop and design products without knowing the target market or understanding customers' needs will lead to inefficiencies and waste. Products are developed on the basis of trial and error because customers' needs are assumed—not known. When this happens, products lack the features, functionality, and price levels that customers want. Many of these products may turn out to be unsuccessful (i.e., they generate less than expected revenues), yet they consume considerable resources, thereby adding to the waste already in the system.

As Cooper and Slagmulder suggest, lean enterprises must develop techniques to manage the costs of future products; *life-cycle costing* and *target costing* are valuable for this purpose.[25] Life-cycle costing "attempts to estimate the product's cost over its lifetime."[26] In doing so, it informs a company about costs and revenues associated with a product from the time it is conceived until the time it is abandoned. Consequently, managers and other employees are forced to think ahead and prepare themselves for activities that might have to be undertaken (and costs that might have to be incurred) during the different stages of a product's life.

Target costing complements life-cycle costing in that it is also used during the planning phase (which includes the market analysis, R&D, and product design) of the value chain. A *target cost* is the cost of a product that provides the desired return on sales after a market-based target price has been determined based on customer requirements and willingness to pay. Target costing forces managers to:

- Identify the intended customers.
- Study the needs and preferences of customers in terms of functionality, features, and price.
- Determine ways to translate customer needs into design specifications, while also attempting to meet the desired cost levels.

To accomplish these tasks, companies use practices such as QFD and *value engineering* (VE). Value engineering is an analytic method for examining the factors that affect the cost of a product, then determining what can be done to achieve the target cost while maintaining the product's features and standards of functionality and reliability.[27]

Employees are constantly challenged to identify ways in which target costs can be met. The Nissan case provides a good description of a target costing system in practice.[28] Nissan spends a great deal of time identifying potential customers and determining their needs; it uses rigorous analytic methods to determine potential sales revenues and margins in order to compute a target cost.

A properly implemented target costing system is valuable to a lean manufacturer, because it helps avoid waste in activities along the value chain. It is important to note that target costing would be useful to both obese and lean systems; however, companies that have obese systems will probably not pay attention to target costing simply because of their push philosophy and lack of attention to waste. Lean companies, on the other hand, will—and must—attempt to identify and reduce waste wherever it occurs, and target costing can be quite useful for this purpose.

From a cost perspective, the R&D and design stage is important, because as much as 90 percent of a product's costs can be locked in (or committed) during this stage.[29]

For example, the materials, components, and parts to be used in a product are decided at the design stage. Therefore, designers must be motivated to think about the downstream implications of the components they include in a product.

Factors such as the number of different components used, the complexity of the components, the function offered by the components and the price of the components all combine to determine whether a product meets customers' needs. A lean manufacturer should compare the implications—including costs—of alternative design specifications on downstream processes. For example, designs that specify the use of common parts can simplify the procurement process—and thereby reduce materials-related costs. The use of common parts allow a company to buy large volumes of the parts, which can lead to bulk purchases and quantity discounts. Designs that use common parts may also be simpler in terms of manufacturing, thereby reducing processing costs.

A well-developed ABC system allows employees to identify the different sets of required activities and their costs, which makes valid cost comparisons possible. In the mid-1980s, for example, Tektronix Corporation decided to use its materials-burdening system to motivate design engineers to reduce the number of different components they used.[30]

Faulty designs can increase manufacturing, marketing, and customer service costs. Moreover, once design specifications are established, subsequent changes can be costly.

*(ii) Production*    Management accounting systems have traditionally paid too much attention to production—perhaps because a majority of most manufacturers' costs are incurred during production. Although the importance of production does not diminish in a lean manufacturing environment, it can no longer be considered in isolation from the other processes in a company's value chain.

Target costing provides a good guideline for the cost expectations from a production process; these expectations must be met. Several types of cost analyses may be required to meet those cost objectives, including supplier cost analysis, production cost analysis, quality cost analysis, and *kaizen* costing.

Traditional product cost systems assume that costs are driven by volume. Most cost accounting textbooks provide examples of traditional cost systems in which overhead is allocated using direct labor, production volume, or some other "volume-based driver."

New developments in management accounting suggest that volume is not the only cost driver that should be considered. For example, using a strategic management framework, Shank introduces the notion of "structural" and "executional" drivers. A structural driver "involves choices by [a] company that drive product cost" and includes scale and scope of operations, experience (learning curve effects), process technology employed, and complexity expressed in terms of product variety.[31]

One could think of structural cost drivers as pertaining to planning, whereas acquisition of resources corresponds to the required levels of scale, scope, experience, technology, and complexity. Arguably, a lean manufacturer should not fix the scale, scope, and complexity levels, because fixed levels may impose constraints on flexibility. On the other hand, it would be difficult for a company to operate without having some idea of the scale, scope, and complexity levels at which it wishes to operate.

One way around this problem might be to keep these levels flexible to a degree. In other words, plan scale, scope, and complexity levels based on existing conditions but be in a position to respond quickly to conditions that may necessitate changes in these levels. To remain flexible, it is important to understand the cost behavior of the resources to be acquired. Kaplan and Atkinson classify resources as *committed* (i.e., acquired in advance) and *flexible* (i.e., acquired as needed).[32]

Committed resources are associated with a planned level of activity; the extent of the commitment to these resources may vary in terms of time. Given the flexibility considerations of a lean manufacturer, it should perhaps acquire more short-term committed resources instead of long-term committed resources. Doing this will allow the company to avoid acquiring excess capacity, which may constitute waste.

The consumption of resources is regulated by executional cost drivers, which determine a company's cost position by focusing on the company's "ability to 'execute' successfully."[33] Aspects such as the commitment of employees to continuous improvement and adherence to TQM beliefs and practices—two examples of executional cost drivers—can help companies reduce the consumption of resources. To the extent that flexible resources are saved, there is a direct cost saving. However, a reduction in the consumption of committed resources translates into increased unused capacity, which must be recognized. Unless these unused resources can be put to other productive uses or eliminated, a company realizes no financial benefits. Therefore, a lean manufacturer must be quick to identify alternative uses for excess resources, or else wisely invest in resources that can be easily disposed of and reacquired later if conditions change (i.e., short-term committed resources).

Reductions in the consumption of resources can be achieved either through *breakthrough* or *continuous* improvements to a process. Breakthrough improvements generally involve major changes to the process (i.e., redesign), whereas continuous or gradual improvements normally take place within the context of the existing processes.

The commitment to gradual, incremental improvements to a process is known in Japanese as *kaizen*. "The essence of KAIZEN is simple and straightforward: KAIZEN means improvement. Moreover, KAIZEN means ongoing improvement involving everyone, both managers and workers."[34] This improvement is achieved simply by improving the standards. *Kaizen costing* takes the notion of *kaizen* one step further by providing information about the cost implications of these *kaizen* activities to employees. These improvements may relate to reductions in materials costs or processing costs.

For example, with respect to materials costs, employees can continuously search for alternative materials that could be used. The benefits associated with other materials may be lower material costs, or easier production and handling.

Manufacturers can also work with suppliers to identify substitute materials that may provide improvement on the dimensions of quality, cost, or time. Several manufacturers have recognized the need to interact closely with their suppliers—the upstream "external constituents" in the value stream of the product or product line.

Dealing with a certified supplier translates into lower costs, because the supplier's materials are guaranteed with respect to quality, delivery, and price. In analyzing supplier performance, a lean manufacturer must look beyond the purchase price of materials and attempt to assess the financial implications of poor reliability. If a supplier is unreliable, additional costs for the following activities may be incurred:

- Inspect incoming materials.
- Conduct additional steps in processing because of the inferior quality of the materials.
- Buy additional material at higher prices because of late deliveries.
- Receive customer complaints because of supplier-related problems.
- Lose goodwill with customers.

A thorough analysis such as this allows a lean manufacturer to determine the true costs associated with alternative suppliers.

An important aspect of lean manufacturing is the minimization of inventory (one form of waste). Companies carry inventory for several reasons:

- To balance ordering and carrying costs.
- To meet customers' on-time delivery needs.
- To avoid shutting down a manufacturing facility.
- To take advantage of volume discounts.
- To hedge against future price increases.[35]

A lean manufacturer must find ways to tackle these reasons for carrying inventory. For example, ordering costs can be reduced by placing blanket orders, which list the needs for longer periods (e.g., six months or even a year) but with staggered delivery. A reduction of inventory levels will automatically reduce carrying costs. With respect to volume discounts, large companies with multiple plants can combine the requirements of all their plants to negotiate lower prices from suppliers. Smaller companies, on the other hand, can "lock in" prices by entering into long-term contracts.

All these practices can help lean manufacturers to reduce the costs associated with acquiring and carrying inventories. However, this can be made possible only by the use of enabling mechanisms, such as establishing long-term contracts, limited or single sourcing, and efficient communication with suppliers.

Having long-term contracts with certified suppliers leads to a win–win situation and allows for experimentation at the supplier's end without the fear of losing a contract. Single sourcing can also result in a win-win situation. Consequently, a strong supplier–customer relationship can be developed, because both parties help one another to reduce costs. Moreover, deliveries are guaranteed at the time the materials are required.

The use of EDI systems can also help in communicating quickly with both suppliers and customers. For example, many auto suppliers have direct computer links with the big-three automakers and know their requirements instantly. Such real-time communication helps the manufacturer receive only what it needs and when it needs it, then deliver to the customer only what the customer needs, and when the customer needs it.

With respect to processing costs, employees must consider the implications of the following improvements to the manufacturing process:

- Reduce setup costs and material handling costs.
- Improve machine efficiency.
- Improve manufacturing cycle-time quality.

PVA is an invaluable tool for analyzing processing activities, identifying value-added activities, and systematically eliminating non–value-added activities. One way to draw the attention of managers and employees to non–value-added activities is by identifying the costs associated with them. A *cost of quality* (COQ) analysis partially accomplishes this task by separately tracking prevention, appraisal, and failure costs (the latter two types of costs are non–value-added). For other activities not included in a COQ report, a simple cost report similar to the one presented in Exhibit 31.8 can be prepared on a periodic basis to capture the attention of managers.

PVA analysis, in conjunction with the cost analyses described earlier, can also help

| Activity | Value-Added | Non–Value-Added | Total |
|----------|-------------|-----------------|-------|
| Material usage | $1,400,00 | $200,000 | $1,600,000 |
| Setups | 0 | 150,000 | 150,000 |
| Material handling | 230,000 | 170,000 | 400,000 |
| Packaging | 310,000 | 30,000 | 340,000 |
| Direct labor | 640,000 | 100,000 | 740,000 |
| Quality | 20,000 | 58,000 | 78,000 |
| Total costs | $2,600,000 | $708,000 | $3,308,000 |

**Exhibit 31.8    Value-Added and Non–Value-Added Cost Report.** *Source:*
**D. Hansen and M. Mowen, *Cost Management,* 2nd ed. © 1997. Reprinted with
permission of South-Western College Publishing, a division of Thompson
Learning. Fax 800-730-2215.**

companies determine where they are inefficient. It makes economic sense to outsource
inefficient processes and eliminate internal resources associated with these processes.
Nonetheless, it is important to note that companies must outsource only those
processes that are not strategically critical; otherwise, they could lose competitive advantage.[36] Strategically critical processes must stay in-house, and companies must continuously strive to increase the efficiency of these processes.

Clearly, the purpose of a cost-management system is to provide managers with much
more than just product cost information. In fact, product cost information is only a
secondary outcome of the system. This is partly because a lean manufacturer does not
depend on product costs for pricing purposes. Because prices are market-based, the
manufacturer uses cost information to assess the outcome of improvement activities on
costs and their potential impact on profitability.

*(iii) Marketing, Distribution, and Customer Service*    The important role of marketing
has already been discussed in section 31.5(a)(I). This section discusses the marketing
process in the three following areas:

1. Attracting and retaining profitable customers.
2. Distribution.
3. Customer service.

According to Foster and Gupta, the notion of attracting and retaining "profitable"
customers is quite different from the traditional role of marketing, which is to attract
customers in order to increase sales revenues. The new role calls for identifying *profitable long-term* customers.[37]

The longevity of customers is especially important in a lean manufacturing company, because the task of attracting customers can be quite expensive. Resources consumed to attract customers are wasted if a customer remains with the company for only
a limited time. Several researchers have noted that marketing costs are a very large percentage of sales revenues—and rising.[38] Given this increase in costs, it only makes sense
to analyze the costs more carefully by using some of the cost management methods developed for manufacturing. However, Foster and Gupta note that there is very little
transfer of these developments to the marketing process.

There are four potential areas that can benefit from a more rigorous cost analysis:

1. Budgeting of marketing costs.
2. Selection of marketing vehicles.
3. Allocation of marketing costs to products.
4. Analyzing customer profitability.

There are two broad methods for budgeting marketing costs: judgmental and analytical.[39] The logic behind using judgmental methods is the supposedly discretionary nature of marketing costs. However, recent research suggests that the use of analytical budgeting methods is increasing. For example, a survey conducted in the early 1990s found that more than 60 percent of U.S., British, and Canadian companies responding to the survey used the *objective and task* method of budgeting.[40] This method, which attempts to recognize an implicit cause-and-effect relationship between marketing activities and their results, budgets based on the objectives established for the marketing process.

Not enough research has been conducted about marketing mix selection in terms of cost management techniques. Perhaps the selection of alternative marketing vehicles is more judgmental than analytical. Morris has undertaken a study to determine what types of information marketing managers of industrial companies in Canada use to select the mix of sales promotional vehicles, and also whether any established management accounting techniques are used to analyze these vehicles.[41] Examples of these techniques include:

- Break-even analysis.
- Cost-volume-profit analysis.
- Net present value analysis.
- ABC analysis.

The results of this study will provide insights into the use of management accounting information and techniques in the marketing process.

Marketing costs have typically been allocated to products or product lines on the basis of the sales revenue or gross margin generated by the cost object. The idea behind the use of these allocation bases is the "ability to bear" criterion of allocating indirect costs.[42] However, the use of these allocation bases does not reflect the extent of marketing resources consumed by the products.

Proponents of ABC have suggested that it should be used to allocate marketing costs.[43] Regardless of whether ABC is used to allocate marketing costs, tracing marketing costs by activity can be valuable for a lean manufacturer, because activity information allows managers and employees to think of marketing as a process rather than as a function. Consequently, they can use PVA to identify the non–value-added marketing activities, then eliminate them. This will allow the marketing process to become efficient or lean.

Kalagnanam and Matsumura studied the order-entry process of a high-technology manufacturing company and found that the process contained many non–value-added activities (which constituted waste).[44] They discovered that errors in the outputs of the process affected downstream activities, all of which translated into the loss of significant amounts of money. The company quickly realized that there were significant improvement opportunities to reduce errors, save costs, and satisfy the internal and external customers.

The fourth area is customer profitability analysis, and it has great significance to a lean manufacturing operation. Identifying the right customer and knowing exactly what actions must be taken to satisfy that customer can help a manufacturer in terms of marketing. Generally, the different customer types demand different services from their suppliers. These services, in turn, give rise to different costs for the supplier or manufacturer. Moreover, different customer types differ in terms of the revenues they bring in. Consequently, the profitability streams of the different customer types vary.

Traditional management accounting systems do not provide the information needed to separate profitable customers from unprofitable ones. Assigning costs on the basis of customer types by using ABC systems allows managers to:

- Identify profitable and unprofitable customers.
- Take steps to keep profitable customers.
- Turn unprofitable customers into profitable ones or else slowly phase them out.

According to Cokins, "with the facts, (unprofitable) customers can than [sic] be migrated toward higher profitability by"[45]:

- Managing service costs.
- Reducing their services.
- Renegotiating prices or shifting their purchase mix to richer products.

In summary, cost management plays a critical role in lean manufacturing companies, because all kinds of waste ultimately translate into costs. The techniques discussed previously help companies to quantify the effects of problems and the benefits derived from their solutions. Cost information, by itself, cannot solve problems; instead, it helps draw management's attention to problems.

Although the framework presented in Exhibit 31.7 appears to suggest that specific cost-management techniques are linked to certain processes in the internal value chain, there is considerable overlap in the use of information across processes. For example, life-cycle profitability and target costing information are useful across the entire internal value chain. The exhibit merely suggests that a particular analysis is most likely to be initiated during the process to which it is linked, though the information may very well be used by people involved in the downstream processes.

*(iv) Accounting Database*    As Exhibit 31.7 suggests, a comprehensive ABC system is essential to providing information for cost-management purposes. Traditional accounting systems capture data by function or department; managers cannot massage this database to obtain information for the purposes of, say, preparing a COQ report or performing supplier cost analysis. But a comprehensive ABC database provides this flexibility to managers and employees, because they can pull the data required and use it for different purposes.

The lesson of "different costs for different purposes" can be very well applied using an ABC database. Information about activities helps employees identify and eliminate waste. As a result, several sources of indirect costs may be reduced, which increases accuracy when assigning costs to cost objects (e.g., processes, products, or distribution channels).

Note, however, that creating and maintaining a comprehensive accounting database is costly. Therefore, a lean manufacturer must find ways to capture data so that tracking costs can be kept low. Advanced computer technology has certainly helped. One Canadian coach manufacturer, for example, uses a palm-held computer with a built-in scanner. This computer transfers information directly from the manufacturing floor to the company's accounting database when a worker scans the parts and components purchased, used, or stored. This technology reduces the cost of tracking information and also greatly improves accuracy and timeliness.

**(b) Management Control in a Lean Manufacturing Environment**   This section discusses the design of a management control system and performance measurement within that system.

*(i) Design of a Management Control System*   In addition to a revitalized cost management system, a lean manufacturing environment also demands a management control system that differs from those used in a traditional mass-production company.

A company that pursues some or all of the principles of lean manufacturing is likely to employ elements of an *organic* control system rather than a *mechanistic* control system. Research suggests that companies pursuing flexibility and JIT manufacturing are using elements of organic control systems.[46] These researchers believe that a lean manufacturer must adopt an organic control system to succeed.

Organic control systems are characterized by:

- A higher degree of delegation of responsibility and authority.
- A participative style of management through lateral communication.
- A network structure of control.[47]

Exhibit 31.5 lists some of the characteristics of an organic control system. Such "loose" systems are critical in a lean setting to maintain the process focus that is paramount. Improvements in processes are possible only in a cooperative environment in which experts share knowledge, employees' ideas are heard regardless of hierarchy, and employees all work toward a common goal.

Ansari et al. call for the following behavioral and cultural changes when a manufacturer converts from a mass-production setting to a lean manufacturing environment[48]:

- Empowerment
- Team responsibility
- Cooperation
- Knowledge-based power

In fact, Johnson argues that a company cannot meet its customers' needs without empowering its employees—not just managers—to make decisions for the benefit of the company.[49]

Empowerment of employees is drastically different from the traditional top-down approach to control; it calls for a redesign of the control system. Empowerment does not translate into freedom for employees to take whatever actions they want to. On the contrary, it calls for employees to act responsibly and be accountable for the consequences of their actions.

Simons recommends the use of four "levers" to manage empowerment[50]:

1. Beliefs systems
2. Boundary systems
3. Diagnostic control systems
4. Interactive control systems

Whereas beliefs systems expose employees to the basic principles or doctrines of a business (e.g., through the vision and mission statements and statements of values and beliefs), boundary systems establish the rules of the game, or limits, with respect to decision making. It is important for employees in a lean manufacturing environment to be aware of the relevant beliefs and boundaries so they can focus on the goals of the company and avoid straying off in undesirable directions, thus adding waste to the system.

Diagnostic and interactive control systems have to do with feedback information for control and improvement purposes. The difference between these two systems is in the way information is used. A diagnostic control system uses the information to track progress against goals and objectives and to take corrective actions (if necessary) to meet these goals. An interactive control system, by contrast, focuses on strategic learning and may influence the realignment of strategies if changes in the environment warrant such a redesign. Whereas the former emphasizes critical performance variables, the latter focuses on strategic uncertainties. Simons argues that all the four levers are required to manage the actions of an empowered employee.[51]

Empowerment does not just happen; it must be fostered in a company, and top managers have an important role in making this happen. Bartlett and Ghoshal argue that the "most basic task of corporate leaders is to unleash the human spirit which makes initiative, creativity, and entrepreneurship possible."[52] According to them, this is possible when top managers are directly involved with key people, because it develops interpersonal relationships and encourages self-monitoring. Clearly, a manager's transformation from a top-down, directional role to a coaching role is not easy and cannot be achieved overnight. Therefore, companies must work at it and facilitate the transformation by focusing on changing the attitudes of employees and nurturing their knowledge and skill levels. Enhanced skills and abilities of employees add to a company's capabilities to execute effectively and improve, both of which are critical in a lean manufacturing environment.

Another aspect of an organic control system that is also important in a lean manufacturing environment is teamwork.[53] Teams can be organized in several different ways, but self-managed teams, or *self-directed work teams* (SDWTs), fit well within an empowered setting.

An SDWT consists of "a group of people performing as valued team members who share common interests and goals."[54] The important features of an SDWT are that team members share common goals, are empowered, manage themselves, and treat one another with mutual respect. An SDWT cannot operate based on hierarchy; knowledge and the pursuit of a common goal are very important. Establishing such teams is particularly important in a lean manufacturing company because of the close communication and interaction required across and within the processes of the company's internal value chain.

Several SDWTs can be established within and across the different processes along a company's internal value chain. These teams can also consist of representatives from suppliers and customers. The control of an SDWT is set by the team itself; it is management's task to determine appropriate measures to motivate the teams and to establish mechanisms to ensure that conflicts do not arise. Eliminating waste is not the responsibility of one individual or one functional area; it is everybody's collective task.

*(ii) Performance Measurement in a Lean Manufacturing Environment*   A second aspect of management control is the design of a performance measurement system. One significant recent development is the *balanced scorecard.*[55] An important aspect of a balanced scorecard is the understanding of cause-and-effect relationships, as shown in Exhibit 31.9.

According to Exhibit 31.9, organizational capabilities influence the functioning of an internal value chain. The value chain's efficiencies can be measured by different process-efficiency measures, which (in turn) influence both the customer and financial outcomes.

Organizational capabilities "are the kind and amount of resources in place with which a company can support its current competitive actions, respond to market change, and maintain growth. . . . [These] characteristics of a company that are not easily bought or re-created are more likely to result in persistent strategic differences from rivals. Capabilities are therefore a potential source of differences among group members that appear alike in their strategy."[56] Therefore, capabilities include not just the skills of individuals, but also the technological capabilities that exist within a company.

Others have argued about the importance of *capabilities* or *competence.*[57] Capabilities are linked to the ability to execute or implement effectively. Measures of this dimension, which are leading indicators in a company, provide valuable information to managers regarding the skill levels in the company. Managers can then take actions to enhance those capabilities. Examples of such measures include skills acquired, hours of training, percentage of employees undergoing team skills training, and technology level within the company (see Exhibit 31.10).

More important than simply tracking the measures is the continuous assessment of the capabilities through comparisons with performance. The important question to be asked is perhaps as follows: "Has the company achieved its desired outcomes with its current

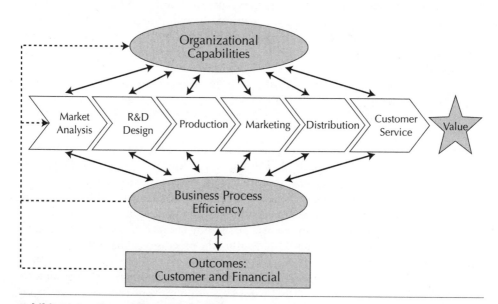

**Exhibit 31.9   Cause-Effect Relationship**

level of capabilities?" If the answer is no, the company must identify gaps (or deficiencies) in its capabilities, establish targets, and work toward achieving them. If the answer is yes, the company must look ahead to new benchmarks (moving targets) and attempt to be the first to reach those benchmarks. This process of self-examination is achieved through the feedback loop (represented by the dashed lines) shown in Exhibit 31.9.

Business-process efficiency measures inform managers how well capabilities have been used to manage or execute the various internal value chain processes. These are interim measures of performance that inform managers how well each process is functioning. In general, these measures pertain to factors such as quality, productivity (efficiency), time, and cost (see Exhibit 31.10). These measures supplement the cost analyses discussed earlier in that they inform about the outcomes of changes to the process. For example, how does selecting supplier A over supplier B affect the number of defects? How does altering the process affect cycle time? Given the nonfinancial nature of most of these measures, they are easily understood by employees and can be reported in a timely manner.

These interim measures are important and valuable because they represent both leading and lagging indicators. They are leading indicators because they influence and inform about the customer and financial outcomes. Good performance with respect to quality and cycle time are likely to translate into more customers and increased revenues, whereas good performance on the productivity and cost fronts should lead to increased profits. They are lagging indicators because they follow organizational capabilities and inform managers about the outcomes of these capabilities.

Customer and financial outcome measures are necessary to obtain information about the market and financial performance of the company. Examples include:

- Number of customers
- Market share

| Organizational Capabilities | Business-Process Efficiency | Customer and Financial Outcomes |
|---|---|---|
| Skills acquired | Percentage defectives | Customer satisfaction |
| Hours of training per person | Percentage rework | Customer returns percentage |
| Percentage of employees undergoing skills training** | Statistical process control (SPC) measures | Customer retention percentage |
| Technology level | First pass yield | On-time delivery percentage |
| Employee satisfaction | Process cycle time* | Market share |
| | Labor productivity | Profitability |
| | Process efficiency* | Return on assets |
| | Process costs* | |

* These measures will be reported for individual processes.
** Could include a variety of skills training (team based skills, SPC skills, negotiation skills, leadership skills, etc.)

**Exhibit 31.10   Examples of Performance Measures**

- Return on assets
- Gross margin percentages
- Growth in sales
- Profits

These measures are used primarily for the purposes of providing feedback to managers and investors about whether the organization's objectives have been met. Additionally, these measures may also be used for rewarding managers and employees.

**31.6 LEAN MANUFACTURING: CONCEPT, METHOD, SYSTEM, OR PHILOSOPHY?**
Previous sections of this chapter have discussed the objectives of lean manufacturing and what these systems do to achieve those objectives. The chapter highlights the many facets of lean manufacturing, which is a collection of techniques and methods that include:

- Small-batch production.
- Reductions in setup times.
- Total productive maintenance.
- Pull production.
- Error-free production.

The objectives of quick, timely, and cost-effective response to a demonstrated need, and then fulfillment of that need (driven by waste removal and continuous improvement), are universal: They extend beyond the shop floor to the entire company.

Each organizational process and system must embrace lean thinking and make the commitment to rethink traditional attitudes about business relationships and work management. Everyone in an organization must view every activity through the lens of the "*lean pentagram*"[58]:

1. Value specification
2. Value stream
3. Flow
4. Pull
5. Continuous improvement

What are the implications for the way in which companies are organized and relate to each other? What are the implications for the landscape of competition in the future when competition is the clash of lean enterprises?

Womack and Jones, for example, note that companies along a vertical chain will establish vertical relationships to form "lean enterprises."[59] The chain is referred to as the *value stream:* Many tributaries flow into the main stream, which ultimately becomes a river flowing into a sea of customers at the mouth. A company can be part of several value streams and thus contribute value to several rivals competing for customers in a common sea. Cooper and Slagmulder point out that the future competitive landscape is likely to be dotted with lean companies, and that competition will be the collision of lean enterprises.[60]

Success in such head-on rivalry will depend on managing the so-called survival triplet of cost and price, quality, and functionality. These are the three essential facets of a product that must be managed by companies that face rivals having similar objectives and capabilities. Intense competition inhibits the choices that companies have with respect to where they position themselves on the three dimensions of the survival triplet. The upshot is that the ability to pursue differentiation as a strategy is severely constrained, which leaves the competitors little option but to focus on cost management.

Porter has a different view; he argues that there will always be a role for strategy. Companies must thus always be concerned with positioning by developing sustainable competitive advantages and isolating niches for themselves.[61]

The principles of lean manufacturing allow operational efficiencies to be gained. But they will not lead to a world in which markets are populated by similar lean enterprises, as Cooper hypothesizes.[62] There will always be differences in the way in which companies absorb and react to the pressures to become lean. Companies may not make the same choices with respect to how they become lean, which facets they make lean, and the degree to which they are made lean. Companies will with respect to capabilities and resources, and also how they absorb and react to the forces in the marketplace. These differences are the foundation for strategy, because they will determine how companies will choose to compete.

Which view will ultimately prevail? Only now can one envision a world of lean enterprises and understand how they can be created and sustained, so the jury is out. The new millennium will certainly bring interesting developments in this area—developments that everyone will watch closely.

## NOTES

1. Society of Management Accountants of Canada (SMAC), "Agile Competition," *Management Accounting Issues Paper 6* (Hamilton: Society of Management Accountants of Canada, 1994).

2. P. E. Drucker, "The Emerging Theory of Manufacturing," *Harvard Business Review* (May–June 1990): 94–102; J. M. Nicholas, *Competitive Manufacturing Management* (Chicago: Irwin, 1998); J. Baron and D. Kreps, *Strategic Human Resources: Frameworks for General Managers* (New York: John Wiley & Sons, Inc., 1999).

3. R. Hayes, S. Wheelwright, and K. Clark, *Dynamic Manufacturing* (New York: Free Press, 1988).

4. Ibid., 185; M. Rother, "Crossroads: Which Way Will You Turn on the Road to Lean?" in *Becoming Lean: Inside Stories of U.S. Manufacturers,* ed. J. Liker (Portland: Productivity Press, 1998).

5. Rother, op. cit. 484

6. J. Womack and D. Jones, *Lean Thinking* (New York: Simon & Schuster, 1996).

7. G. Stalk Jr. and T. Hout, *Competing Against Time* (New York: Free Press, 1990).

8. M. E. Beischel, "Improving Production With Process Value Analysis," *Journal of Accountancy* (September 1990): 53–57.

9. M. Ostrenga, "Activities: The Focal Point of Total Cost Management," *Management Accounting* (February 1990): 42–49, 43.

10. E. J. Blocher, K. H. Chen, and T. W. Lin, *Cost Management: A Strategic Emphasis* (Burr Ridge: Irwin McGraw-Hill, 1999), 105.

11. B. Costantino, "Cedar Works: Making the Transition to Lean," in *Becoming Lean, Inside Stories of U.S. Manufacturers,* ed. J. Liker (Portland: Productivity Press, 1998), 309.

12. M. Finster, *Planning for Quality in New Services & Products,* vol. 2 of *Quality Function Deployment* (Madison: University of Wisconsin, 1995).

13. Baron and Kreps, op. cit., 191.

14. Womack and Jones, op. cit.

15. Baron and Kreps, op. cit.

16. Stalk and Hout, op. cit., 62.

17. Womack and Jones, op. cit., 72.

18. Ibid.

19. Ibid., 71–81, provides a much richer example of this process.

20. G. S. Day, "The Capabilities of Market-Driven Organizations," *Journal of Marketing* 58 (October 1994): 37–52.

21. R. Schmenner, "The Seven Deadly Sins of Manufacturing," in *Strategic Manufacturing: Dynamic New Directions for the 1990s,* ed. P. Moody (Homewood: Dow-Jones Irwin, 1990).

22. R. J. Schonberger and E. M. Knod, *Operations Management: Customer Focused Principles,* 6th ed. (Chicago: Irwin, 1997).

23. U. S. Karmarkar, "Integrative Research in Marketing and Operations Management," *Journal of Marketing Research* 32 (May 1996): 125–133.

24. S. Ansari, J. Bell, T. Klammer, and C. Lawrence, *Management Accounting in the Age of Lean Production* (Burr Ridge: McGraw-Hill, 1997).

25. R. Cooper and R. Slagmulder, *Target Costing and Value Engineering* (Portland: Productivity Press, 1997).

26. R. Kaplan and A. Atkinson, *Advanced Management Accounting* (Upper Saddle River: Prentice-Hall, 1998), 222.

27. Cooper and Slagmulder, op. cit.

28. R. Cooper, "Nissan Motor Company, Ltd.: Target Costing System," HBS Case No. 9-194-040.

29. C. Horngren, G. Foster, S. Datar, and H. Teall, *Cost Accounting: A Managerial Emphasis* (Scarborough: Prentice-Hall Canada, 1997).

30. R. Cooper and B. Turney, "Tektronix: Portable Instruments Division (B)," HBS Case No. 9-188-143.

31. J. Shank, "Strategic Cost Management: New Wine, or Just New Bottles?" *Journal of Management Accounting Research* (Fall 1989): 47–65.

32. Kaplan and Atkinson, op. cit.

33. Shank, op. cit., 57.

34. M. Imai, *Kaizen: The Key to Japan's Competitive Success* (New York: McGraw-Hill, 1986), 3.

35. D. R. Hansen and M. M. Mowen, *Cost Management* (Cincinnati: Southwestern College Publishing, 1997).

36. R. Venkatesan, "Strategic Sourcing: To Make or Not to Make," *Harvard Business Review* (November–December 1992): 98–107.

37. G. Foster and M. Gupta, "Marketing, Cost Management and Management Accounting," *Journal of Management Accounting Research* (Fall 1994): 43–77.

38. L. Percy, *Strategies for Implementing Integrated Marketing Communications* (Lincolnwood: NTC Business Books, 1997); D. Schultz and A. Gronstedt, "Making Marcom an Investment," *Marketing Management* (Fall 1997): 41–49.

39. Foster and Gupta, op. cit.

40. C. Hung and D. West, "Advertising Budgeting Methods in Canada, the UK and the USA," *International Journal of Advertising,* 10 (1991): 239–250.

41. K. Morris, "An Examination of the Accounting Information Used for Selecting, Revising and Evaluating Promotional Vehicles in Industrial Markets in Canada," Master's thesis proposal, University at Saskatchewan, (1999).

42. Horngren et al., op. cit.

43. R. Cooper and R. Kaplan, *The Design of Cost Management Systems,* 2nd ed. (Upper Saddle River: Prentice-Hall, 1999).

44. S. Kalagnanam and E. Matsumura, "Cost of Quality in an Order Entry Department," *Journal of Cost Management* (Fall 1995): 68–74.

45. G. Cokins, "The Cost Management Jungle: Finding Your Way to Successful Solutions," *Profitability and Performance Management Conference,* Conference Proceedings (March 1999), 34.

46. P. R. Duimering and F. Safayeni, "A Study of the Organizational Impact of the Just-in-Time Production Systems," in *Just-in-Time Manufacturing Systems: Operational Planning and Control Issues,* ed. A. Şatir. (New York: Elsevier, 1991); M. A. Abernathy and A. M. Lillis, "The Impact of Manufacturing Flexibility on Management Control System Design," *Accounting, Organizations and Society* 20(1995): 241–258; S. Kalagnanam and R. M. Lindsay, "The Use of Organic Models of Control in JIT Companies: Generalizing Woodward's Findings to Modern Manufacturing Practices," *Accounting, Organizations and Society* 24(1998): 1–30.

47. T. Burns and G. M. Stalker, *The Management of Innovation* (London: Tavistock Publications, 1961); W. L. French and C. H. Bell Jr., *Organizational Development: Behavioral Science Interventions for Organizational Improvements,* 3rd ed. (Englewood Cliffs, N.J.: Prentice-Hall, 1984); R. L. Daft and R. M. Steers, *Organizations: A Micro/Macro Approach* (Glenview, IL: Scott Foresman, 1986).

48. S. Ansari, J. Bell, T. Klammer, and C. Lawrence, *Management Accounting in the Age of Lean Production* (Burr Ridge: McGraw-Hill, 1997).

49. H. T. Johnson, *Relevance Regained: From Top-Down Control to Bottom-Up Empowerment* (New York: Free Press, 1992).

50. R. Simons, "Control in the Age of Empowerment," *Harvard Business Review* (March–April 1995): 80–88.

51. Ibid.

52. C. A. Bartlett and S. Ghoshal, "Changing the Role of Top Management: Beyond Systems to People," *Harvard Business Review* (May–June 1995): 132–142, 132–133.

53. J. Womack, D. Jones and D. Roos, *The Machine That Changed the World* (New York: Rawson Associates, 1990).

54. Society of Management Accountants of Canada (SMAC), "Implementing Self-Directed Work Teams," *Management Accounting Guideline* 38 (Hamilton: Society of Management Accountants of Canada, 1996).

55. R. S. Kaplan and D. P. Norton, "The Balanced Scorecard: Measures That Drive Performance," *Harvard Business Review* (January–February 1992): 71–79.

56. M. W. Lawless, D. D. Bergh, and W. D. Wilsted, "Performance Variations Among Strategic Group Members: An Examination of Individual Company Capability," *Journal of Management* 15(1989): 649–661.

57. K. Cool and D. Schendel, "Performance Differences Among Strategic Group Members," *Strategic Management Journal* 19(1988): 207–223; C. K. Prahalad and G. Hamel, "The Core Competence of the Corporation," *Harvard Business Review* (May–June 1990): 79–91.

58. Womack and Jones, op. cit.

59. Womack and Jones, op. cit.

60. Cooper and Slagmulder, op. cit.

61. M. Porter, "What Is Strategy?" *Harvard Business Review* (November–December 1996): 61–78.

62. R. Cooper, *When Lean Enterprises Collide: Competing Through Confrontation* (Boston: Harvard Business School Press, 1995).

## REFERENCES

Abernathy, M. A. and A. M. Lillis, "The Impact of Manufacturing Flexibility on Management Control System Design," *Accounting, Organizations and Society* 20 (1995): 241–258.

Ansari, S., J. Bell, T. Klammer and C. Lawrence, *Management Accounting in the Age of Lean Production* (Burr Ridge: McGraw-Hill Inc., 1997).

Bartlett, C. A. and S. Ghoshal, "Changing the Role of Top Management: Beyond Systems to People," *Harvard Business Review* (May–June 1995): 132–142.

Baron, J. and D. Kreps, *Strategic Human Resources: Frameworks for General Managers* (New York: John Wiley & Sons, Inc., 1999).

Beischel, M.E., "Improving Production With Process Value Analysis," *Journal of Accountancy* (September 1990): 53–57.

Blocher, E. J., K. H. Chen and T. W. Lin, *Cost Management: A Strategic Emphasis* (Burr Ridge: Irwin McGraw-Hill, 1999).

Burns, T. and G. M. Stalker, *The Management of Innovation* (London: Tavistock Publications, 1961).

Cokins, G., "The Cost Management Jungle: Finding Your Way to Successful Solutions," *Profitability and Performance Management Conference,* Conference Proceedings (March 1999).

Cool, K. and D. Schendel, "Performance Differences Among Strategic Group Members," *Strategic Management Journal* 19(1988) 207–223.

Cooper, R, "Nissan Motor Company, Ltd.: Target Costing System," HBS Case # 9-194-040 (1994).

Karmarkar, U. S., "Integrative Research in Marketing and Operations Management," *Journal of Marketing Research* 32(May 1996): 125–133.

Cooper, R. and R. Kaplan, *The Design of Cost Management Systems,* Second Edition (Upper Saddle River: Prentice-Hall, Inc., 1999).

Cooper, R. and R. Slagmulder, *Target Costing and Value Engineering* (Portland: Productivity Press, 1997).

Cooper, R. and B. Turney, "Tektronix: Portable Instruments Division (B)," HBS Case # 9-188-143.

Costantino, B., "Cedar Works: Making the Transition to Lean," in Liker, J. (ed.), *Becoming Lean: Inside Stories of U.S. Manufacturers* (Portland: Productivity Press, 1998).

Daft, R. L. and R. M. Steers, *Organizations: A Micro/Macro Approach* (Glenview: Scott Foresman and Company, 1986).

Day, G. S., "The Capabilities of Market-Driven Organizations," *Journal of Marketing* 58 (October 1994): 37–52.

Drucker, P. E., "The Emerging Theory of Manufacturing," *Harvard Business Review* (May–June 1990): 94–102.

Duimering, P. R. and F. Safayeni, "A Study of the Organizational Impact of the Just-in-Time Production System," in A. Şatir, (ed.), *Just-in-time manufacturing systems: operational planning and control issues* (New York: Elsevier, 1991).

Finster, M., *Planning for Quality in New Services & Products, Volume II: Quality Function Deployment* (Madison: University of Wisconsin, 1995).

Foster, G. and M. Guptar, "Marketing, Cost Management and Management Accounting," *Journal of Management Accounting Research* (Fall 1994): 43–77.

French, W. L. and C. H. Bell Jr., *Organizational Development: Behavioral Science Interventions for Organizational Improvements,* Third Edition (Englewoods Cliffs, N.J.: Prentice-Hall, 1984).

Hansen, D. R. and M. M. Mowen, *Cost Management* (Cincinati: Southwestern College Publishing, 1997).

Hayes, R., S. Wheelwright and K. Clark, *Dynamic Manufacturing* (New York: The Free Press), 1988.

Horngren, C., G. Foster, S. Datar and H. Teall, *Cost Accounting: A Managerial Emphasis* (Scarborough: Prentice-Hall Canada Inc., 1997).

Hung, C. and D. West, "Advertising Budgeting Methods in Canada, the UK and the USA, *International Journal of Advertising,* 10 (1991): 239–250.

Imai, M., *Kaizen: The Key to Japan's Competitive Success* (New York: McGraw-Hill Publishing Company, 1986).

Johnson, H. Thomas, *Relevance Regained: From Top-Down Control to Bottom-up Empowerment* (New York: The Free press, 1992).

Kalagnanam, S. and R. M. Lindsay, "The Use of Organic Models of Control in JIT Companies: Generalizing Woodward's Findings to Modern Manufacturing Practices," *Accounting, Organizations and Society* 24 (1999): 1–30.

Kalagnanam, S. and E. Matsumura, "Cost of Quality in an Order Entry Department," *Journal of Cost Management* (Fall 1995): 68–74.

Kaplan, R. and A. Atkinson, *Advanced Management Accounting* (Upper Saddle River: Prentice-Hall, Inc., 1998).

Lawless, M. W., D. D. Bergh, and W. D. Wilsted, "Performance Variations Among Strategic Group Members: An Examination of Individual Company Capability," *Journal of Management* 15(1989): 649–61.

Morris, K., "An Examination of the Accounting Information Used for Selecting, Revising and Evaluating Promotional Vehicles in Industrial Markets in Canada," Master's Thesis Proposal, University of Saskatchewan (1999).

Nicholas, J. M., *Competitive Manufacturing Management* (Chicago: Irwin 1998)

Ostrenga, M., "Activities: The Focal Point of Total Cost Management," *Management Accounting* (February 1990): 42–49.

Percy, L., *Strategies for Implementing Integrated Marketing Communications* (Lincolnwood: NTC Business Books, 1997).

Porter, M., "What is Strategy?" *Harvard Business Review* (November–December 1996): 61–78.

Prahalad, C. K., and G. Hamel, "The Core Competence of the Corporation," *Harvard Business Review* (May–June 1990): 79–91.

Rother, M., "Crossroads: Which Way Will You Turn on the Road to Lean?" in Liker, J. (ed.), *Becoming Lean: Inside Stories of U.S. Manufacturers* (Portland: Productivity Press, 1998)

Schmenner, R., "The Seven Deadly Sins of Manufacturing," in Moody, P. (ed.), *Strategic Manufacturing: Dynamic New Directions for the 1990s,* (Homewood: Dow-Jones Irwin, 1990).

Schonberger, R. J. and E. M. Knod, *Operations Management: Customer Focused Principles,* Sixth Edition (Chicago: Irwin, 1997)

Schultz, D. and A. Gronstedt, "Making Marcom an Investment," *Marketing Management* (Fall 1997): 41–49.

Shank, J., "Strategic Cost Management: New Wine, or Just New Bottles?" *Journal of Management Accounting Research* (Fall 1989): 47–65.

Simons, R. "Control in the Age of Empowerment," *Harvard Business Review* (March–April 1995): 80–88

Stalk, G., Jr. and T. Hout, *Competing Against Time* (New York: The Free Press, 1990).

The Society of Management Accountants of Canada (SMAC), "Agile Competition," *Management Accounting Issues Paper 6* (Hamilton: The Society of Management Accountants of Canada, 1994).

The Society of Management Accountants of Canada (SMAC), "Implementing Self-Directed Work Teams," *Management Accounting Guideline #38* (Hamilton: The Society of Management Accountants of Canada, 1996).

The Society of Management Accountants of Canada (SMAC), "Value Chain Analysis for Assessing Competitive Advantage," *Management Accounting Guideline #41* (Hamilton: The Society of Management Accountants of Canada, 1996).

Venkatesan, R., "Strategic Sourcing: To Make or Not to Make," *Harvard Business Review* (November–December 1992): 98–107.

Womack, J. and D. Jones, *Lean Thinking,* (New York: Simon and Schuster, 1996).

Womack, J. P., D. T. Jones and D. Roos, *The Machine that Changed the World* (New York: Macmillan Publishing Company, 1990).

# CHAPTER 32

# Strategic Business Opportunities and Effective Environmental Management Systems

## Steven Pedersen

Seagate Technology, Shakopee, Minnesota

## Christopher H. Stinson

University of Virginia

**32.1 INTRODUCTION**   Many companies now explicitly consider environmental issues when they evaluate their ongoing programs and their strategic plans. In the past, the department responsible for environmental issues in most companies was traditionally concerned only about compliance, not about factoring current and future environmental costs into operational analysis and planning. This traditional approach may have worked in a world in which environmental, health, and safety (EH&S) laws and regulations changed relatively slowly and the public showed little concern about a company's impact on the environment. But this limited scope of EH&S departments is not recommended today for several reasons:

- Environmental health and safety laws and regulations now change frequently.
- Public concern about health and environment has increased, thus raising the expectations that companies will concern themselves with the environment.
- A company's ability to obtain financing, to secure insurance, or to undertake other legal activities is increasingly linked to its environmental record.
- Inattention to EH&S concerns means that valuable expertise will be missing from new-process and product-design decisions.
- Accounting systems that use out-of-date costing methods can obscure the magnitude of environmental costs.[1]

This chapter discusses EH&S issues for three specific audiences:

This chapter is based on "Strategic Business Opportunities," in *1996 Electronics Industry Environmental Roadmap,* ed. The Microelectronics and Computer Technology Corporation (Austin, TX), and sponsored by the Advanced Research Projects Agency (ARPA).

1. Senior management interested in evaluating whether environmental needs and costs are adequately factored into corporate decision-making

2. Midlevel management interested in understanding which environmental needs and costs are likely to affect them and how to respond to these new challenges

3. Managers of EH&S units who need to communicate the effects of strategic decisions on the environmental costs incurred

**32.2 INCORPORATING ENVIRONMENTAL ISSUES INTO CORPORATE DECISION MAKING**    Strategic planning requires managers to set goals, develop processes for achieving those goals, and motivate employees to accomplish the goals. There are distinct financial advantages to incorporating environmental issues into strategic planning, including the following:

- To better understand the sources and cost drivers of current environmental costs.
- To better manage future environmental costs.
- To anticipate issues that could impede product development, distribution, and sales.
- To remain competitive in a world in which competitors are already moving toward greater concern for environmental costs.

Managing environmental impacts must to be part of a company's goals. Companies need to understand what causes these environmental impacts so that they can be considered in process and product design. Environmental performance should also be factored into employee compensation.

**(a) Compliance versus Strategy**    Many industries face the challenge of changing the role of EH&S engineers away from their traditional focus on compliance to an orientation on the future. Compliance is important, but compliance without a strategic evaluation of environmental costs often leads to incomplete—and potentially expensive—decisions.

For example, although the British government gave Shell permission in the 1990s to dispose of a North Sea drilling platform at sea, Shell failed to anticipate the strong public opposition to its plans. Strict compliance was achieved, but strategic planning was evidently limited. Unanticipated international pressures, including a consumer boycott of Shell's products, contributed to a later decision to dispose of the platform differently.

For environmental issues to be incorporated into operations, a reconsideration of the role of EH&S departments is essential. For example, AT&T's Western Electric subsidiary finds that at least 80 percent of the wastes generated by its manufacturing processes are "locked in by the initial design."[2] Analysis of the environmental impacts of *planned* processes often yield greater savings and strategic advantages than does analysis of existing processes. However, incorporating environmental issues into the strategic planning process requires that companies do more than merely comply with existing laws and requirements. Managers responsible for cost control and strategic planning must increase the extent to which they consider the life-cycle impacts of products on the social and ecological environment. Simultaneously, environmental engineers need to increase their consideration of how environmental issues explicitly affect the company's core businesses. Neither strategic planners nor environmental engineers can afford to assume that other groups within the company will take the initiative in controlling and planning for environmental costs.

Many leading companies are modifying their corporate strategic planning and decision-making processes to include prospective consideration of environmental issues. Historically, in many companies, "environmental issues" have been the exclusive responsibility of an EH&S. In these companies, strategic plans were ordained without involving the EH&S department so, after the fact, EH&S would undertake whatever actions were necessary to achieve compliance.

Increasingly, companies are adopting the perspective that "compliance" is only a legal license to operate and that moving "beyond compliance" is one strategy that companies can adopt to achieve advantage over competitors. (The phrase "beyond compliance" does not necessarily mean discharging fewer wastes and emissions than legally permitted; rather, it means that companies have considered the long-term costs and benefits of the activities responsible for its current and future environmental impacts.) The EH&S departments in these companies are evolving their focus away from "pollution prevention" toward "design for environment" and even to explicit consideration of the company's business activities in the context of sustainable development.

Several companies have incorporated environmental performance measures into the presentations at corporate board meetings. For example, as described later, the vice president of B.F. Goodrich's EH&S Management Systems has overseen the transition of his program from a compliance orientation to one that is focused on a systems approach.

**(b) B.F. Goodrich's EH&S Management Systems**    Although often associated with the tire business, B.F. Goodrich is in fact a world leader in aerospace and chemical manufacturing—two lines of business that face substantive environmental challenges. The chemical division has 5,000 employees, and the aerospace division has 8,000 employees. Both units have about $1.2 billion in annual sales. Goodrich's experience with change is now being brought to bear on its EH&S management system—changing it from a compliance-focused system to a strategically oriented management system.

Goodrich has experienced significant competitive advantage from taking this approach. Internal efficiencies have increased because of higher product quality, fewer sick days for employees, and reduced costs of manufacturing. Access to new markets has also improved. For example, an internal culture of environmental and safety awareness facilitates dialogue in developing countries. Outreach to existing customers is promoted by Goodrich, which shares its experiences and information about successful environmental management practices. Goodrich also enjoys a high level of acceptance by public and private stakeholders.

Goodrich's vice president of EH&S, Carl Mattia, reports to a committee of the board of directors that includes four outside directors every six months; this committee, in turn, reports to the full board of directors. Environmental goals for Goodrich must be ratified by the board of directors. Every business unit within the aerospace and chemical manufacturing divisions is responsible for achieving its share of these overall goals.

Corporate environmental performance is tracked using historical, current, and prospective performance indicators. Historical performance indicators include:

- Usage (number and amount) of chemicals listed in Section 313 of the EPA's Toxic Release Inventory (TRI) regulations.
- Number and usage of chemicals included in voluntary regulatory programs (e.g., the Environmental Protection Agency's 33/50 program, in which companies com-

mit to reduce emissions of air pollutants by 33 percent within a certain time period and by 50 percent within a longer period).

- Emissions in excess of permitted levels.
- Number of environmental fines and penalties.
- Total waste, hazardous waste, and chemical waste generated.
- Worker's compensation costs.

Goodrich is currently introducing new performance indicators based on product design. The goal is to add additional cost information to this list, and Goodrich is gradually implementing a "design for environment" program.

Goodrich complies by the six "Codes of Practice" in the Chemical Manufacturer's Association (CMA) "Responsible Care" program and makes an annual report to the CMA (as all member organizations must do; see further discussion later). Furthermore, Goodrich has extended the Responsible Care practices into its aerospace businesses. In the chemical business, Responsible Care is motivated by concerns about product stewardship; in the aerospace business, it is motivated by value-added concerns.

As this program indicates, businesses are both accountable and responsible for their environmental performance. General managers at Goodrich are required to fit these environmental goals into their overall objectives and to ensure that adequate resources exist to meet these goals. The environmental professional is responsible for identifying requirements that make up these goals and for helping businesses comply with their responsibilities. Because of this, Goodrich does not need a large environmental staff; rather, environmental professionals at Goodrich have broad expertise in planning, business processes, and environmental technology.

Goodrich's vice president is especially concerned that all parties—industry, government, and environmental nongovernmental organizations—consider what course of history, regulation, and voluntary actions will most smoothly get the organization to its goals for the future: "Using 20-20 hindsight hasn't worked all that well for us; hopefully, we can use 20-20 foresight to get us efficiently to our desired goals."

**(c) Corporate Environmental Performance**    Society and corporate boards have increasingly higher expectations for corporate environmental performance. These expectations are manifested in the following six initiatives:

1. The Coalition for Environmentally Responsible Economies (CERES) principles.
2. The Responsible Care Program.
3. The International Chamber of Commerce Business Charter's Environmental Management Principles.
4. The British Standards Institution (BSI) Standard BS7750.
5. The European Community Eco-Management and Audit Regulation (EMAR).
6. The ISO 14000 series of standards.[3]

Each of these initiatives is explained in more detail.

**(d) CERES Principles**    The CERES principles were one of the first international standards that addressed corporate environmental performance. The Coalition for Environmentally Responsible Economies is a nonprofit organization whose members include:

- The National Audubon Society.
- The National Wildlife Federation.
- The Sierra Club.
- The Social Investment Forum.
- The Interfaith Center on Corporate Responsibility.
- The U.S. Public Interest Research Group.
- The AFL-CIO Industrial Union Department.

The Coalition for Environmentally Responsible Economies developed the "CERES Principles" (see Exhibit 32.1) in March 1989 in response to the Exxon *Valdez* incident. A business that endorses the CERES Principles commits to becoming publicly accountable for, and to making continuous improvement in, the net environmental impact of all its activities.

About 60 businesses (including corporations such as General Motors, Sun Company, Bethlehem Steel, and Polaroid) have at least partially endorsed these principles. Although the CERES principles were one of the first international standards that addressed corporate environmental performance, other standards and programs (following) are now receiving more attention from corporations, governments, and nongovernmental organizations.

**(e) Responsible Care Program**    The Responsible Care program was organized by CMA in the United States. Adoption of the Responsible Care codes of practice is now required of all CMA members.[4] The Responsible Care program is based on an earlier program developed by the CCPA (Canadian Chemical Producers' Association).

The six codes of practice for the Responsible Care program are:

1. Community awareness and emergency response
2. Process safety
3. Product safety
4. Employee safety
5. Distribution
6. Pollution prevention

These codes establish mandatory programs that are enforced by the chemical industry trade associations in the United States and Canada. These Responsible Care programs apply to any operations in any country in which the company operates. Member companies make an annual evaluation of their own progress toward implementing a complete environmental program.[5]

**(f) International Chamber of Commerce Principles**    The principal functions of the International Chamber of Commerce (ICC) are:

- To represent business at international levels such as the United Nations.
- To promote world trade and investment based on free and fair competition.
- To harmonize trade practices and formulate terminology and guidelines for exporters and importers.
- To provide practical services to business.

### Introduction to the CERES Principles
By adopting these Principles, we publicly affirm our belief that corporations have a responsibility for the environment, and must conduct all aspects of their business as responsible stewards of the environment by operating in a manner that protects the Earth. We believe that corporations must not compromise the ability of future generations to sustain themselves. We will update our practices constantly in light of advances in technology and new understandings in health and environmental science. In collaboration with CERES, we will promote a dynamic process to ensure that the Principles are interpreted in a way that accommodates changing technologies and environmental realities. We intend to make consistent, measurable progress in implementing these Principles and to apply them to all aspects of our operations throughout the world.

### Protection of the Biosphere
We will reduce and make continual progress toward eliminating the release of any substance that may cause environmental damage to the air, water, or the earth or its inhabitants. We will safeguard all habitats affected by our operations and will protect open spaces and wilderness, while preserving biodiversity.

### Sustainable Use of Natural Resources
We will make sustainable use of renewable natural resources, such as water, soils and forests. We will conserve nonrenewable natural resources through efficient use and careful planning.

### Reduction and Disposal of Wastes
We will reduce and where possible eliminate waste through source reduction and recycling. All waste will be handled and disposed of through safe and responsible methods.

### Energy Conservation
We will conserve energy and improve the emergency efficiency of our internal operations and of the goods and services we sell. We will make every effort to use environmentally safe and sustainable energy sources.

### Risk Reduction
We will strive to minimize the environmental, health and safety risks to our employees and the communities in which we operate through safe technologies, facilities and operating procedures, and by being prepared for emergencies.

### Safe Products and Services
We will reduce and where possible eliminate the use, manufacture or sale of products and service that cause environmental damage or health or safety hazards. We will inform our customers of the environmental impacts of our products or services and try to correct unsafe use.

**Exhibit 32.1    CERES principles**

In carrying out these tasks, ICC has prepared and promoted the 16 principles in its "Business Charter for Sustainable Development" (see Exhibit 32.2).

**(g) European Principles and Standards**    Three well-known environmental management-system standards exist or are close to adoption:

1. BSI Standard BS7750
2. The European Union's (EU) EMAR 1836/93
3. ISO 14000 standards

All three of these standards allow for "certification" of a company's compliance with individual standards for environmental management systems.

**Environmental Restoration**
We will promptly and responsibly correct conditions we have caused that endanger health, safety or the environment. To the extent feasible, we will redress injuries we have caused to persons or damage we have caused to the environment and will restore the environment.

**Informing the Public**
We will inform in a timely manner everyone who may be affected by conditions caused by our company that might endanger health, safety or the environment. We will regularly seek advice and counsel through dialogue with persons in communities near our facilities. We will not take any action against employees for reporting dangerous incidents or conditions to management or to appropriate authorities.

**Management Commitment**
We will implement these Principles and sustain a process that ensures that the Board of Directors and Chief Executive Officer are fully informed about pertinent environmental issues and are fully responsible for environmental policy. In selecting our Board of Directors, we will consider demonstrated environmental commitment as a factor.

**Audits and Reports**
We will conduct an annual self-evaluation of our program in implementing these Principles. We will support the timely creation of generally accepted environmental audit procedures. We will annually complete the CERES Report, which will be made available to the public.

**Disclaimer**
These Principles established an ethic with criteria by which investors and others can assess the environmental performance of companies. Companies that endorse these Principles pledge to go voluntarily beyond the requirements of the law. The terms may and might in Principles one and eight are not meant to encompass every imaginable consequence, no matter how remote. Rather, these Principles obligate endorsers to behave as prudent persons who are not governed by conflicting interests and who possess a strong commitment to environmental excellence and to human health and safety. These Principles are not intended to create new legal liabilities, expand existing rights or obligations, waive legal defenses, or otherwise affect the legal position of any endorsing company, and are not intended to be used against an endorser in any legal proceedings for any purpose.

**Exhibit 32.1    Continued**

The BSI Standard BS7750, a currently voluntary standard, has been in effect since March 16, 1992. Facilities operating in Britain can be certified by external examiners to have environmental management systems that meet BS7750. Although other European countries have considered similar standards, most of these have been set aside in favor of the ISO 14000 standards or the EU's EMAR.

The ISO 14001 standards were approved by the International Standards Organization in 1996. Many observers believe that these standards will supplant the British, the EU, and other environmental management standards in other countries and regions. ISO 14001 certification will require that companies have the basic elements of environmental management systems in place.[6]

However, because ISO 14001 is not expected to establish the "performance criteria" necessary to become certified whereas EMAR does, it is possible that companies operating in the European community will have to meet EMAR standards in areas not addressed by the ISO 14000 standards.

The EU passed its EMAR 1836/93 in June 1993. This regulation established an Eco-Management and Audit Scheme (EMAS) that can be voluntarily adopted by industrial

1. *Corporate priority.* To recognize environmental management as among the highest corporate priorities and as a key determinant to sustainable development, to establish policies, programmes and practices for conducting operations in an environmentally sound manner.

2. *Integrated management.* To integrate these policies, programmes and practices fully into each business as an essential element of management in all its functions.

3. *Process of improvement.* To continue to improve corporate policies, programmes and environmental performance, taking into account technical development, scientific understanding, consumer needs and community expectations, with legal regulations as a starting point; and to apply the same environmental criteria internationally.

4. *Employee education.* To educate, train and motivate employees to conduct their activities in an environmentally responsible manner.

5. *Prior assessment.* To assess environmental impacts before starting a new activity or project and before decommissioning a facility or leaving a site.

6. *Products and services.* To develop and provide products or services that have no undue environmental impact and are safe in their intended use, that are efficient in their consumption of energy and natural resources, and that can be recycled, re-used, or disposed of safely.

7. *Customer advice.* To advise, and where relevant educate, customers, distributors and the public in the safe use, transportation, storage and disposal of products provided; and to apply similar considerations to the provision of services.

8. *Facilities and operations.* To develop, design and operate facilities and conduct activities taking into consideration the efficient use of energy and materials, the sustainable use of renewable resources, the minimization of adverse environmental impact and waste generation, and the safe and responsible disposal of residual wastes.

9. *Research.* To conduct or support research on the environmental impacts of raw materials, products, processes, emissions and wastes associated with the enterprise and on the means of minimizing such adverse impacts.

10. *Precautionary approach.* To modify the manufacture, marketing or use of products or services or the conduct of activities, consistent with scientific and technical understanding to prevent serious or irreversible environmental damage.

11. *Contractors and suppliers.* To promote the adoption of these principles by contractors acting on behalf of the enterprise, encourage and, where appropriate, requiring improvements in their practices to make them consistent with those of the enterprise; and to encourage the wider adoption of these principles by suppliers.

12. *Emergency preparedness.* To develop and maintain, where significant hazards exist, emergency preparedness plans in conjunction with emergency services, relevant authorities and local community, recognizing potential transboundary impacts.

13. *Transfer of technology.* To contribute to the transfer of environmentally sound technology and management methods throughout the industrial and public sectors.

14. *Contributing to the common effort.* To contribute to the development of public policy and to business, governmental and intergovernmental programmes and educational initiative that will enhance environmental awareness and protection.

15. *Openness to concerns.* To foster openness and dialogue with employees and the public, anticipating and responding to their concerns about the potential hazards and impacts of operations, products, wastes or services, including those of transboundary or global significance.

16. *Compliance and reporting.* To measure environmental performance; to conduct regular environmental audits and assessments of compliance with company requirements, legal requirements and these principles; and periodically to provide appropriate information to the Board of Directors, shareholders, employees, the authorities and the public.

**Exhibit 32.2 ICC Business Charter for Sustainable Development.** *Source:* **Robert Gray,** *Accounting for the Environment* **(Princeton, NJ: Markus Weiner Publishers, 1993).**

facilities as of April 1995. Nonetheless, the scheme codified by EMAR requires an objective audit of a participating company's environmental management systems (even to the extent of determining compliance with the company's environmental policies) and a public report on the company's environmental performance. Further development of the EU program has been delayed until after adoption of the international ISO 14001 standard on environmental management systems. As of late 1999, the EU was still considering whether to make EMAS mandatory.

The implementation of these initiatives reflects a widespread and increasing public sophistication about the impact of corporate environmental performance. In all likelihood, corporations will continue to be pressured to include environmental issues in their strategic decision making. Furthermore, the potential diversity of international environmental requirements rewards companies that can establish internationally focused management systems. These environmental management systems will be more and more important in establishing a company's public acceptance and competitive position.

**32.3 OBSTACLES TO INCORPORATING ENVIRONMENTAL ISSUES INTO STRATEGIC PLANNING**   Despite the advantages of making environmental issues part of corporate strategy, there may be organizational or psychological barriers to considering environmental issues as a critical component of strategic planning. These barriers may include the perception that environmental issues are primarily compliance problems and that "sustainability" is not fully understood as a source of competitive advantage. Several aids can help companies overcome these barriers to effect a "cultural" change[7]:

- Developing and disseminating strong rationales for incorporating environmental issues into strategic planning.
- Raising corporate awareness of the fundamental importance of environmental issues to strategic planning.
- Starting a training program with the objective of continuously improving strategic planning (as opposed to delaying implementation until a high level of accuracy is assured).
- Basing a training program broadly throughout the organization (instead of primarily within a traditional EH&S department).

With respect to this last point, it is worth quoting Dambach and Allenby[8]:

Design for environment (DFE) is not, and in most companies never will be, a traditional Environment and Safety (E&S) function. This is partly a matter of tactics: financial personnel will put a lot more credence in a green accounting module that comes from the CFO's office than one coming from E&S. Similarly, engineering and technical managers are more likely to trust and use design tools coming from their R&D organizations and product development laboratories, rather than those coming from the E&S organization. In these cases, as in others, this is simply a recognition that the E&S group may be competent in environmental issues, but not in financial methodologies or CAD/CAM tools. The role of the E&S organization will be to provide technical support to the design community as it evaluates decisions, and E&S may be called on to initiate, facilitate, and drive the implementation of DFE.

**(a) Managing Public Perceptions of a Company**   Some companies have used information about environmental performance not only in internal planning but also in external publications. In part, this is done to manage both public and private (e.g., regulatory) perceptions of the company. Because of concern about negative response to private and public information about a company's environmental performance, some companies may be reluctant to publicly report this information (beyond what is required for compliance). However, a purely compliance-oriented reporting strategy may be insufficient if competitors regularly make more extensive disclosures voluntarily.

Consequently, many companies benchmark their environmental disclosures (both in the annual report and, if applicable, in separate environmental reports) against the disclosures of other companies. Environmental reports have been released by at least 70 companies from the United States, Canada, Europe, and Japan.[9] Some companies (e.g., NORTEL) even have World Wide Web (WWW) sites that detail their environmental practices for anyone to see. However, these reports usually describe nonstrategic measures such as toxic release inventory (TRI) emissions and participation in voluntary regulatory programs (e.g., the Environmental Protection Agency's 33/50 program). In the future, measures with added strategic relevance are likely to include such elements as:

- Percentage of recycled (and reused) materials included in products.
- Percentage of recycled (and reused) components included in products.
- Product disassembly time.

**(b) Horizontal Perspective**   Industries are commonly examined from a "horizontal" perspective. For example, the electronics industry can be viewed as composed of manufacturers of electronics equipment, assemblers of electronics equipment, component manufacturers, and a limited number of distribution companies. This perspective is appropriate for developing best industry practices, conducting benchmarking, and for cooperatively developing industry-specific databases.

The alternative "vertical" perspective explicitly includes a company's suppliers and customers. The vertical perspective is appropriate for emphasizing the partnership role that many companies are beginning to develop with suppliers and customers. Supplier partnerships support product design, while customer partnerships provide valuable feedback on product performance.

For many industries, suppliers may be unable to provide necessary components in the required time *without* this explicit vertical integration simply because of short product life cycles. Furthermore, when a manufacturer wants to market a product (and its components) as "green," it may be important to help vertically integrated suppliers develop the appropriate "green" technologies. This supplier-company partnership is reminiscent of the Japanese *keiretsu* system, in which similar "vertical" partnerships are used to help Japanese manufacturers ensure success.

**32.4 IMPROVING STRATEGIC CONSIDERATION OF ENVIRONMENTAL ISSUES**   The wide acceptance of total quality management (TQM) and supplier quality management (SQM) programs in the United States provides an effective model for the environmental arena. These efforts have been accompanied by widely accepted performance standards and guidelines, such as those specified in the Malcolm Baldrige National Quality Awards and the ISO 9000 quality standard.

Local and state programs have emulated the Baldrige Award, and a support industry has grown around process improvement, reengineering, and continuing education.

One important step might be to include environmental *performance* as an additional criteria for the Baldrige Award.

**(a) Parallel with Quality**    Quality programs such as TQM and SQM have led to an evolution in the culture of many professionals who now emphasize systemwide management processes, involvement of management at the highest levels, and measurable, reportable results. This professional evolution is important for those responsible for environmental programs, many of whom have taken a compliance-oriented, reactive approach to environmental management in the past.

As voluntary, prospective initiatives become more common, the opportunity for professional development—and attendant recognition—must also increase. Environmental professionals must expand their expertise to include a broad range of management, financial, and marketing knowledge, and top management must learn to recognize environmental professionals as key contributors to strategic planning and to cost-effective operations.

**(b) Customer-Focused Life-Cycle Analysis at United Defense, L.P.**    Much of the environmental compliance costs incurred by any product's customer (over the product's life) is implicitly determined during the conceptual and detailed design stages of product development. It is critical, therefore, to provide product design teams information about the potential environmental effects of their design decisions and about the life-cycle performance expectations of customers.

This approach has led to a TQM approach for the development of United Defense's Crusader self-propelled howitzer. United Defense recognizes that reducing wastes and emissions in the future should be addressed during the initial design of a product. Preventing defects is more cost-effective and provides more opportunities for improvement than dealing with defects after they occur. TQM analysis naturally leads to a focus on the decisions that are made during the product and process design phase.

In recognition of this path-breaking opportunity, United Defense and the U.S. Army have initiated a *design for environment* (DFE) process to incorporate environmental needs into the design and manufacture of the Crusader system. This design process will build on the lessons learned from the development of past artillery systems.

The plan is to design manufacturing operations and maintenance operations so that the use of hazardous materials is greatly reduced or eliminated. This approach has the potential to reduce life-cycle costs, contingent liabilities for both the manufacturer and customers, potential risk to operators, hazardous-waste generation, and other environmental impacts. These DFE activities reduce both the manufacturer's and the customer's future environmental burdens.

United Defense's Crusader contract stipulates that a DFE approach be used. In particular, the company's Specialty Engineering employees have responsibility to plan, develop, implement, monitor, and maintain an effective *environmental design guide* (EDG) for preferred materials and processes and a *hazardous materials management program* (HMMP) plan, developed in conformance with National Aerospace Standard 411, for materials and processes targeted for elimination or reduction.

The primary objectives of the environmental protection program are:

- To eliminate or reduce hazardous and environmentally harmful materials (as defined by applicable laws or regulation).

- To minimize the cost the government incurs to protect human health and the environment.
- To document that environmental concerns are addressed consistent with essential program mission, performance, schedule, and cost requirements.
- To provide appropriate support to the government's Programmatic Environmental Analysis efforts.

The EDG and HMMP are supposed to influence program design and planning, and to identify and address potential environmental problems that may arise during the program's life cycle, including manufacture, test, operation, and disposal.

Crusader uses product development teams, concurrent engineering, and other TQM-related methods in the design and manufacture of products. This method reduces costs and errors early in the design phase by having design engineers working closely with manufacturing engineers. A similar approach is used when implementing DFE. Design engineers interface with environmental, pollution prevention, process and materials engineers to assure that elimination, substitution, or reduction of environmentally unacceptable materials and processes occurs along with other aspects of the design process. Criteria for the design of products include:

- Use renewable natural resource materials.
- Use recycled materials.
- Use fewer toxic solvents or replace solvents with an alternative material (e.g., using grit blasting instead of solvents for paint removal).
- Reuse scrap and excess material.
- Use water-based instead of solvent-based materials.
- Produce combined or condensed products that reduce packaging requirements.
- Produce fewer integrated units (i.e., more line-replaceable component parts).
- Manufacture recyclable final products.

These criteria require choosing between many alternative design possibilities, especially when considering other design issues such as functionality, cost, and ease of production. Although these choices are not simple to make, the inclusion of environmental criteria in the design process shows the importance of DFE to both United Defense and the U.S. Army.

Another lesson from the quality movement is the necessity of involving the entire supply chain in the process. Environmental programs are not the exclusive domain of environmental engineers. Supply and distribution relationships, raw material sources, and even service providers and customers have a role to play in an integrated, life-cycle–based environmental management process.

**(c) Initial Steps**    The momentum that has grown about TQM can be transferred into attaining environmental excellence. There are many programs that industry can pursue to take the offensive. Here are some of the initiatives or performance metrics that companies, consortia, and trade groups can consider:

- Total costs and benefits of environmental activities (including compliance with current environmental laws and regulations).

- "Social costs" of current and future operations (when regulatory constraints are likely to arise).
- Number of business or governmental partnerships (i.e., a measure of the company's relationship with regulatory agencies).
- Level and content of information shared with the local community.
- Environmental management system certification study.
- Number of supplier audits as a percentage of total strategic suppliers.
- Extent of mentoring relationship with suppliers and customers with respect to an environmental management system.
- Compliance audit results.
- Number of "green" products manufactured or marketed.

**(d) NORTEL Environmental Performance Index**   This section describes how NORTEL created a performance index. Executives in a range of positions across NORTEL are held accountable for meeting environmental objectives and achieving results. In keeping with the maxim that "what gets measured gets managed," the company gathers masses of environmental data across a broad spectrum of programs and operational processes. Typically, the measurements are developed to gauge performance against identified goals.

An *environmental performance index* (EPI) is one way to reduce these data to a manageable score. The index provides a single rating for the company. What prompted NORTEL to undertake the process of developing a company-specific EPI? Senior management and external stakeholders felt it was necessary to begin making business sense of all of the environmental performance information that was being collected for environmental initiatives. When NORTEL began environmental reporting in 1992, little quantitative data was available. In 1994, NORTEL set out to establish specific targets and developed an internal EPI to measure progress.

NORTEL had built a reputation for excellence and leadership in product development and manufacturing. The challenge was to build on those strengths to improve environmental management. Standards and regulations were proposed to the boards of directors in Canada and the United Kingdom to make annual reports about "due diligence" concerning certain nonfinancial concerns, including social and environmental issues. NORTEL expected to increase shareholder value and achieve preferred investment status by demonstrating continuous improvement toward meeting the goals the company had set for environmental improvement and resource management.

The EPI at NORTEL was designed on an Excel spreadsheet that linked all the data. The normalizing factor for the data is cost of sales, which is linked to the producer price index for finished electronic goods. The benchmark year was 1993; later years were normalized and compared against the benchmark year (a 70 percent weighting) and the previous year (30 percent).

Targets were set for a number of environmental media, then a weighted score was developed for each. The target year for achieving reductions was 2000. To achieve the reductions, a total weighted score of 175 had to be reached and maintained (as compared with a neutral score of 100). Scores below 100 indicate increased environmental impact and negative progress toward the target. No advantage is given to maintaining compliance, which is expected as a minimum performance standard. Any permit excursion or notice of violation gives the compliance parameter a negative score.

The EPI is used as both a score card and a tool that provides strategic direction to NORTEL on how to deal with environmental issues. It may have a future use in helping the company review performance across business groups to decide how to allocate resources or make decisions regarding product viability.

**(e) Self-Audits**   The establishment of a self-audit program—whether it is comprehensive or targeted at specific areas of concern—provides an opportunity for a business to demonstrate its commitment to environmental quality and continual improvement. The audit, which should be conducted on a regular basis by qualified internal auditors or an outside auditing organization, should concentrate on a variety of areas or issues essential for effective corporate environmental programs. These areas might include:

- Mechanisms for demonstrating senior management support.
- Processes to ensure that a systems approach is taken.
- Incorporation of environmental concerns in product design.
- Environmental considerations in manufacturing processes and facilities.
- Compliance with existing mandates.
- Community awareness.
- Environmental considerations in marketing and distribution.
- Strategies for addressing disposition or takeback.

Self-audits provide management with an ongoing evaluation mechanism and (to the extent that management is willing to share some portion of the results) present a source for industry benchmarking. In several states, legislatures grant businesses immunity for problems that are identified during self audits and then quickly corrected.

**(f) Improved Understanding of Environmental Costs**   Analysis at many large businesses has revealed that many cost accounting systems do not trace environmental costs to the production processes that generate these costs. This was acceptable historically, because the costs were usually small and the expense of tracing was relatively large. However, the growing magnitude of these costs and the nonlinear form of some cost drivers can cause traditional allocation methods to produce suboptimal financing and investment decisions.[10]

An improved understanding of the impact that environmental issues can have on revenues and expenses provides the following benefits:

- Faster construction of new manufacturing facilities because environmental requirements of construction and operating permits are more quickly satisfied.
- Ability to satisfy demands from corporate customers for manufacturing systems and component products that meet the ecolabeling and product-takeback requirements faced by the corporate customer.
- Ability to maintain existing products and to introduce new products in markets (e.g., the European Union) with ecolabeling product-takeback, and other environmentally based requirements.

**(g) Prototype Facilities**   Companies can collaborate in establishing prototype programs and facilities for managing significant environmental issues. For example, several pilot product disposition programs, such as The American Plastic Council's research program on plastic recycling, are now under way, most with some industrial involvement. Research programs, equipment development, process improvement, and infrastructure development lend themselves to collaborative initiatives, and many are ideally suited for cross-industry cooperation or public/private partnerships.

**(h) Model-Permitting Processes** In some states, electronics and computer companies have worked with state regulators to develop model-permitting processes to accelerate permit approvals. This occurs by specifying certain standards that are acceptable to both industry and regulators. To the extent an individual applicant for a permit meets the stated standards, permit approval is expedited, so substantial cost savings can accrue to the company. Proposals for the elements of these standard permits could be developed on a national basis and made available to regulators through professional channels in an effort to promote consistency among jurisdictions.

Several models exist that could form the basis for innovative model-permitting proposals. For example, the "Dutch Covenant System" encourages self-regulation within a framework developed and agreed upon jointly by industry and government. The framework includes performance-based, quantitative objectives, with emission targets for priority substances apportioned among industry sectors. Industry is then responsible for determining the best approach to meeting the standards and documenting its strategies and tactics in companies' environmental management plans. These plans are incorporated in company-specific licenses and permits, which are updated regularly. A major benefit of the covenant approach is increased communication and understanding among the parties involved in the regulatory process, which yields lower barriers to cooperation in the long run.

**(i) Intel Corporation's P4 Project** In late 1993, Intel, the Environmental Protection Agency, and the Oregon Department of Environmental Quality joined in a partnership to evaluate opportunities to incorporate flexibility and pollution prevention into permits issued under Title V of the 1990 Clean Air Act Amendments (CAAA). The Pollution Prevention in Permitting Pilot (P4) Project was undertaken to develop a facility-specific permit that incorporates pollution prevention as a model permit condition for achieving regulatory compliance. The project's goals are:

- To develop an implementable permit.
- To identify regulatory barriers.
- To document the process.
- To develop options and alternatives that can be useful to others.

The project will demonstrate the ability of pollution prevention to perform equally well in the reduction of air emissions as do traditional, regulatory-specific, "end-of-pipe" controls. The project further showed the value of partnerships between industry and governments in promoting pollution prevention and prospective environmental management strategies that support a company's economic viability while also maintaining a high standard of environmental protection.

In determining the cost of pollution and, in turn, the benefit of pollution prevention, industry examines and balances four factors:

1. The cost of inputs that cause environmental damage.
2. The cost of polluting behavior.
3. The cost of public concern.
4. The cost of adopting pollution-prevention alternatives.

The P4 Project was completed on September 26, 1995, thus becoming the nation's first air pollution permit under Title V that successfully integrates pollution prevention and operational flexibility. The key to this breakthrough was changing the focus from the minor process changes to the overall environmental results.

Under the cooperative model, the sitewide air permit provides Intel the flexibility of adjusting its manufacturing processes on its own—as long as the changes meet specific preapproved permit conditions—without going through an extensive approval process for each individual change. To get this flexibility, Intel agrees to use pollution-prevention practices as the primary method to manage air emissions. In essence, the environmental agencies provide preapprovals of minor changes in exchange for commitments to incorporate pollution prevention.

As explained by Dr. Craig Barrett, Intel's executive vice president and chief operating officer, "this method maintains high standards of environmental protection, encourages efforts for pollution prevention, and creates an opportunity for common sense to be applied to environmental safeguards."

The permit meets all federal and state requirements identified under Title V of the CAAA and Oregon's State Implementation Plan. The permit is environmentally protective and fully enforceable under federal and state law. It contains emission limits for the entire plant site instead of limits for each individual vent or pipe. As long as Intel meets its sitewide emission limits, all minor process changes at the site are preapproved.

**(j) Increased Program Visibility** Some corporations have begun publishing annual environmental stewardship reports. A somewhat less comprehensive effort is to include an environmental section in annual reports. For private corporations (which may not publish an annual report), a statement to stakeholders about environmental objectives and activities could be prepared and distributed instead. Trade associations could also assemble these data from company reports, then disseminate the information to members.

If companies want managers to consider environmental issues, they need to incorporate appropriate incentives into management compensation. Many companies surveyed by Deloitte & Touche (1995) now include nonfinancial measures of divisional or company performance in the variable component of employee compensation.[11]

**(k) Community Outreach** Some corporations periodically invite community leaders to plant sites as an educational activity so that they can learn about ongoing environmental, health, and safety activities. Such "community open houses" can go a long way toward mitigating speculation about environmental conditions or hazards at an industrial site, and they can create informed advocates in the community.

Community advisory councils have also been used effectively to create "community-based champions." These councils bring together a broad range of community interest groups in a setting that fosters communication and understanding. Although some electronics manufacturers have established such councils, the chemical industry provides the best example of successful council operation. Monsanto, for example, operates 14 domestic and 4 overseas councils, serving (in Monsanto's words) as the operating facilities' "ears into the community." These councils provide a forum for education, emergency planning, and communication.

**(l) Development of Educational Curriculum**    Facility managers and EH&S managers can encourage and support the inclusion of environmental topics in the curricula of local educational institutions. This could be as simple as providing guest instructors for existing classes; these instructors can share experiences and explain a company's programs to provide examples of "real-world" environmental management. Other companies could conduct more involved educational efforts, such as working with educational institutions to develop new training programs.

**(m) Internal Continuing Education Programs**    Companies can create educational programs for employees on issues facing an entire industry or a specific operation. These should be technical in nature and address both policy and procedures. Professional certification (or other incentives) can increase the attractiveness of these programs.

Training programs can be modified to facilitate improved consideration of environmental issues in corporate activities. For example, Motorola has developed a well-regarded training program (as outlined later) for its technical education system. Johannson reviews the development of a program for environmental-management training that reversed the typical order of topics in many traditional training programs.[12] Specifically, legal, regulatory, and compliance issues are covered at the end of the program. Programs that emphasize compliance run the risk of teaching managers to focus on current standards rather than to consider potential problems.

**(n) Motorola's Environmental Training Program**    In 1994, Motorola's corporate EH&S group received the chief executive officer's approval and support for a companywide initiative to train all associates on environmental awareness. This training program, which was based on company and personal (i.e., citizen-level) issues, is used to provide a common language and message to all employees. More than 100,000 Motorola employees have completed it. Although Motorola has only about 14 employees in its corporate EH&S group, the company has used this training program to leverage its worldwide influence.

Because of this training program, employees voluntarily began creating problem-solving teams to identify problem areas (at work and in the broader community) where remedies were available.

After the training program was designed and operating, the Motorola EH&S group created four follow-on design for environment courses. Several years later, Motorola initiated a design for manufacturability program. These new courses are regarded as an integral (and continuing) part of Motorola's design for quality commitment. The design for environment courses target both product-oriented issues (e.g., recyclability) and process-oriented issues (e.g., chemical reduction).

In addition to its own employees, Motorola has begun to share these training programs with suppliers and customers. It is critical to have suppliers working from a similar perspective if a corporation is going to implement a design for environment program. Customers have been enthusiastic about Motorola's initiative in these areas as well. Motorola's Cathy Buffington says that, for Motorola, "Compliance with regulations is obviously relevant in offering these programs, but the fundamental course message is that DFE is good business."

Most recently, Motorola has partnered with a nonprofit training organization (the Management Institute for Environment and Business) to develop a program for senior-level decision makers. Motorola's business leaders and environmental managers attend this two-day class on integrating environmental issues into business decisions. The class teaches environmental managers the skills and vocabulary they need to interact successfully with corporate decision makers. The senior-level business managers learn that the environmental managers can provide important information if the EH&S people are sought out early in the strategic decision-making process.

**(o) Technology Transfer**    Companies, acting individually or in concert, can develop models of best practices to be shared with other companies that face similar problems but lack the resources to develop solutions on their own. This approach is especially valuable for large corporations that work with their second- and third-tier suppliers.

Once developed, these guidelines can serve as a basis for industry consensus on operating philosophies and principles. The chemical industry, for example, has established a "Stewardship Initiative" that members of the Chemical Manufacturers Association must adopt to maintain their membership in the association.

**(p) Supplier Environmental Excellence Programs**    Corporations are establishing supplier-recognition awards for quality or performance. Similar awards could be established for suppliers who achieve environmental excellence. Doing so could be part of establishing a standard of performance that suppliers are expected to meet if they want to remain a company's primary supplier.

None of the initiatives discussed earlier is original or unique, and many companies have already embraced some of them. Creativity and communication can certainly help expand the list. But the true test comes in the breadth of acceptance and the willingness of an industry to make its commitment to the environment visible and continuous.

If performance-oriented approaches are effectively implemented, industry can break the cycle of regulation-enforcement-distrust that has inhibited the widespread acceptance of industry-led initiatives. By responding to the growing opposition to ineffective, inefficient government regulation, and while still recognizing and honoring the core environmental values of the community, industry can initiate a new era of partnership. Prospective industry initiatives, accompanied by government-industry cooperative programs and incentives offer significant benefits to all involved.

**32.5 INDUSTRY NEEDS**    A growing set of tools and decision models is now available for incorporating environmental issues into business decisions. Managers who have strategic responsibilities have often ignored environmental issues, and managers who have environmental responsibilities have often been excluded from strategic considerations.

New analytical methods are being developed. For example, computer simulations have been used to conduct sensitivity analysis on the probable outcomes of different decisions.[13] Methods for qualitatively ranking environmental risks associated with hazardous emissions to air, water, and soil have been proposed.[14] However, all these methods must be tested and adapted for each company's specific circumstances.

**(a) Benchmarking Environmental Performance**    Nonfinancial measures of current and future performance include output quality, environmental performance, customer satisfaction, and employee training.[15] However, the various explicit measures of "environmental performance" that have been proposed (and used) are diverse, they are often vague, and they lack widespread industry acceptance. Clearly, therefore, there is a need for environmental performance benchmarks that can be used for internal and external reports.

**(b) Environmental Reports: Independent Evaluation and Certification**    The annual report of a U.S. company often includes some discussion of contingent environmental liabilities in the Management's Discussion and Analysis (MD&A), as required by the Securities and Exchange Commission, and in the footnotes to the financial statements (as required by generally accepted accounting principles). However, discussions of environmental performance in MD&A sections are not audited; auditors merely review the MD&A for consistency with the material in the financial statements that actually has been audited.

Because of this absence of explicit attestation and because the MD&A discussion is usually somewhat limited, a few companies have been experimenting with independent evaluation or certification of their voluntary reports of environmental performance. A few years ago, NORTEL began inserting two pages about environmental performance into its corporate annual report. This is in addition to preparing a separate environmental report describing the company's programs and progress in depth. The environmental report is audited by Deloitte & Touche as a third-party reviewer.

Cahill and Kane point out that "DuPont in its 1992 and 1993 Corporate Environmentalism Reports provided the executive summary, along with DuPont's response, from a third-party evaluation of the company's Corporate Environmental Audit Program."[16] At the present time, however, there is no generally accepted certification that has industry or public acceptance.

**32.6 SUMMARY**    For many years, industry in the United States has advocated voluntary solutions to environmental concerns, while environmental interest groups and government regulators have chosen instead to pursue a policy of mandating the responsibilities, actions, and approaches of private business—sometimes even the specific technology to be used. These regulations have typically been born of legitimate concerns for threats to human health and to sensitive ecological systems. Nonetheless, some regulations have been ill-conceived and politically motivated, thereby creating significant administrative inefficiencies, raising the cost of doing business, and threatening the international competitiveness of U.S. industry.

Some representatives in Congress now promote a different philosophy of government regulation that would require a cost-benefit analysis of new federal rules. Other initiatives at the federal, state, and local government levels seek to eliminate unfunded federal mandates and to reassert local control over a wide variety of matters, ranging from transportation policy to education to the environment. If enacted, these changes would have a profound impact on industry's environmental strategy and management practices.

The potential for a decrease in regulation at the federal level, and indications that similar philosophies may be guiding state and local policymakers, gives industry an opportunity to demonstrate the viability and value of performance-oriented initiatives. Industry must define the scope and nature of these voluntary efforts by seizing the initiative and forming a framework for the actions of individual companies. Collaboration will be required to prevent pollution, improve efficiency, and (ultimately) improve cost structures while maintaining product quality. Leading companies are taking initiative in product design. Through these actions, industry has the opportunity to "reinvent" itself in the eyes of many who have otherwise been adversaries. At the international level, competitive pressures in the global marketplace will require companies to develop universally applied standards of care.

The time has come for industry to communicate the message that performance-oriented efforts work, and that industry can sustain effective environmental management programs. By taking the lead, industry can increase the probability that this regulatory revolution (or, perhaps more correctly, an antiregulatory revolution) will succeed, which would mean that performance-focused programs would become a preferred strategy for environmental managers.

## NOTES

1.  D. Ditz, J. Ranganathan, and R. D. Banks (eds.). 1995. Green Ledgers: Case Studies in Corporate Environmental Accounting (Washington, DC: World Resources Institute); B. Hamner and C. H. Stinson, "Managerial Accounting and Environmental Compliance Costs," *Journal of Cost Management* (1995).

2.  B. F. Dambach and B. R. Allenby, "Implementing Design for Environment at AT&T," *Total Quality Environmental Management* (Spring 1995): 51–62.

3.  L. B. Cahill and R. W. Kane, "Corporate Environmental Performance Expectations in the 1990s: More Than Just Compliance," *Total Quality Environmental Management* (Summer 1994): 409–420.

4.  Ibid.

5.  Ibid..

6.  T. Tibor, *ISO 14000: A Guide to the New Environmental Management Standards* (Chicago: Irwin, 1995).

7.  Dambach and Allenby, op. cit.

8.  Ibid., p. 58.

9.  Cahill and Kane, op. cit.

10. Ditz et al., op. cit.; Hamner and Stinson, op. cit.

11. Deloitte & Touche, "Challenging Traditional Measures of Performance," *Deloitte & Touche Review* (August 7, 1995): 1–2.

12. L. Johannson, "Environmental Training Fosters Bottom-Line Education and Regional Economic Development," *Total Quality Environmental Management* (Autumn 1994): 85–93.

13. D. W. Townsend, "Environmental Portfolio Analysis: An Integrated Strategic Approach to Environmental Management." *Total Quality Environmental Management* (Autumn 1994): 57–66.

14. B. A. Grimsted, S. C. Schaltegger, C. H. Stinson, and C. S. Waldron, "A Multimedia Assessment Scheme to Evaluate Chemical Effects on the Environment and Human Health," *Pollution Prevention Review* 4 (1994): 259–268.

15. Deloitte & Touche, op. cit., 1–2.

16. Cahill and Kane, op. cit., 419.

# CHAPTER 33

# Knowledge Management

## Wendi Bukowitz

**33.1 INTRODUCTION**   Knowledge management might simply be the latest craze to sweep organizational systems—another buzzword destined to be cast aside in a few short years. Or it might have the sticking power of total quality management, activity-based costing, or customer satisfaction, becoming inextricably linked with the way we think about good organizational management. Time alone will tell how profoundly knowledge management influences our ideas about management.

All the talk about knowledge management at office meetings and industry confer-ences—to say nothing about the boatload of articles and books appearing on the topic—makes many managers feel that they ignore it at their own peril. But knowledge management is a slippery topic. It goes by several names (including intellectual capital management and intellectual asset management) and overlaps with many other topics (including innovation, organizational design, information technology, the networked economy, intellectual property, valuation, and measurement, to name a few). Figuring out what knowledge management entails seems problematic enough, let alone figuring out how it can improve organizational performance.

Despite the newness of the term, knowledge management is not new. It goes on in all organizations, all the time. That said, knowledge may be poorly or undermanaged. It may not be managed explicitly but, rather, bundled up in the management of other organizational assets (e.g., relationships with employees, customers, and alliance part-ners) or the value proposition of a service or product. But whether they do so well or poorly, explicitly or implicitly, all organizations manage and use knowledge to get work done. Whether knowledge is managed to great effect is anybody's guess. To a large ex-tent, the growing emphasis on knowledge management is an effort to take at least some of the guesswork out of the equation.

Knowledge management has great appeal in part because practice has preceded the-ory: It does not feel like an idea generated by academics and consultants. Instead, it feels like an emerging business reality to which managers have responded. It just makes sense to people that managing collective know-how will improve the way work gets done.

---

This chapter is freely adapted from Wendi R. Bukowitz and Ruth L. Williams, *The Knowledge Management Fieldbook,* with permission from Financial Times/Pitman Publishing for inclusion in *Guide to Cost Manage-ment,* by Barry J. Brinker, to be published by John Wiley & Sons, Inc.

A handful of organizations have been practicing what could officially be called knowledge or intellectual asset management for more than five years. For some of them, the effort will be a decade old as we reach the millennium. From these organizations and the growing number who have swelled their ranks in the past few years, a body of practice has emerged that observers of organizational management have begun to codify, organize, and analyze.

The approach to knowledge management presented in this chapter is designed to generally acquaint people with the topic by:

- Defining its boundaries.
- Introducing a comprehensive yet simple framework for thinking practically about knowledge management.
- Presenting pressing considerations that confront those embarking on a knowledge management initiative, and also case histories from some organizations that have met those challenges.
- Providing a way of thinking about how to prioritize efforts.

**33.2 BOUNDARIES OF KNOWLEDGE MANAGEMENT**    Many different definitions of knowledge management have been advanced in the past few years, ranging from the philosophical to the tactical. At the philosophical end of the spectrum are disquisitions on the nature of knowledge and its relationship to the knower; at the tactical end of the spectrum is technical gobbledygook about the latest applications of information technology.

**(a) Definitions**    The definition that follows sits squarely in the middle of the spectrum between the high and the low by pointing toward a practical reason why organizations should care about knowledge management: *Knowledge management* is the process by which an organization generates wealth from its intellectual or knowledge-based assets.

This definition creates a need for two other definitions—*wealth* and *intellectual assets*—and at least a few clarifying words about intangibles and knowledge. For these definitions, we first turn to *The American Heritage Dictionary of the English Language*[1]: "Wealth 1.a. An abundance of valuable material possessions or resources; riches. b. The state of being rich; affluence. 2. All goods and resources having value in terms of exchange or use."

The second definition of wealth reveals a specific way of thinking about value—in terms of the ability to exchange a tangible object (or a less tangible resource) for something else, or to put it into use.

Looking back to our definition of knowledge management, we can elaborate on it by saying that it is the process by which an organization generates value from its intellectual assets by creating an ability to exchange them for something else or to put them to use.

To define intellectual asset, we start with the definition of asset from the same dictionary (emphasis added):

> Asset: 1. A *useful or valuable quality,* person, or thing; an *advantage* or a *resource.* 2. A valuable item that is owned. . . . 4. assets. a. *Accounting.* The entries on a balance sheet showing all properties, tangible and *intangible*, and claims against others that may be applied, directly or *indirectly*, to cover the liabilities of a person or business, such as cash, stock, or goodwill.[2]

The emphasis added in this definition highlights key elements that are important in the definition of an intellectual asset: *useful or valuable quality*, *advantage* or *resource*, *intangible*, *indirectly*. To define *intellectual* asset, we merge the common understanding of asset with the accounting definition, emphasizing these key italicized elements, to create a hybrid definition that is specific to assets derived from knowledge:

> *Intellectual Asset:* Anything valued that has no physical dimensions and is embedded in people or derived from processes, systems, and the culture associated with an organization—brands, individual knowledge, intellectual property, licenses, and forms of organizational knowledge (e.g., databases, process know-how, relationships).[3]

**(b) Ownership of Intellectual Assets**    One critical distinction between intellectual assets and traditional accounting assets is that not all intellectual assets can be owned. Companies can own patents and even ideas if they are expressed and codified. But enthusiasm, commitment, and the willingness to express an idea are not as easy to lay claim to. As a result, deriving economic benefit from some intellectual assets is not under the organization's direct control. These assets cannot be relied on to offset liabilities in the same way as traditional assets. For this reason, many accountants and regulators respond squeamishly to the proposition that intellectual assets should be treated in the same way as tangible assets in the financial statements.

Some intellectual assets are better thought of as rented, leased, or borrowed. Gordon Boronow, the president and chief operating officer of American Skandia, an insurance company headquartered in Sweden, suggests that intellectual assets are *volunteered* on a daily basis. They result from discretionary acts on the part of individuals, so they cannot be converted into value in the same way as a warehouse of inventoried parts. Intellectual assets are a different breed of asset. They are not assets in the strict accounting sense, but clearly they are assets of some new type and they demand recognition.

**(c) Individual Knowledge**    In the field of knowledge management the adjectives "knowledge-based," "intellectual," and "intangible asset" are used interchangeably to mean the same thing. The term "knowledge" also appears with alarming frequency. When knowledge refers to organizational knowledge, it falls within our definition of an intellectual asset. But when knowledge refers to individual knowledge, only some of it falls within the boundaries of the definition.

What individuals know may or may not represent assets to the organization. For example, even if what people know is work-related, it may or may not be right or true. If people never use what they know on behalf of the organization, their knowledge is not an intellectual asset according to the definition.

Finally, we can complete our definition of knowledge management by saying that it is the process by which an organization creates the ability to exchange anything without physical dimensions that is embedded in the people, processes, and culture of an organization for something else or to put it to use and thereby generate wealth. With this definition in our hip pocket, we can next think about the elements of the knowledge management process.

**33.3 A FRAMEWORK FOR THINKING ABOUT KNOWLEDGE MANAGEMENT**    The Knowledge Management Process Framework shown in Exhibit 33.1 visually depicts

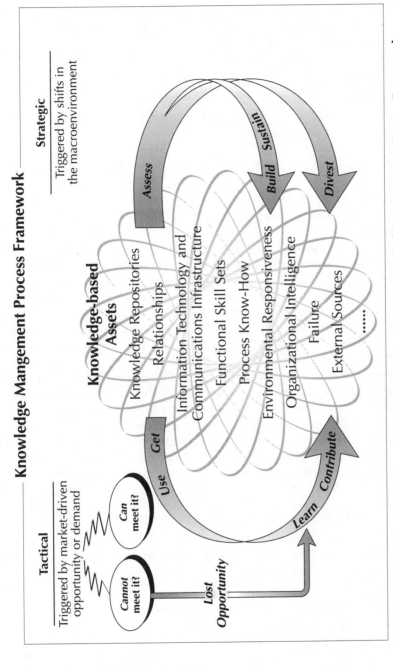

**Exhibit 33.1** Knowledge Management Process Framework. The Knowledge Management Process Framework provides a complete picture of the entire knowledge management process and indicates how its parts are related. The framework is a simplified way of thinking about how organizations generate, maintain, and deploy a strategically correct stock of knowledge-based assets to create value.

the basic building blocks of the knowledge management process and suggests how they interact to create value from knowledge-based assets. It follows two streams of activity that occur simultaneously in organizations:

1. The day-to-day use of knowledge to respond to demands or opportunities from the marketplace.
2. The more long-range process of creating and matching organizational knowledge assets to strategic requirements.

The framework is a simplified way of thinking about how organizations generate, maintain, and deploy a strategically correct stock of knowledge-based assets to create value. All the elements within the process must be managed in relation to one another to achieve the right mix and amount of knowledge-based assets and the capability to sustain and deploy them.

While the process steps flow into one another, thus making the distinctions between them blurred rather than sharp, the activities within each step cohere sufficiently to group them together. (This, of course, is the central lie of any management model—it presents an inherently messy and sloppy process as an organized and segmented set of activities.) Discussing the knowledge management process framework is a bit like learning the grammar of a foreign language. We first have to learn all the rules before we can even begin to grapple with the fact that at least half of the language (if not more) is an exception to those rules.

The first question that comes to mind from study of the process steps of the Knowledge Management Process Framework (Get, Use, Learn, Contribute, Assess, Build and Sustain, and Divest) might be: "How is this process different from the process I go through to generate value from any other resource?" The answer: At the macrolevel of the process steps, it is not very different. But drilling down within the process steps, we can begin to see how trying to extract value from knowledge-based assets invites organizations to experiment with a different set of operating practices. Knowledge management presents an opportunity to view the organization from a different angle, to ponder the changing dynamics of wealth creation, and to ask how the organization might be managed differently to capitalize on them.

**(a) Tactical Process Steps**    The tactical side of the knowledge management process spans four basic steps. Specifically, people:

1. Gather the information they need for their daily work.
2. Use knowledge to create value.
3. Learn from what they create.
4. Feed this new knowledge back into the system for others to use as they tackle problems of their own.

Each step requires the participation of everyone in the organization in some fashion and to some extent for the process to flow. The tactical process steps occur in a decentralized environment in which individuals make decisions about how best to get their daily work accomplished.

*(i) Get and Use*   Getting and using knowledge is old hat for most organizations. People have always scrambled to gather information that can solve problems or inform decisions. However, new technologies that allow tsunamis of information to course through organizations have forever changed these two process steps in some ways and left them remarkably untouched in others.

In the past, many decisions were based on a limited set of information. Time and money constrained how much information could be profitably obtained and used to reach a decision. Now, instead of being forced to take action based on little or no information, people are more likely to find that the challenge is slogging through mountains of irrelevant information to get to the one "nugget" that is critical to their needs. Ironically, the decision-making process with little or with lots of information still looks pretty much the same—shoot from the hip.

How can getting information be more *efficient*? Mainly through the tools and services that an organization makes available to its members. (Throughout this chapter, the term "member" describes those who work for organizations. Member is preferable to employee because the people who generate, maintain, and deploy knowledge in organizations extend far beyond the limits of employees. Temporary workers, contractors, consultants, alliance partners, suppliers, regulators, and even competitors can be part of the organization's membership group.)

By and large, the tools and services that an organization makes available to its members are information technology systems that gather, codify, store, and disseminate documents of some type. The documents may be highly animated and interactive (e.g., those found in computer-based training modules) or they may be limited to text and entirely static (e.g., blueprints or schematics). The services that augment these tools are often the key to their utility. In their electronic form, they come as powerful language-based search engines and intelligent agents; in their human form, as "cybrarians" and knowledge managers. Whether electronic or human, they are a new breed of knowledge guides that intelligently filter out the din of too much information.

When it comes to using information, innovation has become the new standard. With markets narrowed to a unit of one and customer expectations skyrocketing, companies are scrambling to "mass customize" their offerings. But being able to respond to a specific customer request is only half the battle. The other half is anticipating future requests and teaching customers to want your company's products or services. How can members of an organization rise to this challenge of combining information in new and interesting ways to create more *innovative and specific* solutions?

People have to climb out of their silos and look for ideas in places they would not have otherwise considered. The challenge is that when they do, they venture onto another's turf. To counteract the urge to protect turf from outsiders, an organization must establish an environment in which creativity, experimentation, and receptivity to new ideas are encouraged. At the microlevel, it can promote the much-desired practice of "out-of-the box thinking" with approaches such as "mindscaping," which uses graphical representations to stimulate new ways of associating ideas.

Other techniques include playing with toys, theater games, and storytelling to help people connect with the full range of their problem-solving skills. At a macrolevel, work-space design that intentionally causes random encounters and organizational design that messes up the formal hierarchy and forces people to consider who *needs* to know rather than who *is authorized* to know are mechanisms that promote, if they cannot guarantee, behaviors that lead to innovative solutions.

*(ii) Learn and Contribute*    The process steps "Learn" and "Contribute" are relatively new to most organizations. This is not to suggest that in the past no one learned from experience or contributed to the organizational knowledge base. However, the formal recognition of these process steps as a means of creating competitive advantage *is* new.

To conceive of learning as an explicit process step is a particularly formidable shift in thinking for most organizations. The drive toward action—which is understood as doing something visible—so dominates business culture that the act of learning (which is fundamentally invisible) is seen as doing nothing.

Learning is also highly personal and idiosyncratic. Although it is possible to support learning behaviors, it is not possible to ensure that learning occurs. Nor is it possible to ensure that learning that benefits the organization will occur. For these reasons, organizations rely on learning techniques that explicitly link individual insight to organizational strategy, including computer- or board-based simulations and other experiential learning activities, such as the Outward Bound experience. The objective is to provide a focus for learning so that when it occurs, it can be directly related and ultimately applied to the work of the organization.

Getting employees to contribute what they have learned to the communal knowledge base is one of the toughest nuts organizations have to crack. The benefits of a contribution to the company are clear: The organization can save time and money by transferring "best practices" across the organization and by applying knowledge gained from one experience to another.

Technology has made it relatively easy to organize, post, and transfer certain types of information. Creating a knowledge management infrastructure that makes contributing what you know relatively easy can help with some of the tedious requirements of "packaging" information for organizationwide consumption. For example, most people faced with a blank piece of paper will be hard-pressed to list the 10 most important facts they know about their area of expertise. However, these same people can expound for hours on the topic if they are expertly interviewed or if they are asked an interesting question by a colleague who has also thought about the topic. For these reasons conducting executive debriefings and forming "communities of practice" are some of the ways that organizations help people share what they know.

But the benefits of sharing are not so clear to an individual employee: Contribution is time-consuming, and it can even be seen as a one-way ticket out of the organization. If employees share what they know and do not believe that the organization is interested in supporting their transition to other work, they have little motivation to share. It is therefore a great challenge to run an organization in which people believe that contribution will ultimately pay off both for the organization and for themselves.

**(b) Strategic Process Steps**    The goal of the strategic side of the Knowledge Management Process Framework is alignment of the organization's development and deployment of knowledge-based assets with the overall business strategy.

Strategic-level knowledge management calls for a continual assessment of existing knowledge assets; the question is whether those assets seem likely to meet anticipated demands in the future. While individuals and groups are clearly involved in providing the information that eventually has an impact on resource allocation decisions, organizational leadership and specialized groups tend to dominate this part of the knowledge management process. Yet the strategic process steps should not follow a top-down approach. Strategy may be the purview of an organization's leadership, but it is not leadership as usual.

Leaders as coaches who ask questions rather than provide answers and who inspire others to scale new heights have replaced leaders as authority figures who rule from on high. But behind this bright and shiny façade is a gritty reality: The leader who operates in reduced circumstances; the leader who cannot control, but must persuade; and the leader with limits. In this view, leadership is one role among many in the organization. The leader may be the star, but without the bit players, there is no show. This is the reality of the leadership role in the knowledge management process.

Organizations have not traditionally considered intellectual assets part of the strategic planning process, but this is precisely what strategic-level knowledge management entails. We will neatly sidestep the question about whether strategic planning in most organizations occurs at all without becoming subverted by the annual skirmish over budget and assume that, at the very least, a strategic point-of-view influences the annual budget.

The annual budget is important because it is the statement that reflects how an organization intends to allocate resources during its next operating cycle. Investments in intangibles such as training, brands or marketing, and research and development are frequently part of the annual budget discussion. For most organizations, however, it is unclear how investments in these intangibles generate value.

*(i) Assess*    The process step "Assess" requires that organizations understand what creates value and how it is created. One of the most pernicious assumptions in business today is that organizations possess this understanding—a questionable assumption, at best.

In large part, the confusion over what creates value has come about with the dramatic explosion of the "informating" potential of information technology. Shoshanna Zuboff (in her ground-breaking book *In the Age of the Smart Machine*[4]) coined this term to describe how primary information spawns secondary information and often supplants it in terms of usefulness. Since then, others have extended the concept of infomating to describe the growing importance of intangibles as sources of value creation.

For example, some of these thinkers argue that what customers at on-line bookseller amazon.com really purchase is the experience of visiting the company's website. Once there, they can read reviews, chat with other readers, post their own reviews, and maybe even purchase a book. The value that amazon.com offers these readers is an experience. To create that experience, the company has to amass and analyze a huge amount of information about them and other readers. The company's source of value creation lies not so much in its ability to quickly locate and ship books to customers, but rather in its ability to gather and use information that customers freely contribute about themselves.

In this new information economy (as it is often called), the old rules of developing and winning markets seem not to apply. Suddenly product companies feel compelled to expand into services, while service organizations vie to create products. Michael Schrage has named these strange hybrids "prodices" and "serducts." How does leadership in an organization cope with this brave new world of prodices and serducts? How can leadership begin to assess whether its investment in knowledge-based assets will channel activities in ways that create value?

First, leadership must embrace a new theory of the organization that visualizes new sources of value creation. The Intellectual Capital Model is one model that has been widely promoted in the past few years to explain how intellectual capital creates value (see Exhibit 33.2). This model was developed in a collaborative effort that included Leif Edvinsson at Skandia, Hubert St. Onge at The Mutual Group, Gordon Petrash at PricewaterhouseCoopers, and Charles Armstrong of Armstrong Industries. It proposes a scenario in which organizations need to simultaneously manage different types of capital in order to create value.

Components of the Intellectual Capital Model are:

- *Human capital.* Competencies, mind-sets, and the ability of individuals and teams to apply solutions to customers' needs.
- *Customer capital.* The strength of the customer relationship; superior customer-perceived value; increasing customization of solutions.
- *Organizational capital.* Capabilities of the organization, which are made up of codified knowledge from all sources (e.g., knowledge bases, business processes, and the technology infrastructure); the shared culture, values, and norms.
- *Intellectual capital.* The relationships between human, customer, and organizational capital, which maximizes the organization's potential to create value. (This potential is ultimately realized in some form of wealth.)

The dotted lines in the diagram shown in Exhibit 33.2 represent the knowledge flows between the three types of capital. The better these flows are managed, the more the in-

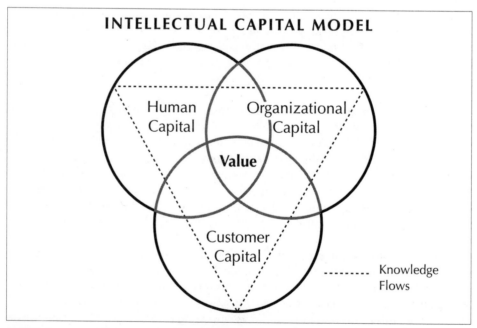

**Exhibit 33.2   Intellectual Capital Model. Organizations need to manage the knowledge flows between these three different types of capital in order to generate value from intellectual capital.**

terrelationships between the three types of capital reinforce one another. As these three types of capital interact in concert, the organization is better positioned to create value. It is also possible for an organization to destroy the potential for creating value if it does not manage in an integrated way the three types of capital that make up intellectual capital.

In addition to a new model of value creation, an organization needs to experiment with a wider range of information sources and analytic methods to assess its stewardship of knowledge-based assets. Metric development for knowledge-based assets is in the experimental stage, which means that the metrics themselves are highly unstable. This can be disconcerting for traditionalists, who want to create a watertight system of metrics that can then be compared over time and rolled up, down, and across the organization. However, not enough is known to propose such a system of measures. (Enough is known to share emerging practices: See the Ramboll case history later in this chapter.)

Knowledge management metrics in use today attempt to complete the picture of how well an organization builds, replenishes, or depletes its total asset base. Some of the metrics are familiar—for example, percentage of sales from new products, number of college graduates, time to market, and employee turnover. They are used as leading indicators of future value creation. Others seek to establish a new way of understanding how well an organization creates and maintains the right knowledge-based assets—for example, return on people, a "rookie ratio," a loyal customer percentage, and the number of ideas generated.

In addition to metrics that are computed from "hard" data, an increasing number of "soft" or qualitative metrics have crept into the repertoire. The precedent of soft metrics was set by customer and employee satisfaction surveys, which have become widely accepted measurement tools. The knowledge management movement has extended the use of soft measures into areas such as organizational capability, including such capabilities as innovation potential and knowledge-absorption capacity.

*(ii) Build and Sustain*   To build future knowledge-based assets that keep an organization viable and competitive, companies must take a fresh look at what it means to manage. Increasingly, organizations are building their intellectual assets through relationships with employees, suppliers, customers, the communities in which they operate, and even competitors.

Relationships are rightly seen as a hedge against the fragmentation inherent in hypercompetition. They have the potential to be more enduring than a discrete transaction. Deriving value from relationships will ultimately force traditional management, which emphasizes direct control of people, to give way to a more facilitative style of management, one that emphasizes the management of environments and enablers. This is especially important because value creation relies increasingly on maintaining a complex and shifting web of stakeholder relationships, both within and outside the traditional corporate boundaries, in which ownership of intellectual assets is rarely exclusive.

A hot debate simmers between those who advocate shareholder value creation as the *sine qua non* of value measures and those who prefer the more diffused stakeholder value creation. Strong and cogent arguments have been made for giving the highest priority to creation of shareholder value. The essence of these arguments is that organizations have a hard time focusing on more than one objective, so they are forced into making tradeoffs between competing objectives. Shareholder value makes the most sense as the number-one objective, because unless owners' needs are satisfied, it will be impossible to satisfy the needs of any other stakeholders. Once owners' demands for value creation are met, everything else can be sorted out.

Although this is a gross simplification of the elegant arguments advanced on behalf of shareholder value creation, it lays out the basic components. In the best postmodern tradition, these arguments deconstruct themselves in the making. It is a fact that organizations have a hard time focusing on more than one objective. But that is precisely the challenge—to be able to see the organization as a whole system with interrelated parts that require simultaneous monitoring and management.

It is true that, at certain times, the needs of owners must take precedence over those of other stakeholders—but not always. The view of how value is created must be flexible enough to respond to varied circumstances, yet still suggest productive courses of action. Always spitting out exactly the same direction—to satisfy shareholder value creation objectives—is one size that may not fit all. A trickle-down theory that indicates that everything else will somehow be sorted out later is, in reality, simply passing the buck. Sorting everything out is what the challenge of building and sustaining knowledge assets is all about.

*(iii) Divest*   Divesting knowledge-based assets conflicts with the tendency of organizations to hold on to assets (whether knowledge-based or otherwise) even if they provide no direct competitive advantage. Political and personal capital are deeply embedded in the development of any organizational assets, and intellectual assets are no exception.

Careers have been built on painstakingly nurturing a specific way of doing business into being. The idea that a company may no longer invest in a particular business by ceasing to fund research and development and not developing the talent needed to continue is frequently met with massive resistance. This idea is especially hard to swallow if the business is successful when the company decides to quit funding it. However, this is precisely the path that more and more companies follow when they try to clear space for the businesses that will keep them viable in the future.

It is a constant effort to remove clutter and provide resources for future sources of value while also running today's operations. In many instances, it is also a painfully difficult effort, because people's lives are disrupted by the continuous shifts that organizations undergo to fit themselves to the contours of gyrating markets.

Who does not know someone who joined a company only to be confronted by a reorganization and asked to relocate within the first six months of employment? Constant reorganizations used to be considered a signal that management did not have a firm grip on the fundamentals of the business. Today it is just business as usual.

Divesting knowledge-based assets is fast becoming part of business as usual, too. Organizations that begin to examine their knowledge-based assets in terms of both opportunity costs—resources spent on maintaining those assets that could be better spent elsewhere—and alternative sources of value are well positioned to realize the benefits of divestiture.

**33.4 HAZARDS AND DETOURS**   Knowledge management has the feel of a "bandwagon": Suddenly everyone, everywhere wants to be *the* knowledge management resource. Xerox is not the document company anymore, it is the knowledge company. So are IBM, Arthur Andersen, Ernst & Young, Compaq Computer, Microsoft, Intel, and so on. The list is endless and endlessly expanding. It extends well beyond consultants and those in the computer industry to include banks, booksellers, and retail boutiques. Why? Everyone has sniffed out the high probability that knowledge really will be the only source of sustainable competitive advantage in the future. No one can prove it, but it makes consummate sense that in a knowledge- or information-based economy, collective corporate smarts will separate the survivors from the has-beens.

And that is precisely the rub: No one can prove it. Current evaluation techniques falter when they try to rise to the level of proof. This means that organizations are vulnerable to finding themselves at a knowledge-management impasse. As organizations navigate through the new territory of knowledge management, what hazards and detours are they likely to encounter? How have some leading organizations managed to bypass or surmount them?

The hazards and detours tend to manifest themselves as institutional debates. Reasonable people take what look like reasonable positions on important knowledge management issues and find themselves locked in opposition, with no way to resolve the stalemate. The way out of this bind is to enlarge the framework so that the picture is big enough to contain the opposites. This may sound like mumbo-jumbo, but knowledge management requires that people look at their organizations from a radically different point of view, because their old views force a dichotomy where none exists. The dichotomies fade away when the frame is wider.

Organizations will encounter many minor hazards and detours on the way to knowledge management, but three of the most problematic are:

1. Philosophy versus practicality.
2. Technology versus people.
3. Faith versus measurement.

In an effort to expand the boundaries of how organizations are traditionally viewed to make room for a new picture big enough to transform these "either/ors" into "both/ands," the sections that follow address each of these topics in turn.

**(a) Philosophy versus Practicality**   This debate starts with what are we talking about and ends with people throwing up their hands and saying that the entire topic of knowledge management is beyond discussion.

Knowledge management is an oxymoron (i.e., a figure of speech in which two contradictory terms are combined). How can we manage knowledge? It is too soft, it is stuck in people's heads, we cannot control it. How can we manage the unmanageable? The business of business is not philosophy; it is creating value and generating wealth. Discomfort levels rise precipitously when businesspeople feel they are venturing into the realm of ivory-tower thought.

Cutting through the anxiety and getting to the core of the problem, the main objection to the term "management" in "knowledge management" seems to be about the stuff that is being managed. The stuff, knowledge, is fluid, mercurial, context-dependent, subjective, relational, hard to pin down, multidimensional, self-organizing, and a lot of other unmanageable-sounding things. It is a lot like people. Yet we have been talking about managing people as long as there have been organizations and no one objects. The fact is, an organization does not really manage people *or* their knowledge: It guides, cultivates, and influences. But it *does* manage processes that support people and their efforts to create value in the organization, and a process exists for knowledge creation and sharing.

Some of the elements of this process can be overtly managed in the way that most organizational processes are managed. Other elements must be managed indirectly, by creating hospitable environments that encourage people to act in specific ways.

*(i) The Dow Chemical Company: A Process for Managing Intellectual Assets*
*The Dow Chemical Company has created a process to respond to the practical demands of knowledge management. Dow has instituted a change to its organizational structure to respond to the philosophical demands of managing the unmanageable.*

In 1992, The Dow Chemical Company launched its Intellectual Asset Management (IAM) group to examine not only patents but also all the company's other intellectual assets. The new IAM group started life as a central staff group, but within two years, most IAM managers were full members of the business units they served.

The IAM group has been instrumental in helping Dow's businesses think about the company's intellectual assets in new ways. The Dow IAM process has played a key role in developing this new perspective. The most significant impact within the larger organization has been in stimulating cross-functional discussions within the business units. The IAM group is developing new ways to leverage the IAM "fishnet" structure (see Exhibit 33.3), which weaves functional expertise with expertise in business strategy to even greater advantage for the company.

*(ii) The Dow Chemical Company's Intellectual Assets Management Process*    The Dow IAM Process (see Exhibit 33.4) has been in use since 1993, when it was launched to improve the company's ability to extract value from its patent portfolio. Its scope has been significantly expanded since then to include trademarks, trade secrets, disclosures of inventions, and key technical know-how (including process methodology, training manuals, and information about critically skilled personnel). Although the major activities of the process have been labeled and organized sequentially for the purposes of explaining the IAM process, in reality the process is continuous, and the steps overlap. The six major initiatives of the process are:

1. *Initiative 1: Portfolio.* The Dow Intellectual Asset Portfolio is created by asking each business to articulate its stock of intellectual assets. These range from patents and trade secrets to technical know-how. This activity ensures that Dow catalogs all existing intellectual assets.

2. *Initiative 2: Assets Classification.* This initiative organizes intellectual assets in terms of their value or potential value to the business. Although the process that Dow uses to manage intellectual assets is complex, for the purposes of an overview it can be simplified into three "umbrella" value categories that each share two dimensions of use. Two of the "umbrella" value categories represent streams within the Dow organization, whereas the third represents a stream to an outside party. Information about intellectual assets is logged into a computer database using common templates and terms to facilitate search and retrieval.

3. *Initiative 3: Strategy.* Strategy is the initiative that ensures that a business strategy includes intellectual assets. The process includes an analysis of how to leverage

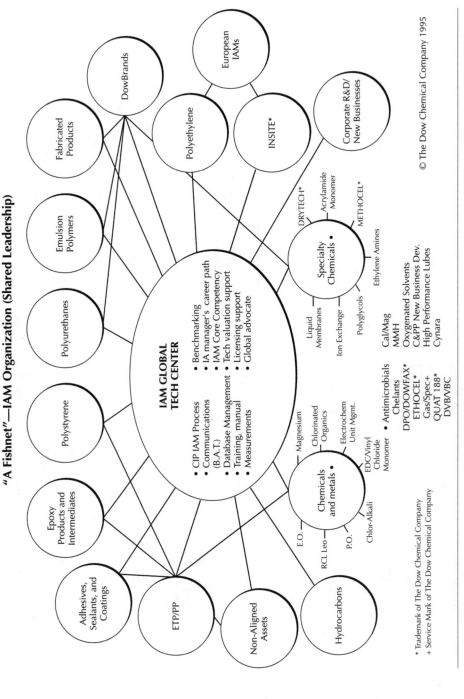

"A Fishnet"—IAM Organization (Shared Leadership)

© The Dow Chemical Company 1995

* Trademark of The Dow Chemical Company
+ Service Mark of The Dow Chemical Company

**Exhibit 33.3** "A Fishnet"—Intellectual Asset Management Organization (Shared Leadership). *Source:* The Dow Chemical Company, 1995. The Dow Chemical Company's Intellectual Asset Management organization started out as a centralized staff function that was transitioned over to the business units. Retaining functional links among the intellectual asset managers who are now part of the business units is one way that the group promotes knowledge sharing.

# INTELLECTUAL ASSET MANAGEMENT PROCESS

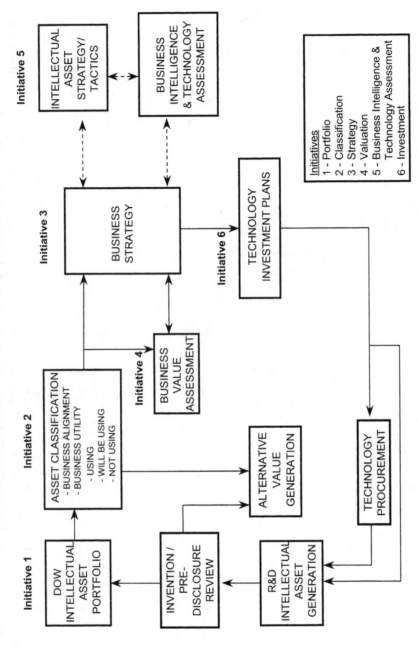

Copyright © The Dow Chemical Company, 1998.

**Exhibit 33.4 Intellectual Asset Management Process.** *Source:* **The Dow Chemical Company, 1995. The Dow Chemical Company's Intellectual Asset Management (IAM) process organizes the major activities that the company uses to strategically manage its intellectual assets.**

full value from existing intellectual assets, develop plans that close strategic intellectual asset gaps, and respond to competitive threats. The intellectual asset management tactics are developed to support the business strategy.

4. *Initiative 4: Valuation.* Valuation approaches at Dow include all standard valuation techniques plus a methodology developed in partnership with Arthur D. Little called the Technology Factor Method (*Technology Factor* is a registered trademark of Arthur D. Little). This activity places a monetary value on intellectual assets based on the plans of a specific business.

5. *Initiative 5: Business intelligence and technology assessment.* Intellectual assets are examined in light of what can be gleaned about the competition's business intentions for its intellectual assets—in terms of both the products that the competition plans to bring to market and the underlying technologies that support those product offerings. In addition, likely competitive responses to Dow's intellectual assets strategy and tactics are considered.

6. *Initiative 6: Investment.* Investment fills strategic gaps by assessing outside intellectual assets or capabilities and determining whether to acquire or internally develop them.

**(b) Technology versus People**   One of the biggest conundrums of knowledge management is that we would not be talking about it if information technology had not so thoroughly altered the landscape, yet knowledge management is not synonymous with information technology. This assertion flies in the face of the many business publications that have substituted the word "knowledge" for "information" in their titles, hoping to hook their stars to the more strategic-sounding knowledge management arena.

Label swapping has confused more than it has clarified. When people hear about knowledge management, they typically ask: "Isn't that what companies are trying to achieve with Enterprise Resource Planning (ERP) systems?" The answer: "Yes and no." The ostensible aim of ERP systems is to deliver more complete and accurate information to decision makers. If we assume that they achieve their objective, the challenge remains—will the decision maker act on the information?

These ERP systems are supposed to deliver information that was previously unavailable and, presumably, not acted on. It is highly likely that when decision makers receive this new information, it will conflict with the way the organization has previously understood its situation. Now, it is up to the decision maker to come forward with this new, contradictory picture of the business and to propose change.

However, in many companies, disturbing the status quo is not well received. Rarely is it in anyone's best interests to shake things up. So, how likely is it that the decision maker will act on this new information? Not likely at all, as personal and organizational agendas diverge wildly. For this reason, information technology solutions are only a piece of the knowledge management puzzle. Encouraging people to behave in ways that are personally challenging but organizationally necessary is another piece that is needed to complete the puzzle. (More on the measurement puzzle piece follows.)

In large part, eliciting changes in the way people behave is important, because the kind of knowledge that can be easily codified and transferred using information technology represents only the tip of the iceberg. Beneath the water line lies a massive body of knowledge that powerfully affects organizational outcomes despite its shadowy, hidden nature. In 1991, Ikujiro Nonaka and Hirotaka Takeuchi wrote *The Knowledge-*

*Creating Company,* which introduced U.S. and European businesspeople to the concepts of explicit and tacit knowledge, which roughly correspond to our tip of the iceberg and its hidden, water-encased mass.

*(i) Explicit and Tacit Knowledge*   What Nonaka and Takeuchi call "explicit knowledge" is knowledge that individuals are able to express fairly easily to the external world using language or other forms of communication. When this knowledge is expressed, it becomes information. What they refer to as "tacit knowledge" is knowledge that an individual is unable to articulate and thereby convert into information. This is the type of knowledge that star athletes possess. It is difficult to dissect their winning style into a set of skills, because the skills have become deeply ingrained through the force of constant practice and blended into an amalgam that is difficult to replicate. This is the type of knowledge that people describe as "gut feel," which is often based on years of experience that comes to the fore at specific moments. It is knowledge that companies intuitively understand will give them a competitive edge. They also recognize that they cannot demand it; they must nurture it. For this reason, creating environments in which people feel inspired receives serious attention these days.

*(ii) False Belief Test*   The existence of tacit knowledge is a fact, not a wish. An experiment that is frequently performed with young children verifies the reality of tacit knowledge. "The false belief test" is described as follows:

> . . . a measure of how well one individual can appreciate that another individual might have a mental geography that differs from one's own. . . . [To conduct the test] . . . a banana is placed in a box while three 3-year-olds are observing. Two of the toddlers are removed from the room and the third is allowed to observe the researcher moving the banana from the box to a basket. The question: When the toddlers who have been removed are returned to the room, will the toddler who remained indicate that s/he knows that they hold a false belief about the location of the banana?
> The results indicate that the toddler who has observed the switch recognizes that the other two hold a false belief—s/he looks towards the box in the belief that this is where the returning toddlers will look for the banana. "Interestingly, when 3-year-olds are asked, . . . where the benighted individuals will look, they say, 'The basket.' Their eyes look at the right place [the box], but they can't yet express their awareness of the deception. . . . They have implicit [tacit] rather than explicit knowledge." By 4, the children make the correct response with language as well as eye gaze.[5]

That said, using information technology as a tool for codifying and transferring knowledge is not to be dismissed. Giancarlo Scoditti, an Italian anthropologist who has studied a particular Melanesian society called Kitawa, has noted the tremendous importance of codifying a language and its stories (which roughly corresponds to business process and best practices).

Kitawa, is an atoll in the Trobriand Island archipelago, about 300 miles from the capital of Papua New Guinea. The Kitawans had no written tradition before Scoditti made it his life's work to codify their language and culture. What he found as he studied the degradation of the Kitawan culture in the more than 25 years he has worked with them is that "oral societies . . . are both tremendously robust and extremely fragile. Until the arrival of Europeans, most Pacific islands had maintained their traditions from generation to generation for hundreds, if not thousands, of years. But contact with other cultures and technologies can cause the chain of knowledge to break down, and if one generation fails to transmit what it knows to the next *millennia of accumulated wisdom can be lost in a few decades"* (emphasis added).[6]

For most contemporary organizations, constant contact with the outside world is the norm. In fact, the "boundaryless" organization is venerated as an ideal. But, as the Kitawan story warns, the absence of boundaries without some form of knowledge codification can subject organizational systems to severe and permanent knowledge loss. This is one reason that organizations must nurture both explicit and tacit knowledge by focusing on both information technology and people.

*(iii) Hewlett-Packard: Connecting People to People Through Information*
*Although the case study that follows falls short of demonstrating that the company has figured out how to use information technology as a conduit for tacit knowledge, it shows how to creatively structure an incentive system that shapes new behaviors. These new behaviors expose people to others with whom they previously might have had little contact through information available on an Intranet. Ultimately, the benefit of this contact through information might serve to connect people to people and boost the transfer of tacit knowledge.*

It is difficult to get people to share what they know, especially with those outside their departments or units. The problem is twofold:

1. It takes time to help out.
2. It is hard to justify when a person is managing to a tight departmental budget.

Hewlett-Packard created a "micropayment" system, in which individuals who wanted to view or download information would be charged a small fee payable to the department of the individual or team that supplies the information.

This approach has helped to erode the barriers of sharing outside departments for several reasons. First, one of the trade-offs of Hewlett-Packard's decentralized structure is a reliance on internal fund transfers to pay for services, from training to travel. However, from an accounting perspective, billing for small services rendered is costly. As a result, many shared services are rolled into overhead; business units are charged a set amount regardless of how often the services are used.

The microeconomy concept eliminates the trade-off for information products that can be accessed electronically. It creates a "pay per view" situation in which consumers of information are charged for precisely what they use.

The microeconomy addressed another problem at Hewlett-Packard: getting people to share information outside their local environment. What blocks sharing is the extra effort it takes to share knowledge with people in different parts of the organization. It often means finding the time to provide additional documentation, context setting, or personal support. Furthermore, the payback is not always easy to trace.

The microeconomy system creates an infrastructure that supports payments of as little as a few cents. Charges can be either transaction-based (in which each instance of access results in a charge) or subscription-based (in which subscribers have unlimited access to material for a specified period of time). The system is a real benefit for contributors because it makes the impact of their contributions visible. In addition, in the past there was no way (other than collecting testimonials) to demonstrate that certain knowledge resources benefited the organization, now the microeconomy systems offers both the proof and the funding to continue supporting them.

**(c) Faith versus Measurement**    Those who espouse the benefits of knowledge management often come across as zealots whose persuasion amounts to little more than a deep faith that these benefits will emerge at some future date. The plain commonsense nature of the entire value proposition for knowledge management is supposed to be a good enough justification for the investment. Yet, as anyone who has tried to justify a budget proposal knows, at the end of the day, numbers talk.

For the knowledge management practitioner, the numbers present an enormous challenge. Although it is possible to figure out the costs of investing in knowledge management initiatives (such as team building, work-space design, best-practices databases, and new positions such as knowledge managers and chief knowledge officers), determining expected benefits and the payback period stymie the best manager.

*(i) Measurement and Valuation*    The Hewlett-Packard example shows how a company might demonstrate payback, but it is limited to one kind of knowledge sharing—information contained in documents (i.e., explicit knowledge). How does one justify investments that create environments in which people are inspired to innovate? Despite a growing body of work in the twin areas of measurement and valuation, the art and science of intellectual asset measurement and valuation are in their infancy within organizational systems.

The distinction between measurement and valuation is not well understood by most managers. In brief, valuation places a monetary value on the expected cash flow from an asset or a group of assets that either currently exists or that is expected to exist with some degree of probability. Measurement covers an entirely different territory. It seeks to describe a particular organizational state by quantifying its inputs and outputs. Measurement is good at understanding what is going on and relating activity to operational outcomes such as effectiveness and efficiency. It is not as good at relating effectiveness and efficiency to financial outcomes. For a true science of knowledge management measurement to develop, the fields of valuation and measurement must be combined to create a new discipline. Academic work from economists and accountants in these areas over the past decade has just begun to penetrate the world of business.

Adding to the problem of organizations accepting these new metrics is the fact that they are trickling into a system already awash in measures. A 1998 study on attitudes and practices about knowledge measurement conducted by Arthur Andersen's Next Generation Group indicated that three-quarters of its global survey group received two or more categories of measures in addition to traditional financial measures on a regular basis. These categories included:

- Customer satisfaction
- Employee satisfaction
- Market share
- Cycle time

- Quality
- Intellectual capital or knowledge measurement

The report concluded that "organizations are swimming in a sea of metric information. Introducing IC [intellectual capital] metrics into the picture may feel like adding more clutter to a battery of metrics . . . [than clarifying the picture]."[7]

However, faith (or at least a new perspective) does enter the picture when organizations face the challenge of envisioning how they create value, which is the first step toward developing measures that matter. As we discussed previously, new models of value creation are essential to understanding the role that knowledge plays in an organization (see the Intellectual Capital Model in Exhibit 33.2, described in section 33.3(b)).

Without a framework to capture the role that knowledge plays in generating value, it is impossible to know what to measure. The traditional business model—as expressed in the financial statements—falls decidedly short of this aim. Its shortcomings are well-known and acknowledged by those who prepare these statements:

> What is a company worth? Accountants all know that a balance sheet is not a guide to value. What are a company's prospects? All accountants know that a historical profit and loss account is not necessarily a guide to sustainable earnings. What risks does a company face? Accountants all know that accounts do not explicitly deal with risks. What are a company's intangible assets (let alone what are they worth)? Accountants know that accounts do not speculate about such matters." (Chris Swinson, President, Institute of Chartered Accountants in England and Wales, Senior Partner, BDO Stoy Hayward.)[8]

Measurement and valuation approaches will ultimately determine whether knowledge management fades into fad or becomes inseparable from good management prac-

### Ramboll's Holistic Accounts

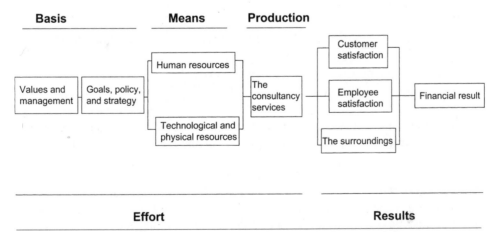

Exhibit 33.5    Ramboll's Holistic Accounts. Ramboll takes a process-based approach to envisioning how the creation and use of knowledge influence financial results.

tice. Although this may seem like a bold claim, numbers are the *lingua franca* of the business world. They are the unifying structure that permits comparison of one possibility to another and can stimulate deep thought about the future. The next decade will be an exciting time for those engaged in building new models and new measurement systems for organizations. These people are pioneering the future, prospecting with analytical tools, seeking gold.

*(ii) Ramboll*

*Ramboll is a consultancy in engineering, management, and related fields with about 2,000 employees. The company is based in Denmark and conducts projects in Europe, Africa, Asia, and Russia. Since the mid-1990s, Ramboll has published a set of intellectual capital accounts that it calls The Holistic Accounts. The Holistic Accounts reflect commitment to the Ramboll philosophy, an expression of the ethical behavior that the company's leadership strives to embody in all organizational activities, by measuring it.*

Ramboll takes a process-based approach to envisioning how the creation and use of knowledge influence financial results (see Exhibit 33.5). It starts with an articulation of how values and management philosophy affect the way in which human, technological, and physical resources are managed to deliver consulting services and then ultimately achieve financial results as well as a high level of employee and customer satisfaction.

Ramboll hooks metrics to each process step as a means of evaluating the company's management of its intellectual assets. Metric information is culled from existing sources because the company does not wish to establish a comprehensive and costly information-gathering system for this purpose alone. Information gathered for other purposes is reused as far as possible. For instance, customer satisfaction and employee satisfaction surveys generate the data required to compute 22 metrics in four categories for customer satisfaction, and 76 metrics grouped in nine categories for employee satisfaction.

For other process steps (such as technology), the metrics are standard and "countable." They include:

- Investment in research and development (projects that develop new methodologies within Ramboll).
- Investment in information technology platform.
- Percentage system failures.

All in all, the Ramboll value-creation process contains several hundred metrics. However, only a subset of the metrics is actively used in any given year, based on the company's strategic focus.

**33.5 PRIORITIZING EFFORTS**    Reflecting on knowledge management in a specific organization raises the question of where to begin. To help answer that question, this section presents a basic diagnostic tool (see Exhibit 33.6). Although it does not go into detail, this diagnostic tool gives a quick picture of where an organization stands in relation to knowledge management today, along with clues about where the organization might benefit the most by making a few changes.

### Instructions

Read each statement below and rate how well it describes your organization by checking the appropriate box:

- Very Well
- Somewhat
- Not at All

When you have finished rating your organization, tally up your total points for each knowledge management process step and plot them on the spider chart that appears below.

| | Describes our organization | | |
|---|---|---|---|
| | VERY WELL | SOME WHAT | NOT AT ALL |
| | ✓ | ✓ | ✓ |
| **GET** | | | |
| People can describe their information needs. | | | |
| People know where to find knowledge resources. | | | |
| People have the tools they need to find and capture information. | | | |
| People with clearly established roles are available to support information seekers. | | | |
| Our knowledge infrastructure is comprehensive and well-organized. | | | |
| **USE** | | | |
| Our organizational structure supports communications and knowledge flows. | | | |
| Our physical environment cross-fertilizes ideas. | | | |
| We treat information as an open resource that flows freely to all parts of the organization. | | | |
| We collaborate on a routine basis with stakeholder communities. | | | |
| People are generally comfortable about acting on new ideas. | | | |
| **LEARN** | | | |
| We consider failure an opportunity to learn. | | | |
| Our organization supports group activities that promote mutual learning. | | | |
| People admit when they fail. | | | |
| Reflecting on lessons learned is an established practice in our organization. | | | |
| When we have a big success, we talk about what we did right. | | | |

**Exhibit 33.6    Knowledge Management Diagnostic Tool**

Once an organization rates itself on the five statements listed for each knowledge management process step, it should compute its score and plot it on the empty "spider" chart that follows the diagnostic. The ideal space for knowledge management is sketched on the spider chart so that an organization can also compare how far from that ideal it stands today.

Another way to use this quick diagnostic tool to stimulate discussion in an organization is to ask a few people to complete it, then have a meeting to talk about differences and similarities among the spider charts.

| | Describes our organization | | |
|---|---|---|---|
| | *VERY WELL* | *SOME WHAT* | *NOT AT ALL* |
| | ✓ | ✓ | ✓ |
| **CONTRIBUTE** | | | |
| There are few barriers to sharing knowledge in our organization. | | | |
| People can find the time to share what they know. | | | |
| We have explicit policies about the use of other people's information. | | | |
| People who don't share what they know, don't get ahead. | | | |
| The communications infrastructure makes it easy to share what you know. | | | |
| **ASSESS** | | | |
| Managers consider knowledge to be one of the primary assets we use to create value. | | | |
| People understand how knowledge contributes to the value of our products (services). | | | |
| We measure our knowledge management process and its results. | | | |
| We routinely share information about the knowledge management process across the organization. | | | |
| Our knowledge management process is linked to our overall business strategy. | | | |
| **BUILD/SUSTAIN** | | | |
| We allocate resources in ways that build strategic knowledge. | | | |
| We use knowledge to strengthen stakeholder relationships. | | | |
| We recognize that what we know about our products and services might be as valuable as the products and services themselves. | | | |
| Our policies, procedures, and cultural norms ensure that people who contribute their knowledge are valued. | | | |
| Our knowledge management process strikes a balance between information technology and people. | | | |
| **DIVEST** | | | |
| We know how to tell the difference between knowledge that can be leveraged and that which has limited applicability. | | | |
| We partner with other organizations to experiment with new types of knowledge. | | | |
| We routinely look for ways to shed non-strategic knowledge. | | | |
| We routinely look for ways to redeploy non-strategic knowledge. | | | |
| People realize that the job they are doing today is not the job they will be doing five years from now. | | | |

**Exhibit 33.6   Continued**

### Scoring

For each process step, count the number of responses in each category, multiply by the value listed in the table and place the total in the indicted box.

| GET | Number of | Multiply by | Total for each category |
|---|---|---|---|
| VERY WELL | | 2 | |
| SOMEWHAT | | 1 | |
| NOT AT ALL | | 0 | |
| TOTAL FOR GET | | | |

| USE | Number of | Multiply by | Total for each category |
|---|---|---|---|
| VERY WELL | | 2 | |
| SOMEWHAT | | 1 | |
| NOT AT ALL | | 0 | |
| TOTAL FOR USE | | | |

| LEARN | Number of | Multiply by | Total for each category |
|---|---|---|---|
| VERY WELL | | 2 | |
| SOMEWHAT | | 1 | |
| NOT AT ALL | | 0 | |
| TOTAL FOR LEARN | | | |

| CONTRIBUTE | Number of | Multiply by | Total for each category |
|---|---|---|---|
| VERY WELL | | 2 | |
| SOMEWHAT | | 1 | |
| NOT AT ALL | | 0 | |
| TOTAL FOR CONTRIBUTE | | | |

| ASSESS | Number of | Multiply by | Total for each category |
|---|---|---|---|
| VERY WELL | | 2 | |
| SOMEWHAT | | 1 | |
| NOT AT ALL | | 0 | |
| TOTAL FOR ASSESS | | | |

| BUILD/SUSTAIN | Number of | Multiply by | Total for each category |
|---|---|---|---|
| VERY WELL | | 2 | |
| SOMEWHAT | | 1 | |
| NOT AT ALL | | 0 | |
| TOTAL FOR BUILD/SUSTAIN | | | |

**Exhibit 33.6    Continued**

| DIVEST | Number of | Multiply by | Total for each category |
|---|---|---|---|
| VERY WELL | | 2 | |
| SOMEWHAT | | 1 | |
| NOT AT ALL | | 0 | |
| TOTAL FOR DIVEST | | | |

### Plot Your Knowledge Management State

Use your totals for each knowledge management process step to plot your organization's knowledge management state on the spider chart. The ideal state is represented by achieving a "10" on each axis. No organization will achieve the ideal. The ideal position merely indicates the extent of the gap between where you are and where you might like to be.

## Knowledge Management State

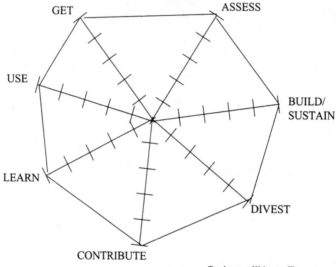

To plot your KM state: The center represents 0, each tick mark represents 2 points with the outermost tick mark defining 10.

**Exhibit 33.6   Continued**

# NOTES

1. *The American Heritage Dictionary of the English Language,* 3rd ed. (Boston: Houghton Mifflin, 1992), p. 2022.

2. Ibid., p. 111.

3. Adapted from W. R. Bukowitz and G. P. Petrash, "Visualizing, Measuring and Managing Knowledge," *Research Technology Management* (July–August 1997), p. 25.

4. S. Zuboff, *In the Age of the Smart Machine: The Future of Work and Power* (New York: Basic Books, 1988).

5. N. Angier, "Evolutionary Necessity or Glorious Accident? Biologists Ponder the Self," The *New York Times,* April 22, 1997.

6. A. Stille, "The Man Who Remembers," *The New Yorker,* February 15, 1999, 52.

7. Next Generation Research Group, *Knowledge Measurement: Phase Three, Global Survey Findings Report, Asia, North America, and Europe* (Arthur Andersen, October 1998).

8. The Institute of Chartered Accountants in England and Wales and The Centre for Tomorrow's Company, *The 21st Century Annual Report* (1998).

# GLOSSARY

**ABC**—see *activity-based costing.*

*Absorption costing*—A method of costing that assigns all or a portion of the manufacturing costs to products or other cost objects. The costs assigned include those that vary with the level of activity performed and also those that do not vary with the level of activity performed.

*Activity*—1. Work performed within an organization. 2. The aggregations of actions performed within an organization that are useful for purposes of activity-based costing.

*Activity analysis*—The identification and description of activities in an organization. Activity analysis involves determining what activities are done within a department, how many people perform the activities, how much time they spend performing the activities, what resources are required to perform the activities, what operational data best reflect the performance of the activities, and what value the activity has for the organization. Activity analysis is accomplished by means of interviews, questionnaires, observations, and reviews of physical records of work.

*Activity attributes*—Characteristics of individual activities. Attributes include cost drivers, cycle time, capacity, and performance measures. For example, a measure of the elapsed time required to complete an activity is an attribute. (See *cost driver* and *performance measures.*)

*Activity-based cost system*—A system that maintains and processes financial and operating data on a firm's resources, activities, cost objects, cost drivers, and activity performance measures. It also assigns cost to activities and cost objects.

*Activity-based management*—A discipline that focuses on the management of activities as the route to improving the value received by the customer and the profit achieved by providing this value. This discipline includes cost driver analysis, activity analysis, and performance measurement. Activity-based management draws on activity-based costing as a major source of information. (See *customer value.*)

*Activity capacity*—The demonstrated or expected capacity of an activity under normal operating conditions, assuming a specified set of resources and over a long period. An example of this would be a rate of output for an activity expressed as 500 cycles per hour.

Source: N. Raffish and P. B. B. Turney, ed., *The CAM-I Glossary of Activity-Based Management, version 1.2* (Arlington, TX: The Consortium for Advanced Manufacturing-International, 1992). Used with permission.

*Activity cost assignment*—The process in which the costs of activities are attached to cost objects using activity drivers. (See *cost object* and *activity driver.*)

*Activity cost pool*—A grouping of all cost elements associated with an activity. (See *cost element.*)

*Activity driver*—A measure of the frequency and intensity of the demands placed on activities by cost objects. An activity driver is used to assign costs to cost objects. It represents a line-item on the bill of activities for a product or customer. An example is the number of part numbers, which is used to measure the consumption of material-related activities by each product, material type, or component. The number of customer orders measures the consumption of order-entry activities by each customer. Sometimes an activity driver is used as an indicator of the output of an activity, such as the number of purchase orders prepared by the purchasing activity. (See *intensity, cost object,* and *bill of activities.*)

*Activity driver analysis*—The identification and evaluation of the activity drivers used to trace the cost of activities to cost objects. Activity driver analysis may also involve selecting activity drivers with a potential for cost reduction. (See *Pareto analysis.*)

*Activity level*—A description of how an activity is used by a cost object or other activity. Some activity levels describe the cost object that uses the activity and the nature of this use. These levels include activities that are traceable to the product (i.e., unit-level, batch-level, and product-level costs), to the customer (customer-level costs), to a market (market-level costs), to a distribution channel (channel-level costs) and to a project, such as a research and development project (project-level costs).

*Activity-based costing*—A methodology that measures the cost and performance of activities, resources, and cost objects. Resources are assigned to activities, then activities are assigned to cost objects based on their use. Activity-based costing recognizes the causal relationships of cost drivers to activities.

*Allocation*—1. An apportionment or distribution. 2. A process of assigning cost to an activity or cost object when a direct measure does not exist. For example, assigning the cost of power to a machine activity by means of machine hours is an allocation, because machine hours is an indirect measure of power consumption. In some cases, allocations can be converted to tracing by incurring additional measurement costs. Instead of using machine hours to allocate power consumption, for example, a company can place a power meter on machines to measure actual power consumption. (See *tracing.*)

*Assignment*—See *cost assignment.*

*Attributes*—Characteristics of activities, such as cost drivers and performance measures. (See *cost driver* and *performance measure.*)

*Attribution*—See *tracing.*

*Avoidable cost*—A cost associated with an activity that would not be incurred if the activity was not required. The telephone cost associated with vendor support, for example, could be avoided if the activity were not performed.

*Backflush costing*—1. A costing method that applies costs based on the output of a process. The process uses a bill of material or a bill of activities explosion to draw quantities from inventory, through work-in-process, to finished goods; at any intermediate stage, using the output quantity as the basis.

These quantities are generally costed using standard costs. The process assumes that the bill of material (or bill of activities) and the standard costs at the time of backflushing represent the actual quantities and resources used in the manufacture of the product. This is important, since no shop orders are usually maintained to collect costs. 2. A costing method generally associated with repetitive manufacturing. (See *repetitive manufacturing* and *standard costing.*)

*Benchmarking*—See *best practices.*

*Best practices*—A methodology that identifies an activity as the benchmark by which a similar activity will be judged. This methodology is used to assist in identifying a process or technique that can increase the effectiveness or efficiency of an activity. The source may be internal (e.g., taken from another part of the company) or external (e.g., taken from a competitor). Another term used is *competitive benchmarking.*

*Bill of activities*—A listing of the activities required (and, optionally, the associated costs of the resources consumed) by a product or other cost object.

*Budget*—1. A projected amount of cost or revenue for an activity or organizational unit covering a specific period of time. 2. Any plan for the coordination and control of resources and expenditures.

*Capital decay*—1. A quantification of the lost revenues or reduction in net cash flows sustained by an entity due to obsolete technology. 2. A measure of uncompetitiveness.

*Carrying cost*—See *holding cost.*

*Competitive benchmarking*—See *best practices.*

*Continuous improvement program*—A program to eliminate waste, reduce response time, simplify the design of both products and processes, and improve quality.

*Cost Accounting Standards*—1. Rules promulgated by the Cost Accounting Standards Board of the United States Government to ensure contractor compliance in the accounting of government contracts. 2. A set of rules issued by any of several authorized organizations or agencies, such as the American Institute of Certified Public Accountants (AICPA) or the Association of Chartered Accountants (ACA), dealing with the determination of costs to be allocated, inventoried, or expensed.

*Cost assignment*—The tracing or allocation of resources to activities or cost objects. (See *allocation* and *tracing.*)

*Cost center*—The basic unit of responsibility in an organization for which costs are accumulated.

*Cost driver*—Any factor that causes a change in the cost of an activity. For example, the quality of parts received by an activity (e.g., the percent that are defective) is a determining factor in the work required by that activity, because the quality of parts received affects the resources required to perform the activity. An activity may have multiple cost drivers associated with it.

*Cost driver analysis*—The examination, quantification, and explanation of the effects of cost drivers. Management often uses the results of cost driver analyses in continuous improvement programs to help reduce throughput time, improve quality, and reduce cost. (See *cost driver* and *continuous improvement program.*)

*Cost element*—An amount paid for a resource consumed by an activity and included in an activity cost pool. For example, power cost, engineering cost, and depreciation may be cost elements in the activity cost pool for a machine activity. (See *activity cost pool, bill of activities,* and *resource.*)

*Cost object*—Any customer, product, service, contract, project, or other work unit for which a separate cost measurement is desired.

*Cost of quality*—All the resources expended for appraisal costs, prevention costs, and both internal and external failure costs of activities and cost objects.

*Cost pool*—See *activity cost pool.*

*Cross-subsidy*—The improper assignment of costs among cost objects such that certain cost objects are overcosted while other cost objects are undercosted relative to the activity costs assigned. For example, traditional cost accounting systems tend to overcost high-volume products and undercost low-volume products.

*Customer value*—The difference between customer realization and sacrifice. *Realization* is what the customer receives, which includes product features, quality, and service. This takes into account the customer's cost to use, maintain, and dispose of the product or service. *Sacrifice* is what the customer gives up, which includes the amount the customer pays for the product plus time and effort spent acquiring the product and learning how to use it. Maximizing customer value means maximizing the difference between realization and sacrifice.

*Differential cost*—See *incremental cost.*

*Direct cost*—A cost that is traced directly to an activity or a cost object. For example, the material issued to a particular work order or the engineering time devoted to a specific product are direct costs to the work orders or products. (See *tracing.*)

*Direct tracing*—See *tracing.*

*Discounted cash flow*—A technique used to evaluate the future cash flows generated by a capital investment. Discounted cash flow is computed by discounting cash flows to determine their present value.

*Diversity*—Conditions in which cost objects place different demands on activities or activities place different demands on resources. This situation arises, for example, when there is a difference in mix or volume of products that causes an uneven assignment of costs. Different types of diversity include: *batch-size, customer, market, product mix, distribution channel,* and *volume.*

*Financial accounting*—1. The accounting for assets, liabilities, equities, revenues, and expenses as a basis for reports to external parties. 2. A methodology that focuses on reporting financial information primarily for use by owners, external organizations, and financial institutions. This methodology is constrained by rule-making bodies such as the Financial Accounting Standards Board (FASB), the Securities Exchange Commission (SEC), and the American Institute of Certified Public Accountants (AICPA).

*First-stage allocation*—See *resource cost assignment.*

*Fixed cost*—A cost element of an activity that does not vary with changes in the volume of cost drivers or activity drivers. The depreciation of a machine, for example, may be direct to a particular activity, but it is fixed with respect to changes in the number of units of the activity driver. The designation of a cost element as fixed or variable may vary depending on the time frame of the decision in question and the extent to which the volume of production, activity drivers, or cost drivers changes.

*Flexible factory*—The objective of a flexible factory is to provide a wide range of services across many product lines in a timely manner. An example is a fabrication plant with several integrated manufacturing cells that can perform many functions for unrelated product lines with relatively short lead times.

*Focused factory*—The objective of a focused factory is to organize around a specific set of resources to provide low cost and high throughput over a narrow range of products.

*Forcing*—Allocating the costs of a sustaining activity to a cost object even though that cost object may not clearly consume or causally relate to that activity. Allocating a plant-level activity (such as heating) to product units using an activity driver such as direct labor hours, for example, forces the cost of this activity to the product. (See *sustaining activity.*)

*Full absorption costing*—See *absorption costing.*

*Functional decomposition*—Identifies the activities performed in the organization. It yields a hierarchical representation of the organization and shows the relationship between the different levels of the organization and its activities. For example, a hierarchy may start with the division and move down through the plant, function, process, activity, and task levels.

*Holding cost*—A financial technique that calculates the cost of retaining an asset (e.g., finished goods inventory or a building). Generally, the calculation includes a cost of capital in addition to other costs such as insurance, taxes, and space.

*Homogeneity*—A situation in which all the cost elements in an activity's cost pool are consumed in proportion to an activity driver by all cost objects. (See *cost element, activity cost pool,* and *activity driver.*)

*Incremental cost*—1. The cost associated with increasing the output of an activity or project above some base level. 2. The additional cost associated with selecting one economic or business alternative over another, such as the difference between working overtime or subcontracting the work. 3. The cost associated with increasing the quantity of a cost driver. (Also known as *differential cost.*)

*Indirect cost*—The cost that is allocated—as opposed to being traced—to an activity or a cost object. For example, the costs of supervision or heat may be allocated to an activity on the basis of direct labor hours. (See *allocation.*)

*Intensity*—The cost consumed by each unit of the activity driver. It is assumed that the intensity of each unit of the activity driver for a single activity is equal. Unequal intensity means that the activity should be broken into smaller activities or that a different activity driver should be chosen. (See *diversity.*)

*Life cycle*—See *product life cycle.*

*Net present value*—A method that evaluates the difference between the present value of all cash inflows and outflows of an investment using a given rate of discount. If the discounted cash inflow exceeds the discounted outflow, the investment is considered economically feasible.

*Non–value-added activity*—An activity that is considered not to contribute to customer value or to the organization's needs. The designation non–value-added reflects a belief that the activity can be redesigned, reduced, or eliminated without reducing the quantity, responsiveness, or quality of the output required by the customer or the organization. (See *customer value* and *value analysis.*)

*Obsolescence*—A product or service that has lost is value to the customer due to changes in need or technology.

*Opportunity cost*—The economic value of a benefit that is sacrificed when an alternative course of action is selected.

*Pareto analysis*—The identification and interpretation of significant factors using Pareto's rule that 20 percent of a set of independent variables is responsible for 80 percent of the result. Pareto analysis can be used to identify cost drivers or activity drivers that are responsible for the majority of cost incurred by ranking the cost drivers in order of value. (See *cost driver analysis* and *activity driver analysis.*)

*Performance measures*—Indicators of the work performed and the results achieved in an activity, process, or organizational unit. Performance measures may be financial or nonfinancial. An example of a performance measure of an activity is the number of defective parts per million. An example of a performance measure of an organizational unit is return on sales.

*Present value*—The discounted value of a future sum or stream of cash flows.

*Process*—A series of activities that are linked to perform a specific objective. For example, the assembly of a television set or the paying of a bill or claim entails several linked activities.

*Product family*—A group of products or services that have a defined relationship because of physical and production similarities. (The term *product line* is used interchangeably.)

*Product life cycle*—The period that starts with the initial product specification and ends with the withdrawal of the product from the marketplace. A product life cycle is characterized by certain defined stages, including research, development, introduction, maturity, decline, and abandonment.

*Product line*—See *product family.*

*Profit center*—A segment of the business (e.g., a project, program, or business unit) that is accountable for both revenues and expenses.

*Project*—A planned undertaking, usually related to a specific activity, such as the research and development of a new product or the redesign of the layout of a plant.

*Project costing*—A cost system that collects information on activities and costs associated with a specific activity, project, or program.

*Repetitive manufacturing*—The manufacture of identical products (or a family of products) in a continuous flow.

*Resource*—An economic element that is applied or used in the performance of activities. Salaries and materials, for example, are resources used in the performance of activities. (See *cost element.*)

*Resource cost assignment*—The process by which cost is attached to activities. This process requires the assignment of cost from general ledger accounts to activities using resource drivers. For example, the chart of accounts may list information services at a plant level. It then becomes necessary to trace (assuming that tracing is practical) or to allocate (when tracing is not practical) the cost of information services to activities that benefit from the information services by means of appropriate resource drivers. It may be necessary to set up intermediate activity cost pools to accumulate related costs from various resources before the assignment can be made. (See *activity cost pool* and *resource driver.*)

***Resource driver***—A measure of the quantity of resources consumed by an activity. An example of a resource driver is the percentage of total square feet of space occupied by an activity. This factor is used to allocate a portion of the cost of operating the facilities to the activity.

***Responsibility accounting***—An accounting method that focuses on identifying persons or organizational units that are accountable for the performance of revenue or expense plans.

***Risk***—The subjective assessment of the possible positive or negative consequences of a current or future action. In a business sense, risk is the premium asked or paid for engaging in an investment or venture. Often risk is incorporated into business decisions through such factors as hurdle rates or the interest premium paid over a prevailing base interest rate.

***Second-stage allocation***—See *activity cost assignment.*

***Standard costing***—A costing method that attaches costs to cost objects based on reasonable estimates or cost studies and by means of budgeted rates rather than according to actual costs incurred.

***Sunk costs***—Costs that have been invested in assets for which there is little (if any) alternative or continued value except salvage. Using sunk costs as a basis for evaluating alternatives may lead to incorrect decisions. Examples are the invested cost in a scrapped part or the cost of an obsolete machine.

***Support costs***—Costs of activities not directly associated with production. Examples are the costs of process engineering and purchasing.

***Surrogate activity driver***—An activity driver that is not descriptive of an activity, but that is closely correlated to the performance of the activity. The use of a surrogate activity driver should reduce measurement costs without significantly increasing the costing bias. The number of production runs, for example, is not descriptive of the material disbursing activity, but the number of production runs may be used as an activity driver if material disbursements coincide with production runs.

***Sustaining activity***—An activity that benefits an organization at some level (e.g., the company as a whole or a division, plant, or department), but not any specific cost object. Examples of such activities are preparation of financial statements, plant management, and the support of community programs.

***Target cost***—A cost calculated by subtracting a desired profit margin from an estimated (or a market-based) price to arrive at a desired production, engineering, or marketing cost. The target cost may not be the initial production cost, but instead the cost that is expected to be achieved during the mature production stage. (See *target costing.*)

*Target costing*—A method used in the analysis of product and process design that involves estimating a target cost and designing the product to meet that cost. (See *target cost.*)

*Technology costs*—A category of cost associated with the development, acquisition, implementation, and maintenance of technology assets. It can include costs such as the depreciation of research equipment, tooling amortization, maintenance, and software development.

*Technology valuation*—A nontraditional approach to valuing technology acquisitions that may incorporate such elements as purchase price, start-up costs, current market value adjustments, and the risk premium of an acquisition.

*Throughput*—The rate of production of a defined process over a stated period of time. Rates may be expressed in terms of units of products, batches produced, dollar turnover, or other meaningful measurements.

*Traceability*—The ability to assign a cost by means of a causal relationship directly to an activity or a cost object in an economically feasible way. (See *tracing.*)

*Tracing*—The assignment of cost to an activity or a cost object using an observable measure of the consumption of resources by the activity or cost object. Tracing is generally preferred to allocation if the data exist or can be obtained at a reasonable cost. For example, if a company's cost accounting system captures the cost of supplies according to which activity uses the supplies, the costs may be traced—as opposed to allocated—to the appropriate activities. Tracing is also called *direct tracing.*

*Unit cost*—The cost associated with a single unit of the product, including direct costs, indirect costs, traced costs, and allocated costs.

*Value-added activity*—An activity that is judged to contribute to customer value or satisfy an organizational need. The attribute "value-added" reflects a belief that the activity cannot be eliminated without reducing the quantity, responsiveness, or quality of output required by a customer or organization. (See *customer value.*)

*Value analysis*—A cost reduction and process improvement tool that utilizes information collected about business processes and examines various attributes of the processes (e.g., diversity, capacity, and complexity) to identify candidates for improvement efforts. (See *activity attribute* and *cost driver.*)

*Value chain*—The set of activities required to design, procure, produce, market, distribute, and service a product or service.

*Value-chain costing*—An activity-based cost model that contains all activities in the value chain.

*Variance*—The difference between an expected and actual result.

*Variable cost*—A cost element of an activity that varies with changes in volume of cost drivers and activity drivers. The cost of material handling to an activity, for example, varies according to the number of material deliveries and pickups to and from that activity. (See *cost element, fixed cost,* and *activity driver.*)

*Waste*—Resources consumed by unessential or inefficient activities.

*Willie Sutton rule*—Focus on the high-cost activities. The rule is named after bank robber Willie Sutton, who—when asked "why do you rob banks?"—is reputed to have replied "because that's where the money is."

*Work cell*—A physical or logical grouping of resources that performs a defined job or task. The work cell may contain more than one activity. For example, all the tasks associated with the final assembly of a product may be grouped in a work cell.

*Work center*—A physical area of the plant or factory. It consists of one or more resources where a particular product or process is accomplished.

## APPENDIX A   CHOICE OF TERMS

### Driver
There is probably no term, other than activity, that has become more identified with activity-based costing than the term driver and its several variations. The problem is that it has been applied to several entities with varying meanings. It is often difficult to understand whether the use of the term driver is related to a causal effect (cost or input driver) or to the output of an activity (cost or output driver). In addition, terms such as first- and second-stage driver have come into use which also describe entities similar to resource and activity driver.

In this glossary we have chosen to use the term cost driver as the causal event that influences the quantity of work, and therefore costs, in an activity. We believe that by restricting the definition of cost driver to one meaning, it will facilitate its understanding.

We also appended the term driver to two other entities. The first deals with the mechanism of assigning resources to activities. That we call a resource driver. The second deals with the mechanism of assigning activity costs to cost objects. That we call an activity driver.

We hope that by limiting the use of the word driver to three clearly defined entities, we can prevent misinterpretation or misuse of the term.

### Non–Value-Added and Sustaining Activities
There are many activities in an organization that do not contribute to customer value, responsiveness, and quality. That does not mean that those activities can be eliminated or even reduced without doing harm to the business entity. Preparing required regulatory reports certainly does not add to the value of any cost object or to the satisfaction of the customer. However, that activity does have value to the organization since it permits it to function in a legal manner. The business community needs to distinguish between activities that are:

—not required at all and can be eliminated (e.g., a duplication of effort),

—ineffectively accomplished and can be reduced or redesigned (e.g., due to outdated policies or procedures), or

—required to sustain the organization and therefore may not be able to be reduced or eliminated (e.g., provide plant security).

**Diversity**
In the definition of this term we listed several examples of types of diversity that could influence cost assignment. We did not attempt to define all the possible types of diversity, or to give examples of each. However, we feel that a good understanding of the issues surrounding diversity is important to ensure that the process of cost assignment is equitable and accurate among cost objects. We would refer the reader to an article published in the *Harvard Business Review* (Sept–Oct 1988), by Robert Kaplan and Robin Cooper entitled, "Measuring Costs Right: Make the Right Decisions," which covers many of the aspects of this topic.

## APPENDIX B    ILLUSTRATIONS

**The CAM-I ABC Basic Model**
The first illustration of the basic model [Exhibit G.1] is an attempt to establish a generic illustration that can be used to assist in explaining the concepts of Activity-Based Costing. The model should be thought of as a template that can be adapted for various purposes. The model should not be thought of as a flow chart of activity-based costing. It is meant to be a conceptual diagram that allows the reader to gain a high-level understanding of the ABC processes.

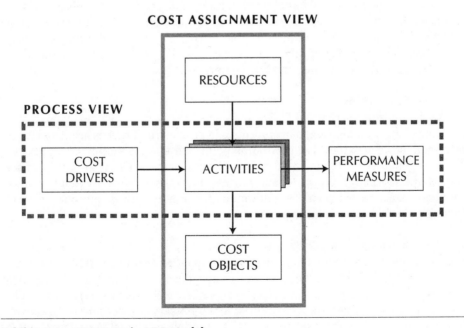

Exhibit G.1    CAM-I Basic ABC Model

There are two axes to the model. The vertical one deals with the classic two-stage cost assignment view. In the expanded model, there are three entities and two processes. The resource entity contains all available means upon which the selected activity can draw. The resource cost assignment process contains the structure and tools to trace and allocate costs to the activity. It is during this process that the applicable resource drivers are developed as the mechanism to convey resource costs to the activity. The activity entity is where work is performed. In this view, the activity is part of the cost structure. It is where resources are converted to some type of output. The activity cost assignment process contains the structure and tools to assign costs to cost objects, utilizing activity drivers as the mechanism to accomplish this assignment.

This cost assignment view is basically a "snapshot" view in the sense that the Balance Sheet on a financial statement is only a view of the business at the moment the accounts were tallied. In this sense, the cost assignment view can be seen as the structure and rules by which cost assignment takes place at some specific time. This time period may be at the end of a month, quarter, or any other time period which may or may not coincide with an accounting reporting period.

The horizontal axis contains the process view. This is a dynamic view, similar to the Income and Expense statement that reports on what has/is happening. This part of the process is initiated by a causal occurrence we call a cost driver. The cost driver is the agent that causes the activity to utilize resources to accomplish some designated work. In this view the activity is some type of active work center. During and after the activity work effort, performance data are collected. The performance measure of activities houses the evaluative criteria by which the organization can determine the efficiency and effectiveness of the activities work effort. It should be noted that there are many other performance measures, such as market share and return on equity, that are not included in the performance measures included in the ABC model.

The process view will constantly be changing. Each time a cost driver initiates work in an activity, new results will be obtained. It is therefore critical that applicable and realistic performance measures be established so that tracking of activity results can be monitored and improved on a continuing basis. ABC, through its reporting and analysis, can become an enabler of other process changes such as synchronous manufacturing, Design for Manufacturing, and Design for Assembly.

**Expanded Process View**

The second illustration [Exhibit G.2] is a more realistic view of what really takes place in an organization. There are many processes in progress, and each is usually made up of several linked activities. The illustration points out that the output (cost object) of any activity may be the input (cost driver) of the next activity. This relationship, of several activities forming a process or sub-process, offers the opportunity to link congruent performance measurements which would offer a more appropriate view of the effectiveness and efficiency of that process.

**CAM-I Expanded ABC Model**

The third illustration [Exhibit G.3] displays an expanded view of the ABC model. Depicted in this illustration are the resource cost assignment and activity cost assignment processes, and their respective databases of drivers. Another addition is an entity called the activity trigger. This term is not defined in the glossary as it pertains to an activity-based costing system rather than to the ABC methodology. The activity trigger is often, but not always, the link between the occurrence of a cost driver and the initiation of ac-

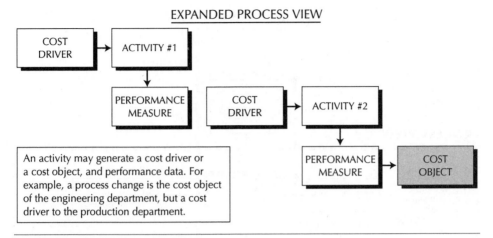

**Exhibit G.2    Expanded Process View**

tion in an activity. As an example, the mere occurrence of scrap does not in itself initiate an activity. There will need to be some management authorization to proceed before a replacement part is produced. In an information system about ABC, the activity trigger will often be the collection point for the information about the cost driver. The other entities depicted are cost drivers, activities, cost objects and activity related performance measures.

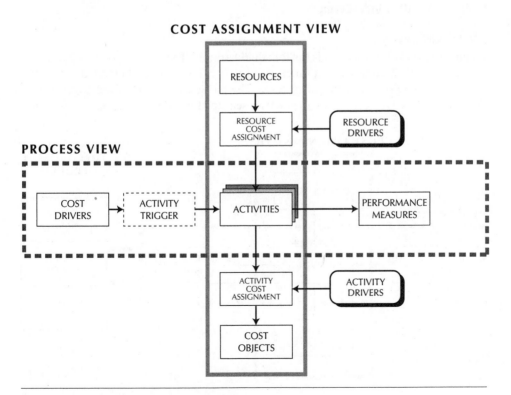

**Exhibit G.3    CAM-I Expanded ABC Model**

**COST ASSIGNMENT VIEW**

TOTAL PROCUREMENT COST POOL — $6,000,000

TRACING AND ALLOCATION — $450,000

**PROCESS VIEW**

MATERIAL REQUIREMENT

*Customer Order Scrap Ticket*

REQUISITIONS

*8,000 per year*

PURCHASING ACTIVITY

PURCHASING PERFORMANCE MEASURES

*6,000 POs per year*

PURCHASE ORDERS

*$75 per PO*
*1,500 PO errors*
*3,500 Expedited*
*6,000 POs per year*
*12 day cycle*

*$75 per PO*

PART

**Exhibit G.4    ABC Model Example**

**ABC Model Example**

Included as well in this section is the fourth illustration [Exhibit G.4] that displays how the model might be applied to a functional activity. The activity illustrated here is the purchasing activity at a department level. The particular task involved is generating purchase orders. One can see by the metrics selected for performance measures, that a

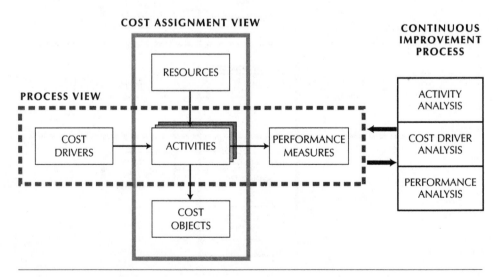

**COST ASSIGNMENT VIEW**

**CONTINUOUS IMPROVEMENT PROCESS**

RESOURCES

**PROCESS VIEW**

COST DRIVERS

ACTIVITIES

PERFORMANCE MEASURES

ACTIVITY ANALYSIS

COST DRIVER ANALYSIS

PERFORMANCE ANALYSIS

COST OBJECTS

**Exhibit G.5    Activity-Based Management Model**

trend analysis could certainly identify candidate tasks for a continuous improvement program.

**Activity-Based Management Model**

The last illustration [Exhibit G.5] is a view of Activity-Based Management. It depicts the key relationship between ABC, and the management analysis tools that are needed to bring full realization of the benefits of ABC to the organization. ABC is a methodology that can yield significant information about cost drivers, activities, resources and performance measures. However, ABM is a discipline that offers the organization the opportunity to improve the value of its products and services.

## APPENDIX C    RERFERENCES

In attempting to use as much of what was available in terms of definitions, there were several reference documents that provided excellent source material. They are:

1. *A Dictionary for Accountants* by Eric L. Kohler, Fifth Edition (Englewood Cliffs: Prentice-Hall, 1975)

2. "Management Accounting Terminology, Statement on Management Accounting Number 2A" (National Association of Accountants, May 1990)

3. *Webster's Ninth New Collegiate Dictionary* (Merriam-Webster, Inc., 1984)

4. *Cost Management for Today's Advanced Manufacturing,* Edited by C. Berliner and J. A. Brimson (Harvard Business School Press, 1988)

Activity-Based Costing has gained a significant measure of development and publicity in the past few years. Several individuals have made significant contributions to this growing body of knowledge. Through their articles, books and lectures, they have influenced almost all of us who have worked in the field of Activity-Based Management. It is also fair to say that their efforts have influenced the content of this glossary.

1. H. Thomas Johnson and Robert S. Kaplan, *Relevance Lost: The Rise and Fall of Management Accounting,* (Harvard Business Review, 1987)

2. Thomas Johnson, a series of articles:
   Activity Management: Reviewing the Past and Future of Cost Management, (*Journal of Cost Management,* Winter 1990)
   Pitfalls in Using ABC Cost-Driver Information to Manage Operating Cost, (*Corporate Controller,* Jan/Feb 1991, coauthors T. P. Vance and R. S. Player)
   Activity Management: Past, Present, and Future, (*The Engineering Economist,* Spring 1991)

3. Robin Cooper, a series of articles:
   Schrader Bellows, (*Harvard Business School* Case, 1986)

The Rise of Activity-Based Costing, in four parts (*Journal of Cost Management,* Summer and Fall 1988, Winter 1989 and Spring 1990)

The Two Stage Procedure in Cost Accounting, in two parts (*Journal of Cost Management,* Spring and Summer 1987)

Cost Classifications in Unit-Based and Activity-Based Management Cost Systems, (*Journal of Cost Management,* Fall 1990)

**4.** Robert S. Kaplan, Union Pacific, (*Harvard Business School* Case, 1987)

**5.** Robert S. Kaplan, One Cost System Isn't Enough. (*Harvard Business Review,* J–F 1988)

**6.** Robin Cooper and Robert S. Kaplan, Measure Costs Right: Make the Right Decisions. (*Harvard Business Review,* S–O 1988)

**7.** Peter B. B. Turney, a series of articles:

What is the Scope of Activity-Based Costing (*Journal of Cost Management,* Fall 1988)

Ten Myths About Implementing Activity-Based Cost Systems (*Journal of Cost Management,* Spring 1990)

The Impact of Continuous Improvement on the Design of Activity-Based Cost Systems, with James Reeve (*Journal of Cost Management,* Summer 1990)

How Activity-Based Costing Helps Reduce Cost (*Journal of Cost Management,* Winter 1991)

**8.** James Brimson, *Activity Accounting: An Activity-Based Cost Approach* (Coopers and Lybrand, John Wiley & Sons. 1991)

**9.** M. Stahl and G. Bound, editors, *Competing Globally Through Customer Value: The Management of Suprasystems.* (Greenwood Press, 1991)

**10.** Charles T. Horngren and George Foster, *Cost Accounting, A Managerial Emphasis* (Prentice-Hall, Inc. 1991)

**11.** Peter B. B. Turney, from a forthcoming book, *Common Cents: The ABC Performance Breakthrough* (Cost Technology, 1991)

# INDEX